914.032   121209
P66e

DATE DUE			

EUROPE
SINCE
1815

UMBERTO BOCCIONI:
UNIQUE FORMS OF CONTINUITY IN SPACE,
1913, BRONZE
MUSEUM OF MODERN ART

EUROPE SINCE 1815

RICHARD PIPES

HARVARD UNIVERSITY

INTRODUCTION

WILLIAM L. LANGER

COOLIDGE PROFESSOR OF HISTORY, EMERITUS
HARVARD UNIVERSITY

A HARPER-AMERICAN HERITAGE TEXTBOOK

AMERICAN HERITAGE PUBLISHING CO., INC.   NEW YORK

HARPER & ROW, PUBLISHERS, INCORPORATED   NEW YORK, EVANSTON AND LONDON

Editors, Alfred E. Prettyman and Stephen W. Sears.
Copy editing, Jere Grant and Annette Welles.
Design and layout, Jean Brock, Harriet Cole, and Karen G. Bowen.
Portfolio text, John Terry Chase and Dennis A. Dinan.
Picture research, Mary Sherman Parsons (Chief) and Margaretta Barton.
Map research, Lucia Scala.
Editorial assistant, Sally Tyson.
Production supervisor, Thomas C. Partis.

Maps and charts by Francis & Shaw.

In addition to the sources listed in the credits accompanying
the illustrations, special acknowledgment is made to the
Service Photographique of the Bibliothèque Nationale, to the
Trustees of the British Museum, and to the European bureau
of American Heritage, Gertrudis Feliu, Chief.

The map on page 38 and those on page 166 were adapted from *Atlas of World History*,
R. R. Palmer ed., © 1957 by Rand McNally & Company.

The author makes grateful acknowledgment to:
Chatto & Windus Ltd., London, England: for the poems "Dulce et Decorum Est"
(pages 327–328) and "The End" (page 337) from *The Poems of Wilfred Owen*, edited by
Edmund Blunden (London: Chatto & Windus Ltd., 1921); also reprinted by permission
of New Directions Publishing Corporation, New York, N.Y.
Thomas Nelson & Sons Ltd., London, England: the poem "1914" (pages 326–327) from
Poems of Rupert Brooke (London: Nelson, 1952). Reprinted by permission of
Thomas Nelson & Sons Ltd.
Siegfried Sassoon: the poem "Attack" (page 327) and a selection from
Collected Poems, 1908–1956, by Siegfried Sassoon (London: Faber & Faber Ltd., 1961).
Reprinted by permission of the author.

Table of Contents

Maps and Charts

Two Centuries in Review

The past two centuries were of epochal importance in the history of Western man and his society. All history is, to be sure, the chronicle of constant change, but never before were the changes as numerous, as rapid, and as far-reaching as in the period following the French Revolution. It is no exaggeration to say that the modern world—the world as we know it—is the product of these two centuries, of vicissitudes at once wondrously impressive and deeply disturbing, marking both beneficent achievements and undreamed-of suffering.

In this Introduction the effort is made to identify and highlight some of the basic political and social features of the recent past. This does not mean that intellectual and cultural factors were less important. On the contrary, they are given rather full treatment in this volume. But they defy brief or general consideration and may therefore be left to the author's own analysis and evaluation.

By the year 1815, which saw the breakdown of Napoleon's empire and the end of French domination of the Continent, several forces of major import were already operative and already transforming the conditions of human society. The ideas of the French Revolution, with their stress on the rights of the individual, on the equality of all before the law and in terms of opportunity, had already sounded the death knell of class stratification and privilege. Never again would the claims of divine-right monarchs go unchallenged, nor the exploitation of the common people—the "black masses"—by feudal landlords and aristocrats be borne without protest. Church hierarchies, traditionally so closely linked to the ruling classes, were in similar disrepute.

Needless to say, the inroads made into the old social order were spasmodic and incomplete, but the new ideas of freedom and equality were to prove themselves insuppressible. Gradually the institution of monarchy, if it was not destroyed and replaced by a republican system, was at least shorn of much or most of its power. Constitutional, representative government spread from country to country. By the eve of the First World War most European states had adopted a democratic system with universal suffrage. First the liberally minded middle classes and then the common man had made their voices heard politically.

Naturally this process of political change was uneven. Social position and wealth still commanded influence or ensured a privileged position. But by the dawn of the twentieth century the rank and file of the population had become literate and thus able to inform themselves through newspapers and other media and to bring the weight of their numbers to bear in political matters. The recognition of civil rights and human freedom, the establishment of equality before the law, the participation of all adult males in political life—these were great achievements of the nineteenth century. So basic and important was this change to popular, representative government that in the twentieth century, when in many countries there was a relapse into some form of authoritarian government, even these reactionary regimes felt it essential to cloak their dictatorship in the trappings of popular government. They called themselves democracies or people's republics; they invariably introduced constitutions and set up representative assemblies; and they encouraged their peoples to exercise the franchise, if only to vote for the one and only ticket submitted by the dominant, totalitarian party. This devotion to democratic forms is a sincere tribute to the political achievement of the preceding century.

Closely akin to notions of individual rights was the rapid development of the idea of the nation and of the right of every people to independence. Cultural nationalism, which stressed community of language, law, and other institutions as well as community of fate as reflected in history, was one aspect of the Romantic movement of the early nineteenth century. By midcentury, however, nationalism had taken on a marked political tinge. The revolutions of 1848–1849 in Central Europe were as much nationalist as liberal and democratic. They aimed at the unification of the many German and Italian states, a program which, though foiled initially by conservative opposition, was to be realized in the 1860s. Thenceforth nationalism was to remain a potent force, for evil as well as for good. In the years preceding the First World War it contributed significantly to the exacerbation of international relations, and in the years between the First and Second World Wars it was rampant especially in the new states of Central and Southeastern Europe. Only the bitter experiences of 1939–1945 brought some deflation of nationalist feeling, at least among the countries of Western Europe, where the notion of regional cooperation and possible union made notable strides in the direction of integration.

Political and military events have traditionally provided the basic material for the historian's narrative. Yet other factors in social development are now generally recognized as important and at times crucial, though they are usually difficult to analyze and evaluate. In the nineteenth century the phenomenal growth of the population and the advent of the machine age were truly epoch-making changes. These two developments may well have been—indeed probably were—related, but what the relationship may have been is still obscure and controversial. The earlier notion that the demands of the new factory system for child labor induced the working classes to raise larger families is now no longer regarded as an adequate explanation. It seems more likely that the impact was the reverse: that the accelerated increase of the population and the attendant multiplication of needs may have stimulated the development of nonhuman power and its application to industrial production, along with the invention of labor-saving machinery.

In any event, the rapid growth of the population was a novel feature and entailed novel problems. Prior to the mid-eighteenth century the population of Europe had grown but slowly and spasmodically. Devastating epidemics, such as the frequently recurring attacks of bubonic plague, smallpox, and venereal disease, had periodically carried off large segments of mankind. Crop failures and famines had contributed to holding population in check. But by 1750 the plague, which was the greatest killer, had disappeared from Western and Central Europe, and notable progress was being made in reducing child mortality through inoculation for smallpox—which at the very end of the century was replaced by vaccination, that is, by the induction of cowpox as a less dangerous method of securing immunity from smallpox. Further advances were to be made in medical science, especially through the discovery of the causes of disease by Pasteur and Koch, in the later nineteenth century.

Another factor in what was nothing less than a population explosion in the late eighteenth century was the rather sudden and widespread adoption of potato culture in northern and central Europe and of maize (American corn) in southern Europe. These highly nutritious plants vastly increased the food supply of the lower classes, enabling large families to subsist on the produce of the merest scrap of land.

In 1803 the Reverend Thomas Malthus, in the important second edition of his *Essay on the Principle of Population,* sounded an alarm by warning that population tends to increase more rapidly than the food supply and that therefore mankind is constantly threatened by overpopulation. Thenceforth the specter of "redundant" population haunted Europe for upward of fifty years, much as the very same specter haunts the whole world today.

During the early nineteenth century widespread unemployment and the ensuing increase of poverty spawned a huge literature, including the varied literature of early socialism, which argued the need for a fundamental redistribution of wealth, if not a complete abolition of private property and the reorganization of society on a communal basis. Most writing, however, was less drastic or visionary. It concerned itself with more limited and more specific remedies for the pressures which were becoming progressively more unbearable. It was soon realized that the promotion of industry would entail more employment opportunities for the lower classes. Governments therefore exerted themselves to this end, at the same time setting up tariff barriers to exclude the manufactures of other nations. Still another remedy was sought in emigration. Governments, traditionally opposed to any loss of population, quickly became converted to emigration programs, even to the extent of providing state support for the emigration of the poor. In the course of the nineteenth century many millions of persons left Europe, mostly to settle in the New World. This great exodus drained off a substantial part of the natural population increase. Thus it served to relieve pressure until industrial development had reached the point of providing employment for all the available manpower. In the process, however, many thousands of sober, hard-working, progressive families were lost to their homelands. It is impossible to determine, in terms of character and ability, what this drain may have meant to European society. In the New World the newcomers certainly provided much of the manpower and brainpower on which its greatness in the twentieth century was to rest.

By the advent of the nineteenth century the so-called Industrial Revolution was already well under way. England, the pioneer country, was largely industrialized by midcentury, and many of the Continental nations had achieved an equivalent stage of development by the end of the century.

The term *Industrial Revolution* is more convenient than accurate, for the change in the mode of production was necessarily gradual. The initial impetus came from a great increase in the demand for goods which, in turn, appears to have derived from the growth of population. What was involved was, firstly, the invention of machinery (chiefly in the textile trades) by which hand labor could perform a number of operations without extra exertion. Mechanical contrivances, in short, made possible a multiplication of production. Contemporaneously, oft-repeated efforts to exploit the expansive power of steam led finally to the invention of a truly efficient steam engine. This quickly rendered the unreliable water power of streams largely obsolete. Steam power was used in mining and in manufacturing, and presently also in transportation. Both the steamboat and the railroad were achievements of the nineteenth century. Their importance in facilitating communication and speeding up transportation can hardly be exaggerated. To speak of the age of steam or of the railway age is altogether appropriate.

Industrialization transformed much of European society in a space of less than a hundred years. In previous ages mankind, excepting for the relatively small upper classes, had lived literally from hand to mouth, that is, on a subsistence level, happy to survive famine, disease, and the devastations of war. Now for the first time in history man's productive power had been greatly enhanced. Steam power and presently electric power, along with so-called labor-saving machinery, enabled him to improve agriculture and increase the food supply. At the same time they enabled him to produce far more than the mere necessaries of life. For the first time there was a potential surplus, in which even the common man was to share in ever greater measure. By the end of the century the real income of the European worker had just about doubled and he was beginning to enjoy some of the good things of life that had hitherto been reserved for the rich and the mighty.

Such fundamental alterations necessarily entailed difficult and painful social readjustments. When governments promoted industry so as to give employment to the indigent, the hungry workers moved in large numbers from the rural areas to the new factory towns. Many historic centers of ten or fifteen thousand population doubled, trebled, and even quadrupled in size within a few decades. They were, naturally, unprepared for this sudden influx. They had no adequate water supply, they lacked housing, they were without anything like modern sewage disposal. For the worker, food and fuel were hard to come by and very expensive. In view of the abundance of labor, wages were shockingly low, while employment was extremely unsteady. Under the circumstances the living conditions of the factory workers were indescribably bad. Reduced to the barest subsistence level, the poor fell easy victims to slum diseases such as cholera, an affliction as horrible as it was painful and lethal, which swept over Europe in several severe epidemics beginning in 1831.

The plight of the inarticulate and unorganized workers inspired the early efforts at trade unionism and led, after the midcentury, to the parallel spread of social as well as political democracy. With the adoption of universal suffrage the workers were able to make their numbers felt. By the dawn of the present century Marxian socialism, originally an out-and-out revolutionary doctrine, had to a large extent fitted itself into the existing democratic structure and tended increasingly to collaborate with other progressive elements in the campaign for peaceful social reform. In Germany, where the Social Democratic party had in 1911 become the strongest single faction in the imperial parliament, the pressure for progressive reform was becoming irresistible by 1914.

The numbers and impoverishment of the lower classes led popular leaders such as Francis Place and Richard Carlile to argue that the workers could hope to raise their wages and improve their standard of living only by limiting their numbers. In the 1820s they launched among the factory workers the first educational birth-control campaign. Their propaganda may well have had a significant impact among the industrial proletariat, but birth control and family planning (more among the middle classes than among the lower classes) was to be widely adopted only during the last quarter of the century. In our own day it is universally recognized as the only effective means to check the headlong population explosion which, reinforced by the tremendous strides in preventive medicine, threatens to engulf the entire world. Many governments are now drafting plans and appropriating funds to educate their peoples in the need for limiting the number of their children.

High though the price of industrialization may have been, the benefits were such as to more than repay society. By the mid-nineteenth century the initial shock of change was being overcome. The new economy was becoming stabilized, while the effects of the new productive system, in terms of increases in food and goods and of greater employment with rising wages, were making themselves clearly felt. As time went on the findings of modern science were more and more being brought to bear on the problems of agriculture and industry. Furthermore, large-scale emigration, as aforesaid, helped to relieve the pressures from which Europe was suffering.

It was partly the continued drain of people—the loss of potential producers to say nothing of the goods and capital that they took with them—that led some governments to search for colonies in which emigrants could be settled without changing their national allegiance. Although the prospective territories, as in Africa and Asia, were mostly unsuited to European settlement, a half dozen European governments quickly became involved in overseas expansion. Fearful lest other powers appropriate the unclaimed parts of the world and then close them to the trade and investments of others, they engaged in a frantic scramble that resulted in the partition of all of Africa, and to the promotion of rival claims to spheres of influence in the Middle East, East Asia, and the Pacific. This spectacular movement, known as imperialism, meant that in hardly more than a generation a few European powers were able to establish direct or indirect control over areas vastly larger than the home countries and with populations infinitely greater.

Phenomena such as imperialism are rarely if ever simple. Psychological and religious factors, as well as political, economic, and military considerations underlay the unbridled expansionism of the Europeans in the closing decades of the nineteenth century. Historically, imperialism was to prove itself short-lived, yet it will always remain convincing evidence of the great superiority attained by a relatively small segment of humanity, and as an impressive demonstration of the vigor and drive that came to the Europeans with better food, improved health, more goods, and more abundant capital—in short, with a higher standard of living resulting from industrialization.

In retrospect, then, the century following the downfall of Napoleon, a period remarkably free of major, prolonged wars, was marked by amazing advances in learning and in economic and social development. The old order of despotic rule and feudal privilege had all but vanished. The middle classes had attained control of political as well as economic life, while the common man, now literate and increasingly organized, was making his weight felt. In terms of health, wealth, and happiness, European society had changed radically and decidedly for the better.

It is naturally more difficult to gain perspective and to evaluate developments of the current century, since we are all still deeply enmeshed in many of its chief problems and have no way of knowing what the outcome of major issues may ultimately be. Men confronted by the personal and social trials which are inseparable from human living tend always to think of their own age as particularly beset by problems, dangers, and tribulations. The very fact that the twentieth century, following on the relatively peaceful nineteenth, has already experienced two great world wars, with their untold loss of life and treasure, seems to many people more than sufficient evidence that things are going from bad to worse and that the present generation is doomed to live precariously in perpetual crisis.

It can be argued with some cogency, however, that the great war of 1914–1918 was the culmination of nineteenth-century forces and developments and really marks the watershed between the two centuries. In a sense many of the woes of the present-day world derive from a conflict whose origins lay in the past. The new age carries a heavy burden inherited from the old.

The First World War had its roots in the rampant nationalism, the imperialism, the bloated militarism, and the tense economic competition that marked the early years of the current century. Furthermore, both Fascism and Communism reach back into the prewar period. But these forces were given enormous impetus by the demands of war, as were certain more recent inventions, such as the automobile, the airplane, the submarine, and the radio.

No one in 1914 believed that the war, once it had come, would or could last more than a few months. It seemed too monstrous an ordeal to be long endured. It stands to reason, then, that after more than two years of desperate fighting all the participants should have been approaching collapse. The British were on the verge of bankruptcy and the French were confronted with formidable mutinies. It is inconceivable that these Allied Powers could have been able to win a victory without the intervention of the United States in April, 1917. This crucial event was, in turn, due to the conviction of the German high command that a decision by traditional land warfare had become impossible and that the deadlock could be broken only by the use of unrestricted submarine warfare against Britain. The Germans knew that they were provoking American intervention, but they fully expected to attain a decision before American power could make itself felt. They gambled and failed, for the submarine operations proved less effective than they had expected. When presently, in the summer of 1918, huge American armies arrived in France to supplement earlier American supplies, the Germans were obliged to follow the example of their allies and accept defeat.

Meanwhile, concurrent with the intervention of the United States in European affairs, the Russian government had been obliged to capitulate to a popular insurrection brought on by the privations of the war. Thenceforth Russia was unable to contribute significantly to the defeat of the Central Powers. On the contrary, the efforts of the Provisional Government to stage a new offensive led only to collapse and chaos, opening the way for the second, or Bolshevik, revolution of October, 1917.

It is most unlikely that Lenin and his Bolshevik party would ever have been able to secure control of the Russian or any other government except in the setting of a militarily frustrating and exhausting world war. The Bolsheviks were the extreme radical, revolutionary wing of Russian Social Democracy and had remained, despite their aggressive efforts, very much a minority. Only through the aid of the German high command had Lenin been enabled even to reach Russia and only through the chaotic situation in the autumn of 1917 had he and his followers succeeded in seizing power. Even then their position was highly precarious, for during three years they had to face civil war in order to maintain their position. Nonetheless, a Communist regime, inexorably hostile to all capitalist countries, had established itself in a major state. It promptly embarked upon a campaign of propaganda and subversion and so initiated the division not only of Europe but ultimately of the whole world into mutually hostile ideological blocs. This basic antagonism quickly became a key factor in all international relations.

Four years of deadly conflict had generated such psychological tensions that nothing short of a vindictive peace would satisfy the victors. The terms imposed on defeated Germany and its allies were admittedly Draconian. The Germans were obliged to acknowledge sole responsibility for the outbreak of the war, to accept heavy losses of territory and resources, and to assume an indeterminate burden of reparations, all designed to paralyze the country for many years to come. In the interests of French security, German territory west of the Rhine was to be militarily occupied, while the Austro-Hungarian Empire was induced to dissolve into a number of national states, many of which then became the allies of France, committed to the task of upholding the new territorial and political order. In sum, the peace treaties left Germany so weakened and humiliated that it barely managed to foil the Communist revolution which the Soviet government had been actively fomenting. At the same time even the victorious countries (notably Italy) were left unstable and the entire Central and Eastern European region disintegrated to the point where none of the governments could, without outside support, maintain itself against domestic or foreign pressures. At home the authorities of the new "national" states had to contend with sizable national minorities clamoring for equal rights. Externally they all lived under the threat of Communist subversion or attack.

The First World War, fought by the Western powers "to make the world safe for democracy," actually undermined democracy in countries where previously it was well established. In Italy the government, unable to cope with the problems left by the war, gave way to the first important authoritarian, totalitarian regime—that of Mussolini and his Fascists. Their victory, in turn, stimulated movements in other countries that were conservative in their aims, although they employed radical methods learned from the Communists. In Germany Hitler's National Socialist (Nazi) movement gained impetus during the 1920s and after the onset of the Great Depression in 1930 soon succeeded in putting an end to the democratic Weimar Republic. Before long most of the Continental countries were under more or less lightly veiled authoritarian regimes.

The Great Depression, the worst on record, spanned the better part of a decade. To some extent it was attributable to the preposterous reparations demands made on Germany and to the financial drain of the war and the dislocations resulting from the territorial settlements. The stagnation of trade and the prevalent unemployment added greatly to the misery, uncertainty and desperation of the 1930s.

Frantic search for markets entailed Japanese aggression against China, which in turn inspired the Italian Fascist government to launch a campaign to conquer Ethiopia. In the heightened international tension, Hitler and the Nazis had risen to power in Germany and had promptly put an end to the disarmament negotiations by resigning membership in the League of Nations. In 1935 Hitler announced the rearmament of Germany and in the spring of 1936 brought Europe to the verge of another great war by further violating the peace treaties and militarily reoccupying the Rhineland. In the same fateful year the Fascists completed the subjugation of Ethiopia while in Spain civil war broke out between the forces of the republic and those of a conservative, military faction. The war in Spain quickly led to the intervention of Italy and Germany on the Fascist side and of Soviet Russia on the democratic, Republican side. Never before had the ideological rift in Europe been so clearly marked nor the antagonism between the Fascist and Communist regimes been so pronounced and so violent.

The aggressions of the 1930s succeeded largely because all efforts to forestall them through international action failed. The peace treaties of 1919 contained an important and promising provision, the so-called covenant of the League of Nations, setting up a permanent international organization for the settlement of critical issues by peaceful means and, when necessary, for checking aggression. The League was inaugurated in 1920 but suffered from the outset through the absence from membership of several key powers. Germany was not invited to join and subsequently was unable to invoke League action with respect to grievances arising from the imposed peace. Soviet Russia, in turn, refused to consort with an essentially "capitalist" organization where it was sure to be outvoted. Worst of all, the United States Senate, in refusing to approve the peace treaties, rejected also membership in the League, despite the fact that the new institution was largely an achievement of President Wilson and that there was strong popular support in the United States for active participation in the project to enforce peace.

Valiant efforts were made by the League during the 1920s to dispose of various international issues. Among other things an international conference was convoked in 1926 (following the admission of Germany to membership) to initiate studies and discussions of the general disarmament envisaged by the peace treaties. This preparatory commission functioned for a number of years. Its labors, though they proved vain, did much to highlight the incredible difficulties in achieving disarmament, due to the fears of every nation for its security and, of course, the suspicions of each as to the designs of the others.

When, in 1933, the League attempted to check Japanese aggression against China, the Tokyo government simply resigned from the organization. Nazi Germany did likewise when, in the same year, it proved impossible for France and Germany to reach agreement on progressive disarmament. Though Soviet Russia accepted membership in 1934, the League was already too enfeebled to act effectively in any major crisis. A supreme effort was made to obstruct Mussolini's policy in Ethiopia by the imposition of economic sanctions, but even this project was wrecked on the shoals of national interest. The failure of the League was one of the great tragedies of the century, yet its history records an important experiment, which showed up the obstacles to the enforcement of peace so long as national sovereignty remained undiluted.

Living as we do under chronic international tension and the threat of imminent annihilation, we naturally think of the immediate past in terms of the great world wars which were so destructive of both material and spiritual values. In the arts and sciences, however, the period preceding 1939 was one of continued and accelerated development. Revolutionary innovations were made in the plastic arts and in music, while in the sciences major advances were made in biology and medicine, in physics and chemistry. The theories of quantum mechanics and relativity called for basic rethinking of many problems and paved the way for rapid progress in atomic science. The foundations of the space age were laid in these years of international unrest and fear.

The threat of renewed war was made more frightening by new techniques of warfare, such as parachute attack and air bombardment of cities and civilians. The British and French governments, troubled by guilt feelings in the matter of the peace treaties and under heavy pressure from public opinion, made repeated attempts to ease the tension through a policy of appeasement—that is, a policy of concessions to meet at least some of the claims of the aggressive powers. But Japan, Italy, and Germany were bound to regard the situation as so favorable to them and the prospect of resistance to their designs so remote that no reasonable offer could attract them. Hitler's aggression against Czechoslovakia and Poland then proved more than the Western powers could bear and in September, 1939 precipitated another cataclysm.

This second war was much more a world conflict than its predecessor, for it was fought on land, sea, and in the air not only on the traditional battlefields of Europe, but on the deserts of North Africa and even on remote islands of the Pacific. Civilians as well as soldiers were in the direct line of attack by planes and missiles. Indeed, the war revealed as had nothing in ages the repressed brutality and ruthlessness as well as the violence of human nature. Among other frightful events was the extermination of some 6 million Jews by the fanatically anti-Semitic Nazis, whose "elite" troops rounded up their victims throughout the territories under their control and then consigned them to gas chambers. The Soviets for their part eliminated the intellectuals and military personnel of the Baltic States and Poland, and in the further course of the war transported whole populations suspected of disloyalty to prison and labor camps in the Arctic or Siberia, where those who survived the ordeal of transfer soon met their end through privation or abuse.

The war machines of Germany and Japan seemed at first irresistible. Poland was overrun in a matter of days, the Netherlands and Belgium were crushed, and the French armies destroyed or captured in a few weeks, and by the autumn of 1940 Britain seemed doomed to invasion and conquest. Only the heroic defense of its air force and the inspiration of its leadership saved it from destruction. In 1941 Hitler, foiled in his designs on Britain, turned eastward, smashing all resistance in the Balkans and then launching a lightning attack on Russia. By December, when Japan provoked the intervention of the United States by a surprise air attack on Pearl Harbor, the Nazi forces were on the very outskirts of Moscow and Leningrad, and their victory seemed inevitable.

But the Soviet armies managed to hold. After repelling ferocious Nazi assaults on Stalingrad, the gateway to the Caucasus, they were able to surround and capture huge Nazi forces and then assume the offensive. At the same time the weight of American power in men and supplies was making itself felt in North Africa and the Pacific. Allied forces invaded Italy in 1943 and forced the Fascist government to abdicate, after which its successor withdrew from the war. A year later American and British forces landed in France. The Nazi armies, under heavy pressure on the eastern as well as the western front, were thrown back and obliged to surrender. Japan held out for a few more months but abandoned further resistance after the devastating atomic attack by American planes on Hiroshima and Nagasaki.

The victorious powers, mindful of the consequences of a punitive peace in 1919, avoided a repetition of such a settlement in 1945. Germany and Japan, though they remained under military occupation for some years, were actually aided by their former enemies in recovering from the worst effects of defeat. The United States, far from again withdrawing from European and world affairs, played an active and indeed leading role, notably in terms of the Marshall Plan, by which the European powers were enabled to recover economically in a remarkably short time.

One very important effect of the Second World War was the deflation of nationalism among many of the Western countries. The results of exaggerated nationalism were all too evident and there was a growing realization that, if Europe were to be saved from total inundation by the Communist tide, the democratic nations must stand together. The United States took the lead in engineering the North Atlantic Treaty Organization (NATO) through which most of non-Communist Europe was united in a defense pact. Within this framework the European governments themselves set up a Council of Europe for political consultation, followed by various experiments in economic cooperation. These culminated in the establishment in 1957 of the so-called Common Market, by which France, Germany, Italy, and the Low Countries were closely bound and integrated economically. Despite some nationalist opposition and occasional setbacks, the future seems to belong to a supranational Western European community, with more than a mere possibility that this may grow into an Atlantic community including the United States and Canada.

The United States government was instrumental also in reviving and strengthening the international organization for the preservation of peace. Now renamed the United Nations, the organization went into operation in 1945 with both the United States and Soviet Russia as members of the directing council. In the intervening years the United Nations has shown itself more effective than its predecessor. Apart from its extensive but less publicized scientific and cultural activities it has provided a forum for discussion and a center for negotiation. Moreover, it has succeeded in setting up an embryonic peace-keeping force which has played a significant part in preventing or restricting hostilities in the Congo, the Middle East, and Cyprus.

Yet with respect to major issues of international relations, the United Nations has been stymied by repeated use of the veto by the Soviet Union. Unhappily the antagonism between the capitalist and communist worlds revived almost immediately after their associated victory over common enemies. During the war the United States had been unstinting in its aid to Soviet Russia, and President Roosevelt had hoped that more trustful relations would result from wartime cooperation. But Stalin on his part never abandoned the conviction that the triumph of Communism required the defeat of capitalism. The Soviet government at once exploited its military position in Central and Eastern Europe to establish satellite Communist regimes throughout that area. Germany became divided into a western democratic Federal Republic and an eastern Communist People's Republic, while Berlin, under joint administration, became a bone of contention and a chronic threat to world peace. After the attempted Communist blockade of Berlin and the subversion of the Czechoslovak government in 1948, the so-called Cold War between the two great world powers and their supporters influenced or decided virtually every important international issue, either directly or indirectly. Only after a decade of flaming hostility were Stalin's successors ready to adopt a policy of "peaceful coexistence" which led to a growing relaxation of tension as a rift opened between the Soviet and Chinese Communist regimes and Russia's European satellites became more and more restless. These developments may presage fundamental changes in international alignments and relations, but for some years to come it seems likely that the ideological division will continue to jeopardize the peace of the world.

The threat of war is the more ominous because of the continued development of atomic and nuclear weapons, the destructive power of which has long since passed the bounds of human imagination. The United States and Soviet Russia are the only states with the resources to have developed and amassed a huge stockpile of these lethal instruments and to have devised methods for their almost instantaneous delivery. Nuclear power, which holds untold promise in its application to industry and communication, has put an entirely new complexion on world affairs. Militarily it constitutes a threat of destruction for the human race. Limitation and control of these fateful machines are certainly the first order of world business and call for the transcendance of the Cold War by the establishment of effective international controls. The opening of the space age, with unimaginable possibilities of further conflict, makes major advances in international cooperation imperative. Through instantaneous communication and fantastically rapid transportation, the planet has indeed been made one. Serious disturbances anywhere and even slight miscalculations could easily lead to universal catastrophe.

By the mid-twentieth century it had become impossible to consider developments in Europe except in their world context. An important aspect of this change has been the speedy liquidation of European imperialism, which for a couple of generations meant European ascendancy in the entire world. The imperial powers, after endowing colonial territories with European ideas of nationalism and self-determination, were unable after two world wars to resist the rising tide of opposition to foreign domination. Willingly or unwillingly, they were obliged to grant their colonies independence, all within a space of some twenty years.

In the broad sweep of world history European imperialism will probably appear as episodic. Yet its permanent effects were of great importance. For if, on the one hand, primitive or undeveloped peoples and their resources were at times ruthlessly exploited, on the other hand the imperial powers provided modern administration and justice. They also established internal peace and ensured external defense. Furthermore, they sank large amounts of capital into the construction of public works and the promotion of public health. In short, they opened up Africa and other areas to the world and, by their investment of money and effort, started that process of development on which the well-being of once "backward" peoples depends. Within less than a generation some fifty new independent states have appeared on the scene and, through membership in the United Nations, have become part of the community of nations. Among the many and varying problems they face is the overriding threat of overpopulation and the ensuing increase of poverty. How to establish a more equitable balance between the rapidly rising productivity of the industrialized nations and the as yet agrarian regimes of the underdeveloped countries is indeed one of the major challenges to modern statesmanship.

The current century presents, then, the dual aspect of amazing achievement, especially in the scientific and technological spheres, and of dismal failure in social relations as revealed by two cataclysmic wars, the antagonisms of the Cold War, the ruinous competition in lethal armaments, and the growing unrest in almost all countries. The present-day student finds himself very much in midstream. Looking back he can see that man has always confronted problems and that the human record is one of both achievement and failure. The study of history, while it supplies no specific key to the future, should give the student perspective and should provide the basis for sounder judgment with respect to the many and dangerous issues that confront him today.

The preceding survey is meant to be nothing more than a preview of the work that follows. It aims to identify the major factors and forces of more recent European history and to set forth their interrelationship. The conditions of life are constantly changing, but never before has change been as rapid or as drastic as over the past two centuries. Never before has mankind been faced with the need for such basic political and social adjustments. Never before have the headlong advances in learning and knowledge presented mankind with such formidable challenges.

Professor Pipes's treatment of this exciting period is comprehensive, yet provides ample detail, notably on the movement of ideas and their impact on historical development. Furthermore, his account is richly illustrated with contemporaneous pictorial material which conveys at least something of the flavor of particular times and events. The general objective of this volume is, above all, to further the student's understanding. Facts are the indispensable building materials of history and the essential facts are here provided. But facts without meaning, that is without interpretation, are soon forgotten. To make sense they must be seen in a broader context and in relation to other events. Emphasis on significance is the aim of this book, which author, editor, and publisher all hope will contribute to a better appreciation as well as to a knowledge of man's recent past.

1

Liberalism and Conservatism: 1815-1848

In 1814, after a quarter of a century of revolution and war, the statesmen of the major powers assembled in Vienna to set the terms of peace for post-Napoleonic Europe. The problems they faced were unlike those any diplomats had coped with since the destructive Thirty Years' War of the seventeenth century. The French Revolution and the conquering armies of Napoleon had internationalized European politics to the point where every problem, domestic and diplomatic alike, had to be dealt with on a Continental scale. Henceforth, no issue of internal politics could be treated within the boundaries of a single state in disregard of the opinion of other states; no conflict between two states could be confined to the parties directly involved. All the issues agitating European opinion from now on—liberalism, conservatism, nationalism, socialism—reverberated throughout the Continent. A rebellion of liberal officers in Spain immediately sparked an uprising of liberal officers in the Portuguese and Neapolitan armies, and sufficiently frightened the Russian tsar in St. Petersburg to consider sending troops to suppress it. The overthrow of the Bourbons in France in July, 1830, induced the House of Commons in England to act on a long overdue parliamentary reform bill. An uprising of Greek patriots against the Turks brought to their aid volunteers from all over Europe. Multinational Europe, divided into numerous sovereign states, was irresistibly fusing into an entity of some kind whose shape and method of functioning, however, were still most unclear.

The central issue of European politics, the controversy that between 1815 and 1848 polarized opinion in all countries into two hostile camps, was the conflict between the ideologies of liberalism and conservatism. The conflict revolved, on its most fundamental, philosophical level, around the question of man's capacity to master his environment and control his destiny.

Ideological Controversies

The roots of the liberal outlook lie in the awareness of the human self, in that individuation which constitutes perhaps the outstanding trait of Western culture. No other civilization has produced an equivalent to the autonomous Western individual: the man who thinks of himself standing face to face with God and nature, possessing the power of independent judgment, and answering ultimately only to his own conscience. Liberal ideology takes this individual as its basic fact. It believes that man has an unlimited capacity for self-development and self-improvement, provided he is free. Personal freedom is a precondition of all progress: with it, man can create on this earth near-perfect conditions. The purpose of liberalism is to remove all the shackles—political, legal, social, economic, even aesthetic—that constrain man and prevent him from giving full play to his personality. At the same time, however, liberalism is not anarchistic. It recognizes that man is a social being and that his quest for freedom, unless somewhat restrained, would impinge on the freedom of others. It devotes its main attention, therefore, to securing for the individual the maximum of liberty that is compatible with the liberty of his fellow men. In politics, it seeks to attain this aim by

Metternich's overriding concern was preserving intact and unchanged the Austro-Hungarian Empire, which he served as chief minister. "Pull one stone out of the structure and the whole will crash," he said. His portrait is by Sir Thomas Lawrence.

subjecting the state to the rule of law and the control of representative institutions and by granting the citizen civil liberties. In economics (discussed in the next chapter), it advocates free trade and manufacture (laissez faire). In art and literature (discussed in Chapter 3), it asserts the right to creativity untrammeled by classical or other norms.

The liberal faith in the individual derives from several distinct sources, including classical and religious humanism. But its principal source is science. Modern scientific endeavor, by penetrating some of the deepest mysteries of nature, accomplished two things. First, it demonstrated the astounding power of human reason, inspiring Western man with great self-confidence. Second, it revealed the existence of a natural order, rationally ordained and therefore capable of being grasped by reason. The discovery of this order also suggested that the operations of society are not arbitrary, but rest on rules and laws that can be discovered and applied to eliminate social friction. It would not be far-fetched to define liberalism as a by-product of the mechanistic concept of nature that dominated Western thought from the seventeenth to the end of the nineteenth century.

The link between liberalism and the mechanistic outlook is especially evident in the notion of "natural harmony." Common to liberal ideologies is the belief that the interests of men coincide and that if they are given the freedom to act on their own behalf, they will contribute, whether they intend to or not, to the general welfare. The liberal economist Adam Smith went so far as to assert that men are more likely to benefit society when they act from selfish motives than when they pursue what they believe to be the common good. Behind this view lay the assumption of a natural order that was prevented from functioning by artificial restraints of all kinds, such as antiquated laws or institutions.

In its practical program, liberalism concentrated on protecting the individual from arbitrary authority, whether of the absolute king or of the unruly mob. Liberal thinkers exalted the law. Their ideal was to transform men from passive subjects into active citizens, protected in their dealings with state and society by legal procedures. They saw the progress of mankind, in the formula of the English jurist Henry Maine, as a development from status to contract. The liberal model everywhere was the English constitution—not as it really was, inconsistent and vague, but as it had been systematized by eighteenth-century thinkers such as Montesquieu and Blackstone. The fact that Britain had withstood the Napoleonic challenge without sacrificing its liberties greatly enhanced the prestige of its system and of liberal causes in general.

The leading theorists of liberalism in its prime were the Germans Immanuel Kant and Wilhelm von Humboldt, the Frenchmen Benjamin Constant and Alexis de Tocqueville, and the Englishman John Stuart Mill. Their writings, translated into the principal European languages, exerted an enormous influence on both political thought and political practice. To such liberals, the state was a necessary evil whose effect was to prevent the natural harmony of interests from making itself felt. To safeguard the individual from the state, they sought, first, to reduce to a minimum the scope of state authority, and second, to subject the authority left the state to a variety of controls.

Liberalism advocated civil liberties—freedom of speech, press, and religion, for example. First formulated in the American Bill of Rights, these liberties were subsequently incorporated in all liberal constitutions. The most fundamental right was that of property, in which liberal theorists saw the surest means of protecting the individual citizen from the encroachments of the state. All these rights were considered inalienable in the sense that no citizen could be deprived of them, except in a national emergency and then only for its duration. They sharply delimited the scope of the state's authority by establishing side by side with the traditional public realm an inviolate private one on which political authority could not trespass. One of the most outspoken defenses of such a separation of the public from the private was made in 1792 by the German scholar and statesman Wilhelm von Humboldt in his essay on *The Limits of the Competence of the State*. The philosopher Kant also wrote persuasively on this subject.

The French liberal spokesman Alexis de Tocqueville, shown in 1844 after the publication of his prescient study of American democratic institutions.

The controls devised by liberal theorists to keep the government within the realm of its legitimate authority may be reduced to three: a written constitution, separation of powers, and legislatures elected by popular vote. A written constitution, one of the hallmarks of nineteenth-century liberalism, was intended to ensure that the political authority functioned not capriciously but in accord with legal norms. The separation of powers—the legislative from the executive and both from the judiciary—was believed to ensure that the government, through a system of "checks and balances," did not grow despotic. (The belief rested on a misunderstanding of the English constitution popularized by Montesquieu in 1748 in his *Spirit of Laws*.) Elected representative bodies were an institutional expression of popular sovereignty—that is, the notion that political authority derives ultimately from the people.

Early nineteenth-century liberals must not be confused with democrats. After the Napoleonic experience, which had shown that the masses could be manipulated to support despots, liberals came to distrust the common people. Benjamin Constant repeatedly warned that democracy could degenerate into despotism, as did Alexis de Tocqueville in his great book, *Democracy in America* (1835, 1840). These considerations induced liberals to oppose the universal vote, preferring to limit the franchise to the propertied classes.

Like other modern ideologies, liberalism was created by intellectuals, but it triumphed because it won the support of the bourgeoisie, the class of property and education. The manufacturer, merchant, or lawyer instinctively sympathized with pleas for individual freedom and understood its advantages. Liberal arguments suited the individualistic entrepreneur, for it promised him a voice in the government—from which he had been excluded alike by the absolutist and aristocratic systems—as well as free scope for his business activities. The European bourgeoisie backed liberal causes, and liberalism achieved its most lasting successes in countries where the middle class was strong—that is, where trade and industry were well developed.

The premises of liberalism seem so reasonable that it is difficult to understand how anyone would oppose them except from the basest self-interest or obtuseness. Yet this was not the case. The conservatives had in their ranks thinkers of great insight and integrity, whose critique of liberal premises merits serious consideration. Many of their arguments have stood well the test of time.

The conservatives took a pessimistic view of man. To them he was not the "measure of all things," but rather, in the words of Horace, "dust and shadow." A fallible, mortal creature, he could neither master nature nor alter his own destiny. All his efforts to do so were doomed. They were symptoms of his "presumptuousness" (a favorite word of conservative publicists), of that self-destructive pride the Greeks called *hubris*. The conservatives saw great danger in man's claim to question everything in the name of reason. In this as in their other views, they were profoundly influenced by the experience of the French Revolution, which began by asserting reason and freedom and ended in bloodshed and despotism.

The conservatives also rejected the liberal view of man as an isolated individual endowed with "natural" rights. For them, man existed only in society; he was born into it and functioned in it. The emphasis on the priority of the social over the individual was characteristic of all conservatism of the late eighteenth and early nineteenth centuries and represented its lasting contribution to political theory. It called attention to the fact, often forgotten by liberals, that man does not exist in the abstract but is always a product of specific historic circumstances. The view was eloquently expressed in the 1790s by Edmund Burke in his *Reflections on the Revolution in France:*

> I cannot stand forward, and give praise or blame to anything which relates to human actions and human concerns on a simple view of the object, as it stands stripped of every relation, in all the nakedness and solitude of metaphysical abstraction. Circumstances (which with some gentlemen pass for nothing) give in reality to every political principle its distinguishing color and discriminating effect. The circumstances are what render every civil and political scheme beneficial or noxious to mankind. . . . As the liberties and the restrictions [on men] vary with times and circumstances, and admit of infinite modifications, they cannot be settled upon any abstract rule; and nothing is so foolish as to discuss them upon that principle.

According to Burke, man, whether he wants to or not, undertakes obligations of all kinds and submits to laws and rules in the making of which he had no part. Concrete duties, not abstract rights, are and must be the political reality; on them rests social life without which man cannot survive. The same views were advanced by such conservatives as the Frenchmen Joseph de Maistre and Louis de Bonald, the Austro-Germans Friedrich von Gentz and Metternich, and the Russian Nicholas Karamzin.

The conservatives regarded the state not as a mechanism but as an organism; it was not something constructed but something that grew. Sound constitutions were a product of historic developments, and it was absurd to propound universal canons of good government. Each society has its own peculiar, time-hallowed constitution, which must not be tampered with. The so-called inalienable rights are a fiction. Liberty, according to Burke, is not a right of nature, but an "entailed inheritance" passed on from generation to generation, exactly as is property or the peerage. In fact there is no one Liberty, there are only discrete liberties. Their preservation depends on the preservation of the inheritance, that is, of the political and social body that binds the living of a nation to the dead in an indissoluble bond, in what Burke called a "kind of mortmain forever." By breaking this bond in the vain pursuit of absolute individual freedom, man falls into the clutches of despotism. To the Continental conservatives, liberty in any form was a chimera. As Maistre once put it, all efforts to gain liberty ended in enslavement.

Conservatives regarded the state as a great creative force. They did not share the liberal view that it was inherently an evil and that the less of it, the better. The state preserved the social order and thereby assured conditions in which man prospered. To be effective, it had to enjoy strong power. Otherwise, the various classes, religions, or ethnic groups would tear at each other and create anarchy. The conservatives preferred the monarchic system as best calculated to ensure authority. Catholic conservatives also stressed the need for a strong universal Church. To Maistre and Bonald, the Papacy was the supreme terrestrial authority.

If liberalism received its principal support from the bourgeoisie, the conservative movement was backed by the nobility, the bureaucracy, and the clergy. These groups feared that the pressures of the middle class for a greater share of political power would encourage the masses to do likewise and eventually cause a complete breakdown of the European order.

In central, eastern, and southern Europe liberalism in the first half of the nineteenth century usually developed in close association with nationalism. In these areas many people lived under governments that were not only arbitrary (that is, subject to no legal restraints) but also foreign. For the Poles, Hungarians, Italians, or Czechs, liberty was, as it were, twice removed: before authority could be subjected to constitutional and other controls, foreign domination had to be thrown off. This was not quite the case in Germany, which, strictly speaking, was self-governing after 1815. But insofar as a large part of the German nation desired a united Germany, the division of the country into numerous principalities was widely considered a violation of national rights; so here, too, nationalism accompanied liberalism.

The conservatives, on the other hand, rejected national self-determination as a fatally divisive principle that would splinter the Western world and destroy its common culture. Metternich, as head of the multinational Austrian Empire, fought it as zealously as he fought liberalism and democracy, for he perceived a close connection among the three movements. The conservatives tended to think in supranational, all-European terms. Metternich often referred to Europe as his "fatherland," and Maistre's last words were "I die with Europe.'"

The argument between liberals and conservatives acquired great relevance after the defeat of Napoleon, when the victors had to decide on a new order for liberated Europe. Not surprisingly, the conservative position was at first dominant, for it had been in great measure the philosophy of the victorious coalitions. But the forces of liberalism were strong and offered constant challenges, especially in countries with a vigorous middle class conscious of its strength and impatient with the bonds of tradition. In England, France, Belgium, and later Piedmont, this middle class supported intellectuals agitating for reforms or constitutions and by midcentury succeeded in gaining access to the sources of po-

At right is J. B. Isabey's preliminary sketch for a painting of Europe's diplomats convened at the Congress of Vienna. Metternich is seated at the right, with his arm on the table; France's Talleyrand stands at the left, in front of the empty chair. At left, a French cartoon attacks the Machiavellian twists and turns of the diplomacy practiced by Talleyrand. He holds a crosier in one hand (he was once a bishop) and a child's toy in the other.

litical power. In countries where the middle class was undeveloped, (e.g., Spain, the Balkans, Russia), the liberal intellectuals either succumbed to the combined weight of bureaucracy, landed aristocracy, and clergy, or adopted more radical socialist and communist ideologies that aspired to a total transformation of the human condition.

The Peace Settlement

The principal task of the statesmen who assembled in Vienna in September, 1814, to draft peace treaties was to prevent France from ever again breaking out of its frontiers and subjugating the Continent. The danger of renewed French aggression was considered very real. France had a record of expansion dating back to the seventeenth century and as a rich and populous state was thought likely to test its strength again. The attempt to contain France took the form of a variety of diplomatic measures: the re-establishment of a balance of power, that is, the distribution of wealth, population, and territory among the states in such a proportion that none would be powerful enough to menace the others; the formation of buffer states—kingdoms and principalities located next to the French frontier and intended to pen France in; and the creation of international institutions perpetuating the practice, introduced during the anti-Napoleonic coalitions, of consultation among the crowned heads.

Containment of France was an aim shared by all the great powers. In addition, each had its own national interests to uphold. England was anxious to keep the Continent open to its trade in order to avert a recurrence of the Continental

System. It had no territorial ambitions in Europe, but its interests required that no one power (especially Russia, whose very size was worrisome) acquire so much land as to endanger the equilibrium. Prussia and Russia had claims to land. Austria, for reasons which will be spelled out below, required the general acceptance in Europe of conservative principles. France wanted as quickly as possible to change its status from that of a defeated state to that of a full-fledged great power.

The peace settlements arrived at by the Congress of Vienna between September, 1814, and June, 1815, represented a skillful compromise of these general and specific needs. They are more admired by historians and diplomats today than they were in their own time, if only because they proved more durable than the supposedly sounder peace treaties drafted after World War I.

The first and most immediate task confronting the diplomats was to set terms for France. In dealing with this issue they showed great restraint, refusing to yield to pressures for revenge that twenty-five years of French conquest and oppression had engendered. The Second Treaty of Paris, signed in November, 1815 (the first, concluded in May, 1814, had been abrogated by Napoleon's *coup d'état* after his escape from Elba), pushed back France to the frontiers of 1790. It also imposed an indemnity and forced France to maintain an allied army of occupation on its soil until the sum was paid. In all, the terms of the treaty were quite reasonable. Talleyrand, the French Minister of Foreign Affairs, had good reason to declare that if France had ceased to be colossal, it was still great. The allies restored the Bourbon dynasty in France and required the king to issue a constitutional charter.

Much time at Vienna was devoted to the fate of the duchy of Warsaw, which Napoleon had created. The Russians were very eager to obtain the duchy as well as other Polish territories, claiming them as reward for their critical contribution to Napoleon's defeat. In this they were backed by Prussia. Both England and Austria opposed this demand, however, for it threatened to bring Russian power dangerously near the center of the Continent. Talleyrand, perceiving in this dispute a chance to improve his diplomatic status, persuaded England and Austria to join France in a secret military convention directed against Russia and Prussia (January, 1815). In the end, the Russians and Prussians had to yield to pressure and be satisfied with smaller acquisitions. The Russian tsar received the duchy on the promise to grant internal autonomy to its inhabitants. However, he had to give up his claim to other Polish lands. Prussia received territories in other parts of Germany, most importantly the rich commercial and manufacturing lands lying on the right bank of the Rhine. These acquisitions greatly enhanced Prussian power and made it a major Western European state. It was now ruler of nearly one-half of all the Germans living outside the Austrian Empire.

The frontiers of Austria also changed. Austria gave up its hereditary possessions in the Low Countries, which were formed into the kingdom of the Netherlands. The new state, embracing Dutch and Belgian provinces, was intended as a buffer against France. As compensation, Austria received holdings in the Italian peninsula: Tyrol and several provinces on the northern shore of the Adriatic (Venice, Lombardy, Illyria). In addition, several Italian principalities were placed in the hands of members of the Hapsburg house, while others were entrusted to monarchs with close personal ties to Vienna. As a result of these arrangements, Austria became the dominant power on the Italian peninsula. Only Piedmont-Sardinia escaped Austrian domination, partly because the great powers wanted yet another independent buffer against France, and partly because they did not wish Austria to enjoy a monopoly on Italy. In time, Piedmont-Sardinia became the center of opposition to Austria, and its rulers led the struggle for Italian independence.

Austrian and Prussian gains at Vienna were in large measure due to Britain's desire to develop them into effective counterweights to France and Russia. Yet the broader "German problem"—the desire of many Germans for unification and national statehood—remained unsatisfied despite these gains. The Congress of Vienna created a Germanic Confederation (*Deutscher Bund*) that embraced all the German-speaking territories, including Prussia and parts of Austria. This Confederation, however, was a paper state. Its unifying organ, a Diet that sat in Frankfort under Austrian chairmanship, had no authority. It was merely an assembly of representatives of the thirty-nine constituent kingdoms and principalities, whose rulers retained full sovereignty over their lands. The only importance of the Confederation was psychological, for by its very existence it kept alive the ideal of a united Germany.

The Congress of Vienna fixed the general outlines of the map of Europe for the next ninety-nine years. The durability of its provisions alone suggests that they were not wholly unsound. Their most glaring weakness was the failure to take into account the democratic and nationalist sentiments that had emerged with such vigor in the preceding quarter-century. The time was past when people and lands could be traded off among major powers like so much real estate, and the Vienna treaties would have had wider acceptance had they taken this fact into account.

The so-called Act of Vienna and the Second Treaty of Paris settled the immediate political problems arising from the defeat of Napoleon and the collapse of his empire. But after twenty-five years of war, there was a widespread feeling that a mere redrawing of the map of Europe was not enough. To keep peace and order, the Vienna settlement required a more permanent basis—nothing less than a regular supervision of the Continent by the great powers, a "Concert of Europe." This conviction resulted in the formulation of important new principles regulating international relations. These principles were embodied in the Quadruple and Holy alliances.

The initiative for both these alliances came from Tsar Alexander, who as early as 1804 had urged the heads of states to subscribe to a code of international ethics. In January, 1814, as Russian troops entered France, he renewed his proposal, calling for a "general alliance to guarantee ourselves and save [ourselves] from the ambition of a conqueror." It so happened that British Foreign Secretary Viscount Castlereagh was thinking along similar lines, although for more pragmatic reasons. Whereas Alexander envisaged a permanent code of international ethics and an alliance to guarantee the *status quo*, Castlereagh thought of keeping alive the coalition that had defeated Napoleon as another safeguard against the renewal of French aggression. At the urging of Alexander and Castlereagh, the four allies signed in Vienna the Quadruple Alliance, which committed them to enforce the Second Treaty of Paris. The Alliance was a diplomatic innovation in that it represented a standing commitment of the great powers to cooperate in time of peace. One of its provisions introduced the novel principle of regular peace-time conferences. Drafted by Alexander and revised by Castlereagh, it read:

> To facilitate and secure the execution of the present Treaty [i.e., the Second Treaty of Paris], and to consolidate the connections which at the present so closely unite the Four Sovereigns for the happiness of the world, the High Contracting Parties have agreed to renew their meetings at fixed periods, either under the immediate auspices of the Sovereigns themselves, or by their respective Ministers, for the purpose of consulting upon their common interests, and for the consideration of the measures which at each of these periods shall be considered the most salutary for the repose and prosperity of Nations, and for the maintenance of the Peace of Europe.

This clause was responsible for several international congresses or conferences held between 1818 and 1822, but it also had long-range implications. It foreshadowed the institutions fully developed in the twentieth century to maintain general peace, not just on an emergency basis, but as a day-by-day concern of the great powers.

Alexander proposed to go even beyond the Quadruple Alliance and to obtain from the heads of state a commitment to abide by Christian principles in domestic as well as international dealings. This wish found expression in the declaration of the Holy Alliance, initially signed by Russia, Prussia, and Austria (September, 1815) and then by all the European powers save Britain, which pleaded constitutional obstacles; the Papacy, for whom it was deemed redundant; and the sultan, who, being a Muslim, was not invited. The Holy Alliance, which Metternich, even though he signed it, dismissed as "loud-sounding nothing," and which the annoyed Castlereagh called "a piece of sublime mysticism and nonsense," pledged the signatories

> both in the administration of their respective States, and in their political relations with every other Government, to take for their sole guide the precepts of [the] Holy Religion, namely the precepts of Justice, Christian Charity and Peace, which, far from being applicable only to private concerns, must have an immediate influence on the council of princes.

This declaration spelled out, in the language of the time, principles of international behavior that in our century found expression in the Atlantic Charter (1941) and the Charter of the United Nations (1945).

Alexander also took the initiative in proposing international disarmament. Although without practical consequences, the suggestion merits attention as the first of its kind to come from a sovereign ruler.

The arrangements made at the Congress of Vienna were conservative but not reactionary in spirit. They were intended to restore peace and order, and so required at least some concessions to the liberal forces released by the French Revolution. As evidence of this, we can point to the fact that in a number of states— e.g., with regard to the duchy of Warsaw, some German principalities, and, above all, France—the peace settlement required the sovereigns to grant their subjects constitutional charters. Nevertheless, within a few years after the peace treaties had been concluded the sentiment of its framers swung violently to the right. The liberal concessions were emasculated, and repression carried the day.

This transformation was largely the personal achievement of Prince Metternich. As Austrian Minister of Foreign Affairs without interruption for almost forty years (1809–1848), Metternich so thoroughly dominated the Continent, especially Central Europe, that the entire post-Napoleonic period has sometimes been named after him. A native of the Rhineland, Metternich rose rapidly in the Austrian service thanks to his diplomatic skills, his loyalty to the House of Hapsburg, and his personal charm. Metternich fully subscribed to conservative ideas, including the primacy of society over the individual, the necessity of firm political authority and rigid social distinctions, and cooperation between the crowned heads of Europe. As Austrian ambassador to Paris under Napoleon, he had come to admire the repressive side of Napoleon's politics, such as police and censorship, which he emulated in Austria and other areas under his influence.

Metternich's success lay in his ability to convince many of the European sovereigns that what benefited Austria also benefited them and Europe as a whole. The Austrian Empire was the only major country in Europe that had emerged from the Napoleonic wars untouched by either revolution or reform. Its government remained a classical eighteenth-century absolutist monarchy, only less enlightened. Authority rested with the German-speaking nobility, from which the monarchy drew its high officials of the administration and church and its army officers. This nobility, in turn, depended on the personal labor or rents of the peasants working their estates. No effort was made to modernize the administration or to allow the citizenry to participate in some kind of partnership with the crown, as had been done in Prussia and in some other European countries. Liberalization spelled loss of privilege to the all-powerful bureaucracy, nobility, and clergy, and for that reason they strenuously resisted it. Furthermore, Austria was a multinational empire in which the dominant ethnic group, the Germans, constituted a minority. Concessions to nationalism within the empire would seriously have weakened the authority of these Germans. Outside it—in Italy and Germany—nationalist principles implied unification and thus the weakening of Austria's influence. The interests of Austria required the triumph of conservative principles. On them depended its survival as a great power.

But all around Austria and even in Austria itself blew the winds of change. To stifle them, Metternich conjured up the spectacle of a vast international conspiracy aimed at overthrowing the existing social and political order. Every unmasked plot, every assassination, every rebellion in Europe drove frightened kings and princes into his arms. Part of his political technique was to deny any distinction between moderate liberalism, aiming at constitutional reform, and

A contemporary engraving depicts the assassination of the German poet August von Kotzebue in 1819. Kotzebue was serving as an agent for Russia.

radicalism, whose goal was political and social democracy. "The husk of liberalism is appearance," he once wrote, "the truth is radicalism; inside the husk lies the reality." The effect of this attitude was on the one hand to magnify the extent of sedition, and on the other, by forcing moderates into more radical positions, to encourage it.

The liberal movement of the restoration era had two principal centers, the army and the universities. In the latter stages of the war against Napoleon, the allies had greatly increased their armed forces. The young officers in Germany, Russia, Spain, and Italy, who had enlisted in 1813–1815 to fight for freedom and national ideals, loathed the conservative system. The universities were even more important as centers of liberal resistance. The beginning of the nineteenth century witnessed a great expansion of institutions of higher learning, especially in Germany. The University of Berlin, founded in 1809 under Alexander von Humboldt (the scientist brother of the liberal theorist Wilhelm), provided a model for modern universities. Open to all comers, it assured to professors and students alike complete freedom of inquiry. Around Berlin and other universities of the new type gathered thousands of young men from various walks of life, their heads filled with political ideas and their hearts eager for action. Some liberal-minded officers and students formed associations to fight the old order. Among the best known of these were the *carbonari*, secret organizations operating in southern Italy against the Austrians. The German student fraternities, known as *Burschenschaften*, although in theory neither secret nor political, in practice often became centers of resistance.

The years 1819–1820 witnessed throughout Europe and in some of the overseas possessions an outburst of liberal and nationalist violence. In 1819 a German student belonging to an extremist republican organization assassinated the reactionary poet August von Kotzebue. The next year another assassin killed the Duc de Berry, the son of the heir to the French throne, the future Charles X. That same year a rebellion of officers broke out in Spain, the rebels forcing King Ferdinand VII to swear allegiance to a new liberal constitution. The

Spanish revolt had immediate repercussions in Portugal and Naples, where liberal-minded officers also overthrew absolutist monarchies and replaced them with constitutional regimes patterned on the Spanish. In response to the Iberian uprisings, several Latin American colonies of Spain and Portugal rose in arms and proclaimed their independence (Mexico, Colombia, Peru, and Brazil, 1821–1822). Finally, in 1822, the Greeks took up arms against the Ottoman Empire.

The closeness with which these liberal and nationalistic rebellions followed one another convinced many conservatives that Europe stood on the verge of another major revolution. Metternich reacted quickly and decisively. After the murder of Kotzebue, he persuaded several German princes, among them King Frederick William III of Prussia, to endorse the so-called Carlsbad Decrees (September, 1819). These ordinances placed German and Austrian universities under the tutelage of curators, dissolved the *Burschenschaften*, severely limited the freedom of the press, and established a commission to look into treasonable activities in the Germanic Confederation. The decrees caused deep dissatisfaction among liberals, but at the same time greatly enhanced Metternich's personal hold on the German governments.

Metternich at first hesitated to intervene similarly elsewhere, for he was afraid of initiating action that could bring Russian troops into Western Europe. For this reason, he rejected Alexander's offer of armies to help suppress the Spanish rebellion. But when the Spanish rebellion spread to Naples and so threatened Austria's hold on Italy, he had to act. Metternich had the brilliant idea of using the system of regular allied conferences, provided for in the Quadruple Alliance, to obtain international sanction for his intervention in Italy. At his urging, the congress of the Alliance, which convened at Troppau and then transferred to Laibach (1820–1821), approved the novel principle of intervention to suppress subversive movements throughout Europe. The key phrases of the Troppau Protocol read:

> States which have undergone a change of Government due to revolution, the results of which threaten other states, *ipso facto* cease to be members of the European Alliance, and remain excluded from it until their situation gives guarantees for legal order and stability. If, owing to such alteration, immediate danger threatens other states, the Powers bind themselves, by peaceful means, or if need be by arms, to bring back the guilty state into the bosom of the Great Alliance.

Castlereagh, who shared Metternich's loathing of revolutions, was taken aback by this interpretation of the congress system of which he had been a principal architect. He had intended the system simply to assure the Continental balance of power. Castlereagh refused to sign the Troppau Protocol on the grounds that it arrogated on behalf of the diplomatic congresses the sovereignty of independent states—a step which he considered both impractical and dangerous. Behind Castlereagh's argument lay some very pragmatic considerations. Britain at this time was in the midst of its great economic expansion, the so-called Industrial Revolution. The products of this expanding industrial economy required markets, and these were easier to obtain when England dealt with independent states and their businessmen rather than with the bureaucracy or

Simón Bolívar, known as the Liberator of South America, was painted in 1823 by Peruvian artist José Gil de Castro.

nobility of large and self-sufficient empires. The national interest of Great Britain thus impelled it to support liberal and nationalist causes much as the national interest of Austria induced that government to fight them.

Britain's refusal to endorse the Troppau Protocol marked the first fissure in the Concert of Europe created at Vienna. The gulf deepened in 1822 when George Canning succeeded Castlereagh as Foreign Secretary. Canning came out openly in favor of national self-determination and promised Britain's help to nations struggling against oppression. He not only refused to join in deliberations, initiated by Metternich, to restore Spanish and Portuguese authority in South America, but proposed to the United States a joint declaration pledging the two countries to keep European powers out of that continent. At Canning's suggestion, President James Monroe formulated his celebrated doctrine in 1823.

In the meantime, Metternich, undeterred by Britain's refusal, initiated with Russian and Prussian support armed intervention in Italy. In March of 1821 Austrian troops crossed the Po River and marched south. They easily dispersed the military forces that the rebel Neapolitan government had sent against them, occupied Naples, and restored the local Bourbon dynasty. The restoration was followed by a massacre in which several thousand persons lost their lives. The Austrians also helped suppress a liberal rebellion in Piedmont. Spain's turn came next. At the Congress of Verona (1822), the allies agreed to intervene in Spain on behalf of absolutism. With their authorization, French armies invaded Spain in the spring of 1823 and once more restored to the throne the ferocious Ferdinand VII. Here too the liberals were slaughtered en masse by the infuriated royalists. Faithful to its principle of suppressing revolutionary movements, the Alliance stood by while the Turks massacred the Greek rebels.

The congresses of Troppau, Laibach, and Verona marked the apogee of Metternich's influence. Having at his disposal, through the machinery of the Alliance, the combined power of Austria, Prussia, France, and Russia, he was in a position to dominate the politics of the Continent. To deal with sedition, real and imaginary, Metternich developed an efficient system of police espionage and censorship that many other rulers copied. A deep gloom descended on Europe.

Metternich was undisturbed by his reputation among liberals, being supremely confident of his rectitude. "I cannot help telling myself twenty times a day," he wrote in 1819, "dear Lord, how very right am I and how very wrong are the others." On another occasion he remarked: "For some years now I have made the singular observation. It is that men who are diametrically opposed to me die. The explanation is quite simple: these men are mad, and the mad die."

The Metternichian system found its purest fulfillment in Russia. Alexander I was too deeply imbued with the ideals of the Enlightenment to embrace Metternich's politics wholeheartedly, but this was not the case with his brother, Nicholas I, who succeeded him in 1825. During the brief interregnum that followed Alexander's death in December of that year, a group of Russian officers staged a mutiny in St. Petersburg and the Ukraine. The uprising had been in preparation for several years. Its leaders were mostly army officers of aristocratic background, some favoring constitutional monarchy, some of republican orientation. In all its principal features, this so-called Decembrist uprising was modeled on similar rebellions in Spain, Italy, and other parts of Europe. But its failure was even more dismal. Energetic military countermeasures by Nicholas squashed the rebellion on the day of its outbreak. This event had a lasting effect in that it strengthened Nicholas' inborn authoritarianism. From the moment of his accession he devoted himself with a single-minded dedication to the cause of absolutism both at home and abroad. Like Western conservatives, he believed that the salvation of mankind rested on the maintenance of order, authority, and a sense of duty. He established in Russia a police state even more repressive than Metternich's, on which it was modeled. It drove into desperation educated society, especially student youth, among whom Nicholas persecuted relentlessly any sign of independence.

In the third decade of the nineteenth century the cause of liberalism on the Continent seemed destined to frustration and failure. But this was only an appearance. The power of the conservative cause rested with the rulers of the three great agrarian monarchies of Eastern Europe, Austria, Russia, and Prussia. With the spread of industry and trade, however, wealth and power passed inexorably to the industrial and commercial nations led by England. And these nations moved toward liberalism.

During the years 1815–1820, the rulers of Great Britain shared the conservative outlook of contemporary Continental statesmen and participated in the Concert of Europe. For them the threat came not from liberalism, since Britain had long realized the basic aims of the liberal movement, but from social unrest. At the end of the eighteenth century, Britain had entered the first phases of its intense industrialization, a process that had created large masses of workers whose livelihood depended on the vagaries of the national and international economy. The Napoleonic wars had stimulated its productivity, but this stimulus ended abruptly with the restoration of peace. The cancellation of defense orders and the simultaneous flooding of the labor market by some 400,000 discharged soldiers and sailors caused considerable unemployment. The industrial crisis was aggravated by an agrarian one. Wheat prices, which had risen steeply during the war, now fell, forcing landlords to abandon much arable land that was no longer profitable to cultivate. These factors caused social unrest in the towns and countryside that at times threatened to explode into revolution.

The British government reacted to this threat with repressive measures. In 1817 it suspended—for the third time in British history—the Habeas Corpus Act, and in 1819 it enacted a series of repressive measures known as the Six Acts which curtailed public assemblies and gave crown officials extraordinary authority to deal with sedition. Sometimes the repression of dissent took violent forms. In August, 1819, a large crowd, gathered at St. Peter's Fields in Manchester to hear speeches in favor of reform, was charged by soldiers. Several participants were killed and hundreds of others injured. This incident was popularly dubbed the "Peterloo Massacre."

In the 1820s, however, the atmosphere in England underwent marked change. For one thing, the economic situation improved, at least in industry. The spread of technical innovations (e.g., steam power and textile machinery) lowered drastically the price of British manufactured goods and permitted them to penetrate Continental and overseas markets. Secondly, the leadership of the dominant

British troops charge a gathering of reform-minded workers in the so-called Peterloo Massacre. The banners call for universal suffrage and for civil and religious liberty.

Tory party passed in 1822 to a new breed of men, some of them of middle-class background, more pragmatic in their outlook and more conciliatory in their spirit than their predecessors. Among them may be singled out George Canning, first Foreign Secretary and then Prime Minister (1827), raised in a banking family; Robert Peel, the Tory leader in 1834–1846, the son of a self-made man; and William Huskisson, president of the Board of Trade (1823–1827). These statesmen were in varying degrees influenced by the ideology of English radicalism, whose leading spirit was Jeremy Bentham.

The term *radicalism* as used in England in the early nineteenth century had little in common with Continental radicalism. On the Continent this word implied political democracy and social equality. English radicalism, on the other hand, was a kind of liberalism, suited to English conditions and temperament. As a young law student in the 1770s, Bentham concluded that the political and legal institutions of his country were a hopeless muddle, bearing little if any relationship to the actual needs of its inhabitants. He had for the English constitution none of the admiration of Blackstone or Burke. Tradition in itself meant nothing to him, but—and in this respect he differed from Continental liberals—neither did abstract rights or liberties. To him, the basic fact was the concrete individual, that is, the individual constantly engaged in pursuit of personal self-interest. Man seeks the greatest amount of pleasure and the least amount of pain, and everything apart from the pain-pleasure calculation—traditions, rights, liberties, and so forth—is meaningless. Those laws and institutions are best that secure the greatest amount of pleasure or happiness to the greatest number of living people. This is the test of "utility." Laws and institutions are justified only insofar as they can meet this test. If they fail to meet it, they must be changed or abandoned. In his numerous writings, Bentham subjected British political and legal institutions to a critique from the "utilitarian" point of view, showing that, whatever might have been their original justification, they no longer satisfied the needs of the majority of contemporary Britons.

Bentham's ideas had little influence on British public opinion during the French Revolution and the era of Napoleon when few were willing to tamper with a system that had proved itself so resilient. But gradually a small band of Benthamites or Utilitarians gathered around the lonely thinker. In 1824 this group put out the *Westminster Review*, in the pages of which they subjected the British constitution and judiciary system to a relentless critique. It was in no small measure due to their efforts that Britain in the 1820s began cautiously to reform its laws. In 1824–1825 the House of Commons repealed the so-called Combination Acts, which had outlawed the formation of labor associations for collective bargaining. In 1828–1829 it also repealed the Test and Corporation Acts and by so doing opened public offices to dissenters and Catholics. All through the decade, the penal system was humanized and the number of crimes carrying capital punishment reduced.

These reforms paved the way for the most important English legislative act of the first half of the century, the Reform Bill of 1832. The electoral system in force in Britain in 1830 was for all practical purposes the same as it had been in the seventeenth century. In other words, it did not make any allowance for the great shifts of population—from the southeast to the northwest and from the villages to the cities—that had occurred along with the industrialization of the country. In many instances, towns that had had large populations in the seventeenth century but had since become mere villages retained the right to send representatives to the House of Commons, whereas cities like Manchester or Birmingham with more than 100,000 inhabitants were unrepresented. This electoral system enabled wealthy politicians to purchase a following in the House of Commons by buying up so-called pocket or rotten boroughs which enjoyed a traditional right to parliamentary representation. Like any system from which men derive advantages, this inequitable arrangement had its defenders. They argued that it had stood the test of time, that it gave a chance to impoverished candidates, through patronage, to gain access to the House of Commons, and that it assured a fair representation to the many distinct groups of the population. Any more rational system of franchise, they claimed, would divide the nation along property lines into two distinct classes, those who had the vote, and those who did not. But the Utilitarians attacked this arrangement as absurd and in time secured the backing of the manufacturing interests, eager to have a voice in the making of laws.

The need for parliamentary reform became urgent in 1830, following the outbreak of the July Revolution in Paris. The Whigs, who at this time formed the cabinet, decided to press for such reform partly to forestall a revolution in England, partly to gain the votes of the newly enfranchised middle-class voters. After long wrangling, Parliament finally passed a comprehensive measure. The Reform Bill of 1832 achieved both a redistribution and an equalization of the franchise. First, it eliminated boroughs with less than 2,000 inhabitants and halved the representation of boroughs with a population between 2,000 and

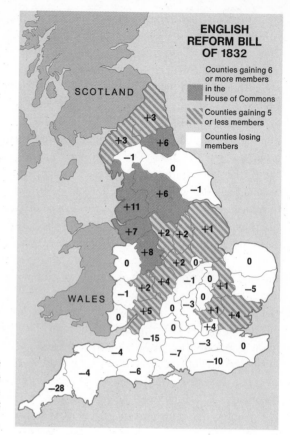

**ENGLISH
REFORM BILL
OF 1832**

Counties gaining 6
or more members
in the
House of Commons

Counties gaining 5
or less members

Counties losing
members

SCOTLAND

WALES

*The most obvious beneficiaries
of parliamentary reform were
the urban, industrialized Midlands and the north; the chief
losers were southern counties.*

4,000. The 168 seats thus gained were assigned to heavily populated areas, particularly the industrial cities. Second, it established uniform franchise in the boroughs and counties, giving the vote to all men who owned or leased a house with an annual rental value of at least £10 and setting precise voting qualifications for rural inhabitants.

The first and most obvious consequence of the act was to enlarge the electorate from 500,000 to 700,000—a figure that by 1866 increased to 1,100,000, thanks to the growth of the population. The increase in the number of voters, however, does not tell the whole story. The elimination of rotten and pocket boroughs and the election of representatives from the new urban centers began the transformation of the Commons from a private club into the national forum it became in the second half of the century. Landed gentry continued as before to dominate it, and rich peers still could manipulate votes, but the reformed House of Commons was broader in its composition and therefore in closer touch with the life of the country.

This triumph of the middle class had its effect on the working population of England, which was to a surprising degree inculcated with the liberal spirit and with liberal ideas. It too wanted a voice in the making of laws and in the 1830s pressed for them with great vigor. The movement for the universal vote, known as "Chartism," was the first significant political effort on the part of the industrial working class anywhere.

The Chartist movement derives its name from the six-point Charter drawn up in 1836 by the London cabinetmaker William Lovett. It called for universal male suffrage, the establishment of equal electoral districts (that is, districts with the same number of inhabitants), abolition of property qualifications for parliamentary candidates, annual Parliaments, the payment of members of Parliament, and the secret ballot. The Charter was widely disseminated, especially among workers and miners in the north. The Chartists held mass rallies, occasionally after dark when they appeared carrying torches and even weapons. The movement was from its beginning torn by quarrels between proponents of peaceful means and proponents of militant means, or, as it was then called, "moral force" and "physical force." The former were led by Lovett, the latter by a demagogic Irish landlord named Feargus O'Connor.

Chartism was formally launched in Birmingham in August, 1838. The following February its adherents held a convention in London, at which they drafted a petition embodying the Charter's six points. This petition, bearing 1,300,000 signatures, they presented to Parliament. In the event Parliament rejected it, the Chartists threatened to call a nationwide general strike.

The government watched these proceedings anxiously and mustered a large force to deal with anticipated violence. But none occurred. The vast majority of the Chartists followed Lovett, and when Parliament in fact did reject their petition (July, 1839), they did nothing whatever. A small local rebellion by a few of O'Connor's followers ended in a fiasco. In the 1840s Chartism, though still alive and menacing, lost some of its impetus, no doubt because the immense prosperity that England now enjoyed temporarily diverted the attention of the workers from parliamentary reform to trade unionism.

Britain's shift toward a more liberal position in the 1820s and early 1830s was accompanied by a similar movement in some parts of Continental Europe, most notably France.

The Bourbons, whom the allies restored to authority in the person of Louis XVIII, did not intend to undo the achievements of the Revolution. The new king, a younger brother of the executed Louis XVI, had concluded in the course of his prolonged wanderings in Europe that monarchical absolutism was a thing of the past. After his return to France, he made a sincere effort to adjust to constitutionalism.

The Decline of the French Monarchy

Louis XVIII ruled by virtue of a constitutional charter hastily drawn up in 1814. The framers of the constitution assumed sovereignty to have come from God and to rest in the king, who "granted" the charter to the nation. The king, vested with extensive powers, was to rule with the assistance of a House of Peers, which he appointed, and a Chamber of Deputies, which was elected by approximately 100,000 voters out of a total population of 29 million. The administration created by Napoleon in 1800 was left intact.

The most important characteristic of the restoration monarchy was the fact that it made no attempt to undo the social achievements of the Revolution. The land taken from the nobles and clergy remained in the hands of its post-1789 proprietors. No citizen could be punished for participating in the revolutionary or Napoleonic governments. The equality of Frenchmen was guaranteed, as

The July Revolution of 1830, as seen by an unknown Parisian artist. The locale is the Pont-Neuf (foreground). At the center a revolutionary scales the statue of Henry IV. In the right background is the Louvre.

were their basic liberties. In short, the middle class and the peasantry retained both the properties and the rights they had acquired after the overthrow of the *ancien régime.*

The political system established in 1814 ran into immediate difficulties, mainly because a large body of French opinion refused to accept its basic premises. The liberals wished to widen the competence of the Chamber of Deputies to the point where, like the British House of Commons, it became the focus of legislative and executive power. The extreme conservatives, on the other hand, wanted to do away with the charter and the parliamentary institutions and re-establish the absolute monarchy. They also desired the restoration to their original owners of the lands that had been confiscated during the Revolution. These conservative elements were dubbed Royalists, Ultraroyalists, or simply Ultras.

The Ultras began to gain ascendancy over Louis XVIII in about 1820. The king, discouraged by the conflicts of political groupings, gradually ceded much authority to the Comte d'Artois, the leader of the Ultras and heir to the throne. It was the Ultras who persuaded Louis to send troops to crush the Spanish revolution in 1823.

The chance of the Ultras came in 1824 with the death of Louis and the accession of the Comte d'Artois as Charles X. From the beginning of his reign, Charles made no secret of his intention to re-establish royal absolutism and the authority of the Church. Even his coronation at the cathedral of Reims was carried out with pomp intended to recall the *ancien régime.* Such acts produced dissatisfaction, especially in Paris. Discontent reached its peak in the summer of 1830 when Charles entrusted the government to Prince de Polignac, the most "ultra" of the Ultras. Polignac, in the so-called Ordinances of July 25, suspended the freedom of the press, appointed several prominent Ultras to high office, and reduced the number of Frenchmen eligible to vote from 100,000 to 25,000.

Two days after these ordinances had been issued, Paris was in rebellion.

Common laborers joined with artisans, students, journalists, artists, shopkeepers, and Napoleonic veterans to fight the detested regime. The royal troops proved unable to suppress the rebels in street fighting in the old quarters of Paris, and Charles abdicated. The republican wing of the rebel forces now wished to abolish the monarchy, but the moderates prevailed, and the crown was entrusted to Louis Philippe, the Duke of Orleans.

Louis Philippe was a very different man from either of his predecessors, both of whom had been products of the *ancien régime*. He had sided with the Revolution and fought in its ranks at Valmy. Afterwards, he had spent several years in the United States, where he had come to know and admire its constitutional system.

The July Revolution led to significant changes in the charter. Louis Philippe became the "King of the French by the Grace of God and the Will of the People," not merely "by the Grace of God," as his two predecessors had been. The constitution, therefore, was no longer a "granted" one. The king lost the monopoly on legislative initiative and the right to nominate and retain ministers; henceforth, a ministry that did not enjoy confidence of the Chamber of Deputies had to resign. Censorship was abolished, and France acquired the freest press in Europe.

The monarchy of Louis Philippe made a conscious effort to rest its power on the upper-middle class. François Guizot, a historian who formulated its political philosophy and served it for many years as a leader, believed the bourgeoisie to be singularly well suited to bear the responsibilities of governing. He defined it as a class combining the leisure of the aristocracy with the industriousness of the common people. The monarchy did all it could to promote the interest of the bourgeoisie and to win its sympathy. The electoral law, though broadened over what it had been, was still narrowly construed, and only 240,000 Frenchmen had the right to vote. The government also established a National Guard, membership in which was restricted to citizens who paid direct taxes and purchased their own uniforms. Both these stipulations limited the Guardsmen ("grocer

Charles Philipon took deadly aim at the jowly Louis Philippe in one of Paris' satirical journals in 1832.

janissaries," as their opponents called them) to the middle class. With characteristic venom but with some justice, Marx defined the regime of Louis Philippe as a "company for the exploitation of French national wealth," of which the king was director and whose dividends were distributed among the ministers, deputies, and 240,000 voters.

Neither his good will and respect for the constitution, nor the freedom which he granted the subjects, nor the great prosperity that France enjoyed under his rule made Louis Philippe popular. France was (and still is) a country of small owners, of several million *propriétaires* of land, workshops (*ateliers*), and stores. These petty bourgeois did not like to be lorded over by the big bourgeoisie and demanded equal rights. Furthermore, the nation as a whole disliked Louis Philippe's efforts to ingratiate himself with the moneyed class by assuming the stance of a "citizen king," mixing with the crowds and displaying good fellowship on all occasions. Nor did it approve of his pacifist foreign policy, which reduced France's influence in the world. Repeated efforts were made to assassinate him, causing the unfortunate man once to remark that on him alone there was no closed hunting season.

By skillful maneuvering, Louis Philippe and his ministers usually managed to secure a working majority in the Chamber of Deputies, but they remained oblivious that a parliament elected by so small a proportion of the country did not reflect public opinion. They made a major mistake in not availing themselves of the support of the conservative peasant-proprietors, so effectively exploited by Napoleon I and by Louis Philippe's successor, Napoleon III. French liberalism had so deep a fear of the masses that it forfeited national leadership to become a narrow class ideology.

This miscalculation provided a fertile soil for various radical movements, which, after July, 1830, made their international headquarters in Paris. Here gathered from all over Europe intellectuals disenchanted with liberalism and the whole social order and aspiring to a fundamental transformation of mankind—patriotic mystics from Poland, German idealists, Italian nationalists, Russian anarchists. The 1830s and 1840s saw the emergence in Paris of modern socialist theory and the development of a break between liberalism on the one hand and democracy and socialism on the other. The ideology of socialism is discussed in Chapter 8; suffice here to call attention to the fact that the modern radical movement emerged at a time and in a place where the bourgeoisie was more firmly in control than it had ever been, before or since.

The triumph of liberalism in Britain and France in the early 1830s destroyed the Concert of Europe. Unity gave way to duality. There were now two contending blocs: a liberal one, led by Britain and France, and a conservative one, consisting of Austria, Russia, and Prussia. The liberal bloc by no means assumed a passive role. It borrowed from its rival the technique of international intervention. As early as 1827 Canning dispatched a British expeditionary force to Portugal to help local liberals in their conflict with the king. After 1830 the British, acting either alone or with the French, intervened repeatedly in various areas on behalf of constitutional causes. *The West Against the East*

The July Revolution produced immediate repercussions throughout Europe, encouraging liberals to fight for constitutions and, in areas under foreign domination, for national self-determination. Their success depended partly on the ability of Britain and France to extend them help and partly on the skill with which absolute monarchs defended their absolutist prerogatives. In August of 1830 a revolt broke out within the southern provinces of the Netherlands. The rebels ejected Dutch forces and proclaimed the independence of Belgium. The Belgian state received the most liberal constitution in Europe, providing for the popular election of both the lower and upper houses of parliament and a king required to act entirely through ministers responsible to the legislature. This constitution, together with that of the United States, served as a model for liberals everywhere during the subsequent revolutionary upheavals of 1848. Liberals also achieved partial successes in the Iberian peninsula. With the help of British and French armies, they overcame absolutist opposition and introduced a semi-constitutional system of government. Denmark and some Swiss cantons also granted constitutions to their citizens at this time.

Elsewhere, the prevailing type of government until 1848 remained that favored by Metternich: absolute monarchy, usually operating through a bureaucracy and police and in partnership with the landed nobility and the clergy. A Polish revolt against Russia in November, 1830, was militarily suppressed with the aid of the Prussian and Austrian troops. The conservative eastern powers stamped out revolts that broke out in the early 1830s in a number of German and Italian principalities. In Sweden and the Netherlands, absolutist rulers, for the time being, also managed to neutralize constitutionalist opposition.

2

The Beginnings of Industrialization

While the French Revolution was shaking the political and social foundations of Europe, a development of equal and perhaps even greater long-term significance for humanity was occurring in Britain. Its consequences were so startling that as early as the 1820s some French publicists were calling it the "Industrial Revolution." The term caught on and entered the general vocabulary after the appearance in 1884 of a book by that title. Although the term is useful in conveying the dramatic effects of industrialization, it is also misleading; from the perspective of our time, the advent of industrialism resembles less a single revolutionary event than a continuous process.

As long as intense industrialization was largely confined to Great Britain—that is, until approximately the middle of the nineteenth century—it was reasonable to treat it as an event localized in time and space. But industrial methods soon began to spread to other countries. Unlike revolutions in the proper sense of the word, the so-called Industrial Revolution had neither a beginning nor a conclusion. On the contrary, industrial methods of production have been gathering momentum since they were first developed. Rather than speak of a "First," "Second," and "Third" Industrial Revolution, some historians in recent times have preferred to use more general terms such as "industrialism," "economic development," or "economic modernization."

The transition from an agricultural to an industrial economy that began in England in the eighteenth century represents one of the most fateful steps in the entire evolution of human society. Obviously, a brief analysis can do no more than call attention to some of its salient features. The adjective *industrial* evokes first and foremost a picture of machines and factories. In one sense, this picture is justifiable, because machines and factories are indeed prominent features of an industrial economy. But they do not constitute its essence. Machinery, including some contraptions that we like to think of as modern, has been known for many centuries. In the late seventeenth century, for example, steam power was experimented with to pump water, propel ships, and even to pressure-cook. Factories, too, are old. Textile and tapestry factories employing hundreds and even thousands of workers were in operation in seventeenth-century France and probably elsewhere in Europe as well. Yet neither early mechanical inventions nor early factories altered in any significant manner the quality of economic life. They were extensions of the human arm, not substitutes for it.

Machines and factories moved from the fringe to the center of economic life only when the pace of economic life quickened to the point where the traditional methods of production no longer satisfied the demand—in other words, when the market for goods outgrew the existing productive capacity. The most fundamental feature of industrialism is the replacement of an economy producing either for immediate consumption or for a local market by an economy producing for a national or world-wide market. This immense broadening of outlets

Steam power's first triumph was in the coal industry. This view of a British mine, by an unknown artist, dates from the 1790s. The Newcomen engine at center hoisted coal from the shafts at far left and right. A cartload of coal is weighed at the right.

for goods that characterizes modern economic life encourages the organization of productivity on an efficient basis and brings about the introduction of machines, new sources of motive power, improved means of transportation, and all the other features of the industrial system as we know it. In short, it is not machines that cause industrial productivity, but the need for intensified productivity that induces the employment of machinery.

Historically, the first reason for the extension of markets was trade. The great maritime discoveries of the fifteenth and sixteenth centuries created unprecedented commercial opportunities for the European states bordering on the Atlantic. The early trade with the West Indies, North America, Southeast Asia, and India enabled Western Europe to accumulate much wealth and at the same time stimulated productivity. Much the same was the effect of the emergence of the national state. The abolition of such restraints on trade as internal tariffs and tolls, accomplished first in England, then in France, and finally in the remainder of Europe, opened up large national markets and also led to improvements in the methods of producing goods. There are at least two other factors responsible for the widening of the market: the increase of population, and defense orders. But these became decisive only later. Early industrialization (from about 1750 to about 1850) occurred against the background of intense national and international trade developed in the preceding three centuries.

The trading opportunities presented by the new markets raised an acute problem of costs; the expanded markets were open to many producers, and, all other things being equal, those who could supply the goods at the lowest price won the business. At bottom, the whole gigantic transformation of human life brought about by industrialism derived and continues to derive from the need to reduce the price of goods and services to make them competitive in the largest possible market. Such was the immediate purpose of all the great inventions: the harnessing of steam and electric power, the construction of machines capable of performing quickly and accurately the most complicated operations, the development of efficient means of transport, the rational utilization of labor. Even in countries where protective tariffs shield native industry from foreign competition, cost is a factor of great importance, because inefficient methods of production drain capital and manpower that can be used to good advantage in some other way.

The overriding concern with costs involves an industrial economy in the life of the country to a degree previously unknown. A truly industrial country is one that not merely imports industrial techniques, but one that gears the entire life of its society to the requirements of more efficient—that is, less costly—productivity.

Industrial progress has not proceeded everywhere at an equal pace, some countries undergoing this process earlier and more intensely. Great Britain was the pioneer, the first country in the world in which the industrial sector of the economy came to outweigh the agricultural one in terms of manpower employed and value of goods produced. It attained this stage by the middle of the nineteenth century. Belgium followed close behind, becoming highly industrialized in the second quarter of the century. Next, industrialism spread rapidly westward to the United States and eastward to France and Germany, the three of which underwent intense industrialization after 1850. There remained large parts of Europe that began to industrialize in earnest either at the turn of the century (e.g., Italy, Russia) or only after World War II (the Balkans). Countries that industrialized late served, until then, as suppliers of manpower, raw materials, and food to their more industrialized neighbors. The United States was an exception in that it industrialized and yet at the same time produced a surplus of food to export to other industrial countries.

Considering the economic prerequisites of industrialization, it is clear why Great Britain should have been the first country to industrialize. To begin with, after the union of England and Scotland in 1707, Britain boasted the largest internal market in Europe. Although inferior in terms of territory, population, and wealth to France, Britain, by uniting with Scotland, had early eliminated those internal restraints on the free flow of goods that continued to obstruct the domestic commerce of France and such other Continental countries as Germany and Italy. Within its insular boundaries, Britain was a free-trade area. This area was further expanded in the seventeenth and eighteenth centuries by virtue of colonial conquests, the territories that Britain acquired overseas providing both a source of raw materials and an outlet for manufactured goods. Lord Chatham, one of the builders of the British Empire, was well aware of the commercial importance of the colonies: "I state to you the importance of America," he once declared; "it is a double market: a market of consumption and a market of supply."

Secondly, Britain enjoyed an unusually rapid growth of population. The population of England and Wales doubled between 1750 and 1832, and this growth, in effect, also doubled the domestic market for consumer goods available to English industry.

In the third place, Britain had the capital to finance the expansion of its productive capacity. This money came largely from overseas ventures, much of it from the slave trade in which Britain played a leading role. In the last two decades of the seventeenth century, British vessels transported 300,000 slaves from

This 1776 engraving shows the Severn River terminus of the Staffordshire & Worcestershire Canal, built by England's canal pioneer, James Brindley. Another of Brindley's canals had no less than 75 locks, 5 tunnels, and 275 bridges and aqueducts.

Africa to the colonies, and after the Asiento Treaty (1713) had opened up South America, traffic in human beings became a virtual British monopoly. The wealth of Liverpool, the main port of Lancashire and the birthplace of the modern factory system, derived largely from its proceeds. England also profited from business in colonial wares, of which it became the chief supplier to the Continent. Many individual fortunes that later helped finance British industry were made in India. Unlike the French, who dissipated much of their wealth on wars or on luxuries, the British tended to invest theirs in trade and manufacture.

Technological Progress

As has been pointed out, technical innovations occurred in close connection with the expansion of the market. Just as the existence of outlets for goods encouraged technical improvements capable of yielding better and cheaper commodities, so in turn the production of better and cheaper commodities made available additional markets. As industrialism developed, the relationship of technology to the market turned out to be not one of simple cause and effect but of constant mutual stimulation.

The classic industry of the early phases of the industrial era was cotton spinning and weaving. Compared to wool, cotton was a relative newcomer to England. Originally, cotton textiles had been shipped from India, but their popularity threatened the woolen interests, which in 1700 pressured Parliament into passing a law prohibiting the importation of printed cotton fabrics. This measure, however, instead of eliminating cotton as a competitor, encouraged the growth of a native cotton industry in Lancashire, a region that enjoyed both the proper climate for cotton spinning and access to good ports. From the beginning the cotton manufacturers had to struggle against the ancient and heavily protected woolen industry, and to survive they had to run their enterprises in a highly efficient manner. For this reason they proved receptive to all kinds of innovations.

The technical inventions that in the course of the eighteenth century revolutionized textile manufacture are difficult to explain because they require acquaintance with the many steps involved in the production of cloth. Basically, these inventions were intended to remedy a chronic imbalance between the two principal phases of this process: the spinning of yarn from fibers and the weaving of this yarn into fabric. In the early days of the Lancashire cotton industry, spinning could not keep up with weaving, and it took at least five spinners to keep one weaver supplied with yarn. This disparity was further increased with the invention in 1733 of John Kay's "flying shuttle," a device that enabled the weaver to increase his output substantially. The spinners now had even greater difficulty keeping up with the demand.

To redress this imbalance, James Hargreaves constructed in 1764–1765 a mechanical spinner named "Jenny" in honor of his daughter. An even more advanced spinning device was produced by Richard Arkwright, the inventor of the so-called water-frame. Combining the Jenny and the water-frame, Samuel Crompton designed the "mule," a spinner that in time acquired great popularity. Thus mechanized, spinning more than met the needs of the weavers. In fact, the balance was now upset in favor of spinning, and efforts were exerted to mechanize weaving so that it could keep up with the flow of yarn. The greatest

Arkwright's water-frame spinning machine (this is his 1769 patent drawing) was so named because it ran by water power.

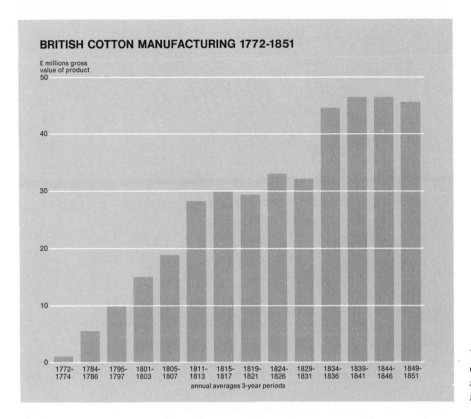

BRITISH COTTON MANUFACTURING 1772-1851

£ millions gross
value of product

50

40

30

20

10

0

| 1772-1774 | 1784-1786 | 1795-1797 | 1801-1803 | 1805-1807 | 1811-1813 | 1815-1817 | 1819-1821 | 1824-1826 | 1829-1831 | 1834-1836 | 1839-1841 | 1844-1846 | 1849-1851 |

annual averages 3-year periods

The transformation of Great Britain's cotton industry is charted here for selected periods. By 1820 cottons had taken the textile lead from woolens.

advance in this direction was made in 1785, when Edmund Cartwright succeeded in building the first practical mechanical loom. But Cartwright's invention gained slow acceptance, partly because of its engineering defects and partly because it required more power than was readily available at the time. The mechanical loom became perfected and began to outnumber the hand loom only in the 1820s.

The ramifications of the major inventions of the industrial age may be illustrated by the effects mechanization of English cotton manufacture had on the United States. The introduction of machinery increased the capacity of the Lancashire mills to the point where the existing supplies of cotton staple from India no longer met their needs. The most obvious alternate source was the United States, but American cotton was uneconomical to process because it was of the so-called short-stapled variety, the seeds of which were difficult to remove. Its commercial value was so low that in the eighteenth century the United States barely grew enough of it to meet its own needs. The situation changed drastically in 1793 when Eli Whitney invented the cotton gin, a machine capable of efficiently removing the seeds. This invention at once made it profitable to use short-staple cotton and led to a startling increase in American cotton cultivation. Two decades after the introduction of the cotton gin, the annual production of cotton in the United States rose from 1.5 million to 85 million pounds. The vast southern plantations on which this cotton grew required masses of cheap labor, bringing about a great increase in the importation of slaves. Thus, technical advances in Lancashire led to an intensification of slavery in faraway America.

The earliest view of the workings of the Newcomen engine was published in 1717 by the English scientist Henry Beighton. Above the brick furnace is the cylinder, with its piston connected to the heavy pumping beam.

The improvements in textile manufacture would not have been so effective were it not that they coincided with revolutionary changes in the methods of supplying motive power. Although not their originator, the textile industry derived from these changes the greatest immediate benefit. Mechanical devices, especially the new looms, required greater power to operate than could be provided by the traditional sources, such as water. The solution was found in steam, the harnessing of which is generally recognized as the single most important invention of the early industrial age.

It had been realized long before 1769, when James Watt constructed the first economical steam engine, that the principles of atmospheric pressure and heat expansion could serve as sources of energy. Engines built on these principles were in operation in about 1700, especially in coal mines, where they were used to cope with the problem of flooding. One such engine, the Newcomen pump (1712), was the direct precursor of Watt's great invention. This pump consisted of a boiler connected to a cylinder containing a piston. Steam was first injected under the piston and then condensed by a jet of cold water to create a vacuum, whereupon the piston descended. A rod connected to the piston operated the pump. The Newcomen engine made twelve strokes a minute, each capable of lifting ten gallons of water. It was an instantaneous success. By 1765 it was in operation in many British collieries and some potteries and had even found its way abroad.

The Newcomen pump had one obvious drawback—it required constant reheating of the cylinder, a procedure that consumed a great amount of fuel. James Watt, a maker of precision instruments and a man of wide learning, set himself to rectify this shortcoming. After much reflection and experimentation, he arrived at a solution that was remarkably simple in its conception and was destined to have incalculable consequences. Instead of cooling the steam within the cylinder, Watt provided for it a separate chamber, or condenser. During this cooling-off period, the cylinder itself remained warm, thus greatly diminishing the amount of fuel needed for the operation. That Watt fully realized this advantage may be gathered from the fact that, in applying for a patent in 1769, he described it as a device "to lessen the consumption of steam, and consequently fuel, in fire engines."

Watt's engine might well have had no immediate economic repercussions had it not attracted the attention of two prominent businessmen. One of them was John Roebuck, a wealthy iron manufacturer and owner of a coal mine. Roebuck's colliery experienced serious flooding that the slow-acting Newcomen pump could not cope with. Impressed by Watt's idea, he entered into partnership with him, undertaking to finance further experiments to improve the steam engine. But Roebuck soon ran into financial difficulties and was on the verge of pulling out of the enterprise when Matthew Boulton appeared on the scene. Boulton, who had made his fortune in hardware, offered to purchase Roebuck's share of the partnership. He saw an immediate use for Watt's "fire engine" in his Soho hardware shop, but he also realized the long-term commercial possibilities in the construction of such engines for sale. In 1768 he and Watt formed their celebrated partnership, Watt providing the technical genius and Boulton the money and business experience. Many difficulties had to be overcome before the steam engine based on Watt's principle of the separate condenser finally became a commercial reality (1776). Boulton invested in it the equivalent of several hundred thousand of today's dollars and probably never realized any profit. But he was a man of great vision, who understood the implications of Watt's invention. When James Boswell, Samuel Johnson's biographer, visited Boulton's Soho foundry in 1776, Boulton proudly declared: "I sell here, Sir, what all the world desires to have—POWER."

Watt's original engine was essentially a pump and as such of limited applicability. But in 1781–1784 Watt patented further improvements that greatly increased the usefulness of his invention. One of these was the so-called double-acting engine, which injected steam on both sides of the piston; another was a device to transform the simple up-and-down movement of the piston into a rotary motion. These improvements made the steam engine more versatile and led to its widespread acceptance. The first to employ it was the iron manufacturer John Wilkinson, who, in return for furnishing Boulton & Watt with cylinders, acquired a steam engine to blow his furnaces. In 1782 Josiah Wedgwood ordered one of Watt's engines to grind pigments and mix clay in his pottery establishment. But the greatest applicability of steam was in the cotton industry. The coupling of Boulton & Watt steam engines to spinning and weaving machines had a startling effect on the price of cotton goods. Between 1780 and 1812 the price of cotton yarn fell by 90 percent. It was such reduction of prices that permitted British cotton goods to flood international markets. Machine-produced cotton textiles were the first clothing material in history available cheaply and in quantities to the mass of the population.

The great advantages of steam over water, above all its economy and independence of geography, soon led to its employment in other industries, where it invariably increased productivity and lowered costs. In 1814 it was installed at the printing shop of the London *Times*, permitting press runs of a thousand copies an hour. Flour mills, breweries, coin mints, and other industries hastened to convert to steam.

One of the most important applications of steam took place in transportation, for the development of railroads and steamships contributed more to the opening of new markets than any other invention of the age. In the early part of the eighteenth century, it took a stagecoach leaving London three days to reach Dover (75 miles) and two weeks to reach Edinburgh (450 miles). Under these circumstances, merchandise could scarcely move from one part of the country to another on land. England, like every other country, consisted of a multitude of small, self-contained economies, each of which satisfied its own needs. In the second half of the eighteenth century, this situation was somewhat improved in England and in some Continental countries by the construction of canals. The pottery manufacturer Wedgwood estimated that one tow horse could pull as much merchandise on a canal barge as could forty horses on land—and with less breakage. But canals had obvious limitations: they were slow, expensive to build, and limited by topography to certain areas, which was not necessarily where they were the most needed.

The first important British rail line linked Manchester and Liverpool in 1830. This is the Mount Olive "cutting" the next year, still being laboriously dug by hand.

Coloured Views on the Liverpool and Manchester Railway, 1833

The railroad was free of these limitations and for this reason it soon dominated land transport. Although English collieries used small steam locomotives in the eighteenth century, the first practical railway engine, George Stephenson's *Rocket*, was not constructed until 1829. Stephenson's achievement lay in applying the motion of the piston directly to the wheels without recourse to the usual rod and crank mechanisms—a procedure that increased the power of the engine and at the same time reduced its fuel consumption. The *Rocket* proved its worth by pulling a thirteen-ton load at a speed of twenty-nine miles an hour. First used to transport coal, railroads soon pulled other loads as well, including passengers. In 1849, only twenty years after the debut of the *Rocket*, locomotives operating between London and Bristol attained average speeds of fifty miles an hour. At this rate, they covered as much distance in half an hour as a typical coach of the 1820s had covered in a day. Naturally, costs of transport dropped, as did prices of the shipped commodities. Wherever it penetrated, the railroad resembled a battering ram that broke down the invisible walls protecting local markets from outside competition. In many instances it became cheaper to buy products manufactured hundreds of miles away than those produced locally, for transport costs were negligible. One of the consequences of this development was regional specialization, each area tending to concentrate on those goods that it could produce most cheaply.

Although it antedated the railroad, the steamship was slow in exerting an impact on the economy. Robert Fulton, an American engineer, ran his paddlewheel steamer between New York and Albany as early as 1807, but the first ocean-going steamships consumed so much coal that they could not compete with the new and improved sailing ships known as clippers, and they only gained acceptance in the 1870s. In the first half of the nineteenth century, they were used largely on inland waterways and other short routes (e.g., coastal waters), where they could stay close to fueling stations.

Most of the technological innovations, particularly the railroads, required large quantities of coal and iron, thus stimulating the search for improved methods of extracting these two basic commodities of the industrial era. The British iron industry was stagnating in the first half of the eighteenth century, for England had depleted its forests and lacked the timber needed for smelting. Early attempts at smelting iron with coal proved unsuccessful, because no way was known of removing the impurities present in coal. Britain, therefore, had no choice but to import iron from such timber-rich countries as Sweden and Russia, though attempts to devise means of employing coal for iron smelting never ceased. In 1781 an important advance was made by Henry Cort, who used coke, a by-product of coal distillation, to produce wrought iron. His method, the puddling process, gained wide acceptance, and within twenty-five years British iron production more than trebled. The Russian iron industry, on the other hand, suffered a corresponding decline. A further improvement was the invention in 1829 of a process that enabled coal to be used successfully to smelt iron. These innovations made Britain the world leader in the production and exportation of coal and iron. How great its lead was may be gathered from the fact that in 1840 it produced ten times as much coal as any of its closest competitors (Belgium, France, and Prussia). By that date, it was clear that a country short of coal

BRITISH COAL OUTPUT 1820-1850
£ millions value at pit head

BRITISH PIG IRON OUTPUT 1820-1854
£ millions gross value of product

annual averages

Whereas British coal output in the second quarter of the eighteenth century (above) showed steady growth, pig iron production (below) rose erratically due to technological problems.

and iron, the two basic materials of industrialism, could aspire neither to economic nor political might.

The Spread of Industrialism to the Continent

Britain, the pioneer in industrial development, was not allowed to enjoy its monopoly for long. Other Western countries, aware of how greatly industrialism had increased British wealth and power, soon emulated its example. At first, Britain tried to thwart competition by passing laws forbidding the emigration of skilled laborers and the export of new machines. But these measures proved unenforceable. Industrial espionage and financial inducements eventually secured for rival powers the designs of the machines and lured to the Continent managers and skilled workers who were instrumental in setting up mechanized textile mills, foundries, and factories of all kinds. The British eventually had to acknowledge their inability to maintain a monopoly on industrial processes and in 1842 repealed the last of the restrictive measures.

In the first half of the nineteenth century, the rest of the Western world profited greatly from British experience, willingly as well as unwillingly proffered. During this time, the United States and several Western European countries laid the foundations of an industrial economy. None, however, became industrialized in the sense that Britain had, for each seemed to lack one or more of the vital ingredients, the fortuitous possession of which had accounted for Britain's early successes. Some lacked the necessary raw materials; others lacked a national government capable of destroying feudal institutions and assuring a large internal market; still others were short of capital. In addition, certain cultural factors inhibited industrial development on the Continent: the attachment to the land here was stronger than in England, as was the viability of old social organizations like the guilds. In most of Europe, it took half a century or more to break down these obstacles to industrialization.

The only Continental country to industrialize in earnest in the first half of the nineteenth century was Belgium, which benefited from a number of unique advantages. First, it possessed large markets by virtue of the fact that from 1793 to 1815 it had formed part of France and from 1815 to 1830 part of the Netherlands and its overseas empire. Access to these markets permitted Belgium to lay the foundations of a sizable industrial complex, which managed to keep going even after it gained independence from the Netherlands, because an exceptionally high concentration of population provided a satisfactory domestic market. Second, Belgium had a progressive government eager to promote industry. The liberal monarchy that emerged from the revolution of 1830 invested its own capital and encouraged the influx of foreign capital. It also assisted in the construction of transport. In 1835 Belgium inaugurated the first complete trunk railroad network on the Continent, and soon the length of its railways, hard-surfaced roads, and navigable waterways exceeded (in proportion to its total area) those of England. Belgium was also fortunate in having good iron and coal deposits, which, until their exhaustion later in the century, enabled it to develop heavy industry.

Until the middle of the eighteenth century, France probably had produced more industrial goods than Britain, but from then on it fell behind. The causes of this lag were partly economic and partly cultural. The soil of France has always been so fruitful that Frenchmen found little inducement to leave it for the cities. The majority of Frenchmen wanted to be and in fact did become owners of agricultural land. Even that part of the population that went to work for industry retained its rural ties and returned to the land when given the opportunity to buy into it. Second, France had poor coal and iron deposits. Third, the French possess a highly individualistic temperament that resents industrial discipline and dissolution in a faceless crowd. They have traditionally preferred small family-owned and -operated shops to gigantic factories. In the middle of the nineteenth century, three-quarters of all Frenchmen still lived on the soil, and as late as 1870 the value of France's agricultural product exceeded that of its industry. The aversion of Frenchmen to large industrial enterprises may be illustrated by the fact that, in the middle of the nineteenth century, 3 million Frenchmen classified as workers were employed by nearly 1.5 million establishments—a ratio of two workers to each business. Although it developed a number of efficient industries (textile, chemical, railroad construction) and acquired an excellent transport network, France remained for a long time a country with a mixed economy.

The states of the Germanic Confederation possessed all of the elements necessary for industrial growth but one: political unity. What became in 1871 the German Empire comprised at the beginning of the century no fewer than 300 sovereign principalities, each with its tariffs and tolls barring the way to the free flow of goods. Farsighted statesmen, realizing that these conditions hindered economic development, concentrated on the creation of a free-trade zone embracing all the German territories, regardless of political divisions. This effort

The completion of Italy's first railroad in 1830, connecting Naples and Portici, was commemorated in a painting by Salvatore Fergola, the official painter to the Italian royal court.

The Zollverein *customs union at its founding in 1834; it later was expanded to take in the northern German states, Baden, and Alsace-Lorraine.*

THE ZOLLVEREIN

culminated in 1834 in the establishment of a customs union known as the *Zollverein*. This bilateral institution developed gradually from tariff agreements that Prussia entered into with neighboring lands. In 1818, when Prussia liberalized its own customs system, a number of principalities that were fully enclosed by Prussian territory lost their customary commercial outlets. At Prussia's suggestion, these states now entered with it into reciprocal tariff agreements, the first of which was signed in 1819. Similar agreements were signed with other principalities that found it expedient to associate with the large Prussian-dominated market. Each of the states entering into such commercial agreements abolished tariffs against the others, but, of course, retained its political sovereignty. In the 1820s other principalities hostile to Prussia established their own customs union, and for a while it looked as if the German lands would be divided into two large commercial blocks, but in the end this group too joined Prussia and its associates. Thus, step by step, the common German market expanded until it embraced all the lands of the Confederation except Austria, which Prussia deliberately kept out as a political rival. The *Zollverein* went into effect on the morning of January 1, 1834, when, all over Germany, carts and barges loaded with goods assembled for the occasion were given the signal to proceed and swept joyfully past the old customs and toll barriers.

The *Zollverein* represents a unique instance of a single national market anticipating the national state. The *Zollverein*, however, only created a market framework; it did not create an industrial economy. This came into existence only after 1850. Despite its internal market, rich mineral deposits, and cadres of excellent scientists and artisans, in the first half of the century Germany remained overwhelmingly agricultural. In the 1840s Belgium produced more iron than the entire *Zollverein*, and coal consumption in the city of London alone exceeded the total coal output of Prussia, Germany's most industrialized state.

The other areas of Europe had only industrial pockets surrounded by traditional agrarian economies. Italy, like Germany, suffered from national disunity but, unlike Germany, created no customs union to remedy it. It has been calculated that merchandise transported from Mantua to Parma, a distance of thirty-seven miles, was subject to no less than six separate custom duties. Italy further suffered from a lack of coal and iron deposits. Its only serious industry was textile manufacture, which was concentrated in the northern regions of the peninsula. The Hapsburg Empire had the rudiments of an industrial center in Bohemia. Russia, although richly endowed with natural resources, a vast market, and an inexhaustible supply of cheap labor, suffered from a shortage of capital and the attitude of its government, which opposed industrialization for fear of social unrest. At midcentury Russia had half a million industrial workers, the majority in the textile industry, the capital and management of which was supplied mainly from abroad. Elsewhere in Europe, mechanized textile manufacture established a foothold here and there, serving as a wedge of industrial culture without significantly altering the quality of life. The varying pace of economic development created a disparity between the predominantly industrial and the predominantly agrarian countries which, in the second half of the nineteenth century, divided Europe into two distinct zones.

Economic Liberalism

In Britain the advance of industry, which had transformed a small and relatively poor island into the world's leading manufacturing and trading power, was attended by a prolonged re-examination of the principles on which the nation's economic life had hitherto rested. The outcome of this re-examination was the triumph of economic liberalism over mercantilism. So great was the influence of Britain at that time that many other countries imitated its liberal economic policy, even though their situation was different from Britain's and called for different measures.

The fundamental principles of economic liberalism had been worked out in the second half of the eighteenth century by the French Physiocrats and by the Scotsman Adam Smith. They rested on the same assumptions of individualism and the natural "harmony of interests" that underlay the philosophy of political liberalism. Their practical recommendations were simple: to reduce to a minimum all interference of state, society, or any other external factor in the free operations of the economy. Tariffs, monopolies, fiscal controls, and guilds all had to go, because they prevented the "natural" order from asserting itself.

The principles of economic liberalism had wide ramifications. Although most directly pertinent to tariff policy, they challenged in one way or another all the basic principles that had guided Western economic life for centuries. In 1787, in his *Defence of Usury*, Jeremy Bentham, who in many matters followed Smith, argued that "no man of ripe years and sound mind, acting freely, and with his eyes open, ought to be hindered, with a view to his advantage, from making such a bargain, in the way of obtaining money, as he sees fit." By proposing free competition for money, Bentham rejected the traditional Christian view that lending money at interest was unethical. Bentham and such French popularizers of economic liberalism as J. B. Say and C. F. Bastiat eventually condemned all restraints on the free economic activity of individuals. "In political economy,"

Adam Smith's portrait medal of 1797 has on its reverse side (opposite) symbols representing Smith's Wealth of Nations.

Bentham wrote, "there is much to learn and little to do." The ultimate triumph of economic liberalism was not due, of course, to the mere force of its arguments. Economic liberalism won in England because it suited the most dynamic and productive class, that of traders and manufacturers.

As we have seen, British industrialists had tried to prevent foreign competition by prohibiting the export of men and machines. But these measures failed, and in any event the more farsighted industrialists preferred to capitalize on the head start that Britain had gained over potential rivals. As early as the 1770s, British manufacturers pressured Parliament to ease tariffs and the Navigation Laws. Their argument was that "from their present ascendancy of skill [they] have nothing immediate to fear from competition, and everything to hope from the speculation of an increased demand." These groups won the ear of Prime Minister William Pitt, who in 1786 signed a treaty with France reducing tariffs between the two countries. But in the protracted conflict between Britain and France that followed the French Revolution, economic warfare provided an important weapon, and economic liberalization had to be postponed.

The agitation for greater freedom of manufacture and trade revived after 1815. Britain's lead was by now so great that British industrialists clamored for the abolishment of the restrictions imposed when British industry had been weak and in need of protection. The manufacturers wanted repeal of the Navigation Laws, which required them to use British ships in trade with British colonies. They objected to duties on the importation of raw materials, especially on wheat, where the duty artificially kept up the cost of bread and forced them to pay workers higher wages. In general, the manufacturers could demonstrate that, with an increasing number of Englishmen gaining a livelihood from industry, the well-being of industry was of vital concern for England as a whole. If their argument did not immediately carry the day, it was because it challenged the interests of the landed aristocracy, which benefited from protection, and the state, which depended on custom receipts for much of its revenue.

The cause of economic liberalism began to make headway with the appointment of William Huskisson to the chairmanship of the Board of Trade. During his tenure of office (1823–1827), Huskisson reduced trade restrictions, proceeding so cautiously that he did not antagonize those whose interests they protected. He based his actions not on general, theoretical arguments, but on concrete evidence. For instance, when reducing tariffs on raw silk, wool, and several additional items, he demonstrated that this action would kill a vast contraband trade in these items. This kind of fiscal pragmatism typified the whole British movement toward free trade. Huskisson also eased the Navigation Laws, enabling the British colonies to engage in direct trade relations with the United States and European countries.

The crucial test in the mounting conflict between economic liberals and protectionists came over grain (or corn, as it is called in England). The early proponents of free trade, the Physiocrats and Adam Smith, had never anticipated such an occurrence; both had regarded the agrarian interests as more open to arguments in favor of free trade than the manufacturers, whom they believed firmly committed to monopolistic practices. As it turned out, however, liberal ideas won increased acceptance among the industrialists, whereas the landlords turned into last-ditch defenders of protectionism. The specific issue over which the decisive battle was fought was the Corn Law.

The Corn Law in force in the 1820s had been passed in 1815 to alleviate the agrarian depression that followed the Napoleonic wars. As long as the wars had been in progress and wheat prices rose, British landlords expanded arable land, even into areas of low productivity where farming would normally have been unprofitable. This had been a main reason for the increase in the so-called enclosure acts, by which landowners evicted tenants in order to consolidate their holdings. The process of enclosures had reached its peak between 1802 and 1815, when acts of Parliament authorized the enclosure of some 50,000 acres annually, most of it for the purpose of transforming pasture land into arable land. With the return of peace, food prices dropped sharply. Wheat, which had sold during wartime for as much as 130 shillings a quarter (a fourth of a ton), fell in May, 1814, one month after Napoleon's abdication, to 73 shillings. To prevent a further decline in prices, the government in 1815 passed the Corn Law, which decreed that if the price of domestic wheat fell below 80 shillings a quarter, no wheat was to be imported; if it rose above that figure, foreign wheat could be admitted free of duty. The intent of the law was to assure the landlords of high prices, but it failed to fulfill this expectation, for domestic wheat prices continued to fall even without foreign competition. The Corn Law was very unpopular among both manufacturers and workers. In the early nineteenth century wheat was still the staple food of the common man. The artificial maintenance of higher wheat prices forced the manufacturer to pay bigger wages and the worker to spend a greater part of his income on food than would have been the case if English wheat had to compete freely with imported wheat.

Huskisson modified the Corn Law by abandoning the absolute 80-shilling figure in favor of a sliding-scale tariff, the amount of the duty charged being proportional to the price of domestic wheat. But this measure did not greatly improve matters from the manufacturer's point of view. During the decade that followed Huskisson's death in 1830 (he was killed in a railroad accident, perhaps the iron horse's earliest victim), nothing significant was done to change further the Corn Law or any other tariff. The issue was reopened only in 1838 with the founding in Manchester of the Anti-Corn Law Association. For the next eight years, the conflict over wheat tariffs fairly dominated English public life.

The Anti-Corn Law Association (or League, as it was later called) was the child of Richard Cobden, a gifted agitator and organizer, who brought to the cause of free trade an almost religious fervor. Cobden felt convinced that freedom of trade would inaugurate an era of unprecedented prosperity for all mankind. At his side stood John Bright, one of the great orators of the time. Cobden, a successful industrialist, devoted his own fortune to the cause of free trade and persuaded Manchester businessmen to make large donations to the league. With Bright's assistance, he poured out a steady stream of pamphlets and books, organized mass rallies, and sent agitators to towns, factories, and even the hostile rural districts to plead for the abolition of duties on wheat. He had an uncanny sense of class interests and appealed to each group in a manner best calculated to win it over. His main argument was of a persuasive simplicity: If England, by abolishing the Corn Law, were to purchase more food abroad, foreigners would use the money thus obtained to buy more English manufactured goods. In this manner, everyone would benefit, except for a small group of selfish landlords.

The campaign—a pioneering effort at modern propaganda—won much popular support, but it owed its ultimate success to the growing awareness of government authorities that tariff reduction would not cut into its revenues. A parliamentary committee appointed in 1840 found that 90 percent of the country's total customs income derived from a mere 19 of the 862 articles subject to duties. These findings caused Tory Prime Minister Robert Peel to lower tariffs on many raw materials and manufactured goods in 1842 and again in 1845. The reductions did not adversely affect customs receipts, because they led to an increase in imports; the revenue lost on individual items was more than compensated for by the larger quantity of imported goods. Evidence of this kind strengthened the hand of the free traders. For the time being, however, the Corn Law remained intact, for it protected the well-being of the landed aristocracy that dominated English social and political life.

The event that gave the final stimulus to the abolition of the Corn Law was the Irish famine. In 1845 the so-called black rot ruined the potato crop of Ireland. England had traditionally bought much foodstuff in Ireland and had no choice but to lower tariffs on food imports to make up for the loss of the Irish produce. Peel now became convinced that the repeal of the Corn Law was inevitable. Despite the fact that his party, the Tories, had been put into office on a platform pledging retention of the Corn Law, he introduced in 1846 a bill calling for the immediate reduction of wheat duties and their abolition three years later. Backed by the Whigs and liberal Tories, the bill passed the Commons.

The repeal of the Corn Law reduced the principal stronghold of the protectionists. The remaining tariffs and other restraints on trade now fell in quick succession. By 1852 Great Britain was for all practical purposes a free-trade country, admitting foreign goods without restrictions of any kind. A series of reciprocal commercial treaties with other countries, notably France (1860), facilitated also the entry of British goods into foreign markets. But although only a handful of countries followed Britain's lead in instituting full freedom of trade

The installation of increasingly complex machinery raised the issue of the safety of working conditions. These calico printing machines, depicted in 1836, have their driving gears and belt systems completely exposed.

E. BAINES, *History of the County Palatine, 1836*

(Holland, Belgium, Switzerland, and Sweden), Britain was not seriously hurt. At midcentury it enjoyed so great an industrial lead that it could compete with protected economies on their home grounds, despite the handicap of tariffs.

As the liberals had anticipated, the establishment of free trade brought immediate benefits to Britain's foreign commerce. The total value of its imports and exports, which before 1846 had fluctuated between £50 million and £120 million a year, rose in 1860 to £370 million and in 1873 to £620 million. But the import-export figures do not reveal the full extent of Britain's commercial relations with foreign countries. Britain derived additional income from two major sources: shipping and investments. British commercial shipping outclassed all competitors and dominated maritime trade, gaining for the country much money. Britain's foreign investments (in government bonds, railroad construction, mines, and other enterprises) also brought large returns. These foreign investments increased from £300 million in the early 1850s to £1,300 million in 1875. Shipping and other forms of "invisible exports" such as insurance, together with income derived from foreign investments, more than compensated for Britain's negative trade balance (i.e., the practice of buying abroad more than one sold there). For example, in 1860, when the value of imported goods exceeded the value of exported goods by £122 million, Britain earned £77 million from international shipping and £75 million from foreign investments. Its net gain was thus £30 million. Britain's principal exports were textiles and products of the metallurgical and mining industries (iron, coal, machines, hardware), and its principal imports were raw materials, chiefly food and cotton.

It should be noted that events refuted the protectionists who had claimed that the abolition of the Corn Law would ruin British agriculture. The landlords and farmers of Britain continued to benefit from the country's general prosperity until the early 1870s, when they were hit by American competition.

The Social Consequences of Early Industrialization

The emergence of industrial economies has everywhere altered the life of societies in a great variety of ways. The most apparent and incontrovertible change involved the growth and distribution of population. The advent of industrialism coincided with an unprecedented growth of the European population. In the middle of the eighteenth century, when rapid industrialization first began, the population of Europe (exclusive of Russia) was estimated to have been only slightly larger than that of Africa. A hundred years later it was twice as large. Roughly speaking (and one has to speak roughly in these matters, for early demographic statistics are notoriously unreliable), from 1750 onward the inhabitants of Europe doubled each century. Human history has never known an increase of similar proportions. We shall discuss the probable reasons and consequences of this phenomenon in a later chapter.

The second important change occurred in the distribution of the population: the shift of inhabitants from the countryside to the city. Urbanization, as this process is called, did not assume dramatic proportions until the second half of the nineteenth century, and for this reason we shall deal with it, too, later. Since the social history of the first half of the nineteenth century cannot be understood without taking urbanization into account, however, some observations about it are in order here.

The reasons for large-scale urban growth were primarily economic. In preindustrial conditions, with low labor productivity, it was more efficient to locate manufactures near the sources of food, that is, in the countryside, because the worker consumed more food (in terms of bulk and weight) than raw materials. This explains why, between 1500 and 1800, manufactures dispersed and the city population of Europe remained static and in some places even declined. The introduction of mechanization and steam power altered this situation. The productivity of labor now increased to the point where the worker required far more raw materials, such as cotton and coal, than food. It became, therefore, more expedient to locate him as close as possible to the sources of raw materials and to bring the food to him. The size and cost of machines, the construction of canals and railroads, and the desirability of concentrating in one place technical, administrative and financial operations contributed further to urban growth—as did the lure of wealth, amusement, and an opportunity for self-improvement.

Britain, the first country to industrialize, was also the first to urbanize. By 1851 its city population outnumbered the rural population, and from then on the urban-rural gap steadily widened. At the same time, the center of the British population shifted from the agrarian regions in the southeast to the industrial centers in the northwest. In Germany and France the growth of cities occurred more slowly, and intense urbanization got under way only in the second half of the century. In Prussia, whose territories included the manufacturing centers and mines of Silesia and the Rhineland, the percentage of urban inhabitants increased between 1815 and 1851 by only 2 percent (from 26.5 percent to 28.5 percent). In France, despite the dramatic growth of Paris, the urban element in the middle of the century accounted only for a fourth of the population. Here and there, however, individual cities expanded at a rapid rate, even in countries with thoroughly agrarian economies.

A far more difficult subject to discuss with any degree of assurance is the effect of early industrialization on the life of the masses of population. To arrive at any convincing conclusions, we would have to examine full statistical data on living standards. Such statistics are scarce and inadequate, even for a country with excellent records such as England. But even if we had complete data on standards of living, the criteria used to evaluate them would be subjective. How can we judge human well-being in statistical terms? How can we compare, for example, the loss of fresh air and a familiar environment with the acquisition of better clothing or more food, or the decline of security with the gain of material goods?

The term *Industrial Revolution* evokes for many people a picture of utter human degradation. It brings to mind children working fifteen hours a day in textile mills; young girls chained to coal wagons in deep underground tunnels and women carrying baskets filled with coal from pits a hundred or more feet deep; families expelled from villages into vermin-infested slums. The picture gains in intensity from the skill with which it was depicted in the popular social novels of the time, such as Charles Kingsley's *Alton Locke* (1850), Elizabeth Cleghorn Gaskell's *Mary Barton* (1848), and Emile Zola's realistic cycle of novels, *Les Rougon-Macquart* (e.g., *The Dram-Shop* [1877] and *Germinal* [1885]). This popular image is not without its elements of truth. The working conditions in early industrial establishments were indeed often appalling and arouse in the modern observer a sense of outrage, as does the indifference of many of the propertied to the suffering of the poor, a subject documented exhaustively by social historians.

Yet degradation and suffering are only a part of the story, and probably not the essential one. In dealing with any social phenomenon, it must be borne in mind that what attracts the attention of contemporaries and historians alike is not the typical, but the new and unusual. An early nineteenth-century observer, who may have passed unconcerned a village hovel, was startled by a city slum. Untroubled (if, indeed, not charmed) by the sight of women and children working from dawn to dusk in the fields or cottage industries, he was shocked when he saw the same women or children tending machines or carrying coal. It is these novel features of industrialization that tend both to dominate and to distort our view of what really happened. But the economic historian must acquire, as Sir John Clapham, a great practitioner of the discipline, once observed, "what might be called the statistical sense, the habit of asking in relation to any institution, policy, group, or movement the questions: How large? How long? How often? How representative?" Applied to social conditions of early industrialism, particularly to England, for which the available evidence is most abundant, these questions provide an important corrective to the traditional view.

Researches undertaken by modern economic historians have convincingly dis-

In rendering industrial subjects, Romantic artists tended to give them a nightmarish, satanic interpretation. This is a British ironworks in 1833.

proved the contention that early industrialism caused a general lowering of living standards among the working population. Employing statistical data rather than the case histories favored by social historians, they have discovered that living standards in Britain, the key country in the debate, improved in the first half of the nineteenth century. (There is no serious question of their improvement in the second half of the century.) The conclusion is based mainly on the fact that, apart from minor fluctuations, real wages (that is, wages adjusted to the cost of living) moved steadily upward. This phenomenon resulted from modern methods of manufacture and transport, which drove down the price of commodities. Thus, even with stable wages, the worker could buy more goods. The authors of a recent study conclude that real wages in Britain rose by some 25 percent in the first quarter of the nineteenth century, and by 40 percent in the second.° Students of French and German working conditions arrived independently at similar conclusions regarding their countries. In addition to a rise in real wages, workers in industrial nations improved their situation by virtue of the fact that modern manufacturing methods required an increasing number of high skills. As more and more workers moved from the unskilled to the skilled category, the median income of the working class went up.

Nevertheless, while the conditions of the working class *as a whole* improved, the conditions of certain of its segments undoubtedly deteriorated. The existence of dire poverty in the midst of general prosperity is a familiar phenomenon. It explains why many contemporaries felt convinced that industrialization had brought impoverishment to the masses. The rise in real wages and wage scales was slow and unspectacular in the nineteenth century, but the misery of certain groups of the population was a shocking reality, visible to all.

The group that suffered most was the unemployed. The introduction of machinery in manufactures that had previously relied on manual labor created havoc in certain trades. Most affected were the hand-loom weavers, who were made obsolete and destitute by the spread of the power looms after 1820. Another cause of unemployment was periodic recession. The industrial economy, producing not for a local and relatively predictable market but for an uncertain national or international market, was subject to wild fluctuations. Each such fluctuation caused layoffs and threw thousands of laborers out of work. The existence of large numbers of jobless, victims of vocational or cyclical unemployment, induces some modern historians to deny that a general improvement in living standards had taken place.†

Statesmen did little to help the unemployed, partly because they did not believe that social ills could be cured by government action, and partly because they considered social welfare measures incompatible with economic progress. Indeed, in 1834 Britain may be said to have taken a step backward in this respect. To curb abuses in the dispensation of public relief to the destitute and unemployed, the House of Commons that year passed a Poor Law that ended

°Phyllis Deane and W. A. Cole, *British Economic Growth, 1688–1959: Trends and Structure* (1962). See also T. S. Ashton, "The Standard of Life of Workers in England, 1790–1830," *The Journal of Economic History,* Supplement IX, 1949.

†See, for example, E. J. Hobsbawm, *The Age of Revolution, 1789–1848* (1962), and E. P. Thompson, *The Making of the English Working Class* (1965).

the traditional "outdoor relief" given by the parishes. Relief was henceforth to be earned in public workhouses. The proponents of this bill argued that there was no real unemployment in the country and that those seeking relief merely wanted to avoid work. In fact, the majority of paupers refused to go into the "bastilles," as they called the workhouses, and found jobs. But in times of severe economic depression (e.g., 1836–1837), the new Poor Law caused great distress in areas where previously parishes had been relied upon to provide relief.

Legislation to protect labor came slowly. It took a long time to realize that industrial workers constituted a distinct social group with specific needs. Nor did the manufacturers favor such protection, on the grounds that it would interfere with the "natural" operations of the economy. Nevertheless, some laws were introduced to curb female and child labor (e.g., the Factory Act of 1833). An important step was the Ten Hours Act, passed in 1847 under the pressure of the agrarian interests, who were eager to revenge themselves on the manufacturers for the repeal the previous year of the Corn Law. This act, applicable to women and children but in practice also extended to men, limited the working day to ten hours. On the Continent the worker remained for the time being entirely unprotected, except in countries like Germany, where the old guild legislation still remained in force.

The initial reaction of workers to the insecurity created by industrialism and economic liberalism was to attack its most visible cause: the machine. In the first quarter of the century Britain was plagued by industrial saboteurs, popularly known as Luddites, who destroyed machinery with a savagery that frightened Parliament into passing a law (1812) making the willful destruction of certain machines a capital offense. In 1831 French workers in Lyons smashed machines used in the manufacture of silk. Violence directed against machinery and factories was a common occurrence in all revolutionary disturbances in the first half of the nineteenth century.

Anti-machine feeling rarely survived the initial impact of industrialism. In time, workers everywhere recognized that the machine had come to stay, and they abandoned industrial sabotage to struggle for economic improvement and sometimes political democracy.

3

——◆——

Romanticism

Historical movements are sometimes easier to identify in terms of what they oppose than what they espouse. The term *Romanticism* has been used to describe so great a variety of attitudes and styles that no single positive definition can give a precise idea of its meaning; indeed, some historians despair whether it has any meaning at all. Yet the Romantic movement certainly existed. Its adherents, whatever their internal differences, were bound by opposition to a common enemy, classicism, the aesthetic doctrine that had dominated Western culture in the seventeenth and eighteenth centuries.

Classicism was a formalized expression of that admiration for the achievement of the ancient Greeks and Romans which had characterized the art and thought of Europe since the Renaissance. But ancient culture, which in the fifteenth and sixteenth centuries had provided a fruitful stimulus, had become by the end of the seventeenth century a rigid doctrine inhibiting free creativity. Underlying the classical doctrine was the belief that there exist absolute, eternal standards of beauty, that these standards had been most closely realized by the ancients, and that, therefore, classical culture provided permanent models for all creative achievement. The aesthetic rules of classicism were formulated in France between 1660 and 1690, most authoritatively by Nicolas Boileau in his *L'Art Poétique* (1674). They embraced, in addition to poetry, other forms of literature, the visual arts, architecture, and music.

The aim of classicism was not so much to please as to instruct; it concerned itself not with the individual and the fleeting, but with the general and the unchanging. Because it assumed that aesthetic rules were absolute and eternal, it imposed on the writer and artist strict limitations. The classical dramatist, for example, was to adhere to the Aristotelian unities of time, place, and action. The poet had to occupy himself with "poetic," that is lofty, subjects and employ an appropriately lofty vocabulary and meter. The painter had to conform to certain rules of composition. One such rule forbade him to depict two figures in a group facing the same direction. That such regulation inhibited creative freedom did not escape the attention of the exponents of classicism, but they saw no harm in it, for they believed that mastery was attained precisely by conformity to prescribed rules. "No one unable to limit himself has ever been able to write," Boileau asserted, and Goethe stated the same principle when he said: "It is limitations that prove the master." Assuming that nothing really new could be said, classicism concerned itself more with form than with content, more with the manner in which an idea or emotion was expressed than with the idea or emotion itself.

Classicism owed its influence in no small measure to the control that its adherents exercised over patronage. Writers and artists require money to support themselves and to display their work to the public. For this reason, unless they have private means, all creative talents depend on a ready market for their prod-

The Englishman J. M. W. Turner was one of the founders of the Romantic school. The Shipwreck (c. 1805), one of his early canvases, is a highly imaginative version of an event he had witnessed. Later Turner's work became more abstract and impressionistic.

Jacques Louis David's Death of Socrates *(1787) is the archetype of classicist painting. The Christ-like philosopher has a final word for his twelve mourning disciples as he reaches for the cup of hemlock.*

uct. In our times, the spread of education and wealth have created outlets for artistic and literary works unknown before the nineteenth century, when talent relied for support on individual patrons: the royal court, the landed gentry, the church, merchants. Much of this patronage was dispensed not directly, through commissions, but through the agency of academies. The model was the French Académie des Beaux Arts, founded in 1648, which secured the remunerative privilege of nominating artists for royal commissions. Similar academies were founded in other countries: the Academia de Nobles Artes de San Fernando in Madrid (1752), the Imperial Academy of Arts in St. Petersburg (1757), the Royal Academy of Arts in London (1768), and so on. These academies, as a rule, maintained schools that trained their students according to classical precepts and held exhibitions to which they admitted only works conforming to these precepts. Drama was similarly kept within classical bounds by subsidized theaters. Printed literature—poetry and the novel—could always appeal over the heads of official establishments directly to the reader and for that reason never succumbed fully to the classical domination.

Conceived in the very broadest terms, Romanticism represented a cultural revolution against the whole classical model on behalf of modern, that is, post-classical, Western culture. Without disparaging the achievement of the ancients, the Romantics claimed equal distinction for the culture created by Christian Europe. This self-awareness of the Romantics as modern Europeans constituted a very important factor in the emergence of the Romantic movement. It lay at the heart of the discussions of a brilliant circle of German writers and critics who in the 1790s formulated the theoretical principles of Romanticism and gave the movement its name. These men constantly discussed the contrast between the "natural" and the "civilized," between feeling and thought, between spontaneity and consciousness. They believed that European classicism had upset this balance by overemphasizing the civilized, intellectual elements at the expense of the natural and emotional ones. From this awareness stemmed their distinction between the "classical" and the modern or, as Frederick Schlegel called it, the "Romantic." The classics, they argued, were rooted in a common mythology and tended to generalize about man and life; they were concerned with the typical. The moderns (by which they meant artists and writers of the whole Christian era), by contrast, were inclined to be subjective, to stress the individual, the unique, the original.

Like all great cultural movements, Romanticism rested on a specific concept of man. Classicism regarded man as a finite, static being, whereas Romanticism viewed him as a being endowed with endless potential. The realization of this potential was, according to the Romantics, the highest purpose in life. Johann Fichte, the German whose writings are among the philosophical foundations of Romanticism, stated that man's supreme virtue was to become himself, and the Englishman Samuel Taylor Coleridge spoke of man as in part "his own creator." This process of self-realization, of the unfolding of one's potential, the Germans called *Bildung*—a term that embraced not only formal education but also the development of one's character, will, aesthetic sensibility, capacity for true friendship, and so on. Frederick Schlegel, one of the founders of Romanticism, put the matter as follows:

> I believe that I live not to obey or to dissipate myself, but to be and to become; and I believe in the ability of the will and of education [*Bildung*] to bring me once more close to the eternal, to free me from the fetters of miseducation, and to make me independent of the limitations of the human kind.

The highest means of self-realization was artistic creativity. To the Romantics, art was not merely an act of craftsmanship, measurable in terms of its ability to cope with well-defined rules; it was an act of reaching beyond "the limitations of the human kind." "The poet is the only true *man*," the German dramatist Johann von Schiller wrote in a letter to Goethe. "Compared with him, the best philosopher is a mere caricature."

Obviously, such a concept of art precluded restrictions on the artist. It demanded that he be free to find the means best suited to his purpose, whether or not they enjoyed the approval of an Aristotle or a Boileau. What mattered was not form but content. The Romantics had nothing but scorn for those who hoped to achieve greatness by adhering to formal rules. "They swayed upon a rocking horse, and thought it Pegasus," Keats wrote of the classicists in his poem "Sleep and Poetry."

For the Romantics, pleasure was the only criterion of art; a work of art must please, not instruct, as the classicists maintained. The French novelist Stendhal defined this principle facetiously:

> *Romanticism* is the art of presenting to different peoples those literary works which, in the existing state of their habits and beliefs, are capable of giving them the greatest possible pleasure. *Classicism*, on the contrary, presents to them that literature which gave the greatest possible pleasure to their great-grandfathers.

An anonymous French spoof at classicism has an actor teaching Napoleon the proper pose for an emperor: the stance of classic Greek statuary.

BIBLIOTHÈQUE NATIONALE; BULLOZ

Also fundamental to Romantic aesthetic theory was the denial of any absolute and immutable standards of beauty; it held that each work is an end in itself and must be judged on its own terms.

Although the flowering of Romanticism occurred at the very time when industrialism was beginning to transform Europe, Romantic writers and artists took little cognizance of it. Indeed, if one were to reconstruct the appearance of England solely from Romantic art and literature, one would imagine it to have been an age of bucolic serenity. The vast majority of Romantic novelists and painters simply ignored the factory or the coal pit, as well as the men working in them. This discrepancy between art and reality suggests how dangerous it is to judge the life of a period from its art.

The Romantics rejected the whole industrial order with its discipline, ugliness, and money-grubbing. They sought escape from it in distant times and distant places that they suitably "romanticized," that is, cleansed of sordid elements. Their favorites were the Middle Ages, the Orient, the Polar regions. They loved the world of children with its spontaneity and sense of wonder. Most of all, they liked to retreat from the city to the countryside, to "nature," as did Childe Harold, the hero of Byron's poem of the same name:

> Where rose the mountains, there to him were friends;
> Where rolled the Ocean, thereon was his home;
> Where a blue sky, and glowing clime, extends,
> He had the passion and power to roam;
> The desert, forest, cavern, breaker's foam,
> Were unto him companionship; they spake
> A mutual language, clearer than the tome
> Of his land's tongue, which he would oft forsake
> For Nature's pages glassed by sunbeams on the lake. . . .
> But in Man's dwellings he became a thing
> Restless and worn, stern and wearisome,
> Drooped as a wild-born falcon with clipt wing,
> To whom the boundless air alone were home.

In general, it may be said that the Romantics avoided the moderation and sensibility that had been the ideal of the classicists and inclined toward extremes of all kinds: experimental literary forms, musical sounds, visual images; extremes of the primitive, grotesque, abnormal. In an effort to transport themselves into the realm of extremes, some Romantic writers (e.g., the German E. T. A. Hoffmann and the Englishman Thomas De Quincey) deliberately induced hallucinations by means of opium and other narcotics.

Romanticism produced its own hero, writes the literary historian Paul van Tieghem, with principal characteristics common in all countries:

The Romantic hero is sometimes a great lord, but more often he is of low or unknown origin. A foundling, an illegitimate child, a plebeian, a valet, clown, or brigand, he feels bitterly the contrast between his social position and his true worth. Everyone owes him something—he owes no one anything. He is full of pride, bitterness, and anger. Isolated in society, he often loathes it. Surrounded by mystery, he is a pawn of an irresistible fatality

The Swiss John Henry Fuseli combined a passion for Shakespeare with a taste for the erotic and grotesque in his Midsummer's Night Dream. *In a trance inflicted by her husband Oberon, the fairy queen Titania embraces a humble weaver masked in the head of an ass.*

which has preordained him for blind passion, for a destiny of adventure and danger, for unavoidable crimes; and yet he is often, at bottom, sensitive and tender. Despite the intensity of his life and the external activism which he unfolds, he remains more passive than truly active; often, like Hamlet, with whom perhaps he has something in common, the Romantic hero hesitates and trembles when confronted with the need for action. In general, he is a frenetic lover, and his love is fatal for its object. He embodies the rights of love against the prejudices of society. Often ironic and haughty, he defies morals and laws.

The Romantic hero was a person estranged from the society in which he was compelled to live and from which he was forever trying to escape. He was the antithesis of the down-to-earth, prosaic, sensible, ordinary man, or "Philistine," as he came to be known later in the century.

The Romantic hero found his incarnation in George Gordon, Lord Byron. Byron not only helped to create the image of his hero in his writings (*Childe Harold, Don Juan*), but he shaped his own life in accord with it. For this reason, he was the most widely emulated person of the whole Romantic era. Between 1815 and 1830, youths all over Europe took to wearing open or "Byronic" col-

Byron designed a helmet appropriate to his role as a champion of Greek independence.

lars, affected "Byronic" haughtiness and spleen, and sought (fortunately, more often in words than in deeds) an early "Byronic" death.° Byron had all the qualifications necessary for his role: he was an aristocrat, a man of great gifts, a victim of social prejudice, and a champion of liberty. Until 1816 he had been very much a member of the English Establishment. He wrote successful verse, had access to the highest social circles, served in the House of Lords, and married an heiress. All was well, but had all remained well Byron would hardly have exerted much influence on Romantic youth. In 1816, just a year after they had been married, his wife sued for divorce. Although her reasons were not and are not to this day precisely known, London society turned against Byron. Deeply hurt, he left England in 1816, never to return. From then on until his death eight years later, he wandered over Europe, deliberately flaunting convention, attacking hypocrisy, and ridiculing the forces of reaction at a time when they were most potent. In his writings he could, when he wished, create lyric verse of the highest order, but much of the time he preferred to assume an air of cynical detachment toward his hero and himself—an attitude that contrasted with the usual solemnities of poetry and won him a great following among the reading public. He died of fever in 1824, fighting in the ranks of the Greek insurgents against the Turks.

The general principles of Romanticism—the assertion of the autonomy of European culture, the stress on individual self-fulfillment and complete creative freedom, the escapism from the industrial and urban toward the exotic and rural—had implications beyond literature and art. The Romantics, in the early phases of their movement, supported liberal causes all over Europe and were in the forefront of revolutionary upheavals directed against the conservative establishment. Romanticism had profound repercussions in philosophy and historical writing, in religious thought, in social theory, and even in science.

Romanticism at its height influenced all the countries within the orbit of Western civilization, from Russia in the East to Latin America in the West. But it was peculiarly a movement of northern Europe. Its home was Germany and England, and its impact was most felt in Teutonic countries. This is not surprising, in view of the fact that classicism, against which the Romantics rebelled, had its roots in Latin culture. Romanticism had difficulty penetrating France, Italy, or Spain; it did so belatedly, and never with the same force as in the north.

Chronologically, the Romantic movement may be divided into three periods: proto-Romanticism of the eighteenth century; Romanticism proper (approximately 1790–1830), with a high point in the 1820s; and decline, which set in during the 1830s, when it weakened and began to lose ground to realism and materialism.

Literature and the Theater   The first flowering of Romantic literature occurred in the late 1790s. To contemporaries, it seemed a strange and sudden phenomenon, but it came not with-

---

° It must be noted, however, that a remarkably large proportion of Romantic writers died young, sometimes of natural causes, sometimes as a result of self-destruction. John Keats died at twenty-five, the Hungarian poet Sándor Petöfi died at twenty-six, the Russian poet Mikhail Lermontov at twenty-seven, Novalis at twenty-nine, and Percy Bysshe Shelley at thirty. Among those who died in the fourth decade of their lives are the German poet Heinrich von Kleist (thirty-four), Byron (thirty-six), Alexander Pushkin (thirty-eight), the Italian poet Giacomo Leopardi (thirty-nine), and Edgar Allan Poe and the Polish poet Julius Slowacki (both at forty).

out warning. European literature of the eighteenth century had running through it a persistent strain of anticlassicism. England produced in the second third of the century an influential Sentimentalist school distinguished by love of nature and the Middle Ages as well as a stress on emotions. Among its best-known works are Edward Young's long poem *Night Thoughts on Life, Death, and Immortality* (1742–1745), Thomas Gray's "Elegy Written in a Country Churchyard" (1751), and the epics of the legendary Irish bard, Ossian, written (or rather, forged) by James Macpherson in the 1760s. Even more directly related to Romanticism were the writings of Jean Jacques Rousseau with their rejection of civilized life. This proto-Romantic tendency culminated in the 1770s and 1780s in the German "Sturm und Drang" ("Storm and Stress") movement, whose leaders were Johann von Goethe and Schiller and whose most influential work was Goethe's *The Sorrows of Young Werther* (1774).

Until the 1790s this current was decidedly subordinated to classicism. The fact that it gained ascendancy in the 1790s was not entirely fortuitous. Classicism had been identified with the absolute monarchy, and especially with the Bourbon monarchy, its principal patron. To many young Europeans, the fall of the Bourbons represented a signal to raise the banner of rebellion against classical authority in the arts. The struggle for the artist's right to create in complete freedom was, psychologically viewed, a counterpart of the civic and political liberties proclaimed by the French Revolution.

The Romantic movement, as we have seen, had its origin in Germany, but its leaders, the most notable being the brothers Frederick and August William Schlegel and the contributors to their journal, *Athenaeum* (1798–1800), distinguished themselves more as critics and theorists than as creative talents. The first significant and truly Romantic literary work appeared not in Germany but in England. It was *Lyrical Ballads*, a small volume of poems published anonymously in 1798. The product of a collaboration between two young poets, William Wordsworth and Samuel Taylor Coleridge, it achieved its effect of novelty by a deliberate violation of one of the cardinal rules of classicism: that under no condition must language appropriate for lofty subjects be used for subjects regarded as common, nor, conversely, must simple, everyday speech be employed for those subjects considered "sublime." Wordsworth and Coleridge had undertaken deliberately to challenge this rule by dealing with everyday matters in sublime language and with fantastic matters in ordinary language. The effect proved too startling for the tastes of the time, and the initial public reaction was unfavorable. Wordsworth's "Idiot Boy," Coleridge's "Rime of the Ancient Mariner," and other poems in the collection were criticized both for their choice of subject and their unsuitability of expression. Nevertheless, the breach in the classical fortress was made. With poets like Wordsworth, Coleridge, John Keats, Percy Bysshe Shelley, and Byron, English poetry, freed from its confines, achieved in the following three decades a level of distinction second only to that of the Elizabethan age.

Poetry was the first of the arts to abandon classicism in favor of Romanticism. After 1800 there emerged in various parts of Europe a new generation of writers who united in opposition to the old literary establishment. Romanticism, by rejecting classical models, stimulated the emergence of national literatures in coun-

A medallion portrait of Goethe done at Weimar in 1829, three years before the poet's death.

The historical novelist Sir Walter Scott is depicted as a Scottish country squire, the role he most enjoyed playing.

tries with weak or nonexistent classical traditions. Russian poets of the eighteenth century, for example, had to follow a classical model that had no roots in their own culture. Adherence to Romantic tenets permitted them to abandon this pretense and to write in a national idiom. Alexander Pushkin, who bridged the classical and Romantic ages of Russian literature, was not only Russia's greatest poet, but also the founder of its modern literary language. Romanticism had a similar effect on other cultures in eastern, southeastern, and central Europe.

While poetry was the principal medium of Romantic literature, prose also was affected by it. Here, the most important innovations were the historic novel and the fantastic tale. The creator of the historic novel was Sir Walter Scott, in his day widely regarded as Europe's leading prose writer. A native of Scotland, he avidly studied his country's past and collected its ballads. Scott's novels combined several elements dear to the Romantic taste: chivalry, the Middle Ages, and a northern setting. Its heroes were vastly different from early nineteenth-century Britons of nearby industrial Manchester. Scott found many emulators, among them the leader of the French Romantics, Victor Hugo, the author of *The Hunchback of Notre Dame* (1831).

The Romantic love for the unusual, especially the fantastic and grotesque, was connected with the belief that life was not what it seemed to mere reason, but instead contained mysteries revealed only to the imagination. This belief found literary expression in fantastic tales. The rage for this genre began in the 1790s with the novels of Ann Radcliffe, which were filled with supernatural incidents against a background of ruined medieval castles and abbeys. The genre was subsequently adopted by writers of major stature, who often heightened the horror by placing supernatural incidents in a realistic environment. Thus, the hero of Adelbert von Chamisso's *Peter Schlemihl* (1814) disposes of his shadow in a commercial transaction with the devil, while the subject of a short story by the Russian writer Nicolas Gogol wakes up one morning to find his nose gone

("The Nose," 1836). *Frankenstein* (1818) by Mary Shelley, the wife of the poet, which deals with a man-made monster, also belongs to this category. Perhaps the outstanding practitioners of fantastic tales were the German E. T. A. Hoffmann and the American Edgar Allan Poe.

The Romantics were much interested in folk literature, which they regarded as a repository of the primitive, "natural" spirit of Christian or "Romantic" culture lost by civilized man. They transcribed the poems, songs, and tales passed by the common people from generation to generation and reconstructed from such oral traditions and literary fragments their national epics. We owe to these efforts the preservation of a great literary heritage, much of which might otherwise have been lost. In Germany the brothers Jacob and Wilhelm Grimm, both professional philologists, collected folk stories, which in 1812–1815 they published in a celebrated book of fairy tales. Finnish folklorists reconstructed the text of their national epic, *Kalevala,* and the Russians transcribed the *byliny,* early heroic poems narrated by village bards. The predilection for the local and native also produced a body of regional literature written in dialects previously regarded as unsuitable for serious literary expression. Poems and stories appeared written in Provençal, Ukrainian, Alamannic, and various other peasant dialects.

Of all the literary genres, the drama succumbed last to the onslaughts of Romanticism. The stage had always been peculiarly in the domain of classicism. The aesthetic doctrines of Boileau found their purest realization in the plays of Jean Baptiste Racine. Altogether, in the theater the connection between classicism and the whole courtly and aristocratic establishment was firmly fixed. It was natural, therefore, that one of the most bitter contests between the old and new literary movements should have occurred in the theater and in France. The contest was climaxed by the so-called Battle of *Hernani,* which took place in Paris in February, 1830.

At issue was Shakespeare, whom the classicists regarded as an uncouth and inferior writer because he had consistently violated the Aristotelian unities, mixed the sublime with the ridiculous, and allowed emotion altogether too much scope. The anti-Shakespearean sentiment reached its greatest intensity in the 1760s and 1770s, when Voltaire attacked the English poet with all his wit and venom. He called Shakespeare a "barbarous charlatan" and described his dramas as a "dunghill containing a few pearls."

All the qualities of Shakespeare that had repelled the classicists endeared him to the Romantics. Indeed, in the early part of the nineteenth century, one's attitude toward Shakespeare became a touchstone of one's position in the whole classical-Romantic dispute. August von Schlegel, who translated Shakespeare's plays into German, regarded the English dramatist as the greatest representative of modern or Romantic genius. Coleridge, in a series of magnificent lectures in which he laid the foundations of modern Shakespearean criticism, extolled him as a peer of the greatest writers of antiquity, and in his book *Racine and Shakespeare* (1823), Stendhal depicted contemporary literary conflicts as a confrontation of the two styles represented by these writers.

The Romantic cause in France received a boost in 1827 when a visiting English theatrical group staged several of Shakespeare's plays. That same year,

Mary Godwin Shelley's Frankenstein *bested the efforts of both her husband and Byron in an informal horror-story contest. She wrote fiction and edited Shelley's works after his death.*

Victor Hugo, the leader of the literary rebels, wrote a play in the Romantic manner called *Cromwell*. He failed to have it staged, but his introduction to it created much stir and became the manifesto of the French Romanticists. Hugo rejected all classical rules, glorified Shakespeare, and called for a theater combining the "grotesque and the sublime, the awe-inspiring and the clownish, the tragic and the comical." "There exists today," he asserted, "a literary old regime, as there once existed a political old regime."

Hugo's opportunity to topple the "literary old regime" came three years later, in 1830, when the state-subsidized Théâtre-Français agreed to stage *Hernani*, his play written in the Shakespearean manner. For the Romantics, the first performance of *Hernani* was the literary equivalent of the storming of the Bastille. The novelist Théophile Gautier, a nineteen-year-old admirer of Hugo, assembled a band of writers, artists, bohemians, and ordinary hobos, for whom he purchased large blocks of seats to the opening night. Several hours before curtain time, Gautier, affecting a scarlet satin vest and green silk trousers, marched his band to the theater, where they amused themselves eating, drinking, and singing. By the time the well-to-do patrons began to arrive for the performance, the interior reeked of garlic and wine, as well as urine, for the Romantics thought nothing of relieving themselves against the walls of the auditorium. Gautier described the scene:

> In spite of the terror inspired by Hugo's partisans, who were scattered about in small parties and who were easily recognized by their peculiar costumes and their fierce looks, there sounded in the theater the low roar of the excited crowd, which is no more to be stilled than the roar of the sea. . . . It needed only to cast a glance at the public to learn that this was no ordinary performance; that two systems, two parties, two armies, two civilizations—it is no exaggeration to put it so—were facing each other, filled with cordial reciprocal hatred of the intense literary kind, ready to come to blows and longing for a fight. The general attitude was one of hostility; elbows were stuck out, the least friction would have sufficed to cause an outbreak, and it was easy to see that the long-haired youth considered the clean-shaven gentleman an atrocious idiot, and would not long refrain from giving expression to his private opinions.

Hugo's partisans had been cued beforehand which passages in *Hernani* had programmatic significance; whenever the actors pronounced these lines, they clapped, shouted, and made such a din that the classicists, if not persuaded, were at least silenced. Five months later came the July Revolution and the final extinction of Bourbon rule, and classicism in its traditional form suffered a defeat from which it has never recovered.

Music, Painting, and Architecture Romanticism found its most characteristic expression and reached its greatest creative heights in poetry and music, because these arts offered the artist the fullest freedom. In this respect, music was a vehicle superior even to poetry, for the musical language is infinite in its variety and utterly personal. In none of the other arts was the conquest of Romanticism so rapid and enduring.

Until Romanticism, music had performed essentially an auxiliary function, serving as an accompaniment or background to religious or social occasions. This functional role limited the freedom of the musician. Romanticism made music an end in itself and thereby emancipated him from such limitations. Musical performance now shifted from the church and salon to the concert hall, and the performer emerged from the obscurity of the organ loft or the orchestra pit into the limelight of the concert stage. Romanticism inaugurated the era of the musical genius, the virtuoso, and the great conductor. From one of the more marginal of the arts, music became, while Romanticism was at its height, the quintessence of art.

The Romantic composer took advantage of his freedom in several ways. For one, he experimented with new musical forms. In addition to sonatas, concertos, symphonies, or quartets, he composed songs, tone poems, incidental pieces, and vast secular works employing choruses and symphony orchestras. To list the names of the works of Frederick Chopin, the greatest Romantic composer for the piano, is to give an idea of the variety of musical forms used by the new school: they include ballades, nocturnes, preludes, scherzos, waltzes, and études. Romantics also took liberties with traditional forms. Beethoven, the greatest of all the Romantic composers, broke precedent by introducing in the second movement of his *Eroica Symphony* a funeral dirge and closing his *Ninth Symphony*

A contemporary engraving gives the flavor of the riotous first-night performance of Hugo's "Shakespearean" play Hernani *in Paris in 1830.*

A highly Romantic subject, the virtuoso violinist Nicolò Paganini, was sketched with a cool insight by Jean Auguste Dominique Ingres, a student of David's and the last great neoclassicist.

with a chorus singing Schiller's "Ode to Joy." In addition to experimenting with forms, Romantics also occasionally violated accepted practices in matters of melody and harmony, introducing combinations of sounds that the classical ear found dissonant and jarring.

Romantic composers favored the piano as an instrument that offered intimacy combined with great tonal range. Beethoven wrote thirty-two piano sonatas, some of which he or his audiences gave such descriptive titles as "Pathétique," "Pastoral," "Moonlight," and "Appassionata." The piano compositions of Robert Schumann also tended to convey emotion and imagery. Chopin composed almost exclusively for the piano, which he endowed with extraordinary intimacy.

Other popular Romantic genres were chamber music and serious songs, the latter often based on contemporary poems. The quartets of Beethoven are generally considered the finest of their kind, and some critics regard the last in the series (Nos. 12–16) as Beethoven's supreme achievement. The leading composers of songs were Franz Schubert and Robert Schumann.

Though they preferred intimate instruments and forms, the Romantic composers, given their penchant for extremes, also wrote for large orchestras. The symphony orchestra as we know it today is in large measure the creation of the Romantic age. It was then that the classical string ensemble of some thirty performers expanded, through the enlargement of the string section and the addition of winds and percussion instruments, to become the modern orchestra of a hundred or more players. The orchestra thus enlarged could no longer perform on its own and required a full-time director to give it cohesion. This was the task of the conductor, who first appeared in the 1820s to coordinate the large body of singers and musicians employed in Karl Maria von Weber's Romantic operas (*Der Freischütz*, 1821, and *Oberon*, 1826). From then on the conductor became an indispensable feature of orchestral performance and a virtuoso in his own right. Romantic composers sometimes went to wild extremes in orchestration. Louis Hector Berlioz was a great innovator in this respect. His *Symphonie Fantastique* (1830), which sought to convey musically the visions of an opium-eater, achieved unusual orchestral brilliance and paved the way for the later innovations of Richard Wagner. In search for even richer effects, Berlioz employed in his *Hymn to France* (1844) no fewer than 1,200 performers. He was also one of the inventors of so-called programmatic music, that is, music intended to narrate a story. Another outstanding Romantic composer for the orchestra was Felix Mendelssohn-Bartholdy. His *Incidental Music to Midsummer Night's Dream* (1826, 1842) and his overture to the *Hebrides* (1830) (also known as *Fingal's Cave*) are superb examples of Romantic music and convey most faithfully the whole spirit of Romanticism with its Shakespearean elves, Ossianic heroes, misty northern islands, and so much else that stirred the imagination of the time.

Of course, one of the basic forms remained the classical symphony, which the Romantics expanded in length and orchestral scope. The nine symphonies of Beethoven, the four of Schumann, the eight principal ones of Schubert, and the last three of Mendelssohn are among the most majestic achievements of Romanticism. They constitute a staple of the modern orchestral repertoire.

Romanticism dominated music throughout the nineteenth century. The great composers of the second half of the century—Richard Wagner, Johannes Brahms, Giuseppe Verdi, Peter Ilyich Tchaikovsky—were Romantics, despite the fact that they lived in an environment that had become hostile to Romanticism.

In the visual arts Romanticism had a less pronounced impact than in either literature or music, for the academies managed to retain their influence over painters by continuing to control art schools, exhibition halls, and commissions. The Romantic school of painting concerned itself most characteristically with nature. The landscape, which in the classical era had served mainly as a backdrop for figures, now became an independent and favorite subject matter. The Romantics neither idealized nature nor reproduced it with realistic accuracy, but sought to penetrate its spirit and to convey its infinite variety of moods. They placed less emphasis on design and more on color, and in this respect they clearly anticipated the Impressionists. The French Romantic painter Ferdinand Delacroix expressed the Romantic attitude accurately when he said a painting should be a "feast to the eye." The pioneers of the Romantic school were two Englishmen, J. M. W. Turner and John Constable. Turner was obsessed with color and went to great lengths to capture it on canvas. It is said that to paint his *Steamer in a Snowstorm* (1842), a work of almost abstract quality, he had himself tied to the mast of a storm-tossed ship. Unfortunately, the colors have deteriorated on many of his paintings and do not render justice to his original visions. Constable's landscapes shimmer and pulsate as few landscapes had ever done before. Both Turner and Constable made sketches in the open, but they painted indoors, because the paints available in their time had to be ground and resolved in oil immediately before use, a task that could be performed only in the studio. Water colors, however, were not subject to this limitation and could be finished on the spot, like a pencil sketch. Early nineteenth-century English water colors convey a freshness and immediacy equal to the best Impressionist works.

In 1828 Paris held an exhibit of English landscape painting that, like the performances by the visiting Shakespeare players the previous year, exerted much influence on French tastes. Constable became the rage. In 1836 Theodore Rousseau launched a native school of Romantic landscape painters when he left Paris for the village of Barbizon in the nearby Fontainbleau Forest to paint in the open. He and his followers founded the Barbizon school, whose greatest representative was Camille Corot, a master of landscapes in delicate silvery gray and pale green hues. Similar Romantic landscape schools arose in other countries, including the United States, where its adherents formed the so-called Hudson River school.

Romantic painters also liked Oriental and Mediterranean themes and painted Arabs, Spaniards, and Greeks, often in settings of violent action. The leading exponent of this genre was Delacroix, who did many colorful canvases depicting scenes from North Africa and episodes from the Greek war for independence (see Portfolio One). A minor school concentrated on grotesque and spooky themes, its adherents painting moonlit nights and ruins, ghosts, and mysterious shapes of various kinds, all calculated to frighten the onlooker. The most popular artist in this genre was the German Caspar David Friedrich (pages 98–99).

The perfection in 1819 of lithography—the art of striking prints from draw-

The English architect James Wyatt designed the emphatically Gothic Fonthill Abbey for an eccentric squire. Completed in 1807, the octagonal tower collapsed in 1825; the whole immense structure was later demolished.

J. RUTTER, *The Delineations of Fonthill*, 1823

ings done with a fatty substance on stone—offered a medium for quick and cheap reproduction. It became one of the favorite media, particularly useful for caricature. Its leading practitioner was Honoré Daumier, whose savage satires of the bourgeoisie under Louis Philippe initiated modern propaganda art.

Concurrently with Romantic painting there developed a movement that is difficult to classify. It was characterized by a desire to return to the simplicity and naïveté of early Italian painting. Its founders, a group of German artists known as Nazarenes, settled in Rome in 1810 and emulated the style of the artists of the fourteenth and fifteenth centuries. A related school, the Pre-Raphaelite Brotherhood, was established later (1848) by Dante Gabriel Rossetti in England. Both these circles were in some respects quite academic in their tastes, but in their admiration for the Middle Ages they resembled the Romantics.

In architecture Romanticism found its main expression in the Gothic Revival, which imitated medieval designs (or what its exponents regarded as medieval designs) and décor. The taste for Gothic building developed slowly, having to contend with a virile classical tradition in architecture, which achieved some of its greatest triumphs in the early nineteenth century. The first significant success of the new style occurred when its exponents won the commission to design a House of Parliament to replace the one that had burned in 1834. The result was exceptionally happy and was widely emulated in other parts of Europe. The Hungarian parliament building, the Vienna city hall, Memorial Hall at Harvard University, and many churches were built in the Gothic style. In Russia, which had no Gothic tradition, this movement yielded a parallel Byzantine Revival. Devotees of these various revivals stopped at nothing. They produced neo-Gothic interiors true to the smallest detail, including "Gothic" kitchens and bathrooms. Ludwig II, the king of Bavaria, constructed between 1869 and 1886 at Neuschwanstein a huge Alpine castle, with innumerable towers, turrets, spires, and all the other trappings of Gothic architecture. Many tourists regard Neuschwanstein Castle as an impressive example of medieval art, but it is actually only the last gasp of Gothic revivalism.

Philosophic Idealism

Romanticism was primarily an aesthetic movement: it concerned itself with art as the highest expression of the human spirit. The Romantics looked down on philosophers, partly because they had been the leaders of the Enlightenment, and partly because they lacked "creative genius." Nevertheless, Romanticism itself rested on very definite philosophical foundations, and it cannot be understood unless one obtains at least a general notion what these were.

The philosophical current associated with Romanticism is known as idealism. It came into existence in Germany between approximately 1780 and 1820 and dominated European thought throughout the Romantic era. It counted among its adherents all Romantics, even those who had never read a philosophical book.

Idealism emerged from a critique of the theories of empiricism, the dominant philosophical school of the eighteenth century. Empiricists such as Locke and Hume maintained that all knowledge derives from experience, that the mind has no "innate ideas." Until experience writes on it, the human mind resembles a clean slate. The most extreme empiricists went so far as to deny the existence of anything not capable of being perceived by the senses. Empiricism broadly

The philosopher Immanuel Kant led a life of almost perfect punctuality, his daily routine so unvarying that his friends set their watches by him.

defined may be said to have been the underlying philosophy of early modern science and owed much of its acceptance to scientific progress.

The most important critic of the empirical school, and the forefather of idealism, was the German philosopher Immanuel Kant. Kant conceded that knowledge derives from experience but argued that this proposition required qualification. He could point, for example, to an important realm of knowledge, mathematics, that has no basis in experience: nothing in our experience teaches us that the corners of a triangle add up to 180 degrees, or that any of the other axioms of algebra and geometry are correct. Mathematical truths obviously belong to a different order of knowledge. Awareness of this distinction induced Kant to analyze in detail the means by which we learn, the principal conclusions of which he presented in the *Critique of Pure Reason* (1781), one of the most seminal books in the entire history of thought.

Kant analyzed the cognitive apparatus and stated that the mind has built into it categories through which and through which alone it apprehends the data that the senses feed into it. The most obvious among these categories are the notions of space and time: we conceive everything by mentally locating it either in space, or in time, or in both. Space and time are, therefore, not qualities of reality itself, but of our mind. The external world as we know it is not the world as it actually is. Its real identity is beyond our grasp; it is the world as it appears after having been processed or filtered through the built-in apparatus of the human intellect. The mind, seen in this light, is not merely a passive recipient of information supplied by the senses. It is a very active organ, filled with understanding that precedes and is independent of experience. Mathematics is an aspect of this non-experimental knowledge.

From the point of view of cultural history, the most important consequence of Kant's theory lay in the shift that it accomplished in the role of the intellect. It was viewed no longer as the clean slate of the empiricists, but as a wonderfully complex apparatus with much understanding—a peer, as it were, of nature itself. This elevated notion of the mind suited the Romantic mood, and the Romantics turned into enthusiastic adherents of Kantian philosophy.

A succession of German philosophers, departing from Kantian principles, constructed individual systems of idealistic philosophy that were exceedingly abstruse and complicated. The most influential of such systems was that of G. W. F. Hegel, formulated in the first and second decades of the nineteenth century. Hegelianism was an ambitious attempt to reconcile "ideas" and "reality" within a single all-embracing scheme. The Hegelian philosophy was dynamic, in the sense that it conceived reality as moving in time and acting through history. Other important idealist philosophers were J. G. Fichte and F. W. J. von Schelling. The various idealist systems had one quality in common, and that was the stress on the creativity of the mind (or "Self" or "Absolute," as it was sometimes called). In this respect they went far beyond Kant. In its extreme form, idealism denied the existence of objective reality altogether and claimed that thought alone had true existence.

Historicism

Until the late eighteenth century history was a branch of philosophy; that is to say, it was regarded as a kind of gloss or illustration of abstract truths. The old saying "History is philosophy taught by examples" perfectly reflects this attitude. A seventeenth- or eighteenth-century reader opened Plutarch less to learn about antiquity than to obtain time-hallowed guidance in the art of statesmanship. In so doing, he denied (whether or not he was aware of it) any qualitative difference between the ancient and the contemporary worlds. Such an attitude conformed, of course, to the whole classicist spirit.

The Romantics, more than anyone else, discredited this view. The modern attitude toward the past, which has come to be called "historicism," is not only one of the most important legacies of Romanticism, but a landmark in the evolution of human thought.

The creator of historicism was Johann Gottfried von Herder, a German philosopher active in the last three decades of the eighteenth century. Herder developed his concept of history in the "Storm and Stress" period, that is, before Romanticism proper got under way. In several works, the most important of which is *Ideas Toward a Philosophy of the History of Mankind* (1784–1791), he spoke of the unique contribution that each culture made to human history. Every nation and every age has its own merit; each is equally near God. "No object in the whole divine order is a means only—everything is both means and goal." Thus there are no "superior" and ":inferior" histories. Man should not aspire to some fixed model, but develop the qualities inherent in the spirit of his own culture or its "ethos." "Every nation has within itself the center of happiness, just as every sphere has its center of gravity." For Herder, the history of humanity was an endlessly varied mosaic, to which each nation makes its own contribution. Although he was not without forerunners, Herder must be given main credit for the concept of world history as a dynamic process involving all mankind.

This concept was further developed by Schelling and particularly by Hegel, who regarded history as a purposeful process whose main phases were marked by the great civilizations. The progress of history represents an irresistible movement toward freedom: in the ancient Oriental states one man only was free; in classical Greece and Rome some were free; in the "Germanic" world all were free. The modern Prussian state represented the culmination of the historic process. This historical philosophical approach, although originally devised for Germany for the purpose of extolling its contribution to world civilization, lent itself perfectly for export and was adopted for their own purposes by nationalists all over Europe.

The basis of historicism is the assumption that every historical phenomenon is unique and self-contained. What the ancient Greeks did helps us understand the Greeks; it tells us nothing about medieval Frenchmen or modern Germans. Historicism denies abstract "man" and eternal truths, much as did Edmund Burke, the British statesman who was one of its progenitors. Its essential quality is relativism, and in this respect it accords with the whole Romantic penchant for the unique and its hostility toward absolute standards.

The historicist outlook exerted its most immediate effect on the writing of history. The school of historians that arose in Germany in the early years of the nineteenth century made a deliberate effort to understand past eras as they actually had been, that is, on their own terms, and not as they appeared from the vantage point of either classical or modern cultures. Barthold Niebuhr's *History of Rome* (1811–1812) is generally recognized as the first work of modern historical scholarship. It owes this reputation to the author's endeavor, by a critical use of sources, to reconstruct Roman events cleansed of the patina put on them by modernizing classicists. The greatest exponent of the new tendency was Leopold von Ranke, who, in a lifetime extending over ninety-one years (1795–1886), produced a vast quantity of works on all epochs, including a monumental *History of the Popes* (1834–1836) and *German History in the Time of the Reformation* (1839–1847). For Ranke, the aim of the historian was to penetrate and to convey the uniqueness, the specific quality of the subject, to seize that essence which differentiates it from all others. Modern historical scholarship rests on the foundations laid by the great German scholars of the early part of the nineteenth century, for what distinguishes modern history writing from pre-Romantic history writing is precisely the belief in the uniqueness of phenomena.

The principle of historicism did not remain confined to professional historiography. In some ways it affected all branches of learning. Let us take law, for example. The concept of "natural law," on which had rested much French revolutionary legislation and the basic liberal doctrine, implied eternal, absolute, immutable standards of good and right. The statement "all men are born free," self-evident as it may seem, in fact silently assumes an abstract "man" whom it contrasts with actual (i.e., non-free) man. The Romantic historicists (as Burke before them) questioned whether this abstract man existed. The founder of the his-

The Englishman William Blake—artist, poet, mystic—portrayed the drama of Genesis; here, a winged, patriarchal God shapes Adam from primordial dust and, literally, the coil of mortality.

torical school of law, Frederick Savigny, maintained that all law was the product of a specific environment and that its roots had to be sought not in abstract rights, but in the "spirit" from which it had emerged. From this point of view, customary (that is, unwritten) law is superior to Roman law, because it derives from and presumably corresponds to the "spirit" of the people who had given rise to it. Similarly striking conclusions were obtained from the application of historicism to other areas of knowledge, such as economics and philology.

Nationalism drew considerable encouragement from historicism. The notion of cultural uniqueness—all nations, as all eras, being equally near God—encouraged intellectuals of small or backward countries to advance bold claims. It is on such grounds that Fichte, in his *Addresses to the German People* (1807–1808), could preach the world supremacy of Germans. Slavic intellectuals, under similar influences, predicted the coming superiority of their race. In Italy Vincenzo Gioberti's book *On the Civil and Moral Primacy of the Italians* (1843) made even more extravagant claims, asserting that Italians had led Europe in all the arts and skills, including warfare. Each such claim rested on different criteria of national greatness, but no one seemed troubled by their mutual incompatibility.

It would be difficult to exaggerate the importance of historicism. It is so much a part of our whole way of looking at things that we may have difficulty realizing how novel the theory was in its day. Some of the most influential ideas of the nineteenth century, including Darwin's theory of evolution and Marxism, derive from it, in the sense that they view reality not as fixed but as dynamic and meaningfully evolving.

One of the characteristic qualities of the Romantics was religiousness. For some of them, Christianity was the essence of all modern or Romantic civilization, the Western counterpart of classical mythology. For others, it was the supreme expression of all the mysterious and beautiful in life. They favored Roman Catholicism, both because it was the religion of the Middle Ages, which they admired, and because it had such splendid ritual.

Religion

Signs of a religious revival became apparent almost immediately after the outbreak of the French Revolution. In the early 1790s Joseph de Maistre and Louis de Bonald, leading conservative theorists, independently and concurrently developed a theory that explained the Revolution as the will of Divine Providence. In 1799 the German Romantic Novalis (Baron von Hardenberg), in an essay called *Christianity or Europe*, extolled the Middle Ages as a period of spiritual unity, when a single Christian faith united all Europe. But the most influential work of the religious revival was René de Chateaubriand's *The Genius of Christianity* (1802), a paean in praise of Christianity as more profound and more beautiful and in every other way superior to classicism:

Of all the religions which have ever existed, Christianity is the most poetic, most human, the most conducive to freedom, to the arts and literature. . . . The modern world owes it all, from agriculture to the abstract sciences, from hospices for the unfortunate to the temples built by Michelangelo and decorated by Raphael. . . . There is nothing more divine than its morality, nothing more lovely, more grand than its dogmas, its doctrine, its ritual. . . . It encourages genius, purifies taste, develops virtuous emotions, infuses thought with vigor, furnishes the writer with noble forms and the sculptor with perfect shapes.

Chateaubriand's book, promoted by Napoleon to justify his Concordat with the Vatican, had a wide audience throughout Europe. It was followed by other works extolling Christianity, usually in its Catholic form, at the expense of antiquity. In its extreme form, the Catholic revival became known as ultramontanism, a movement inspired by Joseph de Maistre that preached the supremacy of the Pope over secular rulers. Many Romantics converted to Catholicism. The early nineteenth century witnessed the re-establishment of the Jesuit order (1814) and the founding of numerous societies for the propagation of the faith. In 1826 King Ludwig I of Bavaria founded the University of Munich to serve as a center of Catholic learning and a counterpart to the Protestant University of Berlin. The Catholic revival even reached Orthodox Russia. There, between 1829 and 1831, Peter Chaadaev wrote a series of *Philosophical Letters* in which he predicted the continued stagnation and backwardness of Russia because it had taken Christianity not from Rome but from corrupt Byzantium. In Poland the cause of national liberation fused with that of Catholicism. The leading Polish Romantic poet, Adam Mickiewicz, extolled his country as the "Christ of nations" whose suffering would redeem the world, as Christ's had redeemed mankind.

In England the religious revival found expression in the Oxford Movement, whose adherents protested against the worldliness and rationalism of the Anglican Church and wished to reinfuse the church with a sense of mystery and beauty, to free it from its dependence on the state, and altogether to give it greater importance in the life of the individual and the nation. The movement was launched in 1833 at Oriel College, Oxford, when John Keble, a newly appointed professor of poetry, delivered a celebrated sermon on "National Apostasy." In it, he protested against the recent emancipation of the Catholics and the subservience of the Anglican Church to the state. Keble was joined by John Henry Newman, with whom he published a series of widely read *Tracts for the Times* (from 1833 on). Newman was not satisfied even with a revitalized Anglicanism, and in 1845 converted to Catholicism. The Oxford (or, as it is sometimes called, the Tractarian) Movement brought ritual back into the Anglican Church and in general stimulated religious sentiment.

In Russia the challenge of Catholicism engendered an important lay religious movement known as "Slavophilism." Slavophilism was more than a religious phenomenon: its doctrines embraced philosophy of history, politics, and social matters. Though it was in effect a theory of Russian national identity, at its base lay a religious doctrine formulated in the 1840s by Alexis Khomiakov. Khomiakov asserted (in answer to Chaadaev) the superiority of the Orthodox faith to both Catholicism and Protestantism, by virtue of its being uncorrupted by worldly concerns and classical philosophy and thereby adhering more faithfully to the spirit of original Christianity. Khomiakov and his circle formulated the first Orthodox philosophy attractive to intellectuals. It became the source of all modern Russian religious thought.

Romanticism also gave rise to mystic movements, most of them variants of neo-Platonism. The discoveries of science, such as magnetism and electricity,

"I was in love with fame as with a woman," wrote Chateaubriand. This 1807 portrait is by Anne Louis Girodet.

also received pseudo-religious connotations and provided the basis of a "Romantic science," some of it silly, some of it plainly dishonest.

The religious revival essentially affected the upper class and the educated. Among the lower classes, the early nineteenth century witnessed rather a loosening of religious ties and a weakening of religious sentiments, especially in countries that underwent significant industrialization. The shift from the village into the city tended to break the bonds linking working families with the church and to encourage a mood of indifference toward religion and its institutions. The English census taken in 1851 found that more than 5 million persons, representing a third of the population of England and Wales, did not attend any church and that half of those who did were dissenters or Catholics. Much the same probably held true of other industrialized and urbanized countries.

Romanticism in the narrow sense of the word was a new literary and artistic style that rejected formalized classicism in favor of spontaneous forms and themes. But in a broader sense it was the beginning of a cultural revolution, the first assertion of an autonomous Western civilization. As the Renaissance had freed Western culture from its subservience to religion and facilitated the emergence of secularism, so Romanticism reduced the authority of classicism and inaugurated an era of artistic and literary freedom, which is the essence of modernity.

The Historic Significance of Romanticism

The full implications of this revolution were not then seen, because the Romantics still adhered to many classical values—more so than they realized, or than one could infer from their anticlassical zeal. But the principle of creativeness as an end in itself and subject only to its own criteria, once launched, has been subsequently pushed to ever greater extremes. Our own culture is a linear descendant of Romantic culture in the sense that it is uncompromisingly individualistic and rejects all restraints on creative freedom.

Romanticism enormously enriched Western art and thought, if only because it enlarged the variety of means available to creative talent. It permitted the use of a vocabulary and a meter, of color combinations, and of harmonies that the preceding age rejected as barbarous. It also opened up to serious inquiry subjects (e.g., folklore or the history of smaller nations) that had previously been deemed unworthy of attention.

But everything has its price. Until the advent of Romanticism, Western culture had rested on a consensus of values and tastes, whether Christian or classical. Romanticism began to destroy that consensus. By rejecting absolute criteria and making self-realization the aim as well as the standard of all creativity, it not only undermined the cultural unity of Western civilization, but contributed heavily to the eventual breakdown of understanding between the creator and his audience. The aesthetic theories of Romanticism, when revived on the eve of the twentieth century, caused a growing estrangement between art and literature on the one hand and the public on the other. For better or worse, twentieth-century modernism derives from the aesthetic of Romanticism pushed to its logical conclusion.

The Romantic Impulse

I will not Reason and Compare: my Business is to Create," wrote the English poet William Blake. On the other side of Europe in Vienna, Ludwig van Beethoven proclaimed, "In a man, music should strike fire from his spirit." In France the painter Eugene Delacroix noted in his diary, "In some people the inner spark scarcely exists. I find it dominant in me. Without it, I should die, but it will consume me (doubtless I speak of the imagination, which masters and leads me)." Though Blake, Beethoven, and Delacroix shared neither a common country nor a common medium of expression, as Romantics they were united in their rejection of the rigid rules of classicism and in their espousal of the unrestricted imagination.

The Romantics viewed imagination both as a purely individual quality and as a "Divine Vision." Blake expressed this double quality poetically: "The Sun's light when he unfolds it/ Depends upon the Organ that beholds it." The German critic Frederick Schlegel made the same claim in prose: "It is precisely individuality that is the original and eternal thing in men. . . . The cultivation and development of this individuality, as one's highest vocation, would be a divine egoism."

The Romantics considered the French Revolution and the meteoric rise of Napoleon the signal for a new era ruled by divine egoism, or genius, as it came to be called. In his poem *The French Revolution*, written in 1804, Wordsworth expressed the elation with which Romantics greeted the opportunities created by the fall of the *ancien régime:* "Bliss was it in that dawn to be alive, but to be young was very heaven!" Joyfully he contemplated the debacle of the old order's "meagre, stale, forbidding ways of custom, law, and statute" and called upon those "who had fed their childhood upon dreams . . . who had made all powers of swiftness, subtilty, and strength their ministers" to create a new order. "Poets," wrote Shelley in full agreement a decade later, "are the unacknowledged legislators of the world."

With the accent on individual vision, the impulses of the Romantics proved highly varied, yet certain themes have come to express the quintescence of Romanticism. In *Mephistopheles Flying Over the City* (left) Eugene Delacroix engraved not just an illustration for Goethe's *Faust*, a favorite Romantic subject itself, he also portrayed the Romantics' relish in the demoniac pursuit of supernatural power. In a like manner, Delacroix's 1827 canvas at right, *Greece Expiring on the Ruins of Missolonghi*, records not just the successful Turkish siege of the insurgent Greeks at Missolonghi in 1826 and the earlier death there of Lord Byron (the poet's still bleeding hand protrudes from beneath the ruins), but the Romantics' highly theatrical devotion to national liberation as well.

Byron the Hero

W hilome in Albion's isle there dwelt a youth,/ Who ne in virtue's ways did take delight;/ But spent his days in riot most uncouth,/ And vex'd with mirth the drowsy ear of Night." Thus in March of 1812, at the age of twenty-four, George Gordon, Lord Byron, introduced himself as the wicked hero of his epic poem, *Childe Harold's Pilgrimage*. By April London society had a new hero. "The subject of conversation, of curiosity, of enthusiasm," wrote the Duchess of Devonshire, "is not Spain or Portugal, warriors, or patriots, but Lord Byron."

The fascination had cause. Born with a deformed foot, fatherless at three, heir to a barony and a Gothic abbey at six, tortured by a sadistic quack, seduced by his nurse, subjected to the violent outbursts of his dour Scots mother, and possessed by a tempestuous mind, young Byron considered himself a fallen angel, a miscreant Mephistopheles. At the age of twenty-one he had left England for the Mediterranean where he swam the Hellespont, chatted with the sultan in Constantinople, and crossed Albania with an outlaw chieftan. Byron refurbished these wanderings of the child and the man as the pilgrimage of Childe Harold.

London's ladies found Byron "mad, bad, and dangerous," but swore in the next breath, "That beautiful pale face is my fate." One scandal followed another, including probable incest and a disastrous marriage. Gossip turned to outrage. In 1816 Byron left England never to return. Abroad, the fallen angel wrote and lived as extravagantly and brilliantly as ever, laying bare "the pageant of his bleeding heart" and rebelling against hypocrisy and tyranny wherever he found them. At the age of thirty-six, "a young, old man," as he put it, Byron sought and found a hero's death aiding the rebellious Greeks against their Turkish masters.

Romantic painters found Byron and his poetry irresistible subject matter. John Martin's 1837 water color above, Manfred on the Jungfrau, depicts the guilt-ridden, oblivion-seeking Manfred (Byron's 1817 literary version of his tormented self) being restrained from suicide by a kindly chamois hunter. At the left is Thomas Phillips' portrait of Byron in Albanian dress, done in England after Byron's return from the Mediterranean. At the right is an illustration from an early edition of Byron's epic poem Don Juan, that shows the hero wooing—and undoing—the Greek maid Haidée.

In 1845, twenty-three years after Shelley drowned, his friend and admirer Joseph Severn painted this memorial canvas, Shelley Composing 'Prometheus Unbound' in the Baths of Caracalla. The Romantic critic William Hazlitt had less love for the expatriate Shelley. "The author of Prometheus Unbound," wrote Hazlitt, "has a fire in his eye, a fever in his blood, a maggot in his brain, a hectic flutter in his speech. . . . His bending, flexible form appears to take no strong hold of things, does not grapple with the world about him, but slides from it like a river."

Sweet Exile

Byron was not alone in swearing "I will not descend to a world I despise" and then thumbing his nose at his native land, its politics, and its customs. Despite the jocular vein of George Cruikshank's 1816 cartoon (below) lampooning Byron's departure from England, or the lush sentimentality of Joseph Severn's painting of Shelley composing verse amidst Roman ruins, exile was serious Romantic business. Almost entirely self-imposed, exile was both a way out of ordinary life—"this cold common hell" Shelley called it—and a way into the incandescent realm of the Romantic imagination. In *Alastor*, writing of his poet hero, Shelley described both the pattern and the reason for exile: ". . . When early youth had passed, he left/ His cold fireside and alienated home/ To seek strange truths in undiscovered lands."

Among the delights of exile was consorting with other exiles. On the shore of Switzerland's Lake Geneva Madame de Staël received a steady stream of precocious and disgruntled fellow Romantics. From Germany came the Schlegel brothers spouting Romantic ideals, from France came Chateaubriand oozing sentimentality, from England came Lord Byron licking his wounds, and the young lovers, Percy Bysshe Shelley and his talented consort and wife-to-be, Mary Godwin. A few years later Shelley set up his own refugee camp for Romantics in Italy, and found it so delightful that he wrote, "Thou Paradise of exiles, Italy!"

But the true bonanza of Romantic exile was the finding of Shelley's "strange truths in undiscovered lands," which foreign soil yielded in profusion. Byron's wanderings, for example, inspired not only *Childe Harold's Pilgrimage*, but also *Manfred, The Prisoner of Chillon*, and *Don Juan*. It was in Italy that Shelley wrote *Adonais, Ode to the West Wind*, and *Prometheus Unbound*, and a soiree of exiles at Lake Geneva prompted one of the stranger "truths," Mary Shelley's *Frankenstein*.

KEATS-SHELLEY MEMORIAL HOUSE, ROME

93

Morocco so delighted Delacroix that he spoke of it as "my Morocco" and filled seven sketch books there. According to the French ambassador, Delacroix made his sketches during the day and then "At night, in the silence of his tent, when everyone was asleep, he would touch them up with water colors." On his return Delacroix painted more finished versions, such as Horsemen Resting Near Tangiers (above). At the right is an 1832 water color, Arab at Prayer. Another 1832 water color, Fantasia (below), records the arrival of his party at Meknes in the desert. "Our entry was a lovely sight." Delacroix noted, "At every turn we encountered groups of armed tribesmen who squandered incredible quantities of gunpowder to celebrate our coming. Sometimes we even heard bullets overhead; they'd forgotten to use blanks!"

The Lure of the Exotic

Like Lord Byron, whom he greatly admired, Eugène Delacroix was fascinated by the Muslim world. For years, in vast canvases filled with color, violence, and sensuality, such as *The Death of Sardanapalus* (overleaf), Delacroix had painted the exotic even though his inspiration came only from Romantic literature and paintings. But in 1832 he made a fateful six-month journey to Morocco. On his arrival in Tangiers he wrote, "I am like a man dreaming, who sees things he is afraid to see escape him."

In fact, Delacroix let little escape. Day and night he prowled the bazaars, slums, and seraglios of Algeciras. Even when he rode 200 miles inland to the desert fortress of Meknes, he continued to sketch, resting his notebook on the pommel of his saddle. The immediate results were the deft water colors on the opposite page, but for Delacroix, as for all Romantic artists, observation was the springboard for imagination. Back in Paris he fused notes, sketches, and memories into hundreds of canvases such as *The Lion Devouring a Horse* (below), painted about 1850, that blended, as Baudelaire pointed out, "dreams and drama in a mysterious reality."

OVERLEAF: *In 1826, inspired by Byron's tragic play, Delacroix painted his own spectacular version of* The Death of Sardanapalus. *On his divan the world-weary and defeated Assyrian king impassively watches the slaughter of his harem and his charger before setting fire to his palace, his treasures, and himself.*

KUNSTHALLE, HAMBURG

The Inward Vision

At the heart of the Romantic impulse lay a profound desire to commune with God or what the Romantics felt to be *the* reality that lay behind reality as observed by the senses. German Romantics had their own version of this theme, the cult of *Sehnsucht*—a dreamlike longing for the ineffable and unattainable. Probably no painter expressed this mood or tasted more fully of the despair it brought than Caspar David Friedrich. With Romantic fervor he cried out against optimistic rationalists: "O, you good-natured people, who do not recognize the inner drive and tension of the soul, and want Man not as the loving God has created, coined, and stamped him, but as time and fashion will have him." To portray the tension-ridden landscape of the soul Friedrich advised artists to "shut your physical eye and look first at your picture with your spiritual eye, then bring to the light of day what you have seen in the darkness." Like many soul-searching Romantics, Friedrich found God "everywhere, even in a grain of sand." But his profound melancholy, which eventually became insanity, turned what might have been joyful pantheistic visions into moody, almost sinister landscapes that fused the natural with the supernatural and beauty with despair.

Deepening melancholy marks Friedrich's artistic development. About 1811 he finished The Cross and the Cathedral in the Mountains (right) using the church as a symbol of redemption from the oppressive forest of life. Man and Woman Gazing at the Moon (below, painted in 1819) shows his growing obsession with the nocturnal aspect of natural phenomenon. In 1821 Friedrich painted The Wreck of the 'Hope' (left), which recorded not only the news of the foundering of a ship and the memory of his brother crushed by ice-floes on the Elbe, but also his own engulfing despair.

Nature Discovered

Dr. Johnson neatly summed up the Enlightenment's attitude toward nature when he said, "A blade of grass is always a blade of grass; men and women are *my* subjects of enquiry." Then came Rousseau, and the race for wood, field, and stream was on. By 1798 William Wordsworth was extolling a new mistress of the mind in a poem entitled, significantly, *The Tables Turned.* "One impulse from a vernal wood," he wrote, "May teach you more of man,/Of moral evil and of good,/ Than all the sages can."

The Romantics considered nature an "active principle" and they felt that she must be perceived by "a heart that watches and receives." Nature not only yielded a profusion of sensations and "thoughts that do often lie too deep for tears," but, in keeping with the active principle idea, she was also seen as a friend and consoler in times of misery. In his poem *Adonais*, commemorating the death of Keats, Shelley gave a vivid example of the Romantic belief in the mystic bond between man and nature when he described how, in a fit of grief, "Morning . . . dimmed the aëreal eyes that kindle day," while the "Pale Ocean in unquiet slumber lay,/ And the wild Winds flew round, sobbing in their dismay."

Believing that "Nature is Spirit visible," the Romantic English landscape painters pursued their subject with unusual devotion. John Constable, whose 1826 painting The Cornfield *is shown at left, believed that "The landscape painter must walk in the fields with a humble mind. No arrogant man was ever permitted to see nature in all her beauty." Constable considered the more impressionistic landscapes of J.M.W. Turner, such as* The Lake of Zug *(above), painted in 1843, "golden visions" which, said Constable humbly, "one would like to live and die with."*

101

The painting above, done by Joseph Danhauser in 1840, is an example not only of the fusion of the arts, but also of sentimental Romanticism. At the piano is Franz Liszt, staring dreamily at a bust of Beethoven. At his right is one of his great loves, the Comtesse Marie d'Agoult. Seated behind Liszt are the novelists George Sand (in man's clothing) and Alexandre Dumas. Behind them Paganini stands between Victor Hugo and the rotund Rossini, the evening's host. Liszt may well have been playing Chopin, whose music he described in true Romantic vernacular: "A bitter and irreparable regret seizes the wildly-throbbing human heart, even in the midst of the incomparable splendour of external nature."

New Forms in Music

"From the heart, may it go to the heart," Beethoven wrote as the inscription to his monumental mass *Missa Solemnis*. In those few words he summed up the credo of Romantic music. When the great composer conducted his *Battle Symphony* following Wellington's victory at Vittoria, "the applause rose to the point of ecstasy"; when Paganini, the Italian violin virtuoso, performed, "screams of delight and astonishment burst from the audience"; when the German writer E.T.A. Hoffmann listened to Chopin, he found himself embraced by "a confusion of colors, sounds, and perfumes . . . as though they all sprang up mysteriously from some ray of light and then united to form a marvelous concert."

The success of Romantic music lay in the wide range of innovations in musical forms developed by the composers. In turn, these changes were facilitated by technical innovations. New fingering mechanisms greatly improved the flute, oboe, and clarinet; valves provided the horn and trumpet with a complete chromatic scale; the iron frame, steel strings, and an improved sounding board turned the piano into a one-man-orchestra; and improved metals added tone and power to the tympany, kettledrums, and cymbals. The range of orchestral possibilities was so great that in his opera *La Muette de Portici* the French composer Daniel Auber did not hesitate to throw in an eruption of Vesuvius.

Romantic composers made use of the almost infinite variety of orchestral possibilities to invent new musical forms that could express the whole gamut of Romantic moods and fantasies. In the course of writing some 700 piano compositions, Chopin expressed every kind of feeling: melancholy, rebellion, exaltation. In his *Symphonie Fantastique* Berlioz blithely combined a delirious waltz, a pastoral fantasy, and a chilling dream of a witches' sabbath. And in opera Wagner fused the whole panoply of orchestral effects with spectacular dramatic action to create grand opera on, quite literally, an earthshaking scale.

THE BETTMANN ARCHIVE

An unknown contemporary did the sketches at the right of Franz Liszt conducting. Liszt employed dramatic facial expressions and explosive gestures to lead the orchestra, and the audience, to dizzying heights of musical excitement.

The Legacy of Romanticism

In 1846 the French critic Charles Baudelaire wrote, "To say the word Romanticism is to say modern art—that is intimacy, spirituality, color, aspiration towards the infinite, expressed by every means available to the arts." Intimacy, color, and complete artistic freedom have indeed been parts of Romanticism's legacy to modern culture. But Romantic idealism has fared less well. In the words of one modern critic, the Romantics who followed Wordsworth's generation "turned from vast mysteries and intoxicating ideas to delicate sentiments and careful description."

If Romanticism proper became overly sentimental and lost its earlier vigor, a new vision was in the making which owed much of its vitality, if little of its intent, to Romanticism. No artist better exemplifies this shift toward Realism than the Frenchman Honoré Daumier. In his *Don Quixote and Sancho Panza* (left), finished about 1860, Daumier painted a Romantic subject with Romantic freedom and expressiveness, yet the painting is realistic in that it portrays rather than praises the combination of the sublime and the ridiculous that is Cervantes' windmill-tilting knight.

By 1860 Europe was in the middle of a revolution as profound as the French Revolution that had fired the imagination of the Romantics sixty years before. Inevitably Romantic idealism proved no match for the Industrial Revolution, yet there remained Romantic masterpieces that even a materialistic age would treasure. In 1819 John Keats (depicted on his death bed in Joseph Severn's drawing above) created such a work in his *Ode to a Grecian Urn.* Describing a love-scene pictured on an ancient Greek vase, Keats wrote,

> What leaf-fring'd legend haunts about thy shape
> > Of deities or mortals, or of both,
> > > In Tempe or the dales of Arcady?
> > What men or gods are these? What maidens loth?
> What mad pursuit? What struggle to escape?
> > What pipes and timbrels? What wild ecstasy?
> Heard melodies are sweet, but those unheard
> > Are sweeter; therefore, ye soft pipes, play on. . . .

4

The High Tide of Liberalism:
1848-1870

The political system prevailing in most of Europe in the 1830s and 1840s was too rigid to respond to the changes that were occurring in European life and thought. It allowed neither for the social shifts brought about by industrialization (the population movement to the cities, the growing power of the capitalist, the increase in the number of wage earners) nor for the emergence of a vocal intelligentsia imbued with new ideas (romanticism, liberalism, nationalism, socialism). The revolutionary disturbances that periodically shook the peace should have served to warn the remaining conservative regimes that they were out of tune with the times. But by and large these signals went unheeded. Aside from a few countries in Western Europe—notably England and Belgium—symptoms of unrest merely hardened the resolve of the conservatives to oppose reforms. Even in France, a country that after 1830 had a moderate government and belonged to the liberal bloc, the clamor for the extension of the franchise was ignored. As a result, beneath the imposing surface of European life there gathered powerful forces ready to erupt and to destroy those political systems that continued to base their authority on a coalition of monarchy, bureaucracy, landed gentry, church, and the uppermost layer of the bourgeoisie, and to install in their places regimes dominated by the whole middle class and the intellectuals.

This eruption occurred in 1848. In the spring of that year the Continent was the scene of a series of related revolutions that were especially violent in those parts (the Austrian Empire, Germany, and Italy), where the conservative system was most firmly entrenched.° These revolutions ushered in a new era in the political life of the West.

The historian Lewis Namier subtitled his book *1848* "The Revolution of the Intellectuals," and, indeed, intellectuals played in it an extraordinarily prominent role. They formulated the revolutionary theories and slogans, led the mobs, and took charge of the national assemblies and provisional governments that came into power once legitimate authority collapsed. These intellectuals came mostly from the universities, the professions (especially law), and journalism—that is, from those institutions and occupations that had experienced unusual expansion in the first half of the nineteenth century.

Intellectuals generally were addicted to what Napoleon I had scornfully labeled "ideology"—all-embracing systems concerned with the betterment of the human race. They not only disapproved of things as they were but believed that genuine improvement had to be total and instantaneous; piecemeal reform or trial-and-error methods were not for them. Ideologies can be defined as secular religions—movements that retain the zeal and chiliasm of true religions but, rejecting God and life after death, direct their energies toward establishing the

The Revolutions of 1848

°Russia, which in the 1840s was the most conservative country in Europe, escaped revolution because opposition was as yet scattered and weak, while the repressive apparatus of the state enjoyed exceptional strength.

The street barricade became the hallmark of the revolutionary outbreaks that convulsed Europe in 1848. As shown in a contemporary lithograph of the Vienna uprising, they were thrown up of whatever was handy—paving stones, timbers, even carriages.

millennium on earth. They flourished greatly in the 1830s and 1840s. François Guizot, Louis Philippe's Prime Minister, watched with bewilderment the scheming of the international intelligentsia headquartered in Paris. "They yearn for events, immense, sudden and strange," he wrote; "they busy themselves with making and unmaking governments, nations, religions, society, Europe, the world." Such ideas intensified the feeling of uncertainty produced by economic and social changes and created an atmosphere propitious for revolutionary upheavals.

The dissident intellectuals, united as they were in opposition to the monarchic-feudal system, differed in their positive programs. Their aspirations had three principal tendencies. One was liberal. A large body of opinion wanted the abolition of all remaining restraints on individual liberties and the introduction of constitutional government with representative assemblies. University professors and members of the professions were especially active on behalf of these goals, from the achievement of which they expected a profound transformation of the human condition.

The second tendency of the intellectuals was democratic. Its adherents fought for the realization of the ideals of the French Revolution. They wanted a republic and the universal vote. A radical wing of the democratic group wanted to go further, toward socialism (the abolition of private property), or anarchism (the abolition of private property and of the state as well), but they were a minority. Many students and journalists adopted the democratic ideology.

The third tendency was nationalistic. Among ethnic groups that either suffered foreign domination (the minorities in the Hapsburg, Russian, and Ottoman empires) or that felt frustrated in their aspirations toward statehood (the Italians and Germans), intellectuals assumed leadership of the cause of national liberation and unification. Their nationalism combined either with liberal or democratic ideologies.

The intellectuals owed their strength in the late 1840s to the fact that their own essentially moral discontent happened to coincide with unrest among the urban lower classes. It would be tempting to ascribe this social unrest to conditions created by industrialization. But if industrialization had indeed been its decisive cause, then England and Belgium, as the industrially most developed countries of the period, should have experienced the greatest violence. In fact, neither experienced a revolution. On the other hand, some of the bloodiest upheavals occurred in countries hardly touched by industrialization, such as Italy and Hungary. Clearly, industrial conditions as such were not the cause of the revolutions of 1848.

A more likely cause was the mass uprooting of populations that accompanied intense urbanization. As we have noted, the first half of the nineteenth century was throughout Europe a period of rapid urban growth. The rural population streamed into the cities partly in search of better-paying jobs, partly in the hope of self-improvement. So great was the influx that between 1800 and 1848 Paris and Berlin more than doubled their populations. One-third of the inhabitants of London in 1851 were not native born. Striking growth occurred also in Vienna, Milan, Budapest, and other metropolitan centers.

Urbanization at this pace and rate inevitably created a variety of problems with which governments of the time were not prepared to cope. Among these, housing was especially acute. Most Continental cities at the time were still confined to a compact area enclosed by the defensive walls of the Middle Ages. The incoming population had to be squeezed into this limited space, into basements or garrets, cheap tenements constructed for quick profit by speculators, or makeshift hovels. The result was enormous congestion. The effects of excessive crowding on human beings are even today poorly understood, but there can be little doubt that they awaken deep-seated anxieties and aggressive instincts. Close contact with wealth in its moneyed, ostentatious form, much in evidence in the cities, aggravated the distress of the new urban population. Little wonder then that it formed a volatile element, receptive to ideological incitement by the intellectuals. In *Vanished Supremacies* Lewis Namier wrote:

> For men rooted in the soil, there is, as a rule, a hierarchy of allegiances: to their village community or estate, to their district, to their "country." . . . Traditional beliefs and hereditary ties persist; class and the way of living determine alignments; things are individual and concrete in the village or the small, old-fashioned town. But in the great modern cities men grow anonymous, become ciphers, and are regimented; thinking becomes more abstract and is forced into generalizations; inherited beliefs are shaken and old ties are broken; there is a void, uncertainty, and hidden fear which man tries to master by rational thought. He starts by proudly asserting the rights of the abstract, average individual freed from the bondage of tradition, and then integrates him into the crowd, a collective personality, which unloads itself into mass movements. The mass is the refuge of the uprooted individual; and the disintegration of spiritual values is as potent a process as the splitting of the atom; it releases demonic forces which burst all dams. The program may be social revolution, or national revolution, or both.

These psychological tensions were exacerbated by economic crises of the kind that recurred periodically in the nineteenth century. The years 1846 and 1847 saw crop failures and industrial layoffs. Many among those hurt by the crises headed for the cities either to seek help or to vent their wrath on the whole urban-capitalist-industrial complex.

The intellectuals and the workers constituted the two main forces of the 1848 revolutions—their brains and muscles, as it were. A force apart were the propertied classes: those industrialists, merchants, professionals, and well-to-do peasants who were committed to no specific ideology, but who nevertheless disliked the *status quo* and supported the revolution so long as it was directed against the absolutist bureaucracy and the feudal nobility. The moment the revolution took a more radical, democratic turn, however, these groups withdrew from it. For this reason, the revolutions of 1848 in every country went through two distinct, consecutive phases: a liberal (or liberal-national) phase, in which intellectuals, workers, and the propertied groups combined to overthrow the existing conservative or conservative-liberal regimes and replace them with typical liberal governments; and a democratic phase, in which the radical and democratic intelligentsia, backed by more desperate working-class elements, pressed on with the

François Guizot, the dominant figure in French politics during the 1840s, was also a historian of great repute.

This daguerreotype of Louis Kossuth, leader of the 1848 revolution in Hungary, was made about 1851 during the exile's tour through the United States.

revolutionary struggle for the purpose of winning full political and social democracy. Once the revolution entered this second phase, the propertied groups invariably threw their support behind the forces of order, usually the army, and helped to suppress the insurrectionary elements. This explains why to many radicals the upheavals of 1848 seemed an unfinished business, and why they so confidently, and vainly, awaited the outbreak of another European revolution.

The first rumblings of revolt sounded in Italy in January, 1848, but the revolutions really began the following month in Paris. In the summer of 1847 French opposition circles, determined to force a broadening of the franchise, launched a campaign of "banquets"—large public dinners at which speakers toasted liberty and criticized Louis Philippe and his Prime Minister, Guizot. The authorities grew annoyed by these doings and outlawed a banquet scheduled for February 22. On that day large crowds took to the streets to demand Guizot's dismissal. Louis Philippe, surprised by the ugly mood of the crowds, yielded and discharged his Prime Minister, but this act failed to placate the populace. The next day the streets filled with an even angrier mob. That evening a procession of students and workers ran into a body of soldiers guarding the Ministry of Foreign Affairs. When one of the demonstrators fired a shot, the troops volleyed and killed fifty persons. During the night the infuriated crowds built barricades all over the city. On February 24 the seventy-year-old king, facing a mutinous capital and no longer confident of his troops, abdicated and sailed for England.

After the king had departed, power passed to a provisional government composed of liberals, democrats, and socialists, who immediately proclaimed the abolition of the monarchy and the establishment of the Second Republic. This done, however, they began to quarrel. The socialists, inspired by the ideas of Louis Blanc (Chapter 8), demanded that the Republic assure jobs to all and found "national workshops" to provide work for the unemployed. The liberals intensely disliked the national workshop project, but for the time being went along with it for fear of the mob. The workshops attracted additional unemployed to Paris and at one time provided relief for a hundred thousand persons. The cost, nearly a million francs a day, was borne by the bourgeoisie and the peasantry, neither of which felt fonder of the Second Republic for making them support what they regarded as an indolent Parisian mob.

Friction between liberal and radical elements came to a head in June, 1848. In the spring of that year the country had voted for a National Assembly. The elections, based on universal suffrage, gave the liberals 500 seats, the royalists 300, and the socialists fewer than 100. The Assembly appointed an executive committee containing no socialists and on June 21 ordered the closing of the national workshops. In reaction to this order, the Parisian workers and unemployed rebelled and seized the eastern half of the city. The uprising threatened to topple the provisional government, but it was suppressed by troops under General Cavaignac, the Minister of War. Except for Marseilles, the rest of France failed to respond to the June revolt.

In Austria the revolution began under nationalistic slogans. It started on March 3 in Budapest, when the popular leader Louis Kossuth demanded a liberal constitution and full autonomy for Hungary. The emperor at first refused to make such concessions, but after rioting had spread to Vienna he had to yield.

März. Mai. October. November. December.

On April 11 Vienna granted Hungary a constitution. Kossuth now pressed for independence, and at the end of July the Hungarians broke relations with Austria. Similar nationalist demands were voiced in Bohemia, where the Czechs founded their own national committee. Italy seethed with rebellion, as did other regions of the Austrian Empire.

The uprisings in Paris and the unrest in the Austrian borderlands emboldened Viennese intellectuals to challenge the detested regime of Metternich. In mid-March mobs led by students caused such a riot that Emperor Ferdinand had to dismiss Metternich and grant Austria a constitution. But the revolution did not stop there. In June it took a radical turn, as artisans and craftsmen set fire to industrial establishments and with their violence helped intellectuals gain control of the city. Ferdinand fled to the safety of Innsbruck. In July a constituent assembly met in Vienna. The deputies, most of them sent from the Slavic areas, passed laws abolishing many feudal rights and granting peasants civil equality.

Having reached its height in the summer of 1848, the tide of Austrian revolution began to recede. The army, which had never wavered in its loyalty to absolutism, now led a counteroffensive. Behind it stood the urban middle class, frightened by radicalism, and the mass of the peasantry, who had gained what they wanted and desired a restoration of order. In June, 1848, the army dispersed the Czech national committee in Prague. In October it captured Vienna and from there proceeded against Hungary, which it cleared of rebels with the assistance of Russian troops. By the spring of 1849 the monarchy had regained control of the empire.

In Germany the years 1848 and 1849 passed under the spell of nationalism. Here the goal of revolutionaries was political liberty and national unification.

The short and unhappy life of a typical 1848 revolutionary: orator and fighter for freedom in March and May, followed by capture (center), summary trial, and the firing squad in winter.

The revolution broke out in Berlin in mid-March. Events followed a pattern familiar in other countries: mass meetings and processions; public clamor for freedom of the press, trial by jury, and other planks of the liberal platform; efforts at suppression; the breakdown of administration. Frederick William IV, impressed by the strength of the opposition, had to agree to the convocation of a constituent assembly, which, like its counterparts in Budapest and Vienna, turned out to have a fairly radical complexion. But by the end of the year, emboldened by the Austrian example, Frederick William used troops to reassert his authority, and the assembly was dissolved. Elsewhere in Germany, local rulers invited liberal statesmen to form governments and granted constitutional charters. The notable exception was Bavaria's King Ludwig I, who preferred to abdicate.

The most dramatic event in Germany was the convocation in Frankfurt am Main of the first all-German parliament. Called the National Assembly, it was organized on the initiative of liberal intellectuals. Elections for it were held in the territories of the Germanic Confederation in the spring of 1848 on a broad, nearly universal suffrage. The voters returned a majority of liberals and nationalists. Since Germany had no regular parties, they cast their ballots for well-known individuals, usually men who had distinguished themselves as champions of freedom. Most of these were academics and members of the professions, and therefore 550 out of 830 deputies turned out to belong to these two categories. The task of the Assembly was to transform the impotent Confederation into an effective all-German government. But the deputies sorely lacked parliamentary experience. Each deputy spoke in his own name rather than for a party, and precious months were spent on rhetoric. The question of admitting Austria into the new state was decided negatively. Much time was spent drafting constitutional projects until an acceptable one was produced in the spring of 1849. At that time the Assembly voted to offer the Prussian king the title "Emperor of the Germans." When Frederick William refused to accept the crown from an illegitimate, revolutionary body, the National Assembly dissolved.

In Italy the revolutionary forces were encouraged by Charles Albert, the king of Piedmont. At heart a dyed-in-the-wool conservative, Charles Albert had personal reasons to dislike the Hapsburgs. Furthermore, he hoped to benefit from the anti-Austrian revolution to augment his territory. Intending to annex Venetia and Lombardy, he declared war on Austria and proclaimed himself leader of an Italian liberation movement. But the Austrians reacted in Italy with more efficiency than had been anticipated in view of their performance elsewhere, and by the summer of 1848 they had brought the Piedmontese offensive to a halt. Frightened by the emergence in several Italian principalities (Venice, Rome, and Tuscany) of radical republics, Charles Albert made peace with Austria. He stood by while the republics were liquidated with the help of Austrian and French troops and reactionary regimes restored throughout the peninsula.

The immediate consequence of the 1848 revolutions everywhere was a conservative restoration. In this sense, the revolutions brought cruel disappointment to many of their participants. The Russian radical Alexander Herzen, who in 1847 had gone to the West expecting to witness the dawn of a new era, was so disillusioned that, in a book published in 1850 (*From the Other Shore*), he

A remarkably candid self-caricature, by Frederick William IV of Germany.

denied human history any meaning. In fact, however, the revolutions of 1848 inaugurated an era of liberal hegemony and of modern mass politics.

The year 1848 marked the end of conservatism in its classical, Metternichian guise as a factor in European politics. After a brief initial reaction, the decades that followed witnessed the unimpeded spread of liberal principles and practices. From Western Europe they penetrated to Eastern Europe and eventually to distant, non-European countries such as Persia and Japan. Liberalism, both political and economic, came into high fashion. It was an up-to-date, operative theory adopted by statesmen of the new generation. In the air were legal reform, civil equality, constitutionalism and parliamentarism, democratic franchise, and national self-determination.

The Causes of Liberal Ascendancy

Why did this occur? Probably the most likely explanation is that rulers and professional politicians alike came to realize that liberal institutions and procedures would strengthen their authority. The examples of the United States (especially after the victory of the North in the Civil War) and Great Britain held much attraction. The wealth and the international prestige of the two liberal powers demonstrated better than could any theories the political benefits that accrued to the state from involving the citizenry in politics. And if those examples were not enough, the revolutions of 1848 served as a reminder that in any event one could not forever freeze the political and social systems nor hope to rule through a bureaucratic-police apparatus. If the art of politics is the art of winning support, then modern life, which in all realms increased the importance of the common man, required that the state gain his support as well.

Another factor in favor of liberalism was its natural affinity with business. Merchants, manufacturers, and investors greatly preferred liberal regimes because they provided a variety of guarantees absent in traditional conservative regimes—notably, safeguards against arbitrary seizure and taxation, and the general protection of law. Governments that wished to increase their wealth and power had, therefore, strong inducements to make liberal concessions as a means of promoting business activity and attracting capital.

The liberalization of European politics in the third quarter of the nineteenth century may be described as an adjustment of the state to conditions created by the spread of industry and the growing social awareness of all groups of the population. The state became liberalized in order to gain new strength and to acquire allies against the radical minorities that in 1848–1849 had shown such destructive capacity. This adjustment did not occur everywhere at the same pace or with the same thoroughness, for conditions varied from country to country, as did the political skill of the rulers. In some countries it hardly touched the surface. But it may be stated as a general principle that only countries that liberalized in earnest subsequently escaped political and social revolutions. Those that did not—among them the Austrian, Russian, and Ottoman empires—went from crisis to crisis until they eventually disintegrated.

We shall now trace the progress of liberalism in the principal countries of midcentury Europe, stressing three issues: the struggle of nationalities for self-determination, the democratization of the suffrage, and the evolution of parliamentary institutions and parties.

Mid-Victorian England   In the middle of the nineteenth century England came closer than any other European country to the fulfillment of liberal ideals: a society that offered the citizen the safe enjoyment of life, liberty, and property. Rich and peaceful, England developed a system of government that most of the world envied. In 1848 the only sedition it experienced occurred in Ireland, where a minor local insurrection was speedily and bloodlessly suppressed.

In England the problems that agitated Continental politics were largely solved. Legislative authority resided firmly in the two Houses of Parliament and executive authority in a cabinet formed by members of the House of Commons. The overwhelming majority of the members of Parliament shared a common political philosophy. Conflicts between them involved not matters of ideology but of practical policy. The two parties remained non-ideological, that is, they had no commitment to a systematic program. The party that happened to be in power at any given time pursued a broad, national line of policy, while that out of power criticized its real or alleged failures. The broad consensus of opinion contributed more than any other factor to the efficient functioning of the British government.

In the late 1840s the political parties underwent realignment. Peel's "great betrayal"—his support of the Corn Law repeal in 1846—broke up the old Tory party that had dominated English politics in the first half of the century. One faction containing Peel's supporters went over to the Whigs. The fusion that resulted was called the Liberal party. The anti-Peel Tories constituted the Conservative party.

The Liberal party consisted of a coalition of two main groups: a smaller contingent of Whig landlords, very close in their outlook and way of life to their Tory rivals, and a larger contingent made up of traders and manufacturers. The latter set the tone. They were the liberals par excellence: they supported full economic liberty, a broad franchise, and the interests of the urban, industrial population. The Conservative party was composed almost entirely of landed gentry, with some backing of shopkeepers and other lower-middle-class elements. It was socially more prominent, and some businessmen, once they had made enough money and could afford a landed estate, switched their allegiance to it. The Liberals completely dominated English politics from the repeal of the Corn Law in 1846 to 1874. During this twenty-eight-year period the Conservatives formed only four short-lived ministries serving a total of fifty-six months. The rest of the time they were in opposition.

The organization of English political parties at this time underwent little change. In the 1830s, in response to the First Reform Act, the two major parties founded their national headquarters—the Tories the Carlton Club, and the Whigs the Reform Club. But since until the mid-1880s most candidates for Parliament ran unopposed and since contests for constituencies were an exception, these headquarters had little to do and functioned as ordinary social clubs.

The English parliamentary system owed much of its excellence to Queen Victoria, who ruled for sixty-four years (1837–1901). She ascended the throne at a time when the popularity of the monarchy was at its lowest, following the mad years of George III and the profligate ones of George IV and William IV. But Victoria quickly won the sympathies of the population by her modesty and by her respect for the constitution. Uninterested in the details of politics, and indeed unable to comprehend them, she left the actual conduct of the government to others. She acknowledged the supremacy of Parliament and adjusted herself as no English monarch had done before to playing a secondary role in the country's political life. Yet at the same time she had no intention of giving up her residual rights. When Lord Palmerston, the powerful Prime Minister, once took the initiative in a foreign-policy matter without bothering to inform her, she reprimanded him; when he repeated the offense, she had him dismissed. Victoria provided just enough leadership to keep the parliamentary system functioning smoothly without ever seeming to threaten the jealously guarded prerogatives of Parliament itself. The result was a balance of power between court, cabinet, and the two legislative houses—that balance which Walter Bagehot in his influential *English Constitution* (1867) described as the secret of the British system of government.

The most important legislative act of the midcentury was the extension of the suffrage, enacted in 1867. The manner in which this bill secured passage is very characteristic of the non-ideological quality of English party politics of the time. The proposal to widen the suffrage was made in 1865–1866 by the Liberals under the leadership of Lord John Russell. It immediately caught the imagination of the working class, especially the trade unions, which took up the old Chartist clamor for the franchise and threatened violence if their demand was not met. The Reform Bill submitted by Lord Russell, however, failed in the Commons, being defeated by an alliance of Conservatives and landed Whig elements among the Liberals. The leading Conservative figure, Benjamin Disraeli, saw in the Liberal defeat an excellent opportunity to restore the fortunes of his power-hungry party. He proposed to the Conservatives that they take the cause of suffrage reform away from the Liberals and submit an even more radical bill in their own

A biting French satire on England's Irish problem shows Queen Victoria, carefully shielded from unpleasant sights, touring the troubled island.

name. In this manner, Disraeli hoped, the Conservatives would win the loyalty of the newly enfranchised voter. Backed by the Conservatives as well as the pro-reform elements within the Liberal party, the Second Reform Bill was passed in August, 1867. It doubled the electorate by enfranchising in effect all house-hold owners and tenants paying taxes above a certain minimum sum. The bill gave England a very broad male suffrage and introduced an era of political democracy.

The Second Empire in France In France the midcentury witnessed a reversion to authoritarian government in the personal rule of Napoleon III. In this respect, France was an exception to the general tendency of the period toward liberalization. But authoritarian regime in its pure form lasted only nine years (1851–1860). By 1860 it became apparent that purely bureaucratic methods could no longer effectively administer France. From 1860 until his deposition in 1870, Napoleon III continuously surrendered power. The whole second half of his reign represented an irresistible sliding toward constitutionalism and parliamentarism, an eloquent proof of the all-pervasive liberal tendency of the age.

The specific political development of France was mainly due to the peculiarities of its social structure. As we have noted, France was a country of small proprietors, extremely sensitive to any threat to their holdings. Whenever they felt such a threat to exist, the French sought protection in authoritarian government. This happened in 1799, in 1850–1851, and in 1958 and 1968. The challenge to property came invariably from the same source, namely the socialist and anarchist elements concentrated in Paris. As soon as these elements seemed to get the upper hand, the majority of the country (that is, the provinces) veered sharply to the right.

The Paris uprising of June, 1848, frightened the countryside in precisely this way. Confronted with a choice between dictatorship and anarchy, it opted for dictatorship and once more entrusted its destiny to a man bearing the name of Napoleon. Louis Napoleon was the son of Louis Bonaparte, Napoleon I's younger brother and king of Holland in the days of the First Empire. In his youth he joined radical causes and imbibed the whole spirit of socialism and nationalism of the Romantic era. During the reign of Louis Philippe he was the principal Bonapartist claimant to the French throne. He twice tried unsuccessfully to overthrow the July monarchy. The second attempt (1840) led to his imprisonment, his eventual escape, and his flight to England.

Louis Napoleon developed an interesting political philosophy, which he outlined in two books, *Napoleonic Ideas* (1839) and *The Extinction of Pauperism* (1844). Underlying his theory were two fundamental thoughts: that modern politics must rest on the masses (rather than on the landed nobility or the moneyed élite), and that the masses must be led by the state. "Today the reign of castes is finished," he wrote; "one cannot govern except by means of the masses. . . . [The masses] must be organized so that they can formulate their will, and disciplined so they can be directed and enlightened about their true interests." In these statements one can detect anticipations of modern totalitarianism, and indeed Louis Napoleon may be regarded as one of its forerunners.

Louis Napoleon was much influenced by the French social thinker Claude

Henri de Saint-Simon. Saint-Simon, whose main activity occurred during the restoration period, maintained that the French Revolution had opened a new age in the history of mankind, what he called the "age of industrialism." By industrialism he meant not so much a specific mode of production, but everything antithetical to the feudal, aristocratic, and parasitic. His industrial class included all who were "productive" or "creative"—bankers, businessmen, engineers, scientists, scholars—as contrasted to the "idlers" (*oisifs*) and "militants," who either lived off the work of others or destroyed that work by war. The new world would be an alliance of industry and science, and all authority would be vested in experts or, as they are known today, technocrats. Inheritance would be abolished, but private property and inequalities in wealth would remain—a provision that disqualifies Saint-Simon from being included among the socialists, with whom his name is customarily linked. He was really an apostle of technological and scientific modernism. His views won him a following among French engineers and bankers, but they were much distorted and subsequently discredited by a group of close disciples who after his death set up a "Saint-Simonian" religious cult.

Louis Napoleon's opportunity to put his own and Saint-Simon's ideas into practice came in 1848. As soon as he learned of Louis Philippe's abdication, he headed for Paris, where the immense popularity of the Napoleonic name helped him gain election to the Chamber of Deputies. In November, 1848, he was nominated to run for the presidency of the Second Republic against General Cavaignac, the suppressor of the June revolt. He won handily.

Under the constitution adopted in 1848, the President's authority was severely curtailed by a single-chamber Legislative Assembly. He could hold office only for a single four-year term. Such restrictions did not suit Louis Napoleon's authoritarian temper, and he awaited an opportunity to be rid of them. In the meantime, he solidified his internal position by skillfully appealing to various social groups. He gained the support of the Catholic hierarchy by backing the Pope in his conflict with the Italian nationalists and by conceding the clergy

"The name Napoleon," said Napoleon III, "is a program in itself: it stands for order, authority, religion, the welfare of the people. . . ." In Constantin Guys' eyewitness sketch, he takes the oath as President of the Second Republic on December 20, 1848.

Baron Haussmann's so-called modernization of Paris inspired these comments by Honoré Daumier. Above, dispossessed tenants; below, hazards of a stroll on the Champs Élysées.

greater influence over the schools. He also won the favor of the royalists by appointing their adherents to high office and of the military by enlarging the army.

The chance for a power seizure presented itself in the summer of 1851 during a prolonged parliamentary crisis caused by an attempt of the Legislative Assembly to do away with universal suffrage. Louis Napoleon now was able to conceal his bid for absolute power behind the mask of a champion of popular freedoms. When the Assembly refused to change the constitution in order to enable him to run once more for the presidency, he illegally dissolved it and ordered a popular plebiscite on the revision of the constitution, coupling it with a proclamation restoring universal suffrage. This *coup d'état* occurred on December 2, 1851, the anniversary of Napoleon I's coronation. There was some scattered resistance, but it was quickly overcome. In the plebiscite that followed, 7,500,000 ballots (against 650,000) approved the President's request to revise—that is, subvert—the constitution.

The new constitution, drafted under Louis Napoleon's instructions, resembled closely the Napoleonic constitution of the Year VIII (1799). It vested in the President, as previously in the First Consul, the essentials of political power. The two legislative chambers had little authority and no control over the ministers. In 1852, once again emulating his uncle, he asked the nation to make him hereditary emperor. Again the country complied, giving him 7,800,000 Ayes against 253,000 Nays, with 2 million voters abstaining. He chose the name Napoleon III.

The new emperor—"Napoleon the Small," as Victor Hugo called him—had nothing but contempt for party politics, considering them a squandering of national energies. Politics were to be authoritarian, legitimized by a broad mandate of national referenda. The center of political authority shifted to the imperial court and to the immense civil service dependent on it. The government of the Second Empire was a government by bureaucracy to an extent unknown in Europe until that time. The bureaucracy controlled local government through departmental prefects who selected reliable pro-government candidates to run for the Assembly and marshaled the vote for them. It could squash any opposition by exercising its right to arrest, detain, and deport political opponents, and to suspend publications. Information gathered by a network of police officials and agents permitted the Minister of the Interior to forestall potential sedition. Under such conditions political opposition did not and could not exist. There is no evidence that the country at large missed political liberties, for the 1850s was a period of great prosperity and a splendid social life. In elections government candidates generally received majorities, and some of the emperor's most solid electoral support came from the working population in the industrial centers.

If Napoleon III had contempt for politics, he was very serious about what we would call today economic development. He surrounded himself with Saint-Simonian technocrats with whose aid he undertook to stimulate economic activity. He founded several large national investment banks, notably the Crédit Foncier to provide mortgages for real estate, and the Crédit Mobilier to finance industrial undertakings. As a result of these and other measures, the value of France's industrial production doubled during the two decades of the Second Empire. From the socialists Napoleon III borrowed the idea of public works as a remedy for unemployment. The most spectacular public works project of his reign was the modernization of Paris carried out under the direction of Baron Haussmann, in the course of which many medieval sections were razed and replaced with broad boulevards. Despite his early interest in the working class, Napoleon III did little to improve France's social legislation. The French working class remained dangerously isolated from the rest of society, bourgeois as well as peasant.

So far, France's course was running against the general liberal trend of the times, but in the 1860s this situation changed as Napoleon's prestige and power, unassailable in the 1850s, began visibly to erode. The main reason for this decline lay in foreign failures. Napoleon III was at heart a pacifist, but this did not prevent him from engaging in an ambitious foreign policy that at times required recourse to arms, for which he had neither heart nor skill. His intervention on behalf of Italy against Austria in 1859 (see below) aroused protests from politicians who preferred a dismembered to a united Italy as a neighbor. Napoleon's commercial treaty with Britain, signed in 1860, alienated many French businessmen who were not prepared to compete with the world's leading industrial power without the protection of high tariffs. In 1861 Napoleon intervened disastrously in Mexico, hoping to found there a Catholic empire. The French candidate, Maximilian, was put on the throne with the help of French troops, but when these withdrew under United States pressure, the Mexicans seized and shot him.

The unpopularity of his foreign policy made it imperative to relax the reins of authority at home, where a liberal opposition was becoming more audible and the bureaucracy less able to guarantee the election of loyal Assembly candidates. As a result, an anti-government bloc took shape. To govern the country as well as to maintain confidence in its finances, Napoleon had to secure the support of the opposition, and to this end he now began to make concessions. In 1860–1861 he increased the financial competence of the legislatures and allowed their debates to be published. In 1867 he granted the Assembly the right of "interpellation," that is, of questioning government ministers. The following year he lifted the most onerous restrictions on the freedom of speech and assembly.

These liberalizing measures, instead of placating the opposition, emboldened it. In the elections of 1869 government candidates received only 4.4 million votes compared to 3.3 million cast for opposition candidates. A majority of deputies now pressed for the creation of a responsible ministry. Napoleon was not prepared to go that far, but in 1869–1870 he further enlarged the authority of the legislatures, granting the Assembly the right to initiate legislation, to vote on the budget, and to demand from ministers a certain amount of accounting. These measures moved France toward an equilibrium between the executive and the legislative, a development that met with the approbation of the majority of the population. In a national plebiscite held in the spring of 1870 the country gave its assent to the new political system with 7.3 million voting for and 1.5 million against.

Despite this impressive triumph, the days of the Second Empire were numbered. A few months later it was shattered by a blow delivered by Prussia, a country that had been quietly gathering strength and now emerged as the first power on the Continent. But before we turn to the story of Prussia's rise, we must deal with chronologically antecedent events on the Italian peninsula.

The Risorgimento   The suppression by the Austrians of the revolutionary governments that had sprung up in northern and central Italy in 1848–1849 left on the peninsula only one liberal state, Piedmont. Unlike the other rulers who quickly retracted the constitutions that had been foisted upon them by the revolutionary mobs, Victor Emmanuel II, the king of Piedmont since 1849, honored the pledges of his predecessor, Charles Albert. The Piedmontese constitution, promulgated in March, 1848, was based on the French charter of 1830. It provided for a bicameral legislature, one appointed, the other elected on a restricted franchise. The ministers were responsible to parliament. Elsewhere in Italy—the Papal domain, the Kingdom of the Two Sicilies, and the principalities of Parma, Modena, Lucca, and Tuscany—the forces of reaction had the upper hand.

Italian nationalism matured slowly. In the 1820s the Italians still lacked any real sense of national identity, and Metternich justly referred to Italy as a "geographic expression." This national sense developed only in the 1830s and 1840s, largely under the influence of Romantic intellectuals and publicists, of whom the most important was Giuseppe Mazzini. A republican and a democrat, Mazzini believed that the unification of Italy would come about through a mass movement of all regions and all classes. To promote such a movement, he founded in 1832 a society called "Young Italy." The goal of this organization, whose membership was limited to patriots less than forty years old, was to stimulate anti-Austrian and anti-absolutist uprisings and help create a united Italian republic. It was linked with a broader international society, "Young Europe," which Mazzini founded two years later with branches among the Swiss, Germans, Poles, and other nationalities to promote democratic, republican, and national goals in the rest of Europe.

Mazzini did much to spread the ideal of Italian unity, but, despite his personal magnetism and courage, his insurrectionary strategy had no success. The Austrians brutally stamped out every uprising organized by Young Italy. The response among Italians, too, was discouraging. Few educated Italians felt as yet sufficient affinity with artisans, shopkeepers, and peasants to join with them in a common struggle for statehood. Young Italy suffered its decisive fiascoes in 1848–1849, when the republics that it had helped to establish were swept away in the subsequent reaction. After that, leadership of the Italian national movement passed to men of a new breed, with another temperament and program.

The greatest figure of Italian politics in the 1850s, and the creator of Italian unity, was Count Camillo Cavour. In contrast to the fiery Romantic intellectual who dashed from insurrection to insurrection, Cavour resembled a typical middle-class English liberal. He admired the constitutional monarchy, believed in industrialism and free trade, and carefully calculated his chances before undertaking any action. Prior to entering politics, he had spent seventeen years running his father's estate, acquiring in this manner a good understanding of management and practical economics.

Cavour entertained no illusions that Italy could win national unity and independence by means of a popular uprising. These aims required a power base at home and abroad. He decided that Piedmont offered the best chance of serving as the national base from which to launch the movement for unification. It was liberal and progressive, fairly prosperous, and enjoyed a strategically advanta-

THE UNIFICATION
OF ITALY

geous position in regard to Austria. In 1847 Cavour founded a newspaper, *Il Risorgimento (Renascence)*, whose name was later applied to the whole Italian unification movement. In it he propagated the idea that Piedmont lead the work of unification. In 1850 he entered the Piedmontese cabinet and two years later took over as Prime Minister, a post he held, with one brief interruption, until his death in 1861. During these years he laid the foundations of Italian statehood. He tackled with great energy the task of economic development in Piedmont, reorganizing finances, lowering tariffs, and promoting the construction of railroads. In a short time his efforts gave Piedmont the most lively economy in Italy. These policies won him much sympathy in England and France. Cavour also firmly reduced the power of the Catholic clergy.

At the end of the 1850s, feeling his home base secure, Cavour undertook negotiations to obtain a foreign ally against Austria. This he found in the Second Empire. At a secret meeting with Napoleon III held in July, 1858, at Plombières, he received the promise of French military assistance against Austria in return for the cession of Nice and Savoy. With this guarantee, Cavour provoked Austria into war by fomenting disorders in its Italian provinces (April, 1859). As soon as Austrian troops crossed the Piedmontese frontier, the French intervened, and in two major battles fought at Magenta and Solferino in June, 1859, defeated them. In the peace treaty that followed (Treaty of Zurich, November, 1859), Aus-

Giuseppe Garibaldi began his career as a military adventurer in South America. After conquering Sicily he was briefly dictator of the island.

tria ceded the rich commercial regions of Lombardy, including Milan, to Piedmont.

Cavour took advantage of the Austrian defeat to organize insurrections throughout Italy. For this purpose he employed the National Society, founded in 1857, which had branches all over the peninsula. In the fall of 1859 uprisings broke out in Parma, Modena, Tuscany, and the northern regions of the Papal domain. Each uprising was followed by a plebiscite in which the population approved a merger with Piedmont. When in the spring of 1860 a rebellion broke out against the Bourbon dynasty in the Kingdom of the Two Sicilies, Cavour encouraged Giuseppe Garibaldi to go to its aid as the head of an expedition of 1,000 "Red Shirts." Garibaldi quickly seized Sicily and from there proceeded to Naples. He intended also to march on Rome, but the French, who had stationed a contingent of troops in Rome since 1849, thwarted this plan. Naples and Sicily, however, were secure and in October, 1860, voted to amalgamate with Piedmont.

In February, 1861, the process of unification, so skillfully directed by Cavour, culminated in the convocation in Turin of the first all-Italian parliament. The assembly proclaimed an Italian kingdom with Victor Emmanuel at its head. The constitution of the new state rested on that adopted by Piedmont in 1848 and retained the principle of ministerial responsibility.

At the time of Italy's founding, two regions still remained outside its borders: Venetia and the Papal domain, with its center at Rome. Venetia was acquired in 1866 after a brief war with Austria. The acquisition of Rome took longer, for the situation was greatly complicated by the French presence. Finally, the French withdrew, and Rome fell under Italian rule and became the capital (1871).

The Papacy

The Papacy was the only power in Europe to resist the midcentury trend toward liberalization. Indeed, it tended to grow increasingly conservative and in the 1860s became the most uncompromising representative of anti-liberal forces.

The Papacy emerged after the defeat of Napoleon Bonaparte stronger than it had been for two hundred years. It profited greatly from the religious revival that had begun during the French Revolution and continued during the Romantic era. In Catholic countries conservative rulers of the restoration era returned to the Church its properties and privileges in recognition of the role that it had performed in resisting the forces of revolution. In addition, at the Congress of Vienna the Popes were awarded the lands that had been taken from them by the French. The Papal States after 1815 embraced much of central Italy, including Rome. In these territories the Popes established an administration, thoroughly clerical and conservative, that collaborated with the Austrian and pro-Austrian princes in stamping out any signs of liberalism and radicalism.

The commitment of the Catholic Church to temporal affairs and its alliance with the conservative states was by no means universally approved by the Catholic community. Some outstanding Catholic writers, such as Félicité Robert de Lamennais, urged the Church to assume leadership of the liberal and democratic movements and to become spokesman of the masses (*The Words of a Believer*, 1834). Others wanted the Church to abandon politics altogether and transform itself into a purely spiritual power.

The liberal tendency in Catholicism seemed to gain the upper hand in 1846 with the election to the Papacy of Pius IX. The new Pontiff had a reputation of being a moderate, liberal man, and he at first justified this opinion by relaxing censorship and granting amnesty to political offenders. But his failure to support the anti-Austrian rebels in Italy in 1848 so enraged the nationalists that they forced him to flee from Rome. Upon his return in 1850 he revealed himself as a stanch conservative, determined to oppose at every point the dominant trends of his age. In 1864 he issued two celebrated encyclicals, *Quanta cura* and *Syllabus errorum*, in which he condemned rationalism, liberal economics, socialism, liberty of conscience, popular sovereignty, and secularism. In 1869–1870 he went further and convoked the Vatican Council (the first since the Council of Trent in the sixteenth century) which, at his urging, proclaimed the doctrine of Papal Infallibility—i.e., the doctrine that the Pope could not err when pronouncing on matters of faith or morals in the performance of his duties.

These developments brought the Catholic Church into direct collision with the secular authorities. The Church resisted the *risorgimento* and rejected the offers of compromise made by Cavour and his successors. As a result, in 1870 it lost its last territorial possession, and Pius IX became a virtual prisoner in the Vatican. He subsequently forbade Italian Catholics to participate in national elections. His reactionary measures evoked protests in Austria and Germany and gave Bismarck a pretext for engaging the Catholic Church in a long-drawn-out political conflict (the *Kulturkampf*, Chapter 9). The relations between the Papacy and secular authorities began to improve only in 1878 with the accession of Leo XIII, who adopted some policies advocated by liberal Catholics.

The Unification of Germany

The difficulty in achieving a unification of Germany lay not so much in an inadequate sense of national identity or in foreign interference, both of which had delayed Italian statehood, but rather in the necessity of reconciling the interests of many sovereign principalities, several of them large and with old traditions. Some of the thirty-nine states of the Germanic Confederation were Protestant, others Catholic; some were industrial and commercial and oriented westward, others predominantly rural and oriented eastward; in some, liberal ideas prevailed, whereas others were thoroughly conservative. To fuse such diverse entities in a single national state required patience and skill. The difficulties were compounded by the rivalry between the two most powerful states of the Confederation, Protestant Prussia and Catholic Austria, either of which had the capacity to perform the function that Piedmont had performed in Italy. One group of German nationalists wanted to unite all the lands with a German-speaking population, including the Austrian, under Hapsburg leadership. This was the so-called "Great German" (*Grossdeutsch*) solution. Another group, proponents of the "Little German" (*Kleindeutsch*) solution, wanted Prussia to lead and Austria to be excluded from the unified German state. The Austrians championed the "Great German" program, of course, but they lacked the power to carry it out. The Prussians therefore triumphed, but the victory of their cause was by no means inevitable.

Prussian political life was characterized by the preponderance of the military. The independent officer corps, which was drawn from the *Junkers*, the land-owning class, formed a tightly knit group with a great deal of *esprit de corps* and

THE UNIFICATION OF GERMANY

a rigid code of social behavior. They had enjoyed great influence in the Prussian state since the eighteenth century and retained it even after Prussia had begun to industrialize, in part because they married into commercial and manufacturing wealth. Prussia was the first country in the world to put modern technology to work for the military. The Prussian General Staff, a highly professional body virtually free of control by the civilian authorities, exploited fully the latest technical innovations, such as railroads, steel armaments, and the telegraph. Helmuth von Moltke, the Chief of the General Staff from 1858 to 1888, was a characteristic specimen of the modern Prussian officer—a romantic visionary for whom war was the noblest expression of the human spirit, and at the same time a pragmatic technician. It was this combination of the feudal and industrial mentalities that made the Prussian and subsequently the German army such a terrible instrument of destruction.

William I, who ascended the throne in 1861, shared the traditional Prussian love of the military. In an attempt to strengthen his armed forces, he approved a series of military reforms, among them measures prolonging the duration of army service and dissolving the popular militia, which was officered by nonprofessionals. These proposals, upon being submitted to the Landtag, the lower house of the Prussian parliament, caused a prolonged parliamentary crisis. (The Landtag had been created in March, 1848, at the height of the revolutionary disturbances in Berlin.) The majority of the deputies at this time were liberals and belonged to the Progressive party. As nationalists, they welcomed measures designed to strengthen Prussia and increase its weight in the Germanic Confederation. But as liberals, they objected to the influence wielded by the military. Interpreting the proposed reform as an attempt by the *Junkers* to gain more power, the Progressives rejected the bill and, to give force to their action, vetoed the budget. The king, hoping for popular support, dissolved the Landtag and ordered new elections. But the voters backed the Progressives, giving them two-thirds of the seats in the new house. William was so dispirited by this turn of events that he was on the point of abdicating, when his military friends persuaded him to seek the help of Bismarck.

Otto von Bismarck came from an old if undistinguished family of Pomeranian *Junkers* and displayed all the virtues and vices of that class. His loyalty to the Prussian monarchy was complete and unflinching, superseding even his loyalty to Germany as a whole. His outlook was fundamentally feudal and rural. He had an instinctive mistrust of people living in the cities, of intellectuals, and of parliamentary institutions. At the same time, however, he understood well how to manipulate for conservative ends liberal institutions and ideas, such as representative assemblies, the universal vote, and nationalism, and even radical ones such as social welfare. He was an outstanding example of the new breed of conservative statesman: a statesman who knew how to exploit liberalism and socialism to strengthen the authority of the state.

When William ran into trouble with the Landtag, Bismarck was serving as Prussian ambassador to Napoleon III. He eagerly accepted William's invitation to take charge of the government and saw as his immediate and principal task to undermine the popularity of the liberals, whom he considered the main threat to royal authority. This aim he achieved by depriving them of their most powerful weapon, namely nationalism. Under Bismarck's leadership Prussia carried out a series of quick and victorious but limited wars, the result of which was to engender enormous patriotic enthusiasm throughout Germany and to give Prussia's claim to hegemony an irresistible impetus. The wars also placed the liberals in a position where to oppose Bismarck was equivalent to opposing the cause of national unification. When Bismarck retired in 1890, German liberalism was demoralized and no longer an effective counterforce to the monarchy.

As soon as he had taken over the Prussian government, Bismarck dissolved the Landtag and imposed a severe press censorship that made it difficult for the Progressives to campaign in the new election. In 1862, between sessions of the house, he introduced new taxes in order to free himself from dependence on the regular budget, which was subject to the Landtag's veto. This unconstitutional procedure was for all practical purposes a *coup d'état*, and for a while there was a danger of a nationwide revolt. But the Berliners were not Parisians, and the expected uprising never came. By his successful defiance of the Landtag, Bismarck dealt a devastating blow to the cause of constitutionalism and liberalism and assured the monarchy of a decisive voice in the country's political life. It was

An attack on Bismarck has the Chancellor carefully making his way toward military dictatorship and war.

at this time that he made his oft-quoted remark: "The great issues of the day will be decided not by speeches and votes of the majority—that was the great mistake of 1848 and 1849—but by iron and blood."

Next, in 1864, Bismarck involved Prussia and Austria in a brief war against Denmark over the disputed territories of Schleswig-Holstein. The victory of the Prussian-Austrian forces greatly raised the prestige of Prussia, which had engineered and directed the engagement.

The crucial conflict—the one that assured Prussia of the lead in the task of unification and guaranteed that Austria would be barred from the united German state—was the Austro-Prussian War of 1866. The pretext was an argument over the administration of Schleswig-Holstein, which the two powers had exercised jointly. But in reality the Prussians wanted war. Moltke later admitted that the conflict had been coldly worked out in the Prussian cabinet. Prussia had to humiliate Austria in order to discredit once and for all the "Great German" solution. In the Battle of Königgrätz (Sadowa), fought in July, 1866, the modernized Prussian army, equipped with the latest breech-loading guns, decisively defeated the Austrian troops, whose guns were of the old muzzle-loading type.

The victory of 1866 unleashed an explosion of nationalistic frenzy in Prussia and many other German regions. To the liberals it presented a dilemma: either to support Bismarck to the hilt and give up hope of establishing a true parliamentary government, or to oppose him and lose influence over the electorate. This dilemma led to a split in liberal ranks. One group formed a National Liberal party, which allied itself with Bismarck and supported his internal policies, even when they violated cardinal principles of liberalism; the other remained in the old Progressive party. The latter gradually lost ground, being squeezed between a right composed of monarchists and National Liberals and a left dominated by the emergent Social Democratic party.

Bismarck promptly capitalized on the pro-Prussian sentiment engendered by victory over Austria. He annexed to Prussia several principalities, connecting in this manner Prussia's eastern and western portions. In 1867 he replaced the Germanic Confederation, which had dissolved as a result of the Austro-Prussian War, with a new political union called the North German Confederation. This association included all of northern Germany, that is, Prussia and most of the Protestant principalities. The constitution of the new Confederation was designed to assure the preponderance of both the Prussian king and the Prussian state. William I became the President of the North German Confederation and the commander of its armed forces. The parliament consisted of two chambers: an upper one (Bundesrat, or Federal Council), representing the principalities, and a lower one (Reichstag), representing the population. Prussia assured itself of sufficient votes in the upper house to exercise an effective veto. The lower house was elected on the basis of universal democratic male suffrage. Bismarck granted this suffrage in the hope of obtaining broad public support against the liberals. (Later on he admitted that this miscalculation had been the worst error of his life.) As Chancellor, Bismarck was accountable only to his king; in other words, there was no ministerial responsibility and therefore no parliamentary system of government. The constitution of the North German Confederation became in 1871 the basis of the constitution of the German Empire.

Under Bismarck the Prussian soldier —well trained and equipped, rigidly obedient—became Europe's best.

To complete the unification of Germany, Bismarck needed one more great victory—over France. Such a victory would assure that the Catholic states of southern Germany would have no choice but to associate themselves with the North German Confederation. Napoleon III himself was not averse to war, partly because he had grown increasingly alarmed over the rise of Prussia and wanted to reduce its power, and partly because a victorious war would bolster his waning prestige at home.

The diplomatic incident that caused the outbreak of the Franco-Prussian War of 1870 was Prussia's promotion of a Hohenzollern candidate to the vacant throne of Spain. The French objected and applied pressure on King William to withdraw it. William agreed to do so. The dispute would have ended amicably, were it not that militant groups on both sides were eager to find a pretext for war. The pretext was provided by the famous "Ems telegram." In the course of private talks with King William at the resort town of Ems, the French ambassador demanded that Prussia not only withdraw its candidate for the Spanish throne but pledge never again to propose a Hohenzollern as ruler of Spain. William refused to give such a pledge. An account of these talks was wired to Bismarck, who released it to the press, but only after having doctored it to make the French demand appear as an insolent ultimatum and the German response as an equally insolent reply. The French, outraged by this action, declared war on Prussia (July, 1870).

The Prussians moved with greater speed and in August thrust through Alsace and Lorraine into France. The French resisted, but a large part of their army found itself encircled and trapped in the Metz-Sedan area. Among the prisoners taken at the beginning of September was Napoleon III himself. Bismarck, who waged war for limited political objectives, had now achieved his aim and wanted to suspend operations. But Moltke and the other military would not agree. They wanted to annihilate the enemy and pursued him deep into French territory, beyond the Loire River. In mid-September the Prussian forces laid siege to Paris, which they had surrounded. Four months later the starving city capitulated.

In January, 1871, while the siege of Paris was still in progress, the Prussian king was proclaimed German emperor.° The new empire, the fulfillment of the dream of German nationalists since the beginning of the century, expanded the North German Confederation to include the kingdoms and principalities of southern Germany, such as Bavaria, Württemberg, and Baden. The empire's constitution derived from that of the Confederation. It gave a preponderant position to Prussia and established the responsibility of the Chancellor (Bismarck) and the other ministers to the emperor. Universal suffrage was retained for the lower house. The constitution made no mention, however, of the "rights of the citizen"—an omission unique in the constitutional charters of the great European states of that time and an evil omen for the political future of Germany. The extent to which the unification of Germany had been the work of the military may be gathered from the fact that among the participants of the ceremonies attending the proclamation of the empire in the Hall of Mirrors at Versailles there

°The proclamation specified that he was "German Emperor" not "Emperor of Germany" in order not to offend the monarchs of the constituent states, who continued to regard themselves as sovereigns of their own territories.

were only two or three civilians. All others, including Emperor William I and Bismarck, wore uniforms.

The events of the 1860s, culminating in the formation of the empire, mark a watershed in the history of the German spirit. Until then the Germans had been universally regarded as a nation of sentimental dreamers: musicians, poets, scholars, craftsmen, and they so regarded themselves. Voltaire expressed the prevailing eighteenth-century view when he said that God, in creating the world, had entrusted to the French the kingdom of the land, to the English the kingdom of the seas, and to the Germans the kingdom of the clouds. This had now changed. Even during the anti-Napoleonic Wars of Liberation (1813–1815), ugly strains of chauvinism had been heard among German intellectuals; they resounded again at the sessions of the Frankfort parliament in 1848–1849. In the 1860s, and especially in the 1870s, following an uninterrupted succession of military victories, nationalism in Germany disassociated itself from liberalism and became arrogant and aggressive. The new nationalism found expression in an exaggerated notion of Germany's past, contempt for the "lesser breeds" (such as the Slavs), and growing reliance on "iron and blood." The theories of Charles Darwin (discussed in the next chapter) with their notions of "struggle for existence" and "survival of the fittest" were readily assimilated by a nation that felt it had finally arrived. As the new mood gained ground, the older idealistic tradition receded into the background. Kant, Goethe, Schiller, and the Humboldts were still greatly admired, but not so much for what they had said as for having said it in German.

The Austro-Hungarian Empire

The Hapsburgs, as we have seen, succeeded in preserving their empire during the revolutions of 1848–1849, despite the severe shocks it had received from nationalists in the borderlands and from radicals in the capital. The Austrian state at midcentury was still a giant, the second power in Europe in terms of territory and the third in terms of population. Its national economy, while not of the first rank, was considerable. Nevertheless, the revolutions of 1848–1849 marked the beginning of Austria's decline. It never regained the exalted international position that it had enjoyed thanks to the diplomatic skill of Metternich and the disunity of Italy and Germany. The unification of these two neighboring countries significantly reduced Austria's influence in Central Europe. Even deprived of such influence, however, the Austrian Empire would have remained a major power had it not been for conflicts among its own ethnic groups that steadily sapped its strength and eventually (1918) assured its dissolution.

The German-speaking population that ruled the Hapsburg domain was numerically a minority group. The non-German nationalities—the Magyars (Hungarians), Slavs (Poles, Czechs, Slovaks, Serbians, Croatians, Slovenes, Ukrainians), Latins (Italians, Romanians), and other ethnic groups (Jews)—outnumbered the Germans approximately three to one, and the proportion tended to increase further to the detriment of the Germans because they had fewer children. During the time when authority was firmly in the hands of the nobility and the autocracy, such ethnic disparity did not much matter. But with liberalization and democratization it threatened the very survival of the state, because, as more citizens received the vote, national interests and antagonisms came to the fore.

The bond that more than any other united this diversified population was religion: three-fourths of the emperor's subjects were Catholics. It was for this reason that Metternich had so closely connected Austria's politics with Catholicism. But in a secular age such a policy had little prospect of success. With each passing decade an increasing number of Austrian subjects thought of themselves not so much as Catholics but as Poles or Czechs or Croatians.

Probably the best solution for Austria's nationality problem would have been federation, a system that would have granted the principal ethnic groups territorial autonomy. But for several reasons this solution was not accepted, despite the strong support it received from some circles. For one, it would have reduced

THE PEOPLES
OF AUSTRIA-HUNGARY

Germans
Magyars

Romanians
Italians

SLAVS

Croatians and Serbians
Czechs
Slovaks

Poles
Slovenes
Ukrainians

.... Dual Monarchy, 1867

the influence of the German element. For another, it would not have satisfied the most radical nationalists among the non-German groups, who refused to settle for anything short of full political independence. Furthermore, with industrialization and urbanization, the various ethnic groups were increasingly intermingled, so that equitable territorial divisions became less and less feasible.

After suppressing the revolutionary movement of 1848–1849, the Hapsburg government veered sharply to the right. The 1850s were a period of black reaction, with authority placed in the hands of the bureaucracy. The Minister of the Interior, Alexander Bach, who exceeded even Metternich in his loathing of liberalism, pursued a policy of Germanization and relied heavily on his officialdom, popularly known as "Bach's Hussars." The new ruler, Franz Josef, was a stanch autocrat, ready to concede political rights to his subjects only when he had no other choice. He ruled even longer than Queen Victoria (sixty-eight years as against her sixty-four).

The first serious breach in the autocratic system occurred as a result of Austrian defeats in the war with Piedmont in 1859. To gain popular support, Franz Josef consented in 1861 to the establishment of an imperial House of Deputies, or Reichsrat. This assembly was elected not directly by voters, but indirectly by regional Diets, each of which had allotted to it a certain number of seats in the Reichsrat. These Diets, in turn, were elected by a quota system or "colleges." The whole electoral system was designed to give preponderance to propertied groups and to German nationals. The franchise was very limited. The Reichsrat initiated and voted on laws (subject to imperial approval), but it did not direct the executive branch: Austrian ministers remained responsible solely to the monarch until the collapse of the empire in 1918.

The Hungarians, whose nationalism was highly developed, refused from the beginning to participate in the Reichsrat and demanded full internal autonomy. Their leading statesman, Count Gyula Andrássy, proposed to Franz Josef that he reject the federal schemes pressed on him by other national groups in favor of a "dual solution" that would make Austrian Germans and Hungarian Magyars equal partners in ruling the empire. The emperor consented to this proposal, partly in order to strengthen his internal position after another military defeat, this time at the hands of the Prussians (1866), and partly to please his pro-Hungarian wife, Elizabeth. In 1867 he approved the *Ausgleich*—the "leveling" or "evening out" of the Austrian and Hungarian portions of the empire. The empire now became a "Dual Monarchy" consisting of an Austrian (or Cis-leithanian) part and a Hungarian (or Trans-leithanian) part. The two were linked by the person of the monarch, who was emperor in Austria and king in Hungary, as well as by three joint ministries (foreign affairs, armed forces, and common treasury). In internal matters the Hungarians received full autonomy. In 1867 the government also issued a decree guaranteeing full civil rights to all subjects, regardless of nationality or religion.

Admirably as the *Ausgleich* may have met the wishes of the Magyar nationalists, in the long run it precluded a satisfactory solution of the national problem for the empire as a whole, for, unless all the ethnic groups received rights similar to those given the Magyars, they were reduced to political subservience to an Austro-Hungarian partnership. For a while, the government seemed ready to

A French traveler sketched the inside of a Russian peasant hut, home to both the family and its livestock.

grant a Hungarian-type arrangement to the Czechs, but in 1871 this proposal was dropped, whereupon the Czechs began to boycott the Reichsrat. From then on, national conflicts in and out of parliament became the principal issue of internal politics in Austria-Hungary.

Of all the countries in nineteenth-century Europe, Russia alone failed to make the transition to constitutional and parliamentary government. It remained an autocracy until October, 1905, long after even some non-Western countries, like the Ottoman Empire and Japan, had experimented with liberal institutions.

The Great Reforms in Russia

Russia's failure to follow the prevalent pattern was due less to the weakness of liberal forces than to the strength of conservative ones. The government and a large part of the educated public had a deep-seated dread of mass anarchy. It feared that the uncouth and unpredictable Russian peasant, who constituted nine-tenths of the country's population, would go on an uncontrollable rampage of murder and arson the instant he sensed a weakening of authority over him. Liberalism seemed to involve precisely such a weakening of authority. The spectacle of dissident political parties, social unrest, and periodic revolutions in the countries of Western Europe indicated to many Russians the necessity of retaining in their own country firm, centralized government. The absolutist state alone could accomplish the enormous task of educational reform and economic development required for Russia's internal stability and external power.

Russian liberalism gained its main support among the Westernized landed gentry. This class, however, was on the decline. In its struggle against the bureaucratic-police regime, it received next to no support from the other groups of the population. To the peasants, the liberals appeared as selfish lords who wanted to limit the power of the tsar in order the better to exploit them. To the young intellectuals, strongly imbued with anarchist ideas, the liberals were anathema because their program—constitutionalism and parliamentarism—would enhance the power of the state that they wished to destroy. As for the bourgeoisie, it was not strong to begin with and in any event tended toward conservatism in gratitude for the protection that the imperial government extended it against foreign competition as well as against the demands of the Russian working class.

Russia's failure to undergo genuine liberalization does not mean, however, that the country did not liberalize at all. The 1860s in Russia was a decade of liberal reform that profoundly altered the face of the country. These reforms were carried out on the initiative of Alexander II (1855–1881), a ruler of essentially conservative views who came to the realization that it was no longer possible to govern a country of Russia's size and international position along purely bureaucratic lines. He therefore introduced a series of reforms intended to increase the participation of society in the country's public life. These "Great Reforms" resembled in their essential features those that Prussia had carried out half a century earlier in response to its humiliation at the hands of Napoleon.

The stimulus to reform, as in the case of post-1806 Prussia and post-1866 Austria, was military defeat. The active policy that Nicholas I had pursued in the Near East from the moment of his accession finally involved Russia in war with the Western powers. Britain, whose commercial interests in that area made it sensitive to Russian encroachments, repeatedly clashed with Russia on behalf of

In an 1853 Punch *cartoon, Britain and France try to diagnose the ills of their patient, the Ottoman Empire, menaced by the Russian scourge.*

the Ottoman Empire. Gradually France too became involved. In March, 1854, Russia found itself at war with a coalition consisting of Britain, France, and Turkey, which was later joined by Piedmont. The allies dispatched an expeditionary force that landed on the Crimean peninsula and after prolonged fighting seized the chief Russian port of Sebastopol (September, 1855). Completely isolated, Russia had to agree to peace terms (Treaty of Paris, 1856) that greatly reduced its influence in the Near East.

Although the Crimean War was in no sense a military disaster for Russia, it discredited the autocratic system enforced by Nicholas I, a stanch supporter of the Metternichian system. It showed that Russia had to modernize or cease to be a great power in any meaningful sense. This realization penetrated even high bureaucratic circles in St. Petersburg and made possible the Great Reforms that got under way with the death of Nicholas I in 1855 and the accession of his son, Alexander II.

Of all the questions confronting the country, the foremost was serfdom. Serfdom had come to Russia, as to most of Eastern Europe, late, having been legalized only in the seventeenth century. In the middle of the nineteenth century, slightly over one-third of the peasant population consisted of private (proprietary) serfs, who had no civil rights and could not legally acquire property. The worst feature of serfdom was not economic—the peasants, by Western standards, had more than enough land to till—but civil and moral: deprived of rights, serfs lacked incentives to improve their lot and felt isolated from society at large. Accustomed since the Middle Ages to treat all authority as hostile, the Russian peasant, for all his devotion to the Church and tsar, indeed harbored powerful destructive instincts.

There was talk of emancipating the serfs as early as the eighteenth century, and it is known that both Alexander I and Nicholas I in principle favored such action, though they did not have the courage to act. After the Crimean War the measure could no longer be delayed. The Emancipation Edict, issued on February 19, 1861, freed the serfs and gave all peasants basic civil rights. It also gave them land. The government reimbursed the landlords for that portion of the land they had lost to their one-time serfs by means of state bonds, which the peasants in turn were required to repay to the government over forty-nine years in the form of annual "redemption payments." For administrative and fiscal reasons, the land was not given directly to the peasants themselves but to village communes. To make certain that he met all his tax obligations and redemption payments, the peasant was forbidden to leave the commune without its permission. Thus, although he was freed from the landlord's authority, the peasant remained tied to the soil and to the commune. Despite these conservative features, the Emancipation Edict was a very bold measure that, without bloodshed, transformed millions of Russians from passive subjects into citizens.

By destroying the legal authority that the landlord had traditionally exercised over the peasantry, the edict necessitated a number of related reforms. In 1864 Alexander introduced into cities and provinces organs of local self-rule (municipal councils and *zemstva*). These institutions were elected by all the groups of the population. They were not meant to compete with the imperial bureaucracy, but to assist it by assuming a variety of responsibilities previously left unattended:

primary education, public health, the maintenance of roads and bridges, and so forth. To fulfill these obligations, the municipal councils and *zemstva* were empowered to collect taxes. Until abolished by the Communists, these organs helped significantly to raise the material and cultural level of the country. They also provided an excellent school of political training for public-minded citizens. Court reform (1864) introduced such advanced Western practices as irremovable judges and trial by jury. The army recruitment procedure was also reformed (1874), the system of draft quotas previously imposed on the serfs being replaced by compulsory military service for all citizens. Censorship was considerably eased. The Great Reforms helped the monarchy obtain a measure of public support in the difficult task of administering so vast a realm and yet did not deprive it of its monopoly of political power. They liberalized the administration without making it liberal.

Even the Turkish government—proverbially the most corrupt and backward in Europe—could not escape the general tendency of the time. In the first half of the nineteenth century, the government of the Ottoman Empire proved itself increasingly unable to cope with the internal and external challenges to its authority. The Greek rebellion of 1821 lasted for a decade and ended with the Turks conceding independence to Greece. In the 1830s Constantinople lost effective control over Egypt. Especially great was the threat of Russia, which in the 1830s established a virtual protectorate over the empire. Had it not been for repeated intervention by Western powers, notably Great Britain, there is little doubt that the Ottoman Empire would have fallen apart, the bulk of its territory being seized by Russia.

The Ottoman Empire

In Turkey, as elsewhere, military defeats provided the most persuasive argument in favor of internal reform. At first, the sultans were content to transplant Western culture, hoping that the adoption of Western manners and techniques would of itself infuse the state with the necessary vigor. Mahmud II (1808–1839), who is sometimes called the Turkish Peter the Great, introduced Western military practices, Western schools, and Western dress for state officials.

The reform movement proper, known as *Tanzimat*, got under way after Mahmud's death. In 1839 the Ottoman government proclaimed the equality of its subjects. The intention of this measure was to create, by decree as it were, a common Ottoman nationality, and in this manner to neutralize national sentiment among the non-Turkish citizens. Its effects, however, were nil, for the overwhelming majority of citizens continued to owe allegiance to their respective religious communities. It aroused much opposition among the Muslims, who could not admit that the Christians, or "Franks" as they called them, were superior to those who followed Islam (literally, "submission to God's will").

Under Western pressure, the Ottoman government carried out further reforms after the Crimean War, the hope being that these reforms would strengthen the empire and make it more resistant to Russian encroachments. In 1856 it issued a far-reaching general reform edict that assured Christian subjects of their civil rights and gave them access to positions in the army and civil service. These measures seemed to point to a steady development toward liberal forms, but, as we shall see, these expectations were not fulfilled.

5

Science and the Scientific Outlook

At the time of its emergence, Romanticism was a great liberalizing force. *The Decline of Romanticism* It helped to emancipate Western culture from the restraints of classicism and restored to the writer and the artist the right to creative self-expression. Politically, it had close affinities to liberalism and nationalism, both of which strove to free man from subjection to arbitrary authority. Early Romanticism was an ally of those who fought tyranny in all its forms.

But time and success killed the generous impulses of the Romantics. As soon as it had dislodged classicism, Romanticism became part of the established order and acquired the status of a new kind of orthodoxy. The poetry of Coleridge and Wordsworth, the novels of Scott and Hugo, and the stories of Hoffmann and Poe became, by the middle of the century, part of a cultivated European's cultural background. Before the century was over, they were included in the secondary-school curriculum—a certain sign of public acceptance. As they grew older, Romantic writers often turned conservative. Coleridge, who in 1789 had celebrated the fall of the Bastille, opposed Catholic emancipation and parliamentary reform in the 1820s. Pushkin, the singer of gypsies and the free Caucasian mountaineers, exhorted Nicholas I in 1830 to suppress the Polish uprising. The late German Romantics grew particularly reactionary.

European youth of the 1830s and 1840s, who found little to admire in the old Romantic idols, sought new heroes and new ideals in the world of science. The first half of the nineteenth century was a period of spectacular discoveries in chemistry, biology, and physics—discoveries that had particular bearing on such traditional philosophic questions as the nature of life and the physical universe. Science had a daring, a freshness, an authority that Romanticism had lost, and gradually talented youth abandoned Romanticism in favor of science and of philosophies based on scientific premises.

The device of the Royal Society of London, the world's oldest scientific institution, *Atoms, Cells, and Energy* bears the words *Simplex sigillum veri* (simplicity is the seal of truth). And, indeed, the quest for the simplest, most economical explanations of the largest number of phenomena is the goal of scientific endeavor. Science seeks to penetrate the screen of appearance which confronts man with a seemingly inexhaustible variety of unrelated objects and processes, to reach the underlying unities. Its progress is marked by ever higher levels of abstraction. To the prescientific or non-scientific mind, for example, breathing, burning, and rusting are unrelated phenomena, each requiring a unique explanation. To the scientist they are merely different manifestations of an identical process, namely combustion. The term combustion permits an abstract (non-sensory) correlation of these three apparently different occurrences.

If abstract principles with the widest applicability are the goal of science, measurement is its means. The scientist learns with the help of quantities. A law

George Richmond's portrait shows Charles Darwin at the age of thirty, at the time the naturalist first formulated his theory of "natural selection." Darwin, wrote the biologist Julian Huxley, shook the world with the "magic force of a single idea."

In his notebook John Dalton sketched representations of two adjacent atoms (top) and below them a molecule, or, as he called it, a "compound atom."

is of little use to him unless it can be expressed in terms of mass, velocity, or some other quantitative unit.

The importance of the scientific discoveries made in the first half of the nineteenth century derives from the fact that they yielded a few fundamental laws capable of embracing an enormous variety of natural phenomena. These laws revealed for the first time the basic structural element of all organic substances and living organisms (atoms, molecules, and cells) and formulated general principles regulating the relations of chemical and physical matter (the laws of the conservation of matter and energy). They also revealed a far greater degree of unity in nature than had been suspected and encouraged philosophers to devise a philosophic system capable of providing a scientific explanation of all phenomena, including the actions of man.

THE STRUCTURE OF PHYSICAL MATTER

The problem of the ultimate structure of matter had troubled thinkers since antiquity. Are there substances in nature, men wondered, which are final and incapable of being reduced to different substances? Among the thinkers who dealt with this question was Aristotle, who postulated that four "elements"— water, air, earth, and fire—were the basic ingredients of all material objects. This fourfold classification or one of its numerous variants survived well into the modern period and was finally abandoned only on the eve of the French Revolution, when Antoine Laurent Lavoisier, the father of modern chemistry, began to investigate the nature of fire. Like Aristotle, eighteenth-century scientists believed that fire was an element, involving the release of a substance called "phlogiston." They expended rivers of ink trying to define phlogiston and to explain why it was so elusive. Experimenting with oxygen, which had been recently isolated, Lavoisier showed that there was no such thing as phlogiston. From his researches he drew two conclusions: that in nature no matter is lost (the law of the indestructibility or conservation of matter), and that Aristotle's elements are not final entities at all but compounds of more basic chemical elements. Lavoisier drew up a table of thirty-two such elements (oxygen, nitrogen, hydrogen, etc.), most of which he identified correctly.

It had long been suspected that elements—that is, substances that cannot be changed into different substances—are made up of identical, minute entities. In the seventeenth and eighteenth centuries, scientists discussed such entities at great length, using the old Greek term "atoms." But the concept had no practical value for want of a method of identifying and measuring its units.

Atoms became an operative concept early in the nineteenth century, thanks to the researches of John Dalton, an English schoolmaster. Pondering the results obtained in experiments on gases, Dalton concluded in 1803 that they could be explained only by assuming that each element was in fact composed of identical atoms. He devised means of estimating the relative weights of the atoms of a number of elements and formulated a theory about the manner in which they combined to form chemical compounds. What distinguished one element from another, according to Dalton, was the weight of their respective atoms.

In the decades that followed Dalton's discoveries, chemists made great progress in ascertaining the precise atomic weight of the elements. This work culminated in the brilliant hypothesis of the Russian chemist Dmitri Mendeleev, who discovered that, if one listed all the then known elements in order of their atomic weight, they seemed to group themselves into several categories, each endowed with common properties. Mendeleev published in 1869 a list of the elements grouped in the form of a "Periodic Table." Some of the categories did not have their full complement of elements—a fact that suggested (for science assumed a symmetry in nature) that other, as yet unknown, elements existed. The Periodic Table in effect predicted the atomic weight of elements not yet discovered. Subsequent researches confirmed Mendeleev's intuition, and in time the empty spaces of the Periodic Table were filled in with elements newly found or artificially produced.

BIOLOGICAL DISCOVERIES

The identification of the atom as the ultimate entity of inorganic matter encouraged a search for a similar entity in living tissue. It had been known since the early seventeenth century, when the microscope first allowed men to take a closer look at tissues, that certain plants consisted of identical cell-like structures. But the "cellular theory" gained general acceptance only as a result of the researches of two German scientists, the botanist Matthias Schleiden and the biologist Theodor Schwann. Schleiden published a paper in 1838 showing the ubiquity of the cell nucleus and suggesting its relationship to the formation of cells. The following year, Schwann demonstrated the cellular nature of animal tissue. It now became evident that plants and animals, from the simplest to the most complex, are constructed of the same elementary "building blocks." Shortly afterward it was shown that all cells consist of protoplasm, a complex of chemical substances that was recognized as the basis of life.

Investigations along these lines yielded important insights into the nature of disease. In the third quarter of the nineteenth century, the German botanist Ferdinand J. Cohn isolated minute plants known as "bacteria," showed that they are responsible for many diseases, and indicated ways of neutralizing them by means of antibodies. On the basis of his findings, Louis Pasteur and Robert Koch developed the science of immunology which succeeded in greatly reducing deaths from communicable diseases.

ENERGY

One of the greatest mysteries confronting physical science in the eighteenth and early nineteenth centuries was the nature of light and heat. Early science had regarded them as material objects, and even Lavoisier listed them in his table as regular elements. This view, however, had one obvious flaw: unlike all other known material substances, light and heat seemed to have no measurable weight. To reconcile this contradiction, some scientists had recourse to the concept of "imponderability." By "imponderables" they meant material objects that were by definition incapable of being weighed. Heat was regarded as an "imponderable" fluid that passed from object to object as if it were some kind of juice. But not everyone was satisfied with this explanation, and experiments continued in the hope of isolating the material substance of heat.

A significant advance in solving this problem was made by Benjamin Thompson, Count Rumford. A native of Massachusetts, Thompson left the United States during the Revolution because of his loyalist sympathies and spent the remainder of his life in the service of various European monarchs. In 1798–1799 he carried out experiments that cast serious doubt on the materiality of heat. In one of these experiments, he placed the tip of a metal borer and the mouth of a cannon in a box filled with water and then proceeded to bore the cannon, at the same time measuring the resultant changes in the temperature of the water. He found that there was no limit to the amount of heat that the action of boring could generate. From this evidence, Thompson concluded that heat was not a material body, for no material body could be produced in unlimited quantities. He suggested instead that it was a "kind of motion."

To James Joule, an English physicist active in the 1840s, belongs the main credit for demonstrating the correctness of Thompson's hypothesis. Joule dissolved a piece of zinc in acid and measured the amount of heat produced by this dissolution. Next, he measured the heat produced by the dissolution of an identical piece of zinc in a battery wired to an electric generator. The second measurement turned out to be smaller. What happened to the missing heat? Joule showed that its exact equivalent could be recovered either in the heat which the passage of the electric current produced in the wire, or in the work performed by the generator which the current had activated. In other words, no heat disappeared, and some heat changed into mechanical motion. These findings led the German Hermann von Helmholtz in 1847 to formulate the law of the conservation of energy. The term *energy* was applied to a variety of phenomena previously regarded as unrelated: first heat, electricity, and magnetism, and subsequently light. These forms of energy were discovered to be interchangeable and capable of being transformed into mechanical work. The law of the conservation of energy (a counterpart of Lavoisier's law of the conservation of matter) held that one form of physical activity can be converted into another, the total amount of such activity in the world remaining unchanged. It is widely regarded as the single most important scientific generalization of the nineteenth century. If conservation of matter gave birth to the science of chemistry, conservation of energy produced the science of physics.

At midcentury there existed in the West a fairly consistent scientific outlook. Its method was defined as inductive and empirical: the careful accumulation of carefully gathered data, and the rejection of anything that could not be verified by the senses or scientific apparatus. Nature, which was regarded as having an objective reality, was seen as operating according to firm, undeviating laws, the most fundamental of which were the conservation of energy and of matter.

The Theory of "Natural Selection"

The theory of evolution, especially in its Darwinian form, exerted the same impact on the biological sciences that the conservation theories had exerted on the investigation of chemical and physical processes. It too linked phenomena previously not considered significantly related to each other, namely the structure and organs of animals and their natural environment.

Until the early nineteenth century, theologians, philosophers, and scientists alike accepted the biblical account that the universe had come into being in the single act of Creation. Every kind of animal and plant, every river and mountain, was believed to have been created in its finished form, exactly as it appeared. This view implied the permanence of animal and plant species. Insofar as everything was eternally fixed, the main function of the naturalist was to classify. The great eighteenth-century Swedish botanist Carolus Linnaeus, true to this concept, devoted his life to the task of classifying and naming the known plants.

However, in biology, as in chemistry and physics, evidence continued to accumulate that could not be reconciled with the traditional view. Toward the end of the eighteenth century, Chevalier de Lamarck, a professor at the Parisian Botanical Gardens, found it impossible to fit some of the plants placed in his care into the accepted classification system. In search of explanations, he concluded that the separation between the species was less clear than the science of the time believed. Gradually, he developed a theory of evolution that he published in 1809 in a book titled *Philosophie Zoologique*. Plants and animals, he argued, were different not so much because God had made them differently, but because in an effort to adjust to their environment they had to assume different shapes and develop different organs. Thus, for example, a whale whose diet consisted of soft plankton shed its teeth, while a giraffe, to reach leaves high up on trees, kept on stretching its neck until it acquired its present monstrous proportions. Lamarck assumed that the characteristics that an animal acquired during its lifetime were passed on to its progeny.

Additional evolutionary evidence accumulated from geology. The existence of layers apparently from differing epochs suggested that the earth also was not created at once in its present form, but underwent constant change. Sir Charles Lyell's *Principles of Geology* (1830–1833) helped to disseminate the view that the earth was not the result of a single act of Creation, but had evolved slowly over a long period of time.

The growing evidence did not for a long time overthrow the static outlook in biology, because no one could satisfactorily explain how the variations of animal species had come about. (Lamarck's theory was regarded as a joke.) The appearance in 1859 of Charles Darwin's *Origin of Species*, which contained a massive body of evidence in support of evolution and a persuasive theory to explain its workings, made, therefore, a tremendous impression.

Darwin's grandfather, Erasmus, had been one of the leading exponents of the theory of evolution, and he himself became well acquainted with it at an early age. Intrigued, as were many of his contemporaries, by its mysterious operations, he accepted in 1831 (at the age of twenty-two) the post of chief naturalist on a scientific expedition exploring the South Pacific and the coast of Latin America in the ship *Beagle*. The *Beagle* cruised leisurely for five years in the southern waters, affording Darwin an excellent opportunity to study closely a number of animal species. On the Galápagos Islands, off Ecuador, he discovered a perfect biological laboratory, for here animals had been able to develop on different islands for millions of years with a minimum of external interference. A comparison of the Galápagos animals with related animals from the mainland of South America or with fossils permitted Darwin to discard the notion of a special Creation. He concluded that animals do indeed evolve with time, and that they do so in response to their environment.

In analyzing the processes of evolution, Darwin found it useful to employ a concept first formulated by Thomas Malthus in his *Essay on the Principle of Population*, published in 1798 (see Chapter 6). Malthus had used this concept

Early in his career the botanist Carolus Linnaeus explored Lapland collecting specimens. He is decked out in his Lapp costume in this portrait.

Ranked as the leading comparative anatomist of his time, Thomas Huxley also made major contributions to physiology, physiography, geology, and cellular study.

—"the struggle for existence"—to explain how the rate of population growth was related to the availability of food supplies. This notion suggested to Darwin the principle of "natural selection," which he formulated (but did not announce) in 1837–1838. Aware that evolution could not gain acceptance unless it was shown precisely *how* animals changed in response to the environment, he spent twenty years after the return of the *Beagle* patiently sifting his data.

In June, 1858, Darwin received a letter and an unpublished scientific paper from Alfred R. Wallace, a young naturalist residing in Malaya, which indicated that Wallace was on the same track. Darwin therefore decided to make his theory public, and the following year brought out *On the Origin of Species by Means of Natural Selection.*

The fundamental assumption of Darwin's theory is that since all organisms live in intimate dependence on their natural environment, to survive and propagate they must engage in a "struggle for existence." Plants fight for light and water, while animals seek to escape their predators and compete for food. To succeed in this endless struggle, organisms must adapt. Adaptation is made possible by the appearance of "variants," that is, some organs or qualities that are particularly suitable to given conditions. As to precisely how these "variants" first occur in organisms, Darwin was not clear. But this was not a fatal flaw in his doctrine, because he was not so much concerned with the problem of why animals happen to be different as with why some differences help them survive and flourish while others cause them to disappear. In other words, he was concerned not with how the fittest "arrive," but with how they "survive."

Given the fact that variants do occur, some are obviously better suited to assist the organism in coping with its particular environment than others. If certain insects, for example, happen to develop coloring that blends with their environment, they can better elude the birds that prey on them and are likely to produce more progeny with similar characteristics. On the other hand, insects whose coloring stands out perish and with time become extinct. In this manner, nature may be said to engage in a constant process of "selecting" those organisms that are most suitable for the particular conditions it creates. This process of natural selection constitutes the heart of Darwin's theory of evolution. He summarizes it in *Origin of Species* as follows:

> If under changing conditions of life organic beings present individual differences in almost every part of their structure . . . if there be, owing to their geometrical rate of increase, a severe struggle for life at some age, season, or year . . . then, considering the infinite complexity of the relations of all organic beings to each other and to their conditions of life, causing an infinite diversity in structure, constitution, and habits, to be advantageous to them, it would be a most extraordinary fact if no variations had ever occurred useful to each being's own welfare, in the same manner as so many variations have occurred useful to man. But if variations useful to any organic being ever do occur, assuredly individuals thus characterized will have the best chance of being preserved in the struggle for life; and from the strong principle of inheritance, these will tend to produce offspring similarly characterized. This principle of preservation, or the survival of the fittest, I have called Natural Selection. It leads to the improvement of each creature in relation to its organic and inorganic conditions of life.

Natural selection explains why we encounter such immense variety of biological forms: variety of forms results from the adjustment of living organisms to that variety of conditions created by nature.

Darwin, of course, did not "discover" evolution. But by the weight of carefully observed evidence, he made what had been a dubious hypothesis a widely accepted scientific theory. The immediate reaction to *Origin of Species* was mixed. A number of scientists found it convincing and accepted it without reservations. Among them was Thomas Huxley, who called himself "Darwin's bulldog" because he championed Darwin's theories wherever they were assailed. (Darwin himself disliked controversy, preferring a sheltered life.) And the opposition was stanch. Evolution challenged the biblical account of Creation and placed man on a par with the other primates such as apes and monkeys. Religious authorities on the whole rejected the theory of natural selection at first, especially in Protestant countries, where the Bible was widely read and often literally interpreted.

A famous early encounter between the Darwinists and their opponents, indicative of the passions that Darwin's theory had aroused, took place in 1860 at Oxford. The leading figure among the opponents was Samuel Wilberforce, bishop of Oxford, popularly known as "Soapy Sam." He had not read Darwin's book, but expected to have an easy time demolishing it by ridicule. In the course of his speech, which the elegant audience received warmly, he turned to Huxley and asked him whether he traced his descent from the apes on his grandfather's or his grandmother's side.

Huxley held his fire until the audience clamored for a reply, then rose to say:

I asserted—and I repeat— that a man has no reason to be ashamed of having an ape for his grandfather. If there were an ancestor whom I should feel ashamed in recalling, it would rather be a *man*—a man of restless and versatile intellect—who, not content with success in his own sphere of activity, plunges into scientific questions with which he has no real acquaintance, only to obscure them by an aimless rhetoric, and distract the attention of his hearers from the real point at issue by eloquent digressions and skilled appeals to religious prejudice.°

In the ensuing pandemonium one lady fainted, another jumped on her chair, and the bishop for once was left speechless.

It would be wrong to regard all opposition to Darwinism as due either to ignorance or prejudice. Darwin himself was well aware that his theory failed to answer many questions. How did variations occur in the first place? How did animals *gradually* develop adaptive organs or features (e.g., the shock-giving organ of the electric eel) that were of no use until *fully* developed and therefore could have no effect on natural selection until then? And why could man produce no new species by selective breeding? Darwin grappled with such problems to the end of his life. Some remain unsolved to this day.

The problem of the emergence of variations, or the "arrival" of the fittest, was in large measure solved around the turn of the century by so-called neo-Darwinian biologists. In the 1890s German biologist August Weismann proved that characteristics acquired by organisms during their lifetime could not be passed on to their progeny. Body cells and germ cells were distinct entities, without influence on one another. These findings fairly finished the old Lamarckian hypothesis that even Darwin had at times found attractive. (Lamarckian theories were revived in Stalinist Russia.) In the early 1900s a Dutch botanist, Hugo de Vries, showed that variants are caused by sudden changes or "mutations" in the germ cells. A mutation produces offspring with some distinct quality that its parents lack. Natural selection then determines whether the variant is useful and worthy of preservation or a freak and doomed to disappear.

Science and Philosophy   The great discoveries in the fields of chemistry, physics, and biology produced a veritable cult of science and engendered something that had no precedent in human history: a scientific culture—that is, a comprehensive interpretation of life parallel to a religious or philosophical outlook. This culture dominated Western thought between approximately 1840 and 1880. It demanded that all opinions accord with the method and the findings of natural science. To gain acceptance, philosophical, religious, political, economic, and aesthetic views had to be "scientific."

The new intellectual current is known by a variety of names, of which "positivism," coined by the French philosopher Auguste Comte (see below), is probably the most widely accepted. Positivism holds that man is not a unique being but an ordinary product of nature. His life, both as an individual and as a member of society, is subject to laws as consistent as those of the inorganic world. He

---

°Leonard Huxley, *Life and Letters of T. H. Huxley,* (1908). Of course, the Darwinists did not claim man's descent from apes, but the descent of both man and ape from a common primate ancestor.

T. H. HUXLEY, *Man's Place in Nature*, 1863

has neither soul nor free will. In the ultimate analysis, he is merely chemical compound. Such a view was diametrically opposed to the Romantic concept of man as his self-creator.

Interestingly, practicing scientists were much more cautious in drawing inferences from their researches than were scientific amateurs and popularizers. Scientists had an instinctive dread of going beyond the evidence at hand. Observation told them nothing about God or life after death or freedom of the will, and therefore they preferred to leave such subjects alone. Darwin himself professed to be an agnostic—one who holds God to be unknowable. Some scientists remained religious. Scientific discovery, instead of destroying their faith, merely intensified it, for it revealed the universe as even more complicated and mysterious than had been suspected. In 1872 the German physiologist Emil Du Bois-Reymond delivered a famous address called "On the Limits of Natural Science" in which he denied that thinking could be explained in chemical terms and asserted that man could never penetrate the ultimate mysteries of nature because he himself was a part of that nature which he was investigating.

The most extreme claims on behalf of science were advanced by the so-called materialists, philosophers who argued that all phenomena without exception are ultimately reducible either to matter or to energy. The idea that man was a mechanism composed entirely of material substances had occurred to philosophers even before the discoveries of modern chemistry and biology. In the eighteenth century there appeared in France "materialists" who denied the existence of the soul. Julien de La Mettrie, the author of *L'Homme-machine* (*Man a Machine*, 1748), pioneered the movement; Baron Paul Holbach's *Système de la Nature* (*System of Nature*, 1770) made it notorious. Both La Mettrie and Holbach defined consciousness and thought as physical phenomena. The influence of these two philosophers, due to persecution by church and state and to the primitive

Thomas Huxley reproduced skeletons of (from left) a gibbon, an orangutan, a chimpanzee, a gorilla, and a man in an 1863 work on man's place in nature, pointing out the similarities and differences in body structures.

condition of eighteenth-century science, was limited, and the triumph of Romanticism put their works into temporary oblivion.

Materialism revived around 1840. Its main propagators were a group of young German philosophers called "Left Hegelians," whose leading spirit was Ludwig Feuerbach. Though Feuerbach himself was not a materialist in the strict sense of the word, he gave the principal stimulus to the emergence of modern materialism. Feuerbach addressed himself to the question: What is the origin of the idea of God, and, by extension, of many other ideas which the senses are unable to perceive? He was not content to dismiss religion as prejudice, ignorance, or mythmaking, as were some of his contemporaries, but investigated the psychological roots of religious sentiment. He was struck that man ascribed to divinity the very qualities that he himself most sorely lacked, for example, omniscience, omnipotence, generosity, beauty, and so on. From this observation he concluded that religion represented what today would be called a "wish fantasy." Man "projected" his own aspirations onto an imaginary being. "Religion," he wrote in *The Essence of Christianity*, "is the relation of man to his own nature . . . but to his nature not recognized as his own, but regarded as another nature, separate, nay, contradistinguished from his own. . . ." By creating this fantasy-wish "other" nature, according to Feuerbach, man estranged or "alienated" himself. The task of modern thought was to return to man all those qualities of which he had divested himself—to recreate "true man." Feuerbach called his system "anthropological" because it freed man from the tyranny of religious and philosophical abstraction with which he had surrounded himself, placed him at the center of the universe, and literally made him his own god.

The Feuerbachian notion of man had great appeal to radical intellectuals and provided the philosophical foundation of both anarchism and Marxism. (See Chapter 8). The vision of a "true man," unencumbered by illusion of any kind, free in the fullest sense of the word, is common to all modern radical movements. In the twentieth century it re-emerged most explicitly in existentialism.

Materialism reached its apogee in the 1850s. Bookstalls were flooded with works condemning idealism and religion and reducing life to chemical processes. The materialists delighted in shocking the public with statements like: "Thought bears the same relation to the brain that bile bears to the liver or urine to the kidneys," and "Man is what he eats." "Is life worth living?," asked one popular pun, whose answer was, "It depends on the liver."

Public opinion was shocked and disturbed by materialism, but not persuaded. Even the educated public of the time found it difficult to accept that man could be scientifically studied at all, let alone that he could only be so approached. Faith in the uniqueness of life processes was deeply ingrained. It was generally believed that living organisms possessed a "vital force," a life-giving substance (not unlike phlogiston) that fundamentally differentiated them from inorganic objects. This belief made people skeptical about the possibility of medicine becoming a "science." The most influential attack on this attitude was Claude Bernard's *Introduction to Experimental Medicine*, published in Paris in 1865. Bernard, a celebrated physiologist, denied the existence of any "vital force" and asserted that living organisms could and should be studied experimentally.

The new concept of man led to the emergence of experimental psychology. In

Leipzig in 1879, Wilhelm Wundt opened the first "psychological laboratory" and proceeded to measure and classify various manifestations of human consciousness.

Once man had been deprived of his unique status and reduced to a mechanism, it was inevitable that the society made up of such mechanisms would also be subjected to scientific interpretation. The study of society became a science, "sociology." Its task was to apply to society empirical methods of investigation, to discover its operating principles, and thus to predict its future behavior.

Sociology originated in the second quarter of the century. Its founder, Auguste Comte, decided that the progress of man from the beginnings of recorded history was essentially a progress of enlightenment involving a gradual transition from lower to higher stages of understanding. All knowledge goes through three phases: theological, metaphysical, and "positive" or scientific. In the earliest phase, man attributes happenings to the will of God or gods. In astronomy, to take one example, he interprets the motions of the planets as responses to divine directives. In the metaphysical phase of knowledge, he discovers that nature obeys firm rules. He still believes that behind these rules lies a will, but he now sees this will as rational and benevolent. Astronomy reached the metaphysical stage in the seventeenth century with the help of Kepler and Galileo. Knowledge enters its final, positive stage when it is realized that nature obeys no superior will, irrational or rational, but its own immutable laws. This happened in astronomy with the discoveries of Newton. The more complex a branch of knowledge, the slower it is to attain this positive stage. Mathematics, being the simplest (in the sense that it depends on no previous body of knowledge), became positive earliest, for no one had ever attributed algebraic or geometric laws to divine volition. The study of society, being the most complex, remained longest in the throes of theological or metaphysical explanations.

Comte felt that the time had come to develop a positive science of society that would reveal the immutable laws governing human relations. In his principal work, *Treatise on Positive Philosophy* (1830–1842), he outlined a grand scheme for the development of knowledge, culminating in the development of sociology. In a society of the future, he believed, human actions will rest on positive or scientific knowledge, and differences of opinion will disappear. Men will no more quarrel over what was right or wrong than they quarrel over the properties of chemical elements. Any disputes that may arise will be settled by experts.

Comte led a sheltered life, refusing even to read newspapers, so as not to be distracted from his supreme task of creating a sociology. But life had its revenge. Three years after he had brought out the final installment of the *Treatise*, he fell in love with a much younger woman, who did not reciprocate his feelings and who soon passed away. Comte was so shaken by this experience that he began to tamper with his admirably lucid system, introducing into it mystical elements that took it right back from the "positive" to the "theological" phase. With some of his followers he created a new "positivist religion" which replaced the worship of God with that of humanity. This religion had its churches, priests, and ritual; Comte's deceased love became humanity's "patron saint." Another group of followers, led by the lexicographer Maximilian Littré, broke away from

Comte, declaring him insane, and remained faithful to pure "positivism." Under Littré's guidance the movement flourished, spreading far beyond France. Because of the importance it attached to knowledge as a factor of progress, positivism had much appeal to intellectuals in non-industrial countries, where indeed knowledge was all that lent itself to development. Positivism boosted the intellectual's sense of self-importance. In Russia, Poland, and Brazil, to mention only three examples, it fairly dominated opinion in the second half of the nineteenth century.

The most promising tool for predicting human behavior seemed the newly developed discipline of social statistics. Henry Thomas Buckle, in his influential *History of Civilization in England* (1857–1861), argued that statistics "reveal the great social law that the moral actions of men are the product not of their volition, but of their antecedents." As an example of the predictable recurrence of human actions, Buckle pointed to the fact that London and Paris post offices received year after year the same proportion of letters bearing neither the name nor the address of the intended recipient. Similar patterns could be found in statistics of marriages, murders, and suicides. Indeed, a French mathematician of the time showed that an occurrence seemingly as haphazard as the proportion of soldiers in the Prussian army who died every year from the kick of a mule remained constant. Statistics and sociology developed from the first in intimate association.

Biological evolution also received social application. This task was attempted by Herbert Spencer and Thomas Huxley. Even before the appearance of *Origin of Species*, Spencer had speculated about the resemblance of society to a biological organism and the possibility of studying history in evolutionary terms. Darwin's book provided him with the necessary theoretical framework to formulate a theory known as Social Darwinism. To Spencer, the "struggle for existence" that Darwin had found in nature was a natural concomitant of social life as well: man, too, was engaged in a constant struggle against his fellows, from which only the fittest emerged victorious. Free economic competition performed the same function in society as natural selection performed in nature. From this analogy, Spencer and Huxley concluded that the less one interfered with the operations of society, the greater the assurance that the fittest, i.e., the best, would come out on top. This was laissez faire at its most extreme, far beyond what Adam Smith and his immediate followers had envisioned. Social Darwinism had great appeal to a part of the business community, for by equating wealth and power with "fitness" and both with "goodness" it provided a pseudo-scientific excuse for disclaiming responsibility for one's less fortunate fellow men. It was rejected by socialists and anarchists, who considered social conflict artificial and transitory and social harmony the natural condition of man. A most persuasive argument against Social Darwinism was made by the Russian anarchist Peter Kropotkin in his study *Mutual Aid as a Factor in Evolution* (1890–1902). Basing his argument on evidence from nature and history, Kropotkin maintained that cooperation was an even more powerful factor in life than struggle, and that it best assured the survival of species.

Darwinism, both in its original and in its Spencerian-Huxleian forms, gave rise to a great variety of pseudo-scientific theories. It lent itself admirably to the justi-

The French philosopher Auguste Comte not only originated sociology as a science but coined the term as well.

fication of oppression or brutality by enabling those on top to claim that the mere fact of being in power proved their greater right to existence. It thus encouraged the mood of violence that became very pronounced after 1870. According to Jacques Barzun,

> No one who has not waded through some sizeable part of the literature of the period 1870–1914 has any conception of the extent to which it is one long call for blood, nor of the variety of parties, classes, nations, and races whose blood was separately and contradictorily clamored for by the enlightened citizens of the ancient civilization of Europe.°

The most pernicious of the hate theories that developed at this time was racialism. Its beginnings antedate Darwin's book, but it flourished best in the atmosphere produced by such concepts as "struggle for existence" and "survival of the fittest" that were popularized by Darwinism. Its founder, the French writer Count Joseph de Gobineau, argued in *The Inequality of Human Races* (1853–1855) that there is a hierarchy of "races." The highest race consists of the Germans (by which term he meant not the population of modern Germany, but the blonde, blue-eyed inhabitants of northern France, Belgium, and England). Because these "Germans" had avoided mixing with "inferior" Semitic and Negroid races, they were destined to rule the world. This theory was later developed by a Germanized Englishman, Houston Stewart Chamberlain, in his *Foundations of the Nineteenth Century* (1899). Chamberlain held that modern-day Germans were the only pure Aryans, and that they alone could save Europe and European civilization from the destructive assaults of such lower races as the Jews, Negroes, and Orientals.

In the long run, the so-called science of society failed to produce anything resembling scientific laws of human behavior, but often buttressed vested interests, social as well as ethnic, and prepared the ground for theories of extermination.

Science and Religion

One of the by-products of the scientific spirit, especially in its Left Hegelian form, was a new interpretation of biblical history.

Textual criticism carried out in the 1830s and 1840s, mostly at German universities, revealed the Bible to be a compilation written at different historic periods. Like the earth and its inhabitants, it now appeared as not having been created at once, but having grown. Readers of the Pentateuch (the first five books of the Bible) had long noted, of course, that it gives alternate and differing versions of a number of events, such as the Creation of man or the Flood. Theologians had exerted a great deal of ingenuity in trying to reconcile these discrepancies. The new, critical school of biblical scholarship, by contrast, sought to peel away the ambiguities and to disassemble the Pentateuch into its component parts. It demonstrated that the Pentateuch consisted of several distinct texts that had been woven together by an unknown editor or editors. Textual analysis of the Gospels raised the possibility that they were not accounts of four separate eyewitnesses. The Left Hegelian Bruno Bauer, in two books written in the 1840s, advanced the proposition that the Gospels according to John,

---

° Jacques Barzun, *Darwin, Marx, Wagner: Critique of a Heritage* (1941).

Luke, and Matthew derived from one common source, namely Mark.

These findings coincided with a new interpretation of the origins of Judaism and Christianity. The new philosophers and historians denied that they were divinely inspired creeds and treated them instead as ordinary legends. In his *Life of Jesus* (1835), David Strauss, another Left Hegelian, presented Christianity as a "myth" unconsciously created by a community raised on Jewish expectations of a Messiah. Others tried to cut through this "myth" to the authentic historical kernel in biblical history. Miracles were rejected in favor of scientific explanations. The most famous attempt to rationalize and humanize Christianity was made by the French positivist Ernest Renan in his *Life of Jesus* (1863). Renan had visited Palestine to depict the story of Jesus against a genuine historical and geographic background. He also tried to provide scientifically plausible explanations of supernatural incidents in Christ's story. His account of Christ's death, for example, rested on medical evidence, providing a clinical account of the hemorrhage that crucifixion would cause in the human body. Although he was a deeply religious person who thought to enhance man's admiration for Christ by his realistic portrayal, Renan so shocked his contemporaries that he lost his university post.

Realism in Literature The aesthetic counterpart of the scientific spirit was known as Realism. A movement based on Realist principles emerged in the 1830s, matured in the 1850s, and dominated Western literature and art from then until the late 1880s.

Realism rested on the premise that man was an intrinsic part of the natural order and a product of his environment. It rejected the Romantic idealization of man as a being endowed with limitless potential. Hippolyte Taine, the founder of positivist literary criticism, assumed that writers—like mankind in general—were molded by three forces: heredity, milieu, and the spirit of their times. Human values, ideals, behavior, and even manner of thinking could always be traced to these three factors. "Vice and virtue," he wrote, "are products like vitriol and sugar." The task of the Realist writer was to penetrate and depict truthfully the human environment in all its complexity. The writer's attention was to shift from the individual and his inner life to the web of circumstance in which this individual found himself and which made him what he was—that is, in effect, to the society within which he lived and worked.

The Realist school demanded from the writer first and foremost a portrayal of the "real" world. By this it emphatically did not mean a world populated by demons, by men who lost their noses or sold their shadows, or by solitary heroes who roamed Alpine peaks or carried a curse for having killed an albatross in the Antarctic. It meant essentially a depiction of nineteenth-century working Europe. Its dramas were small: the cumulative effect of daily misunderstandings, petty squabbles, little injustices committed and suffered without awareness of their ultimate implications. Proceeding from this view, the Realists concentrated on ordinary people, usually from the working class or the petty bourgeoisie, in their ordinary surroundings.

In a world in which little of a dramatic nature happened, action became of secondary importance, and the writer's attention shifted to detail, to things which—insignificant in themselves—in their totality give life its specific quality.

With furious energy Balzac worked as much as 18 hours a day for months on end on his Comédie Humaine. *This study is by Louis Boulanger.*

This detail had to be rendered accurately and objectively. The writer was expected to stay out of the picture and to function as a dispassionate recorder; under no circumstances was he to moralize. Since everything that happens is "natural," in the sense that it has definite causes, everything must be recorded, including the ugly and the repulsive. The novel proved to be the medium best suited to depict the environment in all its realistic detail. In the second third of the century, it was by far the most popular literary form.

Realism originated in France, which had never fully surrendered to Romanticism and now once more assumed its traditional role as the aesthetic leader of Europe. From there it quickly spread to other countries. The founder of Realism was the Frenchman Honoré de Balzac, whose social novels began to appear in the 1830s. Balzac depicted the times so accurately and in such detail that his novels constitute an excellent source of information on social conditions in France under Louis Philippe. In 1842 Balzac brought out the first volume of his monumental *Comédie Humaine* (intended as a modern counterpart of Dante's *Divine Comedy*), which at the time of his death (1850) comprised 47 volumes. One can obtain some notion of the complexity of this narrative from the fact that it has a cast of more than 2,000 characters.

Realism acquired an articulate program in the early 1850s. It was first formulated by the painter Gustave Courbet, who publicly announced that he had his fill of saints and angels and intended henceforth to paint only "the modern and the common." His canvases, including the well-known *Stone Breakers* (page 150), were barred from the official Salon, but he won a circle of supporters, including some writers who translated his sentiments into theoretical manifestoes, and launched literary Realism on its way.

The Stone Breakers *(1849) by Courbet. When the International Exhibition of 1855 barred his pictures, Courbet held a one-man show by the gates under the sign, "Realism—G. Courbet."*

The new movement had its first great success with the appearance in 1857 of Gustave Flaubert's *Madame Bovary*, the story of a lonely provincial woman who betrays her husband and is herself in turn betrayed by her lover. The incident was commonplace (in fact, it was based on an authentic case) and the characters most ordinary, yet the whole had a profoundly moving effect. Flaubert showed that the lives of small people could furnish material for an intensely dramatic narrative. The shock that *Madame Bovary* produced and that caused the book to be impounded by the authorities derived not so much from its description of adultery, a topic frequent enough in literature, but from Flaubert's deliberate refusal to pass moral judgment on it.

From the 1860s onward, the European literary market was flooded with realistic novels depicting an immense variety of human situations previously considered unworthy of serious literature. Readers could learn from them how Swiss shopkeepers, Russian foresters, Polish peasants, Jewish traveling salesmen, Italian fishermen, and Prussian merchants lived. The stress was on the seamy side of life: poverty and drabness when dealing with the poor, immorality and corruption when dealing with the rich.

In England Realism found its main expression in the social novel. Less "objective" than the French Realist novel, it was written with the intention of awakening public conscience and spurring social reform. Some of the novels of Charles Dickens belong to this category, at least in part (for example, the prison scenes in his *Pickwick Papers* (1836–1837) and the description of the workhouse in *Oliver Twist* (1837–1838), as do the novels of Charles Kingsley and Mrs. Gaskell. William Thackeray's and Anthony Trollope's canvases of British life are more typically Realist in the French sense, tending to emphasize description and atmosphere.

Realism reached its greatest creative heights in Russia, a country that had few outlets for its thoughts and feelings besides literature. In fiction it was possible to communicate ideas that censorship would have forbidden in any other guise. Belles-lettres, and in particular the novel, performed in Russia the combined functions of the political pamphlet the religious tract, and the uncensored newspaper.

Russian literature boasts several novels that qualify as Realist in the best sense of the word, among them Sergei Aksakov's *Family Chronicle* (1856), a description of the life of the author's ancestors on the Eastern frontier, and I. A. Goncharov's *Oblomov* (1859), the story of a slothful landlord. But the greatest Russian novelists were adherents of Realism only in a limited sense. While they set their stories in the contemporary world and placed their heroes in a specific social environment, they did not, as a rule, obey the injunction to refrain from moralizing. Count Leo Tolstoy's novels are full of preaching. *Anna Karenina* (1875–1877), like *Madame Bovary*, deals with the theme of adultery, but, unlike Flaubert, Tolstoy does not hesitate to condemn his heroine. Fëdor Dostoevsky's early novels (e.g., *Poor Folk*, 1846) were written in a Realist manner. In his later work, that is, in all his great novels, he turned political pamphleteer. In Ivan Turgenev the moralistic element is least noticeable. *Fathers and Sons* (1862) is a remarkably accurate portrayal of the conflict between generations—the old Romantic-liberal one and the new positivist-socialist one. The author's attitude is so detached that one cannot decide on the basis of the novel where his sympathies lie.

Toward the end of the century, writers in pursuit of extreme realism produced works that were virtually static. In *A Lovely Day* (1881), Henri Céard recounts an abortive affair between a middle-aged, married housewife and her neighbor. The two plan an outing, the woman expecting to be seduced, the man expecting to seduce her. As the day progresses she grows bored with him and he with her. In the evening they return home, separately. The description of that uneventful episode in the life of two completely uninteresting people occupies 200 pages. Realism pushed to such lengths departed from its original intent and imperceptibly shaded into new forms of literary expression that we shall discuss under the heading of Modernism (Chapter 14).

Nineteenth-century Western culture was too rich and too diversified for any single movement to obtain a monopoly on it. If we divide the century into Romantic and Realist periods, it is only to isolate its dominant trends. Just as, at the height of idealism, scientists were quietly pursuing their laboratory experiments, so in the age of scientific hegemony voices of protest were heard inveighing against science and all it stood for. These voices came from thinkers who did not believe that science had all the answers or that man was a mere plaything of forces beyond his control.

The anti-positivist protest movement in the second half of the nineteenth century lacked unity or a formal program. What it had in common were certain general attitudes. It stressed deep-seated, non-rational drives: man's instinct for violence, longing for power, craving for beauty. It glorified those periods in history when these drives seemed to have been best satisfied (such as pre-Socratic

In his diary Leo Tolstoy urged himself to "leave a piece of flesh in the ink-well every time you dip your pen."

Voices of Opposition

Greece and the Renaissance) and looked pessimistically at a future dominated by liberal-socialist egalitarianism.

A leading thinker in this category was Friedrich Nietzsche, an expatriate German philologist and philosopher residing in Switzerland. In the 1870s and 1880s Nietzsche wrote a number of works in which he savagely criticized the moral codes of Christian civilization as stifling natural instincts and leading to spiritual degeneration. He looked back to antiquity and to the Renaissance as great eras of "free spirits." So did his friend and teacher, the Swiss historian Jacob Burckhardt. Burckhardt's *The Civilization of the Renaissance in Italy* (1860) is not only a classic of historical writing and a pioneering attempt at cultural history; it is also a nostalgic evocation of a time when man was an unfettered individual, when people "knew little of false modesty or of hypocrisy in any shape, [when] not one of them was afraid of singularity, of being and seeming unlike his neighbors."

The anti-positivist reaction took many forms, including a cult of the beautiful, an aesthetic revolt whose adherents admired early Christian and Japanese art, neo-paganism, and everything primitive. There was also a current of pessimism, most notably seen in the writings of the German philosopher Arthur Schopenhauer and the Danish philosopher Søren Kierkegaard.

Some of the bitterest criticism of the scientific culture came from Russia, a country exposed to all the intellectual currents emanating from the West, yet sufficiently distinct to entertain the possibility of choosing a different road. Konstantin Leontiev, an original thinker active between 1850 and 1870, felt revolted by the spectacle of contemporary bourgeois Europe. An aesthete, he believed that there could be no morality without beauty. He considered it unthinkable that bourgeois civilization represented the ultimate achievement of history:

> Would it not be dreadful and offensive to think that Moses climbed Mount Sinai, that the Hellenes built their graceful Acropolis, that the Romans waged the Punic Wars, that the handsome genius, Alexander, in some plumed helmet crossed the Granicus and fought at Arbela, that the apostles preached, the martyrs suffered, the poets sang, the artists painted, and the knights dazzled at tournaments, only in order that a French or German or Russian bourgeois, "individually" or "collectively", garbed in his hideous, comical suit should wallow placidly on the ruins of all this past greatness? . . . One would burn with shame for mankind if this base ideal of general utility, trivial labor, and ignominious commonplace were to triumph forever.

Leontiev's ideal was the Ottoman Empire, whose despotic regime prevented the spread of egalitarianism and thus preserved a marvelous variety of life. He advised Russia to "freeze itself" so as to protect its own diversity from the Western solvent.

All of Dostoevsky's mature works are devoted to attacks on the scientific culture of his time. Dostoevsky detested Buckle and Claude Bernard, ridiculed the positivist prediction of a problemless world, and painted a horrifying picture of the moral consequences of atheism and rationalism. Man was not the reasonable creature of the positivists. He was thoroughly evil; only Christianity with its

Dostoevsky's view of the human condition was influenced by his personal experiences with revolutionaries and a sentence to hard labor in Siberia.

gospel of love and promise of afterlife restrained him. Once man begins to question Christian morality and substitutes for it his own reason, he turns into a killer. Such is the message of Dostoevsky's greatest novels, *Crime and Punishment* (1866), *The Possessed* (1871), and *The Brothers Karamazov* (1880). Dostoevsky rejected as preposterous the vision of a world in which men would live in utter harmony according to reason and their own best interests, for he knew within himself powerful irrational and self-destructive drives. In his *Notes from the Underground* (1864), he carried on a fictional dialogue with a positivist in which he made the following point:

> You are firmly convinced that man will accustom himself [to act as reason and science tell him] once the old, stupid habits are shed, and common-sense and science completely re-educate and direct human nature along its normal paths. You are confident that man will at that time *voluntarily* cease to err, and, so to say, be compelled to desire no conflict between his will and his interests. More than that: at that time, you say, science itself will teach man . . . that he has neither will nor caprice of his own and never had any, and that he is nothing more than a kind of piano key or the stop of an organ; and that besides the world has only laws of nature, so that all he does happens not at all because he wants it, but of itself, by virtue of the laws of nature. In consequence, one only has to discover these laws of nature, and man will no longer bear responsibility for his acts and enjoy a very easy life. All human actions, of themselves, will then be reckoned according to these laws, mathematically, like tables of logarithms, up to 108,000, and entered into an index.
>
> As for me, I will not be surprised in the least if suddenly, for no reason, in the midst of all this general future reasonableness, there should appear a gentleman with an ignoble, or better yet, a reactionary and mocking face, plant his arms at his sides, and tell of all you: "What about it, fellows— let's get rid of all this reasonableness, let's kick it to bits, just so that all these logarithms go to the devil and we can again live as we damn please!" That would be nothing yet, but what hurts is that such a man would be certain to find followers: that is how man is made. And all this for the most insignificant reason, the kind one should think unnecessary even to mention: that is, that man, always and everywhere, no matter who he was, liked to do what he pleased, and not at all what reason and interest told him. . . . Man needs only his *free* will, no matter what it costs and where it leads.

In the nineteenth century such warnings received little attention. When Nietzsche lost his mind in 1889, prevailing opinion saw his insanity as the natural consequence of his ideas. Kierkegaard and Leontiev remained unknown outside of a small circle of friends, while Dostoevsky earned himself the reputation of a novelist addicted to the morbid and abnormal. The overwhelming majority of Westerners, optimistic and confident, believed in progress and science.

6

The Industrialization of
the Continent

Until the middle of the nineteenth century Great Britain and Belgium were the only countries in the world possessing sizable industries. As we have noted, the introduction of industrial processes into France, Germany, and some other Continental nations did not at first alter significantly either their social structures or the tenor of their everyday life. This occurred only in the second half of the century, with the intense industrialization of Western Europe and the United States. On the European Continent there now emerged an industrial heartland (northern France, the Low Countries, and western Germany) that closely resembled the older area of heavy industrial concentration in the English Midlands and around London. It had the same density of population and concentration of transport and faced many of the same social problems. Together with England, it constituted something like an industrial core, surrounded by a belt of economically peripheral countries where, apart from isolated industrial pockets, the economies remained rural.

For all the resemblances, however, the industrial development of the Continent showed some important deviations from the pattern originally set by England. To begin with, countries that industrialized after England profited from the English experience. What Britain had acquired by trial and error, others could obtain in finished form. No one, for example, had to retrace the steps involved in the construction of the first steam engine—it could be bought ready-made from Boulton & Watt or their emulators. The result was a telescoping of technological and economic development: processes developed in England in a certain logical sequence became fused and accelerated.

On the other hand, however, Continental industries experienced a problem that had not confronted Britain until much later: a shortage of markets. Britain enjoyed so great a head start that it had little to fear from competition; it had only to produce to sell. But the spread of industrial methods gave rise to a struggle for outlets. Left to their own devices, few fledgling industries could have survived English competition, and for this reason they increasingly turned to the state for protection. After 1879 free trade everywhere went on the defensive, giving way to a policy sometimes called neo-Mercantilism. To the modern state, the possession of an industrial economy became a matter of national prestige and even necessity, for on it depended modern military power. The state could assist the development of native industry in a variety of ways, the most common being protective tariffs, military procurements, and colonial conquests. Every country that industrialized after Great Britain did so with active government support, the extent of this support being directly proportionate to the scantiness of the country's resources and the lateness with which it started along the road to industrialization. State intervention reached its culmination in the twentieth century in Communist states, where governments took over direction of the entire process of industrial development.

Constantin Meunier titled his late-nineteenth-century painting of an industrialized landscape in Belgium The Black Country. *At midcentury, heavily exploiting its natural resources, Belgium outpaced all the Continental powers in industrial growth.*

The second half of the nineteenth century was a period of technological progress of a scope unprecedented in the history of mankind. Inventors and industrialists, exploiting the scientific discoveries made in the preceding century and a half, constructed the foundations for the technical civilization of our own time.

The achievement was international, for all the major inventions resulted from contributions of nationals of many countries. For example, electrical energy, one of the seminal discoveries of the age, was first tapped by Italians, related to magnets by a Dane and a Frenchman, made inductive by an Englishman, turned into an economic source of power supply by Germans, and applied to everyday consumer needs by Americans.

The landmarks in industrial history were the discoveries of new sources of motive power. The first of these was steam, which provided the energy that built the industrial might of Britain. In the second half of the century steam was supplemented by electricity and liquid fuels, both of which became economically exploitable between 1870 and 1890.

The harnessing of electrical power had its origins in scientific experiments carried out in the eighteenth century. It had been known since antiquity that a piece of amber that had been vigorously rubbed attracted other bodies. An English physician in the reign of Queen Elizabeth called this mysterious force "electric" (from the Greek word *elektron*, meaning "amber"). In 1745 two scientists devised a method of collecting "electrical" charges in so-called Leyden Jars, but the energy thus stored was static and of little use. In 1780 the Italian Luigi Galvani accidentally discovered that if he touched a frog with wires connected to a Leyden Jar, the frog twitched. He ascribed this reaction to "animal electricity." Another Italian, Alessandro Volta, showed however that the frog's reaction was due not to any electricity stored in its body, but to the contact of the wires. Utilizing this knowledge, Volta constructed in 1800 a simple primary battery known as the Voltaic Pile. For the next two decades, electricity provided a great deal of amusement at parties and gave rise to a Romantic pseudo-science. The Romantics were attracted to these discoveries because they confirmed their belief in the existence of mysterious forces beyond the grasp of reason.

The next phase in the growth of knowledge about electricity was the discovery of electromagnetism. In 1820 Christian Oersted of Denmark showed that an electric current from a battery transmitted through a wire placed above a magnetized needle had the effect of deflecting the needle. A few years later the French scientist André Ampère devised a method of measuring the relationship between electricity and magnetism. Finally, in 1831, the Englishman Michael Faraday demonstrated that the movement of a coil of wire through a magnetic field produced in the wire a flow of electric current (electromagnetic induction).

Although fully appreciated at the time, these discoveries had no immediate effect on the power supply, because early electromagnetic generators were too cumbersome and expensive to operate. This difficulty was removed only in the 1870s, when a German engineer, Werner von Siemens, produced an efficient generator. In the 1890s the first large high-voltage power stations capable of distributing electricity over large areas made their appearance. From then on electricity became an intrinsic part of modern life.

The discovery of electromagnetism was first utilized in communications. By sending electric impulses over wires it became possible to produce a controlled reaction a great distance away. This was the basis of the telegraph that the American inventor Samuel F. B. Morse constructed in the mid-1840s and for which he devised a special alphabet in a code consisting of dots and dashes. The railroads were the first to employ the telegraph, which found an unforeseen use in 1845 when a murder suspect was reported by railway telegraph to have been seen on a London-bound train. The London police arrested him on arrival, and he was subsequently tried and sentenced to death, the first victim of scientific detection. In 1851 an underwater telegraph cable was laid between France and England, and fifteen years later England and the United States were similarly linked by means of a transatlantic cable. In 1862, 150,000 miles of telegraphic cable were in use throughout the world. The rapidity of communications that resulted from the spread of the telegraph revolutionized warfare, diplomacy, and journalism.

A similar principle to convey voice by electric impulses was utilized in the telephone, patented in 1876 by a Scottish-born professor at Boston University, Alexander Graham Bell.

Electricity found another important use in illumination. Here again, engineers from many countries made essential contributions, the basic ones being those of the Englishman Joseph Swan and the American Thomas Alva Edison. Working independently, Swan and Edison devised the carbon-filament lamp (1878–1881), which eventually replaced other means of providing artificial light, including natural gas and kerosene. Toward the end of the century, most of the big and many of the small cities of Europe converted to electrical illumination. For the first time streets and public buildings were brightly lit at night. Electric lighting provided additional hours of "daytime" and made possible the bustling night life of the late nineteenth-century metropolis. It had particular significance for the working population of the big cities whose hours of leisure previously had coincided with the hours of darkness.

The world had hardly become familiar with electricity when a new source of power made its appearance—gasoline, a product of petroleum that was first used in the 1880s in the internal-combustion engine. Internal combustion, which operates the automobile and many other motors, takes advantage of the pressure produced in the cylinder by an explosion. The principle of internal combustion had been known for some time, but it could not be exploited for lack of a suitable fuel. In 1876–1877 the German engineer Nicholas Otto developed, on lines first indicated by French scientists, the basic four-stroke engine, employing coal gas as a fuel. The internal-combustion engine, however, gained widespread acceptance only after experiments that another German engineer, Gottlieb Daimler, conducted in 1883–1885 with gasoline. The use of gasoline permitted Daimler to design an engine using considerably less fuel than Otto's and thus to construct economical automobiles. In 1894, in a race between Paris and Rouen, gasoline-driven cars defeated all competitors, covering on the average thirty miles per gallon of fuel. Until the outbreak of World War I, driving remained a fashionable sport of the wealthy. Adventurous automobilists organized expeditions across continents: one team of German cars traversed Africa (1907–1909) and another the United States (1908). A further development was an engine

In a daguerreotype of about 1860, the Englishman Michael Faraday holds a bar used in his magnetism research.

fueled by heavy oil, which did not explode but burned gradually. Called the Diesel engine after its German inventor Rudolf Diesel (1892), it found extensive application in industry, railroads, and ocean shipping.

Next to the new sources of power, the most important inventions of the second half of the century resulted from the application to industry of organic chemistry. If the generator and the internal-combustion engine eased the problem of power supply, industrial chemistry provided an entirely new source of raw materials. Like electricity, it had the effect of making man less dependent on nature.

Industrial chemistry originated in the dye industry. Its founder was A. W. von Hofmann, a German scientist living in London. Von Hofmann discovered that coal tar, obtained cheaply by distilling the bituminous coal used in illuminating gas, yielded many new compounds. While experimenting with one such compound, aniline, in 1856, an eighteen-year-old student of von Hofmann's named William Perkin accidentally produced an excellent purple dye. Von Hofmann himself attached no significance to this discovery, but Perkin patented it, built a factory to manufacture the dye, and became a wealthy man. The new synthetic dye found quick acceptance among textile manufacturers. It was also used for a variety of other purposes, including early British postage stamps. Soon, other synthetic colors were produced. Being cheaper as well as more dependable than vegetable and animal dyes, they pushed the latter out of the market. Germany became the world leader in the development and production of industrial chemicals.

Synthetic dyes were only the first of many products subsequently created by industrial chemistry. In the 1860s, for example, the Swedish chemist Alfred Nobel discovered that the addition of kieselguhr, a porous kind of earth, to nitroglycerin made it possible to control that unpredictable and dangerous explosive. The new substance, called dynamite, had an immediate effect upon the design of weapons and greatly influenced military tactics as well as civil engineering. In the 1880s chemists developed artificial drugs (quinine), and in the 1890s synthetic textiles (artificial silk, also known as rayon).

Chemistry also found important uses in agriculture. Justus von Liebig, a German chemist and the author of *Organic Chemistry and Its Relation to Agriculture and Plant Physiology* (1840), analyzed the process by which plants obtain food from the air and the soil and thereby made possible the production of artificial fertilizers. His discoveries freed agriculture from total dependence on the manure of domestic animals, which had never been available in sufficient quantities and diminished further in the nineteenth century as a consequence of the shrinking of pasture land. Countries with a progressive rural economy could now double and triple the yield per acre.

Important technical innovations revolutionized the steel industry. Steel is iron with a carbon content of between 0.1 and 2 percent. It is more malleable than pig iron, which has a higher carbon content (2.5–4 percent), and harder than wrought iron, whose carbon content is lower (less than 0.1 percent). The virtues of steel have been known for centuries as have the technologies of its manufacture, but production costs were always so high that the use of steel had to be confined to expensive items, such as weapons and cutlery. The early railroads employed iron exclusively. So did Gustave Eiffel as late as 1889 in constructing his famous tower for the Paris Exhibition.

The main difficulty in the manufacture of steel lies in the removal of the precise amount of carbon from the pig iron. This problem was first solved by the English engineer Sir Henry Bessemer in his well-known "converter," a device that transformed or "converted" pig iron into steel by injecting a jet of compressed air into the molten iron mass. The air blast oxidized the correct amount of carbon in a matter of minutes, yielding high-grade steel quickly and cheaply. He patented his process in 1855–1859. It had a striking effect on steel prices, enabling Bessemer to manufacture steel costing £5 or £6 a ton, compared to the prevailing rate of £50 to £60. Toward the end of the century, the Bessemer process yielded in popularity to the "Siemens-Martin," or "open-hearth," method, invented between 1864 and 1868.

The Bessemer converter as well as the Siemens-Martin hearth could be used only with a superior nonphosphorus iron ore, because high phosphorus ore, found in abundance on the Continent, resulted in a product too brittle for commercial purposes. In 1876 this problem was solved by two Englishmen, Sidney Gilchrist Thomas and his cousin, Percy Gilchrist, who invented a way of removing phosphorus from iron by adding certain chemicals to the ore and lining the converter with manganese. This invention permitted the exploitation of iron deposits with a high phosphorus content—including those in Lorraine, which Germany had acquired from France in 1871. It made a major contribution to building the great industrial power of modern Germany.

The decline in steel prices led to a sharp increase in demand for steel, which gained acceptance in a variety of industries, such as construction and transport. World production rose from 0.5 million tons in 1870 to 28 million in 1900 and 58 million in 1912.

Innovations in the electrical, chemical, and steel industries by no means cover the range of technical advances made in the second half of the nineteenth century. Photography, sewing machines, refrigeration, canning—all invented in the nineteenth century—caused a great change in human life when they became generally available in the twentieth century.

Mention must also be made of the development of techniques of scientific management and mass production. These techniques, though not strictly technological, had intimate links with technology and influenced productivity and prices as much as did any mechanical device. They were developed in the United States, a country whose perennial shortage of labor induced it to experiment ceaselessly with labor-saving procedures. Scientific management was formulated by the American engineer Frederick W. Taylor and is known abroad as "Taylorism." In two influential books, *Shop Management* (1903) and *Principles of Scientific Management* (1911), Taylor indicated how manufacturing costs could be reduced by putting labor to its most efficient use. The so-called time-and-motion studies that he had conducted in the 1880s for the Midvale Steel Company in Philadelphia pioneered various labor-saving procedures. An important American innovation of this kind was the moving assembly line, designed to reduce to a minimum the movement of the workers by bringing the product to them and limiting their task to a simple repetitive operation. The conveyor belt was inaugurated in the Chicago meat-packing industry, but it found its first important industrial application in the automobile plant that Henry Ford built at Highland Park, Michigan, on the eve of World War I. There in 1913 Ford produced the world's first cheap car, the famous Model T (it sold at $500). The methods of scientific management and standardized production penetrated other industries after World War I and became an intrinsic feature of modern industrial culture.

Emergence of the World Market   In the latter part of the nineteenth century the destruction of the barriers that had obstructed the flow of goods proceeded so relentlessly that for the first time in human history there came into existence a single world-wide market. The expansion of cheap land and sea transport, the search for diverse raw materials, the quest for profitable investments, the growing dependence of the industrial countries on supplies of labor and food from agricultural areas, the demand for ever-new outlets for the goods turned out by industrial economies—all these factors tended to draw countries and continents into an economic unit. The result was an unprecedented degree of international interdependence. The collapse of several banks in Vienna in the spring of 1873 caused a financial panic in Germany, which in turn brought down scores of small railroad companies in the United States, and in New York City led to the dismissal of 200,000 employees. When German agrarian interests persuaded Bismarck to impose a tariff on Russian grain, landlords and peasants on the Volga and Don rivers felt the effects at once. The use of manganese in hardening steel and the discovery by Liebig of the role of nitrates in fertilization led to the development of manganese mining in the Congo and nitrate mining in Chile, bringing industry to areas that in other respects were wholly in a pre-industrial era. Such examples could be multiplied many times.

The factor that contributed most to the economic unification of the world was the spread of railway and steamship lines. Intensive railroad construction began in the 1840s, but the real boom came only after midcentury. (See the chart at right.) Between 1860 and 1878 alone, the railway network in Europe tripled in length. Vast trunk lines were built to connect the great industrial centers with each other and with sea ports. The production of cheap steel made possible by the Bessemer process gave a great boost to this development, because rails made of steel proved many times more durable than those of iron and, by reducing maintenance costs, increased profits.

In Britain railroad construction was left entirely to private initiative; the government not only did not encourage it, but for a long time saw no need to regulate it. One consequence of this attitude was that Britain ended up with two different gauge systems. On the Continent, by contrast, the state took an active part in the process, helping railroads and at the same time imposing on them a degree of control. In Belgium the government initiated the construction of trunk lines and left it to private interests to provide the feeder lines; in the 1870s it reversed its policy, purchased the feeder lines from private owners, and placed the entire Belgian railroad network under state authority. In France public and private interests cooperated, but the government never ceased to exert close supervision. A law passed in 1842 provided that the government would supply the land and the road bed, and private concessionaires would provide the rolling stock, the government reserving for itself extensive authority over the tariffs and the geographic distribution of lines. When the concessions expired, the railroads were to become national property. In 1883 the French government transferred to private interests the lines under its control and guaranteed minimum profits to the companies that assumed responsibility. This arrangement lasted until the eve of World War II, when all French railroads were nationalized. In most of Germany the state built and owned the lines; Prussia, where until 1879 private interests predominated, was a surprising exception. Until 1920 Germany had no formally unified railway system, and the operations of the various systems were regulated by the powerful Imperial Railway Office. In Russia, too, state and private capital cooperated, the imperial government tending in time to gain the upper hand.

If the railway broke down commercial barriers inside continents, the steamship broke them down between continents. The first steamship crossed the Atlantic in the 1820s, but it took time for this mode of transport to become economical because its fuel consumption was so high. The sea-going steamship gained acceptance only in the 1870s when improved engines and the construction of coaling stations along maritime routes permitted its fuel load to be significantly reduced, releasing corresponding space for cargo. Once accepted, steamship transport had an immediate effect on the movement of foodstuffs and mineral raw materials, that is, on bulky and heavy items whose transportation costs had been prohibitive in the days of the sailing ship. It reduced the price of a bushel of American wheat in Western Europe by three-quarters. This price

RAILROAD GROWTH
1850-1910

UNITED KINGDOM
GERMANY
FRANCE
RUSSIA

kilometers
(cumulative)
70,000

60,000

50,000

40,000

30,000

20,000

10,000

0
1850   1870   1890   1910

reduction made possible large-scale grain exports from the Americas to Europe in the 1870s. The simultaneous development of refrigerated trains and ships also permitted transoceanic shipment of meat. Argentinian beef and Australian mutton, which until then had practically no commercial worth for lack of markets, suddenly acquired great value and became the main source of the wealth of these countries. The steamship exerted great influence on the whole economy of the Western Hemisphere, encouraging the development of intense cereal and meat production for export. Conversely, it had a deleterious effect on the agriculture of many European countries, where growing food ceased to be profitable.

The drastic reduction in shipping rates brought about by the steamship led to the development of regional specialization among suppliers of raw materials to the industrial countries. Egypt came to depend on its cotton, Cuba on its sugar cane, Bolivia on its tin, Chile on its nitrates. Such specialization brought sudden prosperity to areas that until then had remained outside the routes of international trade, but it also made them vulnerable to technical innovations and to the slightest fluctuations in the world economy.

During the half century preceding the outbreak of World War I, international trade experienced enormous expansion. Its total volume increased from an estimated $1.5 billion in 1830 to $4 billion in 1850, $14 billion in 1880, and $40 bil-

The noted illustrator Gustave Doré drew this caustic view of stock trading on Paris' bourse.

lion in 1913. The bulk of the trade occurred between the great industrial powers. The complicated financial operations that such a volume of international business required were facilitated by the general adoption of gold as the standard of exchange. The discovery of large gold deposits in California (1848–1849) and South Africa (1886) injected into the international money market vast quantities of bullion. At the beginning of the twentieth century the currencies of most great powers were convertible to gold, a fact that both facilitated and encouraged investments and trade.

Economic activity received another stimulus from two important innovations: the investment bank and the joint-stock company with limited liability. The great expansion of business accompanying industrialization demanded a constant flow of capital for which the traditional sources—private and family fortunes or simple partnerships—no longer sufficed. One device developed to overcome the shortage of capital was the joint-stock or investment bank. Such banks raised the funds for long-term investments in business enterprises either by selling stocks and bonds to the public or by setting aside for this purpose a part of their savings deposits. The model new bank was the French Crédit Mobilier, founded in 1852. It was widely emulated elsewhere, especially in Germany.

In addition to drawing on banks, mid-nineteenth century businesses began to seek capital directly from individual investors by means of stocks or shares, the purchase of which gave the holder a right to share the company's profits. This method of raising funds, simple and advantageous to all concerned, had been known for some time, but it did not gain popularity because partners of companies had been deemed legally responsible for the firm's debts to the full extent of their personal fortunes, no matter how much or little of the stock they owned. Various attempts had been made (e.g., in France under Napoleon I and later in Belgium) to reduce this liability, but the legislation was hedged with so many formalities that it gained little acceptance. The first effective law of this kind was passed in 1855 in England. The law established the principle of limited liability: purchasers of shares in a limited-liability company bore responsibility for the company's debt only in proportion to the amount of their holdings. This law greatly enhanced the popularity of joint-stock companies in England and attracted into industry and trade much new capital. Corresponding laws were adopted in France in 1867, in Germany and Italy in the 1870s, and subsequently in other European countries. The modern stock exchange and its by-product, stock speculation, was one of the results of this legislation.

As the main beneficiary of the expansion of world trade, Europe became the world's supplier of capital. The leader in foreign investments was Britain. By 1914 it had placed abroad the equivalent of $20 billion, a quarter of its estimated national wealth. The bulk of British investments went to self-governing dominions and to the countries of the Western Hemisphere, where they financed a great variety of economic activities. The French preferred to invest in bonds of foreign governments. In 1914 $9 billion, an estimated one-sixth of the French national wealth, was placed abroad, a quarter of it in Russia. Germany had in 1914 investments totaling $6 billion and the United States $2.6 billion. Britain, whose foreign investments exceeded those of all the other countries combined, led in trade, shipping, and insurance and came to perform the function of an

A piece of anti-Semitic propaganda, dating from 1898 and of French origin, caricatures the Rothschild banking house as seeking world dominance.

international clearinghouse. London acquired the status of the world's central money market. Capital, flowing where it was in greatest demand, became something of a commodity. It was bought, borrowed, sold, imported, and exported like any other commercial product.

But the sky was not entirely cloudless. In the overwhelming progress attending the advances of technology, the expansion of markets, and the accumulation of wealth, there were two phenomena that gave cause for anxiety. One was overproduction. As more and more industries developed, it became apparent that sooner or later the markets for their products would become saturated. This fear was a very genuine factor in European economic and diplomatic activities after 1870 and perhaps the single most important motive behind the intense drive for colonial conquests in the last quarter of the nineteenth century (see Chapter 10).

The other was recurrent economic crises. These were not new but never before had they been so frequent, so shattering, and so global in scope. In 1857 the world experienced a major international depression; from then on they occurred every decade or less. On May 11, 1866 ("Black Friday"), a London banking house suspended payments, creating a widespread financial panic that brought down the French Crédit Mobilier. The worst of these crises, which occurred in 1873, brought to a halt the expansion of trade and took many years to overcome. The world was shaken by further depressions in the mid-1880s and mid-1890s. These crises were caused by temporary maladjustments between the productive, commercial, and financial elements of the economy. Businessmen, having had little experience with the workings of the international market and spurred by prospects of immense profit to operate to the limit of their financial resources, easily miscalculated. There was as yet no system of international monetary cooperation, state regulation of banks and of stock exchanges, or market research. Much economic activity was inherently speculative and unstable. At the time, however, these causes were not readily apparent. The socialists won many adherents by their claim that crises were an inevitable concomitant of the capitalist economy and would grow in severity until the whole capitalist system collapsed. Anti-Semitic movements also profited by persuading the gullible that recessions were due to an international Jewish conspiracy.

Industrialism and the National State

The emergence of a world-wide market coincided with the consolidation of national states. The two processes—the internationalization of economics and the nationalization of politics—stood in stark contradiction. As a rule, the conflict resolved in favor of nationalism; that is to say, most states, when confronted with the choice of achieving the maximum of self-sufficiency or raising living standards, chose self-sufficiency. The requirements of national interest caused barriers to be put up against the free flow of goods and men, restricting the world market.

The economic historian W. W. Rostow, after comparing the experience of a number of Western and non-Western countries, discerned three basic common phases in the process of industrialization (chart opposite): "take-off," "maturity," and "high mass-consumption." In Britain "take-off" occurred between about 1785 and 1800, "maturity" was attained around 1850, and "high mass-consumption" after 1930. Using these convenient terms, we may say that the take-off stage—the critical transition from an agrarian to an industrial economy,

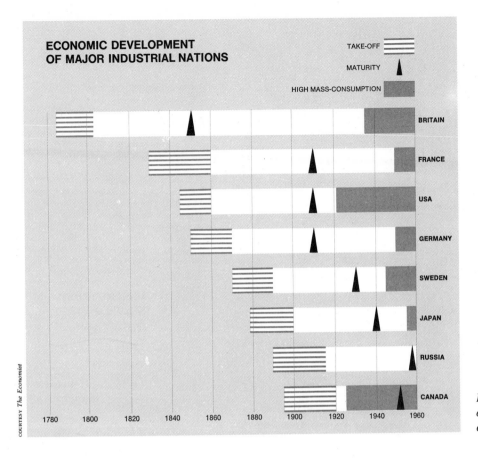

ECONOMIC DEVELOPMENT
OF MAJOR INDUSTRIAL NATIONS

TAKE-OFF

MATURITY

HIGH MASS-CONSUMPTION

BRITAIN

FRANCE

USA

GERMANY

SWEDEN

JAPAN

RUSSIA

CANADA

1780 1800 1820 1840 1860 1880 1900 1920 1940 1960

COURTESY *The Economist*

Patterns of industrial development of leading Westernized nations, as defined by economist W. W. Rostow.

the Industrial Revolution proper—took place in France and Germany between 1830 and 1870 and in Russia after 1890. Yet, in using such general concepts, we must not forget that the experience of each country was unique.

Imperial Germany was the only country on the Continent that fully satisfied all the requirements of an industrialized economy. With these advantages, Germany outpaced its rivals, and on the eve of World War I had surpassed Great Britain in most fields of industrial productivity. The German Empire possessed in the Ruhr, Lorraine, Saxony, and Silesia the richest iron and coal deposits on the Continent. It also had a large and rapidly growing population. At midcentury the Germans outnumbered the French, traditionally the most populous nation in Western Europe. In 1890 Germany had nearly 50 million inhabitants compared to 37 million each in France and in the United Kingdom. Thanks to its tradition of craftsmanship, Germany had numerous skilled artisans who could be shifted from small shops into large industrial establishments. Finally, the state was unusually involved in the country's economic development. The government of Prussia had considerable experience in business, for it owned large properties; it was, for example, the leading producer of coal in pre-1870 Germany. The imperial government set an early example of that marriage between industry and politics that was later to provide the pattern for totalitarian states. Its agencies managed or operated railways and telephone and telegraph lines and exploited forests and mines. In 1913 more than one-half of Germany's state

INDUSTRIALISM AND THE NATIONAL STATE   165

**URBANIZATION
OF EUROPE, 1850**

Population in cities of
100,000 or more

	20%
	6-10%
	5% or less

**URBANIZATION
OF EUROPE, 1910**

Population in cities of
100,000 or more

	20%
	11-20%
	6-10%
	5% or less

revenue derived from its own properties—an income that enabled the monarchy to obtain considerable independence of parliament. The government assisted industry by establishing a network of technical schools that furnished Germany with the largest body of engineers and technical specialists in the world.

The rapidity with which German industrialization progressed once it got under way was indeed staggering, the only parallel being the United States. The charts on page 169 illustrate this growth and require no elaboration. What does call for explanation, however, are two techniques on which the Germans relied to promote their industry: protective tariffs and economic "rationalization."

Until the late 1870s Germany followed the prevalent trend toward free trade. The *Zollverein* was designed less to erect protective walls on the outside than to remove them from inside German territory. With the exception of a few articles, the *Zollverein* imposed moderate external tariffs. When the *Zollverein* was still in its infancy, however, voices began to be heard advocating a radical departure from free trade. The most persuasive argument for such a change was made by the German economist Friedrich List, whose *National System of Political Economy* (1841) deserves to be ranked, in terms of its influence on the course of economic history, alongside Smith's *Wealth of Nations*. If Smith had formulated the theory of economic liberalism dominant until the 1870s, List formulated the principles of economic nationalism which have been dominant since.

List began to champion protective tariffs in the early 1820s, but he developed an economic justification for them only after he had emigrated to the United States in 1825. He arrived in America at a time when that country was experiencing a powerful movement toward protectionism that culminated in the Tariff Act of 1828 (the "Tariff of Abominations"). He read a great deal of the American literature on the subject and was particularly impressed by the writings of Alexander Hamilton, who had been an ardent advocate of tariff protection. On his return to Germany in 1831 (he received an appointment as United States consul in Leipzig), List began to propagate protectionist theories, developing them most fully in his *National System*.

The premise of List's doctrine is that the economy must concentrate not merely or even primarily on the production of goods, but on the development of "productive forces": "The power of producing wealth is infinitely more important than wealth itself." By "productive forces" List meant all the human and material resources involved in economic activity, including knowledge and education, which he regarded as the "mental capital of a nation." On this premise, List proceeded to build a powerful argument in favor of protectionism. Though he agreed with Adam Smith that tariffs prevent a country from obtaining at the most advantageous price industrial goods on the world market and thus indirectly lower living standards, in the long run, he maintained, the sacrifice is worthwhile; protected by tariffs, native industry will mature and acquire the capacity to produce goods at prices below what they would cost abroad. In effect, List advocated a temporary reduction in living standards in favor of long-term economic growth—an argument that would re-emerge in the twentieth century as a central proposition of the so-called economics of development. As for the contention that Britain had become a great industrial power by pursuing a contrary course, List demonstrated that Britain had laid its economic foundations under stringent protectionism and ventured into free trade only when it no longer feared competitors.

List was an "historicist," that is, he viewed phenomena from a dynamic, relativist point of view. He did not regard protective tariffs as an end in themselves, but rather as measures required at a transitional phase. He approved of free trade for backward countries like Spain, to help raise them from a condition of "barbarism," as well as for countries like Britain, which had already attained a high level of productivity. Protectionism, however, seemed to him best suited for countries in the early phase of industrial development.

List had little influence in his own time and, distraught and disappointed, he committed suicide in 1846. But his views gradually won a following among academic economists and those business groups (e.g., iron and cotton yarn manufacturers) that had been hurt by foreign competition during the depression of 1873.

In 1879 Germany formally went over to protectionism. The decisive factor was fiscal: Bismarck saw in customs a good source of revenue (the imperial constitution had made no provisions for levying taxes on the empire as a whole) and yielded to German businessmen who had been long clamoring for higher tariffs. Although in itself quite moderate (it taxed mainly iron, textiles, and foodstuffs), the tariff of 1879 set off a chain reaction. France responded in 1881 with a more severe tariff act, and a few years later Italy, Sweden, and Russia followed suit. The reversion of the great powers to protectionism culminated in the most stringent tariff act of all, the American Dingley Act of 1897.

Although in many cases the motives inspiring protection were narrowly fiscal rather than broadly economic (in List's sense), they everywhere had the effect of promoting national economic development. Of the great powers England alone resisted the new fashion, but even there it had its proponents, especially Joseph Chamberlain, the founder in 1903 of the Tariff Reform League. It is testimony to the dynamism of the European economy at the time that, notwithstanding the emergence of tariff barriers, international trade continued to expand at an intense rate.

Equally important as tariffs for the world economy were the pioneering attempts of the Germans to subject production and distribution to planning or "rationalization." This end was furthered by forming organizations designed either to secure control over the manufacture of a given product (monopolies) or else to reduce or eliminate competition among individual producers (trusts or cartels). Such practices were common in all countries, but nowhere were they

An engraving after an 1833 sketch by German economist Friedrich List pictures an excursion train on one of the railroad lines he envisioned.

as prevalent as in Germany. In Great Britain, for example, agreements for the restraint of productivity or trade, while not illegal, were not legally binding. The United States outlawed them in 1890 by the Sherman Anti-Trust Act. The Germans not only allowed them and enforced them in courts, but regarded monopolies and cartels as superior forms of economic organization. The participation of German banks in much economic development encouraged the formation of cartels, for the banks were interested in reducing as much as possible competition likely to pit one of their clients against another.

German cartels grew rapidly after the passage of the tariff of 1879. In 1905 there were in Germany 385 cartels embracing every major branch of the economy. The larger ones, such as the Rhine-Westphalian Coal Syndicate, were by then organized on a joint-stock basis, with a formal board of directors and regular meetings of members. For a while the Prussian government itself, as owner of collieries, sat on the board of the syndicate. The key unit of the cartels was the Sales Bureau, appointed jointly by the participating firms, which fixed production quotas, prices, or both. Some cartels expanded vertically, that is, they acquired control over the raw materials and means of transport used in their particular field of production. Originally devised as a means of regulating the free capitalist market, cartels furnished models afterward used by countries adopting planned socialist economies.

By virtue of its industrial expansion, Germany began toward the end of the century to give Britain serious competition in markets that until then had been Britain's preserve (Latin America, the Middle East). It also gained a firm foothold in eastern and southeastern Europe. German merchandise, well made and reasonably priced, often suited local needs better than the conservatively designed, high-quality British goods. In 1900 Germany gained second place in world trade, the volume of German business exceeding considerably that of the next two competitors, the United States and France. On the European Continent Germany forged ahead of Britain and captured first place.

Although a great power, France never industrialized in the full sense of the word. In France industrial processes, instead of replacing the agrarian order, accommodated themselves to it, resulting in a mixed rural-urban economy. The attachment of Frenchmen to the land and their individualism, mentioned previously, persisted. As late as 1911, when France was in the "mature" stage of economic development, the majority (56 percent) of its population continued to live in the countryside, and most industrial establishments employed four workers or less. The shortage of coal and iron hindered the growth of heavy industry, while capital tended to flow into luxury goods that did not lend themselves to methods of mass production.

The industrialization of Russia began around 1890, when indexes of economic activity showed a sudden spurt characteristic of the take-off phase of development. Much of the capital, management, and skilled labor came from abroad (France, Germany, Belgium, England). The importance of foreign investments may be gauged from the fact that when the Revolution of 1917 broke out, foreigners directly controlled nearly half of the capital held by Russian banks. The imperial government was divided over industrialization, powerful bureaucratic elements fearing that it would denude the countryside of peasant recruits and

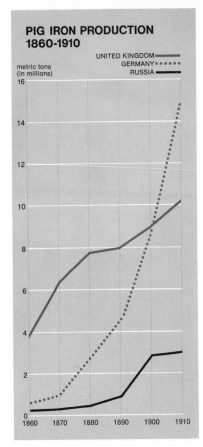

PIG IRON PRODUCTION
1860-1910

UNITED KINGDOM ——
GERMANY ••••••
RUSSIA ——

metric tons
(in millions)

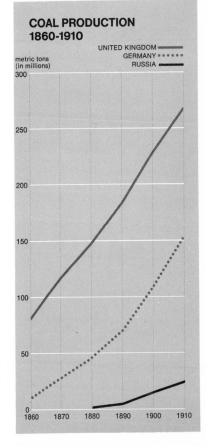

COAL PRODUCTION
1860-1910

UNITED KINGDOM ——
GERMANY ••••••
RUSSIA ——

metric tons
(in millions)

cause unrest in the cities. The main promoter of industry was the Ministry of Finance, headed by Sergei Witte, which had to fight constant battles with the agrarian interests defended by the Ministry of the Interior. The latter opposed industrialization on the theory that, if Russia produced enough manufactured goods of its own to cease buying them in Germany, the Germans would be likely to stop purchasing wheat in Russia. Despite these difficulties, imperial Russia managed in the last quarter of its existence to acquire the foundations of a respectable industrial economy.

In most of the countries outside the industrial heartland (Russia included), industry tended to be consumer-oriented until the outbreak of World War I. It concentrated on the manufacture of textiles and household articles, and on food-processing. Here and there, the presence of rich mineral deposits led to the emergence of industrial nuclei in the midst of agrarian economies (e.g., iron ore in Sweden, copper and coal in Spain, petroleum in Romania, etc.).

Agriculture and Land Ownership

European agriculture was less affected by scientific and technical innovations than was manufacturing. Indeed, in much of Europe farming in the nineteenth century continued to be carried on exactly as it had been since the Middle Ages. The resistance of agriculture to change stemmed partly from the innate traditionalism of the peasantry and partly from the unsuitability of most mechanical, technical, and organizational innovations to rural conditions.

The great shock to European agriculture was the influx in the 1870s of American grain, which was so low in price that, in areas where land was scarce and therefore expensive, growing grain ceased to be profitable. This was the case in England, where agriculture, notwithstanding the abolition of the Corn Law, had continued to enjoy great prosperity until then. The 1870s marked a collapse of English agriculture; with the curtailment of arable acreage, England became now more than ever dependent for its foodstuffs on imports. Denmark experienced a similar crisis but overcame it by switching to dairy farming and exporting to England and other industrial countries milk, eggs, butter, and similar items that could not then be shipped across the Atlantic. Other countries met the overseas threat to their agriculture by resorting to protective tariffs on foodstuffs. The Germans led the way, and before the end of the century most Continental countries had followed suit. Such tariffs hurt countries dependent on agrarian exports and forced them to impose tariffs on foreign manufactured goods. The result was a succession of "tariff wars" in the 1880s, the ones between Russia and Germany and between Italy and France being the most spectacular.

Economic developments in the nineteenth century produced different results on the distribution of ownership in industry and in agriculture. In industry the tendency everywhere was to wipe out small, independent producers and to concentrate ownership in large enterprises. In agriculture—with the notable exception of England—the general tendency was the opposite: large estates were broken up into small or medium-sized holdings. This held especially true of the industrial countries on the Continent, where the one-time serf and tenant farmer gradually turned into an independent proprietor. The transformation was striking in France, the traditional home of the small landowner. Even before 1789 some 40 percent of the arable soil in France had been in the actual (if not legal) possession of the peasantry. The Revolution legalized this ownership and increased further the holdings of the peasants by enabling them to purchase land confiscated from the Church and the *émigrés*. In 1892 France's nearly 5 million individual landholdings measuring 25 acres or less accounted for 90 percent of the farms in the country. Fewer than a thousand properties exceeded 1,000 acres. To what extent the French farmer was also a proprietor may be gathered from the fact that at the end of the century, with a total of 5.5 million holdings, France had only 3.5 million agricultural laborers, that is, peasants working on land not their own. A similar situation prevailed in Germany by 1895, when 94 percent of all the farms were of less than 50 acres and where nearly all of them belonged to their cultivators. Both countries, of course, also had giant holdings; these, in the case of Germany, were concentrated in the east and northeast. In Belgium the parceling of agricultural land reached its extreme. Of a total of 830,000 holdings, 500,000 measured less than 2.5 acres, and only 3,500 exceeded 125 acres. The small farms could survive owing to constant improvement in techniques that increased yields beyond anything known previously. Germany, the pioneer in scientific farming, extracted three times as much wheat from an acre as Russia and twice as much as the United States (1912).

England had a rather special situation. The enclosure acts and early urbanization had decreased the number of small farmers and tenants, giving England the highest concentration of land ownership among the industrial countries. In 1871 approximately one-half the land in Great Britain belonged to 7,400 persons. In 1895, of a total British agricultural area of 32.6 million acres (exclusive of Ireland), 28 million were rented and only 4.6 million were occupied by the owners. The land rent enabled the British aristocracy to maintain a high style of life in the midst of industrial expansion.

In the non-industrialized, rural countries of Europe the bulk of the land re-

French artist Jean-François Millet, himself of peasant background, made the peasantry a frequent theme of his work. This is an 1855 etching.

mained concentrated in the hands of state, church, and large landowners. The peasants in these areas—Ireland, Portugal, Spain, Italy, Austria-Hungary, eastern Germany, and Russia—were predominantly full- or part-time tenants or laborers or partial owners. It has been estimated, for example, that in the central provinces of Spain two-thirds or more of the land was contained in holdings of more than 25,000 acres. In Italy some 10 million men and women worked on land owned by 400,000 proprietors. In Ireland less than 10 percent of the land was tilled by owners; the remaining 90 percent was leased (1904). Such examples illustrate the reason for the acute land hunger that developed in the peripheral countries of Europe toward the end of the nineteenth century. It was a prime cause of the great migratory wave that began to build after 1850.

Population Growth and Migration

From the late eighteenth century onward, the world experienced an unprecedented growth of population. The original cause of this phenomenon is not clear; some scholars ascribe it primarily to a decline in mortality, others to an increase in births. Proponents of the former view maintain that the establishment of firm political order, the introduction of sanitary measures, and improvements in the quantity of food and quality of clothing produced a demonstrable decline in deaths. A. M. Carr-Saunders, an English statistician, has estimated that the death rate (the number of deaths occurring annually for every 1,000 persons) declined in Europe from 32 in 1820 to 20 in 1900. Other authorities, without denying the decline in deaths, ascribe the growth of population to an increase in birth rates. This they account for partly by earlier marriages, made possible by general prosperity and new kinds of crops (e.g. the potato), and partly by a reduction in infanticide and abortions caused by more enlightened legislation pertaining to illegitimacy. They also point out that there were few medical advances in the eighteenth century, when the population growth first got under way.

Whatever the cause, there is general agreement that in modern times the traditional balance between birth rates and death rates has been upset. Before 1800 the birth rate averaged in most countries between 35 and 50 per 1,000 (that is, for each 1,000 inhabitants there were 35 to 50 live births) and the death rate between 30 and 40. The slight surplus of births over deaths was periodically wiped out by one of the traditional enemies of man: war, disease, or famine. This ceased to hold true in the nineteenth century. Mortality rates dropped (in England to as low as 18 per 1,000), while birth rates either remained constant or rose, so that the gap between births and deaths kept growing wider. At the end of the century Italy had an annual surplus of births over deaths of 300,000, Hungary of 230,000, and Russia of more than 2,000,000. As a result, the nineteenth-century population of Europe more than doubled, growing from an estimated 193 million in 1800 to 423 million in 1900. In other words, Europe accumulated more inhabitants in the course of a single century than in all the centuries of its previous existence.

This increase raised fears that the day would come when the earth no longer could house or feed its inhabitants. The leading exponent of this theory was Thomas Malthus, who argued in his *Essay on the Principle of Population* (1798) that the population grew at a considerably more rapid rate than the food supply, with the inevitable consequence that mankind engaged in a constant "struggle for existence" and always faced mass starvation. No real improvement in the condition of the working class was possible. Malthus urged that society abolish social welfare because it encouraged procreation among the poor, and concentrate instead on reducing the marriage rate. Misery and vice (to which he later added "moral restraint") were in his opinion the only efficacious means of preventing an exhaustion of natural resources and ultimate catastrophe. These ideas influenced early liberal thought against social reform and played a part in the passage of the Poor Law of 1834. Though much criticized for their inhumane implications and doubtful scientific premises, the theories of Malthus came back into vogue later in the century. The Malthusian League, founded in London in 1877, initiated the modern birth-control movement.

The dire predictions of Malthus have not been borne out (at least so far), because they made no allowance for the ability of an industrial economy to absorb more people in a given area than an agricultural one. There were several reasons for this phenomenon. First, the introduction of the railroad and steamship facilitated the importation of food from distant areas. Cheap transport, in effect, annexed to Europe the prairies of the American Midwest, Argentina, and southern Russia. Second, the increase in agricultural yields brought about by scientific farming disproved Malthus' fears of an insufficient progression in food production. Third, the harnessing of the energy latent in steam, electricity, and mineral fuels allowed a reduction in the number of horses and freed much pasture land for other purposes. It has been estimated that the steam engines operating in England in 1870 produced the equivalent power of 6 million horses. Thus millions of acres that would have been required to provide fodder for these horses became available for other uses.[*]

These factors enabled countries with advanced industrial economies to maintain population densities that would have proved fatal to purely agrarian ones. Belgium attained in 1900 an over-all density of 589 inhabitants a square mile, and in some provinces of nearly 1,000. By contrast, Spain could barely support 97 and Russia 55 inhabitants a square mile. The growing population provided industrial countries with both a labor force and an expanding domestic market.

But in countries with poorly developed industries, the new population had nowhere to go. For most, land ownership was out of reach, and the cities had few jobs to offer. In such areas in the second half of the nineteenth century, a huge landless proletariat began to emerge. This group might well have caused violent social revolutions had it not been for the safety valve provided by emigration. The excess rural population could migrate to three principal places: to the cities, to other European countries, and overseas. The movement to the cities is an aspect of urbanization that we shall discuss in the next chapter. Within the European Continent, there was a sizable migratory movement of rural inhabitants—some temporary (seasonal), others permanent—to the industrial countries. France was particularly receptive to immigrants, for its own population grew so slowly that there were well-founded fears that France some day would no longer be able to defend itself. To provide labor for its industries and mines, France imported workers from Italy and Poland. Germany also drew on Poland for additional agricultural and industrial labor. But the principal

[*] David S. Landes, in Cambridge Economic History of Europe, Vol. VI (1965).

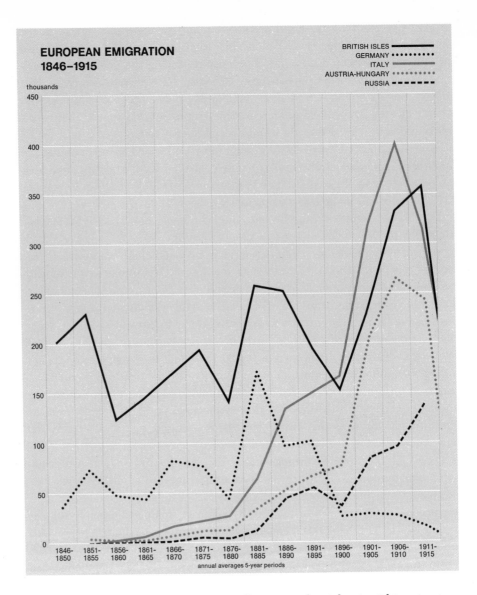

EUROPEAN EMIGRATION
1846–1915

BRITISH ISLES
GERMANY
ITALY
AUSTRIA-HUNGARY
RUSSIA

thousands

annual averages 5-year periods

form of migration was overseas, especially across the Atlantic. This migratory wave constituted the largest population movement in recorded history.

In the first half of the nineteenth century overseas migration was not yet a significant factor in European life. It tended to be sporadic and selective, the majority of the migrants leaving Europe less for economic than for political or religious reasons. The mass exodus began in 1846–1847 with the Irish migration caused by the potato blight. From then on every economic and political crisis sent from Europe fresh waves of overseas migrants. The development of cheap steamship transport contributed to this movement, for ships bringing wheat to Europe, rather than return empty, took on migrants at low fares. In the second half of the century an average of 400,000 persons departed annually from European ports to settle overseas. At the height of emigration (1900–1914), this figure exceeded 1 million. It has been estimated that between 1870 and 1914, 34 million Europeans left for overseas, 27 million of them for the United

States. In this manner Europe lost two-fifths of the additional population that it had acquired during that period.°

Great Britain was the first to experience significant migration overseas. By midcentury it had become customary in England for each economic crisis to be followed by a mass exodus. The Irish famine induced a fifth of that island's population to migrate. Between 1846 and 1860, 3.5 million persons left the United Kingdom (including Ireland). This outflow undoubtedly contributed to the peaceful solution of social conflicts in Great Britain. After the middle of the century, however, the number of migrants from England declined steadily, though it remained large in Ireland.

German migratory statistics show clearly to what extent industrialization increased a country's capacity to sustain population growth. Until Germany had industrialized, its citizens migrated overseas in such large numbers that certain regions showed an actual decrease in population. By the mid-1890s, when German industry attained a high level of productivity, this migratory movement died down, and Germany not only ceased to let out workers but began itself to import them from neighboring countries.

After 1880 few emigrants left industrial Europe: Englishmen and Germans found work at home, while Frenchmen were never inclined to migrate anyway. From then on the bulk of the migrants came from the peripheral countries, especially from Italy and the Slavic regions. The Italian migrants originated mostly in the southern provinces and Sicily, where the rural overpopulation was particularly acute. Nearly half the Italian migrants found work in Europe; the others settled mostly in the United States and Argentina. Between 1880 and 1914 Italy furnished the largest number of overseas immigrants: in 1913 alone 873,000 Italians left home.

Among Russians, despite rural overpopulation, migration overseas was less significant. The overseas migrants consisted largely of Jewish artisans and unskilled workers, inhabitants of the small towns of western Russia who were legally prohibited from either owning land or moving away to other parts of the country. At the turn of the century 15 out of every 1,000 Russian Jews left each year for overseas destinations—one of the highest migratory rates on record.

Migration had a twofold effect. First and foremost, it relieved population pressure and reduced the risk of social upheavals in Europe. Second, it increased Europe's hold on the rest of the globe. Thanks to migration, three continents—North America, South America, and Australia—became Europeanized; a fourth, Africa, acquired compact colonies of European settlers. The problem of "decolonialization" and much of the racial friction afflicting the twentieth century are among the legacies of the great migrations of the nineteenth century.

° It must be noted, however, that an estimated 9 million of the 34 million migrants eventually returned to Europe. The long-term net emigration, therefore, totaled 25 million persons.

The Fruits of Industrialism

In common with any great revolutionary movement, the industrialization of the Western world penetrated areas and produced affects quite beyond what anyone could have expected or predicted. To the poet Wordsworth

> An inventive Age
> Has wrought, if not with speed of magic, yet
> To most strange issues. . . .

As these "strange issues" became more familiar and their potential more widely understood during the second half of the nineteenth century, they inspired hope and fear and every emotion in between. To the Italian Futurist Antonio Sant'Elia the new age promised a dynamic New City; to the German artist Kaethe Kollwitz it meant the ugly exploitation of the mass of mankind; to the Frenchman Ferdinand de Lesseps it brought reality to a dream as old as the pharaohs of antiquity, a canal at Suez. A sampling of the fruits of industrialization, both the sweet and the bitter, appears on the following pages.

Great Britain, as the first nation to industrialize, was first to reap the fruits of the new age. Its landscape was changed (at left, a steam-powered colliery in Northumberland, 1839), its economy revolutionized, its cultural and social patterns altered. It is not surprising, therefore, that Britain made the first effort to assemble in one place—the Great Exhibition of 1851—the most celebrated products of the Industrial Revolution. Prince Albert, Queen Victoria's consort, conceived the Exhibition "to give us a true test and a living picture of the point of development at which the whole of mankind has arrived . . . and a new starting point from which all nations will be able to direct their future exertions." The immense building erected in London to house the exhibits, with its 300,000 panes of glass and its 5,000 iron columns and girders (designed by a greenhouse builder, it was dubbed the "Crystal Palace" by *Punch*), was itself a monument to the new technology. The Crystal Palace was such an attraction that it was disassembled and rebuilt at Sydenham (right); embellished with classic and neoclassic statuary, it was a popular resort until 1936, when it burned to a heap of molten glass and iron.

The Great Exhibition had its detractors, who followed up their visits with predictions of a dim future for Western civilization. According to the Swiss writer Henri Amiel, "The useful will take the place of the beautiful, industry of art, political economy of religion, and arithmetic of poetry." Amiel, however, was in the minority. For most observers at midcentury, the potential promise of the new age greatly outweighed the potential menace. Here, it seemed, was further evidence of the Enlightenment's theory of man's inevitable progress toward perfectibility.

Marvels of the Machine Age

In the six months of 1851 that the Crystal Palace remained open in London's Hyde Park, 6 million people flocked through it to see the marvels of the Great Exhibition The displays by nearly 14,000 exhibitors ranged from the American sculptor Hiram Powers' life-size Greek slave girl, who was not only nude but revolved as well, to the celebrated Koh-i-noor diamond from India, reputedly worth more than all the other exhibits put together, to cuffs "knitted from the wool of French poodle dogs." "I came back quite dead beat," wrote Queen Victoria in her journal, "my head really bewildered by the myriads of beautiful and wonderful things. . . ."

In the machinery sections were great marine engines and printing presses and locomotives and one of Cyrus McCormick's reapers from America, all of them in the process of revolutionizing the way people traveled, what they read, and what they ate. For the most part, the machinery was crisply and simply designed for maximum economy and efficiency; the same could not be said of the machine-made products for the consumer. A contemporary remarked that the "savage population" of Canada showed "more attention to the useful than to the ornamental," but if the Canadians resisted ornamentation, hardly anyone else did. Furnishings swarmed with machine-turned bric-a-brac of every description. There was an iron stove disguised as a medieval castle and a metal bedstead with head and footboards of cast scrollwork in which "the little cupids are prettily introduced. . . ." The Great Exhibition was more than the "authentic voice of British capitalism in the hour of its greatest triumph," as one observer has described it; it was as well the authentic voice of Victorian taste in the machine age.

The articles in the Hardware Section (left) of the Great Exhibition, whether they were "absolute requirements of large industrial populations" or for the "convenience of society," were pleated, plated, tasseled, fringed, and fluted to the maximum. By contrast, Moving Machinery (above), run by steam power from a boilerhouse outside the Crystal Palace, displayed a minimum of frills. In the right foreground is a large British lathe for turning railroad wheels. Below is a portion of the French exhibit, much admired and second in size only to the British. The display of Sèvres vases and porcelain visible at the far left in the print was a particular favorite of Queen Victoria, who placed a large order.

At right is Brunel's Great Eastern ready for launch late in 1857. The huge ship had paddlewheels as well as a single propeller. The launch was broadside and took two lives and four months to complete; great hydraulic rams, chains, and winches "were all broken in regular succession," reported the Times of London. A vessel of greater displacement was not built until 1907. Below is Rain, Steam, and Speed (1844) by the Romantic artist J.M.W. Turner, depicting a train on Brunel's Great Western Railway. On the opposite page, in an 1849 view, a span of a so-called tubular style railroad bridge in Wales is floated into position for lifting by hydraulic jacks.

The Transportation Revolution

Isambard Kingdom Brunel (1806–1859) has been called the Great Engineer, the spiritual father of modern mechanical engineering. An Englishman whose energy was exceeded only by his imagination, Brunel broke new ground in every field he put his hand to; his bridges were the longest, his trains the fastest, his steamships the largest. Among the 2,000 miles of track laid under his direction was the Great Western Railway, running from London into the west of England and carrying in the midcentury period the first great crack trains—*The Flying Dutchman, The Cornishman, The Zulu.* His *Great Britain*, launched in 1843, was the first iron-hulled and screw-driven ocean steamship. Fifteen years later came the *Great Eastern*, accommodating 4,000 passengers and five times the size of any ship afloat, exceeding even the bulk of Noah's Ark as calculated by Sir Isaac Newton. Designed for the long run around Africa to Australia, the "Wonder of the Seas" was made obsolete for that trade by the completion of the Suez Canal, through which she was too big to pass. In the case of the *Great Eastern*, Brunel's vision was too far ahead of his time for commercial success, but the huge vessel proved ideal for the task of laying transoceanic cables, including the Atlantic Cable (1866).

Brunel's engineering accomplishments presaged a growing flood of technological advances in the fifty years after his death that stimulated, and were stimulated by, the spread of industrialization. The year 1869, for example, saw the completion of two remarkable engineering feats in totally different climes, a canal at Suez and a transcontinental railroad across the United States. Railroad mileage doubled and doubled again, until by 1900 it exceeded 170,000 miles in Europe and 600,000 miles in the world. Steel rails, more powerful locomotives, air brakes, refrigerator cars—all in their turn improved service and lowered costs to shippers. In hardly more than half a century similar radical changes took place in ocean-going vessels, changes from sail to steam to steam turbines and Diesel engines, and from wood to iron to steel hulls. Cheaper and stronger steel revolutionized bridge building; new machinery revolutionized road and tunnel construction. Urban transport was altered dramatically by electric streetcars, elevated railroads, the first subways, and the internal combustion engine. Each new development spawned a dozen more until the process had induced a Transportation Revolution.

BIBLIOTECA DEL CIVICO MUSEO DI BELLE ARTI, TRIESTE

Canal at Suez

Many of the major elements comprising industrialism were focused on the problems of building the Suez Canal, so that in time it became a virtual microcosm of the industrial age. It involved the highest engineering skills, steam-powered heavy machinery, the resources of finance capitalism, policy decisions by national governments, the demands of the world market and of imperialism, and, as important as anything else, the single-minded dedication of a promoter-builder. For a decade the Frenchman Ferdinand de Lesseps drew his plans and wheedled support for his dream—a canal through the 100 miles of desert between the Mediterranean and the Red Sea, which, by more than halving the sea journey between Europe and the Far East (cutting, for example, the Marseilles-Bombay route from 10,400 miles to 4,600), would bring nation and nation, mother country and colony, into far closer communication. "It will open the world to all people," de Lesseps promised.

Somewhat more than half the shares in the Suez Canal Company were bought by the French public, the average holding being nine shares. The rest of the money was put up by the Egyptian government. The British, fearing an attempt at French hegemony in the Middle and Far East, opposed de Lesseps every step of the way. "It is the greatest bubble [swindle] which was ever imposed upon the credulity and simplicity of the people of this country," Prime Minister Palmerston told the Commons. (Thirty years later, through a blend of fiscal and diplomatic dexterity, Britain seized control of the bubble.) De Lesseps was backed by Napoleon III instead.

In April, 1859, construction began. The canal itself involved moving some 100 million cubic feet of sand and blasting through three rock ridges. A small canal had to be dug to bring fresh water to the site from the Nile, and a harbor and dock facilities created at Port Said, the Mediterranean terminus. Egyptian laborers with shovels and baskets worked alongside 10,000-horsepower steam dredges. The job took ten years of prodigious effort and weathered repeated financial storms. The total cost came to $100 million.

The print at left offers an aerial perspective. Suez, the southern terminus, is at lower left, Port Said at upper right. At upper left is the Nile Delta. On November 17, 1869, to enormous fanfare, the job was finished and the canal opened to the traffic of the world.

MAURICE WERTHEIM COLLECTION, FOGG ART MUSEUM

EDWIN SMITH

Claude Monet, one of the masters of French Impressionism, painted Gare Saint-Lazare *(above) in 1877. The station, with its vaulted iron and glass roof, was one of the seven great terminals built in Paris. The vista at right was part of the working quarter of Newcastle upon Tyne. Slum houses and tenements were built "of the commonest materials," complained a British Royal Commission, "with the worst workmanship . . : altogether unfit for people to live in." The progressive piling up of housing units in such factory towns as Newcastle reached incredible proportions in the cities. "I have seen the lowest quarters of Marseilles, Antwerp and Paris," wrote French literary critic Hippolyte Taine after a visit to London. "They come nowhere near this. Squat houses, wretched streets, stifling alleys, troops of pale children crouching on filthy staircases. . . ."*

The Birth of Coketown

One of the bitter fruits of industrialism was its physical impact on the urban centers of the world. The centralization so necessary to efficient and profitable manufacture spawned what the urban critic Lewis Mumford has christened Coketown. At night, Mumford writes, "its prevailing color was black. Black clouds of smoke rolled out of the factory chimneys, and the railroad yards, which often cut clean into the town, mangling the very organism, spread soot and cinders everywhere. . . . The manufacture of illuminating gas within the confines of the towns became a characteristic new feature: the huge gas tanks reared their bulk over the urban landscape, great structures, on the scale of a cathedral: their tracery of iron, against an occasional clear lemon-green sky at sunrise, was one of the most pleasant aesthetic elements in the new order."

Of themselves, Mumford notes, the elements of the industrial age "were not necessarily evil; . . . in their segregation they might have been comely." Brunel's viaducts were graceful in their proportions and his tunnel entrances bore pleasing Romanesque designs. In skilled hands the new materials—iron, steel, sheet glass—became original and eloquent structures. But these were the exceptions. In Manchester and Lille and Essen and Pittsburgh and a hundred other cities the slums and factories and railroads spread cancerously, uncontrolled and uncontrollable. In the rush toward profit and in the name of progress the city planner was ignored and aesthetic considerations forgotten. The architect, writes a critic, "suddenly becomes a dim figure . . . retreating into his ivory tower." "Never before in recorded history," concludes Mumford, "had such vast masses of people lived in such a savagely deteriorated environment. . . ."

Captains of Industry

One of the gold medal winners at the Great Exhibition of 1851 in the Crystal Palace was Alfred Krupp of Essen, honored for his design of a 6-pounder steel cannon. At the time Krupp found no interested buyers, but it was not long before the world heard more from the "Cannon King." In the long Krupp dynasty he was known as Alfred the Great. An arms race was music to Krupp's ears. Following the Battle of Königgrätz in 1866, during the Austro-Prussian War, a Prussian general wrote him: "Those children of yours conversed for long hot hours with their Austrian cousins. . . ."

In the course of the second half of the nineteenth century, Krupp and a few score other industrial titans came to wield enormous personal power and influence. Seeming to exemplify the theories of Social Darwinism ("the survival of the fittest"), strengthened by government support or at least non-interference, they formulated or refined the basic elements comprising industrial capitalism. Of particular importance were their techniques designed to "rationalize" the economy. Such devices as joint-stock mergers, trusts, holding companies, and cartels enabled them to regulate markets and curtail competition. These devices soon crossed national boundaries to become international in scope; Alfred Nobel, for example, the Swedish inventor of dynamite, established the Dynamite Trust, Ltd. in 1886 to dominate the explosives markets of five nations.

FOTO KRUPP-HACHETTE

The two sketches above are from the notebook of Alfred Krupp. On the left is his design for a huge 550-millimeter mortar that was used in the siege of Paris in 1870, one of dozens of heavy guns that hurled an average of 300 shells nightly into the French capital during the four-month siege. Above right is Krupp's drawing of an advanced "panzerkanone," dated 1875. The scene below, painted by Otto Bollhagen, is the Krupp foundry in Essen in 1873.

These French advertising posters all date from about 1900. The poster for home furnishings on the opposite page reflects strong Art Nouveau influences, while the one at the right, for bathroom appointments, is strong on snob appeal. Many artists of the day, since famous, tried their hand at posters— for example, Toulouse-Lautrec (pages 306–307) and two represented in color on this page, Albert Guillaume, promoting cigarette papers, and Theophile Steinlen, appealing to lady cyclists.

For Public Consumption

From midcentury on, the benefits of industrialization affected most strongly and most immediately the urban middle class. Possessing the creature comforts before industry began mass-producing them, the aristocracy and the upper classes realized no radical change in their living standards. The lower classes, the masses, gained from the lowering of prices of basic commodities, but only slowly did they reap benefits in areas that the other classes took for granted: sewer systems, water lines, the rudiments of sanitary plumbing, heating units, gas and then electric illumination. In any case, daily life and (except for the upper classes) standards of living were radically altered by the mass and variety of consumer goods that the new technology was inventing, the new factories producing, and the new transportation delivering.

Refrigeration, the ubiquitous "tin" can, pasteurization, and packaging innovations changed eating habits. The sewing machine, the vacuum cleaner, and the washing machine gave housewives a new outlook. Ready-made clothing and machine-made shoes wrought sartorial changes. Carpeting, wallpaper, and furnishings became available in good quantity if not in good taste. The pleasures of the cities came within reach, thanks to street lighting and public transportation. The bicycle, railroad, and steamboat encouraged excursions into the countryside and more elaborate vacations. And simply to reach all these customers required new techniques of marketing and more sophisticated advertising—witness the examples reproduced here.

Pictures of Misery

Europe, remarked the Conservative party's Benjamin Disraeli, was fast splitting into "two nations—the Rich and the Poor. . . . The claims of the future are represented by suffering millions." Commenting on the same phenomenon, Karl Marx observed: "everything seems pregnant with its contrary; machinery gifted with the wonderful power of shortening and fructifying human labour, we behold starving and overworking it." The facts of urban poverty, of a large mass of workers stripped of economic security and defenseless against economic fluctuations, had become a part of the new age.

Disraeli and Marx saw the problem in its broad dimensions; the artist Kaethe Kollwitz, the wife of a Berlin doctor, saw it on an individual, personal level. With much of her husband's practice devoted to social work and a primitive form of socialized medical care for the poor, she witnessed the dreary cycle of illness, unemployment, alcoholism, and desertion, and confided in her diary, "The more I see of it, the more I realize that this is the *typical* misfortune of the workers' families. As soon as the man drinks or is sick and unemployed it is always the same story. . . . For the woman the misery is always the same." Working in charcoal or crayon, limiting herself to browns, blacks, and greys, she strove to capture the blunt images of poverty and exploitation. "I must try to keep everything to a more and more abbreviated form," she wrote, "so that all the essentials are strongly stressed and the inessentials almost omitted."

In the manner of many socially conscious artists (Hogarth, for example), her major work was in series form. Her first series, "The Weavers" (1898), took its inspiration from an abortive revolt by Silesian weavers in 1842, but its individual plates—*Poverty, The Conspiracy, Riot*—had universal, contemporary implications. The series won a gold medal at an exhibition in Berlin, but Kaiser William II squelched the presentation, noting his distaste for "gutter art." (This was not Kaethe Kollwitz' last experience with censorship; after 1933, under Nazi edict, her art was removed from German museums.)

The three examples of her work shown here all date from about 1909. *Lunch Hour* (opposite) is a study of factory workers. The common practice of wives of the poor doing piece work, such as sewing on lace, is the subject of the drawing above right, *The Home Worker*. Below right is *The Homeless*, published in a German magazine in 1909 as one of a series she titled "Pictures of Misery."

A New Dynamism

Historians examining the latter half of the nineteenth century have given the period a variety of labels: the Age of Exploitation, the Age of Progress, the Age of Materialism, the Age of Optimism. Contemporaries were of several minds as well; to the optimists industrialization promised progress, growth, dynamism. "Machinery was indeed dynamic, not static," writes the historian C. J. H. Hayes. "By a kind of parthenogenesis, it multiplied itself; so that everybody was now minded to talk, in the manner of the enlightened Englishman described by Chesterton, 'as if clocks produced clocks, or guns had families of little pistols, or a penknife littered like a pig.'" It was widely believed that in time the material benefits of industrialization would produce an earthly order not unlike the precisely ordered universe Newton had promulgated in the sixteenth century. If the industrial machine still misfired and ran raggedly—and the periodic economic depressions testified that it did—all that was needed was a few adjustments; the machine itself appeared sound.

Dynamism was the credo of a group of Italian artists and writers who founded about 1909 a movement termed Futurism (Chapter 17). Futurists exalted science, technology, and mechanics; the painter Giacomo Balla, for example, sought the speed and movement of the city in his abstract canvases (above). The young architect Antonio Sant'Elia saw the marriage between industrialism and urbanization producing *The New City* (left; 1914). "We must invent and remake the Futurist city to be like a huge tumultuous shipyard, agile, mobile, dynamic in all its parts," he wrote. "Every generation should build its own city."

One of the less felicitous tenets of the Futurists was their glorification of war as "the only health giver of the world"—a belief that was to cost Sant'Elia his life at the front in 1916. Yet without doubt industrialization brought with it a many-fold increase in military power. It was this fact and its implications that has been termed "the lurking nemesis" facing the Western world as it turned into the twentieth century.

7

Urban Culture
and the Middle Class

S ome of the most significant changes in the quality of Western life in the nineteenth century resulted from the process of urbanization, that is, the shift of the population from the countryside to the city. As a consequence of this shift, the city—traditionally an enclave in a rural sea—became for many Western countries the normal place of habitation and for the whole modern world the main source of cultural values. The distinction that we draw between the term *urbane* and the term *provincial* reflects the predominantly urban character of modern civilization, much as the contrast between *noble* and *menial* or *villainous* reflected the rural character of medieval life. The term *urbane* in modern usage is synonymous with *polite, courteous, civil, mannerly,* while *provincial* means *intolerant, illiberal, narrow-minded, insular.* It is not difficult to determine whose values this terminology reflects.

Though the city had grown in importance with the rise of industrialization and the revolutions of 1848, until the middle of the century the urban population was everywhere in a minority. From 1851, when Britain first registered more urban than rural inhabitants, urbanization proceeded everywhere at a rapid pace, especially in countries with developed industrial economies. In 1914 the urban element accounted for 80 percent of the population in Britain, more than 60 percent in Germany, more than 45 percent in France. By that time even countries with relatively weak industries, like Russian Poland and Denmark, had one out of three citizens residing in cities. The increase was particularly striking in large towns. Budapest and Berlin, for example, increased their population tenfold in the course of the nineteenth century. Prior to 1800 not a single European city had a million inhabitants; since then, more than 50 have exceeded that number. The multimillion-person metropolis has determined the course of Western history during the past century.

The typical old European town had been confined to a compact area enclosed by one or more rings of defensive walls. These walls, which remained in place long after they had lost their military significance, artificially constrained urban growth. In the second half of the nineteenth century they were generally pulled down and turned into parks and boulevards. Freed from their confinement, European cities spilled into the adjacent countryside, engulfing villages, farmlands, orchards, pastures, and forests. The outward movement became especially pronounced toward the end of the century, when the construction of streetcar lines and commuter trains made it possible to house the working population far away from its place of employment.

The map of Cologne (following page) will illustrate this development. The area marked with the numerals I through III represents the whole city area as of 1800; it hardly differs from that of the ancient Roman town of Colonia Agrippina that had occupied the same location. The population that gravitated toward this important commercial center in the course of the nineteenth century

W. H. Egley's In the Omnibus, *painted in 1859, manages to capture—in its costumes, its expressions, even in its composition—the very essence of the urban middle class that dominated English social and cultural life during the reign of Queen Victoria.*

PLAN DER STADT KÖLN
mit den statistischen Stadtteilen.

Stadtteil

I	Altstadt-Nord
II	Altstadt-Mitte
III	Altstadt-Süd
IV	Neustadt-Nord
V	Neustadt-Mitte
VI	Neustadt-Süd
VII	Niehl
VIII	Longerich
IX	Merheim (linksrheinisch)
X	Riehl
XI	Nippes
XII	Ehrenfeld
XIII	Bocklemünd
XIV	Müngersdorf
XV	Lindenthal
XVI	Sülz
XVII	Zollstock
XVIII	Bayenthal
XIX	Marienburg
XX	Deutz
XXI	Humboldtkolonie
XXII	Poll
XXIII	Kalk
XXIV	Vingst
XXV	Gremberg
XXVI	Mülheim
XXVII	Stammheim
XXVIII	Dünnwald
XXIX	Holweide
XXX	Dellbrück
XXXI	Merheim (rechtsrheinisch)
XXXII	Worringen
XXXIII	Weiler
XXXIV	Fühlingen
XXXV	Merkenich

Erläuterung:

Wald und Parkanlagen
Wiesen und Grünanlagen
Friedhöfe
Behaute Fläche

Eingemeindet:

1888 die Stadtteile VII—XXII
1910 " XXIII—XXV
1914 " XXVI—XXXI
1922 " XXXII—XXXV

Entwurf und Lithographie angefertigt
von der Vermessungs-und Planabteilung
des Liegenschaftsamts der Stadt Köln
im Jahre 1926.

Maßstab 1:100 000

A plan of Cologne shows the city's growth in stages from 1888 to 1922. I-VI designates the pre-1888 city. The key at upper center delineates (reading down) forest and parks, meadowland, cemeteries, and arable land.

could not be accommodated within these narrow limits and settled in adjacent villages. In the early 1880s Cologne constructed new walls, gaining a bit of additional space (IV–VI), but this space was so quickly filled up that the authorities had to give up the effort to contain the city within definite, neatly drawn boundaries. In the 1890s Cologne burst from its confines, losing the appearance of an enclosed area and acquiring the sprawling, amorphous shape of the typical modern city. Quarters designated VII–XXII were incorporated in 1888, XXIII–XXV in 1910, and XXVI–XXXI in 1914. A similar pattern of growth took place in other European towns. The outline maps of the expansion of London (opposite) resemble ink spots spreading on a sheet of blotting paper.

In the regions of intense industrialization, for example, the western Midlands of England or the Ruhr in Germany, the towns grew so large that they soon absorbed the entire countryside separating them from each other. The result were urban clusters—"conurbia," or "megalopolises" as they are called today. Where this occurred, the usual distinction between town and country lost meaning.

The social group identified with urban life is known as the middle class (in French, *bourgeoisie*). This term is not easy to define, because it is so often loosely used. For our purpose we shall define the middle class as consisting of those who derived their income from non-agrarian property or professional skills and services, and distinguish it from the landed aristocracy and the peasantry on the one hand and from manual labor on the other.

The middle class can be subdivided further into an upper and a lower part. The upper bourgeoisie consisted of industrial entrepreneurs, bankers and wealthy investors, big merchants, and representatives of the free professions. Although it lacked formal criteria of exclusiveness comparable to those the aristocracy had in family ancestry, the upper-middle class did maintain its identity and cohesion by a variety of devices. Until approximately 1870, for instance, it shared with the nobility a virtual monopoly on political representation. It also controlled access to the secondary schools, attendance at which in turn assured entrance to institutions of higher learning and, beyond them, to the professions. And, of course, it controlled capital and credit, the sinews of modern economic life.

The lower-middle class or petty bourgeoisie embraced a large and amorphous body of persons who furnished the aristocracy and upper-middle class with goods and services. It included shopkeepers, artisans, and domestic servants. Wedged between the prestigious upper-middle class and the mass of manual laborers, the petty bourgeoisie was notoriously insecure: eager to climb up the social ladder, dreading proletarianization, it was despised alike by the bourgeoisie proper, whom it wished to emulate, and by the manual workers, from whom it wished to separate itself.

Many large cities had, in addition to the upper- and lower-middle class and the manual laborers, a fourth social group consisting of intellectuals, students, artists, and others, who were usually of middle-class background but detached from it. This "bohemian" element sometimes settled in separate districts, usually on the edge of a slum (e.g., Montparnasse and Montmartre in Paris), and in periods of acute social unrest often allied itself with the working classes against the bourgeoisie.

The rapid growth of cities in the nineteenth century destroyed the cultural homogeneity that had previously characterized urban life. The modern metropolis performs a great variety of economic, administrative, and cultural functions and attracts a corresponding variety of cultural groups, each with its own values and codes of behavior. It is really many towns in one. In dealing with it, therefore, one must distinguish the component groups that, although equally "urban," have differing and often incompatible aspirations. We shall discuss the working class and its supporters among the intelligentsia in the next chapter. Here we shall concentrate on the upper-middle class, the social group that more than any other set its stamp on the nineteenth century.

S. E. RAMUSSEN, *London, The Unique City*, 1937

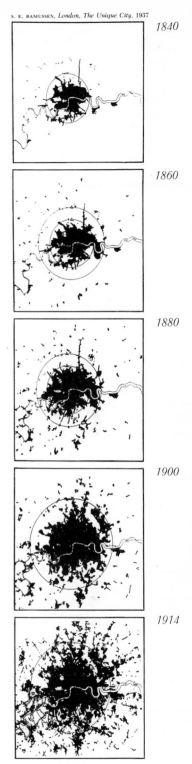

1840

1860

1880

1900

1914

The built-up area of London, traced over three quarters of a century. In 1840 the circled zone was four miles in diameter, in 1914, nine and a half.

The model for the upper-middle class was primarily English, but it was international in scope. The ethics, manners, and tastes of the nineteenth-century bourgeoisie were remarkably uniform. The English Victorian businessman exerted a powerful influence even in countries where life remained largely rural and agrarian, for it was easier to transplant values and modes of behavior than economic or social institutions. The same held true, although to a lesser degree, of the lower-middle class, which also displayed throughout the Western world many common cultural characteristics.

Although the bourgeoisie achieved a dominant position only in the nineteenth century, it is a class with a venerable past. According to the historian Werner Sombart, it originated in Italy in the fourteenth century. It was then that literary works appeared espousing virtues that ever since have been regarded as typically middle class: orderliness, industry, thrift, and the avoidance of sensual temptations and "bad company." Similar ideals were popularized in the so-called merchants' manuals that proliferated between the sixteenth and eighteenth centuries. Among literary works in this tradition are Daniel Defoe's *Robinson Crusoe* and Benjamin Franklin's *Poor Richard's Almanack*. These writings laid stress on the inner purity of the "good man": the "good man" thought cleanly and acted fairly, and by so doing also served best his own interests. In Protestant countries the ideal bourgeois was often depicted as endowed with divine blessing, his wealth being heaven's reward for virtue. His antitheses were the irresponsible, dissipated aristocrat and the slothful, depraved pauper.

Perhaps the most prominent feature of bourgeois culture, in the period of its gestation as well as its maturity, was its inclination to view everything in moral terms. How one disposed of money or brought up children, what relations one established with persons of the opposite sex, and what one did with leisure time testified not only to one's judgment but also and above all to one's virtue. This obsession with morality was a source of both strength and weakness in bourgeois culture.

Thanks to its moral sensitivity, the middle class never remained content simply to bask in its privileges and wealth. It is true that much of the bourgeoisie proved smug and callous and refused to accept responsibility for those less fortunate, treating poverty as punishment for laziness or depravity. But it is equally incontrovertible that the bourgeoisie produced in generation after generation a body of reformers who, by touching its conscience, were able to persuade it to share its advantages. It would be difficult to find in history another social group as firmly entrenched in power as the European bourgeoisie in the first half of the nineteenth century that did not use its power merely to entrench itself further. But the European bourgeoisie abolished serfdom at home and slavery abroad, did away with discriminatory laws against religious and national minorities, extended public education to the masses, and permitted labor to organize and everyone to vote. By these and other similar measures it forfeited both its economic and political monopoly. In a sense, the bourgeoisie undermined its hegemony, but by so doing, it spared most of Europe a revolution.

But there is also another aspect to this moral sensibility. The pre-industrial businessman had lived and worked in a world of relative equals: whether negotiating with another merchant, directing a small body of apprentices, or farming out tasks to domestic craftsmen, he could act in accord with the precepts of justice and charity. This became difficult and sometimes impossible under conditions of industrialism. Industrialization, with its open-market economy, encouraged and indeed forced businessmen to compete, and competition was difficult to contain within ethical bounds, especially if defeat spelled ruin. Free trade brought the abolition of elaborate schemes of price and labor regulations by which early business had enforced fair dealing. Furthermore, industrialization separated the entrepreneur from the mass of wage earners and increasingly left the direction of business to salaried managers who executed but did not initiate policy. All these developments tended to divest economic activity of moral connotations. The businessman of the industrial era had to be aggressive and in his everyday dealings act on principles very different from those that his religious conscience dictated. William Thackeray in his novel *The Newcomes* (1853–1855) offers the following bit of worldly advice, which, even if given tongue in cheek, gives a fair idea of the practical Victorian's outlook:

> To push on in the crowd, every male or female struggler must use his or her shoulders. If a better place than yours presents itself just beyond your neighbor, elbow him and take it. Look how a steadily-purposed man or woman at court, at a ball, or exhibition, wherever there is a competition and a squeeze, gets the best place; the nearest the sovereign, if bent on kissing the royal hand; the closest to the grand stand, if minded to go to Ascot; the best view and hearing of the Rev. Mr. Thumpington, when all the town is rushing to hear that exciting divine; the largest quantity of ice, champagne and seltzer, cold pâté, or other his or her favorite fleshpot, if gluttonously minded, at a supper whence hundreds of people come empty away. . . . Is there a good place at table? Take it. At the Treasury or the Home Office? Ask for it. Do you want to go to a party to which you are not invited? Ask to be asked. Ask A., ask B., ask Mrs. C., ask everybody you know: you will be thought a bore; but you will have your way. What matters if you are considered obtrusive, provided that you obtrude? By pushing steadily, nine hundred ninety-nine people in a thousand will yield to you. . . . If your neighbor's foot obstructs you, stamp on it; and do you suppose he won't take it away?

The code of behavior described by Thackeray contradicted the assimilated canons of religious ethics, and the conflict between "Sunday and Monday," between ethics and reality, ran like a thread through nineteenth-century middle-class life. The conflict was aggravated by the spread of science with its challenge to religious beliefs. In some these conflicts led to a spiritual crisis from which they sought escape in religion, aestheticism, or radicalism. But most members of the middle class resolved the dilemmas by ignoring their existence, that is, acting as though there were no contradictions. Such was the source of hypocrisy, the most outstanding Victorian vice, the natural safety valve of a society whose "practical ideals were at odds with its religious professions, and [whose] religious belief was at issue with its intelligence."*

*G. M. Young, *Early Victorian England, 1830–1865* (1934).

The central upper-middle class institution was the family. This had been the case even in the Middle Ages, as testified by the prevalence of representations of the Holy Family in religious paintings commissioned by medieval bourgeois patrons. One of the earliest middle-class manuals, written by Leon Battista Alberti, a fifteenth-century Florentine humanist, was called *Della Famiglia (On the Family)*; it depicted family cohesion as indispensable to a virtuous life. Alberti called for the submissiveness of wife to husband and children to father, good domestic management, proper education and manners, and sexual purity.

In the nineteenth century economic changes modified the function of the family without depriving it of its traditional importance in middle-class life. When the ideal of the middle-class family first emerged, the family had been an effective economic unit in the sense that its members could and often did engage in joint business activities such as banking, trading, or handicrafts. The modern division of labor and separation of ownership, management, and manual work loosened the economic ties binding the family and transformed it into a primarily cultural unit. It performed this function by a variety of religious, artistic, and literary activities.

Christmas had been originally a purely religious holiday, and had been celebrated in church. During the Reformation in Germany, it first became common

A water color by an unknown artist, dating from about 1865, shows the living room of a well-to-do Lombard family. An engaged couple sits in perfect propriety amidst the ornate furnishings and décor, chaperoned by the girl's mother busy at embroidery.

practice to celebrate Christmas at home. From Germany the custom of domestic Christmas celebrations was transplanted to England by Queen Victoria's German husband, Prince Albert, and from England it spread to the United States. Charles Dickens' *A Christmas Carol* (1843) did much to popularize the custom among English-speaking peoples. It subsequently became in Protestant countries and some Catholic ones an important formal manifestation of family loyalty.

A good middle-class family engaged in cultural activities every day of the year, as well as on weekends and holidays. Very common, especially in England, was the custom of reading aloud. It was both a form of entertainment at a time when there was little of it, and an assertion of domestic cohesiveness. Musical activities were also much in vogue. Middle-class women were expected either to play an instrument or to sing, and in Germany families sometimes formed complete musical ensembles. Culture so relentlessly pursued within the walls of the household inevitably influenced the content and form of literature and art. Books and journals read to the whole family had to avoid subjects unsuited for the ears of children. This consideration accounts in large measure for the well-known prudery of nineteenth-century literature. Older works that did not meet these standards were sometimes expurgated or "bowdlerized," as the procedure came to be known when Thomas Bowdler in 1818 brought out a *Family Shakespeare*.

The genteel life of the middle-class family would not have been possible were it not for the availability of cheap domestic help. The supply came from the overpopulated rural areas. Wages were low and working conditions bad. A full-time chambermaid in mid-Victorian England, in addition to room and board, received a wage of 30 shillings a month—the price at the time of a standard "triple-decker" (three-volume) novel. Domestics were housed in cramped quarters in attics or basements, or even in the kitchen, so as to be available whenever needed. Nevertheless, there was never any shortage of help, because rural girls were lured to the city by its excitements, the hope of marriage, and the opportunity of acquiring a city appearance and manner and thereby improving their social status. The richer middle-class neighborhoods had hordes of domestics. In 1861 England had more persons employed in domestic service than in the textile industry. At the end of the century a seventh of the entire British labor force was engaged in paid domestic work—2,600,000 persons, compared to 1,600,000 engaged in agriculture and fishing.

An important feature of middle-class culture was its attitude toward sex. Here, too, family considerations were decisive. The middle-class household could not tolerate sexual laxity because it threatened its cohesion and even survival: scandal, divorce, an illegitimate child were tragedies afflicting not only persons directly involved, but the entire family. The reaction to the threat was ruthless, both on the part of relatives and society at large; it involved expulsion from the home, disinheritance, and social ostracism. In France the law went so far as to virtually absolve a husband for the murder of an adulterous wife. The bourgeoisie prided itself on its sexual chastity, seeing in it yet another proof of its superiority to the aristocracy and to the lower class. It viewed sex as an unavoidable but regrettable means of procreation and tolerated it only for this purpose.

This attitude had various effects, not all salutary. The sexual life of human

William Holman Hunt painted The Awakening Conscience *in 1853. It depicts the moment when a slightly soiled dove sees her error and leaps in horror from her paramour's lap. The purchaser, however, had Hunt repaint her expression; she now appears to be reconsidering her decision.*

beings is more complicated than nineteenth-century middle-class morals allowed, and it would not stay confined within such narrow bounds. Nowhere was hypocrisy carried farther than in this respect. Middle-class men found it easy to satisfy their appetites with women of the lower classes, and society tolerated such escapades as preferable to family breakup. Prostitution increased enormously in the big cities at the very time when sexual standards were ostensibly at their strictest. The rate of illegitimate births was also high. Records show that in 1851, 42,000 illegitimate children were born in England—a figure interpreted by a contemporary to mean that "one in twelve of the unmarried females in the country above the age of puberty strayed from the path of virtue." In Austria at the end of the century one out of every eight children was born out of wedlock and in France one out of four. How many such children were not recorded and how many were aborted or killed we shall never know.

Sexual escapades were available in the upper-middle class only to men. Women were expected to adhere to prevailing standards and indeed did so to a remarkable degree. They had to be chaste not only in their behavior, but also in their thoughts. If not always as saintly as middle-class imagination depicted them, they were at any rate expected to repress their feelings and conform. This double standard placed a great burden on middle-class women. Only in the 1880s did psychiatry begin to discover the repressive causes of many inexplicable ailments, such as hysteria, and help gain acceptance for a more tolerant attitude toward sex.

In theory, middle-class society was open to anyone with the requisite personal qualities and accomplishments. The criteria were not external (such as ancestry) but internal. It is for this reason that so much importance was attached to good manners, which served as an outward manifestation of inner purity. Etiquette manuals, which proliferated in this era, often identified good manners with religious virtues. One of the most popular manuals, Mrs. H. O. Ward's *Sensible Etiquette of the Best Society*, includes this passage:

> If we examine the laws which good society lays down for our guidance and governance, we shall find without doubt, that they are those which a simple Christian, desiring to regulate the meetings of a number of people who lacked the Christian feeling would dictate. . . . The considerations which dictate [the laws of society] are reducible to the same law, and this law proves to be the fundamental one of the Christian doctrine. . . . The great law of Christianity which inculcates brotherly love and self-denial, finds its counterpart in the first law of politeness—to be agreeable to everybody, even at the expense of one's comfort. Peace is the object of Christian laws; harmony that of social observances. . . . Pride, selfishness, ill-temper are alike opposed to Christianity and good breeding.

Such manuals laid particular stress on the necessity of treating all people as equals and savagely condemned "snubbing," "sniffing," or "cutting." It is easy to understand why a class composed of so many self-made persons, forever dreading the aristocratic sneer, should have attached so much importance to this matter.

Those who did not conform to the accepted norms of behavior were regarded as "bad company," distinguished by such traits as vulgarity, arrogance, and disrespect for public opinion. The "fast woman"—a species of "bad company"—was depicted as a person who flirted, sought out male friends, engaged furiously in sports, and used cosmetics.

Although in theory a "company of equals" and open to all who met its standards of morality and breeding, middle-class society placed many obstacles in the path of those who aspired to rise to it from the lower ranks. Its standards could be attained only by those persons who were successful in the struggle for survival. Money was an unspoken assumption of middle-class morals and manners: money to buy a good education, to secure independence, and to pay for a staff of domestics.

Although such matters are admittedly subjective, there is general agreement that the high tide of middle-class influence (between approximately 1830 and 1890) marked a nadir in taste. The age seems quite to have exhausted its inventiveness in science and technology and to have remained content with borrowing aesthetic guidance from the past. It created no style of its own, preferring to adapt or "revive."

The Upper-Middle Class: Tastes

The tastes of the middle class were influenced by three criteria: realism, moral significance, and ostentatiousness. A pragmatic being, the bourgeois wanted his art to represent life as it was, that is, as perceived by the eye and by common sense. He had little use for allegory, mythology, or the frank sensualism of aristocratic art. Middle-class art was realistic in the sense that it strove at verisimilitude. Yet its realism was diluted by a penchant for moralizing. It was not art for art's sake but art that carried a message. John Ruskin, the most influential art critic of the century, never tired of stressing the moral element in aesthetic experience: The more a work of art elevated the spirit, the greater, according to his *Modern Painters*, was its artistic merit:

> The difference between great and mean art lies, not in definable methods of handling, or styles or representation, or choices of subjects, but wholly in the nobleness of the end to which the effort of the painter is addressed. We cannot say that a painter is great because he paints boldly, or paints delicately; because he generalizes or particularizes; because he loves detail, or because he disdains it. He is great if, by any of these means, he has laid open noble truths, and aroused noble emotions.

Although Ruskin had subtler criteria in mind, most of his contemporaries interpreted his rule to mean that art must convey a moral lesson. This view reached its extremes in Russia, where the radical publicist Nicholas Chernyshevskii had much success in the 1850s with an aesthetic doctrine that judged art solely by its ability to awaken public conscience against social injustice. Leo Tolstoy in *What Is Art?* (1898) rejected all creative efforts that did not make men better Christians. Among the authors he dismissed on these grounds was Shakespeare.

The desire to reconcile realism and morality resulted in a sentimentalized, pseudo-realistic art. Content once more took the upper hand over form and color. In its choice of themes, bourgeois art showed a preference for historic subjects, domestic scenes, and episodes from the life of the peasantry. Because of their

Two examples of popular bourgeois art are offered here. At left is Pierre Auguste Cot's The Storm *(1880), respectable but titillating. On the opposite page is Sir Edwin Landseer's* The Old Shepherd's Chief Mourner. *Such scenes of bathos won Landseer a wide following.*

didactic value, contrasts were in vogue: age and youth, life and death, wealth and poverty, virtue and sin were all depicted in a manner calculated to induce moral reflections. Landscapes and religious subjects declined in popularity, the former because they could not be moralized, the latter because they were difficult to present realistically. Great attention was paid to a smooth finish and faithful rendition of detail.

The names of the nineteenth-century painters whose canvases brought the highest prices are hardly remembered today. Manuals of art history pass them by, and museums store their works out of sight. Yet for the historian they are of the greatest importance as indicators of prevailing taste. The painters most in demand were not the Impressionists, who did not come into their own until the turn of the century, and then only among advanced connoisseurs, but such artists as Sir Edwin Landseer, Sir John Millais, Sir Edward Burne-Jones, Constant Troyon, Rosa Bonheur, and J. L. E. Meissonier. Their works fetched in the latter part of the century today's equivalent of $50,000–$100,000 and more. The buyers who paid these sums were levelheaded businessmen who thought they were making a wise investment. They could hardly have been more wrong. When tastes changed early in the twentieth century, their paintings lost nearly all value. Burne-Jones' *Love and Pilgrim*, bought in 1898 for £5,775 (in purchasing power, the equivalent today of some $120,000), sold in 1941 for £21 (less than $100). Troyon's masterpiece, *Les Hauteurs de Suresnes*, bought in 1889 for £3,045 ($50,000), was disposed of in 1944 for the equivalent of two cases of black-market whiskey. These examples are by no means exceptional, but typical.

The taste of the middle class was most evident in the architecture and home furnishings of the time. The guiding principle was ostentation, for, although in theory money was frowned upon, in reality those who had it liked to display it, especially if they had made it themselves. They strove for heaviness and elaborateness, an effect they achieved with the aid of machines. Until the nineteenth century, an elaborate object was expensive because it required more labor than a plain object. Ornament, therefore, symbolized wealth. The invention of machines able to produce cheaply various kinds of ornament altered this situation, but the basic attitude remained. The bourgeoisie seized on the opportunities that technology offered to surround itself with visible tokens of affluence by decorating everything, including objects of the simplest utility. The result was a veritable orgy of ornamentation. The decorations of this period strike the modern eye as particularly disagreeable because they bear no relation either to function or basic design. The low point was reached at the Great (Crystal Palace) Exhibition of 1851, which demonstrated the possibilities of over-ornamenting every imaginable object from railroad locomotives to bathroom fixtures.

The cluttered appearance of bourgeois interiors was heightened by a predilection for bric-a-brac. Every open space and surface had to be filled. Walls that were not completely covered with paintings encased in rich gilded frames were hung with Oriental swords and shields, carved mirrors, tapestries, and stag heads. Floor space was crowded with cupboards containing china and glass, with potted tropical plants, and endless *objets d'art*. Draperies made of heavy, opaque

Upon careful inspection it is possible to pick out from among the ferns and fretwork and animal skins that decorated her Paris studio the celebrated French actress Sarah Bernhardt.

materials increased the impression of richness and solidity. Windows were seldom opened.

The greatest achievement of middle-class culture was the novel. Although not a new literary genre, it came into its own in the nineteenth century. The novel—especially that which we have described as Realistic—concerned itself with the relationship of individuals to each other and to society at large, and as such admirably suited an age of great social transformations and preoccupations with moral problems. By virtue of its length, the nineteenth-century novel required an audience of leisured readers, which it found largely among middle-class women. It broadened intellectual horizons by exposing the middle class to the life of the lower orders with whom it had little personal contact, and in this manner stimulated social reform movements.

Man for the field, and woman for the hearth;
Man for the sword, and for the needle she;
Man with the head, and woman with the heart;
Man to command, and woman to obey;
All else confusion.

The Emancipation of Women

Thus, in "The Princess," Alfred, Lord Tennyson, the poet laureate of mid-Victorian England, defined the relationship of the sexes. The vision was a man's vision, and one may doubt whether the majority of women willingly subscribed to it. Nevertheless, it is true that in the first half of Queen Victoria's reign the Western middle-class woman was more confined to the household than either her immediate predecessor or successor.

As with so much of middle-class culture, the search for a cause leads back to the family. Woman was the pivot around which this whole institution revolved: it was her task to offer the breadwinner a refuge from the rough competitive world of business, to make sure that the children received a good education and acquired the proper manners, and to supervise the domestics. Ultimately, she guaranteed family cohesion. It was sincerely feared that if women engaged actively in public affairs they would neglect the household, and the home would collapse. The domestication of women stemmed not only from a low regard for their intelligence (which was a factor) but also from a high regard for the home as the basis of civilized life.

Women were expected to be submissive, and this demand was enforced by a variety of discriminatory laws. British and French laws in force in the first half of the century prohibited married women from owning property, even that which they had earned with their own labor. (France, however, did make an exception for real estate.) Upon marriage, a woman's property passed at once to the control of her husband. (According to the English historian G. M. Trevelyan, "The law was in curious contrast to the words of the marriage service, when the man was made to say 'with all my worldly goods I thee endow'; it was really the other way around.") Women were also discriminated against in laws pertaining to the family that virtually barred them from initiating divorce proceedings or claiming legal authority over their children. And, of course, they could not vote.

The discrimination enforced against women violated the tenets of liberalism,

A heavily tasseled, decidedly over-stuffed French rocker, evidence that Victorian taste crossed the Channel.

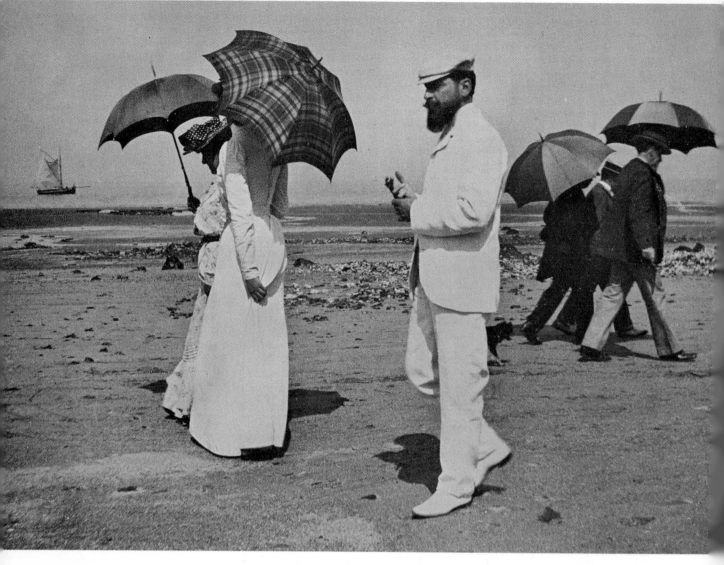

Perfect decorum in beachwear was one of the last bastions of the old social order to fall. This is a beach at Villerville in 1908, photographed by a precocious French youth named Jacques Henri Lartigue, age eleven.

and in a liberal age it was bound sooner or later to be challenged. The challenge, in the form of the feminist movement, emerged in the first half of the nineteenth century, acquired momentum in the second, and gained most of its objectives in the twentieth. Like other movements of the time, it was international in scope.

The first outspoken feminists were the Romantics. As proponents of feeling over convention, they disparaged marriage and extolled free love. Frederick Schlegel did so in his novel *Lucinde* (1799), and virtually every Romantic felt bound to speak up for the rights of love over authority, including that of parents and husbands. Many of the Romantics practiced what they preached, with the result that wife-stealing became among them a common occurrence. Schlegel, for example, stole the wife of a German banker, and Victor Hugo that of his friend, the critic Sainte-Beuve. The Romantic era also produced a number of prominent "emancipated women," including some outstanding novelists. The most celebrated among these were Frederick Chopin's mistress, George Sand, a French novelist who dressed in trousers and smoked cigars, and George Eliot, the author of, among other works, *Silas Marner* and *Middlemarch*.

Isolated feminist symptoms began to coalesce into a movement at the time of Louis Philippe. The Saint-Simonians were particularly active on behalf of female equality, although it is significant that they allowed women no positions of responsibility in their own organizations. Under their inspiration, Parisian women organized feminist clubs and petitioned Louis Philippe to add to his title "King of Frenchmen" that of "King of Frenchwomen."

Feminism got under way in earnest in 1848, when suddenly in Europe as well as in the United States voices were raised demanding equal political and legal rights for women. The leaders of the movement were mainly resourceful and intelligent ladies of middle-class origin. Some joined because they had become aware, through literature or philanthropic work, of the wretched condition of working-class wives; others because they hoped to exert influence on legislatures to curb drinking and gambling; still others because they sought an outlet for their idle energies.

The movement received a great boost in 1869 with the publication of John Stuart Mill's *The Subjection of Women*. With his customary incisiveness, Mill demonstrated the inconsistency of discriminatory legislation. He argued that the subservient position of woman in modern society was a relic of ancient slavery, from which men alone had succeeded in emancipating themselves; that this position was convenient to men, and they therefore brought up women believing that they were by nature submissive the better to dominate them; and that as long as woman remained in an inferior situation her true nature and capacity would remain unknown. "What we now call the nature of women," Mill wrote, "is an eminently artificial thing—the result of forced repression in some directions, and unnatural stimulation in others. It may be asserted without scruple, that no other class of dependents have had their character so entirely distorted from its natural proportions by their relation with their masters."

These arguments, reinforced by current sentiments against Negro slavery, won feminism a fanatical following among a small body of women, but they hardly persuaded public opinion. The humorous English journal *Punch* had a field day ridiculing the new generation of women; if one is to believe its cartoons, by 1870 most of them had turned into Amazons, hardly distinguishable from men. Manuals of etiquette, those reliable guides to current social ideals, rejected woman's claim to political rights. *The Habits of Good Society; A Handbook for Ladies and Gentlemen* (1869) intoned:

> What do women want with votes, when they hold the sceptre of influence with which they can control even votes, if they wield it aright? It is by women that nature writes indelible lessons in the hearts of men. Not only when she fills the sphere of a wife, a mother, a teacher, but in every state of life it is woman who has it in her power to influence for good or evil the men with whom she is thrown.

The anti-feminists replied to Mill's question, "Why can a woman rule over England, but not sit in Parliament?," by forming the Man's League for Opposing Woman's Suffrage.

But even without the vote, the position of women gradually began to improve. One of the best ways for a woman to break out of her domestic confinement was to get a job, and this became easier as the job market expanded. Nursing, which Florence Nightingale had made respectable, was one of the first professions open to women. Later some universities opened their gates to them (those of Italy and Switzerland were among the pioneers). Great gains were made in the United States, a country so short of labor that it had no choice but to allow women into occupations previously monopolized by men, including a large proportion of teaching and secretarial jobs. By gaining financial independence women strengthened their social position, and by the end of the century won in most Western countries the right to own and freely to dispose of property.

After 1870 social attitudes also underwent change. Sports came into fashion, bringing middle-class men and women into freer, more casual contact. In the 1860s a lady's physical exertions had been confined to croquet and archery. In the 1870s women adopted two new sports, lawn tennis and roller skating; in the next decade gymnastic exercises were added to the list. In the 1890s came the bicycle rage. A chaperon could hardly keep up with such strenuous activities and by the 1900s had disappeared, at any rate in England. Ladies were now permitted to travel and to attend theaters and restaurants unaccompanied. Indeed, in high English society it became fashionable to be seen in public without one's husband. Elegant hotels and restaurants came into existence to cater to the socially emancipated woman. It was in one of them, the Savoy of London, that in 1896 the Duchesse de Clermont-Tonnerre made history by becoming the first society lady to light a cigarette in public. Ladies now began to use cosmetics, which in the middle of the century had been restricted to "fast women" and prostitutes.

The change that occurred in the position of women in the closing three decades of the century was reflected in fashions. At midcentury the bourgeois woman had

An 1856 comment by Punch *on the rage for crinolines in feminine fashion bore the caption, "Fragment of an unpublished novel of fashionable life."*

Punch, nov. 22, 1856

deliberately dressed in a manner that precluded any useful work. When the burden of superfluous frills, laces, ruffles, and petticoats had become so great that she was unable to work or even to move, Parisian couturiers invented the "crinoline." This was a bell-shaped frame of metal or whalebone intended to support the overelaborate skirt. Crinolines came into fashion during the Second Empire, providing wits with an inexhaustible subject. A Parisian dramatist even wrote a play called *A Journey Around My Wife*. The crinoline disappeared suddenly about 1870, and from then on female attire became simpler and better suited to an active life. In the 1890s women adopted a skirt-and-blouse costume complete with collar and tie.

Despite these gains in social status and freedom, the right to vote came slowly. The first to grant equal suffrage were frontier areas where women were more active and therefore enjoyed greater freedom. New South Wales in Australia pioneered (1867), followed by Wyoming in the United States (1869) and New Zealand (1886). The first country in Europe to give women the vote was Norway (1907). In the heartland of Western Europe, however, men stanchly held on to their political power. In France women had been promised the vote by the republican government of 1848, but when time for elections came, the idea was quietly dropped. The English Reform Bill of 1832 actually disenfranchised some women who had had the vote under the old system. In 1869 propertied English ladies received the right to participate in municipal elections, but not in parliamentary ones.

To win the vote, the feminists organized toward the end of the century pressure groups modeled on the Anti-Corn Law League. These were the "suffragettes," as they were at first contemptuously called and then proudly called themselves. They agitated and demonstrated, and when these methods failed to bring the desired result, they had recourse to civil disobedience. They accosted public figures, tied themselves to lampposts, and altogether made nuisances of themselves. Some even refused to pay taxes on the grounds that they were taxed without representation. In 1904 the suffragettes formed an International Association for Woman's Suffrage and held regular congresses. But these determined efforts notwithstanding, women did not gain the vote in most countries until after World War I.

Until the 1860s the ability to read and write had been confined in most of Europe to an élite; the majority of the people could do neither. In England at the time of Victoria's accession (1837) a third of the men and half of the women were unable to sign their marriage registers. A similar proportion held in France. In less advanced countries the number of illiterates was much larger: in Italy 61.9 percent for men, 75.7 percent for women (1871); in Romania 78 percent for both sexes (1899); in Serbia 88.7 percent for men and 98.1 percent for women (1874). In effect, the majority of Europeans—from 50 percent in the most industrialized countries to more than 90 percent in the least—were excluded from participation in cultural life. The written word, the chief medium of cultural communication, remained for practical purposes the monopoly of the propertied.

The notion that education is a public responsibility has a surprisingly recent origin. Until the middle of the nineteenth century it was generally assumed that

Education and Literacy

responsibility for education rested on the family or the church. Until 1870 a country so advanced in all respects as Great Britain had virtually no provisions for public education, entrusting the matter to the initiative of private bodies.

Apart from the Jews, who always had taken special care to instruct the young, the first to concern themselves with public education were Protestant nations. In both cases, the ability to read the Holy Scriptures was considered indispensable, and learning to read constituted an essential aspect of a person's religious upbringing. Luther urged compulsory schooling, and a number of Protestant states introduced it. Scotland passed laws requiring every parish to provide a primary school as early as the sixteenth century; Sweden issued corresponding ordinances in the seventeenth century and Denmark and Prussia in the eighteenth. Although not always fully realized, these provisions gave Protestant countries an educational foundation superior to Catholic and Orthodox ones. In states with a religiously mixed population, for example, Switzerland, Protestants as a rule sent a higher proportion of their children to school than did the Catholics.

In the course of the nineteenth century it became apparent that a basic education was indispensable: it simply was not possible to develop the skills necessary for modern technology, military as well as civil, nor to operate democratic institutions with an illiterate population. Since private bodies could not support the burden of educating a population growing as rapidly as that of Europe in the nineteenth century, the state had no choice but to take over.

The first country to assume public responsibility for the education of its citizenry was France. The French had made much progress in this direction during the Revolution and the First Empire, but the most important measure was enacted in the reign of Louis Philippe. This was the Primary School Law of 1833, initiated by François Guizot (who, incidentally, was himself a Protestant), which required every commune to provide at least one primary school for its inhabitants. In the 1870s most European countries followed the example set by France. The result was a network of primary schools, financed partly by the state and partly by the communities, providing compulsory education for children between the ages of approximately six and fourteen. In a number of countries, however, public education remained a dead letter for lack of money and teachers. This was the case, for example, in Spain and Portugal, which had been among the first countries in Europe to pass laws requiring primary schooling.

The progress of education was often slowed by conflicts between proponents of clerical and lay control. The clergy, having enjoyed for many centuries the right of educating children, was loath to surrender this right to the state and insisted on playing a dominant role in public schools as well. The conflict became especially savage in France, where it provided an outlet for the basic hostility between the Republican and Conservative political blocs.

The European educational system tended to separate primary and secondary schooling into two watertight compartments. Even after about 1870, when it had become generally accepted that society owed its children a primary education, it was nowhere acknowledged that society also should assure graduates of primary schools an opportunity to continue their schooling. Secondary schools and the universities remained in effect reserved for the aristocracy and upper-middle

In the view of the French satirist Honoré Daumier, the wide dissemination of popular literature had a negative effect on the social graces.

class. Ordinary citizens were barred from secondary schools by a variety of devices, including tuition fees and language requirements (Latin and Greek). The vast majority of children, therefore, dropped out of school after completing six or eight grades and went to work. Around 1900 the proportion of primary-school pupils who proceeded to secondary schools in most of Europe varied between 2 and 5 percent. The remaining 95–98 percent, if they were persistent, had some avenues open for continuing their studies (e.g., evening schools or the so-called Mechanics Institutes), but such institutions could accommodate only a small minority. The ladder to a higher education, and through it, to professional careers, was only available to those fortunate two to five out of a hundred able to obtain a secondary-school diploma.

Primary education for the masses influenced culture long before it influenced the social structure. In the more advanced countries it virtually wiped out illiteracy. By 1901 the percentage of illiterates in England and France had declined below 6 percent. The decline was even more striking among the young; the proportion of illiterates among army recruits dropped in England and France to around 1–2 percent, and in Germany it was so insignificant that the armed forces ceased to keep illiteracy statistics. In the predominantly rural states the proportion of illiterates at the end of the century remained high: 79 percent in Russia, 68 percent in Spain, 50 percent in Italy and Hungary, 30 percent in Austria. But even here there was evident improvement among the younger generation. The proportion of recruits unable to read and write declined to 27 percent in Russia by 1913 and to 30 percent in Italy and Greece.

We know less about the culture of the lower-middle class than of the upper, because the upper-middle class controlled the institutions of opinion and taste: the influential journals and newspapers, the theater, the art salons, the universities. This fact tends to distort our view of the nineteenth century. We think of it as an age of earnestness, refinement, and gentility, because such were the qualities characterizing the élite. They by no means held true of the age as a whole if we take as our criterion the outlook of the majority. Underneath the surface of what passes for nineteenth-century culture one can clearly discern the seeds of the mass culture of our own time.

The Culture of the Lower-Middle Class

Compulsory primary schooling gave Europe a large body of citizens who were literate without being educated. They could read and write, but they had not been exposed to the humanizing influence of the liberal arts and had no taste for serious novels or informative newspapers and reviews. They preferred a simple and exciting literature that would enable them to escape their humdrum existence. This demand was met by a new literary industry designed specifically to cater to the large, semi-educated petty-bourgeois public of skilled workers, shopkeepers, clerks, and domestic servants.

In the first third of the century the mass reading public, at least in the Protestant countries, still consumed largely religious literature. A religious tract in fictional form, the Reverend Leigh Richmond's *Dairyman's Daughter*, sold 2 million copies within 18 years of its appearance in 1809. The popularity of the propaganda literature spread by the Chartists and the Anti-Corn Law League attests also to a widespread interest in politics. But even then the mass reader

The French popular press capitalized on the notorious affairs of Napoleon III. This is a title page of 1900.

hungered for sensationalism. In 1828 an enterprising English publisher sold over a million copies of a murderer's *Last Dying Speech and Confession* and in 1837 even more copies of an illustrated account of the purported thoughts of another criminal before his execution.

The 1850s mark in England a watershed in the history of mass culture. The increase of prosperity, as well as the spread of scientific views, reduced the interest in political and religious literature and created an insatiable demand for cheap escapist works. Among the principal suppliers of such works was the writer and publisher G. W. M. Reynolds, who regularly outsold Charles Dickens, the most popular author of the Victorian upper-middle class. Reynolds introduced the so-called penny dreadful, a closely printed and garishly illustrated weekly of sensational adventures. These publications provided for the first time exciting literature at a price everyone could afford. Whereas Dickens' family review *Household Words* attained in its best year a circulation of 40,000, Reynolds' penny dreadful *The London Journal* sold in the 1850s around 500,000 copies a week. Reynolds also outsold Dickens with his books. On the day of issue, his *Soldier's Wife* sold 60,000 copies, compared to 35,000 copies sold of Dickens' *Bleak House*. Among Reynolds' books were *The Mysteries of London, The Necromancer, Pope Joan, The Loves of the Harem, Omar, Leila,* and *Agnes, or Beauty and Pleasure*. Had Victorian England kept lists of its "best sellers," our notion of its literary tastes would have to be substantially revised. It seems fairly certain, however, even without such lists, that for every reader of *Vanity Fair* there were ten who read *Wagner, the Wehrwolf* or the *Empress Eugénie's Boudoir*. In France a similar taste was satisfied by the superior novels of Eugène Sue, whose most popular work was *The Mysteries of Paris* (1842–1843).

The literature devoured by the mass reader avoided the moral and social issues preoccupying the middle class. Being frankly escapist, it either skirted real human problems or settled them by means of facile solutions. In the end, love and decency conquered all. The heroes and heroines were generally of humble origin, so that the reader could identify with them. Their personalities were simple and two-dimensional: the heroines pale, weak, and chaste, the heroes virile and courageous. The narrative often introduced characters from the upper classes, but generally class lines were observed. The style inclined toward the turgid and rhetorical, the characters speaking in theatrical sentences that unconsciously parodied the language of the educated.

The success of this cheap, sensational literature did not escape the attention of the guardians of public morality either in England, where it originated, or on the Continent, to which it spread. The upper-middle class in Germany condemned it as "backstairs novels," and the Poles called it "sidewalk literature." Efforts were made to elevate public taste by promoting religious tracts, manuals of self-improvement, and popular "home magazines." Some of these publications gained success, among them the *Family Herald,* known also as "sunshine in the kitchen," a wholesome, low-priced journal that attained a circulation of 125,000. Immensely popular among the lower-middle class, especially skilled workers, was Samuel Smiles' *Self-Help* (1859), a book that advocated perseverance, diligence, thrift, and other traditional middle-class virtues as a road to fame and wealth. *Self-Help* was translated into the major European languages, its popularity attesting to the prevalence of middle-class values among a sizable segment of the working population.

The newspaper was another factor in the molding of mass culture. Until the 1880s its purpose was to serve primarily as a source of information. It was expensive (fourpence was the standard price of a London daily) and hard to read. The *Times*, the leading English paper, achieved in the middle of the century a circulation of 50,000; most of its competitors sold around 5,000 copies.

The emergence of a mass reading public made possible an entirely new kind of news writing that was designed not so much to inform as to distract. Known as "yellow journalism," it stressed subjects that for some reason have come to be known as "human interest": murder, theft, divorce, and scandal, particularly when they involved the rich. Accuracy and truthfulness were sacrificed to headlines and "scoops." The style was brief, simple, and colorful. Originated in the United States in the 1880s and 1890s by Joseph Pulitzer and William Randolph Hearst, it was introduced to Europe by Alfred Harmsworth (later Lord Northcliffe). Harmsworth founded in 1896 the *Daily Mail*, a racy paper selling at a halfpenny that quickly won an immense following among people who previously had not read newspapers. While the *Times* by then had reached a circulation of 70,000, the *Daily Mail* three years after its founding exceeded 500,000 and soon climbed well above 1 million. Harmsworth owed his success to unabashed sensationalism, keeping his readers excited by clever appeals to curiosity and national pride. With the fortune that the *Daily Mail* had brought him, Harmsworth launched other papers and in 1908 bought the *Times*. His success encouraged imitators on the Continent: France produced its *Petit Journal* and *Petit Parisien* and Germany its *Lokal-Anzeiger*, all of which sold over a million copies daily.

Among the diversions available to the masses, mention must be made of competitive sports. Traditionally an amusement of the rich, "games" became "sport" with the introduction of paid public contests. Soccer became a spectator sport in the 1870s; boxing, baseball, and tennis followed suit, and soon virtually all physical contests were commercialized.

Mass culture was not regarded in the nineteenth century as worthy of much attention, let alone respect. But with the steady improvement of the living standards of the Western population, the influence of this culture grew. In the twentieth century the lower-middle class became the most dynamic element in Western society, and its culture gradually superseded that of the bourgeoisie proper.

8

Labor and Socialism

Three distinct groups are involved in modern movements of social protest: the total body of wage earners and self-employed, the minority among them who belong to trade unions, and another minority consisting of socialist intellectuals and politicians. This fundamental distinction is often obscured by a tendency, especially prevalent among socialists, to consider modern history in terms of a dichotomy between the "bourgeoisie" and the "working class" or "proletariat." There is, of course, no homogeneous body of "proletarians." The working class is and always has been a stratified body whose upper ranks mesh imperceptibly with the lower-middle class. There are substantial differences between urban and rural workers, salaried and self-employed workers, skilled and unskilled workers, and between workers in large industrial establishments and those in small artisan shops. Furthermore, there is a basic difference in the condition and outlook of workers in countries with advanced social legislation and those in countries where such legislation is rudimentary or absent. The constant growth of the category of wage earners who provide services instead of producing goods and of the white-collar class—salaried but hardly proletarian— further complicates the picture.

A part, but only a part, of the total working population ever joined trade unions and/or became socialist. Germany, the country with the most developed socialist movement in Europe, had in 1895 an estimated working population of 35 million. Of this number, 850,000 were unionized (1900), and at most 2 million cast their votes for the socialist party. Analysis of German election returns at a time when the Social Democrats were making their biggest advances shows that, even in the most industrialized regions of the country (Silesia, Westphalia, and the Rhineland), no more than a third of the workers voted for the socialist ticket. In Britain before World War I the Labour party never won more than half a million votes, or one vote in fourteen (1910). In France in 1914 the Party of Socialist Unity, which represented most socialist groupings, gathered 1,250,000 votes from an electorate of 7 million laborers; its active membership was 69,000. In the predominantly agrarian countries of Europe the relationship between labor, trade unions, and socialist parties was even more tenuous. In Italy, out of a wage-earning population of 7,700,000, 546,000 belonged to unions (1909), and approximately 1 million voted for the socialists and anarchists (1913). In Russia the Social Democratic Labor party—formed in 1898—did not include among its members a single worker. In view of these facts, both trade unionism and socialism must be regarded as organizations or movements representing only a small, albeit a dynamic and articulate, element of the total working population and intelligentsia.

In the nineteenth century there emerged for the first time a self-conscious labor movement that was determined to advance the interests of the working class. Its leaders were usually skilled, well-paid workers, a kind of labor élite

Jean Jaurès, the leading figure in the French socialist movement, was photographed as he spoke to a party rally in 1913. On the very eve of World War I, as he tried to stem the drift toward war, Jaurès was assassinated by a demented super-patriot.

A membership certificate of the Amalgamated Society of Engineers, Great Britain's first modern trade union.

imbued with liberal values and ideals. Having observed the bourgeoisie wage a struggle against aristocratic privilege and win, these labor leaders insisted on acquiring similar rights for themselves—especially the right to vote and to engage in collective bargaining. The anti-bourgeois spirit among the workers, insofar as it existed, was inspired not so much by animosity toward the middle class and its culture as by resentment against the bourgeoisie for not extending to the rest of the population the rights it had gained. The innate liberalism of the small, self-conscious labor élite presented the main obstacle to the penetration of socialist ideas into labor ranks.

The labor movement usually passed through three phases: mutual-aid associations, trade unions, and political action. The earliest associations of workers were formed by journeymen, that is, members of guilds who had lost the chance of becoming masters and had to resign themselves to the status of lifelong hired hands. These associations were a by-product of the dissolution of the guilds; in countries where the guild system remained strong (e.g., Germany), labor organizations had a slow start. The purpose of the mutual-aid associations was to furnish financial assistance to members in case of illness, accident, or any other emergency. In England in the eighteenth and early nineteenth centuries they were known as "friendly societies," in Italy as "*società di mutuo soccorso*," and elsewhere under similar names. Most governments tolerated such associations, but through "anti-combination laws" forbade them to engage in concerted action against employers for economic benefits.

Trade unionism in the proper sense of the word became possible only when workers received the right to engage in collective bargaining. This right they won first in England. In 1824–1825 the House of Commons repealed the stringent anti-combination laws of 1799–1800. While still forbidding "conspiracy," Parliament now allowed worker associations to organize openly and to engage in peaceful negotiations with employers. In the 1830s British trade unions experienced rapid growth. On the Continent union activity remained illegal for a long time. Piedmont authorized unions in 1848, but most countries did so only after 1860 (France partly in 1864–1868 and fully in 1884, Belgium in 1866, Austria in 1870, Germany fully in 1890, Russia in 1906).

The trade union in its mature form was a counterpart of the capitalist enterprise. It was an organization established for the express purpose of negotiating collectively on behalf of its members with industrial establishments or with a branch of industry. Its aim was not to undermine the industrial or "capitalist" order but to secure within it the greatest share of economic benefits for the workers. In that sense, the trade union was inherently economically oriented and reformist rather than politically oriented and revolutionary. Trade unionism was a by-product of the prosperity created by the industrial and capitalist system; it flourished under conditions of affluence and languished under those of recession or underdevelopment.

The first modern trade union was the Amalgamated Society of Engineers, founded in England in 1850–1851. A wealthy organization with a membership of skilled and well-paid workers, the Society in 1852 demanded an industry-wide abolition of regular overtime and piecework. The employers, interpreting this demand as an infraction of their right to run their businesses as they saw fit, refused, whereupon the Society ordered a strike. For three months the Society supported its striking members. In the end, the employers broke the strike, but the Society had won the admiration of the other trades, and national "amalgamated" societies soon mushroomed throughout Great Britain. Unions of the new type were run by professional labor organizers who had sizable funds at their disposal and directed a staff of full-time lawyers, accountants, field representatives, and clerks. In 1874 British trade unions had nearly 1 million members.

Until the 1890s Britain alone had a significant trade-union movement. On the Continent its development was inhibited by various factors such as government repression, a low degree of urbanization, or by the prevalence of small productive units that were unsuitable for amalgamation on a wide scale. In 1879 when German industry was in full swing, German trade unions had only 50,000 members. (On the eve of World War I, however, they had 4 million members.) The proportion of non-agrarian wage earners belonging to unions averaged 4 percent in France (1906) and 7 percent in Italy (1909).

Trade unions were primarily concerned with securing economic advantages; on the whole, they shied away from politics. In England they hesitated to support the Chartists. After the Second Reform Act (1867), which granted the suffrage to many workers, trade unions preferred to back the Liberals rather than enter parliamentary contests. On the Continent, with some exceptions (the most notable being Germany), trade unions professed either political neutrality (the policy adopted in 1906 by the French and Italian trade-union congresses), or else, as in Spain and Russia, committed themselves to syndicalism, which sought to transfer political authority from the state to associations of producers. The notion that the interests of labor were political and national—let alone international—in scope was as a rule brought to labor from the outside, by intellectuals. It never penetrated very deeply, and for that reason socialist intellectuals mistrusted trade unions, preferring to appeal directly to the "laboring masses." The social history of the last hundred years is marked by constant tension between the economic preoccupations of organized labor and the political preoccupations of the socialists. V. I. Lenin, the most successful revolutionary of modern times, realized this conflict early in his career and built a whole strategy on the assumption that socialism could not be entrusted to workers because, left to their own devices, they would never outgrow the trade-union mentality. Socialism, Lenin held, required a tightly organized body of full-time professional revolutionaries.

Socialism may be described as an ideology whose goal is to change the existing capitalist order, either peacefully and gradually or violently and suddenly, and to create conditions under which labor appropriates all the wealth that it produces. For all their doctrinal differences, socialist theorists of different schools agree that private property should disappear. (By "private property" they usually mean the means of production—that is, natural resources, including land, and the instruments of labor, but not unproductive wealth such as private quarters or personal belongings.) Anarchists and Romantic socialists wish to do away with the state altogether and transfer authority to associations of producers; Marxist socialists wish to have the state expropriate private property and assume control of the means of production.

From its inception socialism has been a doctrine of middle-class intellectuals in rebellion against the middle class. To be sure, among the leaders of the socialist movement one may find a few aristocrats and a few workers, but its most prominent spokesmen have descended from and belonged to the bourgeoisie. They were people raised on liberal values who, unlike the majority of their kind, found themselves unable to accept the disparity between ideals and reality inherent in nineteenth-century middle-class life. Like many conservative critics of liberalism, they rejected the hypocrisy, smugness, ugliness, and dullness of industrialism and looked for a return to a fuller, simpler, more beautiful and satisfying way of life, which they imagined had once existed. Socialism was and remains a normative doctrine: socialist doctrines, including the ostensibly scientific one of Marx, contain strong moralistic elements. They are concerned not so much with life as it is, but as it ought to be.

There is a voluminous and interesting literature that probes into the psychological relationship between intellectuals and socialism. Many middle-class intellectuals converted to socialism because they wanted to serve a cause and could no longer find one in religion. Memoirs abound of youths brought up in conventional bourgeois homes who found in socialism an identification with the masses and a deep moral release. In Russia in the 1870s this phenomenon reached epidemic proportions, with thousands of youths leaving school to seek expiation among ordinary peasants. Contemporary Russian accounts even refer to this "going-to-the-people" movement as a "religious crusade." Other intellectuals turned to socialism because they disliked the disorder of the competitive system and sought a more rational and equitable system of managing the economy. The Belgian sociologist Hendrik de Man argues in *The Psychology of Socialism* (1926) that in a capitalist society, in which everyone is motivated by gain, the intellectuals alone retain the sense of over-all community interest. Socialism attracts them because it banishes the profit motive and replaces it with their own spirit of public service. Finally, for some, especially for ambitious workers eager to exchange the factory bench for an office job, the socialist movement was a means of upward mobility, leading from the proletariat into the ranks of the lower-middle class. In 1915 another sociologist, Robert Michels, observed that "That which the Church offers to the peasant and petty bourgeois, namely, a facility for ascent in the social scale, is offered to intelligent manual workers by the socialist party."

Despite points of contact, the pragmatism of labor and the idealism of the socialist intelligentsia led the two movements toward different goals. The socialists wanted to do away with the bourgeoisie, the workers wanted to become bourgeois. In the end, revolutionary socialism obtained a hold only on the agrarian periphery of Europe where, because of the slow development of industry and democracy, the working class had little hope of raising itself to a higher social status without recourse to violence. In the industrial countries, socialism fused with liberalism and turned reformist.

The theories of the pioneers of socialism are not easy to define. In the first half of the nineteenth century the movement lacked organized parties and formal programs and was composed of an eccentric breed of individuals who gathered around themselves ephemeral bands of equally eccentric disciples. What unites the diverse schools of early socialist thought is their Romantic outlook. They believed in the self-realization of the individual and the brotherhood of mankind (often conceived in terms of a religious renaissance or a "new Christianity"). To the writers and artists of the Romantic movement, the enemy was classicism; to its politicians, the enemy was the *ancien régime*; to Romantic socialists, the enemy was economic competition. They were appalled by the debilitating effect of competitiveness on human character and human relations and felt that, as long as man was compelled by the economic system to fight his fellow man, he was bound to fall far short of his full potential.

Romantic Socialism

The principal purpose of the schemes that the Romantic socialists tirelessly devised was to replace "wasteful" competition with cooperation. They paid surprisingly little attention to that conflict between labor and capital which became the hallmark of the later socialists. What troubled them were not so much the inequalities of wealth as the existing system's failure to make intelligent use of the means of production—not so much the injustice of capitalism as its irrationality. Most of the early socialists opposed revolution, because they felt that the change they desired could not be accomplished by replacing one type of government with another, but only by a slow transformation of the human mind and heart.

There is some question whether Claude de Saint-Simon was or was not a socialist, but because his influence was greatest among bankers and engineers of the Second Empire who were anything but socialists, we discussed him earlier (in Chapter 4). Saint-Simon left behind a large and active body of followers who moved definitely in the direction of socialism but whose influence was dissipated by their erratic behavior.

In the 1830s one of the most influential socialist theorists was Charles Fourier. The son of a merchant, Fourier had been troubled since childhood by the wastefulness of capitalist competition, examples of which he had occasion to observe in his father's business, and by the disharmonies in human relations. In his writings, Fourier concerned himself primarily with finding means to assure for all men work fitted to their individual talents and temperaments. To this end, he proposed the creation of special communities or *phalansteries*. Each *phalanstery*, consisting ideally of 1,600 members, would form working teams to take care of the various needs of communal life. Under this arrangement, members could join the teams that best suited them, achieving the maximum of self-fulfillment in work. The *phalansteries* were to have communal kitchens and nurseries, but families would be allowed to reside together in private apartments. The role of the central government would be reduced to a minimum. Fourier's vision anticipated in some respects the *kibbutzim* established in Israel a century later.

The desire to harmonize social relations was also uppermost in the mind of Robert Owen, the leading socialist in Britain. Owen saw in economic competition the main cause of social conflicts and of the deterioration of human character. Born into an artisan family, he rose rapidly in the world of business and before he was thirty became one of the main manufacturers of cotton yarn in Great Britain. At New Lanark, Scotland, the site of his plant, Owen established a model community that attracted much attention. Later on, he threw himself with great zeal into the task of forming cooperative associations, trade unions, and "labor exchanges" designed to make workers independent of the state and the capitalists. He stood at the height of his influence in the early 1830s, when a vast labor movement arose in Britain, animated by his ideas. Though Owen's schemes (including a socialist community at New Harmony, Indiana) failed, they were not without issue. To Owen belongs much of the credit for having launched in England both the trade-union and the cooperative movements.

Etienne Cabet, a lawyer who once had held the position of attorney general of Corsica, spent many years in England, where he became acquainted with Owen's theories. In his *Voyage to Icaria* (1840) he outlined in minute detail his plan for a totally regulated community. Such imaginary communities had been popular in the eighteenth century, the best known, as well as the most terrifying, having been described in Abbé Morelly's book, *Code de la nature* (1755). In Cabet's vision, as in Morelly's, there was no room for personal initiative of any kind, happiness being attained through the individual's complete integration into the community. Each citizen of Icaria was to be told when to rise in the morning, what to eat, how to dress, what to read, when to marry. It was regimentation carried to the point of madness. For the sake of minimizing social conflict and maximizing productivity, Cabet eliminated freedom. To distinguish it from the socialist and anarchist schemes of the time, Cabet's scheme was called "communist."

Another influential socialist thinker of the Romantic era was Louis Blanc. In his writings Blanc discussed the inability of the worker and artisan to gain economic independence under capitalism because the tools of production were in the hands of the rich. To overcome this handicap he wanted the state to establish "social workshops" that would furnish the workers with all that was required for industrial production. These workshops, operating under the direction of workers and serving their interests, would in time, Blanc believed, prove their superiority over capitalist-owned industries and create conditions of material abundance. Once this occurred society would ask every citizen to contribute according to his ability and reward him according to his needs. Blanc's workshops were instituted in a travestied form in 1848 as "national workshops," less from a desire to make workers self-sufficient than to keep the Parisian unemployed from rebelling. (See Chapter 4.)

Saint-Simon, Fourier, Owen, Cabet, and Blanc are often called "Utopian Socialists." This pejorative term, coined by Marx to discredit his rivals, has no place in a scholarly vocabulary. The early socialists were often eccentric, and their schemes were often fantastic and chimerical. But underneath their wild Romantic visions one can discern a view of the future in many respects less "utopian" than Marx's. They were the first thinkers to realize the social and economic implications of industrialism and the necessity of devising new institutions to cope with them. The disciples of Saint-Simon created sociology, the scientific study of society, and pointed the way to state management of economic development, a concept realized in the twentieth century. Fourier pioneered labor psychology, Owen the cooperative movement, Blanc unemployment relief. As far as the Western world is concerned, their view of the future as a gradual accommodation of society to industrialism proved more realistic than did Marx's prediction of class warfare and revolution.

Robert Owen had an architect friend portray what New Harmony, his model socialist community in the Indiana wilderness, would look like. Public buildings and botanical gardens are enclosed by a rectangle of members' dwellings. Owen's dream never progressed beyond the log cabin stage.

Marxism   Until the middle of the nineteenth century socialist thinkers sought to reduce social antagonisms and to create a world of cooperation. With Karl Marx and his associate, Friedrich Engels, this no longer held true. The ideals of harmony, persuasion, and peaceful evolution yield to programs involving deliberate violence. Marxism is the first modern ideology to advocate conflict as both legitimate and progressive.

Karl Marx was born in 1818 in Trier, a Prussian town near the French frontier, the son of a Jewish lawyer. When he was six years old his family converted to Christianity. Marx began to study law at the University of Bonn, but soon transferred to the University of Berlin, where he engaged in a broad program of study centered on philosophy. In Berlin he drew close to the Left Hegelians and was much influenced by their ideas, especially those of "alienation" and anthropocentrism. Marx had hoped for an academic appointment, but, failing to receive it, he turned to journalism. While reporting for a liberal Rhineland paper he became interested in politics and economics and the relationship between the two. Concern with these matters led him to current French socialist literature, then virtually unknown in Germany. Under its influence he became by 1843 a socialist. Later that year he moved to Paris and from there to Brussels, where he developed in the mid-1840s his own anti-Romantic, "scientific" socialist theory.

Marx detested the bourgeoisie—the "eminent spinners, extensive sausage makers, and influential shoe-black dealers," as he once called them. In Paris he published an essay called "On the Jewish Question" in which he identified the Jewish spirit with that of the bourgeoisie and called on Europeans to overcome both. Marx learned much about class conflict from Friedrich Engels and Lorenz von Stein. Engels, who became his devoted friend, was the son of a wealthy German textile manufacturer. He had spent several years in Manchester and Liverpool as his firm's agent, where he became acquainted with Owenism, Chartism, the Anti-Corn Law League, and the British labor movement. He summarized his impressions in a book called *The Condition of the Working Classes in England* (1845). Stein, a conservative Prussian jurist, brought out in 1842 an important study called *Socialism and Communism in Contemporary France* in which he summarized the teachings of French radicals and argued that the principal issue of the future would be class conflict between the proletariat and the bourgeoisie. Although Stein hoped that by an active social policy the monarchy could prevent class conflict in Prussia, his general historic conception could be used (and was used by Marx) to develop a positive theory of social revolution. Utilizing the knowledge obtained from Engels, Stein, and other sources, Marx developed an original theory based on the notion of class war as a constant and fundamental feature of history. In so doing he had recourse to economic analysis, and was the first socialist to fuse sociology with economics. This specific amalgam constitutes the essence of Marxism and the source of its great appeal.

The fundamental premise of Marxism holds that the relationship of men to the basic means of production determines human actions and institutions. This relationship is for Marx a dynamic, historic one—that is, one constantly in the process of development. Originally, in prehistoric society, goods belonged to all; no one owned anything, and men were equal. Gradually, however, certain people

Karl Marx and his wife, photographed about 1860. Marx fled the Continent after the revolutions of 1848, living the rest of his life in London in modest circumstances and working on Das Kapital *in the British Museum.*

succeeded in seizing control of the land, the basic source of wealth in an agricultural economy. By controlling land, they were able to enslave or otherwise subordinate the majority of the population and force it to work for them. In this manner early communism disappeared, being replaced by the division of society into classes and the exploitation of man by man. Henceforth, all societies have been based on class distinctions. Such societies surround exploitation with an elaborate structure of institutions and ideas designed to justify and perpetuate it. Among them are the state, law, religion, and the church, all of them, according to Marx, serving the interests of the class that at a given time happens to control the means of production.

Although it may appear that the landed aristocracy, having seized control of the basic means of production, could retain its privileged position forever, this did not in fact happen. Every economic system based on a division of classes and exploitation bears within itself the seeds of its own destruction. This is because the means of producing wealth constantly improve, technologically and otherwise, and at a certain stage outgrow the social system constructed on it. Thus, within the feudal system—a term Marx applied to agricultural economies employing unfree labor—there emerged an urban commercial and manufacturing class, the class of capitalists, whose power rested not on land but on money. The capitalist methods of production proved superior and eventually brought down the feudal system.

The triumph of capitalism over feudalism, assured by the French Revolution, did not abolish exploitation; it merely changed its character. The capitalists abolished serfdom and slavery because they found it more profitable to use hired labor, but in his own way the capitalist exploited the hired worker, just as the feudal lord had exploited his serf. To prove this contention, Marx had recourse to the so-called labor theory of value. The notion that value derived from human work was not new (John Locke was among its early exponents). Marx adopted it from the writings of the early nineteenth-century English economist David Ricardo. The theory held that physical labor is the source of all value: the commercial price of a product is directly related to the amount of physical labor that was expended on it. According to Marx, capitalist exploitation operates by appropriating a certain portion of the value that labor creates. The capitalist employer buys labor as he would any other commodity, that is, at the lowest available price, which in the case of labor happens to be the minimum wage necessary to keep the worker alive. This price—or wage—represents only a fraction of the value that the worker actually creates. If, for example, it takes wages of $1 a day to furnish a worker with a subsistence living, but the worker produces in a day goods that can be sold on the market for $5, the difference of $4 represents "surplus value." The capitalist, by appropriating it, commits in effect an act of theft. "Surplus value," which may be defined broadly as the difference between wages paid to the workers and the market price of the goods produced by them, is the basis of the capitalist system and the specific form of capitalist exploitation.

Marx devoted a great deal of attention to demonstrating the inevitable internal disintegration of capitalism. As the feudal system of exploitation had collapsed, so, he said, would the capitalist system. His principal work, the economic treatise called *Das Kapital*, the first volume of which (the only one to appear in Marx's lifetime) came out in 1867, predicted the inevitable collapse of capitalism. Marx's

Among the leading lights of the socialist movement gathered in Zurich in the 1890s are Friedrich Engels (fourth from left) and his friend Eduard Bernstein (far right), theorist of the German Social Democrats.

prediction rested on two related principles, "concentration" and "pauperization," both of which he adopted from the writings of the Franco-Swiss critic of capitalism Jean Sismondi (*New Principles of Political Economy*, 1819).

When it first emerged, according to Marx, capitalism had been a progressive force because it opened new markets and brought to the fore the most dynamic economic elements. Marx greatly admired the achievement of capitalism in its prime in developing an international economy and culture. In contrast to many early socialists, he also welcomed urbanization, having little sympathy for what he called the "idiocy of rural life." But he also maintained that at a certain stage of its history, capitalism became regressive. Under a system of unrestricted competition, the stronger and more efficient producers win out, and the means of production concentrate in fewer and fewer hands. Eventually, effective competition is eliminated. In this manner a fatal conflict arises between the methods of production and the social system resting on it: the method of production, highly concentrated, outgrows the capitalist system that presupposes competition and the diversification of ownership.

In the meantime the laboring force is steadily "pauperized," that is, impoverished. The labor supply increases with the constant accretion of small producers and traders who are ruined by big business. The more workers that are available, the more cheaply can they be purchased and the more ruthlessly can they be exploited. The rich grow richer while the poor grow poorer, a development that compounds the inner contradictions of the capitalist system. The larger the proletariat, the less money needs to be spent on wages; the less money is spent on wages, the more "surplus value" can be reinvested to produce more and more goods for which there are fewer and fewer consumers (insofar as the majority of the wage earners are growing poorer). The result is overproduction and economic depression that grow in intensity and frequency until capitalism crashes.

By the time capitalism is ready to disintegrate the means of production are already so concentrated that nothing is simpler than to nationalize them for the benefit of society as a whole. This event follows a revolution in which the proletariat seizes power and establishes the "dictatorship of the proletariat" of undefined duration. The new government destroys the bourgeoisie, appropriates its ill-gotten wealth, and introduces public control over the means of production. These measures lay the foundations of a new classless society. They open a new era for mankind, an era of return to the freedom and equality of original communism. When that age arrives the state dissolves or "withers away."

Such, in briefest outline, is the theory that Marx and Engels first announced in the *Communist Manifesto* of 1848 and subsequently developed more fully. Engels, in an introduction to a new edition of the *Communist Manifesto* published in 1883, defined Marxism as resting on the following propositions:

> That in every historical epoch the prevailing mode of economic production and exchange, and the social organizations necessarily following from it, form the basis upon which is built up, and from which alone can be explained the political and intellectual history of that epoch; that consequently the whole history of mankind (since the dissolution of primitive tribal society, holding land in common ownership) had been a history of

"Priests, monarchs, statesmen, soldiers, officials, financiers, capitalists, moneylenders, lawyers"—all of them, according to the anarchist Mikhail Bakunin, were "mankind's tormentors."

class struggles, contests between exploiting and exploited, ruling and oppressed classes; that the history of these class struggles forms the series of evolution in which, nowadays, a stage has been reached where the exploited and oppressed classes (the proletariat) cannot attain its emancipation from the sway of the exploiting and ruling class (the bourgeoisie) without, at the same time, and once and for all, emancipating society at large from all exploitation, oppression, class distinction and class struggles.

Critics in Marx's lifetime and since have pointed out numerous flaws in the doctrine: the unfounded historical assumption of an original propertyless and classless society, the inconsistency of certain economic propositions, and the improbability that the proletariat, at the depth of its supposed degradation, would have the capacity to assume power and establish a social order calling for exceptional moral and intellectual maturity. In particular, professional economists have rejected the labor theory of value on which the Marxist theory rests; outside Marxist circles it has become a historical curiosity. John Maynard Keynes, who of all economists has had the greatest influence on twentieth-century economic policy, dismissed Marx and Engels' writings as "out-of-date controversializing." But criticism notwithstanding, Marxism has exercised an extraordinary influence on socialist intellectuals and on much of modern thought in general. In an age dominated by the scientific outlook, it has provided a theory that, even if not considered scientific by professional economists, did use scientific evidence and methods of analysis. Engels, on Marx's death, compared his achievement to that of Darwin, meaning that Marx had provided a key to the process of social evolution as Darwin had done for biological evolution.

In London in 1864 Marx helped organize and acquired control of the International Working Man's Association (popularly known as the First International). Its purpose was to bring together representatives of the world proletariat to prepare for the collapse of capitalism that Marx and Engels believed to be imminent, but from the beginning it suffered from the controversy that developed between the Marxists and their anarchist opponents.

Anarchism Marx predicted that socialism would inevitably replace highly developed industrial and commerical capitalism; thus his ideology had its greatest relevance to countries with advanced economies, such as England and Germany. Anarchism, by contrast, appealed most to the economically underdeveloped countries.

Marxism and anarchism had much in common. Both advocated violence and class war and the replacement of one social order with another. Both desired the abolition of private property. Where they differed fundamentally was in their attitudes to the state and to intellectuals. Like the anarchists, Marx considered the state an instrument of exploitation and oppression and predicted its eventual disappearance. But between capitalism and triumphant socialism, he posited the transitional state called the "dictatorship of the proletariat," during which the new ruling class would use the whole might of the state to destroy forever the apparatus of human exploitation. The anarchists rejected this prospect. They repudiated political authority in all its forms, socialist no less than capitalist. The so-called dictatorship of the proletariat seemed to them certain to degenerate into a new instrument of oppression, a tyranny of intellectuals, the "most aristocratic, most despotic, most arrogant, and most evil of all" as Mikhail Bakunin, their main theorist, once put it. Instead, they advocated the immediate destruction of central government and the transfer of political authority to small communities or associations of producers.

Elements of anarchism can be discerned in the theories of Fourier, Owen, and Blanc, but the most important early anarchist thinker was Pierre Joseph Proudhon. Proudhon was an exception among socialist theorists in that he came from a humble family (his father was a tavern-keeper) and made his living from manual labor (he served as a printer). In 1840 he published *What Is Property?*, a frontal attack on the whole institution of ownership as the basis of man's tyranny over man. In this work and in his subsequent writings Proudhon predicted that property would disappear and give way to a system in which possession of land and productive tools would be vested in the producers, that is, those who actually did the work. (Possession is not a legal right, as is property; it means the right to use but not to sell or bequeath.) These producers would form voluntary associations that would enter into voluntary unions with other associations, until all mankind was linked in a single vast federation. "The twentieth century will begin the era of federations," Proudhon once prophesied, "or it will mark the beginning of a thousand-year purgatory." He opposed the nationalization of private property on the grounds that once the state appropriated wealth, its tyranny would increase: if it owned everything, everybody would depend on it.

Proudhon still envisaged anarchism as emerging gradually and peacefully from within capitalism. But after his death in 1865, leadership of the movement passed to Bakunin, who to an even greater degree than Marx espoused violence. The son of a well-to-do Russian landowner, Bakunin began his career as an officer in the army, but he resigned early and spent the rest of his life (when not in jail or in exile) traveling from country to country in search of revolution. He was an international figure, as well known in Spain as in Russia, in Lyons as in Naples. A huge, burly man with a wild beard and flashing eyes, he personified the archetypical revolutionary. His life was as spontaneous as the one he preached. He never had money of his own, preferring to live on loans that he immediately spent and rarely repaid. "Liberty he always proclaimed the great principle of living," writes a historian of socialism, "and assuredly no one ever lived with more liberty on so little money that was his own."[°]

Bakunin lacked the systematic habits of Marx and left behind no consistent body of doctrine. He believed in the absolute value of freedom, in releasing spontaneous forces held down by the weight of laws, customs, and institutions, above all, the institutions of church and state. He was a determined atheist, believing (as did the Left Hegelians, with whom he was associated in his youth) that religion was the worst instrument of oppression. Bakunin preached destruction, giving little thought to the order that would follow, because he considered destructiveness to be a great creative force in itself.

Although in his revolutionary strategy Bakunin relied on the industrial proletariat, he paid particular attention to the landless peasantry, the unemployed, and other *déclassé* elements. He felt certain that in the masses of the population

°G. D. H. Cole, *Socialist Thought: Marxism and Anarchism, 1850–1890* (1954).

This print was inspired by the suppression in 1843 of a Rhineland newspaper edited by Marx. Portrayed as Prometheus, Marx is bound to his press as the Prussian eagle gnaws at his vitals. The maidens despairing at his feet represent the various Rhineland towns served by the paper.

lurked instinctive social hatreds; it was only necessary to unleash the "evil passions" for the whole world to be engulfed in the flames of class war. He was much encouraged by the prevalence of banditry in the regions he knew best (Russia, Spain, and southern Italy), interpreting it as symptomatic of latent destructive mass instincts. Bakunin was the first radical to have realized the revolutionary potential of the landless peasant. By so doing, he made a unique contribution to socialist strategy, from which the Marxists, despite their rejection of Bakuninism, greatly profited later on. He mistrusted socialist intellectuals, accusing them of a desire to use the revolution as a means of seizing power and replacing the bourgeoisie as the principal exploiting class.

This emphasis on spontaneity was the crux of his quarrel with Marx. To Marx, Bakunin's program was utopian, for it failed to take into account the relentless spread of capitalism and the realities of modern class structure. He considered the anarchists exponents of the interests of the petty bourgeoisie: the small producer, the artisan, the peasant. But for Bakunin, Marx and his followers were laying the groundwork for a "knuto-Germanic empire":

> [The rulers of the socialist state], the Marxists say, will consist of workers. Yes, perhaps of *former* workers. And these, as soon as they become the rulers or representatives of the people, will cease to be workers, and will begin to look down upon the entire world of manual labor from the heights of the state. They will no longer represent the people, but themselves and their own pretensions to rule the people. . . . They [the Marxists] will concentrate the reins of government in a strong hand, because the ignorant people are in need of quite a firm guardianship. They will establish a single State Bank that will concentrate in its hands all commercial, industrial, agricultural, and even scientific productivity: and the mass of the people will be divided into two armies, the industrial and the agricultural, which will be under the direct command of government engineers who will constitute a new privileged class.

The quarrel between the two leaders of socialism often assumed ugly personal overtones. Marx accused Bakunin of serving as an agent of the tsarist police, sent to wreck the International. Bakunin reciprocated by calling Marx a greedy, scheming Jew. Their dispute led in 1876 to the dissolution of the First International.

Labor and Politics   Socialism as an ideology came into being in the middle third of the nineteenth century at a time when the future of the working class was uncertain and the violence of some working-class activities, especially in 1848, suggested the imminence of social revolution. It became an influential movement in the closing third of the century at a time when the laboring class was making unprecedented progress in terms of living standards, education, and political rights. Contrary to the expectation of Marxists and some other socialists, the proletariat (i.e., the impoverished working element), instead of growing in numbers, decreased. In England—the country for which Marx had predicted inevitable pauperization—real wages between 1850 and 1900 increased by an estimated 84 percent. In fact, the period 1850–1875—the very time when Marx was working out his theory of pauperization—witnessed the most rapid rise in real wages. A British parliamentary commission appointed in 1894 concluded after an exhaustive study that the proportion of persons receiving very low wages in England (that is, Marx's pauperized proletariat) had been "very much larger" fifty years earlier; their number had declined partly from general improvements in pay and partly from the tendency of higher skills to replace lower ones. The same held true of the second most industrialized power in Europe, Germany.

These developments confronted European socialists with a dilemma. Insofar as they had the interests of the working class at heart, they had to welcome improvements in its condition, and insofar as they hoped to gain the worker's vote, they had to press for more such improvements. But as they increasingly identified themselves with the cause of social reform, they became tied to the existing social system, and their clamor for revolution turned hollow. If they rejected reforms, they lost labor support; if they advocated them, they integrated themselves into the whole capitalist order and could hardly be taken seriously when they preached its overthrow.

The anarchists were less troubled by this dilemma than the Marxists, for having repudiated parliamentary action in principle, they had no need to adjust their program to please the electorate. Adopting a policy known as "direct action," the anarchists declared war on the existing political order. They boy-

Anarchists twice tried to kill King Alfonso XIII of Spain. This is the second attempt, in Madrid in 1906; a bomb thrown at the royal carriage killed twenty bystanders but did not harm the king or his bride (it was their wedding day). The bomb-thrower shot himself.

Carrying banners and a portrait of Tsar Nicholas II, Russian workers march through the streets of Odessa.

cotted parliamentary elections and sabotaged parliamentary assemblies. They also carried on a relentless campaign of terrorism against heads of state. Anarchist assassins murdered Tsar Alexander II of Russia (1881), President Marie Carnot of France (1894), Empress Elizabeth of Austria (1898), King Humbert of Italy (1900), and President William McKinley of the United States (1901). In addition, they slew scores of high government officials, including Prime Ministers Cánovas of Spain (1897) and Stolypin of Russia (1911).

Alongside sabotage and terror, late nineteenth-century anarchists had recourse to industrial unrest, aiming at the "general strike." The general strike was first conceived in England in the 1820s but was fully formulated toward the end of the century in France. Its goal was a simultaneous and universal work stoppage by all the trades. The "anarcho-syndicalists" expected the general strike to bring the economy to a standstill, cause a collapse of capitalism, and replace the state with a republic based on trade unions. In 1892 the French Congress of the National Federation of Trade Unions formally adopted the general strike as its goal; three years later the first French national trade-union organization, the General Confederation of Labor (CGT), pledged itself to abstain from participation in the country's political life. The French socialist Georges Sorel evolved a theory based on the general strike as a great social "myth" capable of uniting the working class and educating it for the class struggle (*Reflections on Violence*, 1896–1906).

In several European countries it was more than a myth. In 1893 the proclamation of a general strike by left-wing groups in Belgium forced the government to concede universal suffrage. In 1905 in Russia, similar tactics finally persuaded Nicholas II to grant the country a constitution. In 1909 in Spain, the syndicalists seized the city of Barcelona and held it for a week before they were dislodged by government troops. Echoes of the general strike were still heard after World War I in the great English strike of 1926 and in France in 1938.

Anarchism, both in its Bakuninist and syndicalist forms, acquired its greatest following in the non-industrial countries. It enjoyed particular success where democratic traditions were weak and where the population regarded the state as an alien, hostile force (Spain, Italy, Russia). It also won followings in countries such as France that had a large class of artisans and small producers opposed to big industry. These are the same areas that after the Russian Revolution of 1917 developed the most powerful Communist movements.

In the industrially developed countries the influence of anarchism, never great to begin with, waned, while that of Marxism increased. Marxism gained the upper hand over anarchism precisely because it was a more moderate and pacifistic and, one may almost say, a more respectable theory. Instead of throwing bombs, Marxists participated in parliamentary elections. Their leaders were undistinguishable from those of the "bourgeois" parties: neatly dressed, academic-looking gentlemen, in contrast to the disheveled anarchists. Whenever organized labor chose to collaborate with the socialists, it preferred to do so with the Marxists, finding them more stable and politically more adept.

In theory, Marxism should have rejected reformism, insofar as it postponed "pauperization" and, with it, the socialist revolution. But in fact, from the beginning Marxism contained two disparate elements: an uncompromising theoretical one, and a compromising practical one. Marx himself had welcomed the English Factory Laws designed to improve the condition of the workers, although it is difficult to see how he reconciled this approval with the belief that a deterioration of the working class was a necessary precondition of the destruction of capitalism. Be that as it may, his followers also tended to back social reform. By so doing they gained a foothold among the workers.

Germany was the first country in which socialists succeeded in overcoming labor's traditional antipathy to involvement in party politics. This was largely the achievement of Ferdinand Lassalle. Lassalle was less of a theorist than Marx and more of a practicing politician. He became convinced that labor could radically change its condition only by acquiring the vote and forming its own political party. He was instrumental in persuading Bismarck to grant universal male suffrage to Germans by arguing that the enfranchised labor would vote against the Liberals. In 1863 he founded the General German Labor Association, designed to unite all workers in a political party to represent them in elections to the parliament. Lassalle's eloquence and dedication, however, failed at first to break the apathy of German labor to politics, and at the time of his death in 1864 the association had only 4,500 members.

But the seeds were sown. In 1875, at the so-called Gotha Congress, Lassalle's

Proclaiming "The World Is Ours!" a German Social Democratic paper records the unofficial returns in the party's electoral triumph of 1890.

Labor Association merged with the German Social Democratic Labor party founded by several of Marx's followers. This merger laid the foundations of close cooperation between socialism and labor in Germany. The program adopted at Gotha did not entirely please Marx (who also had envied Lassalle's influence over German workers), but insofar as it committed organized German socialism and labor to political action it represented a victory over both anarchism and apolitical trade unionism.

Despite harassment by the government, German Social Democracy gained successes at the polls. It became the first socialist party in the world to carry weight in parliamentary politics. In 1877 it won nearly 500,000 votes and 12 seats in the Reichstag in its first national election. This unexpected strength induced Bismarck to pass an Anti-Socialist Law (see Chapter 9). In 1890, when the Reichstag allowed the Anti-Socialist Law to lapse, German Social Democracy began its triumphant advance. In 1890 it gained 1.4 million votes and 35 seats in the Reichstag, in 1893 1.8 million votes and 44 seats, in 1898 2.1 million votes and 60 seats. Neither various obstacles placed in its path by the government nor attempts to block its progress by National Liberals and Conservatives succeeded in stopping the relentless advance of the socialist movement. In 1903 the Social Democratic party polled 3 million votes and gained 81 seats—nearly a third of the votes cast and as much as the next two parties combined. These electoral triumphs stimulated the emergence all over Europe of Social Democratic parties patterned on the German model.

German Social Democracy owed much success to superb organization. It offered its adherents not only an election ticket and program but a whole way of life. It ran a gigantic publishing enterprise, welfare and insurance agencies, clubs and associations, and even its own taverns. This comprehensive program of activity helped the party gain the loyalty of half the trade-union membership—a figure not duplicated in any other country—and induced it in 1906 to acknowledge trade unions as a progressive force. From its rich treasury the party also subsidized several poorer foreign Social Democratic organizations.

A party of such scope and resources, capable of spending millions of marks on a single national election, required a large professional staff. The more successful its candidates proved at the polls, the fatter its treasury, the longer its membership rolls, the more the party needed a regular bureaucratic apparatus. Robert Michels, in his study *Political Parties* (1915), concluded that Social Democracy did not escape the fate of its conservative and liberal counterparts: like them, it gave rise to a professional élite of organizers and politicians who lost contact with the electorate. He was especially struck by the speed with which socialist politicians of worker background acquired "bourgeois" characteristics.

English labor turned to politics from disappointment with the Liberal party. The first labor candidates made their appearance in the 1870s to protest the passage of the so-called Criminal Law Amendment Act (1871), which gave judges the right to decide when a strike or picketing constituted "intimidation" and was subject to criminal prosecution. To punish the Liberals for sponsoring this law, the trade unions put up candidates for the election of 1874 and gave much support to the Conservatives. The defection of labor voters cost the Liberals this election, and the next year the Criminal Law Amendment Act was repealed.

The trade unions gradually concluded that their interests required political action. In 1899 they decided to participate in elections, though they had as yet no clear idea how to go about it. Labor's resolute entry into British politics is generally attributed to another legal landmark, the Taff Vale judgment rendered by Parliament in 1902. This decision made a union financially liable for the acts of its members, even when they acted without its authorization. Angered by this blow at the essence of trade unionism, the leaders of the unions decided to enter Parliament in sufficient numbers to be able to exert pressure on labor's behalf. The "Labour party" participated in elections for the first time in 1905. It won 29 seats. This election marked the beginning of a fundamental transformation in the structure of British party politics: eighteen years later Labour was to secure a parliamentary majority, form a cabinet, and replace the Liberal party as the main opponent of the Conservatives.

Neither German nor British parliamentary labor deputies worked for the socialist goals of the abolition of private property and the transfer of the means of production to the state. Rather, they fought conventionally for social reforms. The greater were their successes at the polls, the more moderate became their demands, for to win votes they had to appeal to the largest electorate, and this meant toning down radicalism in favor of liberal and democratic slogans. Successful socialist parties tended to liberalize, and in some countries (e.g., Germany and Belgium) they assumed the role traditionally performed by liberal parties.

In the 1880s and 1890s most European countries had their own socialist parties. The majority of these were linked by means of the Second International, formed in Paris in 1889. (Anarchists, however, were excluded.) The Second International advocated active participation of socialists in parliamentary elections where the workers possessed the suffrage and a struggle for universal suffrage where they did not. The Second International dominated the socialist movement during the quarter of a century from its formation to the outbreak of the war. It held regular congresses at which socialists of various nations gathered to discuss common problems and to plan common strategy.

Socialist Revisionism

As the century drew to a close it was becoming apparent that the theory underlying the socialist movement bore little relation to its practices. In theory revolutionary, the movement was in practice reformist. It remained doctrinally committed to the concept of "pauperization," although in reality the gap between the employer and the worker was steadily narrowing. Many socialists realized this discrepancy but hesitated to do anything about it, partly from inertia bred by success, partly from fear of tampering with a doctrine believed scientifically validated for all time.

The first to take cognizance of the changes in social conditions brought about by advanced industrialism was a group of English intellectuals gathered in the "Fabian Society." Composed of outstanding intellectuals led by Sidney Webb and including George Bernard Shaw, the Fabians revived English socialism, dormant since the days of Robert Owen. Constituted into an organization in 1883–1884 for the purpose of propagating socialist ideas, they brought out in 1889 a volume of *Fabian Essays*, the first manifesto of "revisionism" in the socialist movement. (Their name derived from Fabius Cunctator, the Roman general known for his dilatory tactics against Hannibal.) The principal essay in the collection, written by Sidney Webb, represented a reversion to the central idea of the Romantics: socialism would emerge from an evolution of the existing economy, not from its destruction. Webb maintained that the whole development of modern life—the extension of the franchise, the growth of joint-stock companies, the state's assumption of responsibility for social welfare, etc.—steadily broadened the scope of public authority at the expense of private. Society was gradually, inexorably, almost unwittingly taking over tasks once entrusted to individuals. In this manner, and in this manner only, could socialism triumph; it had to grow, it could not be engineered. Since time was working for socialism, they urged slow, "Fabian" tactics.

The Fabians were not Marxists, and for this reason their *Essays* did not cause much stir among Continental Social Democrats. But they impressed Eduard Bernstein, a German socialist then residing in England, a friend of Engels, and a leading theorist of German Social Democracy. In 1898 Bernstein stunned his German colleagues by proposing that the party formally disassociate itself from the "disaster theory," that is, from the view that capitalism would collapse violently from the force of its internal contradictions. In his chief work, *The Premises of Socialism and the Tasks of Social Democracy* (1899; published in English as *Evolutionary Socialism*), Bernstein denied that capitalism continuously disintegrated from economic depressions, that big business was taking over,

Beatrice and Sidney Webb were major figures in the Fabian socialist movement in Britain. The Fabian method —"gradually permeating cultivated people with our own aspirations"— was more intellectual than activist.

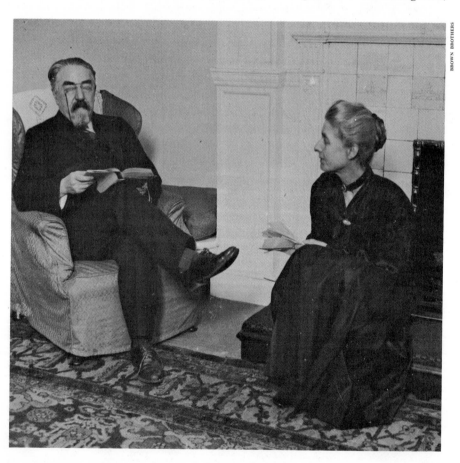

and that the proletariat was becoming pauperized. Capitalist society was fundamentally healthy, he asserted. Drawing on Fabian arguments, Bernstein charged his colleagues with utopianism for adhering to the vision of a sudden leap from capitalism to socialism. Bernstein professed to remain a Marxist but insisted that, like any other scientific theory, Marxism had to be verified by empirical evidence or degenerate into sterile dogma.

A few years earlier the German Social Democrats had adopted a new party program (Bernstein had participated in its drafting) committing them to the "disaster theory." With it they had won several electoral triumphs. Not surprisingly, therefore, they rejected Bernstein's proposal. So did the Amsterdam Congress of the Second International (1904). Nonetheless, Social Democrats everywhere increasingly acted in accord with the principles laid down by the Fabians and the Bernsteinian revisionists. In the happy formula of Karl Kautsky, the leading theorist of German Marxism, Social Democracy was a "revolutionary party, but not a party that made revolutions." Whenever it was expedient, socialists collaborated with "bourgeois" parties; in Belgium (1911–1912) they formed joint electoral blocs. With the growing number of socialist deputies sitting in European parliaments, it was inevitable that sooner or later they would enter cabinets and perhaps even form ministries. The first contingency was in fact realized in France in 1899, when the socialist Alexandre Millerand, to the dismay of many of his colleagues, accepted a post as Minister of Commerce in an ordinary "bourgeois" cabinet.

The myth of proletarian or socialist internationalism was as unrealistic as the myths of "pauperization" and "capitalist collapse." According to Marx, the interests of the working class, and of the socialists as its vanguard, cut across national lines. This belief lay behind the founding of the Socialist International, whose leaders time and again proclaimed their opposition to the diplomatic and military intrigues of their national governments and pledged themselves to resist war. At the height of the Russo-Japanese conflict of 1904, the Russian and Japanese delegates at the Amsterdam Congress of the Second International demonstratively shook hands in front of the assembled audience. The gesture brought a storm of applause, but it merely underscored the unreality of the whole proceeding. The International was a loose association of socialist intellectuals, whose decisions were not binding on their respective socialist parties, let alone on labor as a whole. Its leaders were in their majority sincere internationalists; but the electorate to whom they had to cater was not. The German Social Democrats learned this lesson in the elections of 1907: having condemned the government's brutal suppression of a Negro revolt in an African colony, they lost 28 seats. Industrialism created great differences in living standards, and the working class of the more advanced countries felt less and less affinity with those of the less advanced ones (if indeed it had ever felt such affinity at all). In 1914, with a handful of exceptions, socialist leaders everywhere would vote for war measures they had pledged to oppose, and the workers would proceed obediently to slaughter their proletarian brethren.

E. Vuillard

9

The Crisis of Liberalism:
1870-1914

Liberal ideas and institutions reached the height of popularity in the 1860s. Although they continued to make gains, after 1870 their conquests became increasingly hollow. Long before the outbreak of World War I liberalism entered a phase of crisis.

The basic cause of liberal decline was the steady extension of political democracy. As we have noted in Chapter 1, the early liberals were anti-democratic. They mistrusted the masses, whom they considered ripe for exploitation by despots like Bonaparte, and preferred to keep the franchise restricted to the propertied and educated classes. Nevertheless, the pressures for political democracy proved irresistible, and the liberals had to yield to them. France introduced the universal vote in 1848, the North German Confederation in 1867 and the German Empire in 1871, Great Britain in 1884, Spain in 1890, Belgium in 1893, Norway in 1898, Russia in 1905, Austria and Sweden in 1907, Italy in 1912, Denmark in 1914. The democratization of the franchise altered the whole quality of European political life. Politics became mass oriented. To gain votes, parties had to appeal to the wage earners, who lacked the confidence and the security of the middle classes. These appeals were most successful when based not on individualistic, self-reliant premises of classical liberalism, but on collectivist ideas, whether socialist or nationalist or both in combination.

The extension of the franchise was accompanied by a widening of the scope of state authority. This phenomenon was caused partly by technological and partly by social factors. The railways, telegraph lines, telephone networks, and other utilities introduced in the second half of the nineteenth century required some degree of central control. The state either took over the management of these new services, or assumed responsibility for their regulation. The introduction of compulsory primary education also called for state intervention. So did the adoption of social welfare schemes, pioneered by Germany in the 1880s and emulated in most European countries. Only the central government could initiate, finance, and supervise programs of old age pensions, insurance against sickness and accidents, sanitary regulations, or factory inspection. The whole drift of modern life pointed toward centralization, and away from private initiative, voluntary associations, and local self-rule. It thus ran counter to the liberal contention that the less government the better.

The liberals were not well suited either temperamentally or ideologically to engage in competition for the newly enfranchised mass voter, and kept on losing ground to the collectivist parties of the left and the right.

The socialists have been discussed at length in the preceding chapter. Here suffice it to say that in the latter part of the nineteenth century they succeeded, in large measure, in appropriating the ideas of civil liberty and equality of opportunity which previously had served the liberals so well. In some countries (for example, Germany and Belgium) the Liberal parties virtually disintegrated, their

Édouard Vuillard's drawing L'Affaire Dreyfus, *almost poster-like in execution, depicts a riot in Paris' Place de la Concorde in the 1890s. It symbolizes the violent feelings engendered by the Dreyfus Affair and its divisive effects on the politics of the Third Republic.*

place being taken by the Social Democrats. Elsewhere (for example, Great Britain and Scandinavia) liberalism absorbed so much of socialism that it lost its identity.

To the right, liberalism now faced the challenge of a reinvigorated conservative movement. The conservative doctrines, which we examined in connection with the restoration era (Chapter 1), had been static and backward looking. They had rejected the industrial and urban culture, and the forces associated with it. This no longer held true of post-1870 conservatism. Like its predecessor, the new conservatism gave priority to state and society over the individual and exalted duty and order above rights and freedom. But it proposed to realize its principal aim—a strong state—by different methods.

First, the new conservatives were nationalistic, often virulently so. In the latter part of the nineteenth century nationalism broke its traditional association with liberalism and fused with conservative doctrines: it became a leading weapon in the right-wing arsenal. Modern nationalism no longer aspired to the Mazzinian ideal of an all-European brotherhood of free and equal nations. Rather, it asserted the right of stronger nations or races to dominate the weaker. It was xenophobic. It was usually also anti-Semitic, for the new conservatives saw in the Jew the embodiment of liberalism, capitalism, individualism, cosmopolitanism, radicalism, and many other things they feared and hated.

Second, the new conservatives acknowledged the industrial, urban order and wished to harness its forces in the service of nation and state. In particular, they used social reform as a means of gaining the support of the lower classes against the liberals. They often made common cause with the Church, especially over the issue of secularization of schools advocated by the liberals, but they were not pro-clerical as the old conservatives had been. On the other hand, they maintained close relations with the military establishment.

The post-1870 conservative movement spanned a wide ideological spectrum. In its moderate wing were statesmen like Disraeli—an imperialist and believer in alliance between aristocracy and the working class, but essentially a man with a liberal temperament. Farther to the right stood Bismarck, a typical "strong man" of the time, who defended monarchical absolutism by exploiting parliamentarism, nationalism, and even socialism—yet, for all his ruthlessness in fighting the liberals, a compromiser. On the extreme right were nihilistic nationalists, exemplified by the French publicist Charles Maurras, whose theories anticipated national socialism and fascism.

Socialism on the one hand and neo-conservatism on the other stripped liberalism of its broad ideological appeal. Toward the end of the century liberalism increasingly turned into a movement representing special interests: of the middle class in England, of the free professions in Germany, or of the intelligentsia in Russia.

An important factor in the general discrediting of liberalism was disappointment with parliamentary institutions. The parliament is the central organ of the liberal state, embodying popular sovereignty, and at the same time ensuring that the executive stays within its constitutional limits. Impressed by the achievements of the parliamentary system in Great Britain and in the United States, all European countries had by 1906 introduced parliamentary institutions. Their achievements fell far short of expectations. Except in a few small and rich states, parliaments on the European Continent neither won the prestige nor attained the effectiveness of parliaments in Anglo-Saxon countries.

We can isolate four distinct causes of this failure:

1) *The absence of ministerial responsibility.* The proper functioning of parliamentary institutions requires that those ministers who are charged with administration enjoy the confidence of the deputies, and resign when they lose it.° This principle of ministerial responsibility was not universally adopted. By 1914 it existed in Great Britain (where it had originated), in Belgium, the Netherlands, France, Italy, Switzerland, and the Scandinavian countries. It was absent in Germany, Austria, and Russia, the three conservative monarchies whose rulers refused to concede to representative bodies the crucial right of appointing ministers. Here the cabinet was named by the emperor and held office at his pleasure. This arrangement, under the best conditions, gave the parliament no more than a power of supervision over the executive; under the worst conditions, it produced constant strain between the legislative and executive, which sometimes brought government to a standstill.

2) *The absence of strong and well-organized political parties.* The parliamentary system presupposes the existence of an effective opposition, a kind of shadow government able to assume responsibility the instant the party in power is voted out. This requirement can be met only where there are effective party organizations, able to command parliamentary majorities and to enforce discipline among their members. In most Continental countries such parties did not exist. Instead, there were numerous groupings and cliques representing either specific ideologies, personal followings, or narrow social interests; they were usually small and loosely organized and rarely had the power to assume responsibility for the administration. In such countries the retirement of one cabinet was not followed automatically by another stepping in. Rather, it led to protracted negotiations between statesmen charged with the task of forming a new cabinet, between parliamentary factions, and even between individual deputies for the purpose of securing a workable majority. This procedure vitiated in large measure the parliamentary arrangement in the constitutions of France and Italy, the two major parliamentary states on the Continent. Cabinets composed in such a manner were artificial coalitions and as such inherently unstable. The resignation of a single minister was sometimes sufficient for the whole laboriously constructed cabinet to fall apart. The system also encouraged private deals and corruption among deputies.

3) *The absence of agreement on political principles.* The function of parliamentary bodies is not the resolution of questions of political philosophy; their function is to pass laws. This they can do only if there is broad agreement among political parties on constitutional principles. On the Continent powerful groupings, especially the anarchists and the extreme conservatives, rejected the entire parliamentary system and worked for its overthrow. Furthermore, in countries with minority problems, nationalists sabotaged parliamentary assemblies to gain independence. This was the case with the Irish in the British House of Commons, with the Norwegians in their Storting, and at one time or another with most of the national minorities in the Austrian Reichsrat. The clerical groups

°The American system, whereby the Chief Executive is elected directly by the voters, is rather exceptional.

also sometimes blocked orderly parliamentary procedure out of resentment over the secularization of schools. In France, Belgium, and the Netherlands this issue dominated domestic politics in the latter part of the nineteenth century.

4) *The inability of parliaments to cope with the increased responsibilities assumed by the state.* The extension of the scope of state authority, mentioned previously, required a staff of professional civil servants: parliaments were too unwieldy to deal with the day-to-day exigencies of running social welfare schemes or regulating the economy. As a result, the bureaucracy everywhere made spectacular progress. The German sociologist Max Weber was so impressed by its growth that he foresaw parliaments turning into mere adjuncts of an omnipotent civil service.

For all these reasons, at the turn of the century there was widespread skepticism about the future of representative government. For many Europeans parliaments meant petty squabbles, empty rhetoric, legislative impotence, and graft. Few, even among the conservatives, advocated that they be done away with, but there was a noticeable tendency to treat them as auxiliary institutions, as buttresses of authority rather than its foundation. Some thinkers now argued that the citizenry had neither the knowledge nor the interest to participate actively in political decisions, and that consequently power should be vested in an élite or "ruling class." This idea, later appropriated by twentieth-century dictators, was advanced by the Italian political scientist Gaetano Mosca as early as 1884.

In only one respect did liberalism continue to make significant gains, and that, was in winning increasing acceptance for the idea of civil liberty. In country after country restrictions on freedoms were lifted and the citizenry accorded equal rights. The European of the early twentieth century was freer than he had ever been before. The precariousness of his freedom in view of the steadily growing power of the state was not apparent at the time.

We shall now turn to the political history of Europe from 1870 to 1914, proceeding from countries that established the most successful liberal governments to those in which liberalism fared worst.

Great Britain   The outstanding feature of post-1870 British politics was the steady shift of the political spectrum to the left, toward democracy and socialism. The spread of the franchise accomplished by the Second and Third Reform Bills (1867 and 1884) forced the two major parties to abandon their predominantly aristocratic and middle-class orientations and to court the working-class voter.

As we have noted (Chapter 4), the Conservative party was virtually out of power between 1846 and 1874. After 1874 its fortunes improved considerably, and during the period 1874–1905 it held power for twenty-four out of the thirty-one years.

The driving intellect behind the initial Conservative successes was Benjamin Disraeli. An imaginative statesman, Disraeli offered the Conservatives a program and a sense of direction which they had lacked since the days of Peel. Disraeli's goal was "Tory Democracy," a formula denoting an alliance of the landed aristocracy with the urban proletariat against the moneyed middle class. It was with this alliance in mind that he persuaded his colleagues in 1867 to snatch from the Liberals the sponsorship of the Second Reform Bill enfranchising much of the working population. Despite his intellectual domination of the party, Disraeli had to wait a long time before he was allowed to form a ministry, for, being a converted Jew, a novelist, and something of a dandy, he inspired little confidence in the rank and file of Conservative politicians.

Disraeli headed one short-lived government in 1868, but his great achievements came during his second (and last) ministry. He was nearly seventy when called upon in 1874 to form another cabinet. In the following six years he introduced a series of legislative acts which, moderate as they appear in retrospect, marked a break with the tradition of laissez faire. Among these were laws authorizing municipalities to clear slum areas and construct adequate housing for workers, establishing elementary sanitation procedures, and increasing the power of trade unions. Disraeli also sought mass support by reviving the idea of imperialism, which had fallen into disfavor during the era of Liberal hegemony.

Disraeli's main rival was William Ewart Gladstone, the leader of the Liberal party and the personification of British nineteenth-century liberalism. The son of a wealthy Liverpool merchant, Gladstone had pursued the classical political career, moving from Eton through Oxford to the House of Commons. He hated injustice and oppression, whether at home or abroad, and fought them with a passion rooted in deep moral conviction. At the same time he was a pragmatic politician, skilled at parliamentary tactics and highly efficient in budgetary matters. A combination of preacher and banker, he had great appeal for the Victorian middle class and much of the working population. He failed, however, to win over the queen. Victoria despised him for his self-righteousness and constant moralizing, for addressing her as if she were a "public meeting." She much preferred the companionable Disraeli, who prepared for her political reports that read like novels.

Gladstone headed four ministries (1868–1874, 1880–1885, 1886, 1892–1894). Under his leadership the Commons passed measures extending public assistance to schools, abolishing the purchase of army commissions, introducing examinations for candidates to the Civil Service, and establishing the secret vote. These laws had the common purpose of doing away with privilege and creating equal opportunity. Gladstone also led the fight against the remaining religious restrictions on membership in Parliament. In 1884 he introduced the Third Reform Bill, which gave the vote to four out of five male adults.

Gladstone's favorite cause, the one that offered the greatest outlets for his passion for justice, was Ireland. He did more than any other statesman to curb abuses in Ireland and to pave the road for its eventual independence.

The Irish nationalist movement, which got under way in the 1850s, was heavily supported with men and money by Irish immigrants in the United States. In 1858 they formed in New York the Fenian Brotherhood, the first major organization dedicated to the task of fighting for Irish independence. The nationalists in Ireland gained a strong following in the countryside after the passage of the Ballot Act in 1872 which, by making voting secret, prevented English and pro-English landlords from intimidating the voters. Shortly afterward there emerged in the House of Commons an Irish Home Rule party, which carried out obstructionist tactics designed to force Britain to grant Ireland independence or face a breakdown of parliamentary government.

Benjamin Disraeli, spokesman for the British Conservative party, shown in the 1860s, before his first ministry.

Gladstone set his heart on solving the Irish question. After various palliative measures failed to satisfy the Irish nationalists or to quell disorders, he concluded that nothing short of self-rule would set the matter at rest. He threw his whole prestige behind two Home Rule bills (1886 and 1893), the second of which would have made Ireland virtually sovereign. Both failed to secure a majority in the Commons. Irish politics continued to trouble Great Britain until after much violence it conceded Ireland independence (1921–1922).

The Disraeli-Gladstone rivalry led to an important innovation in British party politics. Until then it had been the practice for British politicians to confine campaigning to their particular constituencies. But in 1879 Gladstone, outraged by Disraeli's support of the Turks, who were then massacring Bulgarians, and by his entire aggressive imperialist policy, decided to storm the country in a railway coach to attack the Conservatives and solicit votes for the Liberal party. This was the so-called Midlothian campaign (named after Gladstone's constituency), a landmark in the evolution of British politics. The Liberals won the election, and from then on both parties regularly conducted national campaigns and put up candidates in as many constituencies as possible, forming regular party organizations. Politics ceased to be an avocation and became a profession.

The Conservatives never had much success with "Tory Democracy," for the working population supported first the Liberals, and then the Labourites. They were more successful with imperialism, the second component of Disraeli's policy. The voters responded favorably to the party's appeal to their pride in Britain's colonial accomplishment. The leading proponent of imperialism after Disraeli's death (1881) was Joseph Chamberlain, a Birmingham manufacturer who had broken with the Liberals over their pro-Irish policy and joined the so-called Liberal Unionist party, which he helped form in 1886. He cooperated with the Conservatives and served in their cabinets. Chamberlain urged closer ties with the overseas possessions, including tariff preferences for colonies. He also urged vigorous expansion in Africa.

The cause of social reform, which the Conservatives had abandoned after Disraeli, was taken up by the Liberals. In identifying themselves with this policy, the Liberals were in some measure motivated by a desire to neutralize the threat of the Labour party, which had emerged at the turn of the century and immediately cut into the workingman's vote. But beyond this pragmatic factor lay deeper reasons. In the second half of the nineteenth century a large part of liberal opinion had become persuaded that one could not depend on diligence, sobriety, thrift, and other middle-class virtues in themselves to solve social problems. The initial handicaps of poverty and ignorance were so great that for a large part of the population the noble ideals of liberalism had no meaning. Genuine freedom presupposed security, and general security could be achieved only if society came to the aid of the less fortunate. The evolution in liberal thought from stress on freedom to stress on equality and social justice can be traced in the writings of the leading English liberal theorist, John Stuart Mill. Beginning as a classic liberal, Mill in his later writings (he died in 1873) urged the state to equalize the distribution of wealth by means of taxation on inherited property and by social laws. The task indeed was great: a contemporary writer estimated that almost one-half of the income of the United Kingdom went to one-ninth of the population, and over half of Britain's capital belonged to one-seventeenth.

The development of the Liberal party occurred along the lines charted in the later writings of Mill and the contemporary German "state socialists" (see below). In the elections of 1906 the Liberals went to the voters with a program that included a bold scheme of social reform, diametrically opposed to laissez faire. They won a sweeping victory and immediately introduced a series of bills that marked the inauguration of welfare measures in Great Britain. The purpose of these measures was frankly declared by a Liberal spokesman to be a "greater equalization of wealth." These laws gave the worker protection against injury suffered during work, allowed him to engage in peaceful picketing, and gave him an old age pension upon reaching the age of seventy. They also fixed procedures for enforcing minimum wages.

This legislation ran into a great deal of opposition, because it violated the fundamental principles of that liberal ideology which had dominated British life for nearly a century. The controversy seethed during the first three years of the new administration and exploded in 1909. In preparing the budget for that year, David Lloyd George, the Chancellor of the Exchequer, found that he lacked money to pay for two extraordinary expenditures: naval construction necessitated by competition with Germany (Chapter 10), and old age pensions. To raise additional revenue, he drafted a "People's Budget," a revolutionary measure designed both to raise revenue and to achieve a certain degree of social leveling. Its most controversial provision called for heavy taxation of so-called unearned income, such as inherited wealth and profits accruing from the rise in the value of real estate. This proposal aroused vehement protests, especially in the House of Lords, which rejected the budget. A constitutional crisis ensued, which

Gladstone disconcerted his opponents and shocked Queen Victoria by conducting a whistle-stop campaign in 1879. He continued to follow the practice; he is shown here in 1885.

only ended two years later with the passage of the Parliament Act (1911) that reduced permanently the power of the House of Lords so that it could thenceforth delay but not veto laws passed by the Commons.

The remarkable pliancy of British parties and institutions gave the country a stability and cohesion that few others possessed. There were strains—the Irish question, industrial unrest (especially acute in 1911–1912), and great disparities in wealth—but all in all the system functioned remarkably well.

The Smaller Democracies   Next to Britain liberalism established itself best in the small states of western and northern Europe: Switzerland, Belgium, Holland, and the Scandinavian kingdoms. Being compact and relatively unpopulous—the number of their inhabitants in 1910 ranged from 2.5 to 7.5 million—these countries were able to preserve the close relationship between voters and government that was no longer possible in the more populated countries. Indeed, in some Swiss cantons government continued to be based on "direct democracy," that is, on the personal participation of the entire citizenry in legislative processes. Prosperity and a high level of literacy also played their part; so did that imponderable, the liberal "spirit"—the attitude of tolerance for dissenting opinion and respect for law without which, in the ultimate analysis, self-government is not possible.

The tendency in these six countries was for liberal forces to move toward political and social democracy, and for the state to gain power.

Switzerland was particularly successful in working out its political problems. In the first half of the nineteenth century it had been organized as a loose confederation of twenty-two cantons, some liberal, others conservative, subject to a bare minimum of central control. By midcentury such decentralization was no longer satisfactory. The country had to construct an exceptionally complex and expensive system of railways and hydroelectric stations, and to organize a national army able to resist the forces of the neighboring great powers—tasks beyond the capacity of the self-governing cantons. Accordingly, in 1874 Switzerland revamped its constitution, adopting a federal system like that of the United States, with a strong central executive. Peculiar to it was the use of national referenda as a means of assuring popular participation in important legislative acts. At the end of the century Switzerland introduced a number of social welfare measures.

In the Low Countries in the latter part of the nineteenth century political conflicts revolved around the issue of school secularization. In the Netherlands the Catholics allied themselves with their arch-enemies, the conservative Calvinists, to prevent the separation of church and state and the assertion of public control over schools pressed by the Liberals. In Belgium the school controversy was long and bitter, and ultimately led to the crushing of the Liberal party. In 1879 the Belgian Liberals passed an education act disqualifying church schools from receiving public funds. This move caused the Clerical party to defect from the Liberals, with whom they had hitherto jointly dominated Belgian politics. In the election of 1880 the Clericals won a majority. They then passed a new education act, extending state support to church schools in predominantly Catholic districts. In 1895 religious instruction in schools was made compulsory. The Liberals rapidly lost strength and virtually disappeared from the political scene, while the traditional anti-clerical forces gathered around the Labor party.

In Scandinavia one of the principal political controversies centered around the desire of Norway to separate from Sweden, to which it had been subjected since 1815. Although enjoying virtually complete autonomy, including a separate parliament and ministry, the Norwegians no longer wanted to be subject to the authority of the Swedish king. For several decades this controversy caused great tension between Oslo and Stockholm. In 1905 the Norwegians unilaterally proclaimed their independence, whereupon the Swedes gave their assent—a unique instance of peaceful separation of one nationality from another.

The Scandinavian countries became converted to liberal and democratic institutions slowly, but at least without the backsliding characteristic of states in which the transition occurred suddenly. In the first half of the nineteenth century Sweden was one of the more conservative countries in Europe. Its liberalization began in 1864 with the promulgation of a constitution and the establishment of a two-chamber parliament. The franchise was restricted. The three Scandinavian monarchies adopted parliamentary government and universal suffrage only in the twentieth century (Norway 1898, 1905; Sweden, 1907; Denmark, 1914–1915).

The Scandinavians were among the first to introduce schemes of social reform modeled on those of Germany. Between 1886 and 1892 the Danes enacted national programs of unemployment and health insurance and pensions for the aged. The Swedes took some steps in this direction in the 1880s, but they did so in earnest only in the decade preceding World War I. At this time they passed laws

A French view of the European scene in 1870. Militant Prussia dominates the Continent, crushing Austria and threatening France, who draws his sword in defense. To the east lurks the Russian giant; to the west the Irish problem worries Britain.

providing for the protection of workers, for the settlement of labor disputes, for assistance in home construction, and for old age pensions.

The Third Republic Superficially, France, with its parliament elected by universal suffrage and a responsible ministry, had a liberal, democratic government, not unlike that existing in Great Britain. No one questions that France was democratic in practice as well as in theory, but there is considerable doubt whether the system prevailing under the Third Republic can be described as a genuinely parliamentary one. For reasons that we shall indicate, the Chamber of Deputies could not exercise the extensive powers vested in it by the constitution, with the result that a great deal of authority devolved on the bureaucracy. The French historian Daniel Halévy goes so far as to state that the Third Republic operated on two distinct constitutional systems:

> Republican France has in reality two constitutions: one, that of 1875, is official, visible, and fills the press—it is parliamentary; the other is secret, silent, that of the Year VIII—the Napoleonic constitution which hands over the direction of the country to the administrative corps.

The fundamental flaws of the French political system—the factors that largely vitiated the parliamentary provisions of the constitution—were the polarization of forces between an intransigent left and right, and the absence of effective political parties.

The Third Republic, born of one German invasion (1870) and killed by another (1940), had two basic political blocs, the Conservative and the Republican. The two differed over basic constitutional principles. Broadly speaking, the Conservatives wanted firm authority, preferably monarchical, allied with the Catholic Church, whereas the Republicans wanted a republic and the separation of state and church. These blocs were not parties, properly speaking, for they had neither structure nor discipline; rather, they were agglomerations of parties, factions, and cliques held together mainly by agreement on the question of church-state relationship. The Conservatives drew their support from the upper-middle class, peasant proprietors, and practicing Catholics. The Republicans had the backing of the lower-middle class, minor civil servants, urban and rural workers, and the intellectuals. The enmity between the blocs was sealed in blood spilled in 1848 in the course of the June uprising and again in 1871 in the suppression of the so-called Paris Commune.

The Commune came into existence as the aftermath of the Franco-Prussian War. Two days after Napoleon III had capitulated at Sedan (September 2, 1870) a group of Parisian politicians proclaimed the establishment of the Third Republic and appealed to France to defend itself against the advancing Germans. But the country at large had no more heart for war. Nearly two-thirds of the deputies sent to the National Assembly elected in February, 1871, favored immediate peace. On the basis of these returns Adolphe Thiers, the leader of the Liberal opposition under the Second Empire, initiated peace negotiations. In the Treaty of Frankfurt, concluded in May, 1871, France ceded to Germany the provinces of Alsace and Lorraine and undertook to pay an indemnity of 5 billion francs (approximately 1 billion dollars).

Among the varied works of the French artist Édouard Manet are portrayals of civil disorders. This is his lithograph of the summary execution of Communards in Paris by loyalists in 1871.

To much of the populace of Paris, worn out by months of siege, the results of the vote for the Assembly and the signing of the peace treaty were acts of national apostasy. Early in March Paris rebelled against France. The uprising was dominated by anarchists who desired the abolition of the centralized state and the transfer of authority to the communes, the smallest unit of French administration. They now proclaimed the overthrow of the Third Republic and the establishment of the Paris Commune. Allied with the anarchists were Jacobin elements. The latter reintroduced the revolutionary calendar of 1793, shut down churches and monasteries, and arrested prominent citizens as hostages.

The legitimate government drawn from the National Assembly and headed by Thiers was at this time sitting at Versailles. Its first reaction to the Commune was to sit back and wait. But when the Communards began to lynch pro-government prisoners, Thiers decided to send troops to quell the rebellion. As soon as the collapse of the Commune seemed certain, the Communards went on an orgy of slaughter and destruction. They set fire to numerous public buildings, and were barely dissuaded from gutting Notre Dame and the Louvre. They executed many hostages, including prominent clergymen. The spectacle that greeted the loyalist troops upon their entry into the city so infuriated them that they launched a massacre of their own. During the so-called Bloody Week (May 21–28, 1871), an estimated 15,000 Communards and sympathizers were killed. Subsequently several thousand more were exiled to a penal colony in the South Pacific. The events of March–May, 1871, left a legacy of hatred between the right and left that has poisoned French politics ever since.

A Conservative paper's comment on the Dreyfus case shows a Prussian officer manipulating a mask of author Émile Zola, a stanch Dreyfus defender, over the face of a Jewish conspirator bent upon the destruction of France.

After the suppression of the Commune France seemed certain to adopt the monarchical form of government, for royalists enjoyed an absolute majority in the National Assembly (400 out of 650 seats). But, unfortunately for them, the leading pretender to the throne was an "ultra," a man of such conservative views that he would not even consent to the retention of the tricolor as the national flag, insisting on the Bourbon white. In the stalemate that ensued, the royalists had to agree to the appointment of a President. In 1875, in view of the continued stalemate, the Assembly passed legislative acts that gave France a new republican constitution. The Third Republic established itself thus almost as if by default. The republican government consisted of a bicameral parliament, whose lower house (Chamber of Deputies) was elected by universal male suffrage. Executive power was entrusted to a ministry formed by a majority in the Chamber. The two houses, sitting jointly, elected a President. His powers were so limited as to make him into a virtual figurehead.

Throughout its existence the Third Republic suffered from the absence of political parties strong enough or organized enough to assume the responsibility of forming a ministry. The formation of a new cabinet each time involved negotiations of the kind described earlier in this chapter, and yielded highly precarious coalitions. The average life of a French cabinet before 1914 was one year; in Great Britain it was five.

The failure of the monarchists gradually sapped their strength and increased that of the Republicans, who for the next forty years dominated French politics. The Republicans put their main effort into reducing the power of the Catholic Church. In the 1880s they issued a number of decrees separating the state from the church, including laws secularizing public schools and requiring their teachers to be laymen. The clergy resisted vigorously, supported by the monarchists and other conservative groupings. Throughout France pro-clerical and anti-clerical elements entered into conflict. This antagonism found expression in the classic French confrontation between village teacher and priest. The Republican drive culminated in 1905 in the repudiation of the Concordat, signed by Napoleon in 1801, and the disestablishment of the Catholic Church. The Republicans also took overdue steps to protect the French working class. In the 1890s they passed laws fully sanctioning trade unions and giving the worker basic security. In 1911 they enacted old age pensions.

The Conservatives, who had once been so near victory, grew embittered by the steady advance of their opponents. They loathed the Third Republic, sought to discredit it, and plotted its overthrow. In the late 1880s the Republic faced great danger from a conspiracy formed around a nationalist general, Georges Boulanger, who prepared to seize the government and assume dictatorial powers. Though everything seemed ready, Boulanger at the last moment lost his nerve, and the plot collapsed. In 1892–1893 the Conservatives exploited the "Panama Scandal" against the government. The scandal resulted from the bankruptcy of a company chartered to dig the Panama Canal, in which a number of high Republican politicians were implicated. But the greatest anti-Republican issue was the celebrated "Dreyfus Affair," around which the whole political life of France revolved for over a decade.

Alfred Dreyfus, a Jew and a captain attached to the General Staff, was arrested in 1894 on the charge of treason. The evidence against him consisted of a document, allegedly in his handwriting and containing military secrets, that was said to have been retrieved from the German embassy by a French agent. Although there was no conclusive proof that the document in question had been written by Dreyfus, he was convicted, dishonorably discharged, and exiled to a penal colony. The fate of an unknown captain would hardly have aroused the whole country had it not become evident from the start that the Conservatives meant to exploit him to convict the Republican government of treasonable activities and to give vent to anti-Semitic feelings. The controversy divided France into two camps, the Dreyfusards and the anti-Dreyfusards, roughly corresponding to the Republican and Conservative blocs. Dreyfus' relatives and friends gathered sufficient evidence to prove that the accused was an innocent victim of a conspiracy to protect another member of the General Staff who had, in fact, committed espionage. Yet Dreyfus was not fully exonerated until 1906, because the Conservative forces had staked so much on his guilt. No other issue in modern French politics aroused so much antagonism.

The collapse of the case against Dreyfus did not destroy the Conservative cause, but led to the emergence of a neo-Conservative movement, whose leading theorist was Charles Maurras. Organized as *L'Action Française* (1899), the new conservatives propagated what they called "integral nationalism," extolling France above other nations. Maurras detested parliaments and democracy, which he considered incapable of providing firm authority. He adopted from the socialists and anarchists the techniques of propaganda and mass politics, and advocated a *coup d'état* leading to the establishment of absolute authority. In the writings of Maurras and his associates one can perceive clearly the roots of modern right-wing totalitarian ideology.

While being challenged by an exasperated conservative right, the Third Republic also confronted a constant threat from the left. The growth of a syndicalist movement dedicated to anarchist ideals and methods severely tested its ability for survival, especially in the early years of the new century.

An Anglo-Saxon observer, accustomed to judging the health of a country by the soundness of its legislature, is likely to underrate the basic solidity of the pre-1914 Third Republic. Owing to its wide distribution of property and an efficient administrative corps, France enjoyed greater political continuity and stability than the yearly shifts of ministries or the irreconcilable hostility between the right and left may indicate. The political system was not satisfactory, but fortunately for France its life depended less on the legislative branch of government than did that of many other countries.

Italy

The constitution of the Italian kingdom resembled that prevailing in republican France. The king, like the French President, was a figurehead, and power rested in a ministry formed by the lower house. The franchise was gradually extended until in 1912 it became universal. The Italian bureaucracy, however, was far less efficient than the French.

Political parties in Italy were casual and formless. The would-be Prime Minister could secure the required majority only by making "deals" with individual deputies, promising them patronage or other rewards in their districts in return for their support in parliament. Known as *trasformismo*, this system of "transforming" the opposition into a malleable body of adherents became in the 1890s the normal method of conducting government. The Italian parliamentary regime, writes H. Stuart Hughes in *The United States and Italy* (1965),

> developed in conformity with neither of the more usual European models. It did not take form as the alternation of two large parties on the English model. Nor did it evolve into a game of constructing coalitions among a number of parties basically ideological in nature, as in France. . . . The Italian Parliament degenerated into an amorphous mass of deputies, dependent on the skillful orchestration of an official majority-monger.

Needless to emphasize, such tactics had little in common with genuine parliamentary procedures. They served to bring discredit to parliament, and it is not surprising that Italian theorists were among the earliest and most outspoken critics of the whole representative system of government.

A bitter issue in Italian politics was the relationship between church and state. As we have seen (Chapter 4), Pius IX had opposed the unification of Italy, and after the Italian kingdom had annexed Rome in 1870, he shut himself up in the Vatican and forbade Italian Catholics to participate in national elections. Leo XIII, who succeeded him in 1878, was a man of somewhat more moderate views. In 1891 he issued the encyclical *Rerum novarum*, which affirmed the concern of the Church for the working class. Nevertheless, on political questions Leo XIII remained fairly intransigent as did his successor, Pius X. The relations between the Italian government and the Vatican remained unresolved until the Lateran Treaties signed in 1929.

Imperial Germany The decline of liberalism occurred nowhere as swiftly and with such disastrous consequences as in Germany. In 1848–1849 the future of that country seemed to rest in the hands of the high-minded intellectuals gathered in the National Assembly at Frankfurt. Fifty years later their heirs, divided, demoralized, and uncertain of their course, formed a minor party, squeezed between a powerful conservative right and an inexorably expanding socialist left. The collapse of German liberalism was a disaster not only for Germany, but for the world at large. In the second half of the nineteenth century Germany set the pace in industry, trade, technology, and science. It seemed to many a model state of the future. The withering of liberalism there contributed heavily to discredit the liberal movement everywhere.

A major responsibility for the destruction of German liberalism rests on Bismarck. Bismarck desired at all costs to preserve the unity of the empire. Afraid of the pull of diverse ideological, social, religious, and regional partisanship, he saw in strong, centralized monarchical authority the best guarantee of national cohesion. He was not against political parties and parliament as such, for he understood that under modern conditions effective government could not be conducted without them. But he envisaged them principally as sources of support. In his view the function of political parties was to speak on behalf of specific social groups, and that of the Reichstag to serve as a channel of loyal opinion and class interest. "I consider parliamentary *cooperation*—if properly

Bismarck, looking no less uncompromising in his retirement, was painted in 1895 by Franz von Lenbach.

practiced—necessary and useful," he wrote, "as much as I consider parliamentary *rule* harmful and impossible." Bismarck viewed resistance to the will of the monarch as an act of disloyalty and crushed it without hesitation. The result of this attitude was to create in Germany a widespread impression that opposition to the central government was morally wrong and unpatriotic. Such an attitude, of course, had fatal consequences for the cause of liberalism in Germany. A great German historian, Friedrich Meinecke, surveying the wreckage of his country after World War II, concluded that Bismarck, by destroying in Germans the capacity for responsible government, bore much of the blame for Hitler's rise to power.

Bismarck was able to pursue his illiberal policies by virtue of the German constitution, much of which he himself had designed. In theory the German Empire was a federation of twenty-five states, but in practice it was a unitary state dominated by Prussia. Prussia had five-eighths of the population of the empire and two-thirds of the seats in the Reichstag; it commanded the armed forces, and controlled much of the agricultural and industrial wealth. The king of Prussia was German emperor, and his chief minister was Germany's Chancellor. The Chancellor owed no responsibility to the national Reichstag. He was appointed by the emperor, and as long as he enjoyed his confidence he could rule the country with near-dictatorial authority. The power of the Prussian king within his own kingdom was unassailable. Whereas the elections to the imperial Reichstag were based on universal vote, the Prussian Diet was elected by a complicated indirect suffrage, which heavily favored the propertied groups and the landed aristocracy. Given the power that he enjoyed in Prussia, and that Prussia in turn enjoyed in Germany, the emperor or a man whom he chose to be his Chancellor could govern the empire with less interference than any head of state of a major European country except the tsar of Russia.

As we noted in Chapter 4, the Progressive party, the principal liberal organization at midcentury, disintegrated in the 1860s. The majority of its members formed the National Liberal party, which stressed the nationalism in its name rather than the liberalism, and supported Bismarck most of the time. It usually spoke for big business interests. The residue, consisting of genuine liberals, formed the Radical party, which enjoyed little influence outside the free professions. The Conservatives represented agrarian interests, mainly the land-owners from the east. The Center party was an organization of Catholics, generally conservative in its orientation, but opposed to excessive centralization and rather progressive on labor questions. Social Democracy formed the most powerful group on the left. Founded as a revolutionary organization, it gradually evolved, as we have seen (Chapter 8), into a party espousing liberal and democratic aims.

Bismarck usually got along with the Conservatives and the National Liberals and had no reason to worry about the weak Progressives. It was the Catholics and the socialists whom he feared. He saw them as foes of the unified and authoritarian German state and fought them ruthlessly, although with little success.

The conflict with the Catholic Church—the so-called *Kulturkampf* ("struggle for culture")—began in Prussia in the early 1870s and in time engulfed most of Germany. The pretext for Bismarck's assault on the Church was the promulgation in 1870 of the dogma of Papal Infallibility (Chapter 4), which he interpreted as a challenge, by the Church, to state authority. Behind his action, however, lay some pragmatic considerations. The German Catholics opposed excessive Prussian power and wished to strengthen the constituent states of the empire. They also maintained close relations with the Austrians and the Polish minorities in Prussia. On Bismarck's initiative the Prussian government expelled the Jesuits, dissolved other Catholic orders and associations, and placed the education of the clergy under state supervision. Recalcitrant priests were forcefully removed from their parishes. By 1876 all the Catholic bishops in Prussia were either in jail or in self-imposed exile. Bismarck also prevailed on the imperial Reichstag to pass a number of laws directed against the Catholics, including a decree requiring civil marriages. The Center party came into existence to resist these measures. Continued persecution of Catholics increased its following, and Bismarck finally had to recognize the folly of an attack on a church claiming the allegiance of more than one-third of the empire's population. In the 1880s he called a halt in his unsuccessful struggle.

While the struggle with the Catholics was at its height, Bismarck launched another political offensive, this time against the socialists. This action was inspired by the success of the newly formed Social Democratic party, which in 1877 had polled half a million votes. He responded to this threat with a double policy: a negative one, designed to repress the Social Democrats, and a positive one, designed to win over their actual and potential supporters.

In 1878, using as a pretext two attempts on the life of the emperor (neither, in fact, involving Social Democrats), Bismarck pressured the Reichstag into passing an Anti-Socialist Law. This act prohibited Social Democrats from holding public meetings, raising funds, or sponsoring publications. It did not, however, prevent them from running for the Reichstag. In response to the law the Social Democratic leaders moved abroad, from where they directed political activities in Germany and put up candidates for elections. It is a telling commentary on the difference between nineteenth-century authoritarianism and twentieth-century totalitarianism that while the Anti-Socialist Law was in effect, German Social Democrats continued to win seats in parliament and from its rostrum publicly to criticize the government.

In his positive program against the Social Democrats, Bismarck availed himself of the ideas of the so-called state socialists. These were mostly academic thinkers—their opponents sometimes called them "socialists of the [professorial] chair"—who accepted the premises of radical socialism but drew from them different conclusions. They agreed that capitalism deprived the worker of a fair share of the wealth he produced. But whereas the radical socialists wanted to right this injustice by nationalizing the means of production, the state socialists advocated social reform carried out under state auspices. They urged the government to achieve a better distribution of wealth by taxing the rich and legislating measures of social security. Their goal was a peaceful achievement of many socialist measures within the framework of the capitalist order. Their program provided the theoretical basis of the modern welfare state.

For Bismarck state socialism offered as effective a weapon against the Social Democrats as nationalism had once been against the liberals. To win the mass voters' sympathies for the monarchy, he initiated measures of social legislation. Most important of these were laws establishing compulsory insurance against sickness and accidents (1883–1884) and unemployment caused by disability or old age (1889). The money for these schemes came from contributions of employers, workers, and the state. These laws gave Germany the most advanced system of social security in existence, and were subsequently copied throughout Europe.

The political results of these policies, however, proved disappointing to Bismarck. Whereas the four other principal parties remained static, the Social Democrats consistently attracted the new voters, especially country people who, upon moving to the cities, first availed themselves of the suffrage. In 1890 the Reichstag let the Anti-Socialist Law lapse. The Social Democrats surfaced and in their first open campaign in twelve years showed that they had not been harmed, for they gained one-fifth of the ballots. In nearly every subsequent election they continued to improve their standing, and in 1912 they won almost as many votes as the other parties combined. Bismarck grew so alarmed by the socialist advances that in his last years in office he considered depriving the socialists of the suffrage, and even abolishing the Reichstag.

Bismarck's career came to an abrupt end in 1890. In that year he was dismissed by the new emperor, William II, who wished to take over the reins of government himself.

In view of the extraordinary power vested in the German emperor, the personality of the new Kaiser was a matter of some consequence. William was twenty-nine when he came to the throne. Raised in the Potsdam Guards Regi-

Britain's Punch, *equating socialism with anarchy, looked with favor upon Bismarck's Anti-Socialist Law of 1878.*

ment, he absorbed the values of the Prussian officer class. He believed in force, and the "survival of the fittest" in domestic as well as foreign politics. For party politics or parliament he had little use. "My *Reichstag* behaves as badly as it can," he wrote on one occasion (in his rough-hewn English) to Tsar Nicholas II, "swinging backwards and forwards between the socialists egged on by the Jews, and the ultramontane Catholiks; both parties being soon fit to be hung all of them as far as I can see." William was not lacking in intelligence, but he did lack stability, disguising his deep insecurities by swagger and tough talk. He frequently fell into depressions and hysterics, and on one occasion, after a humiliating defeat at the hands of the Reichstag, suffered a nervous breakdown. He was also incurably vulgar. An idea of his taste may be gathered from his fondness for practical jokes. The spectacle of his Chief of Staff, dressed in tulle, giving imitations of a ballerina never failed to double him up with laughter.

William's personal instability was reflected in vacillations of policy. His actions, at home as well as abroad, lacked guidelines, and therefore often bewildered or infuriated public opinion. He was not so much concerned with gaining specific objectives, as had been the case with Bismarck, as with asserting his will. This trait in the ruler of the leading Continental power was one of the main causes of the uneasiness prevailing in Europe at the turn of the century.

William did not help matters by his irresponsible public pronouncements. In 1891 he created a sensation with an address to army recruits:

> You have sworn to me loyalty. This means, children of my guard, that you are now my soldiers, that you have dedicated yourself to me body and soul.

Bismarck (center) playing host to the new emperor, William II, at his country estate in 1888. Two years later William dismissed him as Chancellor.

You have now only one enemy, and he is my enemy. Under conditions of present-day socialist disturbances, it may happen—which God forbid—that I shall order you to shoot down your relatives, your brothers, yes, even your parents. Even then you must obey my orders without murmur.

In 1900, when the Chinese Boxers murdered the German minister in Peking, William urged the following advice on an expeditionary corps dispatched to China:

When you encounter the enemy, he shall be beaten! Give no quarter! Take no prisoners! He who falls into your hands is yours! As the Huns under Attila had made themselves a thousand years ago a name that even today covers them with glory in legends and fairy tales, so may you establish in China for a thousand years to come the name of the German, that a Chinese never again as much as give a German a queer look!°

William unfortunately lacked a steadying influence at the court. His Chancellors were, on the whole, weak and ineffective, and the courtiers and military friends mostly yes men. The atmosphere surrounding the Kaiser was a compound of superciliousness and uncertainty in which voices urging moderation tended to be drowned out. A similar mood prevailed among the German middle class; it was elated by the incredible advances of the country in all fields of endeavor, and yet afraid that Germany might not win for itself in the world a place commensurate with its position and needs. The Social Democrats, who stood for democracy and parliamentary rule, were widely regarded as internal enemies; so was much of the working class.

In the Dual Monarchy, created by the *Ausgleich* of 1867, the basic factor of political life was national antagonisms. In the Austrian part the Germans clashed with Slavs and other ethnic groups, which outnumbered them two to one; in the Hungarian part the Magyars fought with the non-Magyar half of the population. The democratization of the franchise in Austria only made matters worse because the electorate among the ethnic minorities, responding to nationalist appeal, sent to the Reichsrat deputies pledged to uphold the national cause. The Magyars noted this fact and refused to widen the suffrage in their part of the state. In Austria real political authority concentrated in the hands of the bureaucracy, and in Hungary in those of the nobility. In neither half of the Dual Monarchy was the parliament an effective instrument.

The issue that aroused especial passion in both Austria and Hungary was elementary education. The introduction of compulsory primary schooling required agreement on the language to be used in the classroom. Minority intellectuals insisted on the use of native languages, sometimes coupling this demand with one for cultural autonomy. There were also disagreements over languages to be used in government offices located in areas inhabited by minority populations.

The imperial government made valiant efforts to satisfy the wishes of the non-German groups in Austria. It conceded them full civil equality, opened up to

Austria-Hungary

°These remarks were the origin of the appellation "Huns" used by the Allies in referring to the Germans in World War I.

them the civil service, and made considerable linguistic concessions in schools and administrative offices. In 1907 the Austrians introduced universal franchise. This was a courageous move, because it gave the non-Germans a majority in the Reichsrat. But nothing really succeeded, and at the beginning of the century there was a widespread feeling that the days of the empire were numbered.

As the century drew toward a close the Austrian Liberals, after taking the lead in enacting anti-clerical measures and legislation favoring the minorities, passed from the scene. The majority of German Austrians now turned toward conservative solutions; a significant minority shifted to the socialists.

The Germans in Austria felt themselves to be a group in danger of being outnumbered, outvoted, and inundated by the Slavs, Jews, and other minorities. They resented both the *Ausgleich*, which had detached Hungary and left them to confront a Slavic majority, and the introduction of universal suffrage, which had reduced their political influence. Some of them looked to the north for help, longing for a "Greater Germany" in which German Austria would be included. But Bismarck gave them no encouragement, for his foreign policy required a strong and integral Austrian Empire. National anxiety, therefore, found its main outlet in a powerful conservative movement dedicated to the assertion of Germanic supremacy.

A distinguishing characteristic of this movement was its anti-Semitism. Behind it lay the fear that the Jews were seizing control over the country's economic and cultural life. After 1867, when they received full civil equality, Jews had moved from all directions into Vienna and the provincial capitals of the empire, many of them fleeing anti-Semitic excesses in Russia. In the following thirty years in Vienna alone, the Jewish population grew from virtually nothing to 150,000 inhabitants, or 10 percent of the population. The influence of the Jews exceeded mere numbers. They controlled much of the banking that financed Austrian economic expansion. They also took over a good part of the urban retail trade. They rarely received gratitude for the economic benefits they brought Austria, but invariably had to bear the blame for economic dislocations and disasters, such as the panic of 1873 (Chapter 6). Much of the resentment of the Austrian middle class and the peasantry against the capitalist-industrial order that penetrated the country at the end of the century focused on the Jew as its symbol. Furthermore, Jews dominated Vienna's culture: they owned most of its daily press, and played a prominent role in literary, musical, and scientific life. Indeed, they were largely responsible for transforming Vienna from a charming provincial town into one of the cultural centers of *fin de siècle* Europe. Although anti-Semitism was on the rise everywhere in the late nineteenth century, it was nowhere as virulent as in Austria. In 1900 a bill was introduced in the Reichsrat making marriage between Gentile and Jew a crime under laws prohibiting relations between man and beast. At the time such a bill had no chance of passage; but it became reality thirty-five years later in the form of the Nürnberg Laws.

In the 1890s the German conservative nationalists founded the Christian Socialist party dedicated to fighting the Slavic and Jewish "danger." Its most popular leader was Dr. Karl Lueger, an anti-Semitic politician whom the Viennese repeatedly elected mayor, despite Franz Josef's refusal to install him in office. When the emperor finally yielded, Lueger launched a vigorous policy of municipalization of public utilities to remove them from the control of Jews and foreigners. The Christian Socialists and their conservative allies held great attraction for the upper and lower German middle classes in Austria. After the introduction of universal suffrage in 1907, the right-wing parties formed the most powerful voting bloc in the Reichsrat. Lueger's political tactics—a combination of nationalism, anti-Semitism, and socialism—greatly impressed a young drifter from Upper Austria named Adolf Hitler, who at the time was unsuccessfully trying to make an artistic career in Vienna. Later he declared Lueger to have been the greatest "statesman" of his time.

To escape the pressures of anti-Semitism many Austrian Jews converted to Catholicism. But a small minority, headed by Theodor Herzl, a Viennese doctor, proposed to solve what had become known as the "Jewish problem" by founding in Palestine a Jewish national home. Herzl's book, *The Jewish State* (1896), although not the first to make this proposal (it had forerunners in Russia and Germany), marked the beginning of Zionism as an organized movement. Thus the ideas that were to lead alike to the destruction of most of European Jewry and to the salvation of its remnant came into being at the same time and at the same place.

After the decline of the Liberals, the main proponents of political and social democracy in Austria were the Social Democrats. Theirs was the single largest party in the post-1907 Reichsrat, but they too were torn by national dissensions, a repetition on a smaller scale of what went on in the empire as a whole.

Russia

The Great Reforms of the 1860s marked a break with the thoroughly autocratic-bureaucratic government in Russia, but they brought no political liberalization. Russians enjoyed basic civil liberties but still lacked political rights. They remained the only citizens in Europe without a constitution or parliament—a situation the educated classes in Russia found intolerable.

In the 1870s the protest against the autocratic system took the form of an anarchist movement. Its leaders, mostly students, were inspired by the belief that the peasantry was ready to rise in rebellion and overthrow the existing political and social order. They were, like anarchists elsewhere, anti-liberal, in the sense that they regarded constitutions, parliaments, and even civil liberties as instruments used by the ruling class to solidify its dominant position. They desired the immediate abolition of state and private property, the transfer of land and tools to peasants and workers, and the shift of authority to associations of producers, as exemplified by the Russian peasant commune.° In their contacts with the peasants, the anarchists quickly discovered that the working people had a deep respect for tsar, state, and church. To undermine it, they launched a campaign of terror against government officials, culminating in the assassination of Alexander II in 1881.

As was often the case, radical excesses strengthened the hand of the reactionaries, who could now claim they had been correct in opposing the liberalization of the 1860s, since liberalism bred anarchy. In the 1880s the government

---

°These radicals are often referred to as "Populists," although they did not so call themselves, preferring the name "Socialist Revolutionaries."

veered sharply to the right. Alexander III, the son of the murdered tsar, was a firm believer in autocratic rule. He revoked many of the powers granted previously to organs of local self-rule, tightened censorship, and repressed any signs of political independence. The same held true of his son and successor, Nicholas II, who came to the throne in 1894. In an effort to win popular support the government condoned and sometimes encouraged anti-Semitism. From the 1880s onward, Jews were occasionally subjected to violent pogroms, which the police made no effort to prevent.

Notwithstanding strict ordinances outlawing them, political parties began to take shape around the turn of the century. The most influential was the party of Constitutional Democrats, formally organized in 1905, but in operation since 1902. It combined demands for parliamentary government and universal suffrage with a rather radical social program, especially on land distribution. To the left stood two socialist parties. The Socialist Revolutionaries continued the older anarchistic tradition: they wanted decentralization of government and the socialization of land, and resorted to terror against government officials. They enjoyed a considerable following among the peasantry. On the other hand, the Russian Social Democratic party was built on the model of its German counterpart. It demanded political democracy as its immediate aim and a socialist order as its long-term objective. Its principal adherents were among intellectuals and skilled urban workers. Russia had no single conservative party, but instead various reactionary, nationalistic groupings whose adherents treated all demands for change, whether moderate and liberal or extreme and radical, as conspiracies of Jewish, Polish, or "Masonic" origin. Although even smaller in the number of active members than parties of the left, right-wing groups enjoyed considerable influence on policy by virtue of their connections at the court.

Like Austria-Hungary and Turkey, Russia was a multi-national empire with numerous minority groups, some of which began to evidence stirrings of nationalist sentiment.

The most troublesome of these minorities were the Poles. Descendants of a nation that in the seventeenth century had dominated Eastern Europe, the Poles would not reconcile themselves to the loss of independence. The Russians had made several efforts to arrive at an accommodation with their Polish subjects, most notably in 1815 when they granted the duchy of Warsaw a constitution with broad internal autonomy. But these efforts failed, because the Polish leaders refused to accept any status within the Russian Empire. They not only insisted on independence, but on independence within the frontiers of 1772, before the First Partition, when Poland had extended "from sea to sea"—from the Black Sea to the Baltic. The Russians on their part could not acquiesce in a demand that would cut off their western provinces, with the result that through the century relations between the two nations remained extremely strained. A Polish rebellion in 1830–1831 caused the Russians to suspend the 1815 constitution; another in 1863 moved them to abolish Poland as an administrative entity and to incorporate it into Russia. At that time tens of thousands of Poles were expelled from the western provinces of Russia and sent into penal servitude in Siberia. The defeat of the 1863 uprising temporarily cooled nationalist passions in Poland. Many Poles felt that instead of fighting for ephemeral independence, they should concentrate on raising the economic and cultural level of the nation. The 1870s and 1880s were an era of such practical concerns. But in the 1890s nationalism in its political form re-emerged, this time in close association with socialism. And as the century drew to a close Poles and Russians once more began to clash.

In addition to the Poles, Russia had many other minority groups: Ukrainians and Belorussians, both of them Slavic and Orthodox, culturally close to the Russians but by no means identical; and numerous Finnic, Jewish, Turkic, Iranian, and Caucasian groups. At the end of the century, Russians proper (without Ukrainians and Belorussians) constituted somewhat less than 45 percent of the population of the empire. Although many of the minorities were not yet sufficiently self-conscious to advance national demands, most of them produced, early in the twentieth century, a thin layer of nationalistic intelligentsia. Influenced by the example of the nationalists in Austria-Hungary, these intellectuals began to think in terms of cultural or territorial autonomy for their ethnic groups. To these claims the imperial government usually reacted with repression and Russification.

Until 1904–1905 the imperial government managed to beat off challenges to its authority. But the failure in the war against Japan (Chapter 10) so weakened it that it was no longer able to do so. The military debacle encouraged urban unrest, which the government could not suppress because its armed forces were many thousands of miles away. By the autumn of 1905 the autocracy lost control of the country. Political parties, though still technically outlawed, began to meet in the open; censorship broke down; workers formed strike committees; the countryside blazed in revolt as peasants burned estates and seized private land. In October, 1905, the tsar, faced with the threat of a general strike, capitulated. He now issued an "October Manifesto" granting Russian subjects full civil liberties and promising the establishment of a representative legislative body. Having by this measure won the support of moderate groups, the government used the returned troops to stamp out disorder.

Conservative politician Peter Stolypin headed Russia's government from 1906 until his assassination in 1911.

The October Manifesto marked the second phase in the liberalization of Russia, the era of constitutional rule. The constitution ("Fundamental Laws") of 1906 provided for a parliament—the first in the country's history—consisting of an upper and lower chamber. The latter, called the Duma, was elected by universal and secret male ballot. The Duma had the right to debate and vote on legislation. No law could become effective without its approval. It also voted on the budget. But it lacked the power of appointing and dismissing ministers, who remained responsible to the tsar. The tsar retained other prerogatives, including the right to declare war and to direct the armed forces. In its principal provisions, the Russian constitution resembled those in force in contemporary Germany and Austria, on which it was modeled.

Although a phenomenon without precedent in Russian experience, the constitutional regime engendered great enthusiasm in the country. In the elections to the first Duma, held in April, 1906, the liberals (Constitutional Democrats) won a stunning victory, capturing more than one-third of the seats. The constitutional experiment thus seemed off to a good start, for, unlike the parties of the extreme left and right, the leaders of this party accepted the new order. But the imperial government, having regained its footing, had second thoughts about the concessions it had made when under duress. The tsar and his closest advisers never reconciled themselves to sharing authority with the Duma, and indeed tended to treat its very existence as something of an affront. The first Duma was dissolved after a session of ten weeks; the second, meeting early in 1907, after one of fifteen weeks. Furthermore, various devices were invented to bypass its authority.

Finally, in June, 1907, the government ventured on a virtual *coup d'état*, reminiscent of Bismarck's action in 1862. While the country was preparing for its third election in fourteen months, the government promulgated a new electoral law. Its purpose was to reduce the representation of the peasants, workers, and minorities and to increase that of the Russian propertied classes. The measure was incontrovertibly illegal because, according to the constitution, changes in the electoral system required the approval of the Duma.

Management of policy in the new government was entrusted to an able conservative politician, Peter Stolypin. Stolypin, who in many ways emulated Bismarck, believed that the function of parliament was to assist the monarchy. The new electoral law gave him what he wanted, a docile majority, and the next two Dumas lasted out their normal terms of five years each. With Duma support Stolypin took energetic steps to solve the persistent agrarian crisis. He abolished the laws requiring the peasant to belong to the commune, enabling him to consolidate his land holdings, and made various provisions to promote the emergence of a vigorous rural middle class, which he hoped would stabilize the countryside. But he had many enemies, and in 1911 he fell victim of a bullet fired by a terrorist on the police payroll.

On the eve of World War I Russia was a vigorous and dynamic country saddled with a backward-looking monarchy and an anarchistic peasantry. The economy had expanded greatly since the 1890s, the currency was stable, and the education of the citizenry was making rapid progress. But the political situation seemed insoluble, despite the great hopes awakened in 1905-1906. The failure of the imperial government to treat the popularly elected Duma as a genuine partner created constant tension, which benefited the revolutionaries. The hostility between the leaders of public opinion and the bureaucracy created for the revolutionaries a propitious atmosphere for agitation among the politically inexperienced peasants and workers.

Spain   It is an exasperating task to seek any meaningful trend in the political life of nineteenth-century Spain. Revolutions, restorations, followed by more revolutions and restorations, succeeded with monotonous regularity and without any discernible sense of progression. These events never failed to produce a great deal of excitement for those engaged in them, but they had little effect on the life of the population at large. In the second half of the century, while Spain ostensibly enjoyed parliamentary government and even intermittent universal suffrage, a traveler venturing into Andalusia was still well advised to engage a retinue of bodyguards.

Early in the century Spain had had a vigorous constitutional movement; the constitution drafted in Cádiz in 1812 by the anti-Napoleonic rebels had provided a model and an inspiration for a whole generation of European liberals. But the country, strongly influenced by one of the most conservative church establishments in Europe, repudiated liberalism and time and again helped reactionary elements to suppress attempts at genuine representative government. The army, which earlier in the century had been a liberal force, also gradually evolved toward the right.

Under such conditions the constitutional system established in 1876 after the accession of Alfonso XII turned out to be a farce. The guiding spirit behind it was Antonio Cánovas, a cultivated man with genuine liberal sympathies. Cánovas admired Disraeli and Gladstone but felt that his own country was not yet ready for a true parliamentary system. Until the population was sufficiently educated and prosperous, it had to be ruled by the rich. And since the rich themselves were divided into two camps, Liberals and Conservatives, Cánovas devised an ingenious plan. Under his prodding, the two parties decided which at a given time would govern and which would provide the opposition—an arrangement that saved them the trouble and expense of campaigning. Elections were mere formalities, which gave returns in accord with instructions sent from Madrid. On one occasion (1886), the government newspaper even carried the election results before the election itself had taken place. This elegant system of conducting government survived until 1931.

A complicating factor in Spanish politics was the tenacity of regional sentiments. Although Spain had no minority problem in the strict sense of the word, in some provinces, such as Catalonia, there existed a great deal of hostility to Madrid. These regions were also centers of Spain's incipient industry, where the anarchists obtained a powerful hold on the urban and rural proletariat and caused the government a great deal of trouble by organizing strikes and carrying out acts of terrorism. The country tended thus to split in two: a conservative and Madrid-oriented center and north, and a more radical, federalist east and south. In the Spanish Civil War in the 1930s the battle lines between the Nationalists and Loyalists would run approximately along the divide between these two zones.

The pseudo-parliamentary government, instead of reflecting the realities of the situation, papered them over. Power actually rested in the landed aristocracy, clergy, and army, which showed little interest in the common citizenry and lived as if Spain were still the proud possessor of the Netherlands and Latin America. Only a handful of intellectuals concerned themselves with public matters.

The Balkans and Turkey

The history of the Balkan peninsula was that of the disintegration of the Ottoman Empire. To stem this disintegration Turkish reformers tried to liberalize and modernize their government. They failed, and from the possessions of Turkey emerged several new national states. By 1914 Turkish holdings in the Balkans were reduced to the area immediately surrounding Constantinople.

At the beginning of our period, that is, around 1870, the Ottoman Empire still controlled most of the Balkan peninsula, except for Greece, independent since 1829. But its control over this domain was weak, for the Christian nationalities, incited by Russia, were growing increasingly restless. The attempt to establish a common "Ottoman" nationality embracing both Muslims and Christians (Chapter 4) bore no fruit whatever.

In 1876 the Turkish reform movement, or *Tanzimat*, reached its apogee. The

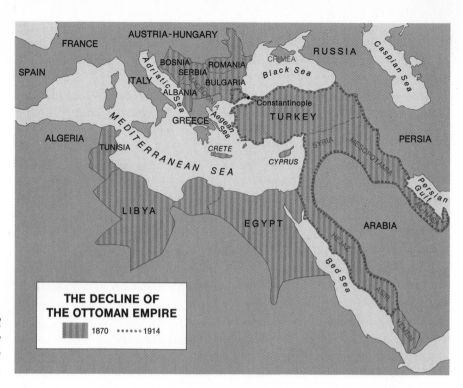

The Ottoman hold on Egypt, nominal at most by the 1830s, was broken by Britain in 1882. Tunisia went to France (1881), Libya to Italy (1912).

Balkans were then in the midst of a rebellion, and to quell the disorders an attempt was made to transform the empire into a constitutional monarchy. This measure was the work of Midhat Pasha, an experienced civil servant, who saw in liberalization a means of consolidating the empire. The Ottoman constitution promulgated in 1876 on his advice was patterned on the constitutions of Germany and Austria. It reserved considerable authority for the sultan, but it also created a parliament with a voice in passing of laws and budgets. The constitution aroused general dissatisfaction. The new sultan, Abdul-Hamid II, a ruthless man and an authoritarian ruler, resented the loss of absolute power. The clergy, Muslim and Christian alike, were displeased by the new arrangement because it deprived them of their authority over their respective religious communities. The bulk of the peasantry, of course, cared little about the whole matter. The main support of the constitutional regime came from the Westernized officials, burghers, and intellectuals—elements which the rest of the population called by the pejorative term *effendis*. The new parliament barely assembled when it was permanently adjourned by Abdul-Hamid. Midhat, who had been dismissed, was presently murdered, and the absolutist regime came back.

A critical event in the history of the area was the Russo-Turkish War of 1877–1878 (Chapter 10). Turkey lost the war, and at the ensuing Congress of Berlin had to acquiesce to painful territorial losses. Romania and Serbia, previously semiautonomous principalities carved out of Ottoman lands, were given recognition as independent states. An autonomous Bulgarian state was created, and Bosnia and Herzegovina were occupied by Austria. After 1878 Turkey's holdings in the Balkans consisted of little more than Albania and Macedonia.

The new Balkan states were in theory constitutional monarchies, but any resemblance to constitutional states as known from Western experience was coincidental. The usual method of settling political disputes was by recourse to arms. Disaffected groups frequently resorted to assassination and abduction. On one occasion the Bulgarian king himself was kidnapped. National and territorial disputes provided a constant source of friction.

The deterioration of the Ottoman Empire caused a succession of constitutional crises, none of which, however, resulted in stable and effective government. In 1908 Abdul-Hamid was forced by an army rebellion to restore the constitution of 1876 and to convene a parliament. For a while Turkey seemed at long last to be on its way toward a truly liberal regime. But the hope proved deceptive. In 1909 Abdul-Hamid encouraged a Muslim conservative rebellion against parliamentary institutions. The uprising was suppressed by the army, which deposed and exiled him. During the next four years, power was exercised by a weak sultan, Mohammed V, assisted by a cabinet and an assembly. The new government also failed to stop the disintegration of the empire. In 1912–1913, in the course of two successive Balkan wars, Albania became independent and Macedonia joined with Greece. In 1913 a group of politically-minded officers known as "Young Turks" seized power, and by ruthless means sought to suppress opposition in the center and borderlands. The intervention of the army in political life as a result of ineffective parliamentary institutions, first observed in Turkey, was to become a common phenomenon in Europe after World War I, and in Africa and Asia after World War II.

The instability of the Balkans was a source of great international concern, because it encouraged Russia and Austria to seek influence there. As we shall see, the conflict between these two powers over Serbia provided in 1914 the immediate cause for the outbreak of World War I.

The Ottoman ruler Abdul-Hamid was known as the Red Sultan for his ruthless methods and bloody repressions, a view reflected in a French print.

History has a built-in bias in favor of "crises." The historian cannot help but select incidents and trends indicative of conflict or disorder because they make for change, and change causes the flow of events, which is his concern. A narrative of political history between 1870 and 1914 may suggest a more desperate state of affairs than in fact was the case. To correct any such false impression, we must keep in mind developments other than political: the unprecedented progress in industry and trade, the constant rise in living standards, the spread of civil liberties, the remarkable achievements in thought and art. We shall then understand why, notwithstanding serious doubts about basic issues of domestic politics, the majority of Europeans looked confidently to the future; and why, in all, it was a good time to have been alive.

10

Diplomacy and Imperialism: 1870-1914

The period of fifty-five years separating the Congress of Vienna from the Franco-Prussian War (1815–1870) was one of relative international stability. During this time the great powers devoted their principal attention to domestic problems resulting from industrialization and the introduction of political democracy. Expansion was not fashionable. There was a widespread belief that mankind stood at the threshold of a new era in its history. As Herbert Spencer put it, the age of "industry" was replacing that of "militarism." International conflicts of that period—as, for example, over the legacy of the Ottoman Empire, or the unification of Italy and Germany—involved objectives of a specific and limited nature, usually territorial, and as such were negotiable. They caused shifts in frontiers without upsetting the European state system as a whole.

This no longer held true of international relations in the years 1870–1914. Issues dividing the great powers now became both more basic and ill defined, involving vague aims such as "spheres of influence" or "a place in the sun." The extraordinary growth of population and of industrial productivity gave rise to fears that outlets capable of absorbing the excess people and goods would soon become saturated. These fears pushed statesmen to the conquests of new land and markets. The spread of racial and Social Darwinist ideologies encouraged such tendencies by providing them with a seemingly scientific justification. Expansionism revived in a more ambitious and brutal form than ever, and the world entered a period of disequilibrium from which it has yet to emerge.

The most persistent cause of diplomatic tension throughout the nineteenth century was Russia's pressure southward, toward the Mediterranean, the Persian Gulf, and the Indian Ocean. This pressure encroached on British commercial interests and on Austria's territorial ambitions, and transformed the whole long southern frontier of the Russian Empire into a focus of keen international rivalry.

Russia's primary interest centered on the eastern Mediterranean, or, to be more precise, on Constantinople and the Straits. This concern is often explained in terms of a search for warm-water ports, but this reasoning is questionable, for Russia had neither a fleet nor a foreign trade of such dimensions as to require vigorous expansion. The matter may be better explained in terms of cultural factors. To Russia Constantinople was the source of its Christian faith and the fountainhead of its monarchy. Furthermore, Russians felt close kinship to the Balkan Christians, most of them Orthodox and Slavic. The European holdings of the Ottoman Empire were thus a natural object of aggrandizement, especially to the Russian Pan-Slavists who advocated a supra-national state embracing all Slavs under the scepter of their tsar.

The British reacted to Russian exertions in this area with an alarm that today seems quite out of proportion to the danger it posed and that can be explained only by the exaggerated notion they held of Russian military might. They tried a

Great Power Rivalry in the Balkans and Middle East

Germany's Kaiser William II (left) and Britain's King George V, in full panoply, leave the royal palace at Potsdam to review the garrison. The occasion was the wedding of William's daughter in 1913; it was the last meeting of the two cousins.

variety of methods to stop the Russians from taking over European Turkey. On some occasions they cooperated with them against the Turks (e.g., in 1827–1829, during joint action on behalf of the Greek rebels). At other times they rallied diplomatic support behind the sultans to forestall Russian designs (as was done in the 1830s and 1840s). When neither method succeeded, Britain had recourse to arms (the Crimean War, 1854–1856). All along, the British applied pressure on the sultans to carry out internal reforms as a means of solidifying their empire and making it more resistant to Russian pressures.

Farther east, the British and the Russians competed over the approaches to India. The border separating that area from Russia was not well known at the time, and there was genuine fear in London that Russian expansion into central Asia could endanger Britain's hold on the Indian subcontinent. The swift conquest of Turkistan by Russian armies in the 1860s caused consternation in England, which deepened in the early 1880s when the Russians began from there to press on Afghanistan.

The constant need to resist these advances created an unfavorable view of Russia in England and other parts of the English-speaking world. Indeed, most of the preconceptions held about Russians today in England and the United States were formed in the Victorian era, in the heat of competition over the Middle East.

Notwithstanding their defeat in the Crimean War, the Russians soon renewed their pressures on Turkey. The event that gave them an opportunity to do so was

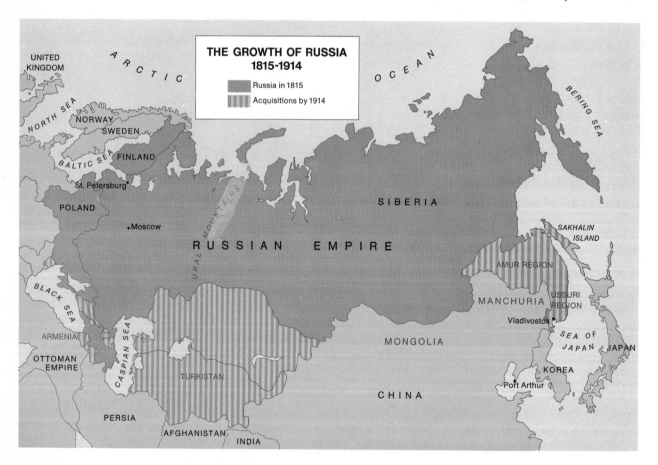

THE GROWTH OF RUSSIA
1815-1914

Russia in 1815

Acquisitions by 1914

the outbreak in 1875 of an anti-Turkish uprising among the Balkan Christians. The Turks reacted to the revolt with brutal massacres, which outraged people throughout Europe. There were great pressures on the tsar to come to the aid of the persecuted Balkan Christians, and in April, 1877, he declared war on Turkey.

The war at first went badly for the Russians, but eventually they broke Turkish resistance, and in January, 1878, approached Constantinople. The sultan, in the Treaty of San Stefano (March, 1878), had to accept humiliating terms. Among them was the creation of a "Greater Bulgaria," a Russian vassal state carved out of Turkish territory. The treaty virtually eliminated the Ottoman Empire from the Continent and assured Russia of undisputed influence in the Balkans.

The Russian victories and especially the peace terms caused consternation among the great powers. As the Russian troops approached Constantinople, Disraeli ordered British naval units to the Bosporus as a warning that he would not tolerate seizure of that city. The Austrians, too, showed annoyance, and threatened mobilization, although they had originally consented to the Russian attack in return for the Turkish provinces of Bosnia and Herzegovina. The Russians had no choice but to yield to British and Austrian pressure. In secret talks with London and Vienna, carried out in the spring of 1878, they consented to reduce substantially the proposed Bulgarian state and to give up some other claims to the Balkans. An international congress convened by Bismarck shortly afterward (Congress of Berlin, June, 1878), ratified these earlier accords.

Until the war of 1877 Russian expansion into the Balkans had run mainly into British opposition. From then on it met increasingly with the resistance of Austria.

Austria's interest in the Balkans was an unexpected result of the unification of Italy and Germany. The emergence of strong national states south and north had deprived Vienna of its traditional spheres of influence and forced it to seek outlets for its ambitions elsewhere. Such an outlet it found along its southeastern frontier, in the unstable regions adjoining the Ottoman Empire. From 1877 onward Austria pursued its claims in the Balkans with increased vigor, sometimes with active British and German encouragement. In 1881 Austria, by means of a secret accord, established a virtual protectorate over Serbia, and two years later it signed a military alliance with Romania. These diplomatic moves greatly perturbed the Russians. They were even more angered by Austria's interference in 1885 in the internal affairs of Bulgaria, a state the Russians regarded as their dependency. The rivalry over the Balkans in the 1870s and 1880s led to a deterioration in relations between Russia and Austria, and ultimately had profound consequences for the whole diplomatic alignment of Europe.

The tension in the Balkans, for all its implicit dangers, presented less of a threat to the general peace than did the post-1870 antagonism between France and Germany. The latter involved two leading powers with great military establishments. The quarrel between them, moreover, concerned not territories belonging to third parties, as was the case in the Balkans, but general issues that could hardly be settled except by a clear-cut victory of one over the other.

At stake, fundamentally, was hegemony over Europe. France had aspired to this hegemony since the seventeenth century and on one occasion, under

The Alliance Systems

Russia's royal family poses for an official portrait in the early 1890s. At center is Tsar Alexander III; behind him is future Tsar Nicholas II.

Napoleon I, had actually attained it. Except for distant Russia it had been traditionally the largest, the most populous, the richest, and therefore the mightiest state on the Continent. In the second half of the nineteenth century it had ceased to be all these things. The German Empire equaled its territory, vastly surpassed its population (64 million to France's 39 million in 1911) and industrial productivity, and, as 1870 had demonstrated, excelled it in military power. The two rivals for European supremacy eyed each other with suspicion, and their leaders grew convinced that the final settlement of their disagreements required another war.

In France this *revanchist* sentiment was especially widespread within the Conservative bloc, which favored action against Germany to revenge the defeat at Sedan and to recover Alsace and Lorraine. In the 1880s the anti-German movement gained great momentum; it played a prominent part in both the Boulanger and Dreyfus episodes (Chapter 9). Nor were the Republicans immune to these sentiments.

The German attitude toward the Third Republic was at first essentially defensive. Bismarck considered his country to have attained its natural limits: it was "satiated," as he put it. The principal task of his foreign policy was to safeguard what had been won, that is, to protect the unity and the integrity of the empire. The greatest threat to this aim was France. France endangered the empire both because of its inherent hostility toward Germany, and because of its capacity, by means of alliances with Germany's neighbors, to force it into a two-front war. Bismarck, therefore, concentrated on diplomatically isolating France: "We require that France leave us alone," he wrote in 1872, "and we must prevent it from securing allies should it fail to remain still; as long as it is without allies, France poses to us no danger."

The most effective way of depriving the French of allies was to bind any potential friend of France to Germany. These were, first and foremost, Russia, Austria, and Italy. (England, a naval power without a significant army, was not a serious factor in these calculations.) Proceeding on this premise, Bismarck engineered two major alliance systems—the League of the Three Emperors (1873: Germany, Austria-Hungary, Russia; after 1881 known as the Alliance of the Three Emperors), and the Triple Alliance (1882: Germany, Austria-Hungary, Italy).

The League of the Three Emperors, the basic instrument of Bismarck's diplomacy, committed the signatories to come to each other's aid in the event one of them was attacked by a fourth power. It was valid for three years and could be renewed. The League served German interests superbly well, isolating both Austria and Russia from France and assuring Germany of their help should Bismarck's nightmare—a French attack—materialize. Russia gained least, since neither of its allies could offer it effective assistance against its main rival, Great Britain, in the Middle East. The Triple Alliance came about as a result of Italy's rivalry with France over North Africa. Piqued by French seizure of Tunisia in 1882, the Italians cast their lot with the Germans and Austrians. The Alliance also bound the three powers to help each other against external attack.

The two alliances constituted the foundation of the Bismarckian diplomatic system, which dominated international diplomacy during the years of his chancellorship. France was in fact isolated: it could initiate no action against Germany without rousing against itself virtually the entire Continent.

For all its seeming solidity, Bismarck's system had one fatal flaw: the incipient hostility between Austria and Russia, Germany's principal allies. Bismarck exerted great efforts to keep this antagonism from breaking into the open, for he was aware that should such a breach occur he would be forced to make a formal choice between them and thereby automatically drive the spurned ally into French arms. The task proved to exceed even his exceptional diplomatic skills.

The fissures in the League of the Three Emperors began to appear in the wake of the Russo-Turkish War of 1877. The unfriendliness that Austria had demonstrated during and after the conflict, and the neutrality displayed by Germany, produced in Russia strong dissatisfaction with the League. Political writers of a conservative and Pan-Slavic orientation began now openly to question the value to Russia of an alliance with the two empires, and to call for a general reorientation of Russia's foreign policy. Indeed, a good case could be made that the League brought Russia no returns for its very real services rendered Germany and hence should have been abandoned in favor of an alliance with France. But neither Alexander II nor his son and successor, Alexander III, were as yet prepared to alter radically Russia's diplomacy. Personal friendship with Kaiser William I and admiration for Bismarck and things German, combined with a loathing for the republican form of government, inhibited a *rapprochement* with France. In 1881, and again in 1884, Russia renewed the alliance to Bismarck's great relief, although in a watered-down version that permitted it greater freedom of action in regard to Germany.

Bismarck always attached great (perhaps excessive) importance to public opinion in the formulation of foreign policy. The outburst of anti-German feeling in Russia after the Russo-Turkish War of 1877, coupled with the helplessness of the tsarist government in dealing with its revolutionary movement, persuaded him that the League did not furnish a sufficiently stable basis for Germany's foreign policy. He now decided to negotiate, behind Russia's back, an additional treaty with Austria. In 1879, on his initiative, the two countries signed an accord committing them to help each other if attacked by Russia or a power supported by Russia and to preserve neutrality if attacked by any other country. The alliance in effect committed Austria to help Germany against a potential Russo-French alliance in return for a freer hand in the Balkans. Because the treaty was concluded in utmost secrecy, both countries could continue to adhere to the League of the Three Emperors.

Despite the secrecy of the Austro-German alliance of 1879, the growing affinity between the two countries did not escape Russian diplomats. When in 1887 the Alliance of the Three Emperors came up for its periodic renewal, the Russians made difficulties. To keep the tenuous link with St. Petersburg from snapping, Bismarck resorted now to a desperate move. He proposed to the Russians a secret "Reinsurance Treaty," committing Germany to maintain neutrality in the event of an Austrian attack on Russia in return for Russian neutrality in the event of a French attack on Germany. This treaty, which was signed in June, 1887, was clearly incompatible with the spirit of the Austro-German alliance of 1879. Bismarck's single-minded obsession with isolating France led him into a system of such complexity and inner contradiction that its collapse became inevitable.

The Reinsurance Treaty notwithstanding, Russo-German relations deteriorated steadily, causing a simultaneous improvement in Russo-French relations. In 1888 Bismarck issued a directive to the German Imperial Bank to refuse Russian state bonds as collateral for loans. This measure made it difficult for the Russian government to obtain funds on the German money market and compelled it to turn instead to France. The same year the French government authorized the floating of the first Russian state loan, and thenceforth the imperial government secured in France the bulk of its foreign capital. This financial dependence inevitably made the Russians more responsive to French pressures for a political and military accord. The decisive event in the relations of the two countries was the refusal of William II in 1890 to renew the Reinsurance Treaty. Convinced that autocratic Russia and republican France would never get together, and offended by the anti-Austrian implications of this treaty, William allowed it to lapse. By this action he paved the way for a Russo-French *rapprochement*. In 1894 the two countries concluded a military convention calling for the immediate mobilization of French and Russian armies in response to a mobilization order by any member of the Triple Alliance and for mutual military help against Germany if either country were attacked by Germany or one of its allies.

From 1894 onward, Europe stood divided into two hostile blocs. One, dominated by Germany, embraced Austria and Italy; the other joined France and Russia. The agreements binding the two blocs assured that if one of the signatories became involved in a war with another, the other signatories would become involved as well; in other words, that any clash between two major powers would inevitably turn into a general war. England, for the time being, stayed outside these pacts.

The Revival of Imperialist Sentiment

The dangers implicit in the rivalry over the Balkans and the antagonism between the Franco-Russian and Austro-German blocs were aggravated by conflicts over colonies. These became intense in the last quarter of the nineteenth century. The great powers, having attained their national borders in Europe, carried their struggle for territory and influence overseas to areas in which statehood either was unknown or in a condition of decay.

Great power competition for overseas possessions is defined by the term *imperialism*. This term has today a pejorative meaning, but this was not the case before the twentieth century. In the ancient Middle East, where they originated, "empires" had been superior forms of political organization, permitting the coexistence within one state of diverse races, nations, and religions. The Persian Empire represented a great advance over earlier states that had annihilated or enslaved conquered nations; so did the Hellenistic and Roman empires, the latter of which had survived as an ideal in Western tradition until the Napoleonic era. Imperialism acquired its bad name only around 1900, following a sudden outburst of Western expansionism. At that time it came to mean ruthless aggrandizement and the exploitation by whites of the colored races.

From the late eighteenth to the late nineteenth century, European opinion had been opposed on purely pragmatic grounds to colonial expansion. Along with other mercantilist notions the liberals rejected the view that a state gained power and wealth from the acquisition of overseas possessions. Their attitude rested partly on political and partly on economic arguments. The Frenchman Turgot stated the political case against the colonies even before the outbreak of the American Revolution when he compared them to fruits that "clung to the tree only until they ripened." The subsequent separation of the North American colonies from England and of the Latin American ones from Spain and Portugal having confirmed this expectation, liberals concluded that sooner or later all colonies would demand and obtain independence. The economic argument against imperialism held that the costs of administering and defending overseas possessions exceeded the profit they brought. Adam Smith, Bentham, Cobden, and other liberal theorists maintained—and had evidence to prove it—that a country gained more from trading with other sovereign states than from exploiting its own colonies. Since colonies brought no economic advantages and were certain to separate, there seemed little point in keeping those one had and none in acquiring others.

Such considerations were responsible for the loosening of bonds between the European states and their colonies in the course of the nineteenth century.

Although English Liberals were not prepared to quit the overseas possessions, they were willing to go quite far in conceding them self-rule. The process of emancipation, of transforming dependent colonies into virtually independent states, began in the 1830s. In 1837 a rebellion broke out in the Canadian provinces as a result of a prolonged conflict between crown-appointed officials and representative assemblies. Rather than suppress the rebellion by force, as it would have done in the past, the British government dispatched to Canada a new governor, Lord Durham, a man of moderate views prepared to conciliate Canadian opinion. Durham submitted to London in 1839 a *Report on the Affairs of British North America,* a document that provided the basis for a new kind of relationship between Britain and its possessions. It proposed to grant the Canadian legislatures nearly complete authority in domestic matters, and to confine that of the crown and its officials to Canada's foreign policy and foreign trade. On the basis of Durham's report, the House of Commons passed in 1840 a Union Act with Canada. Before long, similar arrangements were made with other overseas territories inhabited by European populations (Australia, 1850; New Zealand and Cape Colony in South Africa, 1852). In this manner a new type of self-governing colony came into existence. Later known as "dominions," they represented a transitional stage between colonial status and full independence.

In 1834 Britain abolished slavery in its possessions. Although enacted largely under pressure of philanthropic and religious groups, this measure owed its passage to the relative indifference of statesmen and businessmen of that time to colonial affairs.

The anti-imperial sentiment prevailing in liberal England was echoed on the Continent. Bismarck, although not unappreciative of the value of the colonies, showed little enthusiasm for overseas ventures. He preferred to encourage other powers to seize colonies so as to divert their attention from Germany. The French Empire also remained stationary after 1830, the year France had seized Algeria.

Evidence of a shift in sentiment made itself felt first in Russia in the 1860s. Partly from economic considerations (the desire for potentially rich cotton-

"Radical Jack" Lambton, Lord Durham, by Sir Thomas Lawrence. Durham called for Parliament to establish "responsible government" in Canada.

PUBLIC ARCHIVES OF CANADA

growing areas), and partly under pressure from the military, the imperial government authorized in 1865 an invasion of Turkistan. In a few years three Muslim central Asian principalities were conquered, and Russia established itself firmly in the heart of Asia. From there it carried out expeditions south and west, toward the Persian and Afghan borders, until it was finally stopped by British intercession.

In England in the late 1860s several writers began to speak up on behalf of the imperial cause, and to exhort Britons to greater appreciation of the achievements of its explorers, conquerors, and settlers. The movement gained impetus with the conversion of Disraeli to its tenets. In 1872, in his Crystal Palace speech, Disraeli accused the Liberals of a deliberate effort to dissolve the empire, and urged Britain to reforge its links with the colonies:

> The issue is not a mean one. It is whether you will be content to be a comfortable England, modeled and moulded upon Continental principles and meeting in due course an inevitable fate, or whether you will be a great country, an Imperial country, a country where your sons, when they rise, rise to paramount positions and obtain not merely the esteem of their countrymen, but command the respect of the world.

In an 1876 Punch *cartoon, Prime Minister Disraeli offers Victoria the crown of India. The next year the queen took the title Empress of India.*

Disraeli conducted a vigorous imperial policy, being especially concerned with checking Russian threats to the "imperial lifeline" extending from London to India. It is with this in mind that he acquired for Britain a dominating voice in the control of the Suez Canal (see below). At the end of the century imperialist sentiment was widespread in Great Britain. Joseph Chamberlain built his political career on it, and Rudyard Kipling owed to it the immense popularity of his stories and poems glorifying the colorful colonial life. Nevertheless, British enthusiasm was always somewhat checked by deeply rooted liberal convictions about national self-determination and free trade.

On the Continent the imperialist movement got under way somewhat later, but once started it was not greatly inhibited by liberal traditions. In the 1880s publicists and politicians throughout Europe began to extol the need for colonies and to call for colonial conquests. Very active on behalf of the imperialist causes were lobbies in the form of colonial societies, the first of which had been founded in Britain (Royal Colonial Institute, 1868). Imperialist enthusiasm even spread to the United States, a country born in rebellion against colonial rule, where President Theodore Roosevelt propagated it with all the vigor of his ebullient personality. Nor was the movement confined to Western countries. The Japanese became converted to it as well, and at the turn of the century participated alongside European powers in acquiring territory and spheres of influence on the Asiatic mainland. As a rule, the socialist parties furnished the most consistent opposition to imperialist ventures.

The Causes of Modern Imperialism

Before proceeding to trace the history of late nineteenth-century imperial expansion, we must ask what caused the shift in opinion and induced the great powers to put so much effort in establishing themselves in the poor, backward areas of Africa and Asia.

There is a widespread belief that the reasons for modern imperialism are economic: the search for outlets capable of absorbing excess goods, capital, and population. This view owes its prevalence to the fact that it was shared by both the advocates of imperialist expansion and its opponents. The former, in an effort to persuade a reluctant public to back overseas ventures, promised the acquisition of colonies would solve all economic and social problems. They claimed that "trade follows the flag" and that enterprising men would find overseas unlimited opportunities to better themselves. Such an appeal was explicit in Disraeli's speech cited above. The critics of imperialism, mostly socialists, accepted the premise but turned the argument around. They charged that imperial conquests were carried out solely for the private advantage of the bourgeoisie while at the same time diverting public opinion from pressing domestic problems. Pro-imperialists and anti-imperialists agreed that imperialism was economically profitable. They only differed in their judgment as to whom it benefited: the country as a whole or special interest groups. In view of this basic agreement, it is not surprising that the public at large accepted the general economic interpretation of imperialism.

Dispassionate analysis of the data, however, reveals that the economic benefits of colonialism were insignificant and that the liberals were more correct in their estimate of the matter. Colonies were significant neither as outlets for goods and capital, nor as centers of emigration.

As concerns trade, the available figures indicate that business with the colonies, especially those acquired in the late nineteenth century, represented a small part of the total trade of the imperial powers. This held true even of Great Britain, which of all the imperial powers did the most business with its possessions. Trade within the empire accounted for one-quarter of Britain's external commerce. Half of that trade, however, was with the self-governing dominions, such as Canada and Australia, which had been acquired long before 1870. Only one-eighth of the imperial trade was with the colonies proper, and the bulk of that was with India, a British possession since the eighteenth century. In the case of the other powers, the share of the colonial market in their total foreign trade was smaller yet: it was 11 percent for France, 4 percent for Japan, 0.4 percent for Germany, and 0.3 percent for Italy.° The colonies were simply too poor to absorb a significant quantity of industrial goods. The industrial powers did the greatest volume of business with one another, not with the underdeveloped colonies. Great Britain sold in the United States goods twice the value of those disposed of in India, its richest colony; and Germany, in turn, found Britain its best customer. From the strictly commercial point of view, the interests of the great powers required them to cooperate, not to engage in rivalry over colonies.

As concerns capital investments, the argument that colonial expansion was undertaken in an effort to find outlets for excess capital was popularized by the English economist John A. Hobson in his study *Imperialism* (1902). In a statement of breathtaking sweep, Hobson asserted: "It is not too much to say that the modern foreign policy of Great Britain has been primarily a struggle for profitable markets of investment." This theory was afterwards accepted by many socialists, including Lenin, and explains why the Communists attach so much importance to expelling Western powers from the colonies: to them, colonies are the last bastion of the whole capitalist order.

° Figures from Grover Clark, *The Balance Sheet of Imperialism* (1936).

The wickedly ironical Max Beerbohm portrayed the arch-imperialist Rudyard Kipling enjoying an outing "along with Britannia, 'is gurl."

Statistical evidence, however, indicates no meaningful relationship between capital investments and colonialism. The great years of overseas expansion (1875–1895) were, in the case of Britain, a low point in the rate of foreign investment. Britain exported more capital in the era of anti-imperial sentiment than in the heyday of imperialism. Nor is there any indication that British investors were guided by imperial preferences. Only 13 percent of all British foreign investments on record in 1914 were placed in the colonies proper (as distinct from the five older, self-governing dominions), compared to 20 percent placed in the United States and Latin America. France invested less than 10 percent of its foreign capital in its colonies; 90 percent went to sovereign states. France's investments in Russia exceeded two and a half times those placed in its own possessions. Germany's investments in its African colonies represented about 4 percent of its foreign capital commitments. Clearly, as in the case of trade, capital followed not the flag but economic opportunity: it went where the returns were best, regardless of who was in political control. In an age when currencies were readily convertible to gold, it made no difference to an investor in what currency he drew his profit. It may also be noted that two among the most aggressive imperialist powers, Russia and Japan, not only had no excess capital looking for investment opportunities, but borrowed heavily from their imperialist competitors.

In drawing up the economic balance sheet of imperialism, it is necessary also to take into account the cost of administering and defending the colonies. These charges cannot be exactly computed, but they were high. In the case of Germany, Italy, and Japan they must have considerably exceeded the negligible returns from trade and investments.

The expectation that colonies would absorb migrants was not borne out either. The territories suitable for settlement had been seized before 1800. Those taken between 1870 and 1914 did not lend themselves to this purpose. The total net migration of Europeans to all their overseas colonies between 1885 and 1935 was 500,000 persons—less than the United States sometimes received in a single year. European migrants settled on the American continents, not in Africa and Asia where the scramble for colonies took place.

To deny that economic necessity required colonial expansion, however, is not to deny the existence of economic factors behind it. It can be shown that *objectively*, imperialism did not significantly solve any of the problems confronting advanced economies. At the same time, *subjectively*, economic considerations played a very important role in the revival of imperialism. It was widely believed that imperial expansion could permit the absorption of excess goods, capital, and population, and this belief—even if now proven to have been unfounded—stimulated imperialism. One must keep in mind the deep anxiety felt by many Europeans as they observed the incredible outpouring of goods made possible by modern technology. Their worry over markets was genuine and understandable, the more so as with each decade new countries industrialized and thereby entered the list of potential competitors. The economic crises of 1873 and 1885, each severe and prolonged, gave substance to these fears. It was no coincidence that imperialist sentiment emerged in England around 1870, for that happened to be the very time when Britain, hitherto the unchallenged leader in world trade, for the first time confronted serious competition from Germany and the United States. To farsighted statesmen it seemed imperative that Britain expand: "Little England" had to become "Greater Britain" or the country would decline and perish. The fear was particularly acute in Germany, whose production rose at a staggering rate, much beyond the needs of the domestic market. The hunt for colonies began as a kind of preventive action or insurance against future crises from overproduction and overpopulation. Once it got under way every country that aspired to great power status had to join in, if only because the other great powers did so. Russia and Japan, countries with rudimentary industries, engaged in imperialist rivalry not because their economies required it, but because it was thought that unless they did so, their future generations would experience insurmountable economic and social difficulties. Not the needs of the existing economy but faulty economic calculation concerning the future constituted the economic factor in imperialism.

Modern historians tend also to stress heavily the political side of imperialism. They see it as expansion for the sake of power, strategic advantage, national glory, and many of the very same goals that had inspired national conflicts in Europe itself. Some among them also ascribe the outburst of late nineteenth-century expansionism to irrational drives in man, such as aggressive tendencies inherited from primitive ancestors.

Colonial competition in the late nineteenth century was global in scope. Every region not claimed by a power able to assert its sovereignty was open to seizure. But the two areas that attracted the most attention from the great powers were Africa and China. They were at the center of the imperial rivalries.

Overseas Expansion

The Struggle for Africa

The rush for Africa began with the completion in 1869 of the Suez Canal. The new waterway cut the route from Europe to the Indian Ocean in half and immediately acquired great commercial and military value, especially for Britain. Britain had failed to participate in the construction of the canal because its experts doubted its feasibility. The undertaking had been launched by the French, who thereby strengthened their already solid position in the eastern Mediterranean. Britain could not tolerate this situation, for control over the Suez gave France mastery over the route connecting Britain with some of its most important overseas possessions. An opportunity to redeem the mistake presented itself in 1875 when the khedive (viceroy) of Egypt, faced with bankruptcy, offered for sale his shares in the Suez Canal Company. On learning the news, Disraeli immediately borrowed 4 million pounds from the Rothschild bank (he was afraid to miss the chance by waiting for a regular parliamentary appropriation) and with it purchased the khedive's shares.

Disraeli's move not only gave Britain 44 percent of the stock in the Suez Canal Company, and thereby the strongest voice on its board, but also a base from which to establish hegemony over northeast Africa. After the khedive had suffered further financial reverses, England and France compelled him to abdicate and placed Egypt under joint rule. In 1882 the British took advantage of a nationalist uprising to occupy Egypt and establish a protectorate over it. From there they extended their authority southward, into the Sudan. By 1900 northeast

Africa was British, except for two Italian enclaves (Somaliland and Eritrea), French Somaliland, and independent Ethiopia.

The French, ousted from the northeast, realized their imperial ambitions in the northwest. In 1881 they seized Tunisia, and then expanded into Morocco and the Sahara. Despite strong native resistance, by 1914 France had established its authority over this territory.

The most intense imperialist competition occurred in the central regions of Africa. This area, believed to harbor great mineral wealth, became the object of keen rivalry involving colorful explorers, chartered companies, and, behind both, the foreign ministries of the great powers.

In the 1860s central Africa was still an unknown territory, penetrated only by a few intrepid missionaries and explorers. Its opening to Western influence was due to the enterprise of an Anglo-American journalist, Henry M. Stanley. Stanley first went to Africa in 1871 as a correspondent for the New York *Herald* to locate David Livingstone, a British missionary lost in cannibal country. Having completed this celebrated mission, he became fascinated with the economic potentialities of the vast and unchartered Congo River basin. He returned there on several exploratory expeditions, first on his own, then on behalf of the Belgian king, Leopold II, whose interest he had aroused. In 1878–1882 Leopold founded the International Association of the Congo—ostensibly a private company, but in fact an instrument by means of which he established control over the area. In time Leopold secured international recognition of the Association as the sovereign authority in the Congo under his personal rule. This arrangement benefited most the businessmen interested in the economic exploitation of the region, for it exempted them from Belgian parliamentary control. It led to such abuses and protests, however, that in 1908 the king felt compelled to transfer sovereignty over the Congo to the government of Belgium.

Belgian advances in central Africa aroused German interest. The first German explorations there were carried out by individuals acting without Bismarck's encouragement or authorization. In 1884–1885 they claimed on behalf of their country extensive territories in eastern and southwestern Africa. At first reluctantly, and then with increasing enthusiasm, the German government assumed responsibility over these colonies.

A German satirical magazine included these drawings in a "special issue" in 1904 devoted to colonialism in Africa. At the right, the German propensity for regimentation is applied to the local fauna. Opposite, the British utilize whisky and religion to gain a favorable balance of trade.

BOTH: Simplicissimus, 1904

France, Portugal, and Britain were also active in central Africa, exploring and setting forth claims. The absence of fixed frontiers of any kind made friction unavoidable. The most serious incident occurred in 1898 when British and French expeditions, racing from different directions to secure control of the upper Nile, ran into each other at Fashoda in the Sudan. After a tense period of diplomatic maneuvering, which for a time threatened war, France yielded and ordered withdrawal of its forces. Britain's triumph in the "Fashoda Crisis" assured its hegemony in that part of Africa, but the bad blood it created delayed for several years a Franco-British diplomatic understanding in Europe.

In South Africa the colonial problem was complicated by the presence of white settlers, descendants of seventeenth-century Dutch and Huguenot colonists, known as "Boers" (a Dutch word meaning "farmers"). The Boers engaged in agriculture and cattle breeding, employing Negro slave labor. Imperialism here, therefore, involved not the conquest of a native colored people, for these had already been subjugated by an earlier colonial wave, but the establishment of one white authority over another.

The British had seized South Africa from the Dutch in 1806, at which time they renamed it Cape Colony. From the beginning of their rule they clashed with the Boers over slavery, which the British first limited and then (in 1834) abolished. Once slavery was outlawed, 10,000 Boers left Cape Colony to migrate to the north and northeast (the "Great Trek," 1835–1837). Here they founded two independent republics, Transvaal and the Orange Free State, in which they built plantations worked by slaves.

The Boers were not permitted to enjoy their way of life in the new land for long. The discovery of the world's richest diamond deposits in the Orange Free State (1867) and of gold in Transvaal (1886) attracted to the two republics hordes of European fortune seekers. By the end of the century these outsiders, or *uitlanders*, most of whom settled in boom towns of which Johannesburg was the largest, outnumbered the Boers in both republics. The Boers refused to grant the newcomers political suffrage and discriminated against them in other ways as well.

Rivalry between the British and the Boers reached a high level of intensity in the 1890s. At that time, the Prime Minister of Cape Colony was Cecil Rhodes, an

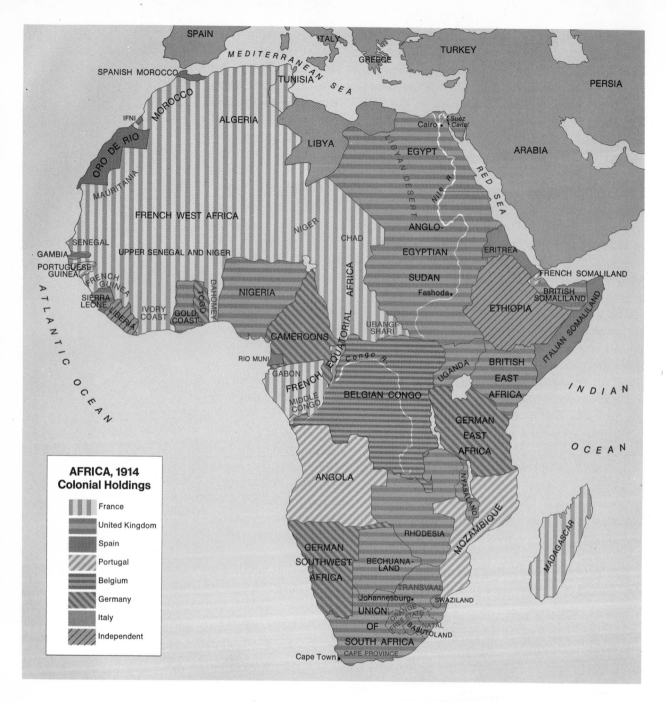

AFRICA, 1914
Colonial Holdings

- France
- United Kingdom
- Spain
- Portugal
- Belgium
- Germany
- Italy
- Independent

immensely wealthy entrepreneur with a directing voice in the South African diamond and gold syndicates. Rhodes was an ardent empire builder. His great dream was a solid British domain extending from Cape Town to Cairo. In 1889 he obtained a royal charter to form the British South Africa Company, through the agency of which he obtained control of Bechuanaland. This region he later renamed Rhodesia and attached to Cape Colony. After being appointed Prime Minister in 1890, he exerted constant pressure on the Boer republics hoping to bring about their collapse. With the aid of a few friends, among them a certain

Dr. Jameson, he formed a plan calling for a coordinated internal and external attack on the Transvaal. It involved an uprising of *uitlanders* in Johannesburg, to be followed by the dispatch of an armed expedition under Jameson to its aid. Unfortunately for Rhodes, Jameson bungled his assignment by penetrating the Transvaal before the *uitlanders* had revolted. He suffered defeat and capture (January, 1896), and Rhodes had to resign as Prime Minister. Despite its failure, the strategy that Rhodes devised for the subversion of the Boer republic is of historic interest, for it anticipates the methods used later on, with more success, by totalitarian rulers in Europe.

In 1899 Britain and the Boer republics went to war. The British quickly disposed of the regular enemy armies, but they required over two years to suppress the guerrillas who continued the struggle. In 1902 the Boers finally capitulated and acknowledged British sovereignty.

The African continent was so thoroughly carved up by the great powers that in 1914 only two countries, Ethiopia and Liberia, retained their independence.

THE PARTITION OF CHINA

In the Far East the situation differed from that in Africa in that imperial competition was not over territories unclaimed by internationally recognized powers, but over the legacy of one of the most ancient of states. In the end, however, the results of imperialist rivalry were analogous to those observed in Africa. The great powers established definite claims to specific regions of China, and were it not for the outbreak of World War I, which diverted their attention, China's collapse and partition could hardly have been averted.

Until the nineteenth century China and Japan alike had isolated themselves from Western influences. But Japan's resistance to the West collapsed much sooner. After 1868 the Japanese rejected traditionalism and turned toward Europe. They modernized their political system, introduced compulsory military service, adopted European educational methods, and launched the beginnings of an industrial economy. The speed and thoroughness with which the Japanese Westernized has no historic parallel. Because of this they were not only able to resist encroachment by European states, but before the end of the century to join the ranks of the great powers and to become involved in imperialist ventures themselves.

The Chinese did not follow this road. Why Japan Westernized and China did not is a question beyond the scope of this survey. It may be mentioned, however, that one of the reasons for China's refusal to do so was the antiquity and accomplishment of its native culture. Japan's culture had been borrowed from China; its Westernization involved the substitution of one alien cultural influence for another. China's culture was indigenous, and Westernization implied a renunciation of the country's national identity and heritage. For a long time the Chinese refused to acknowledge the superiority of Western techniques, even when militarily defeated. They responded to humiliation not by acquiring these techniques and turning them against external powers, as the Japanese had done, but by indulging in fanatical xenophobia. The Chinese government proved less and less capable of exercising effective authority over its vast domain, which included several large dependencies (Sinkiang, Manchuria, Mongolia, and Tibet) and tributary states (Korea, Indochina, and Burma).

The French cemented their grip on Indochina in 1884 with a victory, painted here by a Chinese artist, over the Chinese near Hanoi, capital of present-day North Vietnam. The French troops holding the two forts at top, supported by warships, repelled the Chinese advancing from the right along the river.

Western penetration of China, spearheaded by Britain, initially took commercial and military forms. In 1842, following a brief war, Britain compelled the Chinese authorities to open several ports to trade, and to cede Hong Kong to them. The British soon strengthened their position and in the middle of the century gained additional privileges for their merchants and missionaries after the suppression of the so-called Taiping Rebellion, a violent anti-imperial and anti-foreign uprising.

After this rebellion the Chinese government began to lose control over its territories. The uprising had revealed the weakness of the regime and encouraged foreign claims to territories traditionally regarded by the Chinese as under their sovereignty. The territorial encroachments were inaugurated by the Russians, who appropriated the Maritime Province. There, in 1860, they constructed a port they named Vladivostok—literally, "Master of the East." The French began exploration in Indochina, which in the 1880s they appropriated as a colony. In 1886 Britain took over Burma. The greatest threat to China, however, came from Japan, which in the 1870s established a foothold on the Asiatic mainland. Japanese intrusions into Korea led in 1894 to the Sino-Japanese War. The modernized Japanese forces won without much difficulty. In the Treaty of Shimonoseki (1895) China had to cede Formosa to Japan and grant independence to Korea. The latter became a Japanese protectorate.

So far, encroachments on the Chinese domain had involved China proper less than its tributary states. The Sino-Japanese War of 1894 initiated a veritable scramble for native Chinese territories. The competition at first took the form of economic concessions. Through financial inducements and military blackmail, the great powers forced the Chinese government to lease them port cities and grant licenses to construct railroads and engage in mining. By means of such concessions, the holder assured himself of a "sphere of influence" over a region. In time, it was expected, such "influence" would lead to outright ownership. The Russians obtained the first important concession in 1896 in the form of a privilege to extend the Trans-Siberian Railway across northern Manchuria to Vladivostok. This arrangement gave them a claim to the entire Manchurian province, an important and rich dependency of China. Other powers won from the Chinese government similar economic concessions. The United States did not seek such concessions but instead exerted pressure on the other powers to accept the so-called Open Door policy guaranteeing all countries free access to Chinese markets (1899).

In 1897–1898 the Germans and Russians undertook joint action for the purpose of occupying the Chinese port cities of Kiaochao and Port Arthur, respectively. These seizures marked the beginning of the territorial partition of China proper. Their example was soon emulated by France, Britain, and Japan.

These constant encroachments by foreign powers stimulated in 1900 the outbreak of a second, even more violent anti-foreign uprising, the so-called Boxer Rebellion.° The movement was fundamentally religious, being directed against Christians, especially Chinese converts. The Boxers were so much imbued with fanaticism that they regarded themselves as immune to foreign bullets. They were crushed largely by intervention of foreign armies, including a detachment from the United States. As compensation, the Chinese government had to make further concessions as well as pay an exorbitant indemnity.

°The name derives from "Righteous and Harmonious Fists," a patriotic organization dedicated to exercises as a means of steeling the mind and body for combat.

This photograph was carefully posed to emphasize the international nature of the foreign armies that intervened in the Boxer Rebellion in China in 1900. The troops are, from left, British, American, Russian, Indian, German, French, Austrian, Italian, and Japanese.

Rivalry in the Far East led in 1904 to the outbreak of a war between Russia and Japan. At the turn of the century a group of unscrupulous adventurers, interested in exploiting the lumber resources along the Yalu River in northern Korea, persuaded Nicholas II to back their claims. These activities encroached on the Japanese sphere of influence. Japan proposed negotiations, but the tsar, egged on by militant circles at the court, refused, whereupon the Japanese in February, 1904, attacked Port Arthur. Subsequently, they inflicted a series of humiliating defeats on Russia's army and, in the Battle of Tsushima, sank a good part of its navy.

In 1911 a group of Westernized reformers in China overthrew the imperial government and proclaimed the establishment of the Chinese Republic. The leader of the group, Sun Yat-sen, had been educated in an English school in Hong Kong and had spent many years in Europe and the United States. The republican regime which he headed did not possess adequate resources for effective administration or for the implementation of its program of Westernization. There seemed little chance that it would be able to check the ambitions of Japan which, after its victory over Russia, appeared destined to dominate the Far East.

Anglo-German Rivalry   At the beginning of the twentieth century the international situation presented the following picture: in Europe two major blocs confronted each other, one linking Germany with Austria and Italy, the other linking France with Russia. The main rivalries pitted Russia against Austria over territory and influence in the Balkans, and Germany against France over general primacy on the Continent. The powers also engaged in competition over African and Asian possessions.

Britain so far had stayed out of alliances, preferring "splendid isolation" to military commitments. A pre-eminently commercial country, it needed peace; and as an insular state without a standing army it could neither benefit from the armed forces of potential allies, nor contribute much to them. Its foreign policy was flexible, sometimes backing the Austro-German bloc, sometimes the Franco-Russian.

The factor which finally caused England to abandon its isolation was the same that had moved it a century earlier to form anti-Napoleonic alliances: the fear of a single power becoming so overwhelmingly powerful as to be in a position to dominate the Continent. This danger now came from Germany.

Bismarckian diplomacy, as we have noted, had been defensive. In the 1890s this conservative foreign policy no longer suited the mood of Germany, which observed with frustration the overseas conquests of rival powers. Kaiser William II formally abandoned Bismarck's defensive Continental diplomacy in 1896 when he committed Germany to what became known as *Weltpolitik* or "world politics." The term had no precise meaning, but as used, it implied that Germany would no longer concentrate exclusively on self-defense. Instead it would engage actively in international competition for colonies, markets, and influence.

The trouble with *Weltpolitik* was not its general aim, which was pursued by all the great powers, but the absence of specific objectives. The theorists and executors of *Weltpolitik* had no clear notion of what they wanted, except to make Germany's weight felt. As a result they seemed to want everything and to threaten everybody at once. This applied especially to Britain. The Kaiser's irresponsible sallies into international affairs challenged Britain's position in a number of widely separated areas of the world without any hint of the conditions on which it would be possible to come to terms. In 1896 the Kaiser surprised and outraged Britain by sending the President of Transvaal a telegram congratulating him on his victory over the Jameson raiders. The move seemed to indicate an intention to enter South African politics, but this goal was not pursued. Instead, two years later William challenged Britain's whole Middle Eastern position by declaring himself, in a public address, ready to act as "protector" of the world's Muslims, the majority of whom lived under British rule. This threat of subversion was not carried out either, because the Kaiser's attention was soon diverted to the Far East, where his seizure in 1897 of Kiaochao had accelerated the scramble for Chinese territory.

Such actions, coming in rapid succession and lacking a definite purpose, caused consternation in England. Yet the breach between England and Germany was not inevitable. Britain had greater disagreements with Russia, and even with France, than with Germany, and some British statesmen advocated an alliance with Germany. In 1898, at the height of the Fashoda Crisis in the Sudan, Joseph Chamberlain opened exploratory talks with Berlin to this end. The Germans, however, cold-shouldered British advances, and the negotiations collapsed. The Germans saw themselves as holding the balance of power between Britain and the Franco-Russian bloc and believed that by procrastinating they could exact from Britain greater concessions in their bid for a greater role in "world politics."

The critical event in the rupture between England and Germany was the naval race that broke out in 1900.

Under the influence of the books of the American historian Alfred T. Mahan, who depicted naval supremacy as the decisive factor in modern warfare, and of the German Minister of the Navy, Alfred von Tirpitz, William II undertook to construct a large battle fleet. The intention was to create an offensive navy of sufficient strength to menace the British Isles, in the expectation that such a threat would force Britain either to withdraw a good part of its navy to home waters and thereby imperil its empire, or yield to German demands for territory and commercial advantages. The navy, in other words, was to serve as an instrument of diplomatic blackmail. With this goal in mind, Germany enacted in 1898 and 1900 naval laws authorizing the construction of a high-seas fleet.

The British were highly perturbed by these measures, especially the Second Naval Law (1900), which provided for the construction, over a period of twenty years, of 38 battleships. For Britain, naval superiority was not a matter of mere ambition or prestige, but of survival. Since the early nineteenth century the British Isles had come to depend for their basic necessities on imports. Four-fifths of the wheat consumed in Great Britain, for example, came from abroad by ship. By obtaining control of the high seas, a hostile power could force Britain into submission without setting foot on its soil. It was to prevent this from happening that Britain in 1889 proclaimed the so-called "two-power standard," a formula committing it to maintain a naval force superior to that of the two next most powerful navies combined. Any country that challenged this rule invited the enmity of Britain.

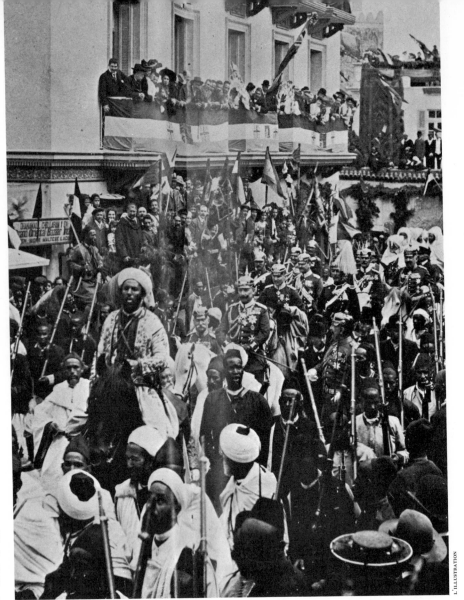

Kaiser William II (at center, mounted on the white horse) initiated the First Moroccan Crisis in 1905 with a visit to Tangier, hoping to split the Anglo-French Entente Cordiale.

To meet the German threat Britain took diplomatic and military counter-measures. In 1902, abandoning its traditional policy of nonalignment, it signed a defensive alliance with Japan. Two years later it entered into an Entente Cordiale with France—a loose act of friendship without specific military commitments. At the same time the British government authorized the construction of a new class of battleships, the so-called dreadnaughts, superior to any warship then in existence. The first of these vessels was launched in February, 1906.

The Germans, viewing these moves as portents of a hostile alliance directed against them, sought to break the tightening noose by detaching from the anti-German bloc first England, then Russia, but their efforts backfired. An attempt to test and loosen the Entente Cordiale by intervening against France in Morocco (the so-called First Moroccan Crisis, 1905) yielded the contrary result: it so appalled the French and British that they initiated secret military talks.

When in May, 1906, the German government passed the Third Naval Law providing for battleships capable of matching the dreadnaughts in displacement and firepower, an Anglo-German breach became inevitable. British statesmen now became convinced that nothing short of acknowledging German superiority on the Continent and on the high seas would satisfy the Germans, and that it was essential for Britain to safeguard its vital interests by extending full support to the Franco-Russian bloc. In 1907 Britain settled its outstanding differences with Russia over the Middle East and signed with it a treaty similar to the Entente Cordiale. The agreement did not call for automatic military assistance, but it left no doubt with whom Britain would side in the event that the Austro-German and Franco-Russian blocs went to war.

After 1907 relations between the great powers underwent a succession of dangerous crises in scattered parts of the world, each capable of causing a major war. Of these the gravest occurred in 1908 in consequence of the Austrian annexation of Bosnia and Herzegovina, and in 1911 in the course of a Franco-German confrontation in Morocco.

Austria originally occupied Bosnia and Herzegovina in 1878 as a result of a deal with Russia (see above), later confirmed by the Congress of Berlin. Such de facto possession, quite satisfactory to Vienna, seemed threatened in 1908 by the deposition of Sultan Abdul-Hamid and the assumption of power in Turkey by nationalistic officers (Chapter 9). The Austrians now feared that the Young Turks would demand a return of the occupied territory. A group of aggressive Austrian statesmen, headed by Aehrenthal, the Minister of Foreign Affairs, therefore urged the annexation of Bosnia and Herzegovina to forestall such an eventuality. In secret negotiations with the Russians the Austrians secured their agreement to the annexation in return for a pledge to support the right of Russian warships to pass through the Straits. While the Russians made vain efforts to obtain British and French agreement to a revision of the Straits convention, Austria announced its annexation of Bosnia and Herzegovina (October, 1908). The Turks, who considered these regions their property, as well as the Serbs, who coveted them, were outraged; the Russians, having received nothing from their secret accords with the Austrians, now publicly ranged themselves against Vienna. For several months there was danger of war between a Russo-Serbian bloc and Austria, the latter backed to the hilt by Germany. But although for the time being war was averted, the Bosnia and Herzegovina incident left a lasting legacy of hostility in Eastern Europe, aggravating in particular the relations between Russia and Austria.

The Second Moroccan Crisis flared up in July, 1911, when William II ordered a German gunboat to Morocco. The ostensible purpose of his move was to protect German business interests during civil disturbances in this area, generally recognized as a French sphere of influence. The true reason was to force France to concede the French Congo to Germany. Britain firmly backed France. Germany ultimately obtained a part of the French Congo in return for a recognition of French rights to Morocco, but at the price of driving England and France closer together.

Incidents of this kind tended to solidify each of the two great alliance systems and to widen the gulf separating them from one another.

La Belle Epoque

ROGER VIOLLET

The Franco-Prussian War officially ended on June 28, 1871. Bismarck's Prussian legions had captured Napoleon III; Paris was shell-torn and occupied, Alsace-Lorraine lost, and the new government of the Third Republic found itself saddled with a massive indemnity. From March until the end of May the convulsions of the Paris Commune had revived all the horrors of civil war. The French capital presented a desolate landscape of "gaping roofs, battered walls, and charred frontages. . . . The theaters were closed and the shops were shuttered; no one even cried newspapers."

Paris was battered, but her spirit was unbroken. When the government floated a loan for Bismarck's 5 billion franc indemnity, Paris alone subscribed 12 billion of the astonishing total of 42 billion francs raised. More important, a new spirit was in the air. "War, revolutions, military intrigues; strategy, tactics, artillery, shells, petrol, we've had enough of them," wrote the popular journalist Philibert Audebrand. "The theaters are open again, ladies and gentlemen, the Parisiennes are more seductive than ever, visitors are arriving in crowds, and *gaiety is in the air.*" Rapidly the indoor world of the genteel salon gave way to the varied pleasures of the outdoor cafés, the café concerts, the parks, the circuses, the racecourses, the banks and islands of the Seine, the streets, the Opéra, the ballet, the theaters. *La belle époque*, the beautiful years, had begun. All Paris was to be a stage.

History's image of *la belle époque* is largely the work of a succession of bold artists who dared, as one contemporary critic wrote, "To compose the picture not in the studio but on the spot, in front of the subject; to shake off all conventions; . . . to give a meticulous interpretation of the impression, of the raw sensation, however strange it may seem; to present the living being, in gesture and attitude, moving in the fugitive, ever-changing atmosphere and light; . . . to make the figures inseparable from their background, as though they were the product of it. . . ."

La belle époque had many aspects, but at stage center of this theatrical age were the café concerts, a unique blend of music hall and night club featuring entertainers who aroused, shocked, and delighted all Paris. At the right is Edgar Degas' delicate yet lusty pastel, *Le Café-Concert aux "Ambassadeurs"* (1876), and at the left, Toulouse-Lautrec's 1894 lithograph of Montmartre's most famous dance team, La Goulue and her partner Valentin le Désossé, performing at the celebrated Moulin Rouge.

It was there that La Goulue made a gesture that in its own way epitomized the age. Executing a high kick, she knocked off the top hat of the visiting Prince of Wales, and said archly, "Hullo, Wales, are you paying for the champagne?"

Believing that "the motif should be observed more for shape and color than for drawing," Pissarro portrayed Paris with the bright palette and "comma" brush strokes of the Impressionists. Below is one of the many views Pissarro did of the Avenue de l'Opéra. At right is his rendition of the Pont-Neuf, looking across the Seine from the Île de la Cité.

The City of Light

The Paris that served as a stage for the festivities of *la belle époque* was the favored creation of nature, history, and the determined efforts of a slightly spurious baron. Nature provided Paris with a gentle climate, rolling wooded hills, and the broad reaches of the Seine. History left the city a rich legacy of buildings, monuments, and bridges such as the Pont-Neuf (above), built in 1607 by Henry IV. But it was reserved for Napoleon III's Préfet de la Seine, Baron Georges Eugène Haussmann, to turn Paris from an impenetrable labyrinth of sewerless alleyways and decayed tenements into a modern metropolis of broad, tree-lined boulevards, with spacious plazas setting off such elegant landmarks as the Opéra (left).

Between 1853 and 1870 Haussmann ruthlessly revamped Paris. By tearing down slums and ramming new boulevards through the medieval fortifications that girdled and cramped the city, Haussmann not only opened Paris to itself, but to the country and the suburbs as well; by making two huge parks, the Bois de Boulogne and the Bois de Vincennes, just outside the old walls, he gave the city racetracks, riding trails, and ice skating rinks. An 81-mile aqueduct brought fresh spring water and 300 miles of tiled sewers made perfume a luxury rather than a necessity. Mindful of beauty and a varied social life, Haussmann flanked his boulevards (which were wide enough for a troop of cavalry) with trees, spacious sidewalks, and buildings featuring multi-class residency and a consistent architectural style. No more than six stories high, each building had shops and offices on the ground floor, apartments for the wealthy on the floors above, and, following a pattern of gentle decline in social status with each ascending story, garrets under the eaves for artists and the poor. When the Second Empire fell Haussmann lost his job, but once the Franco-Prussian War was over Paris hurried to complete his grand scheme. By 1880 the result was a city that was at once spacious and intimate, efficient and beautiful.

The man who best caught the changing aspects of this new light-filled Paris was Camille Pissarro who, when conjunctivitis threatened his sight in the 1890s, turned to painting dozens of views of the city he loved from behind his closed windows.

Above: In the Conservatory (1879) *was one of Manet's few paintings to win official acclaim. "This is a most attractive modern work," wrote one art critic. "The air moves, the figures are marvelously projected."*

In 1876 Manet made the informal portrait at the left of his friend, the Symbolist poet Stéphane Mallarmé. Mallarmé was one of the few art critics to proclaim the virtue of Manet's abandonment of academic finish. "What is unfinished about a work," wrote Mallarmé, "if all its elements are in accord, and if it possesses a charm which could easily be broken by an additional touch?" This charm is evident in the scene on the Rue Blanche (right), where Manet skated.

La Haute Bourgeoisie

At the center of Parisian society were the wealthy, well-educated, and fashionable citizens of the upper-middle class, or *haute bourgeoisie*. Thoroughly respectable, moderately republican, and mildly progressive, they were the natural center of the Third Republic as it steered a precarious course between the radical left and the Bonapartist and monarchist right.

From the self-satisfied midst of the *haute bourgeoisie* there appeared a painter who dressed like a dandy, detested bohemianism, and sought official recognition, but who, nevertheless, dealt conventional art a blow from which it never recovered. A revolutionary in spite of himself, Édouard Manet thought it only natural that a painter "must be of one's own time and paint what one sees." His attitude toward the neoclassical convention of copying Renaissance models was equally straightforward: "We are not in Rome and don't want to go there. We are in Paris; let us stay there."

Manet painted many aspects of Paris, but none with surer knowledge than his own world of the *haute bourgeoisie*. In works such as *In the Conservatory* (left) he caught the essence of middle-class well-being by picturing a fashionable young couple as they posed calm and self-assured in their winter garden. In *Skating* (below) and *Bar at the Folies-Bergère* (overleaf) Manet skillfully mirrored the pleasures of the fortunate as well as the less amusing lot of those who served their "betters."

Suffering from an advanced case of locomotor ataxia, Manet began his last great canvas, *Bar at the Folies-Bergère*, in 1881, only two years before his death. A fancy music hall featuring elaborate revues, the Folies was one of Paris' more egalitarian institutions, catering not only to the wealthy bourgeois with "overworked digestions and underworked intelligences," but also to "foreigners, shop assistants on a spree, and little ladies on the make." Shown in the Salon of 1882, the picture was dubbed dull and in bad taste, but one critic realized what Manet had accomplished and prophetically wrote, "He does not immobilize forms . . ., he surprises them in their effective mobility. It is a very new formula of art, very personal, very piquant, a direct conquest of the artist which will not be lost on the future."

Degas believed "A picture is a thing that demands as much cunning, astuteness, and vice as the perpetration of a crime." He practiced this credo using candid-camera-like poses and techniques such as blowing steam over pastel, to catch, as on the facing page, the ephemeral vision of a ballet skirt in motion. At the right is an 1873 painting of Vicomte Lépic and his two daughters strolling along the Place de la Concorde. Below is a pastel study of a gentleman on his way to the hunt.

The Rich at Play

With the opening of the Paris Exposition of 1878 *la belle époque* moved into high gear. "The prosperity of the city is staggering," exclaimed the journal *Siècle*. "The hotels are full, the restaurants are turning people away, and the boulevards are crowded with visitors leisurely examining the beauties of the capital." From a city of charred ruins, in seven years Paris had become the playground of the world, especially of the rich—American millionaires, European nobility, the new industrial aristocracy. Their pleasures were numerous, sociable, and always fashionable: strolling along the boulevards, riding in the Bois de Boulogne, consuming quantities of truffled game and poultry along with vintage wines at an endless round of dinner parties, going to the races at Longchamp and Auteuil, attending the Opéra, reveling in the night life of the *demimonde*.

In keeping with the Victorian double standard, "ladies" were expected to find music halls "mostly unsuitable," and the cafés of Montmartre were "to be avoided." The gentlemen were freer even if their freedom was lightly disguised. "Men, of course, went to the Opéra for the ballet, or rather to talk to the *danseuses*," wrote one aristocratic Englishman. Indeed the gentlemen so much enjoyed the ballet at the Opéra that its director was unofficially known as "Procurer to the Republic."

The almost gluttonous delight which the rich took in the best things in life was easily matched by the open-armed yet extraordinarily sensitive and rigidly disciplined passion of Edgar Degas for capturing the beauty of this society. "To produce good fruit," wrote Degas, "one should be like a tree trained on an espalier; your arms stretched out, you stay put all your life, your mouth open to gobble up whatever comes your way." A master at portraying an exact impression of movement and light, as in *Ballet Seen from a Loge* (right), or *At the Races* (overleaf), Degas sought to go beyond "instantaneous impressions" in order to "get hold of the customs of a race, that is to say, its charms."

Degas finished *At the Races* around 1880 when horse racing was at its most fashionable. The painting is probably of Longchamp in the Bois de Boulogne; the mustachioed jockeys are gentlemen riders, and the race may well be the *Prix de Drags*, a very smart occasion which the *beau-monde* viewed from a variety of elegant and stylish carriages. At the center of this enthusiasm for horse racing were the Prince of Wales, who sparked a craze for things English, and Paris' ultra-fashionable Jockey Club, which by 1905 included the reigning monarchs of England, Holland, Belgium, Denmark, and Serbia among its members. Keeping up with royalty was an expensive pastime and soon American millionaires—the Goulds, the Vanderbilts, the Biddles—became familiar figures on the turf and throughout the chic world of the very rich.

Joie de Vivre

Paris was of course more than a playground for the rich; it was also a spirit of *joie de vivre* —an optimistic, almost childlike love of life which the English language has never been able to precisely or adequately translate. *Joie de vivre* expressed itself in the optimism with which Parisians rebuilt their devastated city, in their love of fun and pleasure, even in their response to the influenza epidemic that followed the World's Fair of 1889. Parisians laughed off the deadly disease with a cheerful cabaret song that ended in the chorus "Everybody's got the influe-en-za-ah!"

Joie de vivre was a common quality, but it took an uncommon artist to catch its full-bodied character. In the 1860s, when Pierre Auguste Renoir began to study painting, his teacher, on seeing one of his lighthearted efforts, caustically asked, "No doubt it's to amuse yourself that you dabble in paint?" Unabashed, Renoir answered, "Why, of course, if it didn't amuse me, I wouldn't do it." Not only the dreary poses but also the dark pasty colors of the neoclassical masters seemed to him a betrayal of life. "No shadow is black," he wrote. "It always has a color. Nature knows only colors." For years a struggling but happy artist, Renoir, in vivid, lively paintings such as the two reproduced here, and in sketches such as *Anglers Along the Seine* above, created scenes of Parisian gaiety that have given *joie de vivre* a visual if not a verbal translation.

In 1908 at the age of sixty-seven, when rheumatism had forced him to paint with his brush strapped to his wrist, Renoir summed up his technique by saying, "I arrange my subject as I want it, then I go ahead and paint it, like a child." For instance, in Bal à Bougival *(left; 1883) he posed his brother and the Impressionists' favorite model, Suzanne Valadon, as typical summertime Parisians enjoying outdoor dancing. In* Luncheon of the Boating Party *(right; 1881), he again posed friends (including Alice Chirigot, his wife-to-be, playing with a puppy) in order to mirror the festive joy which Renoir knew both as a child and as an exponent of his era.*

The year 1885 marked a turning point in the history of *la belle époque*. It was a moment of equipoise before Paris plunged into the frantic excitement of the *fin de siècle* and before France was rocked by the string of political crises that began with General Boulanger and ended with the First World War. No painting expresses this moment of balance more convincingly than Georges Seurat's monumental, frieze-like masterpiece, *A Sunday Afternoon on the Island of La Grande Jatte*, painted in 1885 when Seurat was only twenty-five. Artistically Seurat's work broke new ground. His pointillist technique of spreading tiny dots of pure color that combined not on the canvas but in the eye according to optical laws led to the search for new visual perspectives and uses of color that were to so fascinate the *avant-garde* after the turn of the century.

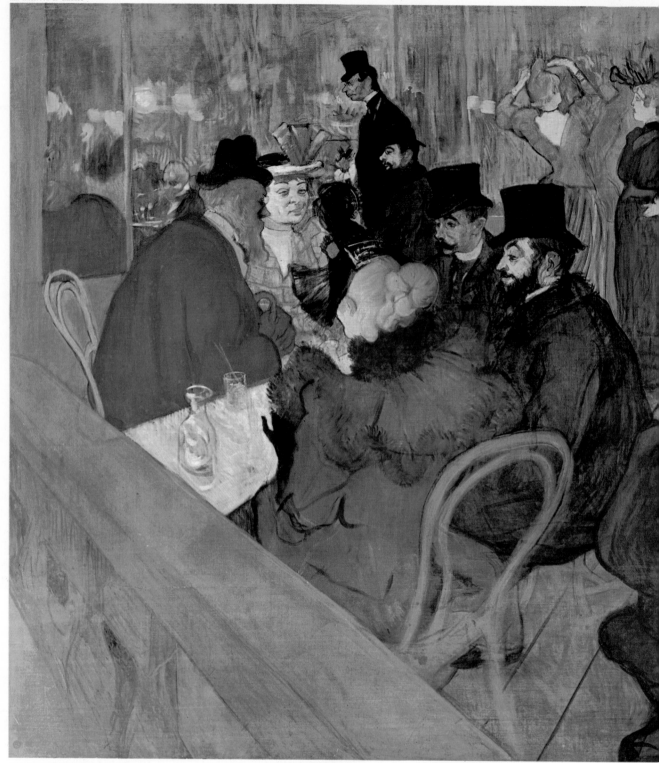

Toulouse-Lautrec finished his "autobiographical" painting, Au Moulin Rouge
*(above), in 1892, three years after the cabaret had opened its doors to the
demi-monde. Seated at the table are some of his closest friends. Behind them
are the dwarf-like Lautrec, his towering cousin-companion Tapié, and, re-knot-
ing her famous orange bun, Lautrec's favorite subject, the dancer La Goulue.*

Demi-Monde

I n the 1860s Montmartre was a rural wooded hillside dotted with windmills on the outskirts of Paris. A generation later it was the center of the city's thriving night life, of the *demi-monde*, where nothing was illegal and everything available. As the nineteenth century drew to a close, a frenzy for fast living and good times gripped the City of Light. The triumph of realism in literature had encouraged a flood of lurid novels, scandalous journals, and a taste for forbidden fruits. In Montmartre dandies such as the *boulevardier* at right consorted with cabaret singers, comics, and chic and not so chic prostitutes to create the hybrid society of the *demi-monde*.

One of the fixtures of this society was a stubby, bearded, well-dressed gentleman, his figure cruelly deformed by stunted legs, who almost nightly clambered down from his horse-drawn cab, sniffed the air, and then, propped up by his cane, advanced unsteadily up one of Montmartre's narrow streets in search of a café and a drink. Born the son of the hard-riding, hard-drinking Count of Toulouse and prevented by his deformity from living a sportsman's life, Henri de Toulouse-Lautrec felt that "nature" had betrayed him. Montmartre, whose singular people were full of gaiety and eccentricity that bordered on monstrosity, made Toulouse-Lautrec feel at home and provided an unexplored terrain for his genius. A prominent figure of the world he pictured, he painted the *demi-monde*, himself included, with a relish that inevitably had little to do with idealized beauty. "I have tried to draw realistically and not ideally," he said. "It may be a defect, for I have no mercy on warts, and I like to adorn them with wanton hairs, rounding them off, and giving them a bright surface."

Working in gouache on cardboard, Lautrec painted Monsieur Boileau *in 1893. The artist's absinthe-drinking friend was one of Paris' better-known gossip columnists.*

Unlike the Impressionists who preceded him, Toulouse-Lautrec believed that "the figure alone exists." In his prints and posters he concentrated on strong, rhythmic lines enclosing areas of bold, contrasting colors. Some critics were dismayed and wrote of his "curious and evil talent" which "dissects his models in a sort of moral and psychological nakedness," but the artist was unmoved. When an actress asked, "Lautrec, why do you always make women so ugly," he replied, "Because they are." His caustic style was, however, in part a reflection of the rough-and-tumble nature of fin de siècle entertainment. Among Lautrec's closest friends was Aristide Bruant, proprietor of the cabaret Le Mirliton, where Bruant specialized in insulting the demi-monde. "Here's something fancy coming," Bruant would bellow as customers arrived. "No dregs this time. Something choice, three star tarts. And the gentlemen behind are undoubtedly pimps or ambassadors." Society loved it. In 1895 Lautrec did the lithograph at right of his colorful, haughty friend. The sketch below right, Yvette Guilbert en diseuse, is one of a series Lautrec did of the queen of the café concerts. She accepted the unflattering likeness philosophically, but added, "For the love of God, don't make me so appallingly ugly! God knows, everyone cannot see its value as a work of art!" Below is an 1896 sketch in which Lautrec featured his friends Chocolat the dancing clown and Achille the bartender.

Troupe de
Mlle ÉGLANTINE
Eglantine   Cléopatre
   Jane Avril   Gazelle

The Entertainers

Occasionally Toulouse-Lautrec ventured into the dignified society of his class, but only long enough to call it "a crush of gloved hands manipulating tortoise-shell or gold lorgnettes." Soon his familiar figure would again be seen waddling exuberantly and with seemingly inexhaustible vitality through an endless round of Parisian pleasures. No amusement, from the ballet to the brothel, was too refined or too crude for his taste. Armed with a sketchbook and a hollow cane filled with "refreshments," he made a second home of theaters, circuses, cabarets, and brothels, becoming friends of the dancers, singers, bareback riders, actors, and prostitutes who entertained a generation bent on having its fling.

Fascinated by the artificiality of Paris' show business élite, Toulouse-Lautrec made thousands of drawings, many of which he later turned into lithographs, posters, and paintings of such famous show people as the singers Yvette Guilbert and Aristide Bruant (left) and the circus clown Chocolat (far left). His posters, such as *Troupe de Mlle. Églantine* (above), became the rage and revived the art of print making. In turn the entertainers paid homage to his genius. "The more one sees of him," wrote one friend, "the taller he grows. In the end he assumes a stature above the average."

The Charm of Everyday

While Toulouse-Lautrec was recording the gay, often bizarre, and sometimes lurid night life of *fin de siècle* Paris, another artist, who was just three years Lautrec's junior but who was to outlive his fast-living friend by nearly half a century, was quietly painting a wholly different facet of *la belle époque*. In his canvases Pierre Bonnard celebrated the thousand and one scenes of daily life that made Paris a synonym for charm. Unlike Lautrec, who feasted on the exotic and the forbidden, Bonnard cultivated the familiar and the natural. As one of his friends wrote, "He understands, loves, and expresses everything he sees, the pie for dessert, the eye of his dog, a ray of sunlight coming through a window blind, the sponge in his bathtub."

Although Bonnard showed a marked preference for familiar subject matter, stylistically he was an important innovator. As a member of a small group of artists who called themselves the Nabis ("Prophets" in Hebrew), Bonnard championed freedom from rational restraints so that painting might partake of the freshness of childlike perceptions. His work effectively communicated his intent. As early as 1893 one critic observed, "M. Bonnard catches the most fleeting expressions; . . . and in support of this gift he is able to draw upon a delicate sense of humor, sometimes ironic, always very French."

Bonnard had a fondness for maxims: "True importance is an unexpected impression"; "Its faults are sometimes what gives life to a picture"; "The unlikely is often the real truth." The Cab Horse, Boulevard des Batignolles (below), painted in 1895 while Bonnard was living in the Batignolles district, and Movement in the Street (left), finished in 1900, are examples of his maxims as well as delightful expressions of his private yet common vision.

The Avant-Garde

P aris celebrated the beginning of the twentieth century with yet another World's Fair. The year 1900 was, as one artist later wrote, "a time of great tranquility, employment, and money." However, a new world was being born. Electricity was making Paris literally as well as figuratively the City of Light. The Métro (subway), the telephone, and the automobile signaled an era of rapid transportation and communication, and Alexandre Gustave Eiffel's great iron tower proclaimed the triumph of the industrial age. The twentieth century was on its way, but few realized that the new century would be more of a departure from than an extension of the nineteenth. Among those few was a loose-knit international coterie of artists, writers, musicians, and thinkers who, attracted by the Paris of *la belle époque*, began to experiment with radically new artistic ideas.

Avant-garde painters owed much to the individualistic tradition that had begun with Manet forty years before, yet their bent was fundamentally different. Willing to believe that "Nature is only a hypothesis," they created new visual experiences where color no longer necessarily represented color as seen by nature, or shapes natural shapes, or experiences happenings as perceived by the rational, conscious mind. Using brilliant, broad strokes of color, as in André Derain's portrait of Henri Matisse (below), or the difficult visual perspectives of Cubism, as in Pablo Picasso's portrait of the art dealer Kahnweiler (lower right), or the dream-like vision of Henri Rousseau (far right), they abandoned the logical clarity of a century gone by for the revolutionary dimensions of a new age.

In his 1905 portrait of Matisse, André Derain made the same free use of explosive colors as Matisse himself. The Salon was scandalized; a critic labeled them "Fauves," wild savages.

In 1906 Picasso painted his patron, the American writer and grande dame of the avant-garde, Gertrude Stein.

Later, in 1910, Picasso portrayed his dealer and friend, the German Henry Kahnweiler, in his new Cubist style.

Henri Rousseau's Poet and His Muse is an allegorical portrait of the poet and critic Guillaume Apollinaire.

End of an Era

When the *avant-garde* painter Maurice Vlaminck wrote his memoirs, he pictured Paris at the beginning of the new century as a place where "life was more engrossing than one's career or one's prospects." Though it was the center of the West, Paris still retained a "happy provincial routine." Times were good, people were friendly, and "half of Paris seemed to be perpetually strolling around with a little cash in its pockets."

It was this intimate, charming, unruffled world of little pleasures which Edouard Vuillard pictured in canvases such as *The Park* (left). Like his fellow Nabi, Pierre Bonnard, Vuillard painted only those scenes which familiarity had made a part of himself. Shy and retiring, he would say, "I prefer to be humble rather than to pretend to understanding." His subtle, intricately colored paintings prompted the novelist André Gide to write in his review of the 1905 Salon, "I do not know what I like most here. Perhaps, Monsieur Vuillard himself. I know few works where one is brought more directly in communion with the painter." Vuillard's success, wrote Gide, "is due to his emotion never losing its hold on the brush . . ., to his speaking in a low tone, suitable to confidences, and to one's leaning over to listen to him."

By 1905, however, events already threatened Vuillard's world. In that year the First Moroccan Crisis led to a rising flood of *revanchist* sentiment against Germany. By 1912, after the Second Moroccan Crisis, French nationalists could hardly wait for hostilities to begin. "The man of arms has taken revenge upon narrow ideologues and windy pacifists," wrote Etienne Rey in his popular book, *The Renaissance of French Pride*. "Once again men have come to realize the essential virtue of war, the exaltation which it induces in the spirit of mankind." When war did come in August of 1914 the French jubilantly greeted the news. As troops marched past Versailles, bedecked with flowers as in the photograph above, women shouted gaily, "Don't forget to send me the Kaiser's moustache!"

11

❖

World War I

Napoleon III once observed that one can do anything with bayonets but sit on them. Weapons, both military and diplomatic, invite use. In August, 1914, the tensions generated by international rivalries exploded into general war.

The immediate cause of World War I, the spark that led to the explosion, was the conflict between Austria and Serbia. Serbia, small but vigorous and highly nationalistic, stood in the path of Austrian expansion into the Balkans, competing with it for the legacy of the disintegrating Ottoman Empire. On occasions when the Serbians had gained territory from the Turks, the Austrians applied pressure and forced them to renounce it. Gradually, influential circles in Vienna concluded that Austrian interests required Serbia to be crushed and looked for an opportunity to open hostilities.

The occasion presented itself in June, 1914, when a Serbian terrorist assassinated Austrian Crown Prince Francis Ferdinand during the latter's visit to Sarajevo. Although the assassin was an Austrian subject, and Sarajevo, located in Bosnia, was Austrian territory, Vienna charged Serbia with responsibility for the crime. The dispute initially appeared to be leading to yet another Balkan crisis of the kind the world had learned to take in stride. But this time the outcome was different because the intricate chain of alliances forged in the preceding thirty-five years was brought into play.

Before attacking Serbia, Austria requested German assurances of support against Russia should Russia come to Serbia's aid. The request placed the Germans in a quandary. On the one hand, they were not eager to place themselves at the mercy of Austrian diplomacy, which could involve them in war with Russia and therefore with France. On the other hand, the trend of international relations since 1890 had made them increasingly dependent on Austria. Austria, in fact, was the only ally on whom they could count, for Italy, the other member of the Triple Alliance, seemed to waver in its loyalties. The Germans thus could not let Austria down without risking complete diplomatic isolation—a fact the Austrian diplomats exploited to the utmost. On July 5 William II yielded to their pressures and gave the Austrians the desired assurance—the so-called "blank check"—of unconditional support against Serbia. The Germans counted on this assurance to intimidate Russia and forestall its intervention. But if this device did not work, they were prepared to fight. Many German generals believed that time was working against Germany because the Russians were making great strides in modernizing their armed forces, and that the sooner war came, the better.

With the German guarantee in its pocket, Austria issued an ultimatum to Serbia on July 23. The Austrians made their terms intentionally unacceptable, for they were seeking not a peaceful solution to the quarrel but a pretext for an invasion. The next day Germany came out in Austria's support, making public a note in which it warned the other powers to keep out of the Austro-Serbian dispute or face "incalculable consequences."

Beginning with the Crimean War and the American Civil War and reaching new peaks of skill in World War I, documentary photography revealed to the world the true face of war. These are German troops breaking the Allied line along the Somme in 1918.

The Russians could not acquiesce in the destruction of Serbia, for to have done so would have meant forfeiting all influence in the Balkans. But they too did not want to act without consulting their ally. The French, like the Germans, felt that they risked isolation if they failed to honor their treaty obligations, and on July 25 pledged to the Russians support against Austria.

On July 28, encouraged by the Germans, the Austrians declared war on Serbia, despite Serbian willingness to accept all but two of the most insolent demands of their ultimatum. The very next day Austrian artillery bombarded Belgrade. Austria's haste was due to its desire to destroy Serbia before the other powers had a chance to arbitrate and settle the dispute.

In response to the Austrian attack, Russia ordered a general mobilization (July 29). At that period a mobilization order was tantamount to a declaration of war. The call to the colors of reserves and the activation of reserve units required several weeks. The country that completed the process first enjoyed a decided advantage over its adversary because it could commence hostilities whenever and wherever it wanted. No country, therefore, could allow a potential enemy to mobilize without immediately following suit. Once mobilization was under way, military operations ensued almost automatically, since each power sought the benefit of strategic initiative.

At this juncture several last-minute attempts were made to stop the drift to war. The Russians proposed submitting the dispute over Serbia to an international court, but the Austrians would not hear of it. Next, the British tried to mediate. Their proposal, containing a thinly veiled threat to support Russia and France in the event of war, had an effect opposite to the one intended. William II, his head filled with racial doctrines, interpreted the British move as evidence that the "Anglo-Saxons" had decided to join the "Slavs" and "Gauls" in encircling and destroying the "Teutons." He became nearly hysterical and made up his mind to fight. In both Berlin and Vienna war parties silenced the more conciliatory groups.

At this point events got out of control. On July 31 Austria ordered a general mobilization, followed the next day by France and Germany. At 7 P.M. on August 1, Germany declared war on Russia, and that very night, without a formal declaration of war against France, sent its troops into Belgium and Luxemburg on their way to Paris.

Europe, in the midst of the summer holidays, was not aware of what these events portended. Contemporary sources agree that the outbreak of the war caught the Continent by surprise.

Ever since 1894, when France and Russia concluded their treaty of alliance, Germany had had to prepare for the contingency of a two-front war. To meet this

On the opposite page are Austrian Crown Prince Francis Ferdinand and his wife (rear seat) minutes before their assassination in Sarajevo. The picture above was made in Berlin as war was announced; the news was greeted with similar enthusiasm by all the belligerents.

Military Preparations and Plans

Alfred von Schlieffen, Chief of the German General Staff from 1891 to 1905, author of the celebrated strategic plan to defeat France.

situation, the German General Staff formulated a strategic plan involving two rapid, closely coordinated thrusts—first against France, then against Russia. The success of this plan depended on speed. France had to be crushed in less than six weeks, the time it was estimated the Russians would require to complete their mobilization. This consideration explains why the Germans so seriously viewed the Russian mobilization order of July 29 that they declared war on Russia three days later. Any delay in reacting to it spelled ruin to their entire strategic plan.

A fundamental difficulty with this concept was the fact that France could not be knocked out in six weeks by an attack across the Franco-German frontier, for this frontier was short (150 miles) and heavily fortified. The French could be struck decisively only by outflanking their fortifications, that is, by crossing the Low Countries. It was with these thoughts in mind that Count Alfred von Schlieffen, the Chief of Staff, had formulated his famous strategic plan in the early 1900s. The "Schlieffen Plan" called for a wheeling movement by an overwhelming right wing across Belgium, coupled with a holding operation by the center and left disposed along the Franco-German frontier. The operation that Schlieffen envisaged has been likened to a swinging door, the right wing serving as the door, the center and left as its hinge.

The French had a general notion of what the Germans intended. To meet their anticipated thrust through Belgium, they devised "Plan XVII." Rather than collide head-on with the swinging door, they decided to concentrate forces in the center; as soon as the Germans launched their wheeling movement, they intended to strike at the German positions in Lorraine at the pivot of the swinging door, so as to separate it from the hinge. Thus one offensive was to be met with another offensive.

The German strategy had an obvious flaw in that the violation of Belgian territory was certain to bring Britain into the war on the Franco-Russian side. But the Germans were not much perturbed at this prospect. As the only major European power without conscription, Britain had only 160,000 men under arms—a minuscule force compared to Germany's 5 million or France's 4 million. Bismarck once expressed German contempt for Britain's military might when he threatened to order his police to arrest any expeditionary force the British might land on the Continent. The British navy was another matter. But the navy could make its weight felt only in a protracted war, and the Germans felt certain that by crossing Belgium they could finish the war in two or three months.

The Germans and the French alike believed that the decision would be reached on the Western front. Until then, Russia and Austria were expected to keep each other balanced in the East. The French rather overestimated the effectiveness of the Russian army because of its modernization, for which they had advanced much money. The Russian command was generally of low quality, and transport and communications were of a most primitive kind. Much the same may be said of the Austro-Hungarian army, which, in addition, suffered from the disloyalty of the Slavs who formed the majority of its conscripts.

Although it was not immediately apparent, the war that broke out in 1914 differed fundamentally from all other wars that had preceded it. The best way to define the difference is to say that World War I was the first industrial war—the first in which the manpower and technology of the industrial era were applied to the slaughter of human beings. In the second half of the nineteenth century the major European powers (Britain excepted), emulating the example set by Prussia in the Napoleonic era, had introduced universal military service coupled with reserve systems. This practice virtually transformed the entire male population into a potential fighting force. Within a few weeks after the outbreak of war in 1914, 6 million men stood poised to fight. Behind them were many more millions who could be drawn upon as the need arose. Such masses of soldiers could not be equipped and armed by conventional arsenals; they required the services of the country's entire industrial plant. Countries like Russia, Italy, and Austria-Hungary, which had the manpower but lacked the industrial backing, found themselves now at a great disadvantage. By contrast, Great Britain and the United States, even though they had no peacetime conscription and therefore lacked a ready pool of reservists, managed quickly to mount efficient armed forces thanks to their superior industrial capacity and the industry-bred discipline of their citizenry.

The application of industrial methods to warfare accounted for the unprecedented destructiveness of World War I. Battle experience gained in the wars of the nineteenth and early twentieth centuries (the American Civil War, the wars waged by Prussia against Austria and France, and the Russo-Japanese War) yielded a variety of new weapons of great destructive power, such as the breech-loading rifle and the machine gun. These instruments of death could now be put into mass production. So could the automobile and airplane, which with a few changes became suitable for military purposes. Warfare acquired a new dimension: it became total, calling for the full commitment of human and economic resources.

The Germans had little trouble overcoming Belgian resistance, stanch though it was, and pushing on toward Paris in accord with their timetable. Shortly after Germany had sent troops across the Belgian frontier, Britain declared war.

The Major Campaigns,
1914–1916

In response to the German offensive, the French put into execution their Plan XVII, launching an attack against Lorraine. But German resistance there proved stronger than had been expected, and the drive soon faltered. The failure of this offensive placed the whole French army in grave peril. The Germans carried out their drive through Belgium on a broader front and with more numerous forces than the French had anticipated. The French had disposed only 31 divisions on their Belgian flank against the 52 which the Germans employed in the wheeling movement, and these they grouped along the eastern half of the Franco-Belgian border, leaving the western portion virtually undefended. The German right wing moved forward with astounding speed. On August 27 advance units crossed into France, on September 3 they captured Reims, and two days later they were 15 miles from Paris. The bulk of the French army, vainly battering against German positions in Lorraine, now faced the danger of being trapped in a gigantic nutcracker formed by the enemy's steadfast center and irresistibly advancing right. How near collapse France was at the beginning of September may be gathered from the fact that the government at this time evacuated to Bordeaux.

To relieve the pressure on the French, the Russians hastily mounted an offensive against Germany in East Prussia. But the attack was badly executed and ended in disaster. The German forces, led by their two ablest generals, Paul von Hindenburg and Erich Ludendorff, met the Russians in early September in the Battle of Tannenberg, and inflicted on them a crushing defeat.

At this point, when the war seemed over, there occurred what became known as the "Miracle on the Marne." The Allies expected the Germans to keep their extreme right wing moving forward, first to the west and then to the south of Paris, so as to isolate the capital from the rest of the country and outflank the French armies of the center. But the Germans shifted the direction of the extreme right, sending it instead north and east of Paris. Their intention was to close the gap that developed between their extreme right and the other armies taking part in the offensive. The astonished French saw the Germans, instead of executing the dreaded flanking movement, exposing their own flank. With superb confidence, General Joseph Joffre launched on September 6 a general counteroffensive along the Marne River. The Germans, exhausted and confused, stopped their advance and then withdrew. Both Paris and the French army were thus saved from a disastrous encirclement.

**THE WESTERN FRONT
1914-1917**

German advance, Aug.-Sept., 1914
Stabilized front, 1914-1916
German attacks and gains, 1915-1916
Allied attacks and gains, 1915-1916
Hindenburg Line, 1917

This turn of events ended Germany's hopes of crushing France in six weeks and forced it into a protracted two-front war, which it had sought so desperately to avoid. The failure of the Schlieffen Plan has been subsequently blamed on the German command's unwillingness to adhere strictly to its creator's recommendations. It has been said that Schlieffen's successors lost courage at the last moment and weakened the right wing to reinforce the left, and then deflected the right from its appointed course around Paris. Recent researches, however, have shown such criticism to be unfounded. They reveal that Schlieffen himself had considered a variety of alternatives in troop dispositions, and that he had actually intended to route the extreme right north of Paris. Furthermore, it appears today that his famous plan was not realizable under the best of circumstances. It ignored modern railroad transport and the advantages that it gave the retreating side, with shrinking and therefore faster lines of communications, over the advancing side whose lines became increasingly extended and slower. The plan was simply a desperate gamble. One can only marvel at the recklessness of a government willing to risk the fate of 68 million people on a strategy so rigid in its timing that a delay of a week or two spelled the difference between victory and defeat.

Walking wounded of the British Expeditionary Force, photographed in the retreat from Antwerp in 1914.

The following two months (October and November, 1914) of military operations on the Western front are known as the "Race to the Sea." The two opponents were not so much trying to reach the coast as to outflank each other. As each effort failed, they moved farther north and west, until the Channel put an end to their maneuvers. In Flanders the Germans had the disagreeable experience of running into the small but superbly trained British Expeditionary Force (BEF) consisting of regulars. At Ypres the BEF lost 50,000 men, the bulk of its contingent.

By Christmas, 1914, the Western front was stabilized, and a solid line stretched from the English Channel to Switzerland. This line was to remain virtually unchanged for the next two and a half years. Despite offensive operations that cost millions of casualties, neither side succeeded until March, 1917, in denting the front by more than ten miles either way. Flanking movements in the West were no longer possible. The enemy had to be assaulted frontally, that is, in the most difficult and costly manner. This fact helps explain the enormous casualty lists of World War I.

Although their great offensive had failed, as 1914 drew to a close the Germans were in a better position than their rivals. In the opening stage of the war they had augmented their economic capacity considerably by securing control of industrialized Belgium and the northern regions of France, the latter containing over half of France's coal and nine-tenths of its iron. No enemy soldiers stood on German soil. Under these circumstances, the Germans could adopt a defensive strategy on the Western front.

In the course of 1915 the battle lines in the West remained relatively static as both sides turned their attention to the East. On the French front troops installed themselves in trench complexes. Attempts at a break-through produced no significant results. In April, 1915, the Germans succeeded in opening a gap in the Allied lines by the use of a new weapon, poison gas, but the breach was soon sealed and the front re-established.

The Central Powers achieved their gains in Russia in 1915 against the forces of six-foot six-inch Grand Duke Nicholas. He was relieved by the tsar, who took command himself.

In drawing plans for 1915, the German General Staff decided to make a major effort on the Eastern front to help their hard-pressed Austro-Hungarian ally. Although the Russians had suffered a severe defeat at Tannenberg, their simultaneous offensive launched against Austria-Hungary had gone well. In the fall of 1914 Russian armies had conquered Galicia and threatened to break across the Carpathian Mountains into the Hungarian plain. Czechs and other Slavic conscripts were deserting the Austro-Hungarian armies in droves. The position of the Dual Monarchy was further aggravated by Italy's defection from the Triple Alliance. After a period of wavering, the Italians in May of 1915 declared war on Austria-Hungary and launched an offensive along the Isonzo River near Trieste. Pressed along its extended frontier and shaken by the disloyalty of its minorities, Austria, which had irresponsibly begun the war, stood on the verge of collapse. To forestall this disaster, the Germans withdrew eight divisions from France, and in May, 1915, launched an attack against the Russians. Confronted with superior firepower and better command, the Russians had to withdraw, evacuating both Galicia and central Poland.

Among the Allies, the stalemate obtained on the Western front in the winter of 1914–1915 caused deep differences of opinion. One group, including the majority of the generals, continued to believe that the war would be decided in France and favored building up forces there until they were strong enough to launch an overwhelming offensive. Another, led by David Lloyd George and Winston Churchill (then First Lord of the Admiralty), felt that it was useless to throw men and matériel against the well-entrenched Germans. Instead, they wanted a diversion against Germany's weak allies, especially the Ottoman Empire, which had joined the Central Powers in December, 1914. The Churchill-Lloyd George plan was to seize the Dardanelles and Constantinople by means of a sea-borne invasion force in order to open up a convenient sea route to Russia and wreak havoc in Germany's and Austria's backyards. But the military was not prepared to gamble precious divisions on such a risky venture. The Australian and New Zealand troops landed in February, 1915, at Gallipoli, near the entrance to the Dardanelles, proved insufficient for their task. The whole operation was badly bungled, and in December of 1915, after suffering heavy casualties, the Allied troops withdrew. Churchill had to resign from the cabinet.

The entrance of Italy and Turkey into the war greatly extended the scope of military operations in 1915. There was fighting in the provinces of the Ottoman Empire, especially in Transcaucasia and Mesopotamia, where the Russians and the British respectively made good progress. The British also ejected the Germans from most of their colonial possessions. The Bulgarians sided with the Central Powers, and the Romanians went over to the Allies (1916). In this manner a secondary front came into existence in the Balkans, pitting the Italians, Romanians, and Serbs against the Austro-Hungarians, Turks, and Bulgarians.

In the course of 1915, while engaging in relatively minor skirmishes elsewhere, the Germans, French, and British were marshaling their resources for a supreme effort on the Western front in 1916. With great energy, Britain made up for its peacetime lack of military preparations. A call for volunteers brought to arms over a million enthusiastic men, who were speedily trained and dispatched across the Channel. In January, 1916, when the flow of volunteers seemed to dry up,

Britain took a step without precedent in its history by introducing compulsory military service. Lloyd George, appointed Minister of Munitions, overcame the shortages that had developed early in 1915 and placed the entire munitions production on an efficient basis. France and Germany also recruited masses of men and geared their industrial production to military uses.

In 1916 both sides expected to achieve a break-through by concentrating an enormous superiority of men and artillery on a short sector of the Western front. These expectations, however, were cruelly disappointed. Under technical conditions prevailing at the time, the defender had a decided advantage over the attacker. The critical factor was the machine gun. Placed behind lines of barbed wire, it exposed the attacking forces to a deadly barrage that mowed them down and sooner or later forced them to stop. Gradually the trenches on both sides developed into elaborate subterranean fortifications: on the surface, barbed wire, mines, and a maze of trenches; underground, command posts, living quarters, and supplies. An attack against such a line was not so much a charge as a siege, but it took the generals a long time to realize this fact.

The first great battle of 1916 was inaugurated by the Germans early in the year in the area of Verdun. They struck at this relatively unimportant fortress with the deliberate intention of "bleeding white" the French army. For reasons best known to themselves, they counted on inflicting five French casualties for every two of their own. They intended to force France to keep pouring men into combat

Several of the reasons why the carnage of World War I exceeded that of all previous conflicts are shown in this German photograph: entrenchments, poison gas, the machine gun.

BAYERISCHES HAUPTSTAATARCHIV, MUNICH

THE EASTERN FRONT, 1914-1918

—— Farthest Russian advance, 1914-1915
--- The front, 1915
▨ Brusilov offensive, 1916
━━ Armistice line, 1917
▨ Area occupied by Central Powers under Brest Litovsk Treaty, 1918

by the hundreds of thousands until it could do so no longer and collapsed from sheer exhaustion. The Battle of Verdun in fact exceeded in ferocity and casualty rates any previously fought. Much of it was waged by pockets of isolated units that held on to the last and exacted a frightful toll from the opponent. As the French solidified their positions, German losses increased. Of the 500,000 men who lost their lives at Verdun by July, 1916, when the forces finally disengaged, nearly one-half were Germans.

The Battle of Verdun sapped the strength of the Allies while they were preparing for a great summer three-front offensive to end the war. The French, exhausted by Verdun, had to yield the initiative to the British, whose large and fresh forces concentrated in the area of the Somme River. The Italians were to launch an attack on the Austrians, while in the East the Russians undertook to mount a powerful offensive in Poland.

The first to strike were the Russians. They moved early in June, in time to relieve the hard-pressed defenders of Verdun. Commanded by Aleksei Brusilov, the ablest Russian general of the war, they advanced with great vigor, especially against the Austrians. Their victories in the summer of 1916 were the most brilliant won by the Allied armies in the entire course of the war. Had the drive not been allowed to bog down from lack of decision and political bickering, it might well have caused the collapse of the Central Powers. In the Brusilov offensive the Russians lost an estimated 1 million men.

While the Russians were rolling forward in the East, the British were preparing a major offensive on the Somme in northwestern France. They had assembled not only an eager army of volunteers but a quantity of weapons and supplies of all kinds exceeding anything previously seen on a battlefield. Among them were airplanes and new armored vehicles known as tanks. This superb fighting force, buttressed by French divisions, stood concentrated along a 23-mile front. The Allied intention was to pulverize the German lines by an artillery bombardment, and then send in the infantry simply to "mop up" what had survived the shelling. In other words, the artillery was to conquer, and the infantry to occupy ground.

On June 25, 1916, Allied artillery—one gun for each 20 yards of front in the British sector—opened fire. The bombardment went on without interruption for seven days and seven nights. Then it suddenly stopped, and the Allied troops went over the top. What was intended as a mopping-up operation soon turned out to be a "race with death." The Germans, concealed inside their excellent fortifications, had survived in considerable numbers. As soon as the artillery barrage lifted, they emerged and manned their machine guns. The attackers, especially the British, were severely handicapped in their dash toward the German positions, for each of them had to carry 66 pounds of supplies and ammunition—they could barely walk let alone run across the cratered no man's land. Their chances of survival were further diminished by being required to advance in orderly waves with fixed bayonets. The German machine gunners cut them down as they approached, wave after wave. On the first day of the Somme offensive the BEF lost 60 percent of its officers and 40 percent of its rank and file—the highest casualty rate of any battle recorded in history. Despite these losses, the Allies pressed their advance into the murderous fire in the ensuing weeks, until the onset of winter put an end to the operation. The Somme offensive gained the Allies a maximum penetration of seven miles. The total cost to both sides was over a million killed and wounded, approximately one casualty for every four square yards of contested ground.

The results of the Italian offensive along the Isonzo River in 1916 were also disappointing to the Allies. Despite strenuous efforts, the Italians did not succeed in denting the Austrian line or significantly pushing it back.

The great battles of 1916, especially Verdun and the Somme, attained a level of horror and sheer destructiveness never before experienced. They were simply "battles of attrition," in which the aim was no longer to outmaneuver, outflank, or break through enemy lines, as had been the case in previous wars, but systematically to drain the opponent's human and material resources. In such combat, casualties were computed on the same basis as expenditures of matériel: no matter how high, they were considered justifiable as long as they inflicted greater losses on the enemy. Human lives became statistical quantities, accounted for like shells or fuel.

A German artist sketched dispirited Russian troops captured as the Brusilov offensive was blunted in 1916.

Morale   The depersonalization of warfare, which began in 1916 and continued until the armistice, profoundly depressed the morale of the troops.

Difficult as it is to believe today, the outbreak of hostilities in 1914 had aroused widespread enthusiasm. The vast majority of Europeans knew of war only from books, for the Continent had been spared prolonged warfare for nearly a century, and in consequence they tended to romanticize it wildly. For many it brought a welcome change from the routine of factory or office. War was seen as the adventure of a lifetime, an escape from a "world grown old and cold and weary," in the words of Rupert Brooke, the most popular of the early English war poets:

1914

Now, God be thanked Who has matched us with His hour,
And caught our youth, and wakened us from sleeping,
With hand made sure, clear eye, and sharpened power,
To turn, as swimmers into cleanness leaping,
Glad from a world grown old and cold and weary,
Leave the sick hearts that honour could not move,
And half-men, their dirty songs and dreary,
And all the little emptiness of love!

Oh! we, who have known shame, we have found release there,
Where there's no ill, no grief, but sleep has mending,
Naught broken save this body, lost but breath;
Nothing to shake the laughing heart's long peace there
But only agony, and that has ending;
And the worst friend and enemy is but Death.

In the first two years of war, the combatants on both sides, many of them volunteers, fought with incredible discipline, fervor, and bravery.

After Verdun and the Somme the situation changed. The discipline remained, at least on the Western front, but the fervor disappeared and for bravery there was less and less scope. Burrowing for months on end in damp, rat-infested trenches, exposed to constant danger from gas and artillery, surrounded by decaying corpses, the fighting man gradually lost his identity and turned into a dull cog in an impersonal war machine. His thoughts concentrated on survival. His best chance of survival was receiving a wound serious enough to send him to the rear for a long convalescence.

To obtain a flavor of the war of attrition we can do no better than turn to the later war poets who, unlike Brooke and his contemporaries, depicted warfare in its true horror. The first poem cited below, written by Siegfried Sassoon, conveys the sensations of the soldiers moments before going over the top; the second, also by Sassoon, depicts the appearance of a battlefield after an attack; and the third, by Wilfred Owen, relates an incident which occurred during a routine gas bombardment.

At dawn the ridge emerges massed and dun
In the wild purple of the glow'ring sun,
Smouldering through spouts of drifting smoke that shroud

The menacing scarred slope; and, one by one,
Tanks creep and topple forward to the wire.
The barrage roars and lifts. Then, clumsily bowed
With bombs and guns and shovels and battle-gear,
Men jostle and climb to meet the bristling fire.
Lines of grey, muttering faces, masked with fear,
They leave their trenches, going over the top,
While time ticks blank and busy on their wrists,
And hope, with furtive eyes and grappling fists,
Founders in mud. O Jesus, make it stop!

⋄ ⋄ ⋄

The place was rotten with dead; green clumsy legs
High-booted, sprawled and grovelled along the saps

And trunks, face downward, in the sucking mud,
Wallowed like trodden sand-bags loosely filled;
And naked sodden buttocks, mats of hair,
Bulged, clotted heads slept in the plastering slime.

⋄ ⋄ ⋄

Bent double, like old beggars under sacks,
Knock-kneed, coughing like hags, we cursed through sludge,

*Part of the grisly harvest of the
Somme offensive of 1916, a slaughter
on a scale that moved English poet
Siegfried Sassoon to write, "I am
staring at a sunlit picture of Hell."*

Till on the haunting flares we turned our backs,
And towards our distant rest began to trudge.
Men marched asleep. Many had lost their boots,
But limped on, blood-shod. All went lame, all blind;
Drunk with fatigue; deaf even to the hoots
Of gas-shells dropping softly behind.

GAS! GAS! Quick, boys!—An ecstasy of fumbling,
Fitting the clumsy helmets just in time,
But someone still was yelling out and stumbling
And floundering like a man in fire or lime.—
Dim through the misty panes and thick green light,
As under a green sea, I saw him drowning.

In all my dreams before my helpless sight
He plunges at me, guttering, choking, drowning.

If in some smothering dreams, you too could pace
Behind the wagon that we flung him in,
And watch the white eyes writhing in his face,
His hanging face, like a devil's sick of sin;
If you could hear, at every jolt, the blood
Come gargling from the froth-corrupted lungs,
Bitter as the cud
Of vile, incurable sores on innocent tongues,—
My friend, you would not tell with such high zest,
To children ardent for some desperate glory,
The old Lie: Dulce et decorum est
Pro patria mori.°

In the spring of 1917 many armies experienced mutinies. A serious revolt took place in April in the French army, when many regiments refused to go into battle. Disorders also occurred in Italian and Russian units. The forces of the most industrialized countries, England and Germany, succeeded in maintaining excellent discipline. But according to Ludendorff, the German army lost at the Somme its old fighting spirit, never to regain it.

Mobilization of the Home Front

When the war had broken out no one anticipated either its intensity or its duration. The issue was expected to be settled in a matter of weeks or, at most, months, and therefore no provisions had been made beyond the usual military kind.

This attitude underwent radical change as the war went on, seemingly without end, making increasing demands on manpower and resources. In static trench combat, ultimate victory came to depend less on the skill of the men under arms than on the ability of the nation to furnish them with an uninterrupted flow of weapons, ammunition, and replacements. Since the resources of every country had their limit, this task could not be entrusted to the normal operations of a

°"It is sweet and proper to die for one's country."

peacetime economy, the more so as the war had disrupted the intricate commercial links connecting all countries with the world market. The economy had to be centralized and managed so that all the resources—human and material alike—were employed in the most efficient manner. In response to this need, the belligerents devised a variety of institutions and procedures, which in the most extreme case, that of Germany, brought the country close to a kind of state socialism. This development is of utmost historical importance. The economic measures devised during World War I as temporary remedies outlived the war, providing a new model of economic and political organization. This model was utilized fully by subsequent totalitarian systems and to some extent also by the democratic countries.

Germany, a country especially short of resources, pioneered this process. Before the war a large proportion of its raw materials, food, and labor had been imported from abroad, from areas which after 1914 came under enemy control or were inaccessible because of Allied command of the high seas. Without putting its resources to the most rational use, Germany would have been unlikely to remain in the war for long. German industrialists realized this fact sooner than did German generals, who relied entirely on force of arms and showed little awareness of the economic aspects of modern warfare. Walther Rathenau, the director of electrical industries, was the first to grasp the need for organizing Germany's domestic resources for war. At his urging, the Prussian government established in August, 1914, a War Raw Materials Department to stock and allocate raw materials on a priority basis. In November staple foods were placed under controls, and in 1915 food rationing was instituted. The Germans also carried out intensive experiments with chemical substitutes for scarce raw materials, including food. A spectacular result of these efforts was the discovery of a method of "fixing" nitrogen present in the atmosphere—a discovery that freed Germany from dependence on nitrates, previously obtained from Chile, and provided its industries with an essential of both high explosives and chemical fertilizers.

Sound management and applied science permitted Germany to overcome to some extent the shortage of raw materials. But there remained an acute shortage of labor. The armed forces continued without interruption to siphon off white-collar and manual workers to the point of endangering both the economy and the administration. The losses suffered in 1916 at Verdun and the Somme necessitated especially severe encroachments on the labor force. The problem was solved by a drastic method. In the fall of 1916 the Kaiser placed Ludendorff in charge of the entire German war effort. Ludendorff grasped much better than most Prussian generals the necessity of harnessing the total national resources to the war effort. He requested and obtained from the Reichstag in December, 1916, the passage of the National Service Act that mobilized the entire male population of the country for war service. The law required every male between sixteen and sixty years of age and not on active military service to take a job in an occupation officially designated as critical, be it in a factory or office or on a farm. A special war office (*Kriegsamt*) was established to supervise the execution of this law. In time, the *Kriegsamt* became the central agency for the management of the war economy. To augment its manpower further, Germany began forcefully to deport workers from occupied territories in Belgium, France, and Poland. In Octo-

Posters and prints played an important role in mobilizing public opinion against the enemy. This 1915 print, captioned "A Fine Victory," was inspired by reports of German atrocities against Belgian civilians.

ber, 1916, on Ludendorff's recommendation and with the enthusiastic backing of the industrialists, the German government established special concentration camps to receive the deportees and distribute them to factories, farms, and military construction sites. In all, 60,000 foreign laborers were brought in by February, 1917, at which time protests in neutral countries forced the cancellation of the program. Both the National Service Act and the deportations represented a significant innovation in the relationship between the state and the individual. The introduction of forced labor brought Germany the closest of all the belligerents to total mobilization.

The Allies acted more slowly in mobilizing the home front, in part because they lacked Germany's tradition of economic centralization, and in part because they never experienced equally severe shortages. Unlike the Central Powers, they had at their disposal the inexhaustible resources of the United States and the British Empire. But they too in time found it necessary to organize. Having centralized the manufacture of munitions and introduced conscription, the British government in February, 1916, passed the Defence of the Realm Act, authorizing it to purchase raw materials at set prices. By the time the war ended, all the belligerents had put into effect some control measures, among which the following may be mentioned: fiscal operations freeing currency from its dependence on gold; centralization of foreign trade; priorities on raw materials; price and wage controls; rationing of all kinds; restrictions on agriculture; and labor conscription. Merely to list these measures is to indicate how much the economic policies of the war period departed from traditional liberal practices and foreshadowed the regulated economies of more recent times. It was during World War I that the productive resources of a country first began to be viewed as an economic whole, and statesmen began to think in terms of production "crash programs" and national economic development.

What did the belligerents expect to gain from all their efforts and sacrifices? On what conditions were they prepared to make peace? Until January, 1917, no one knew. Incredible as it may seem, two years after the outbreak of hostilities neither the Allies nor the Central Powers had formulated anything resembling their war aims, anything that could serve as a basis for peace negotiations.

This became apparent in December, 1916, when President Woodrow Wilson, believing the conflict deadlocked and hoping to bring the belligerents to the conference table, invited both sides to formulate their intentions. It was only in response to his request that the statesmen of the great powers diverted their attention from the pursuit of war long enough to define their goals—and even then they did so more from a desire to appease American opinion than from an earnest belief in the value of such an exercise.

The Allied terms included the following demands: the evacuation by the Central Powers of all the territories occupied by them since August, 1914; the surrender of Alsace and Lorraine; the expulsion from the Continent of the Ottoman Empire; and the reorganization of Europe in accord with the principle of national self-determination—in other words, the disintegration of Austria-Hungary. The Central Powers could have accepted these terms only if they were ready to capitulate—which in December, 1916, they definitely were not.

The German terms were even stiffer. In their formal reply to Wilson, the Germans asked only for a vague "zone" lying between Germany and Russia, colonies, and financial compensation. (They were silent on Belgium.) But their actual aims were much more ambitious. Recent studies based on documents captured in Germany after World War II reveal that nothing short of European domination and possibly even world hegemony would have satisfied William II and his associates. They expected from the war a considerable expansion of German territory, including full political control over Belgium and the industrial regions of France in the West, as well as over Poland, the Baltic region, and the Ukraine in the East. In addition, they envisaged the formation of a large Central European Customs Union embracing Germany, Austria, Holland, France, and the Scandinavian countries. These political and economic gains would have given Germany a solid base for the conduct of *Weltpolitik*, as well as assuring it of an enormous market for its industrial goods.

Clearly, with such unacceptable aims in mind, neither side thought seriously of peace. The war had become a sheer contest of wills—a primitive struggle for national survival.

> There was absolutely no definable area of disagreement and therefore no problems to be solved, the solution of which would mean peace. It was this that turned the First World War into an insane orgy of destruction. With the lack of any rational declaration of intentions, the formulation of the whole conflict was left to the apocalyptic imagination. Blind hatred reached the level of delirium, because there was nothing, no handhold, to which articulate thought might cling.°

The only serious peace move was initiated by the Austrian emperor, Charles I, who in 1916 succeeded Franz Josef. Determined to save the Austro-Hungarian

°Herbert Lüthy, "The Folly and the Crime: Thoughts on 1914," *Encounter* (March, 1965).

General Erich Ludendorff became a virtual dictator in both the military and civilian spheres in Germany. Fiercely opposing any course short of total victory, he urged unlimited submarine warfare in 1917.

WELTKRIEGSBÜCHEREI, STUTTGART

Empire even if it meant betraying Germany and signing a separate peace treaty, he opened secret negotiations with Allied representatives early in 1917. He even offered meaningful concessions; but the Italians considered them insufficient, and the negotiations collapsed.

The War at Sea The operations of the fleets, especially Britain's Royal Navy, were less spectacular than the great offensives on land, but they had a critical influence on the outcome of the war. Command of the high seas assured the Allies of steady supplies of raw materials, industrial products, and men, and enabled them to deny these very things to the enemy. In short, it permitted the Allies to bring to bear the resources of five continents against that portion of the sixth which was controlled by the Central Powers.

Its role as the guardian of the Allied supply routes demanded of the Royal Navy a cautious, defensive strategy. It strove to keep the high seas free of German vessels and to enforce a blockade of the Central Powers, while avoiding major engagements with the German battle fleet stationed in its home ports. There was little to be gained from a victory over the German navy, and everything to be lost from defeat at its hands. As Churchill once put it, the commander of the Royal Navy was the only man on either side capable of losing the war in an afternoon. The one major naval engagement of the war—the Battle of Jutland, fought in May, 1916—resulted not from design but from the confusion of British and German admirals. It ended indecisively.

The only serious challenge to British naval supremacy was the submarine. Cruising undetected on the high seas, it proved deadly to the unescorted, unarmed merchant ships on whose cargoes Britain's war effort depended. In February, 1915, in retaliation for the British blockade, the Germans proclaimed

English artist Joseph Pennell made this sketch of submarines in port in 1917. So effective was the Allied convoy system that of every thirteen ships sunk by German submarines in the final year and a half of war, only one was under convoy.

a counterblockade, threatening to sink on sight all ships entering British waters, including those displaying a neutral flag. This policy, ruthlessly carried out, aroused much anti-German feeling in neutral countries. The sinking of the passenger ship *Lusitania* (May, 1915) off the coast of Ireland with a loss of 1,200 lives, many of them American, nearly brought the United States into war against Germany. To mollify foreign opinion, in September, 1915, the Germans temporarily suspended such attacks on neutral ships, though they continued to dispatch Allied vessels at a disturbingly high rate.

In February, 1917, the German government reversed itself once more and decided to resume unrestricted submarine warfare. At that time it announced its intention of sinking any ship, regardless of flag, that entered the waters designated as a "war zone" around Allied ports in the Atlantic and Mediterranean. This step was a desperate gamble, not unlike that taken with the Schlieffen Plan. Superficially, the situation of the Central Powers early in 1917 looked sound: the great Allied offensives of 1916 had been beaten back, Romania had been defeated and occupied, and Russia seemed on the verge of collapse. But the long-run prospects were dim, because the Central Powers had at their disposal fewer human and material resources than did the Allies. The Allied blockade was making itself increasingly felt, causing serious food shortages in Germany and Austria. The German high command realized this fact, and considered defeat inevitable if the war lasted much longer. The only chance of victory lay in a supreme effort to knock out Britain, thereby freeing Germany and Austria from the asphyxiating blockade. The German navy thought it possible, by means of the submarine, to sink 600,000 tons of shipping a month, at which rate Britain would run out of food by the autumn of 1917. Unrestricted submarine warfare, of course, virtually assured America's entry into the war, because the United States would not stand by and tolerate the wanton destruction of its merchant and passenger ships. This risk, however, was considered worth taking because the United States was so unprepared militarily that the war could end before its power had made itself felt. As it turned out, the German leaders once more underestimated political and psychological factors in international relations, and placed too much trust in sheer force and chancy timetables.

At first, unrestricted submarine warfare was successful beyond Germany's most sanguine expectations. In April of 1917 the U-boats sank 850,000 tons of Allied shipping. The figure declined somewhat during the summer but remained sufficiently high to cause deep anxiety among British statesmen. With food reserves sufficient only until October, the island faced the prospect of starvation. But as is always the case with new offensive weapons, countermeasures were soon devised. Depth charges and mines proved effective, and even more so were convoys in which British (and later, American) men-of-war escorted fleets of merchant vessels. These methods eventually brought the submarine under control. How thoroughly the Allies commanded the seas by late 1917 may be gathered from the fact that in the last year of the war, Allied navies transported across the Atlantic over two million American soldiers without a single casualty.

As generally anticipated, unrestricted submarine warfare caused the United States to declare war on Germany (April, 1917). America's entry at first had negligible effects on the military situation (except for naval operations), but it

THE WESTERN FRONT
1918

━━━━ The front, March, 1918
▬▬▬▬ German spring offensive
━━━▶ Allied counteroffensive
••••• Armistice line, Nov., 1918

exerted, from the beginning, an important psychological influence. In the long run, it assured the defeat of the Central Powers.

The Campaigns of 1917–1918   Although the experience of the first two years of war had demonstrated the futility of frontal attacks against entrenched positions, such attacks were repeatedly resorted to in 1917 and 1918. The generals always hoped that surprise, new tactics, or more devastating weapons would smash the enemy lines; and, in any event, they could think of no alternative. French generals, true to the Napoleonic tradition, were particularly fond of head-on assaults.

In early 1917 the French prevailed on their allies to launch another coordinated offensive. This major effort, from which great things were expected, also failed. During the preceding winter the Germans had constructed a heavily fortified defense system in depth (the so-called Siegfried or Hindenburg Line), to which they withdrew on the eve of the Allied attack. The British and French troops sent against it suffered frightful losses—30,000 killed in the first 48 hours—without being able to break through. The Russian offensive, launched on Allied insistence despite the grave internal crisis in Russia (Chapter 12), was the last gasp of a dying army. In the fall it dissolved, and the new Bolshevik government, which seized power at the beginning of November, sued for peace. The Italian offensive also went badly. In the Battle of Caporetto the Austrians and Germans threw back the attackers, capturing 300,000 prisoners and nearly destroying the Italian army.

During the second half of the war, the Western front became increasingly mechanized. If the Germans proved masters in the art of fortification, the British showed the greatest ingenuity in applying to warfare advanced industrial technology. It is they who first developed the tank, which was destined to play so critical a role in World War II. Having tried it with some success in the Somme offensive, the BEF secretly gathered a large number of tanks near Cambrai, and in November, 1917, sent them against the unsuspecting German trenches. The attack—the first in which tanks were used in massed columns—succeeded in achieving a break-through; but since no preparations had been made to follow up the assault, the Germans rallied and closed the breach.

The British also led in the production and use of the airplane. Originally employed mainly for reconnaissance, the plane came to fulfill a variety of functions in the latter stages of the war: for example, to bomb supply depots behind enemy lines, and to provide tactical support of troops. The Germans, for their part, initiated the practice of bombing the civilian population with the intention of disorganizing industrial productivity and lowering morale. From October, 1915, onward they subjected eastern England, especially London, to systematic bombing by Zeppelins (dirigibles) and airplanes. These air attacks strained the nerves of British civilians and brought about a certain decline in production. In retaliation, the Allies bombed German industrial sites. When the war ended, they were readying one-ton aerial bombs to drop on German cities. Such bombing further obliterated the distinction between the military and home fronts.

The last major offensive of the war was launched by the Germans in March, 1918. Russia's withdrawal from the war the preceding winter had enabled Germany to transfer forces from the East and to mount the final supreme effort aimed at capturing Paris. Timing was once more essential to the German plan: the offensive had to succeed before American troops could reach the Western front in sizable numbers. Ludendorff, who directed the operation, was prepared to lose a million men to achieve his objective. The main brunt of the offensive fell on the British sector, which nearly caved in. The situation seemed desperate, and the Allies finally agreed to establish a unified command under the leadership of Marshal Ferdinand Foch—a step they had not been able to decide upon previously. At its height, the German offensive came to within 40 miles of Paris. But the Allies, reinforced in May by several fresh American divisions, fought back furiously. In July, 1918, they counterattacked, breaking through the Siegfried Line and sweeping toward the pre-1914 frontiers.

In September, 1918, the Bulgarians sued for peace, followed in October by the Turks. One by one the ethnic minorities of Austria-Hungary proclaimed their independence, and on November 3 the Austrians capitulated. The next day violent revolts and mutinies engulfed Germany. The Kaiser abdicated and fled to Holland. Finally, on November 11, 1918, a German delegation appeared at Allied headquarters to request an armistice.

Marshal Foch (left), Allied supreme commander, with General John Pershing, head of the American forces.

The Effects of the War   In assessing the consequences of World War I, we must distinguish between short, medium, and long-term effects.

The most immediate and tragic consequence was the loss in lives. There were about 10 million dead and nearly twice that number wounded, many of them permanently mutilated.° A generation of European youth had been wiped out. The war also caused immense material losses, destroying much of the wealth accumulated during the preceding century. The financial losses alone were staggering. To pay for the cost of the war, the belligerents had to spend most of their capital reserves to liquidate a part of their foreign investments. Europe, before 1914 the world's banker, became by 1918 its debtor.

Among the middle-term effects, the most important was the change in the international position of Europe. The war deprived Europe of the world hegemony it had enjoyed throughout the nineteenth century. Gone were the days when a conference of half a dozen European ministers could decide the fate of distant continents. There emerged in the course of the war two vast powers with large populations that threatened to take over leadership in world affairs. The United States came out of the war as the strongest Western state, in no small measure because sales and loans made to the other belligerents had gained it a great deal of wealth. In Eastern Europe the Russian Revolution had brought to power a radical regime that immediately declared war on the entire Western political and economic system. The international position of Europe was further weakened by provisions of the peace treaty (Chapter 15) which, by penalizing the defeated powers, perpetuated the hatreds and suspicions awakened by the war.

In the long run perhaps the most profound consequence of the war was the demoralization of Western man. The senseless destruction of life and property carried on for four long years by nations regarded as the most advanced in the world destroyed confidence in rationalism and progress, two basic tenets of modern Western civilization. In the course of the war there emerged influential intellectual movements that openly preached the irrationality of life. It is symptomatic of the mood of postwar Europe that one of its best sellers was a turgid treatise by Oswald Spengler, a German school teacher, bearing the title *The Decline of the West*. The success of the Bolsheviks, who proclaimed the old order bankrupt and called for a revolution, also owed much to this widespread mood of despair and futility.

The postwar atmosphere was ripe for power-hungry demagogues to exploit the accumulated resentments, especially among the war veterans, by focusing them on concrete objects. Some of them blamed the carnage or defeat on the capitalists, others on the Jews, yet others on the Communists. And since life had become terribly cheap, it became possible to clamor for mass extermination of the classes, races, and political groups allegedly responsible for the war. For if a million men could have been sacrificed for a few square miles of no man's land, why could not a similar number be liquidated to assure a "constructive" aim such as the creation

---

°The known dead (in millions) were as follows: Germany, 1.8; Russia, 1.7; France, 1.4; Austria-Hungary, 1.2; the United Kingdom 1.0; Italy, 0.5. Serbia lost 360,000 men, the Ottoman Empire 325,000, Romania 250,000, and the United States 115,000. The actual fatalities were certainly much greater, and have been estimated as high as 13 million. There were also heavy civilian losses, the worst in Anatolia, where in 1915 the Turks massacred nearly 1 million Armenians as retribution for their alleged treachery.

British soldiers blinded by poison gas during the German spring offensive of 1918 wait for medical aid.

of a classless or racially pure society? In other words, why not kill off all the bourgeois or all the Jews or all the Communists? Such solutions were not generally acceptable in the immediate postwar years, when people still adhered to the older, pre-1914 values, even if unsurely; but for the first time they were openly proclaimed by some public figures.

The world of 1919 stood stunned and uncertain. Wilfred Owen, the greatest of the English war poets (he was killed one week before the armistice), expressed thus the deep doubts of the generation that had lived through the war:

THE END

> After the blast of lightning from the East,
> The flourish of loud clouds, the Chariot Throne;
> After the drums of Time have rolled and ceased,
> And by the bronze west long retreat is blown,
>
> Shall life renew these bodies? Of a truth
> All death will He annul, all tears assuage?—
> Fill the void veins of Life again with youth,
> And wash, with an immortal water, Age?
>
> When I do ask white Age he saith not so:
> "My head hangs weighed with snow."
> And when I hearken to the Earth, she saith:
> "My fiery heart shrinks, aching. It is death.
> My ancient scars shall not be glorified,
> Nor my titanic tears, the sea, be dried."

And French essayist Paul Valéry wrote in 1919: "We, modern civilization, know now that we are mortal. . . . We realize that a civilization is as fragile as a life."

12

The Russian Revolution

H ad it not been for World War I, tsarism might well have muddled through and peacefully yielded to some kind of parliamentary regime. Despite the existence among Russian intellectuals of a strong radical wing, the mood of the country was not revolutionary, and the 1906 constitution, for all its shortcomings, did provide a basis for a genuinely representative system of government. But the war precluded such a peaceful evolution. It subjected Russia to enormous strains that aggravated inherent political weaknesses and social tensions. All the belligerent states of Europe experienced such strains, and by 1917 most of the countries on the periphery of the Continent were near collapse. Russia collapsed first because its government (for reasons discussed below) proved both unable and unwilling to obtain the cooperation of the country in the war effort. By 1916 it became evident even to extreme conservatives that Russia could not remain in the war without major political changes. The events that led to the abdication of Nicholas II and the revolution that followed were thus originally a by-product of World War I—an unexpected consequence of what had begun as efforts to invigorate the pursuit of the war.

The war at first engendered great patriotic fervor. Initially it proved popular with most political groupings: with those of the right because it seemed to promise Russian hegemony in the Balkans, and with those of the center and left because the alliance with the Western democracies seemed to assure the country of a liberal future. The industrial workers showed their dedication to the war effort by suspending strikes. A wave of patriotism sweeping Russia temporarily reconciled tsar and nation.

But the mood did not last. Economic difficulties and the incredible ineptitude of the monarchy in all matters of organization reopened old wounds, and within a year after the outbreak of hostilities, government and society confronted each other once again in a spirit of traditional hostility.

Russia's wartime problems were partly due to inherent economic causes, and partly to mismanagement.

Although an ally of Britain and therefore in theory able to gain access to resources throughout the world, Russia was during the war more effectively blockaded than Germany or Austria. The Central Powers had severed Russia's principal land routes to the West, and by naval control of the Baltic and the Straits had closed its maritime routes as well. The only links with the outside were through distant Vladivostok and the northern port of Archangel, the latter connected with the interior by means of a single railway which was completed only in 1917.

Russia's isolation was not necessarily fatal, for the country had immense internal resources. But poor organization, combined with inadequate transport facilities, prevented their exploitation. When in the autumn of 1914 the military requisitioned railroad cars, Russian cities at once experienced a food shortage,

The Petrograd garrison, a key factor in the Bolshevik seizure of power, is shown demonstrating by the light of bonfires. This water color is by an American-born artist, E. B. Lintott, who was a witness to the revolutionary events in the Russian capital.

notwithstanding abundant harvests in the agricultural provinces. Such shortages became chronic during the war years. The country's industrial plant also never fully geared for the war effort. Of all the belligerent countries, imperial Russia did least to mobilize its home front.

Such mobilization as did take place was carried out by the Duma and the organs of local self-rule. In 1914–1915 these bodies appointed committees that took the initiative in organizing the domestic side of the war effort. They established military hospitals, assisted refugees, and helped retool industry for military needs.

The failure of the imperial regime to cope with the domestic side of the war was only partly due to incompetence. It also had deeper causes of a political nature. Harnessing the nation for war involved a partnership between government and citizenry, and thereby inevitably increased the power of society. Both the court and its bureaucratic-police apparatus feared such a development almost as much as they feared an Austro-German victory. For if the Duma, municipal councils, and *zemstva* (Chapter 4) obtained an active voice in the war effort, they could not be put back in their place once peace had been restored. For this reason, the imperial government hesitated to request or to accept public assistance. It may be said that it waged a war on two fronts: externally against the Central Powers, and internally against contenders for a greater share of political influence.

Nicholas II himself had anything but an autocratic personality. Simple and modest, he was temperamentally better suited for the life of a country squire than for that of an absolute ruler. His real passions were his family and the outdoors. If Nicholas defended autocracy with such stubbornness, it was not from an appetite for authority but from an almost mystic sense of duty: he believed himself to have a sacred obligation to maintain and pass on intact to his successor the autocratic system he had inherited from his father. He never really became reconciled to the constitution that had been wrung from him in the turmoil of 1905.

In this attitude he was strongly encouraged by his wife, Alexandra. Born in Germany but raised in England, the empress had a congenital loathing for parliamentary government. She regarded as a conspiracy all attempts by the Duma to assist in running the country and urged her weak husband to oppose them with all his might. Her letters to him were full of exhortations to be strong and masterful—to be another Peter the Great. Because of her superior strength of will and undeviating political outlook, Alexandra gained increasing ascendancy over Nicholas until in the end she took away from him the reins of government.

The imperial couple's political isolation was compounded by a domestic tragedy. After giving birth to four daughters, the empress finally produced an heir to the throne. The boy, however, turned out to be suffering from hemophilia: the slightest cut or bruise caused him painful hemorrhage and threatened death. The despair of the parents knew no bounds. They tried every possible remedy to no avail, and when medicine failed, sought help from quacks and charlatans.

The only person able to stop the tsarevitch's bleedings turned out to be one Grigori, an itinerant preacher and healer. He was by origin an uneducated Siberian peasant, whose dissoluteness had earned him the nickname Rasputin—

A German cartoon on the Duma's attempt to gain power in 1915: the tsar looks up from his grim playthings to exclaim, "How my dolly has changed!"

the "Depraved." How Rasputin succeeded where everyone else had failed is not known, though it has been suggested that he used hypnosis. Because of his healing powers he became a household fixture at the court. The empress, temperamentally inclined to mysticism, came to regard him as a messenger sent by God to save the dynasty from extinction; and Nicholas, who deeply loved his wife, acquiesced in the presence of a man whom he disliked and mistrusted. As his prestige at the court rose, Rasputin indulged in every conceivable vice with impunity. The police could take no measures against him, for the empress treated all reports of his misdeeds as slanders spread by unfriendly politicians.

The critical moment in the relationship between the monarchy and the nation occurred in the first half of September, 1915, when Nicholas made two decisions: to assume personal command over the army, and to prorogue the Duma.

By departing for the front, Nicholas intended to bolster the morale of the troops who that year had suffered great reverses at the hands of the Germans. But another, and perhaps more important reason for his action, was the wish of the empress to remove him from Petrograd in order the better to be able to handle the detested Duma.

The Duma, in fact, grew increasingly discontented with the conduct of the war. In August, 1915, a group of parliamentary leaders ranging from monarchists to moderate socialists formed a coalition known as the "Progressive Bloc." On September 7 this bloc published a program; its principal demand was the introduction of parliamentary government, that is, the appointment of a cabinet responsible not to the tsar but to the Duma. The bloc asserted that only such a government could enjoy the confidence of the country and carry the war to a successful conclusion. To the imperial couple this demand was intolerable. Their reply was to prorogue the Duma. By taking this step, Nicholas deprived himself of the one institution capable of organizing Russia under trying wartime conditions, and virtually assured his downfall.

After September, 1915, political authority devolved into the hands of Alexandra and her sinister companion. They made and unmade ministries, appointing to the highest positions men whose sole qualification for office was their unquestioned loyalty to the imperial couple. In a short time the two disorganized the whole higher civil service.

In 1916 Russia was in deep crisis. The cities, their population grown in two years from 22 to 28 million, suffered acute food shortages. The army still fought with magnificent courage, winning in 1916 its greatest victories. But its morale was being undermined by ugly rumors. It was openly said at the front that the empress and her Prime Minister, Stürmer, were German sympathizers, that Rasputin was the empress's lover, and that all three betrayed military secrets to the enemy. In the Duma, which was reconvened in November, 1916, the leader of the Constitutional Democrats made a speech in which he virtually accused the government of treason. Even the Grand Dukes pleaded with Alexandra to get rid of Rasputin. She, however, remained deaf to all such entreaties, urging Nicholas instead to exile meddling politicians to Siberia.

Finally, in December, 1916, a group of conspirators which included a close relative of the tsar, a member of an aristocratic family, and an ultra-conservative Duma deputy lured Rasputin to a private residence and there murdered

A Russian cartoon, titled "The Russian Ruling House," depicts Nicholas and Alexandra posed puppet-like on the knees of a dominating Rasputin.

L'ILLUSTRATION

A photograph made in March of 1917, when the tsarist government was toppled, shows soldiers of the Petrograd garrison patrolling the streets.

him. The empress never recovered from the shock. To her it meant the end of the dynasty and of Russia.

Neither Nicholas nor his wife reacted vigorously when on March 8, 1917, disturbances broke out in Petrograd. It was as if they had expected heaven's wrath to descend on the country to avenge the murder of Rasputin. The riots started in the breadlines and from there spread to factories and army barracks. The city had at the time a swollen garrison of 170,000 men, many of them raw recruits recently drafted in the villages. They did not want to go to the front and took advantage of the riots to mutiny. Such disturbances were common among belligerent countries in the second half of the war. Indeed, at this very time a large part of the French army also refused to go into battle (Chapter 11). But the difference was that Russia had an inept and discredited government, completely isolated from the nation. Government troops brought in to deal with the rioters at first fired on them but then refused to do so and fraternized instead. Chaos spread unchecked, and before anyone knew what had happened, the mobs were in control of the streets. On March 12 a group of Duma deputies constituting a Provisional Government assumed interim responsibility for public order. Three days later a delegation of deputies journeyed to the army headquarters to inform Nicholas that the well-being of the nation and the successful pursuit of war required his abdication. He complied readily, almost happy to be rid of the heavy burden, and abdicated in favor of his brother, Michael. The following day Michael decided against accepting the crown, abdicating in turn in favor of the Provisional Government. Thus, on March 16, 1917, the Romanov dynasty came to an end, and Russia lost the pivot around which its political life had revolved for centuries.

The March Revolution was received in the cities with unbounded enthusiasm. The Provisional Government
The streets filled with joyous crowds. They demonstrated, paraded, or simply
milled around, intoxicated with their new freedom. It was as if a great load
had been lifted, and everyone could at last breathe freely. All hopes seemed
near realization.

The first Provisional Government was a coalition of the same groups that in
1915 had formed the Progressive Bloc. It was committed to the pursuit of the war.
It also had a deep commitment to civil liberties, and immediately after assumption of authority abolished all limitations on individual freedom, including the
restrictions on ethnic or religious minorities. But beyond these measures the
Provisional Government did not feel itself empowered to go. As its name implies,
it regarded itself merely as a transitional authority, something like a trustee of
national sovereignty until the convocation of a Constituent Assembly. This
legalistic attitude determined its subsequent fate.

The Provisional Government faced formidable problems. The country was in
the throes of an acute economic crisis: the treasury stood empty, the ruble continued to fall, transport was disorganized, food deliveries lagged. The administration was also in disarray. Shortly after assuming power, the new government
abolished the detested police, replacing it with an ineffective "peoples' militia."
The imperial civil service dissolved. The result was an administrative vacuum,
which well-meaning but inexperienced intellectuals tried to fill by forming various councils and committees to assume responsibilities for local government.

But beyond economic and political problems lurked even graver ones—problems that may be described as those of excessive expectations. The country had
awaited "democracy" for so long and so fervently that it expected miracles: it was
to cure all ills, resolve all disputes, and make everyone happy. The peasantry
wanted "democracy" to confiscate at once the land belonging to non-peasant
proprietors and distribute it among them. The workers demanded better wages,
shorter hours, and a voice in the running of factories. The national minorities
insisted on immediate autonomy. The radical intellectuals called for far-reaching
reforms leading toward a new social order. The demands of one group instantly
provoked demands of other groups, each fearing to lose out in the great scramble
for goods and rights. What happened was that wants and aspirations repressed
for decades under imperial rule suddenly rose to the surface, and no appeal to
reason, patience, or patriotism could stifle them any longer.

The Provisional Government would have had a difficult task controlling these
pressures even under the best of circumstances. But if it had any chances of
success, it spoiled them by committing two serious mistakes.

The first was to forget that a government must rule. The legalistic argument
that it was only a "provisional" authority meant little to a nation desperate, after
years of imperial mismanagement, for firm authority, the more so because the
government kept on postponing the elections to the Constituent Assembly to
which it intended to transfer sovereign powers. This failure is not surprising. The
leaders of the Provisional Government had a background of parliamentary
opposition which had taught them how to criticize authority but not how to
exercise it. On some occasions, when provincial representatives came to Petrograd
for instructions, they were told by ministers that in a democracy policy decisions

THE PROVISIONAL GOVERNMENT   343

should be made locally, and therefore no instructions from the center would be forthcoming. Such an attitude invited anarchy.

The Provisional Government's second mistake was to remain in the war. It was apparent even in March, 1917, that the country had no strength to carry on. Nevertheless, the government not only decided to continue fighting but undertook to launch a major offensive. In making this disastrous decision, it was motivated by two desires: to secure Constantinople and the Straits, promised Russia by the Allies in secret agreements of March, 1915, and to participate in the general peace settlement. But Allied pressure also played its part. Allied statesmen, their eyes riveted on the Western front, knew little and cared even less about the desperate internal problems confronting the new Russian government. All they wanted was another offensive on the Eastern front to divert German forces. The Provisional Government, dependent as it was on its allies for military and financial support, could not resist these pressures, and promised to throw its last available forces against the external enemy. When later the time came to defend its authority from an internal enemy, the government found it no longer had any forces at its disposal.

From the beginning of its existence, the Provisional Government had to cope with a dangerous rival on the left, the so-called soviets. The first soviets (the word means "council") emerged in the Revolution of 1905 as strike committees of industrial workers. In the course of that first revolution, they had expanded through the admission to their ranks of soldiers and sailors from nearby garrisons and thus became popular organs of political action. Their organization was informal, not unlike that of the American town hall meeting. Socialist intellectuals quickly realized the value of soviets as instruments of mass agitation and bases for revolutionary activity. They joined them, providing leadership and ideologi-

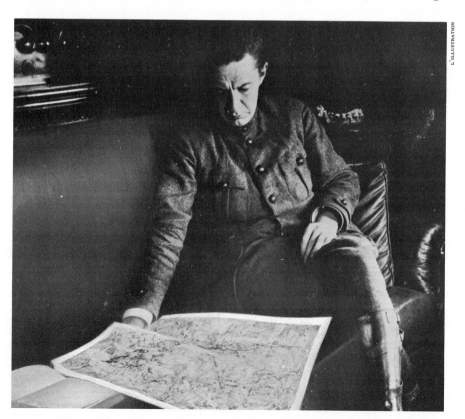

Alexander Kerensky was photographed examining a military map in the fall of 1917, shortly before the Bolsheviks overthrew his Provisional Government.

cal guidance. The Social Democrats in 1905 were especially active in the soviets. They saw them as a means of exerting "socialist" pressure on the "bourgeois" government if and when the middle class succeeded in overthrowing "feudal" tsarism.

The Petrograd Soviet, liquidated in December, 1905, re-emerged on March 12, 1917, the very day the Provisional Government came into being. In its early days it was a committee representing the mutineers of the Petrograd garrison. Its first act was to issue the celebrated "Army Order No. 1," which contributed much to the collapse of discipline in the Russian army. This self-styled decree deprived officers of nearly all their authority and created in every military unit soldier committees endowed, among other rights, with exclusive control over weapons. The order was jubilantly received by the soldiers, who in many regiments proceeded to arrest and even lynch officers accused of "undemocratic" behavior toward them. Like its 1905 predecessor, the new Petrograd Soviet soon broadened its composition and transformed itself into the Soviet of Soldiers' and Workers' Deputies. It claimed the right to issue decrees and to countermand ordinances of the Provisional Government. The Petrograd Soviet, and the soviets that sprang up in the other cities of the empire, enjoyed close links with the troops and industrial workers, and from the very beginning assumed the prerogatives of a shadow government.

Until the fall of 1917 leadership in the soviets was everywhere in the hands of moderate, democratic socialists belonging to the Socialist Revolutionary party or the Menshevik faction of the Social Democrats. Their policy was inconsistent in the extreme and contributed greatly to the breakdown of the Provisional Government. On the one hand, they favored continuation of the war; on the other, they insisted on social reform measures that made the pursuit of the war all but impossible. They could conduct such a contradictory policy because they had no political responsibility and sought none; they were content to use the soviets as organs of pressure on the "bourgeois liberal" government. But the passions they aroused among the masses with their calls for a social revolution soon got out of hand, and in the end the moderate socialists found themselves swept aside by the very forces they had helped to unleash.

The dyarchy between the Provisional Government and the Petrograd Soviet reflected the profound cleavage that had long existed between Russian liberals and radicals. It courted disaster, and responsible statesmen made great efforts to overcome it and to consolidate political authority. In May, 1917, the coalition cabinet resigned, yielding to a ministry of a more radical complexion. Its outstanding figure was a young lawyer, Alexander Kerensky, who assumed the post of Minister of War. As a prominent agrarian socialist, Kerensky enjoyed a following in the Petrograd Soviet. It was hoped that he could bridge the gulf between the two centers of power and rally the country for the forthcoming summer offensive.

However, instead of subsiding, the acute internal crisis that developed in the spring became further aggravated upon the arrival in Petrograd of Lenin, the most radical and most ambitious of the socialist intellectuals.

The novelist Turgenev once divided mankind into two categories: the Hamlets and the Don Quixotes—those who think without acting, and those who act

The Bolsheviks

without thinking. Most Russian revolutionaries fell neatly into one of these two groups. There were those who theorized, engaged in hair-splitting arguments, and drafted endless programs, manifestoes, and protests, but in the end did nothing. They loathed bloodshed, and for all their talk about class war or terror always recoiled when it came to employing force. The others detested talk and extolled action. They believed in a direct assault against the existing order, even at the sacrifice of their lives. They carried out terrorist acts with incredible bravery, usually ending their days either on the gallows or in exile.

Lenin belonged to neither category. He esteemed theory but only a theory linked to action. He had no aversion to violence, considering it a natural concomitant of life. Among his intellectual heroes was the Prussian military theorist Clausewitz, the author of the theory of strategic annihilation. But at the same time Lenin rejected useless self-sacrifice. He believed that force should be used with circumspection so as to yield the best results. No politician of his time had a better appreciation of the nuances of power: how to obtain it when weak, and how to augment it when strong.

Lenin was born in 1870 under the name Vladimir Ilich Ulianov in a middle-class family. His father was a school inspector in Simbirsk, the same town where by a remarkable coincidence the father of Kerensky, his future adversary, served as school principal. When he was seventeen his older brother was executed for participation in a plot to assassinate the tsar. After completing school, Vladimir Ilich went on to study law at the University of Kazan. There, like many students of his time, he became involved in political activity, joining a terrorist organization and taking part in a mass student protest, for which he was expelled. But he managed later on to pass examinations at the University of St. Petersburg where in 1891 he received his law degree.

During Lenin's university days Marxism became a serious intellectual force in Russia. Lenin became passionately converted to it. He accepted the theories of Marx and Engels literally, without doubts or reservations, in a spirit nothing short of fanatical—with greater dedication than Marx himself, who frequently asserted his theories were a method, not a dogma. He had a religious, ascetic disposition, incapable of tolerating either dissent or weakness. A century or two earlier he might well have been the leader of some extreme fundamentalist sect. Once he had grasped the historic mission of the proletariat as seen by Marx, he fully identified himself with it, and came to believe with an utterly sincere conviction that he embodied its spirit. Anyone who opposed him was by definition an enemy of the working class, a scoundrel whose life had no value.

In St. Petersburg Lenin joined an illegal circle of Social Democratic propagandists, for which in 1895 he was arrested. The years 1897–1900 he spent in rather comfortable exile in Siberia, studying and writing for legal Marxist journals. When he regained his freedom, he found the Social Democratic movement in disarray. The revisionist theories of Eduard Bernstein (Chapter 8) had persuaded many socialists to reject social revolution in favor of peaceful evolution. Other socialists, impressed by the rise of trade-unionism, decided to confine themselves to helping workers improve their economic condition. Such views revolted Lenin. He saw in them a betrayal of Marxism, an opportunistic surrender to the bourgeoisie. In 1900–1901 he experienced a profound spiritual crisis.

When he emerged from it, his mind was made up: he decided that neither the peasantry, nor the working class, nor the intelligentsia could be depended on to carry on a revolution, and that it was necessary to found a small, tightly organized, fully independent party of professional revolutionaries.

In 1902 Lenin brought out in Germany, where he had temporarily settled, his most important theoretical work, *What Is to Be Done?*, outlining the tenets of what was to become Bolshevism. The working class of itself, Lenin maintained, was not capable of developing a proletarian class consciousness or of maintaining revolutionary zeal. Of itself, it could not progress beyond trade-unionism, that is, the striving for peaceful economic self-improvement. The ideal of the socialist revolution had to be carried to the workers from the outside, from a body of professional, full-time revolutionaries. Like priests of some religious order, the socialist intellectuals had to guard the true faith.

In 1903 in London the Russian Marxists convened a congress of the Social Democratic Labor party. In the course of debating its statutes, Lenin insisted that the party should be a highly centralized and disciplined body, open only to persons prepared to place themselves without reservation at the disposal of its Central Committee. Many of the other participants rejected this concept as élitist and undemocratic; they preferred a party organized on another model, with easy admission and autonomy of local cells. In the complicated struggle that ensued, Lenin carried the majority and formed a faction that called itself "Bolshevik" (from the word *bol'she* meaning "more"—hence the "Majority"). Its opponents became known as "Mensheviks" (from *men'she* or "less"—hence the "Minority"). Thus, within a short time of its foundation the Russian Social Democratic organization split into two hostile wings, one centralist and the other democratic. Lenin's majority did not long survive the London congress, but with characteristic political acumen he retained the name "Bolshevik" as psychologically more appealing. His following consisted mostly of middle-brows, who admired him and accepted his leadership without question. The Mensheviks, on the other hand, claimed the major theoretical lights of Russian Marxism, and enjoyed closer ties with the labor movement. Lenin ran his organization with a strong hand. He vehemently attacked his opponents, including one-time associates, accusing them of opportunism, treachery, corruption, and all other manner of sin.

When the war broke out, Lenin joined a small international band of socialists who opposed the fighting and urged the soldiers of all countries to transform the war between nations into a war between classes. He spent the war years in Switzerland, impoverished and isolated. Before 1914 his activities had been financed by a few eccentric millionaires and by bands of Bolshevik youths who carried out daring holdups of Russian banks. Now these sources were dried up, and Lenin had to search desperately for literary jobs to support himself and his wife. He cut a rather pathetic figure as he buttonholed Russian travelers passing through Zurich to fulminate against the bourgeoisie and the Second International (Chapter 8), for which he had developed a consuming hatred. He had little hope of seeing a socialist revolution in his lifetime.

The German authorities had their eye on émigrés like Lenin, considering them potentially useful in sowing defeatism among Russian troops. In 1915, on the initiative of one Parvus, a Russian renegade socialist in their service, they established contact with Lenin, though apparently without any concrete results. (It may be mentioned, in passing, that the Germans pioneered in the use of political propaganda and spent much money and energy in efforts to undermine the morale of their various enemies.)

When the March Revolution toppled the imperial regime, Lenin was impatient to return to Russia. At the urging of Parvus the German authorities gave permission for a special sealed train, carrying Lenin and a number of other Russian revolutionaries, to cross Germany on their way to neutral Sweden. Their intention was to let loose in Russia the most outspoken opponents of Russia's participation in the war, and thereby to accelerate the demoralization of the Russian armies.

Lenin reached Petrograd via Stockholm in mid-April, and at once attacked the Provisional Government. He demanded the transfer of all power to the soviets,

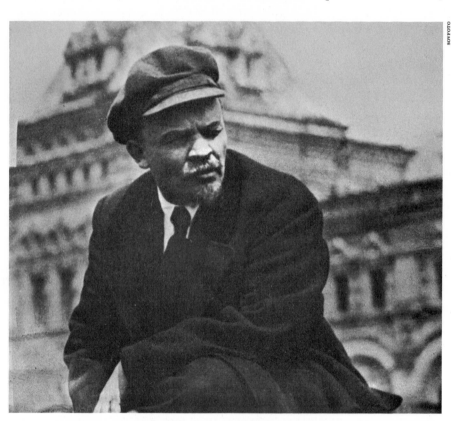

"There is no other man," an observer remarked of Lenin, "who is absorbed by the revolution for twenty-four hours a day, who has no thoughts but the thoughts of the revolution. . . ."

the nationalization of land, the abolition of the army and the civil service, and the cessation of hostilities. In effect, he wanted nothing less than an immediate socialist revolution. Other socialists, including most of his own Bolshevik followers, were aghast at the thought of cutting short the "bourgeois" stage of the revolution. But Lenin was not to be restrained by theory. He realized instinctively that the Provisional Government was foundering, that no one wanted political responsibility, and that the country would soon be ripe for a *coup d'état*. When pressed for a theoretical justification, he could fall back on the concept of "permanent revolution" formulated before the war by Parvus and Leon Trotsky, according to which the bourgeois revolution immediately, without a halt, would deepen into a socialist revolution. In any other country at war, Lenin's public pronouncements would have landed him in jail or before a firing squad. In France that same month the government executed 23 persons for propagating defeatism and inciting mutinies. But in Russia, in its noonday of democracy, any restraints on speech were regarded as an intolerable violation of human liberties, and Lenin was allowed to speak and publish freely.

Lenin's ultimate aims—the disorganization of the army, subversion of the Provisional Government, and seizure of power—required money. This he now obtained from the Germans. The German high command was so delighted with Lenin's relentless criticisms of Russia's war effort that it placed at Parvus's disposal considerable sums for transfer to him. In April Parvus turned over to Lenin's representative in Stockholm 5 million marks. With this and subsequent subsidies from the same source, Lenin financed the party newspaper *Pravda*, flooded the trenches with antiwar propaganda, and built up a Bolshevik paramilitary force in the form of Red Guard units composed of workers.°

In mid-July, after the failure of the great military offensive, rioting troops demonstrated in the streets of Petrograd, demanding the transfer of power to the soviets. Even though the Bolshevik party did not organize these disturbances (it judged its forces too weak as yet for a seizure of power), the Provisional Government accused it of complicity and proceeded to arrest those Bolshevik leaders it could lay its hands on. Lenin, however, escaped in disguise and concealed himself in Finland.

The Bolshevik Seizure of Power

By July Russia for all practical purposes had ceased to have a government. The cabinet having resigned, it took most of the month to replace it. The new Prime Minister was Kerensky, a dedicated democrat and excellent orator, but a man short on political skill. Despite the fiasco of the July offensive, he kept on exhorting the troops to fight in the unrealistic hope that victories at the front would somehow reunite the nation and quell social conflicts. Rather than address himself to urgent domestic issues, he spent his time at army headquarters. Kerensky satisfied no one: conservative opinion condemned him for tolerating anarchism, while the left taunted him as a servant of the international bourgeoisie.

At this time (August, 1917) there began to take shape to the right of the government a loose coalition of liberal and conservative elements. It included army officers disgusted with the destruction of discipline among the troops, businessmen afraid of economic collapse, and various political figures. These elements had no formal program or organization. What bound them together was alarm over the rapid disintegration of political and social institutions and the conviction that unless this process was checked, Russia faced civil war. They accepted the March Revolution, in the making of which they had played a decisive role, but they felt that at this point the establishment of order was more important than further extensions of freedom or equality.

°That Lenin received money from the Germans had been suspected as early as 1917, but proof of the fact became available only after World War II, with the capture by the Allies of the archives of the German Ministry of Foreign Affairs.

General Lavr Kornilov, appointed and then dismissed as head of the army by the Provisional Government.

In countries with unstable government it is common for the armed forces to assume political responsibility. Unlike political parties, armies by their very structure require an effective chain of command that enables them to carry out decisions. In late summer of 1917, therefore, those who sought a way out of the chaos instinctively turned to the generals, around whom there now emerged a movement of national restoration. Its great hope was the colorful Cossack General Lavr Kornilov, Kerensky's new Commander in Chief. Like some other professional generals of the Imperial Army, Kornilov came of peasant stock, and mistrusted monarchs and aristocrats. But he disliked the socialists even more. He expressed contempt for the Provisional Government, which he accused of yielding to anarchist pressures, and talked openly of leading troops on Petrograd to restore order.

The Russian left was much disturbed by this development. Well versed in the history of the French Revolution, it tended to interpret the events of 1917 in the light of those of the 1790s. Radical intellectuals knew that at a certain point a revolution faced the danger of a right-wing reaction. When Kornilov began to menace the Provisional Government, the leadership of the Petrograd Soviet decided to back Kerensky to resist the "danger from the right" and to prevent a Napoleonic coup. The "danger from the left," that is, from Lenin and the Bolsheviks, was considered at this point to be the lesser of the two evils. With the concurrence of Menshevik and Socialist Revolutionary leaders, Bolsheviks were admitted to the military formations established by the Petrograd Soviet to defend the city against Kornilov. Thus unexpectedly Lenin's party, nearly shattered in July, re-emerged in the center of events.

Kerensky's difficulties with the army came to a head in the second week of September. Convinced that Kornilov was plotting a *coup d'état*, Kerensky dismissed him from the post of Commander in Chief and himself assumed supreme civil and military powers. Kornilov refused to obey the dismissal order. There ensued complicated political maneuvers, some of which remain obscure to this day. In any event, on September 9, Kerensky openly broke with Kornilov, and Kornilov issued an emotional appeal announcing his intention of saving Russia from the Germans and their agents among the radicals. Simultaneously he dispatched troops toward Petrograd. But the Petrograd Soviet saw to it that the transport and communications of the advancing rebels were disorganized. Kornilov's units simply melted away as they approached the capital.

After the Kornilov affair the position of the Provisional Government became hopeless. By allying himself with the Petrograd Soviet against Kornilov, Kerensky had alienated a large part of his officer corps, without thereby gaining authority in the Soviet. Quite the contrary. The Soviet, regarding itself as the savior of the country from a "counterrevolutionary" plot, was less than ever disposed to obey the government. From early September onward the cabinet did not even hold meetings, all power being vested in Kerensky. To make matters worse, a violent rebellion broke out in the countryside, where peasants, abetted by military deserters, began to burn estates and seize land.

At the height of the Kornilov crisis the Provisional Government had released from jail the Bolshevik leaders arrested after the July disturbances, in order to create a common "democratic front" against the "Bonapartist" threat. Among the Bolsheviks who profited from the amnesty was Leon Trotsky. (Lenin, charged by the Provisional Government with being a German agent, had to remain in hiding.) An outstanding orator and publicist, Trotsky had had an irregular political past, sometimes allying himself with the Mensheviks, sometimes with the Bolsheviks, but generally pursuing an independent policy. In 1905 he had been a leading figure in the first Petrograd Soviet. Afterward, while in exile, part of which he had spent in the United States, he published penetrating essays on such subjects as the nature of the future revolution and the role in it of the soviets. In July, 1917, Trotsky cast his lot with Lenin. The two men complemented each other admirably. Lenin had a narrow intelligence and an unprepossessing exterior but a tremendous will power and a genius for organization. Trotsky, by contrast, had a brilliant mind and a charismatic personality, but he sorely lacked perseverance and patience.

While Lenin remained in his Finnish hideout, Trotsky assumed leadership of the Bolshevik cause. In this he was greatly aided by winning the election to the chairmanship of the Petrograd Soviet on October 3. He at once employed his energies to push the Soviet toward a decisive conflict with the Provisional Government.

On October 23 the Central Committee of the Bolshevik faction held a clandestine conference in Petrograd, attended by Lenin, to discuss the feasibility of a power seizure. Several participants were opposed to this proposal. They pointed to reports from party cells indicating poor morale and organization and predicted that a coup would fail and destroy the party. They preferred to wait until the Bolsheviks had obtained a solid majority in most of the country's soviets. Lenin, on the other hand, insisted on immediate action. He felt that the government was at its lowest ebb and that the Bolsheviks, enjoying majorities in the Petrograd and Moscow soviets and having at their command a force of Red Guards, were strong enough to strike and succeed. After acrimonious discussions Lenin's view prevailed. The committee resolved to prepare for the coup, without fixing the strategy or setting the date. Since Lenin had to remain in concealment, Trotsky took charge of the preparations.

Trotsky was certain it would be disastrous to carry out a power seizure in the name of the Bolshevik party. The country simply would not have tolerated any one party assuming political power. Even the most pro-Bolshevik workers and soldiers felt loyalty not to the party as such, but to the soviets, which the Bolsheviks had proclaimed as the country's legitimate authority. For this reason, a coup d'état had to be disguised as an assumption of authority by the soviets, or, more specifically, by the Second All-Russian Congress of Soviets, scheduled to assemble in Petrograd at the beginning of November. Until then, Trotsky's strategy was to incite the Petrograd Soviet (many members of which belonged to other socialist parties) against the government and at the same time surreptitiously to create a suitable power apparatus.

Trotsky implemented his plan superbly well. From the rostrum of the Soviet he kept on taunting the government, accusing it, among other things, of conniving with Kornilov and the Germans. He claimed that Kerensky, in order to rid himself of revolutionary Petrograd, had secretly arranged its surrender to the German armies. This treacherous plot had to be thwarted. Trotsky persuaded the Soviet to veto a government order sending troops from Petrograd to the front, and to constitute, under his chairmanship, a Military-Revolutionary Committee. Ostensibly, the committee's task was to organize the defense of the capital against the alleged government-inspired German occupation. In fact, it was intended to serve as the instrument through which the Bolsheviks, acting in the name of the Soviet, were to secure control of the military garrison and arsenals of Petrograd. It mattered little that Trotsky's charges were sheer inventions. His rhetoric held crowds spellbound and enabled him to manipulate them at will. Here is Nikolai Sukhanov's eyewitness account of Trotsky's effect on the mob on the eve of the Bolshevik power seizure:

> The mood of the audience of over three thousand, filling the hall, was definitely one of excitement; their hush indicated expectation. The public, of course, consisted mainly of soldiers, though it had not a few typical petty bourgeois figures, male and female. The ovation given Trotsky seemed to have been cut short, from curiosity and impatience: what was he going to say? Trotsky at once began to heat up the atmosphere with his skill and brilliance. I recall that he depicted for a long time and with extraordinary force the difficult . . . picture of suffering in the trenches. Through my mind flashed thoughts about the unavoidable contradictions between the parts of this rhetorical whole. But Trotsky knew what he was doing. The essential thing was the *mood*. The political conclusions had been familiar for a long time. . . . Soviet power [Trotsky said] was destined not only to put an end to the suffering in the trenches. It would provide land and stop internal disorder. Once again resounded the old recipes against hunger: how the soldiers, sailors, and working girls would requisition the bread from the propertied, and send it free of charge to the front. . . . But on this decisive "Day of the Petrograd Soviet" Trotsky went further:
> "The Soviet government will give everything the country has to the poor and to the soldiers at the front. You, bourgeois, own two coats? give one to the soldier, freezing in the trenches. You have warm boots? stay at home. Your boots are needed by a worker. . . ."
> The mood around me verged on ecstasy. It seemed the mob would at any moment, spontaneously and unasked, burst into some kind of religious hymn. Trotsky formulated some short general resolution or proclaimed some general formula, on the order of: "We will defend the cause of the workers and peasants to the last drop of blood."
> Who is in favor? The crowd of thousands raised its hands like one man. I saw the uplifted hands and burning eyes of men, women, adolescents, workers, soldiers, peasants, and typical petty bourgeois figures. . . . [They] agreed. [They] vowed. . . . I watched this truly grandiose spectacle with an unusually heavy heart.

Lenin, cut off in his hideout from day-to-day developments, burned with impatience. He feared that unless the Bolsheviks acted quickly, the military would overthrow the Provincial Government, restore order, and forever cut the ground from under his party. He wanted the Central Committee to start an insurrection at once, without bothering to wait for the Congress of Soviets. "The

Leon Trotsky, architect of the Bolshevik coup d'état, *was photographed at his Red Army headquarters in 1919.*

people [i.e., the Bolsheviks] have a right and a duty to decide such questions not by voting but by force," he wrote to the Central Committee. But Trotsky procrastinated, keeping opponents in and out of the Soviet in a state of constant suspense: one day he would hint that insurrection was near at hand, the next he would deny that any insurrection was intended. The resultant confusion was so great that neither the Provisional Government nor the groups in the soviets opposed to a coup took preventive measures. Trotsky's handling of the situation provided a model subsequently imitated by many dictators, and especially by Hitler in his foreign policy dealings. The technique of charging the opponent with one's own intentions and alternating between threats and promises became a stock in trade of modern totalitarian leaders.

On November 6—one day before the opening of the Congress of Soviets—the Military-Revolutionary Committee issued an appeal to the population of Petrograd. It claimed that the followers of Kornilov were assembling forces with which to suppress the Congress and to prevent the convocation of the Constituent Assembly. In order to meet this alleged threat it took upon itself the responsibility of defending the "revolutionary order." This fabricated accusation provided the pretext for the Bolshevik insurrection. That night detachments of the Military-Revolutionary Committee and the Red Guard (both under Bolshevik control) took over key buildings in Petrograd and arrested the ministers of the Provisional Government (Kerensky, however, eluded them and escaped). In contrast to the days of March, 1917, there was virtually no bloodshed, except at the Winter

Lintott's water color shows the Red Guard storming loyalists in the Winter Palace in Petrograd, the only violence in the Bolshevik take-over.

Palace, where a small body of loyalist troops held out until the following day.

In the early hours of November 7 Lenin emerged from his hideout, and together with Trotsky made a triumphal appearance at the Congress of Soviets. The Congress, representing about half of the country's soviets, approved of a Bolshevik resolution proclaiming the passage of all power to the soviets. The resolution said nothing about the Bolshevik party or its role in the new system: what that was emerged only later. At the time, the vast majority of the delegates, including many leading Bolsheviks, had no idea that Lenin intended a one-party dictatorship and thought they were merely formalizing the dissolution of the Provisional Government.

The leaders of the Menshevik and Socialist Revolutionary parties, however, sensed what lay behind the passing of "all power" to the soviets. Denouncing the resolution as a fraud perpetrated by the Bolsheviks to subvert democracy, they walked out of the Congress, accompanied by catcalls, over which could be heard Trotsky's taunt, "Into the dustbin of history!"

Lenin took charge of the government in November of 1917 with the same assurance Napoleon had shown in November of 1799. His problem was similar: how to restore stability to a completely disorganized society. But the conditions were different, and so were the means. Where Napoleon achieved stability by sanctifying property and reviving old institutions, Lenin did so by destroying property and creating a completely new institutional framework.

Civil War

In the first months Lenin gained the appearance of being master of the situation by identifying himself with those processes over which he had no control: anarchy on the land and in the factories, and mass desertions in the army. Rather than try immediately to establish order, he legitimized, as it were, disorder. On November 8, 1917, he signed a decree requisitioning without compensation landed properties belonging to the crown, church, monasteries, and wealthy landlords, for immediate distribution to the peasants. This decree changed nothing: it merely sanctioned the existing situation, for peasants were seizing estates anyway. Later that month Lenin authorized another *fait accompli*, namely worker control over industries. Both these measures were taken bodily from the anarchist program, but this did not trouble Lenin, who viewed them merely as stop-gap remedies, to be undone once he was more firmly established in power.

Similar considerations induced Lenin to sign a humiliating peace treaty. The Germans posed stiff demands: they wanted, among other things, Finland, Poland, the Baltic Provinces, and the Ukraine—regions containing over one-quarter of Russia's population and much of its wealth. Lenin's colleagues objected to making such concessions, but Lenin saw no choice: Russia had no army left to continue the war, and any attempt to recruit a new one would topple his government. Peace at any cost was the price of political survival. After bitter debates that threatened to split the party, Lenin won, and in March, 1918, the Russians signed at Brest Litovsk a peace treaty conceding the Central Powers their demands.

Where Lenin was not willing to make any concessions whatever was on the monopoly of political power. Although all through 1917 he had clamored for a Constituent Assembly and had publicly stated his willingness to accept the voters' verdict, even if unfavorable to his party, when the occasion presented itself he did not keep his word. The elections to the Consituent Assembly held late in 1917 gave a majority to the Socialist Revolutionaries. The Bolshevik party obtained only one-quarter of the seats. Lenin allowed the Assembly to convene and sit for one day and then ordered units of soldiers and sailors to disperse it (January 18, 1918).

Having secured in early 1918 a modicum of internal authority, Lenin could now concentrate on the main external threat to his regime, the so-called White movement.

After the Bolsheviks had seized power, a number of generals made their way south, to the region inhabited by the well-to-do and conservative Don Cossacks. There in January, 1918, they formed a volunteer army to "oppose the impending anarchy and German-Bolshevik invasion." The initial force was small, around 3,500 men, mostly commissioned and noncommissioned officers. It had no money and found it difficult to recruit volunteers in a nation heartily sick of war. But gradually its numbers grew, and by the end of 1918 the Whites had at their command an effective fighting force. It consisted of three principal armies: one in the south, under General Denikin; another in the Urals, under Admiral Kolchak; and a third west of Petrograd, under General Iudenich.

The White movement is often described as "counterrevolutionary," but the label is inappropriate. Unlike France in the 1790s, Russia had no significant movement for the restoration of the monarchy. The White leaders in all theaters of war pledged themselves to reconvene the Constituent Assembly and to respect the government chosen by a popular vote. They entrusted the political management of their forces to Constitutional Democrats or Socialist Revolutionaries, members of parties wholly committed to the democratic achievements of the March Revolution. On the other hand, it is true that the actual temper of the Whites was more conservative than their official pronouncements indicated. The officers, shocked by the tragedy that had befallen their country, sought scapegoats, and often found them in liberals and socialists, whom they treated as identical and sometimes refused to distinguish from the Bolsheviks. Had they won the Civil War they almost certainly would have established, at least temporarily, a military dictatorship of some sort.

To meet the White danger, the Bolsheviks formed the Red Army in the summer of 1918. Its organization was Trotsky's second great contribution to the Bolshevik cause. The original military force at Bolshevik disposal was an undisciplined rabble, mainly occupied with looting and extortion. Such troops could not hope to defeat the professional soldiers of the Whites. In April, 1918, Trotsky therefore suggested founding a regular armed force, based on compulsory conscription and staffed by ex-tsarist officers. Lenin and the other Bolshevik leaders received this proposal skeptically, fearing that an army might turn around and overthrow their government; but in the end, Trotsky's view prevailed. In the summer of 1918 decrees were issued introducing compulsory military service for all members of the working class. At the same time former imperial officers were ordered to accept commissions in the Red Army or face confinement in a concentration camp and the detention of their families as hostages. By the end of the year the Red Army had 800,000 men under arms, including nearly 50,000 ex-imperial officers. Throughout the Civil War, the command of the Red Army was entrusted to these officers, but they were subjected to close supervision by "military commissars" drawn from the ranks of loyal Bolsheviks. The soldier committees introduced in 1917 by Army Order No. 1 were abolished, and strict discipline, with the death penalty, was restored. In November, 1918, the government formed a Council of Workers' and Peasants' Defense to direct the entire war effort. Trotsky, as Commissar of War, had the responsibility over military operations, but he did not interfere with strategy, preferring to leave this matter to specialists.

The war was fought with incredible savagery. There was no stable front, and some areas changed hands dozens of times, each change being followed by bloody repressions. Murder of prisoners and hostages, torture, and mutilation were daily occurrences. Particularly vicious were the so-called "Green" armies, composed of anarchistic peasants who rejected alike the Reds and Whites, and murdered with impunity anyone they disliked, especially urban inhabitants.

A controversial aspect of the Civil War was the so-called Allied intervention. In the summer of 1918 contingents of Allied troops, largely British and Japanese, landed respectively in Archangel and Vladivostok. Their primary purpose was to safeguard the enormous stores of war supplies—over 1 million tons—that had been dispatched by the Allies in 1916–1917 to the Russian armies but for lack of transport had remained stockpiled in the ports of entry. Their secondary purpose was to reactivate the Eastern front against the Central Powers. By the end of 1918 the total Allied contingent in Russia was about 10,000 to 15,000 strong. Since such a force could not seriously undertake military operations against the Central Powers, the Allies extended support to the Whites, who were committed to the pursuit of the war. This support at first took the form of financial assistance, resembling that extended by the Germans to the Bolsheviks.

After the signing of the armistice in November, 1918, there was no longer any military reason for keeping troops in Russia, but there was an economic one. In February, 1918, the Soviet government had declared that it would not honor debts incurred by preceding Russian governments. At the same time it had

An incident photographed during the Civil War: a White lynching party hangs Bolshevik captives as a warning against aiding the Communists.

An American soldier at a snowy outpost near Archangel in north Russia during the winter of 1918–1919. The United States contributed some 5,000 men to the Allied intervention force.

expropriated major industries and all banks, in which Western investors had a large interest. These measures represented a serious loss to Western countries, already impoverished by the war. Since the Whites promised both to respect Russia's foreign obligations and to compensate owners of confiscated properties, in 1919 the Allies offered them military assistance. It would be tempting to believe that in so doing they were motivated by a desire to suppress Bolshevism. But there is no evidence to show that they, in fact, thought of Bolshevism as a long-term danger. The Allied leaders, especially Lloyd George and President Wilson, were ill informed about events in Russia and tended not to take seriously the Bolshevik government with its amateurish leadership and unorthodox policies. Among influential Western statesmen, Churchill alone urged a vigorous military intervention to stamp out Bolshevism; but in this he had no more success than he was to have in the 1930s with his pleas for a firm stand against the Nazis. While helping the Whites, both France and England had their ears tuned to Moscow for any signs of willingness to make financial compensation for loans and investments. The help extended to the Whites was too small and too sporadic to assure a White victory, but just sufficient to enable the Bolsheviks to rally much Russian national sentiment behind their cause. With the exception of a few minor engagements, more accidental than intentional, the Allied troops did not fight the Red Army. The Civil War was throughout a fratricidal struggle between Russians.

The Whites came nearest to success in October, 1919, when they launched a four-pronged offensive against Moscow and Petrograd. Denikin's army approached to within 250 miles of Moscow, and Iudenich's troops penetrated the suburbs of Petrograd. But later that month, when the Red Army counterattacked, the overextended White forces simply disintegrated. In the spring of 1920 the Whites were left holding only the Crimea, from which they were expelled in November of that year. This action ended the Civil War.

In the course of the war the Bolsheviks reconquered some of the borderlands that had proclaimed their independence during the Revolution. They had no success along the Western frontier, where direct Allied support helped protect the political integrity of Finland, Poland, Lithuania, Latvia, and Estonia. But they overcame local resistance of the nationalists in Belorussia and the Ukraine, and in 1919 transformed them into Soviet republics. In 1920 the Red Army conquered Armenia and Azerbaijan and in 1921, after bitter fighting, Georgia. These three areas were forcefully fused into a Transcaucasian Soviet Republic.

The victory of the Reds over the Whites was not due to their superior social program or greater appeal to the masses. Programs counted for little in those years, nor did the masses show greater liking for the Bolsheviks than for their opponents. According to Soviet statistics, over 2.5 million desertions took place in the Red Army during the war. The Bolshevik victory can be better explained by their superior understanding of modern warfare. The White leaders were essentially old-fashioned staff officers who viewed combat in strictly operational terms and had little patience with politics. The Bolsheviks, on the contrary, waged "total war," one that fused military operations with economic and psychological (propagandistic) activities. They also enjoyed the advantage of a unified command and of a centralized transport system.

While the Civil War was in progress Lenin instituted in Russia a one-party dictatorship—an entirely new political system that subjected the whole citizenry to the authoritarianism previously established within the Bolshevik party and that provided a model for all subsequent totalitarian regimes.

Constitutionally, the new state was a republic of soviets. The structure and operating procedure of the soviets was normalized, and they received constitutional status as organs expressing the will of the working population. The people's will, theoretically, filtered upward: from the numerous local soviets of workers' and peasants' deputies, through provincial congresses of soviets, to the country's highest legislative organ, the All-Russian Congress of Soviets. The latter appointed a cabinet called the Council of Peoples' Commissars. This government structure existed in the Russian Soviet Republic, as well as in the three borderland republics of Belorussia, Ukraine, and Transcaucasia. In 1924 the four were fused in a single Union of Soviet Socialist Republics.

The idea of a state composed of soviets was anarchist in inspiration. The Bolsheviks adopted it partly because of the role that the Congress of Soviets had accidentally played in their power seizure, and partly because it provided a convenient democratic façade for their profoundly undemocratic manner of government.

From November 7, 1917, onward, the true source of sovereignty resided in the Bolshevik party, or, as it became known in 1918, the Communist party. The party was organized in an authoritarian fashion, from the top downward. At the top stood the self-appointed and self-perpetuating Central Committee. The Central Committee made decisions by majority vote, but Lenin always had his way because a mere threat of resignation brought his recalcitrant colleagues into line. The orders of the committee were binding on the lower organs of the party, including the Communist parties of Belorussia, the Ukraine, and Transcaucasia. In fact, they were also binding on all of the country's institutions without exception. The party viewed itself as the "vanguard of the proletariat," that is, the embodiment of the aspirations and interests of the most advanced social class, the class destined to abolish forever all classes. It was subject to no legal restraints. Any opposition to it, whether from within or without, even that coming from the working class itself, was by definition counterrevolutionary. In its capacity as the "vanguard of the proletariat," the party reserved for itself exclusive control over the organs of the state. The composition of the Central Committee and the Council of Peoples' Commissars was virtually identical, Lenin chairing both. Key positions in all soviets, from the lowest to the highest, had to be occupied by Communists. In other words, the whole *state* apparatus built around the soviets was merely a casing that concealed the operations of the true power mechanism vested in the *party* apparatus.

To assure its monopoly of political power, the party had to eliminate competitors. This process makes melancholy reading, less shocking to us than it was to contemporaries. One by one, political opposition was suppressed. As early as December, 1917, political parties were deprived of an opportunity to make themselves heard by a law that suspended (with two exceptions) all non-Bolshevik newspapers. Next, the rival parties were liquidated. The first to be outlawed was the liberal Constitutional Democratic party (December, 1917). The Socialist Revolutionaries and Mensheviks were harassed but tolerated for a while, because their following among peasants and workers made it dangerous to take open action against them. But with the end of the Civil War, they too were subjected to persecution. In 1922 prominent Mensheviks and Socialist Revolutionaries were arrested or expelled from the country. A sham trial of Socialist Revolutionaries held in the summer of 1922 condemned twelve of the party's leaders to death—a sentence without parallel in the entire history of imperial Russia. The liquidation of parties was accompanied by destruction of private and civic organizations. By the time the process was completed in the early 1930s, there was no organization of any kind left in Russia that was not either closely supervised or directly run by the Communist party. Society was atomized into its individual components, and unable to resist pressures from above.

The basis of the party's power was economic. Its decrees had force because the party acquired control over all the capital and all the productive resources of the country—a control that enabled the party to decide who should eat and how much, who should wear a warm coat, and who should have a roof over his head. This fusion of political monopoly with economic monopoly, inaugurated by the Bolsheviks, is a distinguishing feature of all modern totalitarianism.

The economic policy pursued between 1918 and 1920 is known as "War Communism." In some of its techniques it was influenced by the domestic policies of the Germans during World War I and represented a belated mobilization of the Russian home front. But it went much further. Its ultimate purpose was not so much economic as political: to undercut the economic basis for any resistance to the Communist party. Indeed, as we shall see (Chapter 16), War Communism proved to be an unmitigated economic disaster, lowering productivity below anything Russia had known before or since. Politically, however, it was eminently successful.

War Communism was an attempt to centralize in the hands of the party the country's entire productive and distributive processes. Its policies may be grouped under five headings:

1) *Land.* The peasants, having seized the available land, were loath to supply produce to the cities and army in exchange for worthless paper money. To extract the produce from them, the government in the summer of 1918 undertook forceful requisitions. The Commissariat of Food acquired the exclusive right to stock and distribute foodstuffs and to confiscate them wherever found. These confiscations were usually carried out by armed detachments, originating in the cities or the army, that in effect robbed the peasantry of produce. In November, 1918, all land was nationalized.

2) *Industry.* A decree of June, 1918, revoked the earlier anarchist law authorizing worker control, and nationalized, without compensation, a great part of the industrial and mining establishments. Nationalizations continued during the next two years, so that by 1920 nearly the entire industrial plant of the country was in the hands of the party. It was administered by a Supreme Council of National Economy.

3) *Banking and trade.* In December, 1917, private banks were closed and their resources taken over by the State Bank. In April and November, 1918, the right to private foreign and internal trade, respectively, was abolished; commerce became

a state monopoly. Attempts were also made to replace money by barter and wages in kind.

4) *Labor*. Emulating the wartime National Service Act of Germany, the Communists introduced compulsory labor: everyone was required to work. Strikes were outlawed. Workers and peasants were conscripted to perform service and in 1920 were occasionally organized into "labor armies." A decree of July, 1918, singled out members of the "bourgeoisie" for the obligation to perform hard and menial physical work.

5) *Expropriations*. Monastic and church properties, as well as properties of the crown, were confiscated. A law issued in May, 1918, abolished inheritance and appropriated for the state properties of deceased citizens. Individual decrees expropriated many private possessions, including those of a "nonproductive" kind, such as jewelry and art collections.

It would be a great mistake to think that Russians accepted these political and economic repressions with equanimity. They resisted, and did so more fiercely than any other people subsequently subjected to totalitarian controls. Terrorism revived: Socialist Revolutionary gunmen killed individual Communists and gravely wounded Lenin himself. The peasantry fought so energetically against food requisitions that in 1920 almost half the Red Army had to be assigned the task of suppressing agrarian rebellions. In 1920–1921 serious dissensions developed within the Communist party among members dissatisfied with the muzzling of freedom. The climax of the resistance came in March, 1921, when the garrison of the Kronstadt naval base near Petrograd—one of the citadels of Bolshevism in 1917—revolted against the Communist dictatorship and proclaimed a "Third Revolution" in the name of true soviet democracy.

Lenin responded to this resistance with pitiless terror. Neither he nor Trotsky delighted in blood; but their ideal was to remake man and society, and to achieve

ANNE S. K. BROWN MILITARY COLLECTION

The expropriation of church treasures by the Red Army in Petrograd in 1922, viewed by a Russian artist.

it they felt compelled to remove enemies as swiftly and coldly as a surgeon removes morbid tissue. To Lenin all politics was a battle in which one either destroyed one's opponent or perished at his hands.

In the first ten months of Bolshevik rule repression was sporadic. But in September, 1918, after an assassin had shot the chief of the Petrograd secret police, Lenin proclaimed the inauguration of a systematic "Red Terror." This meant in practice giving state security organs the unlimited right to search, arrest, imprison, torture, and execute without trial persons accused of a broad range of activities deemed "counterrevolutionary." The weapon of Red Terror was the Extraordinary Committee for the Suppression of the Counter-revolution, or Cheka, established in December, 1917. Its head was Felix Dzerzhinskii, the son of a Polish landlord, a revolutionary mystic who sent his victims to the firing squad with the joyless cruelty of a Grand Inquisitor. These victims included persons of all social groups, among them peasants who had concealed food and workers who had gone on strike. How many persons perished in the Cheka's compounds will never be ascertained, for Lenin apparently ordered its records destroyed. The number must have been enormous. For example, after an anti-Bolshevik uprising in Iaroslavl in 1918, the Cheka shot 350 prisoners. Several hundred of the survivors of the Kronstadt rebellion suffered a similar fate. Among the early victims of terror were Nicholas II, his wife, and their five children. In July, 1918, the Bolshevik guards holding them imprisoned in the Urals butchered them, burned the bodies, and dumped the remains in an abandoned mine shaft.

As the prisons overflowed, the police began to send convicts to forced labor camps, the first of which was established in April, 1919, in northern Russia. Here White prisoners of war, ex-tsarist officers, political dissenters, and economic "saboteurs" did hard labor side by side with common criminals. These early camps were the nucleus of a vast concentration camp system that was to develop later under Stalin.

A by-product of Bolshevik dictatorship and terror was mass migration from Russia. During the Civil War an estimated 2 million persons left the country to seek refuge abroad. Among them was a large proportion of Russian intellectuals, including some of its greatest writers and artists.

The Communist International

It was a fundamental tenet of Marxism that the socialist revolution had to begin in countries with the most highly developed capitalist economy. By Western standards, imperial Russia certainly did not qualify as an economic power of the very first rank. How then could one reconcile with Marxism the fact that the first socialist revolution had occurred in Russia? Lenin explained away the contradiction by treating the Russian Revolution as the act of "snapping the weakest link" in the capitalist chain. He assumed that before long the other links would break too. He asserted more than once that unless the Russian Revolution was followed shortly by revolutions in the great industrial countries, it would fail in its historic mission.

Immediately upon assuming power, the Bolsheviks launched an intensive program of international revolutionary propaganda and subversion. But the opportunity for large-scale activity of this kind came only with the November, 1918, armistice. The demoralization that spread in Europe after the war, es-

A powerfully drawn Communist poster of about 1919 calls for workers and peasants "to defend your power, your land, your will!" against the exploitation of ruler, church, and capitalist.

pecially among the defeated Central Powers, provided fertile ground for social upheavals. Many people who before 1914 had turned deaf ears to radical agitation were now prepared to believe that the "bourgeois" order was indeed rotten and that the time had come to do away with it. This mood permitted the Communists to achieve some striking, if transitory, successes.

In early November, 1918, even before Germany had formally capitulated, Communist groups composed of radical workers and intellectuals initiated mutinies and formed soviet-like councils of workers' and soldiers' deputies in several German cities. (This was to provide the Nazis later on with a pretext for the claim that Germany had lost the war from a "stab in the back.") In January, 1919, the Communists staged an uprising in Berlin, and in April they proclaimed a Soviet republic in Bavaria. Throughout 1919 Communist agents and sympathizers promoted violent disorders in Austria. In Hungary in March, 1919, Lenin's associate Béla Kun overthrew a progressive liberal government and founded a Hungarian Soviet Republic. These revolutionary attempts were promptly suppressed by conservative military or paramilitary self-defense units, with the exception of Béla Kun's republic, which managed to survive for half a year.

Lenin had decided as early as 1914 to break with the Second International (Chapter 8) and to found a new socialist body, genuinely dedicated to the cause of world revolution. In March, 1919, when Communist-sponsored revolts in Central Europe were at their height, Lenin realized this ambition by launching in Moscow the Third, or Communist, International (Comintern). The task of this organization was everywhere to stimulate and assist revolutionary movements. Its head was Grigori Zinoviev, Lenin's closest collaborator and in 1917 his companion on the train from Switzerland. In deference to Lenin's belief that modern capitalism depended for survival on its colonies (see Chapter 10), the Comintern paid great attention to the so-called national liberation movements in colonial areas. In the first year of its existence, the membership of the Comintern was small and haphazard, consisting mostly of Spanish, Italian, and French anarchists. In 1920, when contacts with the rest of Europe were re-established, its composition broadened. On Lenin's instructions, in every country the Communists initiated a policy of splitting the existing socialist parties so as to detach from them their most radical elements and form them into national Communist parties. These, in turn, were linked with the Comintern. This method attained a certain measure of success, especially in Germany.

The optimism of the Communists at that time knew no bounds. Every minor crisis abroad, every strike, every manifestation of sympathy for Soviet Russia portended to them an imminent revolution. Zinoviev made the following prediction on May Day, 1919:

> The [international revolutionary] movement progresses with such dizzying speed that one may say with assurance: a year from now we shall begin to forget that Europe had undergone a struggle for Communism, because in a year all Europe will be Communist. And the struggle for Communism will move on to America, and perhaps also to Asia and the other parts of the world.

Shortly after its founding, the Comintern experienced an internal conflict over two issues: the relationship of foreign Communist parties to the Communist International and to their own "bourgeois" governments.

Lenin envisaged the Comintern as an international Communist party, endowed with the same unquestioned authority over its constituent parties as the Central Committee of the Russian Communist party enjoyed over its regional branches. But many foreign Communists would not acquiesce in such authoritarianism.

The Germans especially resented being compelled to submit to Russian rule. The anarchists quit in large numbers over this issue. Lenin, however, would not yield. In 1920 the Comintern formulated a twenty-one point program to which all foreign Communist parties and affiliated organizations had to subscribe. In this fashion began the domination of the international Communist movement by the leaders of Soviet Russia, which continued until the mid-1950s.

On the question of domestic politics, a vociferous section of the Comintern membership—its so-called left wing—desired an uncompromising conflict with the bourgeois order. They wanted neither cooperation with other parties nor participation in parliamentary elections. Lenin repudiated this strategy. In an important treatise, *Leftism, a Childhood Disease of Communism* (1920), he outlined the manner in which Communists were expected to exploit all conflicts within non-Communist societies, exactly as the Bolsheviks had done:

> The whole history of Bolshevism both before and since the Revolution is *full* of examples of zig-zagging, accommodations, compromises with other parties, including those of the bourgeoisie! To wage war for the overthrow of the international bourgeoisie . . . and in advance to reject zig-zagging, the exploitation of conflicts of interest (even of a temporary kind) among the enemy, accommodation and compromises with possible . . . allies—is this not an infinitely ridiculous thing? . . . After the first socialist revolution of the proletariat, after the bourgeoisie of one country had been overthrown, the proletariat of that country will remain for a *long time weaker* than the [international] bourgeoisie. . . . One can defeat a more powerful opponent only by the greatest concentration of forces and the *imperative*, most circumspect, careful, cautious, skilful exploitation of every, even the smallest "crack" among one's enemies, of every conflict of interest among the bourgeoisie of various countries, among the various groups or species of bourgeoisie within individual countries—as well as of every opportunity, even the smallest, to win a mass ally, even a temporary, wavering, unsteady, unreliable, conditional one. . . .

The concept of world-wide revolution introduced a new and explosive element into international relations. It implied the rejection of the existing state system and the deliberate refusal to recognize peace and stability as goals of foreign policy. Like the *Weltpolitik* of William II, it challenged everything and everybody, but in a manner infinitely more ambitious and even less capable of being satisfied by concessions. The aim of the "overthrow of the international bourgeoisie" meant that the Russian people, whom the new government had in 1917 promised peace and bread, found themselves harnessed in the service of a messianic cause that would deprive them, for a long time, of both.

13

---◆---

Modern Thought

The great political and military events that occurred at the beginning of the twentieth century must not be allowed to obscure for us a development of comparable if less palpable importance. The years 1890–1910 (the dates, of course, are approximate) witnessed a veritable cultural revolution. This event is still too close to be grasped in full. Indeed, we do not even have a name for it, except the vague term *Modernism*, which, for lack of a better term, we shall have to use. But its reality is all around us. The twentieth century cannot be understood without taking into consideration this revolution.

Modernism represents a renewal of the Romantic impulse: it is, in Edmund Wilson's phrase, the "second flood of the same tide." Like Romanticism, it proclaims the right of every man to his own values and taste, unfettered by classical or other models. But in making this claim it goes much further than did Romanticism, whose spirit of revolt, retrospectively, appears timid. Modernism is anti-traditionalist without reservations. It sheds impatiently the burden of the past and draws its material directly from raw life. It frowns upon "civilization" with its rules and inhibitions, lavishing admiration instead on whatever is simple and spontaneous. Innovation is not only permitted, as it was under the Romantics, but encouraged, being regarded as the test of true creativity.

Allied to the modern admiration for the simple and spontaneous is the frank acceptance of uncertainty. In this respect, twentieth-century culture differs from all that has preceded it. It has no fixed image of human nature, it recognizes no universal standards of morality or beauty, it even rejects the notion of objective reality. It views everything as in flux and devoid of permanent qualities. These attitudes represent an extreme reaction against the entire positivistic outlook dominant in the mid-nineteenth century.

The collapse of positivism was due to a number of causes. One was the doubts that affected the West toward the end of the century as a result of political, social, and economic crises. The irrationality of World War I played a critical role in the breakdown of the complex of ideas based on the assumption that reason will inevitably rule mankind. Another factor was boredom. In the 1880s the European public, tired of earnestness and purposiveness, began once more to experience pleasure in "art for art's sake," in mysticism and idealism, and in everything else that midcentury opinion had frowned upon. But in the long run, perhaps, the decisive causes were developments that occurred within science. In the 1890s physicists uncovered a vast realm of nature which they could not satisfactorily explain in terms of traditional science. Phenomena of this order called for explanations based on concepts and rules that differed from—and sometimes stood in stark contradiction to—those of traditional science, previously considered validated forever. Suddenly the notion of an all-embracing realm of "nature," obeying definable and unexceptional laws, began to dissolve. Positivism, pushed to its logical conclusion, turned against itself. Subjectivism, un-

Three leaders of the modern revolution in science were photographed in California in 1931. The experiments of A. A. Michelson (left) led Albert Einstein (center) toward his theory of relativity. Robert A. Millikan was an important contributor to subatomic theory.

certainty, chance, believed banished from Western thought, re-entered the scientific vocabulary. This development was fatal for the whole positivistic-materialistic point of view, which had rested on the belief in the existence of one nature and of one set of laws regulating it. It may be said, therefore, that scientists betrayed the positivistic-materialistic outlook on life and unexpectedly joined the ranks of its enemies.

Modernism was flourishing by the time World War I had broken out, though it did not penetrate popular culture until after World War II. Our contemporary thought and art are fundamentally a development of intellectual and aesthetic principles formulated in the period 1890–1910. This period is likely to be seen by future generations as one of the most creative ages in the history of man. (By so saying, we do not pass judgment on the quality of modern culture, but merely state its historic significance.)

We shall divide the discussions of this subject into two parts. In the present chapter we shall discuss the changes that physics and psychology brought about in man's view of nature and of himself. In Chapter 14 we shall deal with the effect these changes had on art and literature. It must be borne in mind, of course, that such a division is an artificial one, for the Modernist revolution took place concurrently in all realms of thought and taste.

The New Conception of Matter

The contrast between the views of nature held by the scientist and the common man has never been as great as today. It is no exaggeration to say that in the twentieth century, a century in which science is dominated by concepts of relativity and quanta, even well-educated men profess a common-sense, mechanistic outlook that would have brought them no credit three hundred years ago.

The main cause of the discrepancy between science and general culture is the widening gap between scientific concepts and everyday experience; and this gap, in turn, derives from the growing preoccupation of scientists with objects and processes that are too big, too small, or too fast for unaided observation. The realm beyond man's sensory perception is enormous: it is enough to realize that the unaided human ear perceives sounds only within the frequency of 16 to 20,000 cycles, whereas scientific instruments can detect sound waves in a range of 100,000,000 cycles. Similarly, what the human eye perceives as light is but a narrow, intermediate band of a vast radiation spectrum that includes invisible radio, infrared, and X-ray waves. Common sense, based on sensory experience, is therefore merely a crude, rule-of-thumb set of guidelines for that particular and limited environment in which man happens to find himself. The instant we leave the realm of familiar dimensions and velocities, common sense loses relevance. It tells us no more about objects that are smaller than the atom or move at speeds near that of light than life in the water teaches the fish what it is like on land or in the air.

Early science did not encounter this conflict with experience with the same intensity because it concerned itself mainly with man's immediate environment. Even seventeenth-century mechanistic science did not depart radically from common sense: its laws may have taxed the imagination, but by and large they did not contradict rules applicable to everyday life. Galileo and Newton, for all their revolutionary influence, viewed objects in a framework of absolute time and space, exactly like that known to ordinary man. It was the investigation of optical and electrodynamic phenomena carried out in the last quarter of the nineteenth century that first uncovered an entirely different realm of nature, one to which human experience proved largely irrelevant. To explain phenomena of this kind it was necessary to have recourse to abstract mathematical formulas and to laws which often make mockery of daily experience. Indeed, what are we to make of such propositions as: matter is only another form of energy; an object increases its mass as it increases its velocity; and time runs faster or slower depending on the speed with which the clock travels?

The discrepancy between science and experience, although extreme in our time, is not peculiar to it; nor is there reason to fear that it will always remain so wide. Max Planck, the discoverer of quanta, once said that the world of science differs as much from that of the average adult as the world of the average adult differs from that of the child. All growing up, whether of individuals or of civilizations, involves the weaning away from a total commitment to immediate experience and common sense, and the acceptance of many rules and principles that contradict them. An infant, when it reaches for the sun, acts on the common-sense premise that it can touch whatever it sees. As it grows, it learns that this is not the case, that the circumference of the sun and the distance that separates it from the earth are so great that nothing in man's immediate environment can give any meaningful equivalent for purposes of comparison. In maturing, people come to accept such abstractions as infinity, eternity, the number zero, and the strangest fact of all, the inevitability of their own death. Many opinions that we consider based on plain common sense are actually articles of faith that we have assimilated to the point where they seem natural and self-evident. The same holds true of mankind at large. That the earth is flat and stands still is common sense—it is a concept that accords with experience; that the earth is round and revolves around the sun is a scientific proposition that contradicts experience. How many habits of thought had to be broken before man would admit the possibility of people walking feet up and heads down on the other side of the earth! There is good reason to believe that the basic discoveries of modern physics will in time enter the mainstream of general culture as firmly as has the heliocentric theory of Copernicus.

In the 1860s no one entertained the suspicion that the view of nature then accepted would ever be questioned. Physics and chemistry seemed to have arrived at a conclusive understanding of matter. There was general agreement that matter consisted of irreducible atoms, that there was a different kind of atom for each of the 92 chemical elements, and that one element could not be transformed into another. Furthermore, it was believed that matter and energy were qualitatively different, each subject to a different law of conservation. These explanations accorded perfectly with the prevalent mechanistic philosophy of the period and were regarded as eternally validated. Yet the twentieth century found reason to question every one of them. Mechanistic physics now appeared inadequate to explain a vast range of phenomena, for which it had to be replaced by the quantum theory of Planck (1900) and the relativity theories of Einstein (1905 and 1916). It was gradually realized that atoms were not in fact the smallest, irreducible components of matter, but agglomerates of yet smaller particles; that these particles were identical in the atoms of all the elements; and that the elements themselves were not immutable. Matter and energy were discovered to be different aspects of the same phenomenon and subject to a single law of conservation. The notion of absolute time and space also had to be abandoned.

At the beginning of the twentieth century it was thought that these discoveries had overthrown traditional physics. Today this is no longer the accepted view. Science in general progresses not by abandoning older theories but by showing the limits of their validity. "The new world picture does not wipe out the old one," Max Planck observed, "but permits it to stand in its entirety, and merely adds a special condition for it." The discovery that the earth was round did not affect medieval road maps or navigation charts, which had perfectly served the purposes for which they had been designed. By analogy, modern or mathematical physics has not invalidated older physics. For this reason a leading physicist even denies that one can speak of a "revolution" in modern physical knowledge. In *Philosophic Problems of Nuclear Science*, Werner Heisenberg writes:

> Columbus' discoveries were immaterial to the geography of the Mediterranean countries, and it would be quite wrong to claim that the voyages of discovery of the famous Genoese had made obsolete the positive geographical knowledge of the day. It is equally wrong to speak today of a revolution in physics. Modern physics has changed nothing in the great classical disciplines of, for instance, mechanics, optics, and heat. Only the conception of hitherto unexplored regions, formed prematurely from a knowledge of only certain parts of the world, has undergone a decisive transformation.

Twentieth-century physics has abandoned a unified view of nature: it accepts the existence of several distinct physical realms, each subject to different sets of explanations. As yet no formula has been found to bridge these sets and to re-establish that unity of nature which underlay mechanistic science. This is one of the reasons why it can be said that modern science has helped to destroy the notion of an objective reality.

The most important achievements of modern physics have been the discovery of the structure of the atom and the formulation of two theories: relativity and quantum.

THE DISCOVERY OF ELECTRONS AND OF RADIATION

The subatomic structure of matter was first revealed in the course of experiments conducted with electricity. In 1876–1878 electrical current sent through low-pressure gas tubes was observed to generate curious rays from the negative, or cathode, pole. These "cathode rays," as they were named, illuminated the gas, heated objects standing in their way, and even caused these objects to throw shadows. They obviously consisted of some kind of matter, but what it was no one knew. Curiosity about the phenomenon increased with the discovery made by Wilhelm Roentgen in 1895 that cathode rays released penetrating rays. Because of their enigmatic nature, Roentgen called them "X rays."

In 1897 the Englishman Joseph John Thomson finally solved the mystery. He identified cathode rays as particles of negative electricity and showed that they had an extremely small mass, 1/2000th that of the hydrogen atom, the smallest

ROGER-VIOLLET

Marie and Pierre Curie in their Paris laboratory about the turn of the century. She was awarded Nobel Prizes in both physics and chemistry.

material object previously known. He called these particles "electrons." Thomson's analysis demonstrated not only that the negative electric current consists of corpuscles, but, more importantly, that there exist material bodies smaller than atoms. Further researches also revealed the existence of other particles, which were named "protons." Before long it was realized that electrons and protons were constituents of all atoms, although their relationship to each other remained obscure. In any event the atom lost its position as the irreducible, minimal "building block" of matter.

Shortly after Thomson had identified electrons, two French scientists, Pierre Curie and his Polish-born wife, Marie, made the discovery that elements such as uranium and radium had the property of "radioactivity"; that is, they spontaneously discharged electrons and other particles and rays. The radioactivity of radium was so great that the energy it released could, within an hour, raise the temperature of an equivalent quantity of water from freezing to boiling. The process of radiation upset some seemingly impregnable laws of physics. It violated the principle of the conservation of matter, since radioactive elements were shown to disintegrate spontaneously. It blurred the distinction between matter and energy. It also disproved the whole notion of the immutability of elements: for in the course of their disintegration radioactive elements changed their atomic weight and moved down the Periodic Table.

These findings threw physics into disarray. They confused the picture of physical matter and its relationship to energy, and challenged the universal validity of mechanistic science.

THE THEORY OF RELATIVITY

Albert Einstein, who with Max Planck made the greatest contribution to modern physics, was the son of a German-Jewish businessman. In the early 1900s he held a job as a clerk in the Swiss Patent Office. The position was undemanding and left him much free time for scientific studies and speculations. Like the other great physicists of modern times, Einstein was not a laboratory technician but a thinker, whose only equipment consisted of pen and paper. He was much interested in philosophy, especially the writings of the contemporary Viennese, Ernst Mach. Mach, an extreme positivist, criticized Newton's concepts of absolute space, time, and motion on the grounds that they could not be empirically verified and therefore represented unscientific, metaphysical assumptions.

Reflecting on the contradictions introduced into the picture of the physical world by recent discoveries, Einstein concluded that these contradictions were due to the application of mechanistic concepts to phenomena not subject to mechanistic laws. In particular, mechanistic physics was not applicable to light and objects traveling at a speed near that of light.

According to the mechanistic view, light consisted of waves (which James Maxwell in 1864–1865 proved to be electromagnetic in nature), transmitted through a material but weightless substance known as "ether." This ether was thought to fill empty space in the universe and to permeate matter. It was regarded as motionless, providing a stable point of reference against which all motion was measured.

The experiment that cast doubt on the whole notion of ether, and a good deal of traditional physics besides, was performed in the 1880s by A. A. Michelson and E. W. Morley. By means of an ingenious apparatus these American scientists determined that the speed of light, known to be in the neighborhood of 300,000 kilometers (or 186,000 miles) a second, did not change, regardless of the direction in which light traveled—whether with the motion of the earth or at an angle to it. For if the motion of the earth (30 kilometers a second) indeed occurred through static ether, a light beam sent along its course should have traveled correspondingly more slowly. At first the paradoxical results of the Michelson-Morley experiment were thought to be due to imprecise measurement, but every subsequent test yielded the same negative result. Light, it was found, has a constant speed.

In 1905 Einstein published in *Annalen der Physik* a 30-page paper under the unassuming title "On the Electrodynamics of Moving Bodies." It was an early fruit of his speculations, known as the "special theory of relativity." In this paper Einstein showed that such findings as obtained in the Michelson-Morley experiment necessitated the abandonment of the whole concept of ether. This conclusion had far-reaching implications. For if ether did not exist, it was no longer possible to find a stable frame of reference in the universe: there was no longer any fixed coordinate to provide a standard for measuring absolute space or time. Space and time turned out to be not absolute, but relative—different for each "system."

To illustrate what Einstein meant when he spoke of the relativity of time, we may ask (as he did): What do we mean when we say that two events occur at the same time? Let us suppose that a person traveling on a train sends, exactly midway between two stations, two beams of light, one forward, and one backward. Since the speed of light is constant (that is, it is not affected by the motion of the train), an observer *outside* the train will see the two beams strike the stations at precisely the same instant. For him, they will be simultaneous events. They will not be simultaneous, however, for the person *inside* the train. Since he is in motion toward the forward station, for him the beam sent ahead will strike the station sooner, because in the interval between his sending the beam and receiving its reflection, he will have traveled some distance forward. Here we have an example of two "systems," each with its own timing.° In daily life, of course, such problems do not arise, because we deal with slow-moving objects; but they become very real when we turn to objects moving at a velocity approaching that of light. The same holds true of space, which is also relative. Einstein demonstrated that the length of material bodies cannot be objectively measured, for it depends on the speed with which they move in relation to the observer.

The special theory of relativity had an unexpected bearing on the puzzling connection between matter and energy. In his paper Einstein showed that mass, like time and size, depends on the object's velocity: the greater the velocity, the greater the mass. Mass he defined as "latent energy," showing that all mass has energy and all energy contains mass. Both are controlled by the same law, the law of the conservation of energy. The relationship between mass and energy Einstein defined in his formula $E = mc^2$—that is, energy equals the product of the mass multiplied by the square of the speed of light.

The special theory of relativity applied to all physical phenomena except gravitation. For the latter, Einstein devised in 1916 his general theory of relativity. One of its predictions was that light waves (which Einstein had previously identified as corpuscular) were subject to gravitational attraction. In 1919, as soon as the termination of hostilities permitted it, the British sent scientific expeditions to South Africa and Latin America to test this hypothesis. The photographs taken by these expeditions during a solar eclipse confirmed Einstein's predictions by showing that light "bent" in the vicinity of the sun. These findings captured public imagination as did no other scientific discovery of modern times, and brought Einstein unrivaled international fame.

THE STRUCTURE OF THE ATOM

The discovery of electrons, protons, and radiation, and the formulation of the special theory of relativity helped physicists to construct the model of the atom. In 1910–1913 Ernest Rutherford and Niels Bohr formulated the so-called solar model of the atom, according to which atoms consist of a positively-charged nucleus (proton) surrounded by negative particles (electrons), orbiting around it much as the planets orbit around the sun. The chemical elements were distinguished from each other not, as had been thought earlier, by the properties of the atoms, for these were identical in all the elements, but by the quantity of electrons or protons. The more of them in a given atom, the greater its atomic weight. In 1932 physicists discovered a third subatomic particle, which, because it had neither the negative charge of the electron nor the positive charge of the proton, they called the "neutron."

In 1919 Rutherford took another important step toward the understanding of

°This example is drawn from Leopold Infeld, *Albert Einstein* (1950).

ULLSTEIN

Albert Einstein was photographed (opposite) in Berlin in 1920, when he was director of theoretical physics at the Kaiser Wilhelm Institute. He worked in the modernistic tower shown above, designed by the German architect Eric Mendelsohn, who was much influenced by Expressionist painters.

Physicist Max Planck, photographed just before World War I, developed his quantum theory during his long tenure at the University of Berlin, where he taught for thirty-nine years.

atoms. He bombarded nitrogen atoms with helium nuclei and found to his amazement that in this manner he could disintegrate the atom of nitrogen and transform it into an atom of oxygen. This experiment marked the birth of nuclear physics. Subsequently the nuclei of other atoms were split with apparatus of increasing complexity.

In the 1930s it was realized that the splitting of atoms could release enormous energy. In 1938 the German physicist Otto Hahn found that the bombardment of the nucleus of uranium, the heaviest natural element, with neutrons caused a chain reaction yielding millions of volts of energy. These experiments, announced promptly in the journal *Nature*, aroused great curiosity in the international scientific community. On their basis, three years later, the United States government authorized work leading to the manufacture of the first atomic bomb.

THE QUANTUM THEORY

There is general agreement today that Max Planck's discovery of quanta was the single most important event in the development of twentieth-century physics. No theory, not even that of relativity enunciated by Einstein, has exerted a comparable influence on the modern conception of nature and the scientific method.

In studying the light effects of radiation, Planck noticed the absence of high-frequency light waves. This observation led him to the hypothesis that the exchange of energy between mass and radiation occurred not in a continuous stream, but discontinuously, in packets or quanta of energy. He formulated the manner in which this exchange took place in a mathematical equation.

Science was slow in realizing the full implications of the quantum theory. At first it attracted attention because it challenged one of the most firmly established principles of science, namely that natural processes occur continuously, without gaps or jerks. As the Latin proverb has it, *natura non fecit saltum*, "nature does not leap." But in time the quantum theory completely changed scientific thinking. Analysis of quanta revealed that in dealing with extremely small and fast-moving particles it is in principle impossible simultaneously to locate them in time and space and to determine their speed. We can know at any one instant only half the qualities of such objects, and therefore we cannot with certainty predict their behavior. Determinism had to be abandoned. "Indeed, the present quantum theory furnishes us only with laws of probability, allowing us to say what, the result of the first observation being given, is the probability that a later observation will furnish us such and such result."°

Mechanistic science conceived nature as an objective reality outside man: it was monolithic and subject to ironclad and universal laws. Man was seen to confront this reality as he would an unknown continent. By using accurate instruments to carefully assemble and process data, he was believed capable of obtaining a complete understanding of all natural phenomena without exception. According to the mechanistic view, if one could ascertain the position and movement of every particle of matter in the universe, he would be able (theoretically) to predict all future events from the present into eternity. This view struck deep

The Implications of Modern Physics

°Louis de Broglie, *The Revolution in Physics* (1953).

The Dane Niels Bohr reconciled the quantum theory with the solar model of the atom that he developed with Ernest Rutherford.

roots in the Western consciousness, and contributed much to that sense of self-confidence that characterized Western culture in the nineteenth century.

Modern physics, while leaving intact mechanistic explanations of certain natural phenomena, shattered the overall mechanistic conception of nature. It destroyed the notion of an objective reality with all that it implied: the unity of nature, the universality of natural laws, the determinism of physical processes, and the ability of science to solve all problems of the natural world. Its impact on general culture was therefore bound to be great, even greater than that of biology in the mid-nineteenth century.

Einstein struck the first telling blow against the concept of an objective reality —a concept that assumes the existence of universal time and space into which nature fits, independently of the observer. Einstein showed that there is no single spatial and chronological frame of reference. Every observer is confined to a specific and relative time-space system. As Einstein once put it, before relativity it had been thought that if one removed from the universe all material objects, time and space would remain; according to relativity, however, time and space would disappear along with the objects. Relativity replaced one objective reality with many subjective realities.

The quantum theory and quantum mechanics which issued from it in the 1920s had an even more devastating effect on the traditional concept of reality. They demonstrate that we cannot know both the position and the motion of certain particles and therefore we are not able to predict their behavior. In such cases, statistical probability replaces determinism. This means that some physical phenomena are exempt from that absolute and unexceptional certainty that had been considered the hallmark of science.

The implications of these discoveries profoundly influenced the whole intellectual climate of the twentieth century.

Old-fashioned empiricism with its belief in "facts" and the power of induction—the ability to elicit general laws from a mass of evidence—is not generally shared by modern scientists. No one heaped more scorn on it than did Einstein. He thought that scientific understanding is achieved only through insight and deduction, and went so far as to agree with the ancient philosophers that "pure thought" could grasp reality.

Gone today too is the belief in the capacity of science to unravel all enigmas of nature. Modern physicists are cautious and even humble in their claims:

> The knowable realities of nature cannot be exhaustively discovered by any branch of science. This means that science is never in a position completely and exhaustively to explain the problems it has to face. We see in all modern scientific advances that the solution of one problem only unveils the mystery of another. Each hilltop that we reach discloses to us another hilltop beyond. . . . The aim of science . . . is an incessant struggle toward a goal which can never be reached. Because the goal is of its very nature unattainable. It is something that is essentially metaphysical and as such is always again and again beyond each achievement.°

With the disappearance of the concept of objective reality, there disappeared

°Max Planck, *Where is Science Going?* (1932).

also the old dichotomy: man-nature. In *The Physicist's Conception of Nature*, Werner Heisenberg has observed that the physicist of today does not view nature as something existing independently of him, and concerns himself, to an extent unthinkable among scientists a century ago, with philosophical questions, especially problems of knowledge:

> The common division of the world into subject and object, inner world and outer world, body and soul is no longer adequate and leads us into difficulties. Thus even in science *the object of research is no longer nature itself, but man's investigation of nature. . . .* Science no longer confronts nature as an objective observer, but sees itself as an actor in [the] interplay between man and nature.

The effect of these diverse implications of modern physics has been to render obsolete the whole positivistic outlook. Positivism had rested on the assumption that, unlike religious and philosophic "pseudo-knowledge," scientific knowledge was objective and certain. But as science itself abandoned objectivity and certainty in favor of relativity and probability, positivism in its classical meaning lost sense.

It would certainly be farfetched to assert that the twentieth century has consciously assimilated the findings of modern physics. For most people the discoveries of Planck and Einstein are a form of magic that they do not understand and therefore fear. But science plays too large a part in Western culture not to exert its influence, even when misunderstood and resented. Modern physics has radically altered the attitude of man to himself and to his environment, throwing him back on his own resources: by destroying the fixed conception of an objective reality it has also destroyed, especially for those who lack religious faith, external bearings, casting people adrift in a sea without charts or landmarks. Such is the main intellectual source of what is called the "alienation" of modern man. "For the first time in the course of history modern man on this earth now confronts himself alone . . . he no longer has any partners or opponents," writes Heisenberg. These words, uttered by a physicist, could as well have been spoken by an existential philosopher, a psychoanalyst, or an abstract painter. They touch on the most vital aspect of modern culture, that quality that lends it its sense of unity.

The New Conception of Man

As we have seen (Chapter 5), the mid-nineteenth century had produced a view of human nature that was in accord with the prevailing materialistic and mechanistic outlook. It treated man as a physiological entity pure and simple, and thinking as a by-product of chemical processes. In the second half of the century this view began to break down. The emergence of psychology as an independent discipline, freed from the tutelage of philosophy, led to intense investigations of human behavior which soon revealed the need for subtler methods of analysis than those provided by natural science. The growing dissatisfaction of natural science itself with mechanistic explanations and with materialism in its cruder forms further encouraged a revision of psychological assumptions. Gradually, a new conception of man emerged, as different from the traditional conception as new mathematical physics was different from its mechanistic predecessor.

American psychologist William James, brother of the novelist Henry, taught anatomy, physiology, and philosophy as well as psychology at Harvard.

The distinguishing feature of modern psychology is its abandonment of the notion of the "soul" as the central agency of mental and psychic processes. The traditional Western view held that man consisted of two separate entities, a body and a soul, the one responsible for physiological and the other for mental and spiritual functions. Nineteenth-century materialists, of course, denied the existence of an immaterial soul, but they in fact retained it in another guise. Academic psychology of the 1870s and 1880s assumed that mental processes originated in sensations, and that these sensations produced in organisms a sense of "consciousness," which was merely another term for "soul." The task of psychology was to localize in the body the organs of sensation and consciousness, to separate consciousness into its elementary components ("ideas," "concepts," "feelings," "emotions," and so forth), and to describe how these components interacted to produce higher states of mind. Much attention was also devoted to measuring psychological phenomena, such as the intensity of sensations. This view had a great deal in common with the whole mechanistic outlook, because it regarded higher psychological processes as resulting from the combination of lower ones. There was agreement that consciousness was an entity, that it had distinct properties, and that it could be analytically separated into its constituent elements.

The first forceful attack on this view of consciousness was launched around 1890 by the American psychologist William James and the French philosopher Henri Bergson. Both of these influential thinkers denied that consciousness could be broken down into its components, on the grounds that mental states constitute an indivisible totality. The mind is in constant flux—it is a living stream, not a building constructed of individual bricks.

In his *Principles of Psychology* (1890–1892), James included a chapter entitled "Stream of Consciousness" in which he eloquently described this psychological continuum. Bergson, in his popular books and lectures, laid stress on the inner logic of mental operations. He showed that these obey not formal categories but their own rules in which associations play an important part.

James and Bergson helped to emancipate psychology from its subservience to natural science by depicting the unique quality of mental processes and demonstrating their immunity to analytic methods. But although they criticized academic psychology for its treatment of consciousness, they did not deny that a single state of consciousness existed. This notion was rejected by their successors after the turn of the century.

The modern conception of man, as we have said, abandons altogether the view that man possesses a single "soul" or "consciousness," in favor of one of two alternatives. One school, originating in the United States and Russia and continuing the older positivist tradition, maintains that "consciousness" is a metaphysical abstraction that cannot be scientifically studied. It concentrates its attention instead on behavior. The other, born in Central Europe and more closely connected with the literary and philosophic tradition, maintains that the conscious is merely an outer shell for the real motor of the psyche, the unconscious.

The first of these two schools has its original source in American pragmatism, whose leading figure was William James. James developed a celebrated theory

The French philosopher Henri Bergson in 1905. "There are general problems which interest everybody and must be dealt with in language comprehensible to everybody," Bergson maintained, and this ability to popularize broadened his influence.

according to which our mental states are not causes of our actions but responses to them. In his view the physiological precedes and has priority over the psychological. An extreme formulation of this theory is James's aphorism: "We do not weep because we are sad, but we are sad because we weep." James laid great stress on the ability of the will, by guiding behavior, to influence the general condition of the mind. The so-called Behaviorist School of psychology, founded by the American John Watson, concentrated entirely on the study of human actions. An extreme development of this tendency occurred in Russia. The psychologist Ivan Pavlov demonstrated by experiments on animals the existence of what he called "conditioned reflexes," that is to say, responses to external stimuli independent of volition and any conscious process. These experiments caused fears, apparently unfounded, that by exploiting such conditioned reflexes it should be possible to transform human beings into soulless automata.

The second modern school of psychology, that which stresses the unconscious, has had a growing influence both on science and on public opinion in the twentieth century.

The idea that the psyche is divided into two separate compartments is by no

The Cry (1893), *by the Norwegian Expressionist painter Edvard Munch, is a visualization of subconscious fears like those in a nightmare.*

means new. It was a commonplace among Romantics, who habitually distinguished between what they called "imagination" and "understanding"—the former grasping reality instinctively and therefore deeply, the latter grasping it formally and superficially. It is quite incorrect to claim, therefore, that modern psychology "discovered" the unconscious. Even the most determined adherents of nineteenth-century academic psychology could not entirely dispense with it. What modern psychology has done, however, is to shift the unconscious from the periphery to the center of psychological explanation.

Much of the credit for popularizing the concept of the unconscious belongs to Henri Bergson. He drew a sharp distinction between "intelligence" (in which he included science) and "instinct." Man develops intelligence to cope with the problems of life. It is a practical instrument, concerned with reality only insofar as it can be used. It systematizes experience by means of formal logic and such categories as physical time and objective space. Instincts, by contrast, are free from such utilitarian influences. They are spontaneous drives, deeply buried in our subconscious. Bergson devoted much attention to memory, showing it to be a rich storehouse of knowledge which surfaces only when not restrained by intelligence, in dreams, hallucinations, or delusions.

The most influential modern theory of the unconscious is that associated with the psychoanalytic method of Freud, which, because of its present-day popularity, requires a more extended discussion.

Sigmund Freud was born in Vienna in 1856 in a middle-class, assimilated Jewish family—a biographical fact not without bearing on his intellectual development. The environment in which he grew up was exceptionally inhibiting. As a member of the bourgeoisie, he had to adhere to a demanding code of morals, especially strict in all that pertained to sex. As an assimilated Jew, he faced in addition the conflict between the inner awareness of being Jewish and the need outwardly to conform to a hostile, Catholic milieu. Such inhibitions also affected most of his friends and early patients, who came from a similar background and faced similar problems of adjustment. Undoubtedly this circumstance heightened Freud's sensitivity to tensions between inner drives and outward restraints. Like all theories claiming universal validity, Freudian psychology is the product of a specific place, time, and social environment, that is, of unique historic conditions, and remains most relevant to them.

In the 1880s Freud, then a medical student, participated in experiments carried out in Paris and Vienna to cure hysterical patients by means of hypnosis. It was discovered that in a hypnotic trance patients relived situations from their life, and that when being confronted with this information upon awakening they sometimes were cured of hysteria. For Freud this discovery had great significance, revealing the existence of an empirically verifiable subconscious level, a vast repository of hidden information that seemed to control the intelligence. It also suggested to him a central theory of psychotherapy: that the mere identification of the cause of a nervous sickness may result in its cure.

Freud's predecessors and contemporaries treated hypnotic experiments primarily as a method of healing nervous disorders. For Freud it served as an inspiration for a systematic study of the unconscious. The fact that hysterical patients concealed from themselves certain experiences, usually those that were in stark conflict with prevalent moral norms, suggested to him the existence of a "repressive mechanism." He was the first to study systematically, and in all its manifestations, the conflict between the conscious and unconscious and particularly to call attention to the ingenious methods by which the psyche resolves this conflict. This was the truly new contribution of his theory.

Freud began to investigate repression by analyzing dreams. Like Bergson, he believed that dreams convey messages from the unconscious; but unlike Bergson, for whom the unconscious was passive, he assumed it to be full of drives. Dreams embody wishes, but wishes disguised in a symbolic form, for the conscious "censors" the unconscious and forces it to express itself in an indirect, circuitous way. By relentlessly probing into his own dream recollections and those of his patients, and then connecting them with incidents from life, Freud concluded that dreams spoke in an elaborate code, which, if properly deciphered, permitted an insight into the deepest recesses of the mind. He found, in particular, that many seemingly innocent or nonsensical dream sequences disguise sexual fantasies. He published the results of these investigations in 1900 in his most famous book, *The Interpretation of Dreams.*

From dreams, Freud proceeded to analyze art and literature, religion, politics, and many other kinds of human activity, seeking in each case to identify the manifestations of the repressed unconscious. In this manner he gradually constructed a comprehensive theory of human behavior and culture centered on the concept of repression. Although he began his investigations with persons suffering from nervous disorders, in time he concluded that the distinction between the normal and abnormal is one of degree, and sometimes merely one of social convention.

Freud distinguished in the psyche three distinct components: the *id,* the center

"Insight such as this falls to one's lot but once in a lifetime," Sigmund Freud wrote in his celebrated study, The Interpretation of Dreams *(1900)*.

of unconscious drives; the *ego*, the seat of reason—that which we call "I" in ordinary speech; and the *superego*, the locus of conscience. Both the ego and superego are molded by culture, and exert a restraining influence on the unconscious id. They have the ability to keep out of consciousness that which they dislike.

The most important repressions involve sexual drives, because these drives are both extraordinarily powerful and subject to strict cultural taboos. Freud believed that the repression of sexual instincts begins early in childhood. (His assertion that children experience strong sexual desires conflicted with the prevalent view of the time that preadolescents were asexual, pure creatures, and brought his theories into early disrepute.) According to Freud, all male children suffer from what he called the "Oedipus complex," that is, from a conflict brought about by their being in love with their mothers and desiring to kill their fathers. Girls, on the other hand, suffer from a sense of sexual inferiority. Childhood neuroses are unavoidable. They are the main cause of psychological troubles experienced in adulthood.

The task of psychoanalysis is to probe deeply into the memory in order to retrace all the way to childhood the chain of repressions, make the conscious aware of the unconscious, and thus resolve psychic conflicts. This task it accomplishes in a variety of ways, including the analysis of dreams and free-thought associations.

Freud believed that psychoanalysis provided the key to the understanding of all human phenomena, and would in time become the keystone of the humanities. It explained everything that man "makes or does." In view of this claim, it is not surprising that he likened himself to Copernicus and Darwin.

Freud's influence on Continental thought has never been very strong. On the other hand, it has been great in England and even more so in the United States, where a whole cult has arisen around his theory. Critics of Freud point out that his "topography of the mind," with its threefold division, is purely metaphysical, since the id, ego, and superego cannot be empirically verified; that his interpretations in psychoanalytic categories of phenomena such as religion and primitive society are speculative to the extreme; and that the usefulness of psychotherapy remains to be demonstrated. For all their novelty, Freudian theories can be shown to rest on old-fashioned, nineteenth-century premises. They assume the power of reason to control irrational drives, the unchangeability of human nature across the ages, and the acquisitiveness and individualism of man. A sympathetic student of Freud calls psychoanalysis

> the last great formulation of nineteenth-century secularism, complete with substitute doctrine and cult—capacious, all-embracing, similar in range to the social calculus of the utilitarians, the universal sociolatry of Comte, the dialectical historicism of Marx, the indefinitely expandable agnosticism of Spencer.°

Needless to say, Freud's adherents think otherwise. Although they have subjected the master's theory to many revisions, they regard it as the most profound insight ever gained into the human mind.

°Philip Rieff, *Freud: The Mind of the Moralist* (1961).

Carl Jung was a disciple and close collaborator of Freud's from their first meeting in 1907 to 1913, when the two strong-willed men parted bitterly to follow divergent paths.

Among Freud's students and associates, the most influential was Carl Jung, who broke with Freud and founded his own psychoanalytic school. Jung was nearly twenty years younger than Freud, a Swiss whose background was free of the inhibitory factors so significant in Freud's case. His psychology is more affirmative and optimistic, and in some respects more modern. In contrast to Freud's positivistic-mechanistic outlook, Jung adopted a conception of nature close to that of modern physics, complete with nuclear analogies. If to Freud man was fully conditioned by his past, to Jung he was constantly made and remade by the free exercise of his will. Jung's psychology was therefore less deterministic.

Jung divided the psyche into two categories, the conscious and unconscious, the ego sharing in both. The conscious and the unconscious are in constant conflict because their relationship is inherently antithetical. When the conscious is outgoing, interested in the external world—"extrovert"—then the unconscious is withdrawn, self-centered—"introvert"; on the other hand, when the conscious

The logical positivism of Bertrand Russell (left) and the existentialism formulated by Martin Heidegger (right) dominate twentieth-century philosophy.

is "introvert," the unconscious turns "extrovert." This disharmony causes psychological tension, especially acute in middle age; it can be a source of creativity, but it can also cause neuroses and nervous breakdowns. Jungian psychology strives to harmonize the conscious and unconscious parts of the psyche and to bring the two drives into some kind of equilibrium.

Jung's conception of the unconscious was broader than Freud's. To Jung it was not only the seat of appetites, but also of religious and other spiritual needs. He viewed it as twofold, consisting of the "personal unconscious" and the "collective unconscious." The latter—a central concept for Jung—is the repository of memories that all men share. It consists of "archetypes," images common to all humanity, that appear in dreams of individuals as well as in works of primitive art and in mythology. Examples of archetypes are the mother-goddess, paradise, the wandering hero, the number three. To Jung, symbols, whether personal or collective, were not substitutes for repressed drives, but primordial images that force their way to consciousness because we live not only as individuals but also as members of humanity, and as such share in mankind's unconscious.

If Freud's psychology dominates psychotherapy, Jung's has had fruitful application in the study of primitive and mass cultures.

Modern Philosophy In the twentieth century physics and psychology have appropriated the two central concerns of traditional philosophy—the nature of matter and the nature of thought. Philosophy in Western culture has correspondingly lost status, and has become an academic discipline of limited influence.

The leading philosophical movement of modern times is logical positivism (or logical empiricism). This school originated in Vienna in the early 1920s under the influence of the writings of the British philosopher Bertrand Russell. Today it dominates professional philosophic thinking, especially in Great Britain and the United States. Like the older empirical tradition from which it descends, logical positivism rejects metaphysics, and acknowledges only propositions that can be either empirically verified (e.g., scientific facts) or shown to have logical validity (e.g., mathematical equations). The Viennese Ludwig Wittgenstein, who with Russell is the most influential philosopher of the century, argued in his *Tractatus Logico-Philosophicus* (1922) that the majority of philosophical propositions constitute verbal deceptions, which, when subjected to strict logical analysis, turn out to be devoid of meaning. The adherents of this school concentrate their attention on the use of language, seeing in it the key to the understanding and critique of philosophical concepts. Rudolf Carnap, a leading figure of this movement, sought to develop an artificial logical language that would avoid the pitfalls of everyday speech and achieve the precision of mathematics. The tendency of logical positivism, like that of modern philosophy in general, has been to shun humanistic preoccupations, especially moral concerns, on the grounds that they lead to conclusions that are either self-evident or unverifiable, if not absurd. Instead, it has turned its attention to logical and mathematical problems closely related to those confronting physical science, with which it maintains close contacts.

The only important modern philosophical movement to continue the traditional concern with moral questions is existentialism. This movement was founded by the German thinker Martin Heidegger, whose main work is *Being and Time* (1927). From Germany it penetrated into France, where, during and immediately following the German occupation (1940–1944), it acquired an influential following grouped around the writer Jean-Paul Sartre. (Heidegger, like Jung, compromised his reputation by collaborating with the Nazis; Sartre, on the other hand, always has been sympathetic to the left.) Existentialism is a philosophy born of the desperation caused by two world wars and the breakdown of traditional values. It provides guidance for the uprooted, "alienated" individual, cut off from religion and any other system of stable, absolute values, by showing him how to establish his identity through involvement in life.

Like modern physics and psychology, existential philosophy views the individual not as a finished product with set qualities, but as a creature in the process of becoming. Life is meaningless, absurd. Man finds himself in it utterly alone (existentialists profess atheism), without any stable frame of reference. The elemental facts of life are boredom and anxiety—a view that the existentialists have adopted from the nineteenth-century Danish philosopher Søren Kierkegaard. To overcome both, man must act, he must become "engaged"; in so doing he acquires an identity. "Man is potential" (Heidegger); he is "nothing else but that which he makes of himself" (Sartre). The intellectual idols of the existentialists, in addition to Kierkegaard, are Nietzsche and Dostoevsky (Chapter 5), leading critics of mid-nineteenth century Western culture.

The analogy between the new view of matter and the new view of man must not be pressed too far, but it is apparent that the two have close affinities. Just as modern physics has abandoned the older view of matter as a final substance with fixed qualities, so has modern psychology abandoned the older view of the "soul." The study of nature and the study of man simultaneously lost sight of their respective objects.

14

◆━━◆◉◆━━◆

Modern Taste

The Modernist movement in art and literature began once artists and writers sought to push the positivistic view of reality to its logical extreme and to locate a "real" reality behind the veil of appearance. This quest led them to tamper with the conventions of space and time. But gradually they abandoned altogether the notion that their task was to render reality. Modern art and literature create their own reality—a fact which accounts both for their tremendous inventiveness and their difficulty in communicating with the public at large.

The history of modern painting divides itself into three successive periods, each characterized by increased dissociation from visual realism. The first period (approximately 1860–1886) was Impressionist; the second (1886–1910), Post-Impressionist; and the third (1910 to the present), Abstract. The innovations achieved between 1860 and 1910 had a decisive effect on all subsequent painting. The history of visual arts since the introduction of Abstraction represents little more than an elaboration of themes and techniques developed in the preceding half century. Once a revolutionary movement, the modern style has itself gradually become orthodox and conservative. Today it dominates artistic expression and commerce as thoroughly as classicism had done in its time.

Impressionism

As we mentioned before (Chapter 3), Romantic artists failed to reduce significantly the power of the academies for the reason that the purchase of a canvas or a statue, unlike the purchase of a book or a ticket to the theater or a concert, involves a considerable investment of money, and investors like to seek the advice of experts. This was especially true of the bourgeoisie, the main patron of the arts in the nineteenth century, whose keen appreciation of money was not matched by a corresponding aesthetic judgment. The Academy of Fine Arts met this need for expertise. By selecting a painting for exhibition at the Salon, it stamped on it, as it were, a seal of approval and thereby emboldened middle-class patrons to buy. In making its selections, the Academy tended to favor works that in terms of content met the middle-class preference for the narrative and the morally uplifting, and in terms of technique adhered to the classical criteria of draftsmanship and finish. The more money invested in paintings conforming to these standards, the greater grew the intolerance of patrons and dealers of any innovation, for the triumph of a different aesthetic spelled to them great financial loss.

The rebellion against the academic art establishment broke out in the 1860s in Paris. As we have seen, its slogan, "Realism," paved the road for an anti-Romantic rebellion in literature (Chapter 5). The leader of the rebels was Courbet, around whom had gathered an articulate body of admirers, ready to proclaim his principles of painting as universally valid aesthetic laws. Repeatedly rejected by the Salon, Courbet organized anti-Academy exhibits, and in 1862 opened a school where young artists, bored with copying antique models at the

The modern artist's quest for "true" reality took on new dimensions with the advent of Abstract Expressionism, which rejected the traditional canons of representational art. Its pioneer was Vasili Kandinsky, whose Black Lines, No. 189 *(1913) is reproduced here.*

The Impressionists were particularly intrigued by the effects of light on water. This is Alfred Sisley's Flood at Port-Marly *(1876), one of a series of paintings he did of the effects of spring floods on the Seine near Paris.*

Ecole des Beaux Arts, could paint from live models. The following year Napoleon III authorized a *Salon des Refusés* to exhibit works rejected for the official Salon. Clearly, the monopoly of the Academy was on the wane.

The founders of what later became known as Impressionism—Claude Monet, Alfred Sisley, and Camille Pissarro—spent their formative years in this atmosphere of rebellion and developed early a strong sense of artistic independence. At the beginning of the 1860s the future Impressionists turned their backs on studios and museums and took to the country. Scattering around Paris—Pontoise, Argenteuil, Barbizon—they painted nature directly, under the open sky. The recent invention of a method of storing ready-mixed paints in metal tubes enabled them to complete their canvases on location. The imagination of these painters was captivated by the role of light in determining the appearance of objects. They never tired of observing and reproducing light effects in their infinite variety. They concluded that in nature all was color—they saw neither white nor black, nor the halftones prized by academic painters, and therefore discarded them. They also paid little attention to the line, that is to drawing, because like Romantic painters they found that the eye did not distinguish sharp borders between objects. Their main effort was directed at capturing the living, fleeting instant in its totality as expressed in light effects. We can obtain an excellent notion of their aims and methods from the advice Pissarro gave a fellow artist:

> Look for the kind of nature that suits your temperament. The motif should be observed more for shape and color than for drawing. . . . Precise drawing is dry and hampers the impression of the whole, it destroys all sensations. Do not define too closely the outlines of things; it is the brush stroke of the right value and color which should produce the drawing. . . . Paint the essential character of things, try to convey it by any means whatsoever, without bothering about technique. When painting, make a choice of subject, see what is lying at the right and at the left, then work on everything simultaneously. Don't work bit by bit, but paint everything at once by placing tones everywhere, with brush strokes of the right color and value,

Claude Monet painted La Grenouillère *in 1869. It was a popular bathing spot on the Seine frequented by the Impressionists, who found its rippling waters an ideal subject to depict with unrefined strokes of color.*

while noticing what is alongside. . . . The eye should not be fixed on one point, but should take in everything, while observing the reflections which the colors produce on their surroundings. Work at the same time upon sky, water, branches, ground, keeping everything going on an equal basis and unceasingly rework until you have got it. Cover the canvas at the first go, then work at it until you can see nothing more to add. Observe the aerial perspective well, from the foreground to the horizon, the reflections of sky, of foliage. Don't be afraid of putting on color, refine the work little by little. Don't proceed according to rules and principles, but paint what you observe and feel. Paint generously and unhesitatingly, for it is best not to lose the first impression. Don't be timid in front of nature: one must be bold, at the risk of being deceived and making mistakes. One must have only one master—nature; she is the one always to be consulted.°

The painters of this group did not confine themselves to landscapes. They also depicted contemporary genre, especially everyday scenes in Paris and its environs. They loved big city life. They frequented cheap cafés and dance halls on the Montmartre, then still a village overlooking Paris, the parks, playgrounds, market places, and any other location where life could be caught in its uninhibited spontaneity. One of their favorite haunts was La Grenouillère on the Seine, where they swam and engaged in rowing, then a sport newly come into fashion. In general, their subject matter was popular rather than aristocratic: they preferred people at work and at play to the frozen attitudes of the well-to-do—a fact which did not endear them to the art patrons.

In the handling of genre subjects, the future Impressionists were strongly influenced by Japanese prints, knowledge of which had penetrated to the West in the 1860s. (The influence of Japan, paramount for all modern art, began with the so-called Meiji Restoration of 1868, when Japan abandoned its isolation and opened regular contact with the outside world.) The deliberate disregard of perspective by the Japanese in favor of a two-dimensional, flat effect, their

°Cited in John Rewald, *History of Impressionism* (1961).

unorthodox manner of placing figures off-center, their use of primary colors and avoidance of shadows—all fascinated the young painters and encouraged them to take similar liberties. Degas, perhaps the greatest of the group, was especially influenced by Japanese examples.

The Salon from time to time accepted works of the young rebels, but it did so capriciously. In 1874, tired of fighting the Salon, they organized their own exhibit. The event was what the French call a *succès de scandale*. The public, which came in droves, found the exhibition an outrage. What shocked it most was the lack of finish, the seeming "sloppiness" of the exhibited works. The Impressionists, in their effort to render the vibrations of light, deliberately avoided the satin-smooth gloss that convention demanded. As a rule they did

Edgar Degas' L'Absinthe (1876) is a striking study of withdrawal, set in a café on the Place Pigalle patronized by many of the Impressionists.

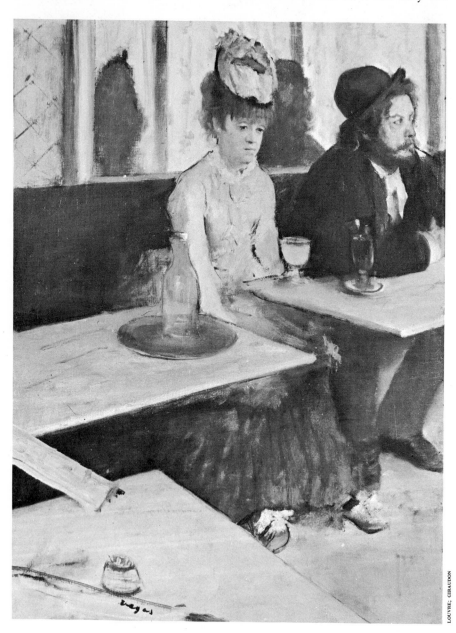

not coat their canvases with the customary base and sometimes even squeezed the paint directly from the tube, spreading it with a spatula. To the visitors at the 1874 exhibit the canvases resembled rough sketches or essays for paintings rather than genuine works of art. In addition they complained that the subjects were trivial, the models ugly, the colors unrealistic, and the draftsmanship amateurish. One journalist, reporting on the exhibition for a satirical magazine, borrowed the title of a canvas by Monet, *Impression, Sunrise,* to label the whole school "Impressionist." The name stuck, although those to whom it applied disliked it, preferring to call themselves "Independents."

Impressionism reached its peak of creativeness during the decade following the first exhibition. Its adherents formed a closely knit group. Confident of their method, they experimented ceaselessly, discovering ever new subjects and techniques, and creating in the process a new vision of man's environment. Even today, nearly a century later, one is amazed by the inventiveness of the Impressionists, for nearly all their paintings are in some measure original and contain surprises for the viewer. But this was not apparent at the time, and the public remained hostile. Dealers boycotted the Impressionists except for one in particular, Durand-Ruel, a loyal friend who bought their works when no one else wanted them and advanced them money for living expenses and art supplies.

In the mid-1880s the Impressionist group began to break up. Some of its members left Paris for the Côte d'Azur (Riviera) in search of more intense light contrasts; others quarreled on personal or doctrinal grounds. In 1886 they held their last joint exhibit. This date is generally taken to mark the end of Impressionism as an original, living force.

The year 1886 also marked Impressionism's first commercial successes. That year Durand-Ruel, exasperated by the hostility of the French public, organized an exhibit of his friends' works in New York. The show enjoyed an unexpected success. American patrons purchased a number of Impressionist paintings, and continued to do so in subsequent years—a farsighted attitude that permitted the United States to acquire in time the best collection of Impressionist paintings in the world. In 1891 Monet's nearly abstract *Haystacks*—fifteen successive images of the same subject under different light conditions—were purchased at high prices. From then on the Impressionists were "in" with discerning connoisseurs. The general public was not won over until after World War I.

Coincidentally with their first successes, the Impressionists found themselves under attack from a new generation of painters who accused them not of being too radical but of being not radical enough.

Post-Impressionism and Abstract Painting

Impressionism carried the seeds of its own destruction. In one respect it was "realistic," and belonged to the whole positivist trend that characterized science and the scientific outlook (Chapter 5). But in another and deeper sense, it rejected realism. By denying the objectivity of nature and concentrating on optical effects, it cast doubt on the whole notion of visual reality. If the task of painting was not to reproduce things as they were "in themselves" but as they struck the viewer, why confine oneself to external, that is, sensory impressions? Why not look deeper, into the mind's eye, into reality as it appeared to the inner self? Or, for that matter, why bother with objective reality at all? Why not concen-

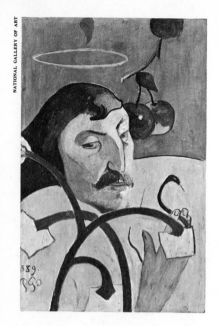

In an ironic self-portrayal as a saint, painted on a door in a favorite Brittany inn, Paul Gauguin jibed at symbolism in painting he had helped initiate.

trate entirely on the subjective world of the artist? By shifting from objective reality to subjective response, the Impressionists paved the way for a complete withdrawal of the artist from his traditional task of depicting the external world about him.

Impressionism was followed by a movement usually called Post-Impressionism, and sometimes Expressionism. This movement marked the shift from a purely sensory, visual perception to a psychological perception of reality. The Post-Impressionists were concerned not with the surface appearance of objects but with their reflections in the viewer's mind. They were especially influenced by the literary concept of "symbols," understood as words or images by means of which external reality is suggested to and assimilated by the mind.

Impressionism was a French movement; Post-Impressionism was international. Although originating in France, it spread rapidly to other countries, notably Germany and Russia. It had much less coherence than Impressionism. The Impressionists constituted a well-identified group which held together for nearly a quarter of a century, adhered to a fairly concrete aesthetic program, exhibited jointly, and sold through one dealer. The Post-Impressionists formed small, ephemeral bands, which rarely survived a couple of seasons. By the time Post-Impressionism yielded to Abstract art (around 1910), the whole notion of movements and schools disintegrated. Painting became thoroughly individualized, each artist developing his personal style or mannerism.

Post-Impressionism was launched by Paul Gauguin, Georges Seurat, and Paul Cézanne, and included among its adherents the Dutch painter Vincent van Gogh.° In contrast to the Impressionists, born mostly in the 1830s, the leading Post-Impressionists (with the exception of Cézanne) belonged to a younger generation, born around 1850.

Gauguin led the attack on the Impressionists, whom he dismissed as the "official painters of tomorrow." He rejected their illusionism as superficial and sought a deeper grasp of reality in the psychic unconscious and in the mysteries of primitive life. In revolt against modern rational civilization, he fled in 1887 to Central America and in 1891 to Tahiti, to paint unrealistic works, almost medieval in their mysticism. He pioneered in the discovery of primitive art, claiming that it expressed the sense of wonder that civilized man no longer possessed. The taste that the twentieth century has acquired for African and pre-classical Greek art owes a great deal to Gauguin. So does the whole current of "modern primitivism," contemporary painting in a deliberately childlike manner by amateurs, the most gifted of whom was Henri Rousseau.

Seurat's main contribution was the technique of "pointillism." Study of scientific light theories convinced him that the mixing of colors ought to occur not on the painter's palette but in the viewer's eye. He worked out an elaborate system of conveying both shape and hue by means of carefully juxtaposed dots of primary color. In a sense, Seurat was at one with the Impressionists in seeking to capture the effects of light. But his method was fundamentally incompatible with Impressionism, because it required the artist to compose slowly and methodically, and this could only be done in the studio. Seurat's works are

°These painters are often mistakenly called "Impressionists." The term, however, should not be applied indiscriminately to all modernistic painters of the second half of the nineteenth century.

classical in their static quality. They contradict every principle stated by Pissarro in the passage quoted above.

Cézanne is today generally recognized as having had the greatest influence on twentieth-century painting. He was older than Gauguin and Seurat, belonging to the generation of the Impressionists. But even while Impressionism was at its height, he stood to the side, pursuing his own individual path. Cézanne was fascinated not by light but by form. "Nature," he once asserted, "must be treated in terms of the cylinder, the sphere, the cone." This principle he applied to landscapes, figures, and especially to still life. His colors were deliberately dull, the emphasis being placed on the shape and spatial relationship of objects. He pioneered the transition from the visual to the intellectual grasp of reality, from appearance to underlying structure.

The Post-Impressionists, unlike the Impressionists proper, paid great attention to composition, which they worked out as carefully as the academic painters. This held less true of van Gogh, who adopted their emphasis on the "inner" reality of objects, but in matters of composition preferred to follow the Impressionists and the Japanese. Toulouse-Lautrec, another outstanding Post-Impressionist, also adopted Japanese models in his works, especially in his brilliant drawings, lithographs, and posters.

Gauguin's The Day of the God *is composed around the Maori god of creation. For Gauguin the South Seas idyll he painted was a mockery; he died there in 1903, nearly blind, a victim of syphilis and alcoholism.*

Julien Tanguy was one of the few dealers (Durand-Ruel was another) who saw the promise of modern painting. Vincent van Gogh painted Tanguy (left) against a backdrop of the Japanese prints much admired by the Post-Impressionists. Opposite is one of the carefully structured landscapes of Paul Cézanne, a view of Mont Sainte-Victoire in Provence.

In the early years of the twentieth century painting fell into as great confusion as physics. The notion that the artist's task was to represent "reality" became meaningless, for no one seemed certain any longer what reality was. The aversion of post-1900 painters to visual realism was heightened by the spread of photography. Although invented in the 1830s, photography did not become a popular pastime until half a century later, when George Eastman produced the first Kodak (1888), a cheap and simple amateur camera. Now that everyone could produce naturalistic portraits and landscapes with a snap of a shutter, it no longer made sense to do so laboriously by paint and brush. Painters increasingly began to think of a canvas not as a reproduction but as an end in itself:

> Beginning in 1905 the great goal was an art that would express human inwardness without recourse to metaphors drawn from the outside world. The essential was no longer to reproduce objects, *but to make the picture itself into an object* which, through the resonance inherent in its construction, would awaken a feeling similar to that aroused by the things and processes of visible nature.°

The picture thus tended toward an autonomous existence, its purpose being not to mirror reality but to create it.

The possibilities inherent in this aesthetic led to the emergence of a bewildering variety of pictorial schools. Each appeared on the scene with great fanfare, accompanied by a manifesto, worded in high-flown but imprecise terms, which

°Werner Haftmann, *Painting in the Twentieth Century* (1960). Italics added.

rejected the past and promised an entirely new art. It shocked the public for a season or two, until pushed into oblivion by another even more radical school equally intolerant of all that preceded it and equally short-lived.

In 1901 the great sensation were the painters of a group dubbed "Les Fauves" (the Savages), which included Henri Matisse. They announced that the purpose of painting was to depict not things but "emotions." They used color without reference to natural appearance, for the mere sake of effect—like "sticks of dynamite, exploding them to produce light," in the words of one of their adherents. The French Fauvists had their counterpart a decade later in the German "Expressionists."

Around 1907 the new sensation was Cubism, whose leading exponent was the Spaniard Pablo Picasso. Pushing Cézanne's geometric view of reality to its logical conclusion, the Cubists painted geometric designs with the intention of having them serve as visual "stimuli" to recreate reality in the viewer's mind. They liked to experiment with collages, that is, paste-ups of material objects like newspaper clippings, scraps of wood or metal, pieces of string, and anything else that was handy.

The flight from visual reality culminated in 1910–1911 with the introduction of "Abstraction." Cubism still paid some obeisance to reality by aspiring to stimulate the viewer into "imagining" physical objects not depicted on the canvas. Abstraction gave up reality altogether. It regarded a painting as a completely self-contained, self-justified object—an end in itself, like a tree or a house. The pioneer of Abstract painting was the Russian Vasili Kandinsky, who lived and worked in Germany. Under the impression of Monet's *Haystacks*, Kandinsky concluded that the subject matter of a painting was irrelevant—decisive was the arrangement of shapes and colors. The movement caught on, especially in Moscow, which, on the eve of World War I, became the international center of Abstraction. It achieved its ultimate fulfillment in the work of another Russian, Casimir Malevich, whose *White Square on a White Background* represents the culmination of the whole Abstract movement.

After 1910 it is no longer possible to generalize about the history of painting. Although Abstraction dominates, side by side there exist other schools. Some painters, notably Picasso, have traversed a great variety of styles in an unending search for the new. Others formulate their personal techniques and adhere to them. With the triumph of extreme subjectivism, aesthetic standards have disappeared: since every artist is acknowledged to have a right to his own "reality," there can be no generally acceptable criteria to help distinguish good art from bad. One of the by-products of this whole development has been a decline in professional skills, especially of draftsmanship. Nineteenth-century artists, even when they rebelled against the line (as did the Romantics and Impressionists), knew how to draw well. This no longer holds true of most contemporary painters, who do not undergo the long and exacting training necessary to achieve mastery of drawing.

Much of the misunderstanding of Abstract art derives from the desire to apply to it standards of traditional representational painting by inquiring about its meaning. Abstract art bears close kinship to Byzantine and Muslim art. It no more "means" anything than does a stylized icon, a Persian carpet, or a Turkish tile. It must be liked or disliked as an object in itself, not as a reproduction of something else. Fundamentally, visual art as it had been understood for hundreds of years in the West has disappeared in our time, giving way to a purely decorative style.

The evolution of the visual arts from conventional realism to abstraction has had a powerful influence on the applied arts, producing a veritable revolution in design. The essential feature of this revolution is a merger of art and engineering.

In the nineteenth century art and engineering were natural enemies, one belonging to the realm of beauty, the other to that of utility. The function of art

Modern Design

BOTH: MUSEUM OF MODERN ART

Les Demoiselles d'Avignon *(1907) was Pablo Picasso's first venture into Cubism. It has been called "a battlefield of trial and experiment" (the two faces at right, for example, are suggestive of African sculpture). The title is an ironic reference to a cabaret or brothel in Barcelona.*

was to conceal by all available means, mostly ornament, the true appearance of ordinary objects, especially those produced by industrial methods. John Ruskin, the high priest of Victorian taste, even declared ornament to be the essence of art. The majority of engineers probably shared this sentiment. But in the course of their work they sometimes had to employ expedients that violated it. When constructing a cheap bridge or factory building, they occasionally dispensed with ornament, leaving the structural elements exposed to the eye. These unpretentious, utilitarian buildings, some of which have survived, strike the viewer as remarkably modern. "Artlessness" of this kind, of course, was tolerated only in buildings of little importance. It was unthinkable in public buildings and private residences. These were the domain of "art," that is, of skills designed to disguise true structure and function.

The essential quality of modern design is rebellion against aesthetic camouflage. It marks the positive acceptance of industrialism and the reunification of art with engineering, identifying beauty with that design which best—that is, most economically—fulfills the function of a given object. It refuses to disguise a load-bearing pillar as a Greek column, to conceal an ordinary toilet inside a pseudo-Gothic chair, or to distort the shape of a sewing machine with wrought-iron tracery. It exiles ornament from objects of utility, leaving it to art. (This fact has further encouraged the visual arts to abandon the representational in favor of the ornamental.)

The pioneer of modern design was the English poet and artist William Morris. Morris married in 1859, and like a good middle-class citizen proceeded in an earnest manner to furnish his household. He found to his disgust, however, that the wares offered by commercial stores consisted entirely of ugly machine-made "antiques." He then founded, with a few associates, his own workshop to produce various household goods, such as furniture and wallpaper. By standards of the time his products were remarkably plain and functional. He grew so enthusiastic about the mission of improving public taste that he transformed the workshop into a commercial enterprise. Later on he designed his own house. He also founded the Kelmscott Press, which pioneered modern book design. Morris was inspired by an anti-industrial animus: like a typical Victorian, he idealized the Middle Ages and wanted a return to guild production. Nevertheless, his efforts anticipated Modernism in the sense that they posed, and in some measure solved, the question of preserving beauty under industrial, mass production, conditions.

A notable phase in the development of modern taste was a movement that originated in the 1890s in Germany and Belgium and today is generally known by its French name, "Art Nouveau." (In Germany it is called *Jugendstil*—"Youth style.") Like Morris, the artists of this movement were steeped in the mentality of their time, and yet departed from it, moving toward Modernism. Art Nouveau was essentially a decorative style, highly flamboyant, characterized by sinuous floral lines, asymmetry, and the use of unshaded colors. It involved the transfer of some of the visual effects of Post-Impressionism to the applied arts. Art Nouveau had its furniture, posters, jewelry, bookbindings, and many other objects of use, usually exquisite in workmanship and expensive. It also had an architectural style, whose greatest exponent was the Spaniard Antoni Gaudí,

An Art Nouveau chair, made c. 1900 by the Frenchman Hector Guimard.

the designer of fantastic churches and apartment houses in Barcelona. By its stress on ornamentation, Art Nouveau ran contrary to what we have defined as the essence of modern design, but it is regarded as pre-Modernist because of the boldness of its design and the use of ornament not to conceal but to accentuate structure.

The greatest innovations in architecture were made in the United States. Toward the end of the century the unprecedented expansion of industry and population in America necessitated the development of cheap and fast building methods. There was no place for the classical temple or the Gothic cathedral styles in the office buildings and residences designed for booming Chicago, where modern architecture was born in the 1890s. The so-called Chicago school, led by Louis H. Sullivan, made use of the latest technical innovations, such as steel frames and safety elevators, to construct office buildings, warehouses, and department stores of great height and almost free of ornament.° These buildings revealed honestly their structure as well as purpose. The Chicago style spread to England and to the Continent, where it found even more radical application. Here, as in the United States, business proved most receptive to innovation, being attracted to it by considerations of economy and efficiency.

Antoni Gaudí's Casa Milá apartment in Barcelona, with its avoidance of straight lines and its improbable shapes, looks like a pastry cook's masterpiece. It is built of cut stone.

°Chicago's great fire of 1871 necessitated rapid rebuilding and created an atmosphere conducive to architectural experiments.

Public institutions and private builders remained, on the whole, resistant until after World War II.

In the early 1900s the principles of Modernism were also extended to domestic appliances. The tendency here too was to discard superfluous ornament and to reveal function. The pioneering work in this field was done by Germans, especially by the gigantic electric cartels, which, even before World War I, streamlined such domestic objects as lamps, irons, and tea kettles. At the time the Germans excelled in industrial design, that is, the application of advanced aesthetic standards to mass-produced consumer goods.

The whole evolution of modern design from William Morris onward reached a

Walter Gropius wrote that buildings must be "receptacles for the flow of life which they have to serve." He practiced what he preached in his Bauhaus at Dessau, combining in one complex workshops, classrooms, offices, dormitories, and social areas.

synthesis in the "Bauhaus"—a collective of designers founded in Germany in 1919 by Walter Gropius. Its purpose was to bridge, institutionally, the distinction between art, craftsmanship, and industry by gathering under one roof in creative companionship craftsmen, artists, architects, and engineers. The Bauhaus produced buildings, furniture, and appliances, and sometimes even outfitted complete households. Its orientation was democratic in the sense that it aimed at providing well-designed industrial goods for the mass market. It dissolved in 1928, and shortly afterward, with the advent of Hitler, leadership in industrial design passed to the Scandinavian countries and the United States.

In music it is not possible, of course, to speak of "reality" quite in the same sense in which the word is used in the visual arts and literature, for music does not depict. And yet there is a musical equivalent of realism, and that is the rendering of emotions. Emotion may be described as the musical counterpart of visual and literary reproduction. Modern music, through a succession of technical innovations, has tended to move away from emotional expression and toward pure sound that pleases the ear and sometimes appeals only to the intellect.

The crisis of traditional music began in the mid-nineteenth century. Its immediate cause was the exhaustion of the possibilities inherent in the traditional idiom. By then, Romantic music had said everything it had to say, and composers found it increasingly difficult to create without repeating Beethoven, Schubert, or Chopin. A traditionalist of such genius as Brahms agonized for fourteen years over his *First Symphony* (1876) because he did not want to repeat his predecessors. The trouble with Romantic music was that it had not departed radically enough from the conventions of classicism. Although Romanticism had increased the independence of music, broadened the range of its forms, and permitted a certain degree of harmonic freedom, it never challenged the basic premises of classical music. Technically, Romantic composers continued to adhere to the canon of a Bach or a Mozart. Their harmony was "tonal," that is, based on a seven-note scale with major and minor keys. A trained listener can tell immediately from a few bars of classical or Romantic music the key in which it is written and the note on which it will end.

The first important departure from the classical-Romantic musical tradition is associated with the name of the German composer Richard Wagner. To begin with, Wagner had a novel conception of music, envisaging it as only one ingredient in a total artistic experience. In his "musical dramas" he fused music with poetry and visual effects to produce an experience of this kind. He dispensed with the customary recitative and arias, giving each character or event an identifying theme. Second, Wagner took great harmonic liberties, frequently departing from strict tonality. Though he had a great gift for melody, he did not indulge in it, preferring to concentrate on musical moods. Wagner's *Parsifal* and *Tristan and Isolde*, written in the late 1850s, were seminal works that even today seem remarkably *avant-garde*. His friends, headed by the king of Bavaria, established at Bayreuth a Wagnerian center, where his musical dramas were performed in a setting calculated to create an impression of utmost reality. Apart from a small coterie of fanatical devotees, however, the public was scandalized by his works, considering them jarring and formless.

Musical Impressionism originated in Russia, but reached its heights in France. Its founder was the Russian composer Modest Mussorgsky, whose *Pictures at an Exhibition* (1874) represents the first successful attempt at transposing pictorial images into sound. Claude Debussy, however, was the greatest composer of this school. Like the contemporary Impressionist painters, he sought to re-create in musical terms the fleeting impressions of nature. This he did not by means of such naïve sound-effects as imitating the chirping of birds or the clap of thunder but by establishing an overall sound-mood. He virtually abandoned melody and often ignored tonality. Among his outstanding works are *La Mer* (The Sea; 1905) and compositions for the piano with such typical im-

MARCEL BREUER

Tubular steel chair (1925) by Marcel Breuer, an alumnus of the Bauhaus.

Picasso sketched Igor Stravinsky in 1920 after the première of his ballet Pulcinella, *for which Picasso designed the costumes and settings.*

pressionistic titles as "Gardens in the Rain," "Reflections in the Water," "Bells Through the Leaves," and "The Sunken Cathedral."

Musical Impressionism faded out around 1910 and was replaced by a new fashion comparable to Fauvism. As Matisse and his friends delighted in color for its own sake, so the composers of this new trend found pleasure in sheer sound. Expressionism in music was also a Russian invention, the product of the musical genius of Igor Stravinsky and the organizational talent of the greatest of modern impressarios, Sergei Diaghilev. Diaghilev succeeded in assembling the best musical, choreographic, and decorative talent in Russia around the Ballet Russe, with which he revolutionized the art of the dance. This group turned its back on nineteenth-century choreographic conventions, with their predictably tulle-clad ballerinas performing predictable steps to predictable music, in favor of violent effects: fantastic costumes and unrealistic backdrops splashed with wild colors, dramatic leaps, and violent rhythms. The most sensational work in the repertoire of the Ballet Russe was Stravinsky's *Le Sacre du Printemps*, a work that made free use of primitive sounds and beats. Its first performance in Paris in 1913 created a theatrical scandal comparable to the Battle of *Hernani* of 1830 (Chapter 3). The public, outraged by the savagery of the music and dancing, booed so loudly that it nearly drowned out the sound of the orchestra. The assimilation of primitivism into serious music, however, proceeded apace, being accelerated during World War I when American troops imported Negro jazz to Europe. The total effect of these innovations was not only to broaden the range of musical expression but, more fundamentally, to free the composer from the obligation to convey emotions and impressions by allowing him to indulge in pure sound.

For all his innovation, Stravinsky still adhered to a harmonic reference system

—that is to say, he wrote in a definite key. The most radical of modern musical innovators, the Viennese Arnold Schönberg, went a step further and abandoned tonality altogether. Rather than treat all notes in a composition as tied to a common key, he decided to treat each as an independent entity. In his musical system the scale consists of twelve independent notes, unrelated to a tonal key. The purpose of such "atonal" music is simply to organize sounds. In this respect it is closely akin to Abstract painting, which took a similar attitude toward visual images. Schönberg composed the first "atonal" work in 1907–1908 (*The Second String Quartet*) and continued to experiment with this mode until his death in 1951.

After 1910 music, like painting, lost its unity and broke up into a bewildering variety of individual tendencies. Some composers, such as Richard Strauss and Jan Sibelius, continued to write Romantic music. Others, for example the Hungarian Béla Bartók, adopted no particular musical system, experimenting ceaselessly with techniques and forms. The same holds true of Stravinsky, who left Russia after the Bolshevik seizure of power and settled in the West. Yet others followed Schönberg and proceeded relentlessly toward extreme abstraction. Modern music has encountered even stronger resistance than painting, and hence contemporary concert managers usually schedule modern compositions in the middle of the program to prevent audiences from avoiding them by either arriving late or leaving early. The achievement of modern composers, however, has been considerable because they have greatly extended the range of their art. The time may well come when music will be regarded, along with design, as the most original aesthetic contribution of the twentieth century.

All that has been said above concerning modern thought and art applies, with minor modifications, to literature as well. We find here the same withdrawal from objectivity, the same uninhibited experimentation, and the same creative individualism. The attention of modern writers has shifted from the external to the internal: from society and man's place in it to the inner world of the individual. A characteristic feature of modern prose and poetry is the abandonment of the rigid chronological framework. It takes similar liberties with time that modern painting takes with space and modern music with tonality. Concentration on the inner states of the mind has encouraged the adoption of subjective, psychological time in place of objective, physical time.

Modern Literature

The rebellion against literary realism began in poetry. In the heyday of positivism poetry had been out of favor with the public because it was less suitable to rendering the social environment than was prose. It regained favor in the 1880s, and before long poetry experienced a veritable renaissance. The revival began in France, but it quickly spread to the rest of the Continent, and from there, with some delay, to England and the United States.

The most influential poetic movement of the second half of the nineteenth century and the fountainhead of all literary Modernism was Symbolism, a movement that began in France. The Symbolists reacted against the so-called Parnassians, the poets of the positivist era, who stressed purity of form and precision of language as the highest aesthetic virtues. The founder of Symbolism, Stéphane Mallarmé, developed a poetic theory pithily summarized in the following sentence: "It is not *description* which can unveil the efficacy and beauty of monuments, seas, or the human face in all their maturity and native state, but rather *evocation, allusion, suggestion*." "Evocation," indeed, was the key concept of the entire Symbolist school. Symbolism strove to penetrate beyond the formal meaning of words to their evocative connotations. It also sought evocation by word combinations and rhythms that produced something akin to musical effects.

The contrast between the Parnassians and the Symbolists may be illustrated in their respective treatment of the same theme, the classical image of faun and nymphs. In his poem "Pan," the leader of the Parnassians, Leconte de Lisle, treats the subject as a tableau in two scenes: a faun is surrounded by dancing nymphs and falls in love with one of them; when darkness descends he carries the nymph away. This poem lends itself perfectly to pictorial treatment, for it concerns itself only with external appearance, telling us nothing about the subject's thoughts or feelings. By contrast, Mallarmé, in "The Afternoon of a Faun" (1876), his most celebrated work, deals with nothing but the confused flow of the faun's consciousness after the sudden and fleeting glimpse of two nymphs. Mallarmé's poem is not pictorial or descriptive but musical, evocative. Debussy, in setting "The Afternoon of a Faun" to music, is said to have followed the poem line by line.

Symbolism immensely enlarged the vocabulary of the writer by breaking with the tradition that held that each object or occurrence has one and only one word that most accurately renders it. It encouraged writers to invent allusions, word combinations, symbols, and other oblique devices that bore no definable relation to the object depicted, yet engendered in the reader's imagination and emotion the desired response. On this principle a great modern school of poetry came into existence. Among its leading practitioners may be mentioned Paul Verlaine and Arthur Rimbaud in France, W. B. Yeats and T. S. Eliot in England, R. M. Rilke in Austria, Alexander Blok, Boris Pasternak, and Anna Akhmatova in Russia.

In extending the means of expression available to the poet, Symbolism caused poetry to become obscure and unapproachable. In pre-Symbolist days any literate person could approach a poem with the assurance that a modicum of concentration would be rewarded with a modicum of understanding. Symbolist and post-Symbolist poetry requires more than concentration. It calls for knowledge of the author and his personal language, for without such knowledge the allusions cannot be understood and the poem appears meaningless. As a result, poetry has ceased to play a part in popular culture; it has become instead a secret language understood only by initiates.

Although its greatest impact was on poetry, Symbolism also had a powerful effect on prose. This, together with the influence of modern psychology, did much to discredit realistic and naturalistic techniques in prose.

In the typical realistic novel of the nineteenth century, the characters were endowed with definable personalities and orderly minds. A representative realistic hero had a "character" with a fixed set of qualities, which permitted the reader to anticipate the hero's reaction to a given occurrence. His ideas, insofar as they were spelled out, formed themselves as a matter of course into grammati-

Marcel Proust (center), shown in the 1890s at a picnic, was rather a dilettante before sequestering himself to write Remembrance of Things Past.

cally correct and logically consistent sentences. Such a conception of the literary personage accorded with the mid-nineteenth century view of the human psyche with its "states of consciousness." Toward the end of the century *avant-garde* writers found this whole conception unsatisfactory. Bergson and James had made them aware that the mind does not operate in a neat logical manner: consciousness is formless, hazy at the edges, flowing in a continuous stream. In real life thoughts jump from subject to subject in accord with an informal logic of psychological associations, the key to which lies buried in the individual's past experience. The notion of character as something static dissolved further under the influence of psychology. It now appeared not as a fixed condition but a process—a battlefield on which the conscious waged constant war on the unconscious. According to the English novelist Virginia Woolf, one of the leaders of the new school of novelists, "life is not a series of gig-lamps symmetrically arranged, but a luminous halo, a semi-transparent envelope surrounding us from the beginning of consciousness to the end." The task of the novelist therefore is to "convey this varying, this unknown and uncircumscribed spirit, whatever aberration or complexity it may display, with as little mixture of the alien and external as possible."° To achieve this aim he must have recourse to methods different from those employed by the realists.

One of these methods has been for the writer to isolate himself entirely from active life in order to delve undisturbed into the innermost recesses of his memory and to bring to the surface its unconscious recollections. Marcel Proust spent ten

°Virginia Woolf, *The Common Reader* (1948).

Above left, James Joyce with Sylvia Beach, whose Paris bookstore was a haven for expatriate writers and who published Joyce's Ulysses in 1922. Above right, Anton Chekhov (in black hat) with Count Leo Tolstoy in 1900.

years (1909–1919) in a cork-lined apartment in Paris in an effort to achieve this. The result is *Remembrance of Things Past*, an incredibly detailed evocation of past experiences.

Proust followed Bergsonian psychology, but the majority of innovators preferred the "stream-of-consciousness" technique derived from late nineteenth-century psychology. This technique seeks to render verbally the spontaneous flow of thought with all its capriciousness, fragmentariness, and imprecision. The most celebrated novel of this genre is James Joyce's *Ulysses*, published in 1922. Joyce tells in it the story of a single uneventful day—June 16, 1904, to be precise—in the life of ordinary citizens of Dublin by following the flow of their "internal dialogue." Memories, wishes, and impressions fuse in one inseparable whole. The narrative has that indeterminate quality that modern psychology finds in the operations of the mind. The method attracted many other practitioners, among them Virginia Woolf (*Mrs. Dalloway*, 1925) and the American novelist William Faulkner. It has the great virtue of permitting the writer to depict his characters not only as they presently are, but as they were in the past and as they are likely to be in the future. It thus accords with the modern view of the personality as something in the process of becoming.

The stress on inner psychological processes is responsible for the most radical innovations in the art of novel writing, but it has been by no means universally adopted. Side by side with the psychologically oriented school of writing there exist other tendencies, of which two are especially noteworthy.

One group of writers has pursued the older tradition of the social novel by using the device of grand family chronicles, which permits them to show the

evolution of society as revealed in attitudes and actions of successive generations. Among the outstanding novels in this category are Thomas Mann's *The
Buddenbrooks* (1901), John Galsworthy's *The Forsyte Saga* (1906–1921), and
Roger Martin Du Gard's *Les Thibaults* (1922–1940). The Nobel Prize Committee has always shown partiality for authors of this genre, but their popularity
has declined, and today they are more esteemed than read.

The other tendency may be described as visceral writing. Its exponents scorn as
decadent the whole psychological orientation, preferring to write in a vigorous
language taken from everyday life and stressing violent physical experience. The
English novelist D. H. Lawrence, a leader of this school, considered "understanding" to be the greatest calamity to have befallen mankind and appealed for a revival of the dormant senses. "I stick to the solar plexus," he wrote. "Your solar
plexus is where you are you." The Italian Gabriele D'Annunzio and the American
Ernest Hemingway were leading representatives of this tendency.

The withdrawal of much of modern prose literature from contact with social
reality has thus not gone unchallenged. Although Proust, Joyce, and the other
writers of the psychological school dominate the current high-brow literary
scene and academic criticism, strong voices nevertheless are heard condemning
this trend. Some critics maintain that modern techniques like the "stream of
consciousness" obscure instead of clarifying the processes of the mind and make
much modern literature unintelligible. Others accuse modern writers of having
forfeited the writer's traditional function as an intermediary between the reader
and his fellow men. Some of the greatest prose writers of the post-Symbolist era
—for example, Anton Chekhov and Thomas Mann—though not immune to modern trends, continued to write in a traditional manner.

In the theater the greatest innovations were introduced by Chekhov, who has
had overwhelming impact on dramatic art in the twentieth century. Chekhov
wrote what can best be described as "undramatic drama"—plays that have no
plots and that derive dramatic tension from psychological conflicts within the
characters themselves. Chekhov once said that life's real tragedies occur when
one opens an egg at breakfast—that is, the tragic is the commonplace. His characters are frustrated people, constantly torn between their awareness of reality
and their aspiration to some higher ideal that is unattainable, and that, even if
it were attained, would not make them happy. In his *Seagull* (1896), *The Three
Sisters* (1901), and *The Cherry Orchard* (1904) almost nothing happens, and
yet there hovers over the proceedings a sense of deep disaster. The principles
that Chekhov introduced were developed by successive dramatists and led to
the emergence of the modern *avant-garde* theater. The plays of this genre take
as great liberties with the formal dramatic unities as the modern psychological
novel takes with the tradition of the narrative.

Interesting experiments along these lines have also been made in the cinema,
which from a form of cheap amusement has developed into one of the liveliest
arts. The technical flexibility of the moving picture permits great freedom in
distorting formal time and space for narrative purposes. Efforts to utilize modern
techniques in cinematography, initiated in Russia in the early 1920s by Sergei
Eisenstein and revived in France after the Second World War, represent an attempt to transfer to the screen the methods of the psychological novel and drama.

15

The Twenties

The two decades separating the end of the First World War from the outbreak of the Second witnessed a disastrous decline of liberal attitudes and institutions. The liberal crisis, noticeable at the end of the nineteenth century, came to a head in the twentieth—what had been a sickness turned into an agony. By 1939 liberal regimes survived only in the few countries in which they had struck the deepest roots: Great Britain, the Low Countries, Switzerland, Scandinavia, and France (and in the latter, only until the summer of 1940). Elsewhere the rule of law, constitutional safeguards, and parliamentary bodies collapsed under internal or external pressure. Their place was taken by authoritarian regimes ranging from relatively innocuous, old-fashioned dictatorships to the most ruthless and destructive totalitarianisms.

The disaster that befell liberalism had several causes, all of which had made themselves felt before the Great War. Of these the most important were national and social antagonisms and the erosion of the middle class. The World War and the Russian Revolution gave added impetus to these processes. Disoriented and demoralized, liberal governments (including those composed of democratic socialists) proved unable to cope with their tasks and at the same time withstand a growing challenge from left and right extremists: Communists, Fascists, Nazis, and their many imitators. In country after country they fell under the onslaught of groups determined to seize power and exercise it without any constitutional or even moral restraints. The story of this dark episode in Western history is the subject of this and the following two chapters.

The principal peace terms concluding World War I were drawn up at a conference held at Paris in the first half of 1919. The Treaty of Versailles, signed in June, set the conditions for Germany and at the same time provided for the establishment of a League of Nations. Supplementary treaties with the other defeated countries were signed later: with Austria in September, 1919, at St. Germain; with Bulgaria in November, 1919, at Neuilly; with Hungary in June, 1920, at Trianon; and with Turkey in August, 1920, at Sèvres. (All these are localities in the vicinity of Paris.)

Although the representatives of many countries participated in the deliberations and were consulted in cases directly involving their interests, the terms were in large measure set by the big powers, the so-called Council of Four, composed of President Woodrow Wilson and the Prime Ministers of Great Britain (David Lloyd George), France (Georges Clemenceau), and Italy (Vittorio Orlando). The defeated powers, Germany included, did not participate in the negotiations and had to sign conditions in the framing of which they had taken no part. Soviet Russia, which had dropped out of the war in March, 1918, by signing a separate peace treaty with the Central Powers, was not represented either.

The Council of Four intended to lay the groundwork of a lasting peace, but

The Peace Settlement

Woodrow Wilson acknowledges the cheers of Parisians as he arrives for the peace conference. With him is French President Raymond Poincaré. Wilson made brief tours of Britain, Italy, and France before the conference and was lionized everywhere.

its members differed greatly on how to go about it. Two general approaches were discernible: the "hard" line, espoused by the French, and the "soft" line, advanced by the United States. The Italians sided with France, while the British vacillated between the two positions.

Clemenceau, the head of the French delegation, saw the main cause of international instability in German aggressiveness, and considered it essential to weaken Germany to the point where it no longer would be able to wage effective war. Concretely, this meant creating a buffer state along the Rhine separating Germany from France, and breaking up Germany into a number of smaller states and demilitarizing it. It was on his insistence that the British maintained their blockade of Germany, preventing the flow of food into a country on the verge of starvation, so as to soften it and force it to accept onerous peace terms.

President Wilson, by contrast, did not regard Germany as the principal source of instability or as the country responsible for the outbreak of the Great War. To him the cause of the war lay in fundamental flaws of the system regulating relations between states: in secret diplomacy, thwarted aspirations to national statehood, and, above all, the absence of institutions capable of peacefully resolving international disputes. He was less concerned with punishing or disarming specific aggressors than with establishing a new order that would remove the causes and eliminate the means of aggression in general.

The peacemakers of 1919 lacked that freedom of action that their predecessors had enjoyed at Vienna in 1815. Each of the Four, in addition to serving as a diplomat, also headed a political party dependent on a democratic electorate. This electorate, by and large, had little understanding of the broader issues of international relations, and responded readily to the appeals of demagogic politicians and irresponsible journalists for vengeance (in the case of the European Allies) or withdrawal from foreign commitments (in the case of the United States). Public opinion thus exerted an invisible but ever-present influence on the negotiations. How disastrous this influence could be is evident in the example of Lloyd George. In December, 1918, in the course of a parliamentary election, the British Prime Minister found himself making extravagant promises to the discharged soldiers and recently enfranchised women voters. Before he knew what he was committing himself to, he had pledged to extract from the Germans all the money that Britain had spent on the war. "We will get out of her all you can squeeze out of a lemon and a bit more," a close associate of his promised the voters; "I will squeeze her until you can hear the pips squeak." Such incautious promises forced Lloyd George after his re-election to follow the "hard" line more than he really wished to do, especially on the issue of reparations. In the case of the United States, as we shall see, the failure of public opinion and congressional leaders to support Wilson had an even more disastrous effect on the fate of the peace treaty.

The Germans had originally agreed to an armistice on the basis of Wilson's "Fourteen Points," a general peace plan which he had made public in January, 1918. The French, British, and Italians did not much care for the proposal, but they went along for fear that unless they did, the United States would sign a separate peace treaty. The Fourteen Points called for national self-determination for all peoples and the redrawing of European frontiers to conform with it.

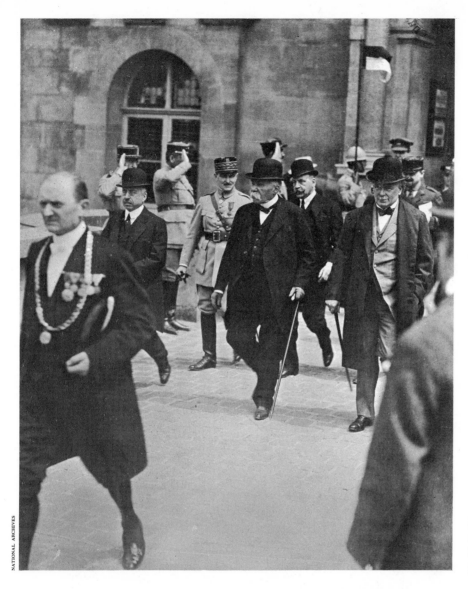

Lloyd George (right) and Clemenceau were photographed in June, 1919, at St. Germain after delivering their peace terms to the Austrian delegates.

They also urged freedom of trade and of navigation, open diplomacy, and the establishment of an international organization to guarantee the security of states. Wilson made no mention of any punitive measures against the Central Powers, and in his public speeches explicitly disavowed them.° The Fourteen Points constituted the legal basis of the peace negotiations, but they were promptly lost sight of. Later on, the Germans and Austrians could therefore claim with some justice that they had been tricked into signing an armistice.

The negotiations at Paris were conducted in an atmosphere of acrimony and tension. Clemenceau, pressed by the French generals, pursued relentlessly and with great cunning his main objective, the emasculation of Germany. Wilson tried to frustrate these designs, but he was not a skillful diplomat, lacked knowledge of foreign languages, and was handicapped by the absence of domestic sup-

°The European Allies, however, in accepting the Fourteen Points, did reserve for themselves the right to claim full compensation for damages to civilian property.

port. At one point he became so angry that he threatened to break off talks and sail for home. Orlando, peeved at the failure to win territory for Italy, actually did pack up and leave. Lloyd George, ignorant of European history and geography, shifted his position frequently. The spectacle was not a pretty one, and it contributed heavily to the general sense of postwar disenchantment.

Finally, in June, 1919, after much wrangling, the peace treaty was ready for submission to the Germans. Its provisions bearing on Germany may be grouped under three headings:

1) *Territorial.* In the west, Germany was to surrender Alsace and Lorraine and evacuate territories occupied during the war. American and British opposition forced Clemenceau to drop his plan for a buffer state in the Rhineland and the breakup of the rest of Germany. Instead, German territory west of the Rhine and within a belt thirty miles deep to the east of it was declared permanently demili-

The map of Europe as redrawn by the 1919 peacemakers; also shown are areas of subsequent dispute.

EUROPE AFTER WORLD WAR I

German Empire, 1914

Austro-Hungarian Empire, 1914

Russian Empire, 1914

Ottoman Empire, 1914

Disputed areas after Treaty of Versailles

tarized. Here the Germans could neither station troops nor build military installations. The Saar region was placed for fifteen years under international administration, to be followed by a plebiscite. In the east, Germany was to cede to the new Polish state the area of Posen as well as a "corridor" to the Baltic. East Prussia and Upper Silesia were to be polled whether they wished to join with Germany or with Poland. German overseas colonies were taken away and placed under the League of Nations. These provisions deprived Germany of one-seventh of its territory in Europe and one-tenth of its population. The lost territories had considerable economic value, for they contained three-fourths of Germany's iron resources and one-fourth of its coal.

2) *Military.* Apart from an army of 100,000 men and a minuscule navy, Germany was to be disarmed. It was to have no heavy artillery, tanks, military aviation, or submarines. Military conscription was abolished.

3) *Reparations.* Originally it had been the intention of France, Britain, and Italy to recover from Germany in the form of an indemnity all the money they had spent in waging war. Unyielding American opposition forced the abandonment of the proposed indemnity. Instead, the European Allies contented themselves with reparations, that is, repayment of the losses that German military action had inflicted on civilian property. Germany's legal liability for these losses was fixed in a separate article.° A Reparations Commission was appointed to determine the extent of the civilian property losses. In 1921 it reported its findings, fixing the reparations at $33 billion; half of this sum was to go to France.

No peace treaty in modern times has evoked sharper criticism and produced more controversy. The German delegates confronted with these terms protested loudly but to no avail. They were told that if they refused to sign, Allied troops would occupy Germany and the British would maintain indefinitely their naval blockade. A scathing critique of the treaty, and especially of its reparations provisions, appeared in early 1920 from the pen of John Maynard Keynes under the title *The Economic Consequences of the Peace.* Keynes called Versailles the "Carthaginian Peace of M. Clemenceau." It was "neither right nor possible": in the first instance because it degraded the Germans to long-term economic servitude, in the second because its territorial and other punitive provisions prevented them from fulfilling the demands of that servitude. Keynes's acid sketches of the negotiators, his persuasive economic arguments (we shall encounter him later as the outstanding economist of modern times), and his moral indignation did much to discredit the Versailles settlement.

In recent years scholars have taken a more tolerant view of the matter. As for the moral issue, it has been pointed out that if Germany had won the war it would have almost certainly imposed harsher terms on the Allies. The extent of Germany's territorial ambitions was suggested by the Brest Litovsk Treaty (Chapter 12) by which Germany forced Russia to yield territories containing one-fourth of its population and much of its industrial and agrarian wealth. Financial exactions,

°The article (No. 231) reads: "The Allied and Associated Governments affirm and Germany accepts the responsibility of Germany and her allies for causing all the loss and damage to which the Allied and Associated Governments and their nationals have been subjected as a consequence of the war imposed upon them by the aggression of Germany and her allies." This controversial article does not, as has been often claimed, place on the Central Powers exclusive moral responsibility for the war. It was drafted by a young American lawyer, John Foster Dulles, to provide a legal basis for reparations.

L'ILLUSTRATION

Escorted by war veterans, Thomas Masaryk enters Prague in 1919 to take office as head of the Czechoslovakian republic.

too, were not immoral in themselves, since it had been a custom of long standing in Europe for the loser to pay: Napoleon imposed an indemnity on Prussia in 1806, and the Germans, in turn, collected from France after the war of 1870. As for the feasibility of the treaty, a French economist, Étienne Mantoux, demonstrated in a book called *The Carthaginian Peace, or the Economic Consequences of Mr. Keynes* (1946) that after Hitler had come to power Germany easily raised for rearmament the money and goods that it had been allegedly unable to provide for reparations.

Whatever the merits of the case, there can be no doubt that Versailles was widely regarded as a harsh and punitive peace. The bad conscience over Versailles weakened the will of Europeans later to resist Hitler, who rode to power on slogans pledging to rectify the treaty's real and alleged injustices.

The terms for the four other Central Powers involved essentially territorial changes. The application of the principle of national self-determination formalized the dissolution of the Hapsburg Empire and gave recognition to the emergence in Eastern Europe of a number of new states. Serbia, united with several Austrian provinces inhabited by Slavs, became Yugoslavia ("the country of southern Slavs"). The Czechs and Slovaks merged to form the Republic of Czechoslovakia. Farther north, Poland regained its independence lost in the eighteenth century. Its territory consisted of lands partly ceded by Germany and Austria in the provisions of the peace treaty, and partly won from Soviet Russia in a war waged in 1920. Romania enlarged at the expense of Hungary, acquiring the province of Transylvania. Hungary separated from Austria and became fully independent. The Italians gained several Austrian regions, including southern Tyrol and the port city of Trieste. As a result of these losses Austria, which in 1914 had been the second largest state in Europe, was reduced to the status of an insignificant power, smaller in size than Bulgaria. All that remained of its former glory was Vienna, once the capital of a vast empire, now a head without a body. The Treaty of St. Germain explicitly forbade Austria to unite with Germany.

One of the main criticisms leveled at the post-World War I settlements is that by destroying the Austro-Hungarian Empire they created in the East unviable and unstable states that endangered the peace of Europe. It is true that the Allies encouraged independence movements in this area, but the process unrolled on its own anyway. By the time the peace negotiations opened, the Austro-Hungarian Empire had already fallen apart and its constituent nationalities had proclaimed their independence. Nothing short of armed intervention by the Allies could have re-established the Hapsburg Empire, and such intervention was, of course, inconceivable.

The Russian Empire escaped wholesale disintegration because the Communists reconquered most of the separated borderlands by force of arms (Chapter 12). In addition to Poland, only Finland and the three Baltic states—Estonia, Latvia, and Lithuania—succeeded for the time being in asserting their independence. The Ottoman Empire, on the other hand, lost its remaining possessions, including Palestine, Syria, and Iraq, which came under British or French control. All that Turkey retained was Anatolia and Constantinople with its environs.

Woodrow Wilson made many concessions to his colleagues on questions of territory and reparations in order to secure what mattered to him most: the League of Nations, on which he pinned his hopes for a lasting peace. Clemenceau realized this fact and exploited it to wring concessions from the President. Wilson, in turn, succeeded in making the League an integral part of the peace treaty with Germany.

The League of Nations

The idea of a permanent supra-national body to settle disputes between countries before they erupted into war was not new. As we have seen (Chapter 1), the Congresses of the Quadruple Alliance, convened after the defeat of Napoleon, were originally designed to meet this need. Throughout the nineteenth century an increasing proportion of activities involving many states—communications and treatment of prisoners of war, for example—were entrusted to international regulatory organizations such as the International Postal Union and the Red Cross. In 1914 over thirty such international bodies were in operation. In 1899, on the initiative of Tsar Nicholas II of Russia, a conference was convened in The Hague to discuss disarmament. Although no agreement was reached on arms limitations, measures were adopted limiting the use of certain weapons and assuring protection of civilians in wartime. The conference also established a permanent court of international arbitration to sit in The Hague and to pass on disputes submitted to it by the concerned parties. Neither the regulatory international organizations nor the Hague Court—a body of legal experts rather than judges—infringed on the sovereignty of independent states; but they were indicative of the growing need in the modern world for institutions whose competence cut across national boundaries.

Wilson received valuable support in his efforts from Jan Christian Smuts, a member of the South African delegation to the peace conference. In his booklet

The League of Nations (1919), Smuts outlined clearly the scope and functions of the proposed body. The League, he maintained, should be viewed not only

as a possible means for preventing future wars, but much more as a great organ of the ordinary peaceful life of civilization, as the foundation of the new international system which will be erected on the ruins of this war. . . . It is not sufficient for the league merely to be a sort of *deus ex machina*, called in in very grave emergencies when the spectre of war appears; if it is to last, it must be much more. It must become part and parcel of the common international life of states, it must be an ever visible, living, working organ of the polity of civilization. It must function so strongly in the ordinary peaceful intercourse of states that it becomes irresistible in their disputes; its peace activity must be the foundation and guarantee of its war power.

The League, as created by the peace treaty, was conceived not as a supergovernment but as an association of free sovereign states—a fact not always understood by its friends or opponents. Its members merely undertook to help each other to repel aggression and pledged to submit to arbitration their own disputes. The League was intended to act as an organ of collective security, obviating the need for military alliances, considered one of the main causes of the war.

The widespread revulsion against war is expressed in Théophile Steinlen's 1922 poster calling for a "War on War" on behalf of an international labor federation.

The League of Nations consisted of two chambers: a General Assembly, composed of representatives of member states and convened annually; and a Council with executive functions made up of representatives of the five great powers (the United States, Great Britain, France, Italy, and Japan), as well as those of four additional states, elected by the Assembly. The headquarters of the League was to be located in Geneva. Operating under the League's auspices were numerous international offices (labor bureau, economic bureau, and so on). Its day-to-day business was carried out by a Secretariat. Among the important responsibilities imposed on the League were trusteeship of the colonies taken away from the Central Powers, and the supervision of plebiscites in disputed areas.

The success of the whole peace settlement of 1919–1920 depended in large measure on the willingness of the United States to help with its execution. The French had consented to moderate their claims on Germany only because the United States and Great Britain assured them of joint protection against German attack. A defensive treaty to this effect was signed by the three powers on the same day the Germans affixed their signatures to the Treaty of Versailles. Furthermore, the League of Nations had been from the beginning an American idea. Indeed, many European statesmen viewed it skeptically, and agreed to the League only as a means of ensuring the permanent involvement of the United States in European affairs.

Unfortunately, the American public was not yet ready to assume that world leadership which the self-destruction of the great European powers had thrust upon it. From the beginning of its history the United States has viewed itself as an antithesis of the Old World. Its reluctant entry into the war had been predicated on the assumption that the intervention would be short and decisive. In the words of a popular American war song, the boys would be back "when it's over over there." But, of course, nothing was or could be over. The bickering at Paris and the subsequent conflicts among big and small powers reinforced the deep-seated aversion that the majority of Americans had toward lasting involvement abroad.

Wilson did not help his cause by his unskillful handling of the opposition. He failed to secure cooperation of congressional leaders before making his commitments, and rejected their suggestions for emendations afterward. Such a policy was imprudent, for he had to contend in both houses with a Republican majority whose leaders were isolationist. When the Versailles Treaty came up for ratification, considerable opposition developed. Exasperated, Wilson took his case for the treaty and the League of Nations to the country. In September, 1919, in the midst of a speaking tour, he suffered a paralytic stroke that removed him from active politics.

Two months later the Senate refused to ratify either the Treaty of Versailles or the mutual-assistance pact with France. The most essential element of the entire peace settlement was thus knocked out: the League lost its main champion, and France lost the principal guarantor of its security.

The difficulties in enforcing the peace settlements began almost immediately. National self-determination, accepted as one of the bases of the peace treaties, proved exceedingly difficult to carry out in practice. In many areas, after cen-   *Boundary Disputes* turies of coexistence within larger multi-national empires, the various ethnic groups had become so thoroughly intermingled that even the best of will (often absent) could not produce a formula able neatly to separate one from the other. The usual solution was for the stronger nation—as a rule, the one on the winning side in the World War—to decide the issue in its own favor.

The new Polish Republic was particularly troublesome in this respect. Having lost its independence in 1795, Poland lacked frontiers on which to fall back and had to carve its territory out of what had been German, Austrian, and Russian possessions. With French encouragement (the reasons for which are stated below) it expanded in all directions, seizing in the process regions to which its ethnic claims were highly doubtful. The Poles ignored the results of the plebiscite in Upper Silesia, which had rendered a majority in favor of union with Germany, and sent troops to occupy this territory. Later on, Upper Silesia was divided between the two countries, Poland retaining the most valuable industrial and mining districts. The Poles also seized the region of Vilno, claimed by Lithuania. In the summer of 1920 Polish forces invaded Soviet Russia. Their aim was to detach from Russia the Ukrainian and Belorussian territories and to create out of them a buffer region against the Soviet Republic. However, the Russians threw the offensive back. They now swept forward into Poland, reaching the gates of Warsaw, to be stopped and thrown back in turn. By the Treaty of Riga (1921) Poland secured lands containing large Ukrainian and Belorussian minorities. As a result of all these acquisitions, one-third of Poland's population consisted of minorities.

Another area of keen boundary dispute was Transylvania, a district with a mixed Romanian and Magyar population. The Allies had promised Transylvania —a part of the Hungarian monarchy—to the Romanians as a reward for their entry into the war against the Central Powers. In January, 1919, the Romanians proclaimed the annexation of this territory, an action subsequently confirmed by the Treaty of Trianon. But the Hungarians would not reconcile themselves to the loss of a region inhabited by 2 million Magyars and continued to hope for its reacquisition. The Transylvanian question poisoned relations between the two countries throughout the interwar period.

Farther to the south the Italians engaged in a protracted feud with the Yugoslavs over the Trieste-Fiume region, another legacy of the defunct Austrian Empire. The Italians occupied this region on the evacuation of Austrian troops in November, 1918. President Wilson, however, refused to acknowledge Italy's claim to Fiume, a predominantly Slavic area, and it was this issue that caused Orlando to withdraw from the peace conference. Fiume kept on changing hands until the Yugoslavs in 1924 finally conceded it to Italy.

A particularly savage conflict broke out in 1919 between the Greeks and the Turks. The Allies had assigned to the Greeks numerous islands in the Aegean as well as the Smyrna region on the Ionian coast, territories with a predominantly Greek population. The Turks, who had reconciled themselves to the loss of their empire, refused to give up territories that were geographically a part of the Turkish homeland. A nationalist army formed in Anatolia by a one-time Ottoman officer, Kemal Atatürk, began to resist Greek encroachments. For over two years Greeks and Turks engaged in full-scale war, in the course of which the Greek population of Anatolia was partly massacred and partly expelled. Peace was restored only in 1922.

The League of Nations made valiant efforts to settle peacefully these and similar disputes, but it had neither the authority nor the machinery to enforce its decisions. Its judgments were effective only when both parties in a boundary dispute found it expedient to accept the League's verdict. The border disputes left a legacy of resentment which persistently troubled international relations, especially in Eastern Europe, and undermined respect for the peace settlements. The losers tended to view the principle of national self-determination as a fraudulent formula devised by the strong to rob the weak.

Heavy as had been its losses in the war, Britain emerged from it sufficiently intact to nourish the illusion that nothing had changed and that it could revert to its old routines. The desire to return to "normalcy," that is, to pre-1914 life, was the dominant trait of British public opinion in the interwar period, to be finally shattered only by the Second World War. It was a self-deception that served to conceal the gravity of the problems confronting Britain and to delay the application of drastic remedies.

Great Britain

The crisis was fundamentally economic in nature. British prosperity, and the social stability resting on it, were uniquely dependent on foreign trade. Before the war one-third of Britain's entire national product had been sold abroad. After the war Britain found it increasingly difficult to recapture its old markets. Some countries, notably Germany, once Britain's leading customer, were too impoverished to make significant purchases. Others, such as the United States, had developed during the war great industrial resources of their own, and imported proportionately less. The decreasing foreign demand affected precisely those industries that had traditionally provided the bulk of British exports: coal, iron and steel, textiles, and ships. Britain's ability to sell abroad was further diminished by high prices, caused partly by antiquated methods of production and partly by the decision in 1925 of the Exchequer, headed by Winston Churchill, to restore the gold standard. In some areas overpriced British goods were pushed out of the market by Japanese merchandise manufactured at substantially lower costs. The net effect was a steady decline in British sales abroad: in 1924 the share of the national product sold through exports fell to one-fourth. The gap between exports and imports became wider than it had been before the war, although for the time being the unfavorable balance of trade was righted by shipping income, returns on foreign investments, and other "invisible exports."

The decline of foreign sales in the staple industries, employing the bulk of labor—mining, metals, shipbuilding, and textiles—caused chronic unemployment. Throughout the 1920s a tenth or more of the British labor force was regularly out of work. There were never fewer than 1 million unemployed, and sometimes their number exceeded 2 million.

Persistent unemployment caused social unrest of an intensity and on a scale not experienced in Britain since the early decades of the nineteenth century. There were frequent strikes and demonstrations, sometimes violent. The coal miners were especially disaffected. The example of the Russian Revolution encouraged the emergence in the British labor movement of a radical wing hostile

Workers parade by the Marble Arch in Hyde Park during the British general strike of 1926. Visible second from left is the banner of the Amalgamated Society of Engineers (page 218).

to the whole social and economic system. Social unrest culminated in May, 1926, in a general strike. The strike, which began with a work stoppage by the miners, expanded as several sympathetic trade unions joined in. It collapsed after nine days, but not without leaving a legacy of mutual mistrust between the upper and lower classes.

The social unrest of the postwar era provided the background to a major realignment in British politics. Until 1922 Great Britain was ruled by a coalition government formed in the midst of the war. Although Prime Minister Lloyd George was himself a Liberal, the coalition rested on Conservative support because much of the Liberal party had refused to follow Lloyd George's leadership. In 1922 the Conservatives decided to withdraw from the coalition. Three major parties participated in the elections that followed: Conservative, Labour, and Liberal, the latter split into pro- and anti-Lloyd George factions. The Conservatives won, polling 5.5 million votes and gaining 347 seats in the Commons. The Liberals suffered a crushing defeat. While they polled a respectable 4.1 million votes, in the individual constituencies they won more second and third places than first and ended up with only 117 seats. Labour, on the other hand, which polled only slightly more votes (4.2 million), captured 142 seats, and became, for the first time in history, His Majesty's Opposition party. The Liberals were never to recapture their old position, and have remained to this day a minor third party.

British politics in the interwar period was dominated by the Conservatives. The tone in the party was set by wealthy, rather unimaginative and tradition-bound businessmen. They believed in deflation, that is, dear money, strict economy in government spending, and the minimum of activism in foreign affairs. They refused to recognize the fact that Britain no longer was the leading industrial power in the world. They rejected bold fiscal measures advocated by farsighted Britons as a means of radically improving the country's economic position and blamed social unrest on Bolshevik agitation. The leaders of the

Conservative party believed all problems facing Britain to be problems of postwar readjustment. This attitude conformed to the mood of the majority of British voters, who longed for the pre-1914 world, and who liked being reassured that it would soon return.

The Labour party consisted of several disparate elements. The bulk of its support came from conservative trade unionists, from whose minds nothing was farther than class warfare or revolution. It was they who repeatedly rejected offers of affiliation with the British Communist party, founded in 1920. But the Labour party also had a radical wing, mostly from the depressed areas with high unemployment, whose representatives sympathized with Soviet Russia and had no aversion to class conflict. Finally, there was a small but influential intellectual faction of socialist professors and writers who, like their Fabian forerunners, injected an ideological element into the party. Although British Labour was more radical now than it had been in the late nineteenth century, its leadership, on the whole, was just as responsible and willing to operate within the British political tradition as it had been then. The two Labour cabinets—one in 1924 and another between 1929 and 1931—produced no revolutionary legislation. Indeed, they proved rather timid. This caution frustrated the more radical elements in the party, but it gained Labour the reputation of respectability that it had previously lacked among middle-class voters, and established it as the normal alternative to the Conservatives.

The 1920s marked the climax of the movement for Irish independence. During the war the Irish nationalists, who openly sympathized with the Germans, staged a rebellion against British rule. Violence erupted again in 1919, and for the next two years Ireland was in the grip of a savage civil war between the followers of the Sinn Fein and regular British forces. Finally, in 1921–1922, Britain agreed to a compromise. Ireland was divided, the smaller northern part remaining British and the remainder receiving dominion status. In the next few years the latter severed all political ties with Britain and became an independent republic.

France and French Diplomacy

The main concern of French statesmen in the 1920s was containment of Germany. Victory had given France for the first time since the middle of the nineteenth century an upper hand over its rival, and it worked feverishly to take advantage of its temporary superiority. France's long-term prospects were not favorable: its population was smaller and declining; its industrial capacity inferior, despite its acquisition of Lorraine; its political life unstable. The refusal of the American Senate to ratify the defense pact against German aggression had released Britain from a similar commitment and left France to fend for itself. All these factors encouraged French statesmen to adopt an intransigent attitude. They aimed at nothing less than to emasculate Germany internally and to isolate it externally, and they pursued both ends without much regard for their impact on the world at large.

The French government more than any other insisted that Germany fulfill punctiliously its reparations commitments. It had borrowed heavily to reconstruct the areas devastated by war on the assumption that it would recover the equivalent from reparations, and was unwilling to acquiesce in any German requests for the easing of terms or delays in deliveries. Early in 1921, even before the Reparations Commission had made its report, French troops occupied three German cities on the Rhine to ensure prompt payments. In January, 1923, on the excuse that the Germans had defaulted on coal deliveries, a Franco-Belgian force occupied the Ruhr, Germany's most productive industrial area. By then the French exercised direct or indirect control over most of the lands lying along the Rhine.

French diplomacy simultaneously pursued a policy of alliances designed to block Germany in the East. Before 1914 France had relied on Russia to provide the threat of a two-front war. Now, however, Russia was no longer its ally. Indeed, France was the most anti-Soviet country in Europe, for it had suffered the greatest losses from Communist expropriations and defaults on foreign debts. To replace Russia it now sought friends in Central Europe and in the Balkans, among the states that had profited at the expense of Germany and the Austro-Hungarian and Russian empires. These states welcomed French financial assistance and guarantees against potential future German, Austrian, or Russian claims, offering in return dubious promises of support in the event of German aggression. The anchor of France's alliance system was the "Little Entente," a coalition formed in 1920–1921 between Czechoslovakia, Romania, and Yugoslavia. France also cultivated Poland, whose territorial claims against Russia and Germany it supported militarily and diplomatically. The alliances with the smaller states of Eastern and Central Europe had for the French also a secondary function of a *cordon sanitaire* against Soviet expansion.

France's strong-handed methods on the Continent could succeed only as long as both Germany and Russia lay prostrate. This was certain not to be forever, and in retrospect French foreign policy of the early 1920s appears to have been exceedingly shortsighted. It played right into the hands of German militarists and nationalists bent on revenge, and undermined the democratic government then in power in Germany. Furthermore, it encouraged an alliance between Germany and Russia, the two outcast nations of Europe. In 1922 these countries surprised the world by signing at Rapallo a treaty pledging them to remain neutral should one of them be attacked by a third power. Rapallo marked the beginning of economic and military cooperation between Soviet Russia and Germany. Russia obtained from Germany credits and technical advice and in return provided facilities on Soviet territory for the *Wehrmacht* to carry out secret tank and aviation exercises which had been forbidden by the Versailles Treaty.

In 1925 France at last obtained international guarantees of its security. At a conference held in Locarno, Great Britain and Italy committed themselves to protect the existing frontier between France, Belgium, and Germany. In separate mutual defense treaties with Poland and Czechoslovakia, France obtained and gave the promise of help in the event of German attack. Locarno created the illusion of ushering in a new era of international good will and collective security. But that the French did not place excessive trust in it may be gathered from the fact that in 1929 they began construction of a massive chain of fortifications along the German frontier, the so-called Maginot Line. It was intended as an impregnable wall to stop the invader should all the guarantees fail and France find itself alone face to face with German might.

The government that succeeded the Hohenzollerns was appointed by a National Assembly popularly elected in January, 1919, and convened in the town of Weimar. In the Assembly, the Social Democrats had the largest bloc of seats (38.5 percent) and, together with the associated Catholic Center party, held a comfortable majority. The German Republic was therefore in large measure their creation. The constitution adopted by the Assembly in 1919 gave Germany a parliamentary democracy, with a strong executive. The President and the Chancellor received wide emergency powers to use against subversion, including the right temporarily to suspend civil liberties. The authority of the central government was increased, that of federal governments diminished. It was the most liberal and democratic constitution Germany had ever had, and an excellent one by any standards.

The Weimar Republic had from its inception to contend with the opposition of rabid anti-democratic elements on both the left and the right.

On the left, the most dangerous enemy was the Communist party, whose aim was to replace the republic by a Soviet-type government in which it would exercise dictatorial powers. In January, 1919, a proto-Communist group of "Spartacists" staged an uprising in Berlin, and before long Communist groups raised the banner of rebellion in other German cities. In Munich in April the Communists proclaimed a Soviet Republic of Bavaria.

The Weimar government reacted to radical subversion with great vigor and succeeded in suppressing it. Defeat, however, did not discourage the Communists from keeping up a steady offensive against the republic so as to undermine its popularity among the masses of workers.

The Weimar Republic

Spearheaded by a tank obtained from the British, German troops advance into Berlin to quell the Spartacist revolt in 1919.

In coping with the Communists the government had to rely on the help of right-wing elements, especially of paramilitary formations composed of discharged soldiers and civilian volunteers. The leaders as well as the rank and file of these groups had no love for the republic. They detested the Social Democrats, the leading party in the government, whom they accused of having "stabbed in the back" the German army in the last months of the war by fomenting strikes and mutinies. They also refused to recognize the action of the National Assembly in ratifying the Versailles Treaty and scorned the government for complying with the Allied demands for reparations. The right-wing opposition consisted of two disparate elements: traditional monarchists and nationalistic radicals, who temporarily cooperated with each other out of hatred of the Weimar Republic. The two groups murdered political opponents and staged repeated uprisings. On one occasion they even succeeded in seizing temporary control of Berlin and forcing the government to flee (Kapp *Putsch*, March, 1920). The Weimar authorities tended to treat right-wing subversives with greater indulgence than the Communists, probably because they regarded the latter as more dangerous.

The socialist-liberal consensus that had prevailed in Germany at the end of the war evaporated remarkably fast, and soon political life began to polarize. Extremist parties did surprisingly well in the first postwar elections to the Reichstag (June, 1920), the Communists gaining one-fifth of the seats and the most militant nationalist party one-sixth (see chart, page 445). This election marked the beginning of the steady disintegration of the liberal-democratic center.

Weakened by a narrowing domestic mandate, the Weimar Republic had also to contend with steady pressure from its neighbors, especially France. Immediately after the cessation of hostilities Germany was required to surrender to the Allies the bulk of its merchant navy, as well as considerable quantities of gold and raw materials. Then came regular reparations payments. The occupation of the Ruhr by French and Belgian troops in 1923 caused an outburst of national resentment that carried with it even the working class: in the occupied areas workers refused to work and carried out acts of sabotage. Throughout Germany there was dissatisfaction with the inability of the Weimar Republic to stand up to what were widely considered unreasonable and degrading foreign demands.

In 1923, on top of all its other troubles, the republic experienced an inflation the likes of which had never been seen. The steady outflow of gold in the form of reparations payments or transfers of private capital, as well as the adverse balance of trade resulting from the need to import industrial raw materials and food, caused a steady depreciation of German currency. In the spring of 1921 one United States dollar equaled 65 marks; in September, 1923, it was worth 9 million marks, and in November, 1923, 4.2 trillion! By then, several hundred paper mills and printing establishments worked around the clock to supply the treasury with banknotes. The mark became worthless—and so did bank savings, investments, securities, and loans. The German middle class, whose livelihood had depended on such values, grew to detest the republic which had in effect expropriated it, and swung to the right, toward monarchistic and nationalistic movements.

A German magazine's bitter comment on American loans going directly to the French for reparations payments.

Simplicissimus, JUNE 28, 1922

In the fall of 1923 the Weimar Republic seemed on the verge of collapse. In October the Communists staged an uprising in Hamburg, and the following month right-wing extremists, led by General Ludendorff and Adolf Hitler, attempted a coup in Munich. Both revolts were contained, but the danger of sedition remained.

In 1924, however, the situation unexpectedly improved. A clever monetary reform introduced a new and stable mark to replace the worthless old currency. The Allies realized at last that it was not possible to keep on squeezing Germany without regard to its ability to pay. In 1924 they appointed a commission headed by the American financier Charles G. Dawes to draw up a plan for the economic reconstruction of Germany. Dawes's report established a schedule for reparations payments and recommended that Germany receive sizable international loans. Earlier in 1924 the French had pulled out of the Ruhr. Soon private and public funds from abroad began to flow into the country. The Germans used a part of these to meet their reparations obligations, thus easing the strains on their economy.° The treaties of Locarno further eased Franco-German relations. One of its consequences was Germany's admission into the League of Nations.

The stability and prosperity that began in 1924 re-established for the time being the prestige of the moderate parties and restored a certain degree of confidence in the republic. Nevertheless, the position of the Weimar government remained precarious because the majority of Germans in principle opposed the republican-democratic form of government. This became apparent in the presidential elections held in 1925. At this time 48.1 percent of the voters cast their ballots for the monarchist General von Hindenburg and 6.2 percent for the Communist candidate. A minority—45.2 percent—of the voters backed the candidate of the Social Democratic, the Catholic Center, and other parties supporting the regime. Hindenburg's election, made possible by the Communist refusal to join forces with the republican parties, had tragic consequences for the republic, for Germany, and for the world. As we shall see, it was Hindenburg's political naïveté that enabled Hitler in 1933 to become Chancellor and to acquire dictatorial powers.

The 1924 poster of a Nazi coalition makes an anti-Semitic appeal to the "exploited" German working classes.

The Drift Toward Dictatorships

The instability of postwar conditions placed stresses on parliamentary institutions which the weaker among them could not withstand. Ethnic, social, and political strife, either separately or in combination, created a demand for firmer authority than that provided by the liberal system with its multiplicity of rival parties and cumbersome parliamentary procedures. An increasing proportion of the citizenry of postwar Europe came to question the efficacy of liberalism and to seek salvation in dictatorships. This held especially true of countries where the parliamentary system either had failed to sink deep roots before World War I, or where it had had only come into being since the war.

Among the first countries to shift toward authoritarian forms was Hungary. Its first postwar administration, formed in January, 1919, was liberal and progressive, but two months after its formation it was overthrown by a Communist

---

°"The U.S.A. lent money to Germany which enabled her to pay reparations to the European ex-allies, which enabled them to make war-debt payments to the U.S.A.—and so the circle continued." William Ashworth, *A Short History of the International Economy Since 1850* (1962).

Marshal Josef Pilsudski, who assumed dictatorial power in Poland in 1926.

regime sponsored by Soviet Russia (Chapter 12). The Communist leader, Béla Kun, antagonized a large part of the population by his anti-religious policy and a program of land nationalization. In the summer of 1919 the Communists were ejected, in turn, by invading Romanian troops, who freely plundered the country. At the same time right-wing terrorists exacted revenge on the Communists and their suspected sympathizers, and carried out anti-Jewish pogroms. Finally a semblance of order was re-established in 1920. A nationally elected parliament nominated Admiral Nicholas Horthy as regent, to exercise supreme executive powers until the restoration of the monarchy. Since the Allies, however, prevented such a restoration, Horthy remained permanent regent with all the usual royal prerogatives.

In the next few years several other countries took the road to authoritarianism. In 1923 Kemal Atatürk, the commander of the Turkish national army, became dictator of the Turkish republic. The Republican People's party, which he headed, was declared the only legitimate political organization. The same year a military coup in Spain brought to power Miguel Primo de Rivera, who dissolved the parliament, suspended the constitution, and proceeded to rule the country by decree. In 1926 neighboring Portugal came under a dictatorship in which authority eventually fell into the hands of Antonio Salazar. In Poland Marshal Josef Pilsudski, commander of the armed forces which had fought for independence during the war, carried out a coup against the parliament in which the Peasant party had obtained a majority (May, 1926). Pilsudski left parliamentary institutions intact, but by assuming the combined functions of Prime Minister, Minister of War, and Chief of Staff, he enjoyed virtually dictatorial powers. Opposition parties were tolerated but harassed. In 1929 King Alexander of Yugoslavia, exasperated by endless friction among Serbs, Croats, Slovenes, and other minorities, suspended parliamentary government temporarily.

The only one among the successor states to resist the general trend toward authoritarianism was the Republic of Czechoslovakia. A country with a high level of culture and a relatively well-developed industrial economy, it created a democracy in no way inferior to the most advanced Western models.

Italian Fascism

In turning to the Fascist government established in Italy by Mussolini, we are moving into a gray zone separating ordinary dictatorship from totalitarianism. The differences between the two systems will be discussed in the next chapter. Here suffice it to note that totalitarian regimes are not content to deprive the citizen of his political rights, but also rob him of his civil liberties. Mussolini claimed to be a totalitarian ruler and tried to be one, but he never really carried out a totalitarian revolution of the kind accomplished by Lenin and Hitler, and for this reason his place is not among them.

Fascism arose against a background of violent social unrest that broke out in the industrial centers of northern Italy at the end of the war. This area had old traditions of syndicalism and anarchism, which the news of the Russian Revolution revivified. Beginning in 1919 Italy experienced a wave of massive strikes, culminating in September, 1920, in seizures of whole factories by syndicalist workers in Milan and Turin. From the cities the unrest spilled into the countryside, where tenants seized estates and refused payment of rents. In 1919–1920

Italy tottered on the brink of social revolution, which the frequently changing socialist and liberal governments seemed unable to do anything about. It was this situation that gave Mussolini his chance.

Benito Mussolini was born in 1883. His father, a poor village blacksmith, was a professed anarchist, and Mussolini spent his childhood in an atmosphere of rebellion against government, church, private property, and the whole culture of the middle class. As a youth he tried his hand at teaching and other occupations, including bricklaying, but his real passion was politics. He read avidly, showing a predilection for such modern prophets of violence and élitism as Nietzsche, Sorel, and Pareto.

He gained his initial political experience in the Italian Socialist party, where his literary and speaking ability helped him make a rapid career. In 1912 he was elected member of the party's Executive Committee and editor of its official newspaper, *Avanti.* Two years later, however, he was expelled from the Socialist party because as an ardent patriot and militarist he had objected to the party's pacifist policy and agitated for Italy's entrance into the war. In 1915 he went to the front, from where he returned in 1917 with grave wounds. He still remained a socialist, but of a militant kind, who, like Lenin, despised the liberal, reformist tendencies prevalent among European socialist parties. Unlike Lenin, however, he also rejected their cosmopolitanism.

Mussolini (center, wearing the national colors across his chest) and his Blackshirts parade in Rome after their takeover.

Mussolini at first admired the Bolshevik Revolution, but he quickly became disillusioned with it, and after the Communists became involved in fomenting industrial strikes and violence, turned against them. He gathered around himself students and ex-soldiers whom he organized into combat units, called *fasci di combattimento.*° Beginning with April, 1919, these black-shirted squads engaged in street brawls and attacked the offices of radical organizations and newspapers. Claiming that he was saving the country from communism and anarchism, Mussolini persuaded frightened industrialists and landlords to give him financial support. His movement gained momentum, especially after the factory seizures of 1920. It attracted nationalists embittered by the failure of Italy's allies to accede to all its territorial demands, unadjusted war veterans, poets and artists won over by Mussolini's romantic activism, and ordinary people who simply wanted an end to the anarchy. The situation was not unlike that prevailing in Germany at the same time, except that the Italian socialists, who dominated the government, were much less energetic in dealing with extremists.

Until the end of 1921 Mussolini lacked a party organization, and indeed denied any need for it. Fascism was a "doctrine of action" not to be confined by organizational fetters. But in November, 1921, he decided, against the advice of his more radical followers, to found a regular party organization, the *Partito Nazionale Fascista.* Its membership was then around 300,000.

His ambition was to acquire dictatorial powers. The Fascist following in parliament was small: with their allies, they controlled less than one-tenth of the seats. But the Italian parliamentary system being what it was, lack of a majority was not an insurmountable obstacle to a prime-ministership. It had been traditionally the task of the Italian Prime Minister to constitute a majority only after assuming office by making deals with individual deputies. In 1922 Mussolini demanded that the king appoint him to form a cabinet. The king, a weak and confused man, hesitated, and so did the leaders of the moderate parties. The trouble was that no one, Mussolini included, really knew what he stood for and what he would do once in office. To force the issue, in October, 1922, Mussolini organized a "March on Rome," a coordinated advance on the capital by thousands of Fascist Blackshirts. (Mussolini himself stayed behind in Milan.) Nothing was done to stop them. Even before the Fascists had control of Rome, the king agreed to Mussolini's demand.

Mussolini, like Hitler after him, subverted democratic institutions only after he had succeeded in legally becoming head of government. Although he had risen on an anti-Communist, anti-anarchist platform, his real enemy was the liberal state. He skillfully exploited its weaknesses to destroy it from within.

In December, 1922, Mussolini obtained from parliament dictatorial powers for the period of one year to restore order in the country. Almost immediately turbulence subsided: strikes were either broken up or called off, factories were restored to their owners, street fighting and brigandage were suppressed, the civil service was infused with new life. The pacification was remarkably successful, and in the elections of 1924 the "National List" presented by the Fascists received an absolute majority (63 percent) of the popular vote. Although here

°The term *fasci,* from which derives the word *fascism,* refers to *fasces,* a bundle of rods containing an axe, which in ancient Rome symbolized authority. It was widely used in Italy by both radical and nationalist movements.

and there the Fascist militia used strong-arm methods, there is general agreement that the elections were honest, and represented a genuine vote of confidence in the new regime. With a parliamentary majority Mussolini could proceed to acquire permanent dictatorial powers. In 1925–1926 he issued a series of decrees that transferred to him, as Leader, *Duce*, all the essentials of legislative authority. In 1928 a new electoral law was introduced which abolished universal suffrage and limited eligibility for parliamentary elections to candidates officially approved by the Fascist Grand Council.

Like Soviet Russia, Fascist Italy was ruled by a single party that controlled the legislature and the administration. The party, in turn, was under the personal authority of the *Duce*. Mussolini, emulating Lenin, combined the functions of head of party and of government. He also closely followed Lenin's system of meshing the party and state apparatus. After 1926 other political parties were outlawed. The Fascist party also controlled numerous ancillary organizations, including youth organizations (*Balilla* and *Avanguardisti*) and trade unions. But the Fascists never attempted to establish control over the entire organized life of the country. The Catholic Church, relations with which were regularized by the Lateran Treaties of 1929, was left its autonomy and allowed to carry on many activities. The monarchy, too, was left intact. Nor did the Fascists tamper with the judiciary: they respected the independence and irremovability of judges, and made no attempt to interfere with court procedures except for political cases tried by a special tribunal. Thus Mussolini's power was never "total."

In their social and economic policy the Fascists displayed little initiative. Private property, including ownership of industry, was retained. Mussolini made an effort to tamper with the economy only in 1934, in the wake of the great depression which threw 1 million Italians out of work. At that time he introduced the system of "corporatism." The country's entire economy was divided into twenty-two branches, in each of which the employers and employees formed a "corporation," regulated by a National Council of Corporations. The ostensible task of this arrangement, which aroused much attention at the time, was to correct the faults of the free economy and to eliminate class conflict. Although clearly modeled on the Soviet Five-Year Plan (see Chapter 16), the corporations did not signify the introduction of economic planning. Insofar as the "Corporate State" had any reality, it meant a greater role of the state in the running of the economy —an anticipation of that mixed system of state direction and free enterprise which became common everywhere after World War II.

It would be vain to seek in fascism any fixed ideology. Mussolini himself repeatedly insisted that the essential quality of fascism was dynamism—a sense of constant movement, daring, excitement. A popular Fascist motto, *Me ne frego* ("I don't give a damn"), typified the attitude that Mussolini desired of his followers. There was much stress on youth, and *Giovinezza* was made the anthem of the Fascist party. Mussolini made a great deal out of the imperial tradition, exhorting the Italians to re-establish in the Mediterranean a modern Roman Empire, but it is doubtful that he took this aim seriously. He was too intelligent to believe the slogans with which he confused the Italian public. At bottom he was a great cynic—a modern *condottiere* for whom life was a game. He thought to get the most out of it by living recklessly.

Striking a typically bombastic pose, Mussolini was photographed at a ceremony in the Italian colony of Libya.

16

Totalitarianism

The term *totalitarianism* was coined by Mussolini to describe the kind of regime he sought to establish in Italy: a regime in which one party monopolizes all power, dissolves or subordinates all independent institutions, and asserts complete, direct authority over all its subjects and all their activities. Although totalitarian governments may differ from one another in some particulars, they represent a distinct political type, as consistent in their essential features as were the diverse enlightened despotisms of the eighteenth century or the parliamentary democracies of the nineteenth.

Totalitarianism is the antithesis of liberalism, and its most implacable enemy. It rejects the philosophical principles on which the liberal order rests (as defined in Chapter 1). It denies the ultimate worth of the individual, valuing him only insofar as he is useful to the state or national community. Consequently it has no use for freedom or for law, whose purpose it is to protect the individual. It also denies the fundamental harmony of human interests, stressing instead the universality of conflict, whether social, national, or racial. From the point of view of these assumptions, totalitarianism is a conservative creed. At the same time, however, it borrows from socialism its techniques of mass appeal. It is a mass-oriented movement, harnessing the emotions and aspirations of the multitude not to satisfy them but, with their help, to destroy resistance to the leader's total power whether at home or abroad. It is conservative in its aims and radical in its means.

Totalitarianism is not only a political system but a whole set of values, a way of life. In economics it rejects laissez faire in favor of state controls. In culture it is usually anti-modernist.

To understand totalitarian regimes and to distinguish them from ordinary dictatorships, we must keep in mind the dual nature of the liberal state. The classical liberal state rested on twin foundations, political and civil. Liberalism in politics subjected the government to legal restraints (constitutions) and the authority of elected, representative institutions (parliaments). Liberalism in civil matters ensured the individual citizen the protection of the law and a great variety of personal freedoms. While ideally political rights and civil liberties went together, it was possible to have one without the other. As a matter of fact, most Europeans enjoyed civil liberties long before they had constitutions and the right to vote.

The dictatorships that spread in Europe in the wake of World War I, as described in the preceding chapter, cut down only the political pillar of the liberal state. They resulted from disenchantment with party politics and parliamentary procedures which seemed unable to provide the firm national leadership required under conditions of postwar instability. The purpose of these dictatorships was merely to remedy what was seen as a fatal flaw in the traditional liberal system, not to uproot liberalism as such. A Pilsudski in Poland, a Salazar

At a Nazi party rally at Nürnberg in 1934, American correspondent William L. Shirer described an audience listening to Hitler. "They looked up at him as if he were a Messiah," he wrote, "their faces transformed into something positively inhuman."

in Portugal, or a Horthy in Hungary were "strong men": they abrogated constitutions, reduced parliaments to virtual impotence, and appropriated executive and legislative powers. But they did not—and this distinguishes them from a Stalin or a Hitler—strive for total power. The political authority they exercised stayed within traditional limits. They left their citizens recourse to law; nor did they challenge on the whole their right to form independent associations, to criticize the government, or to travel abroad. Even in Mussolini's Italy the independence of judges and courts was respected to a considerable extent.

In totalitarian states such lines are no longer observed. The barriers separating the individual from society, and both from the state, fall down. Civil liberties are dispensed with. In a mature totalitarian regime, such as Soviet Russia was under Stalin after 1933, or Germany during the last three years of Hitler's rule, the citizen turns into an object devoid of any rights whatever.

Totalitarianism emerged at a time when the ideas and social classes on which liberalism had traditionally relied were in a state of collapse. The pessimism and the mood of violence that had appeared before World War I, and which the war had intensified, undermined the faith in reason and progress and the respect for human life which constitute the essence of the liberal outlook. The simultaneous decline of the middle class (discussed in the next chapter) deprived liberalism of that social group which had traditionally served as its main support. The worldwide economic depression that began in 1929 further weakened the liberal cause by souring a large part of the working class on democracy and democratic socialism. By the early 1930s liberalism seemed spent, a thing of the past, and totalitarianism the wave of the future.

The first totalitarian state, and the universal model, was Soviet Russia during the period of War Communism, 1918–1920 (Chapter 12). It is not that Lenin assumed dictatorial powers, dissolved the duly elected Constituent Assembly, and transformed the Congresses of Soviets (proletarian parliaments) into a mere rubber stamp. It is not even that he suppressed rival parties. Had he done this and nothing more he would have been merely another garden variety postwar dictator. But Lenin went much farther in that he refused to be bound either by law or by inherent rights of the individual. Following Marx he regarded law and human freedoms as deceptions by means of which the class in power suppresses those it exploits, and he declared at once his intention of denying them to his opponents in the name of the proletarian dictatorship. The will of the party—that is, in effect, his will—was to Lenin superior to rights and freedoms and to law. The Communist party was not bound by any objective norms, not even those of its own making. All that remained, therefore, was the sheer will of the leader, unlimited in scope and unrestrained in application.

Although, as we had occasion to point out, the power of the liberal state after 1870 had increased steadily, nothing had prepared the world for such a startling development. The Bolshevik Revolution shattered the traditional conception of what was properly within the limits of state authority. Everything came within the purview of the state, and therefore everything acquired political significance. The many barriers which, since the American Revolution, had been carefully constructed to prevent this from happening, crumbled in Russia. The politicization of life characterizing totalitarianism finds succinct expression in the

The Nazis early attempted to capture the loyalty of German youth. This photograph was taken at a youth rally held by the party in Munich in 1925.

paraphrase of Christ's words that the ruler of the African state of Ghana, Kwame Nkruma, had engraved on his monument: "Seek ye first the political kingdom and all other things shall be added unto you." Or, in the words of Mussolini, "Everything within the state, nothing outside the state, nothing against the state."

Lenin's successes in establishing his power and especially his use of the Bolshevik party to obtain control over the government and the citizenry impressed ambitious politicians in other parts of Europe. Here the teachings of neo-conservatism (Chapter 9) had created in certain groups an intense anti-liberal sentiment. First Mussolini, then Hitler, and finally some dictators of smaller countries learned to combine neo-conservative ideas—nationalism, anti-Semitism, and mass action—with the Leninist technique of one-party politics to create a Western version of totalitarianism or semi-totalitarianism.

The central institution of the totalitarian state is the party. The word "party" applied to the Communist or National Socialist organizations is a misnomer, for they have next to nothing in common with what is ordinarily meant by that term: a voluntary association of persons with similar opinions or interests formed to exercise pressure on the government or to assume temporarily political responsibility. The totalitarian party forms the very essence of the state, penetrating everywhere and controlling everything. In Mussolini's words, it is "the capillary organization of the regime," invading the tissues of the body politic as the blood vessels spread through a living organism. The party not only assumes responsibility for government; it becomes the government. If in the liberal state the party in power is a temporary lessee of sovereignty, in a totalitarian state it is its permanent owner. Membership in such a party is not open to everyone: it is bestowed on the select in conformity with strict standards, being regarded a privilege.

The totalitarian party owes responsibility only to its leader—*vozhd, duce, führer*—who may or may not also serve as the formal head of the government, but who invariably directs its affairs. His powers are unlimited, though they are rarely legally defined. This following description of Hitler's powers, voted by the Reichstag in 1942, gives a good idea of what they in fact are:

> The Führer must . . . at all times be in a position—without being tied to existing legal restrictions—in his position as Führer of the nation, supreme commander of the armed forces, head of the Government and supreme possessor of executive power, senior judiciary and Führer of the Party, to urge every German . . . to fulfill his duties by all means that he considers suitable, and, on violation of such duties, to inflict the punishment that he considers suitable.

What does the totalitarian state want? What does it offer the individual in return for his loss of rights and freedoms? The question is a difficult one to answer. While totalitarian regimes spend much effort on formulating and propagating their official ideologies, they rarely commit themselves to firm rules, for to do so would limit the leader's freedom. Even Lenin, who devoted a great deal of attention to theoretical writings, left no consistent body of doctrine, and his ideas can be cited to justify completely contradictory policies. Totalitarian movements prefer ideological flexibility, which allows constant shifts to meet changing conditions. They all, however, demand sacrifices: they invariably appeal to the present generation to give up whatever it cherishes for the sake of the generations to come. Despite their secular, anti-religious bent, they are therefore every bit as other-worldly as are traditional religions, for the blessings they promise are never to be enjoyed here and now, but only in some mythical future.

Instead of a fixed ideology totalitarian leaders prefer a sense of drive, of forward motion, of what Mussolini described as the "state of highest ideal tension" and called the most important ingredient of fascism. Liberalism tended toward a static situation in which state, society, and individual each would function within its proper sphere, and the whole body politic revolve like a well-oiled mechanism. Such an ideal is utterly alien to the totalitarian spirit. It seeks constant action. It thrives on enemies, and cannot do without them, whether they be designated as Jews, capitalists, Communists, imperialists, or "the Establishment." When no enemies exist they are invented, for crises alone justify the power and obedience that leaders of such movements claim. In this sense totalitarian regimes are inherently dynamic, expansive, and unsettling.

To maintain itself in power a totalitarian regime needs a large police apparatus invested with broad powers. Its task is not only to ferret out actual opponents but to prevent sedition in advance. To this end it employs terror, striking alike at the guilty and the innocent, so as to create an atmosphere of pervading fear. (At the height of the Stalinist terror, Moscow furnished provincial police authorities with quotas indicating what percentage of the local population was to be arrested.) Naturally, a police enjoying such powers acquires control over the party that had created it, for to stand up to it is to invite the charge of disloyalty. In both Stalinist Russia and Nazi Germany the police in the end superseded the party and ran the state. The ultimate fulfillment of totalitarianism is the concentration camp, a self-contained, isolated realm where "enemies of the people" are incarcerated, to live, to suffer, and to die at the pleasure of their police masters.

A common feature of totalitarian regimes is their loathing of both the middle class and the intellectuals, two elements that resist dissolution in an amorphous mass. Representatives of these two groups often initiate anti-liberal revolutions, but they usually perish at the hands of those they raise to power. The social group that profits most is the lower-middle class. In the Communist, Fascist, and Nazi parties the people who made the best careers and who set the tone were small businessmen and functionaries of all kinds. Their ambition was to displace the bourgeoisie, and it is they who lent totalitarian movements their hostility to the propertied, the titled, the well-educated. Yet at the same time they wished to separate themselves as sharply as possible from the working class, and as a result they ruthlessly destroyed democratic socialism within and without their parties.

Totalitarianism, insofar as the historical record is any indication, can be stopped only before its adherents seize the state apparatus. Once in power a totalitarian regime cannot be dislodged, except by defeat in war. Its control is so pervasive and its vigilance so keen that internal opposition against it has no chance of establishing a foothold.

After peace had been restored in 1919 the Western economy tended spontaneously to revert to the system that had prevailed before 1914, that is, to a free, self-regulating world market. For a while the effort succeeded, and by 1925 world productivity and world trade attained to their prewar levels. But the economic reconstruction rested on fragile foundations. In 1929 the collapse of values on the New York Stock Exchange caused a world-wide chain reaction leading to the most severe economic depression in history, and producing disastrous social and political consequences. No single factor contributed so heavily to the triumph of totalitarianism.

The World Economic Crisis

As we have pointed out previously (Chapter 6), international prosperity before World War I had depended on the existence of a world market in which goods, money, and labor moved virtually unobstructed to where they were in the highest demand, that is, where they were the most productive. This movement was not entirely free, for it had to contend with protective tariffs, especially toward the end of the nineteenth century. But prior to 1914 these tariff barriers were not high enough to impede significantly the natural flow of the international economy.

The disruption of this economy began in earnest during the war. The Central Powers were from the beginning cut off from their usual sources of supply and forced into self-sufficiency. In 1917 Russia, one of the leading commercial nations, withdrew from the world economy. All the belligerents had to channel their productive capacities to military purposes, overdeveloping industrial sectors which with the restoration of peace would be of little use. The neutrals, on the other hand, especially the United States, expanded their general production at a feverish pace to keep up with the demands of the belligerents, much beyond the needs of the normal world market. The war thus unbalanced the economic life of both belligerents and neutrals.

After the cessation of hostilities it proved difficult to reforge the disrupted trade links and to restore the economic balance. The immediate problem was the

The German artist Kaethe Kollwitz (pages 190–191) did this charcoal study, Unemployed, *in Berlin in 1925.*

uneven distribution of gold and "hard currencies," that is, currencies that were internationally accepted (e.g., the dollar, pound sterling, Swiss and French franc, etc.). Wartime purchases had siphoned off a great deal of the European gold to the neutrals: in the 1920s the United States alone owned 40 percent of the world's gold reserve. Furthermore, the newly independent countries of Eastern Europe began statehood with such small reserves that their currencies never gained international status. Germany, burdened with large reparations payments, had little gold to spare. As a result of these factors, convertible currency —the lifeblood of international trade—was in such short supply that many European countries were unable to engage in significant foreign trade. Their currencies turned into tokens with a strictly internal circulation.

To remedy this situation and to stimulate trade on which the health of their own economies depended, the capital-rich countries—the United States, Great Britain, and France—poured in the 1920s a great deal of money in the form of loans and investments into the capital-poor countries, especially Germany. Another means of overcoming the shortage of capital was acceptance of the so-called Gold Exchange Standard, introduced in 1922. A country that adopted it backed its currency not with gold proper but with gold-backed currencies or securities of other countries. These measures succeeded in stimulating trade, but they also created an unhealthy dependence of much of Europe on the continuous flow of outside capital, especially from the United States, as well as on the economic stability of the gold-holding countries.

A second factor that inhibited postwar trade was the steady rise of tariff barriers. To protect its overexpanded industries from competition, the United States passed in 1922 a very stringent tariff act, thereby making it even more difficult for capital-poor countries to secure gold and dollars. Furthermore, the dissolution of the great empires in 1918 had produced numerous successor states, each of which immediately established its own tariff system. The total length of European frontiers in 1920 was exactly double that of 1914; each new mile of frontier represented another hurdle to the movement of goods. These successor states exacted higher duties than had the empires. It has been estimated, for example, that the Czech and Hungarian republics charged tariffs 50 percent in excess of those collected by the Austro-Hungarian Empire of which they had formed a part.

The shortage of gold and convertible currencies and the simultaneous increase of tariff barriers created a vicious circle: to raise gold or hard currency each country sought to obtain the most favorable balance of trade, that is, to sell abroad the most and to buy abroad the least. Obviously, the less it purchased from other countries, the less the latter could purchase from it in return. Gradually, the international economy began to move toward "autarchy," or self-sufficiency of individual states, which vitiated the whole idea of an open world market.

In the meantime productivity was rising everywhere. By 1925 world manufacture of goods, having surpassed that of 1913, continued to climb upward. It was only a question of time before productivity outpaced demand. For the time being (1925–1929), however, trade kept pace with output, thanks to constant injections of capital.

In October, 1929, the main source of this capital suddenly dried up. The collapse on the New York Stock Exchange of a stupendous speculative wave in common stocks caused a shortage of capital in the United States. Credit became difficult to obtain. United States imports and foreign investments shrank and by 1932 were only one-third of what they had been in 1929. Many European banks and enterprises whose credit had been overextended or that had relied on the currencies or securities of other countries now went bankrupt, pulling down other banking and commercial institutions. In May, 1931, when the Creditanstalt, the principal bank of Austria, declared its insolvency, Europe experienced a grave financial crisis. A few months later several German banks suspended payments. Soon gold disappeared: in September, 1931, Great Britain went off the gold standard, and two years later the United States followed suit.

Trade declined. Most countries carefully guarded their limited reserves of gold and hard currencies and confined their foreign dealings as much as possible to agreements with individual countries, that is, in effect, to barter agreements. Between 1929 and 1932 world trade declined in value from $68.6 billion to $26.6.

The reduction in trade necessitated a corresponding reduction in productivity, since there was no point in manufacturing goods that could not be sold. World productivity of raw materials and manufactured goods decreased by more than one-quarter; in the two leading countries (the United States and Germany), the output of industrial goods declined by nearly one-half. Workers had to be laid off or dismissed. The world had never experienced unemployment of such dimensions. In 1932, when the depression was at its worst, an estimated 22 percent of the world labor force, or 30 million people, were jobless. In the nineteenth century many of these unemployed could have migrated overseas, but this became much more difficult now because some of the leading recipients of immigrants in the past, notably the United States, severely restricted the inflow of foreigners. °

The depression occurred at a time when confidence in liberalism and all it stood for was already severely shaken. Liberalism had proved itself incompetent to cope with postwar political and social instability; now it also showed its economic impotence. In the early 1930s the only way out of chaos seemed to lie in strong, purposeful "total" authority. The depression completely discredited liberalism and gave the critical impetus to totalitarian regimes that were to dominate the next two decades.

Stalinist Russia War Communism had secured Bolshevik power, but it left the country economically and spiritually shattered. Between 1918 and 1920 an estimated 7 million people died in Russia from sickness, hunger, and the cold. The peasantry, outraged by food expropriations, refused to produce beyond its own immediate needs, and in 1920–1921 a terrible famine afflicted the country. Only thanks to the American Relief Administration, organized by the future President Herbert Hoover, were hundreds of thousands of additional Russians saved from certain starvation. Compared to 1913 the productivity of heavy industry in 1920 declined four-fifths and real wages of workers two-thirds.

Lenin, confronted with this catastrophic situation, acted in a typically resolute manner. In March, 1921, he abandoned War Communism and adopted the New Economic Policy (NEP). The NEP was primarily designed to placate the peasantry and to restore agricultural productivity. Forced food requisitioning was replaced by a tax in kind. The peasants were allowed to lease land and hire labor, and to dispose of their produce on the free market. A good deal of private initiative was also permitted in trade and manufacture. The results of this policy were spectacular. By 1928 Russian agricultural and industrial productivity attained their pre-1914 levels. Never before or since was the Soviet government as popular, especially among the peasantry, which at long last realized the age-old dream of having at its disposal all the country's arable land.

The NEP awakened widespread expectations that the Communist experiment was over, and that Russia, like France after the fall of Robespierre, was entering its "bourgeois" stage of development. Such hopes proved deceptive. The Communist leaders never gave up their monopoly either of political power or of what

° In 1921 Congress passed an Immigration Act which established quotas by country of birth: the annual number of immigrants from any country was limited to 3 percent of the number of that nationality who were foreign-born United States residents in 1910. As a result of this and subsequent laws, the number of immigrants coming to the United States in the 1930's sank to one-tenth and less of what it had been before the war.

Russian peasants line up for bread during the 1920–1921 famine. The American Relief Administration distributed in Russia nearly half a million tons of food, clothing, and medicine.

they called the "commanding heights" of the national economy, that is, heavy industry, banking, and foreign trade. The NEP was merely a breathing spell, a period of national convalescence before the next phase of the revolution from above got under way.

In December, 1922, Lenin suffered a paralytic stroke that incapacitated him completely. He died in January, 1924. Even before his final illness the question of his successor arose in acute form. One of the weaknesses of a regime that comes to power by violence and maintains itself in power by violence is that it lacks a legitimate procedure of succession. Lenin's heir could be selected only by a process of ruthless in-fighting within the party hierarchy, with the victory going to him who gained the support of the party's functionaries.

On the face of it Trotsky had all the attributes of an heir-apparent. He had been the organizer of the October Revolution and the creator of the Red Army. He was the most intelligent of the Bolshevik leaders; he was also the best orator, and, next to Lenin, the most familiar figure in the country. He headed the armed forces. He had the assets, but he lacked the essential personal qualities: will to power and the ordinary talents of a politician. Trotsky had no patience for the details of administration, nor did he know how to pretend interest in the little bureaucrats who came to the center for guidance and leadership. He preferred to speak and write on behalf of world revolution, hoping to maintain his leadership by appealing to the emotion and imagination of the masses as he had done in 1917.

But times had changed. The masses no longer counted. What counted were the millions of functionaries of the party and government who carried responsibility for the day-to-day administration of what had become a large and relatively stable state. These "men of the apparatus," or *apparatchiki*, had had enough of turmoil. They craved normalcy, an opportunity to enjoy the fruits of the power they had won since 1917. They were now a ruling class. Why should they endanger their position on behalf of a world revolution to which Trotsky

SOVFOTO

Lenin (left) and Stalin were photographed together in Moscow in the summer of 1922. In December of that year Lenin suffered a paralytic stroke.

was exhorting them? An increasing proportion of these *apparatchiki* came to distrust the clever Jewish intellectual and turned instead to a stolid Georgian named Joseph Dzhugashvili, known in the party as Stalin.°

Stalin was born in 1879 in an artisan family. After receiving a sketchy education in a religious seminary, he associated himself with the Bolsheviks and became a full-time revolutionary. He had no literary or rhetorical gifts, but he was loyal, dependable, and ready to carry out Lenin's instructions without raising the kind of moral or theoretical questions that troubled most other Russian Social Democrats. In the Revolution he played a minor role. However, after the Soviet state had been established and administrative problems multiplied, Lenin came increasingly to rely on him. Stalin could always be counted upon to attend to details for which Lenin and Trotsky, preoccupied as they were with major political or military decisions, had no time. Gradually, he built up within the party a personal following consisting of non-ideological careerists. By the time the Civil War had come to an end, a great deal of the party apparatus had quietly slipped into Stalin's hands. Trotsky paid no attention to the inarticulate Georgian, whom he once characterized as a "grey blur." By 1922 Stalin grew so powerful that he had the temerity to ignore Lenin's instructions and even to

°The Georgians, who inhabit the Caucasus, have been under Russian rule since 1801. They are Orthodox Christians, but have nothing in common with the Russians either ethnically or linguistically.

insult Lenin's wife. One of Lenin's last acts was to break personal relations with Stalin.

By then it was too late. Skillfully exploiting personal rivalries among other Communist leaders, Stalin organized party coalitions against Trotsky, his main rival. He depicted Trotsky as an unprincipled opportunist who had repeatedly betrayed Lenin and who now wanted to lead the country into dangerous adventures. Rather than exert efforts to promote revolutions abroad, as Trotsky desired, Stalin counseled "socialism in one country"—the concentration of all efforts and resources on developing in Soviet Russia a huge industrial economy. Trotsky's arguments that "socialism in one country" was a contradiction in terms because socialism (in the Marxist sense) could triumph only as an international movement fell on deaf ears among the party rank and file. In 1927 Trotsky was expelled from the party and two years later exiled from the Soviet Union. After long wanderings he settled in Mexico, where in 1940 he was murdered by a Stalinist agent.

Stalin's victory over Trotsky marked the beginning in Russia of a new phase of totalitarian rule. Combining talents for incredible intrigue and sadistic destructiveness with outstanding administrative abilities, Stalin eliminated his rivals one by one and emerged in the late 1930s as the absolute master of 170 million people. No other man in history had ever held such power.

Stalin's rule may be divided into three phases: the basic economic transformation of Russia (1928–1932), political terror (1932–1938), and war and external expansion (1939–1953). We shall deal with the last of these phases in the chapters that follow and here concentrate on the first two.

The main aim of Stalin's economic measures was to provide Soviet Russia with an industrial base on which to erect a modern military machine, which World War I had revealed was alone capable of winning twentieth-century battles. To realize this aim it was necessary to centralize the productive resources of the country and to direct them in a rational manner toward specific economic goals. In other words, a wartime economy was to be introduced in peacetime.

In 1928 the NEP was abandoned and replaced by rigidly controlled economic planning. In that year Russia adopted the Five-Year Plan, a crash program concentrated on building up heavy industry. Emphasis was placed on coal and iron, electrification, and machine construction. Each branch of the national economy was assigned specific production targets, and detailed schemes were drawn up for the movement of capital and resources. The country, especially its youth, responded enthusiastically to this gigantic constructive undertaking whose ultimate purpose, as depicted in a massive propaganda campaign, was abundance of consumer goods and a socialist society.

The results of the first Five-Year Plan were indeed spectacular. Upon its completion a second Five-Year Plan with similar objectives was launched. In 1936 Russia produced three times as much iron and oil and four times as much coal and steel as in 1913. The electrical output was sixteen times that of 1913. Many new industries were established—for example, automobile and tractor plants and industrial chemicals—which had not previously existed in Russia.

The class that paid most dearly for the forced industrialization was the peasantry, which in 1926 constituted 78 percent of the population. Soviet Russia did not have enough resources to launch its industrial drive and at the same time to provide the consumer with anything beyond the barest necessities. The anticipated reduction in consumer goods, however, raised the danger that the peasant would once more refuse to sell his food to the cities and industrial centers because he could receive in return nothing but worthless paper money.

To prevent this from happening Stalin cajoled the party into launching simultaneously with the first Five-Year Plan a massive program of land "collectivization." The government now took over the peasant's land, that which he had acquired before and since the Revolution, as well as his livestock and agricultural implements. These were turned over to "collective farms" (*kolkhozy* and *sovkhozy*) supervised by party-appointed managers. The peasant became in effect a hired hand, tilling for the state what had been until then his own land. In return for his labor, he received that part of the produce that remained after the collective had met the quotas set by the government. If the village did not produce a surplus above the required state deliveries, it had to go hungry. The city's supply was assured in any event.

The peasants furiously resisted this expropriation which reverted them to the condition prevailing before the Emancipation Edict of 1861. Rather than surrender their cattle they slaughtered and ate them. In many villages armed resistance reminiscent of 1920 broke out. Army and police units had to surround such villages and shoot the peasants into submission. Rich peasants, the so-called kulaks, or "fists," who were also the most productive elements in the countryside, were forcefully removed from their properties and either killed or exiled to concentration camps. How many people perished in this action cannot at present be established. During the war Stalin, in an expansive moment, confided to Winston Churchill that collectivization affected 10 million peasants, "the great bulk [of whom] were very unpopular and were wiped out by their

The propaganda directed at the Russian peasant included such newspapers as The Collective Farmer, *shown being printed on the back of a truck in a Ukrainian wheat field at harvest time.*

laborers." We may therefore assume that close to 10 million peasants lost their lives. Peasant resistance lowered production of food to the point where in 1932–1933 Soviet Russia suffered its second major famine since the Revolution. The cities had their food quotas delivered, but many villages starved, especially in the Ukraine. Peasants quit their villages in droves and moved into the cities.

By 1932 virtually the entire industrial and agricultural resources of Russia were in the hands of the state—that is, of Stalin. The dictator's next task was to secure this personal power against any potential contenders. Beginning in 1932 Stalin launched a reign of terror, initially directed against the Communist party apparatus but later broadened to encompass the entire population. He had to rid himself of those who took their Marxism and Communism seriously, whose memories reached back to Lenin and Trotsky, who had links with foreign socialists, and to replace them with a new generation of functionaries—men from the lower strata who owed everything to him and who knew and believed only what he allowed them to know and believe.

This process was launched in 1932 with a mass purge of the party, in the course of which one-third of the party effectives were dropped from the rolls. The reign of terror proper began in the winter of 1934–1935. The pretext was the assassination of Sergei Kirov, the popular party chief in Leningrad. Stalin claimed that Kirov's murder was the work of a vast counterrevolutionary organization and that vigorous measures were required to root it out. (Today it is virtually certain that Kirov was assassinated in the best gangland fashion on the orders of Stalin himself.) In the years 1936–1938 the astonished world witnessed in Russia what looked like the enactment of some ghoulish scenario by Dostoevsky: a succession of show trials at which the men who had made the Revolution and helped found the Soviet state confessed to the basest crimes, including espionage on behalf of foreign powers. Each trial ended with mass executions. By 1938 not one of Lenin's close friends and associates was left alive. In the 1930s elaborate theories were advanced in the West to explain these proceedings, often with reference to alleged peculiarities of the Russian "soul." (Some Westerners, of course, accepted the trials at face value.) But in 1956 Nikita Khrushchev, Stalin's successor, explained the confessions in a very simple manner:

> How is it possible that a person confesses to crimes that he has not committed? Only in one way—as a result of methods of physical pressure, of tortures, which bring him to a state of unconsciousness, deprivation of judgment, which rob him of human dignity. [Stalin's] "confessions" were secured in this manner.

Before being brought to trial the victims were subjected to such inhuman beatings and tortures that they agreed to anything and looked forward to death as relief.

The show trials were only public spectacles behind the scenes of which unrolled a wholesale terror. Millions of party and state functionaries, army officers, trade unionists, intellectuals, simple peasants, and workers were arrested by the secret police, speedily "investigated," forced to sign fabricated "confessions," and either shot or sent to concentration camps. Both Bolsheviks and their one-time opponents now shared a similar fate. The Russian intelligentsia was virtually annihilated. The secret police, concentrated in the Ministry of the Interior (NKVD, later renamed MVD), replaced the party as the ruling organization. Even its chiefs, however, were not immune from persecution, each in turn being accused of treason and executed, until in 1938 Stalin settled on a fellow Georgian, Lavrenti Beria.

In 1938 the whole gruesome process finally ground to a halt. The old Communist apparatus lay in shambles, and a new generation had come into power: crude and ignorant, but totally dependent on Stalin and presumably loyal to him.

Neither the horrors of collectivization nor those of the terror discouraged Western pro-Communists. Indeed, in the 1930s the popularity of Stalin and Soviet Russia grew. Many foreign intellectuals, appalled by the economic depression and the rise of fascism and nazism, idealized the Soviet experiment, and saw in it a blueprint of the future. In the 1930s there was a widespread tendency in the West to dismiss any evidence unfavorable to Soviet Russia. "You cannot make an omelet without breaking eggs" was frequently heard in justification of Stalin's actions.

The more his power grew, the more Stalin withdrew from the public eye. Stalin was not a "charismatic" leader, that is, one able to command a fanatical following by the force of his personality. He had no rhetorical gifts whatever: he spoke with a monotonous voice and in a heavy Georgian accent, which to a Russian has a very comical sound. Instead of exposing himself personally he projected his identity through an enormous propaganda campaign that impressed on the public the image of an all-knowing, all-present, all-powerful, and, indeed, immortal being.

The Nazi Seizure of Power

The economic crisis of 1929–1932 undercut the last remaining props of the Weimar Republic. Exports declined by two-thirds, and by 1932 over 6 million Germans were unemployed. German workers were now in as desperate straits as the middle class had been during the inflation of the early twenties, and as discontented. Many defected from the Social Democrats and joined extremist parties.

One group that profited from this situation was the German Communist party. Well-organized, purposeful, aggressive, it continued to whittle away votes from the Social Democrats, the mainstay of the republic. Its share of the parliamentary seats grew steadily, especially during the depression (chart, opposite). The Communists were not concerned by a much more spectacular gain of the parties at the opposite end of the political spectrum, the traditional conservatives and the National Socialists. At the time they regarded the Social Democrats as their main enemy, the principal rival for the workingman's vote, and concentrated all efforts on their destruction. With Stalin's backing, German Communist leaders acted on the premise that Hitler was less dangerous, indeed preferable, to the liberal, reformist socialists.

The greatest benefit from the disintegration of the liberal center accrued to the Nazis, the German National Socialist Labor party (NSDAP). Between 1928 and 1932 they picked up 11 million votes and increased their share of parliamentary seats thirteenfold.

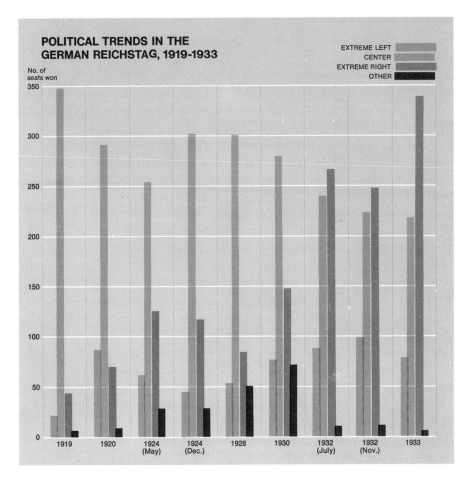

POLITICAL TRENDS IN THE GERMAN REICHSTAG, 1919-1933

EXTREME LEFT
CENTER
EXTREME RIGHT
OTHER

No. of seats won

350
300
250
200
150
100
50
0

1919　1920　1924 (May)　1924 (Dec.)　1928　1930　1932 (July)　1932 (Nov.)　1933

The NSDAP came into existence as one of the numerous Austrian neo-conservative parties that would have vanished without a trace were it not that in the person of Adolf Hitler it acquired a leader of singular demagogic gifts and utter nihilistic unscrupulousness. Hitler was born in 1889 in the family of a petty Austrian customs official. As a youth he tried desperately to make an artistic career, but the Vienna Academy of Fine Arts rejected his application for admission on the grounds that he did not know how to draw. Temperamentally unable to hold a job, Hitler became a tramp. Living in Viennese flophouses, he earned just enough from casual manual work and peddling his landscapes to keep his head above water. During these years he developed a consuming hatred for the cultivated bourgeois society of Vienna that had rejected him and condemned him to the life of an anonymous cipher, and most of all for the Jews who were so prominent in Vienna's cultural life. He dreamed of gaining power and exacting revenge for his humiliations. Hitler had no political ideas either then or later, but he studied attentively the techniques of mob manipulation. He admired greatly the Christian Socialist mayor of Vienna, Karl Lueger (Chapter 9), for his ability to appeal simultaneously to German nationalism, anti-Semitism, and anti-capitalism to gain votes. He also observed closely the activities of the Austrian Social Democrats, especially the mass rallies at which orators whipped up their followers. Hitler knew that he could only realize his wild ambitions by mastering crowds. His intellectual baggage was common currency of right-wing

Austria in the turn-of-the-century period: Social Darwinism, racism, anti-parliamentarism.

From his youth onward Hitler evidenced a hysterical personality. He was subject to frequent, ungovernable outbursts of rage, which later astonished even his intimate associates. His utter confidence in himself and his cause, combined with overpowering emotionalism, made him into a spellbinding orator; and on his rhetoric he built his political career. Notwithstanding his extreme skill in utilizing political and military means to gain his objectives, there can be no doubt that he had a deranged mind: medicine is familiar with psychopaths who pursue totally irrational ends in a highly calculating manner.

During World War I Hitler served in the German army on the Western front. (He had earlier abandoned his Austrian citizenship out of disgust with the vacillating policies of the Hapsburgs, especially their leniency toward their non-German subjects.) After demobilization he joined the disaffected veterans who were plotting the overthrow of the Weimar Republic. His skill in rabble-rousing in Munich beer halls secured him contacts with nationalistic generals who needed popular support for their subversive plans but did not know how to go about obtaining it. In 1920 Hitler and his friends—a casual assortment of war veterans, journalists, ideologists, and plain thugs—formed squads of street fighters to assault Social Democrats and Communists. These units, modeled on Mussolini's *fasci di combattimento*, were organized in 1921 into regular Storm Troop detachments (*Sturmabteilungen*, or SA). In 1923, when the French occupation of the Ruhr seemed to have dealt the republic a fatal blow, Hitler joined Ludendorff in an abortive *coup d'état* in Munich. For this he was arrested and sentenced to five years in prison. There, comfortably installed, he began to write his main political work, *Mein Kampf* (*My Struggle*).

After the fiasco of 1923 the Nazis came to the conclusion that power had to be secured not by violence, that is, by a direct assault on the republic. Like Lenin and Mussolini, Hitler decided to make his "revolution" only after having come to power and now began to stress legality. The Weimar Republic played into his hands by dealing leniently with him and his followers, although the Nazis made no secret of their ultimate aims. Hitler himself was released from prison after serving only one year. Later, when the Nazis stood at the pinnacle of power, Hitler's Propaganda Minister, Joseph Goebbels, recalled the Weimar days:

> Until 1932 our political opponents did not realize where we were going, that our respect for legality was only a trick. We wanted to come to power legally, but we certainly did not intend to use power legally. We did not want to tolerate parties that in a year would deal with us as we intended to deal with them. They could have suppressed us. This would not have been so difficult. But this was not done. In 1925, a few of us could have been arrested, and everything would have been over. But we were allowed to cross the danger zone.

The Nazi program must be viewed on three distinct levels: the official party platform, most explicitly formulated in 1920; the concealed political aim—totalitarianism—which became apparent only in 1933, after Hitler had secured the chancellorship; and the ultimate racial goals, hinted at in the 1920s and

The biting Social Democratic poster below asks, "Do you want these to rule you?" The 1932 Nazi poster opposite equates a vote for Hitler with the fight against hunger and despair.

partly realized in the 1930s, but revealed in all their insanity only after the outbreak of World War II. The gradual, piecemeal manner in which the Nazis unraveled their program was one of the reasons for their success in deceiving the public at home and abroad.

The formal party platform of 1920 was designed to appeal to the broadest strata of opinion. It advocated nationalism based on race (rather than on culture) and called for the unification of all Germans in a single state, the renunciation of the humiliating treaties of Versailles and St. Germain, and the expulsion from Germany of residents with foreign citizenship. Its nationalism was fortified by unabashed anti-Semitism: German Jews were to be denied the status of Germans on the grounds that they did not and could not belong to the German "racial community." The platform also contained strong socialist elements. It favored state guarantees of employment, the confiscation of war profits and of income not earned by work, the nationalization of big business, and profit-sharing. To the peasants the Nazis promised land reform and to the lower-middle class (which they courted especially assiduously) the expropriation of department stores, the great competitor of the shopkeeper. The platform was emphatically anti-bourgeois and anti-liberal, making a strong appeal to the sentiments hostile to industrialization and capitalism among the lower-middle class and the working population.

The 1920 program also pledged to "abolish the corrupt parliamentary order," but it did not specify what would replace it. Nothing was said about the intended one-party dictatorship, the abolition of political rights and civil liberties, or the omnipotence of the police. Following the example of Lenin and Mussolini, Hitler was most reticent about the most essential.

He was more explicit about his ultimate, long-range racial aims, but these were so fantastic that hardly anyone, even among the Nazis, took them seriously. What he had in mind was no less than the physical destruction of a considerable part of the European population and its replacement by a new breed of human beings. These were to be sired by the purest representatives of the "Aryan" race and brought up in the spirit of National Socialist ideas: industry, thrift, and unquestioned loyalty to Hitler as the incarnation of the "Aryan" spirit. The "inferior" races and "defective" human specimens were to be enslaved or pitilessly destroyed.

Hitler succeeded in coming to power in a perfectly legal manner by taking advantage of the widening rift between right and left to present himself as the leader of a "revolution" leading to national unity and renascence.

In 1930 the government was assumed by the Catholic Center party, which at last took firm action against both the anti-republican parties, the Communists and Nazis, and outlawed their strong-arm squads. The extremists, however, continued to do well in elections: in July, 1932, the Nazis won the largest number of votes and became the strongest party in the Reichstag. They demanded that Hitler be named Chancellor, but President von Hindenburg refused on the basis that the Nazis were a divisive party, likely to exacerbate social conflicts. Soon new elections were held (November, 1932). This time the Nazis lost 2 million votes, while the Communists made another advance. The good showing of

*The Establishment
of Nazi Totalitarianism*

the Communists frightened the traditional conservatives and induced them to seek an alliance with the Nazis. In January, 1933, Hitler was invited by the monarchists to head a coalition government. The men who engineered this deal had little sympathy for the Austrian upstart, but they believed that by bringing Hitler into the government they could thwart the Communist danger and at the same time exert a moderating influence on the Nazis. On January 30, 1933, Hindenburg appointed Hitler Chancellor of a cabinet in which the Nazis held only two additional posts.

Hitler at first kept up the pretense of being a good parliamentarian and insisted on holding new elections, the third in a year, to secure an absolute majority in the Reichstag. In the electoral campaign SA squads ruled the streets, intimidating opponents and fighting Communist gangs. The Nazis offered no specific program; they merely asked the country to give them four years to show what they could accomplish toward a national revival. Their brutal electoral techniques did not bring them the anticipated majority, but they secured a respectable following nonetheless: 17 million votes, or 43.7 percent of the ballots. With their allies, the Nationalists, they now controlled 51.9 percent of the Reichstag seats. This was a sufficient basis on which to make a bid for total power.

By 1933 the totalitarian model was well established. What Lenin, Mussolini, and Stalin had learned by trial and error, Hitler could put into practice in fin-

A picture made in 1933 shows the senile "Wooden Titan," German President von Hindenburg, taking the salute of SA troopers as his masters march behind him. Hitler is visible at center in mufti, next to the bemedaled Goering.

ished form. Within a few months after taking office as Chancellor, he gained enough authority to assert unlimited personal power over the German people.

The first step was to abolish civil rights protecting the opposition. This step was taken even before the Reichstag elections, in the guise of defending the country from an alleged Communist conspiracy. On February 27, 1933, unknown arsonists (most likely Nazis) set fire to the Reichstag building in Berlin. Hitler immediately blamed it on the Communists. He demanded that Hindenburg invoke constitutional emergency provisions and suspend civil liberties to safeguard the security of the country. On his Chancellor's advice, the President issued on February 28 an "Ordinance for the Protection of the People and the State" that indefinitely suspended civil liberties, authorizing

> restrictions on personal liberty, on the right of free expression of opinion, including freedom of the Press, on the rights of assembly and association; violations of the privacy of postal, telegraphic, and telephonic communications; warrants for house searches; orders for confiscations as well as restrictions on property.

Since the police, who were charged with carrying out these sweeping provisions, were by then largely in Nazi hands, the ordinance enabled Hitler legally to dispose of his opponents. The Communists now paid dearly for their shortsighted tactics: their party was the first to be outlawed and their leaders went to jail or to concentration camps, where most of them later perished; with them went many Social Democrats and other outspoken anti-Nazis. Regular courts were enjoined from interfering with the police and confined to civil suits. "Political" and "criminal" offenses (as defined by the Nazis) were handed over to the police and to "People's Courts," created in 1934. The Ordinance of 1933 remained in force until the collapse of the Nazi regime in 1945 and provided the legal basis for the repressions and executions of German citizens in the intervening period.

After the March, 1933, elections, Hitler turned his attention to the destruction of political rights. His aim was to be invested by the Reichstag with full legislative authority, that is, to usurp from the nation's elected representatives the right to issue laws. Such an amendment to the constitution required approval of two-thirds of the deputies. The Nazis persuaded the Catholic Center party to support their resolution, and by arresting Communist deputies they secured the necessary majority. On March 23–24 the Reichstag passed an "Enabling Act" divesting itself for a period of four years (but in fact permanently) of legislative authority. As Chancellor, Hitler could henceforth issue laws, even those violating the constitution, without consulting the Reichstag. The Social Democrats were the only major political party to vote against this self-imposed sentence of death that simultaneously destroyed German parliamentarism and German constitutionalism.

With the authority he now possessed Hitler could rapidly proceed to establish control over the whole of state and society. This process, euphemistically called *Gleichschaltung* (Coordination), involved the penetration by the NSDAP and its subsidiaries of all facets of German life, and the elimination of most foci of independent power. Among the first to go were the governments of the federal states. Their authority was severely abrogated, with the result that Germany be-

Heinrich Himmler, one of Hitler's earliest adherents, headed the SS and the Gestapo, eventually directing the entire Nazi police apparatus.

came for the first time in its history a centralized, unitary state. In the spring of 1933 all political parties, including those that had invited the Nazis into the government a few months earlier, were disbanded, and the NSDAP was declared the only lawful political organization in the country. The once powerful trade-union organizations were abolished and dissolved as well. So were most other associations, including cultural and recreational ones. At the end of 1933 Goebbels could thus describe what the Nazis had achieved in the course of the year:

> The Revolution which we have accomplished is a total one. It has seized all the realms of public life and transformed them from the ground up. It has completely altered and reformed the relations of men toward each other, toward the state, and toward problems of existence. . . . The system which we have overthrown found in liberalism its most accurate representation. If liberalism took as its starting point the individual and placed the individual man in the center of all things, we have replaced the individual by the nation and the individual man by the community.

At the beginning of 1934 only three institutions were still outside Hitler's complete grasp: the SA, the church, and the army.

The Storm Trooper organizations, which had proved so useful in the Nazi march to power, at this time numbered over 2 million members. Among them were genuine radicals who had taken at face value the socialist slogans of the Nazis, as well as ambitious politicians who wanted a "second revolution" to bring to heel big business and the largely middle-class army. But for Hitler the concept of "revolution" had lost its usefulness, and in 1934 he publicly declared Germany would have no more revolutions for a thousand years. Furthermore, he needed the support of big business and the officer corps to launch the program of rearmament, now his immediate goal. After some hesitation he therefore decided to liquidate the SA. In June, 1934, on his orders, several hundred SA leaders were massacred. Henceforth this organization lost influence.

Like other totalitarian leaders, Hitler was anticlerical. He saw in Christianity a "Jewish swindle," and he privately expressed his ultimate intention of wiping out the church. But in the first years he was not yet strong enough to tackle the powerful Catholic and Protestant establishments, and contented himself with a demand for strict separation of church and state. In July, 1933, he signed a Concordat with the Vatican in which the Catholic hierarchy recognized the new regime and renounced all activity in Germany save that of a purely religious and philanthropic kind. The Protestant churches, however, from the beginning offered strong resistance to the Nazis on ideological and moral grounds. Later, as the Nazis began to interfere with Catholic organizations, they, too, resisted. In 1937 the Pope issued an encyclical in which he voiced his anxiety over Nazi policies. By then the Nazis and the two major churches were locked in a grim struggle that lasted until the collapse of the regime.

The army, or *Reichswehr*, remained autonomous for the time being, for Hitler and the generals happened to have had common interests: both wanted to rearm. It was only in 1938, when basic rearmament was completed, that Hitler took personal charge of the *Reichswehr*. (See Chapter 18.)

The Nazi party did not differ fundamentally either in its structure or in its functions from the Communist party of the Soviet Union, or the Italian Fascist party, and therefore need not be described. The NSDAP created a whole hierarchy of offices that duplicated and controlled the regular state apparatus. It was officially described as "the bearer of the idea of German statehood, indissolubly bound with the state." When Hindenburg died in 1934, Hitler assumed the title of President, thus uniting in his person, like Lenin and Mussolini (but unlike Stalin), the positions of party chief and head of government.

To assure his personal power Hitler established an élite corps, the *Schutzstaffel* (Guard Detachment), or SS, which was placed under Heinrich Himmler, a one-time chicken farmer and the most pathologically sadistic among the Nazi leaders. The SS began as a bodyguard whose members took the oath of personal loyalty to Hitler and swore to carry out without question any orders he issued. Into it were recruited the most vicious elements of the Nazi movement. They staffed police posts, both overt and secret, and gradually penetrated much of the party and state machinery. From their ranks were drawn the concentration camp guards and, during World War II, the mass murderers. The powers of the SS grew steadily and eventually came to approximate those that the NKVD enjoyed under Stalin in Russia.

Anti-Semitism occupied a very special place in Nazi doctrine and practice; indeed, it was the only constant element in National Socialism, the one policy that never changed. Hitler and his associates were rabid anti-Semites, to whom the Jew was a satanic figure, a bloodsucker and invidious despoiler of Aryan purity, the lowest of subhumans. Their attitude toward the Jew was of a most primitive kind, in which sexual anxieties and historic traditions, rooted in the darkest Middle Ages, played a significant part. But Hitler also exploited anti-Jewish feelings in a cold-blooded fashion, for he needed a racial foe, much as the Soviet Communists needed their "class enemy."

The advent of the Nazis to power led immediately to the issuance of anti-Jewish laws. These culminated in the infamous Nürnberg Laws of 1935, which in effect deprived Jews of German citizenship and forbade them to marry "Aryans." The law defined as Jewish anyone who professed the Jewish faith or who had at least one-fourth of Jewish blood in his veins. Subjected to constant indignities and gradually deprived of their livelihood, many Jews had to migrate, leaving their possessions behind. In November, 1938, the anti-Semitic policy entered a violent phase with an organized nation-wide pogrom and burning of synagogues. These anti-Semitic acts were merely a prelude to what was intended as an eventual annihilation of the Jews and other "lower races" in Europe.

Hitler's main objective, once he had secured dictatorial powers, was to give Germany a powerful armed force with which to conquer "living space" and subjugate the Continent. The rearmament program required the maximum concentration of the country's resources, not unlike that introduced by imperial Germany during World War I. Shortly after the Nazis came to power the German economy was put on a wartime footing. Private enterprise was left intact because it proved efficient and cooperated with the Nazis, but it found itself subjected to stringent controls. Production soared: between 1932 and 1935 alone German steel production trebled. In 1936, emulating Stalin, Hitler introduced a Four-Year Plan. Its purpose was to make the German economy self-sufficient in

Hitler at a carefully staged Nazi party rally at Nürnberg. "You have to go through one of these," correspondent Shirer wrote, "to understand Hitler's hold on the people, to feel the dynamic in the movement he's unleashed and the sheer, disciplined strength of the Germans."

strategic war materials, such as rubber and gasoline, by the development of substitutes. In 1940, when the plan was to be fulfilled, Hitler expected the armed forces and the economy to be fully geared for war.

In their social policy the Nazis spoke of creating a one-class society, but they did not pursue this aim with anything like the determination they displayed in their destructive policies. In 1934 they formed a "National Labor Front," uniting employees and employers in a single national organization. This institution, modeled on Mussolini's "corporations," did not greatly alter society, for the retention of private property kept intact the traditional social distinctions.

The Nazis owed much of their early popularity, especially among the workers, to the elimination of unemployment. The rearmament program absorbed many of the jobless; others found work with large public work projects, such as the construction of a network of superhighways (*Autobahnen*), ultimately also destined for military uses. Within a year of Hitler's coming to power the number of unemployed dropped by half; gradually unemployment disappeared. But pay was low, and the standard of living remained stationary, below that of 1929. The government made determined efforts to win labor support by means other than high wages. Especially popular with the working population was the "Strength through Joy" program, which combined vacations, education, and entertainment with Nazi indoctrination. A "People's Car" (*Volkswagen*) was designed to provide cheap transportation for the Nazi citizen. Of course, nothing came of the socialist promises, for the government could not afford to alienate the industrialists who furnished the military hardware.

Among the party's auxiliary organizations mention must be made of the Hitler Youth (*Hitlerjugend*). It was a copy of the Union of Communist Youth (*Komsomol*), founded by Lenin in 1918, and later emulated by Mussolini in his *Balilla* and *Avanguardisti*. Its purpose, too, was to indoctrinate the new generation with the party ideology and a sense of obedience, and to furnish cadres for the party and police.

No account of nazism can ignore its public spectacles. The party showed great skill in manipulating visual and auditory effects to hearten supporters, sway doubters, and overwhelm opponents. Parades, organized with a precision and on a scale never before seen, hypnotized participants and, through the radio and movies, audiences all over Germany. The greatest of those was the annual party rally at Nürnberg. There assembled tens of thousands of stalwart Nazis, lined up like so many identical automatons, with their insignia, banners, and battle gear, facing their leader, high up on a podium. Hitler's speeches to those and other gatherings, in which threats and promises always alternated, kept Europe in a state of constant tension. The synchronized roar of the crowds with their *Sieg-Heil!* (Victory-Hail!) and *Ein Volk, Ein Reich, Ein Führer!* (One People, One Country, One Leader!) created the impression of an elemental force that nothing could stop.

Stalin and Hitler were the only truly totalitarian leaders. But their seeming success in coping with domestic problems encouraged elsewhere a further move away from liberalism toward totalitarian forms. A number of dictatorships veered in the 1930s toward more restrictive policies, suspending or violating civil liberties and establishing governments of a semi-totalitarian kind. In Austria the threat of Nazi subversion induced the authorities in 1933 to suspend parliamentary government and many civil liberties. In the same year Portugal adopted a new constitution, based on the Fascist model. In Spain a civil war that broke out in 1936 (Chapter 18) brought to power a Fascist government with totalitarian aspirations. And in Poland, after the death of the dictator Pilsudski in 1935, authority passed into the hands of army officers who increasingly repressed political opposition and imprisoned people they disliked.

Repercussions

In other countries democratic institutions, hitherto intact, weakened appreciably and sometimes collapsed under the assault of conspirators. In 1934 democracies were done away with in Latvia and Bulgaria; in 1936 in Greece; and in 1938 in Romania.

In many instances this anti-liberal, anti-democratic subversion was financed by the Nazis, who exploited various sources of discontent and played on anti-Semitism abroad to undermine political stability and prepare the soil for eventual conquest.

In the 1930s traditional institutions and political morals were disappearing everywhere in Europe with dizzying speed. The world headed for a catastrophe that no one seemed able to prevent: another war, but one that could be also a revolution and possibly mark the end of civilization as it had been known in the West.

17

The Dissolution
of the Middle Class

Behind the collapse of liberalism lay not only specific political and economic factors but also deeper social and cultural ones. Liberal institutions throughout the European Continent caved in with such speed and finality because of the coincident collapse of the middle class, that social group which traditionally had provided its backbone (Chapter 7). In the twentieth century the bourgeoisie suffered both impoverishment and demoralization. Its money went or lost value; the family, its fulcrum, fell apart as women asserted their independence and sought self-fulfillment outside the confines of the home; its moral scruples and its gentility appeared increasingly ridiculous in a world subjected to mass slaughter and the horrors of totalitarianism. Already in 1920 Keynes noted a drastic shift in the bearing of the once-proud middle class:

> [Twenty-five years ago] the capitalists believed in themselves, in their value to society, in the propriety of their continued existence, in the full enjoyment of their riches and the unlimited exercise of their power. Now they tremble before every insult; call them pro-Germans, international financiers, or profiteers, and they will give you any ransom you choose to ask not to speak of them so harshly. They allow themselves to be ruined and altogether undone by their own instruments, governments of their own making, and a press of which they are the proprietors.

This led Keynes to conclude that perhaps it was true "that no order of society ever perishes save by its own hand."

An essential aspect, perhaps the main cause of the decline of the European middle class, was its impoverishment. This was brought about in three ways: taxation, inflation, and expropriation.

Impoverishment

Taxation

Until the end of the nineteenth century, income taxes were virtually unknown: whatever a man earned, he kept. Governments, national and local alike, derived their revenue from taxes on property, from customs duties, monopolies, state properties, or indirect taxes. The notion that the greater a man's earnings the more he should pay contradicted the whole liberal ethos, since it seemed to penalize industry and thrift. On occasion, during national crises (for example, in France and England during the French Revolution, and in the United States during the Civil War), income was taxed, but only for the duration of the emergency. The absence of an income tax made it possible to amass enormous fortunes in a short time; it was an essential in the ascendancy of the middle class.

Regular taxation of income was introduced only in the second half of the nineteenth century. It was necessitated by rapidly rising government expenditures on armaments and social welfare. Great Britain inaugurated a regular graduated

The disintegration of the European middle class was well under way in late 1921, when this drawing appeared in the German satirical journal Simplicissimus. *"We cannot socialize with these nouveau poor," the beggars complain. "They have nothing!"*

income tax in 1874, Prussia in 1891, France in 1909. At this time the treasuries of the great powers came increasingly to depend on this source for their operating revenue. In 1909 Lloyd George stated that the income tax, previously an expedient, had become "the center and the sheet anchor" of the British fiscal system. Germany, which had introduced a particularly efficient scheme of taxing income, derived from it early in the twentieth century one-half of its revenue.

But important as the income tax may have been for the budgets of some states, until 1914 it bore rather lightly on the individual citizen. In the 1890s an Englishman paid the equivalent of 3 cents on each earned dollar; in Prussia the wealthiest contributed 4 percent of their earnings. Elsewhere in Europe the income tax was usually lower, and in any event, it was rarely collected.° It has been estimated that prior to 1914 the total tax burden (income, local, and property taxes) even of the most affluent European did not exceed 8 percent.

Taxation became burdensome only after the outbreak of World War I. It was especially heavy in Great Britain, which had made an early decision to pay for military expenditures not from loans (as was done in France and Germany) but from taxing income. In the middle of World War I an Englishman contributed to the government 15 percent of his income, and at its conclusion an unheard-of 30 percent. With the restoration of peace the rate was somewhat reduced, but it never again reverted to its pre-1914 level. During the Second World War the British tax climbed once more, to claim one-half of earnings. Englishmen were, in addition, liable to a heavy inheritance tax (death duty), which on wealthy estates amounted to 50 percent. Understandably, it became increasingly difficult for an Englishman to make a fortune and virtually impossible to pass it on to his heirs. This fact greatly demoralized the middle class, removing an important traditional motive behind its economic drive: the prospect of accumulating capital for oneself and one's family.

The British income tax and death duties, exacting as they may have been, were at least legally enacted. On the Continent in most cases the middle class was shorn of its property by less legitimate and less predictable means.

INFLATION

A considerable part of the income of the nineteenth-century bourgeois derived from capital investments. The income which these investments brought was meaningful only as long as prices remained relatively constant; that is, as long as a given sum of money brought year after year a corresponding return in goods and services. It so happened that in the nineteenth century, especially in its second half, the Western world enjoyed exceptional monetary stability. Prices rose, but so slowly—on the average 1 to 1.5 percent a year—that the rise was not felt. A European living on capital had reasonable assurance that the income it yielded would enable him to live in the accustomed style for the remainder of his days.

World War I inaugurated the great modern inflation, which is still in progress. Its original causes were the classical ones of all inflations: too much money and too few goods. During the war governments everywhere to some extent helped cover their extraordinary military expenditures by printing paper money. Even Britain, which followed a conservative financial policy, between 1914 and 1918

°The United States introduced a modest income tax in 1894, but the Supreme Court voided it. It came back in 1913 with the ratification of the Sixteenth Amendment.

Worthless German marks are baled for scrap paper after the currency reform of 1924.

quadrupled the quantity of pounds in circulation. In Germany, in the same period, the amount of circulating banknotes increased five times, in Russia twelve times, in Austria-Hungary fifteen times. At the same time, with the economy working primarily for the military, consumer goods became scarce, and their prices steadily climbed upward. Between 1913 and 1920 wholesale prices more than doubled in the neutral European countries (e.g., Holland and Switzerland), tripled in Great Britain, quintupled in France, and sextupled in Italy. A person living on fixed income now found that he could buy less and less for his money; he was doubly hurt in countries with heavy income taxes, where he had less of the depreciated money to begin with.

Nowhere was the inflation more calamitous than in postwar Germany. The inflation of 1922–1923, which reduced the mark to the absurd level of 4.2 trillion to the United States dollar (Chapter 15), utterly ruined the German middle class. It now had to dispose of its treasured possessions—art works, libraries, musical instruments, furniture—merely to obtain money to buy food. In a few years the class of property and education which had been the supporting pillar of imperial Germany was reduced to a standard of living below that of the working class. The following random observations of a contemporary give some idea of the effects of the great postwar inflation on the lives of middle-class Germans:

I know a former high government official. One day I noticed the leather covering on his big easy chair had been removed and cheap cloth substituted. I spoke about it. He smiled apologetically. "The children needed shoes." In October of 1922 the mark salaries of lower government officials were sixty-nine times as high as in 1914; of middle officials, sixty-two times

The sale of art treasures by the hard-pressed to gain stable dollars was of widespread concern in postwar Europe. The anguished figures represent Holbein, Dürer, and Cranach.

as high; and of higher officials, only fifty-seven times as high. Meanwhile, a bricklayer made one hundred and forty-seven times as many marks as in 1914. A skilled workman was paid more than three-quarters of the income of a principal of an elementary school or a medical officer. For a two-hour university extension lecture, the lecturer is paid the equivalent of ten cents, enough for a meal for himself and his family. One of the foremost economists in Germany writes newspaper editorials which bring in from a half-dollar to a dollar each. In November of 1922 the monthly stipend of a lower official would barely buy the coat and vest of a suit of clothes; trousers had to await the next pay check. A higher official was fortunate; *he* could buy the whole suit and a pair of paper shoes. . . . If the lower official's income all went for butter, he could buy two pounds every three days.

A middle-class widow in Berlin is writing of the hardships she had to undergo. In January of last year her monthly pension of 6,000 marks just sufficed to supply her with milk and two pounds of fat. Her other expenses for herself and her daughter, who is ailing from a disease caused by undernourishment, amounted to 80,000 marks—obtained by letting rooms, sewing, and teaching. No meat was included in the diet. She says: "I am still forced to work hard from six o'clock in the morning until ten o'clock at night. . . . We live entirely upon potatoes, bread and margarine, and a little soup.°

Persons disposing of hard currencies could make fortunes in postwar Germany buying up belongings of the hard-pressed bourgeois. During this time, approximately one-quarter of the apartment houses in Berlin passed into the hands of foreigners. The resentment that this wholesale loss of its property caused among a people notable for their industry and thrift can be readily imagined. It played no small part in the subsequent swing of much of the middle class to the Nazis, who promised them retribution and recompense.

The effects of inflation were only slightly less devastating among the successor states of the dissolved East European empires. The Austrian crown, which in 1914 had been worth twenty U.S. cents, sunk in 1922 to 1/700th of one cent. In Poland it took 8 million Polish marks to buy one dollar. In those countries with runaway inflations, profiteers and speculators who possessed dollars had a field day.

The inflation in France and Italy was far less calamitous (here disaster was to come only during World War II), but it was serious enough to subvert the life of the middle classes. In both countries the currency (franc and lira, respectively) lost in the decade 1914–1924 between two-thirds and four-fifths of its purchasing capacity. What this meant concretely may be illustrated by the example of a hypothetical French family disposing of a capital of 500,000 francs. Before the war this capital yielded an annual income of 23,000 francs. Of this sum 14,000 went to meet living expenses, the surplus being available to be added to the capital. In 1924, partly due to the natural increase in the capital and partly to the rise in interest rates, the family's annual income rose to 30,000 francs. But because of the increase in living costs, it now required 40,000 francs to maintain

°F. A. Ross, "The Passing of the German Middle Class," *The American Journal of Sociology* (March, 1924).

its accustomed standard of living. The family had an option of either lowering its standards (for instance, by firing domestics) or eating into its capital.° Neither alternative permitted in the long run survival of middle-class life: either comfort or long-term financial security had to be sacrificed.

EXPROPRIATIONS

The middle class suffered the greatest economic disaster in Russia, where after the Bolshevik seizure of power nearly all private property was nationalized. Several million people, from wealthy industrialists, bankers, and landowners to shopkeepers and self-employed artisans, were made destitute overnight. The collectivization of agriculture carried out in 1928–1932 completed the proletarianization of this class by expropriating the land and livestock of the small rural proprietors.

The only other part of Europe where such drastic measures against property owners were instituted was Nazi Germany. During their twelve-year reign the Nazis expropriated the wealth of the Jewish population under their control.

Land reforms carried out in several East European countries after World War I often took the form of expropriations. The governments of Latvia, Romania, Yugoslavia, Czechoslovakia, and Poland established norms for maximum landholdings by one individual and declared properties exceeding them liable to confiscation. Where such land reform was actually carried out, the owners (especially if they were of a foreign nationality) usually received only a fraction of the true market value of their properties. The same held true of the proprietors of major industries, for example, the Romanian oil fields or the Czech Škoda works, which were nationalized in the 1920s.

Finally, rent controls often served as a concealed form of expropriation. During or immediately after war many governments passed strict regulations fixing the amount owed by tenants for their rooms or apartments. In countries subjected to extreme inflation, the real value of fixed rents sunk so low that they did not suffice to pay for basic house maintenance. Under these conditions real estate became a financial burden instead of a source of income, and many hard-pressed owners had to dispose of their property for much less than it had originally cost.

A price guide for the well-turned-out gentleman—admittedly temporary, as the dollar shines brightly and the mark sinks out of sight. Both cartoons are from Simplicissimus, 1922.

The Breakdown of the Middle-Class Family

On top of its financial disasters, the middle class suffered another misfortune: a loosening of the bonds that held the family together.

This process was in part brought about by economic developments. The family business, passed on from father to sons, and providing employment for needy relatives, could not withstand the competition of large, publicly financed corporations. It either collapsed or went public, entrusting its management to salaried executives brought in from the outside. The basic entity of modern enterprise is not the family, but rather on the one hand the impersonal corporation and on the other the salaried individual. The family as such has ceased to perform any meaningful economic function.

At the same time, the family has also gradually been deprived of its cultural and social functions. Public schooling has everywhere taken over the education of youth. Gone are the tutors and governesses who in the heyday of the bourgeoisie had filled middle-class households. Entertainment, too, has largely

°This example is drawn from Lucien de Chilly's *La classe moyenne en France après la guerre, 1918–1924* (1925).

ceased to be sought within the confines of the home. The middle class, which in the nineteenth century had spent its leisure hours at home in reading, conversation, music, or games, has acquired the habit of seeking amusement outside. Movies, sports, dances, night clubs, cocktail parties, and other modern forms of entertainment have in common that they all lure the individual out of his house and away from his family.

But perhaps the single most important cause of the weakening of family bonds has been the progressive emancipation of women from their traditional confinement to the home. In the course of the present century, women have come to demand a full life of which the family forms only one aspect, and not necessarily the central one.

The older feminist movement attained most of its goals between the First and Second World Wars: the right to vote (apart from a few countries—Italy, France, Switzerland, and Yugoslavia), as well as legal equality. But the feminists did not stop there, content with their gains. Already in the 1870s there emerged among them a radical faction that wanted to move beyond political and legal parity with men to full social and sexual equality. This radical tendency originated and won its greatest following in northern Europe—Scandinavia and Germany—but in the course of the present century its influence spread throughout the Western and even the non-Western world.

To begin with, the radical feminists challenged the institution of marriage. They did so not merely on the grounds that in its actual workings it discriminated against women—grounds a John Stuart Mill might have chosen (Chapter 7)—but because they considered the whole institution inherently wrong. Marriage, they argued, created a false relationship between the sexes because it institutionalized love, a volatile and changing thing, and forced people to live

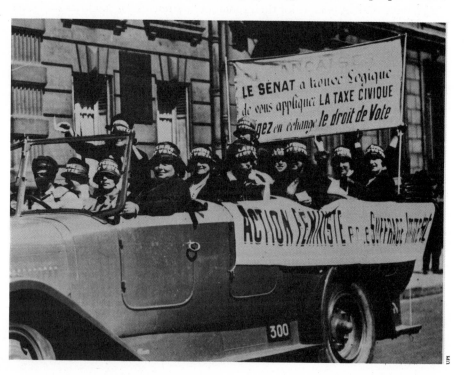

A women's suffrage demonstration in France during the 1920s. French women did not gain the vote until 1945.

together even after they had ceased to care for each other. Emotional honesty was more important than marriage vows and contracts.

Such sentiments were expressed in the influential plays of the Norwegian dramatist Henrik Ibsen. He penetrated behind the conventions and hypocrisy surrounding middle-class family life to reveal the dissembled frustrations, tensions, and suffering. Ibsen demanded for the wife the right to self-fulfillment, even at the risk of breaking up the family. Nora, the heroine of his *Doll's House* (1879), leads a seemingly content existence in a conventional middle-class household, until a crisis occurs which reveals the superficiality of her whole family relationship. She is wrongly accused of having forged a signature on a bond, whereupon her husband is ready to abandon her. After the mistake had been realized, he wants to forgive and forget, but Nora revolts. She now realizes how little she had known about herself, her husband, and her children. She tells him:

> Our home has been nothing but a playroom. I have been your doll-wife, just as at home I had been papa's doll-child, and here the children have been my dolls. . . . I am not fit for the task [of bringing up children]. There is another task I must undertake first. I must try and educate myself—you are not the man to help me in that. I must do that for myself. And that is why I am going to leave you now. . . . I must stand quite alone if I am to understand myself and everything about me.

To her husband's reproach that she cannot leave him because of her "sacred duties" to her family, Nora retorts that she has "other duties just as sacred . . . . duties to myself." In another Ibsen play, *Lady from the Sea* (1888), the heroine chooses in the end to remain with her husband but only after he consents to let her depart with her lover.

The quest for self-realization, of course, did not necessarily take the form of love affairs. It could involve the decision to pursue a higher education, to acquire a profession, or to take a paying job. What it meant in all cases, however, was a shift in prime responsibility from the family to oneself.

From criticism of marriage there was but one step to the advocacy of free love. One of the leading exponents of this theory was Ellen Key, a Swedish writer active at the turn of the century. She called loveless marriage a crime, and exhorted men and women alike to seek their happiness wherever they found it, in or out of wedlock.

The critique of marriage and the stress on woman's right to self-fulfillment was reinforced by revolutionary changes in the understanding of sexual life. As we have noted previously (Chapter 7), the nineteenth-century bourgeoisie held sex to be a necessary evil, which it tolerated only insofar as it was essential to procreation. Anything pertaining to sex beyond procreation (within marriage, of course) was thought debasing, repulsive, and physically harmful. Women, like children, were considered non-sexual beings. There was a widespread belief that women were organically incapable of experiencing sexual satisfaction. In general, all that pertained to sex was taboo and shunned.

The veil of mystery surrounding sex was lifted at the end of the century. Medical investigations revealed the enormous complexity of human sexual experience, the variety of its outlets, and the prevalence of drives and practices previously regarded as abnormal. A pioneering contribution was a work by the English physician Havelock Ellis, *Studies in the Psychology of Sex*, the first installment of which appeared in 1898. It described in a clinical manner all the known aspects of the sexual impulse, avoiding the customary moralizing: Ellis treated its varied manifestations as neither good nor bad, but simply as natural. Although the book scandalized the public and caused legal proceedings to be instituted against its author, it initiated a serious scientific investigation of sexual behavior.

An important by-product of Ellis' and related studies was the discovery that woman possessed as strong sexual instincts as did man. The view of woman as a pure, ideal creature who suffered with resignation man's advances was completely shattered by medical evidence. Indeed, as the researches of Freud showed, female sexual drives were so powerful that their repression could bring about nervous and physical disorders. As a result of these findings, advanced scientific and intellectual circles in early twentieth-century Europe began to acknowledge that woman, no less than man, had a right to seek sexual gratification.

In the course of World War I the social and sexual emancipation of Western woman made dramatic strides. Many women, including those from middle-class homes who had previously disdained gainful employment, took jobs to replace the men who had gone to the front. In Britain nearly 1 million found work in industry, and in Germany the National Service Act enrolled 6 million. These women earned their own pay, acquired an independent social life, and found themselves less tied to the household and the family. The war enhanced their sense of independence and self-reliance.

After the armistice the majority of women had to give up their jobs to the returning veterans, but the attitude of employers toward them underwent a lasting change. An increasing number of positions in business and industry became regularly available to women, and some—e.g., secretarial and sales positions—have turned into their preserve. The modern middle-class woman regards it as perfectly natural to take work outside her household even if she has no financial need to do so.

The First World War also affected sexual morals. The relations between men and women, whether those working side by side in industry or those meeting casually in places of entertainment, became freer, more spontaneous, less inhibited. Fighting men on furlough from the trenches were in no mood to respect the old codes of behavior. Sexual relations became very casual. An important contributing factor was the spread by the armed forces of contraceptive devices. Their main purpose was to safeguard the health of the troops, but their main effect was to remove the fear of pregnancy, a factor which more than any other had inhibited extramarital relations in the past. In the 1920s contraceptives became for the first time widely available in Europe.

During the war the loosening of moral codes was not assigned much importance because, like everything else that had happened then, it was considered a temporary deviation from the norm. But the revolution in morals only intensified with the restoration of peace. In the 1920s suddenly everything that had been regarded as right and proper in the nineteenth century was dismissed as hope-

The new French fashions for 1925, from Harper's Bazar *(as it was then spelled); the celebrated "flapper" of the 1920s was then evolving.*

lessly out of date. The older ideal of the self-effacing wife and mother yielded to a new ideal of an aggressive, self-seeking "bachelor girl" who lived fast and free without thought of the future, getting out of life all it had to offer. The term "sex appeal" was coined in the 1920s. The physical type of the ideal woman changed: she was rather boyish with her hipless and bosomless figure, her short hair, and her athletic carriage—the very antithesis of the young lady of the mid-nineteenth century. Smoking and drinking in public became fully accepted. There was little room for husbands and children in this ideal world of modern womanhood, which very few realized but to which many women aspired and took as their model.

The decline of the family after the war can be demonstrated statistically: it became smaller and less stable. Impoverishment forced many bourgeois to limit themselves to one or at most two children, because they could not afford properly to bring up and educate more. "Birth control," devised in the early twentieth century for the benefit of the poor, was in fact practiced largely by the upper classes. In Great Britain in 1927 the number of births per 1,000 inhabitants dropped to one-half of what it had been fifty years earlier. In France, the classical country of the propertied middle class, more people died each year than were born, so that the population actually declined. As the century progressed it became less common for relatives to live under the same roof, and the size of household units diminished.

Middle-class families became less stable due to the easing of divorce laws and procedures. These had once been both strict and costly. In most of Europe until the end of the nineteenth century adultery was the only legally recognized grounds for divorce. In Great Britain, prior to 1857, it required a private act of Parliament to terminate a marriage; this was so difficult to obtain that there were only fifty divorces granted in Britain in the whole first half of the nineteenth century. Toward the end of the century the variety of grounds on which a divorce could be obtained was much increased, and at the same time the legal procedures were simplified and made less costly. Divorce now came within the reach of a moderately well-to-do person. In France the new laws recognized, in addition to adultery, habitual drunkenness and violence as grounds for divorce. Sweden went further, authorizing divorce on grounds of "unconquerable aversion." Soviet Russia in its early years went furthest of all, requiring nothing more than mutual consent and official notification. (Later on, under Stalin, Soviet divorce laws were considerably tightened.)

As a result of these developments there has been a slow but steady rise in divorce rates. In France the number of divorces increased fivefold in thirty years (1874–1904). In the United States, which always had the highest divorce rates, it more than doubled over the same period. In Great Britain divorces were uncommon at first, but gained momentum later. Two out of every 1,000 British marriages ended in divorce in 1911; in 1921 the number rose to 8; in 1937 to 16; and in 1950 to 71. Among the affluent in urban, industrial, Protestant areas marriage has in fact become a conditional arrangement such as the radical feminists had preached.

A final factor requiring mention in connection with the weakening of family bonds is the shortage of domestic help. Young girls who would have previously served in private homes preferred after World War I to take employment in industry or trade, not so much because it paid better but because it gave them more independence and a higher social status. The industrial countries experienced, therefore, a severe shortage of domestics. The number of girls in domestic service in Great Britain declined from 1.4 million in 1911 to 352,000 in 1951; male servants all but disappeared. On the Continent the supply of servants remained adequate, but there inflation had so lowered incomes that many middle-class families could afford no more than one domestic, or none at all.

Neopaganism Apart from economic and social blows, the middle class in the twentieth century suffered also a serious loss of self-confidence. The typical bourgeois had viewed everything in moral terms, and these morals in turn rested on religious foundations. The motive that inspired the nineteenth-century businessman was not only or even primarily greed, but the conviction that he was doing good: that he bettered the world by creating employment, producing wealth, raising living standards, and bringing nations into peaceful concourse. It was this assurance of the élite and the responsibility and discipline that it gave rise to that permitted the extraordinary economic achievement of the West in the nineteenth century.

The grandsons of the men who had built industrial empires and forged trading links between the most distant parts of the world, however, came to doubt the value of this activity. The socialists told them they not only did not produce wealth, but stole it from the working man, its true creator, and furthermore that they bore responsibility for wars which were simply struggles for resources and markets. Scientific discoveries upset their fathers' religious beliefs and commonsensical outlook. Taxes, inflation, and expropriations made it seem utterly pointless to accumulate capital that sooner or later was bound either to end up in the treasury or depreciate to nothing. Combined, these factors engendered in the middle class the mood of hedonism typical of periods of great uncertainty. A new morality emerged which preached the unrestrained enjoyment of the present, the surrender to everything that gratified the senses, that gave the sense of total fulfillment, of being fully alive.

The desire to live it up had made itself felt among the wealthy aristocracy and uppermost middle class already at the turn of the century. The "Edwardian Era"—the brief reign of Edward VII (1901–1910)—was a period of unprecedented elegance and luxury. The money then squandered belonged to a generation that thought of itself as the last one able to afford such a life. After the war this attitude spread to the broader layer of the bourgeoisie. The pursuit of pleasure took many forms, all strenuous and frenetic. In the 1920s a dancing mania swept the Western world, not unlike that which had followed the Napoleonic wars a century earlier. The tango and the fox trot, imported from the Americas, replaced the traditional waltz, and Dixieland acquired great popularity. Cocktail parties came into vogue; night clubs mushroomed. Outdoor sports like tennis, swimming, skiing, and mountain climbing were vigorously pursued. There was great interest in professional athletics, such as boxing. *Avant-garde* intellectual and artistic circles in Europe, in their search for new forms of excitement, took to using opium, morphine, and other drugs.

The postwar generation rediscovered the human body, which had been carefully concealed during the era of gentility. Sunbathing, previously considered unhealthy, became the rage in Europe after German physicians had discovered that it helped undernourished children overcome deficiencies in vitamin D. Swimming suits became skimpier, more revealing.

Max Beckmann's bitter comment on the social mores and nihilism prevalent in the between-wars period; the scene is a Baden-Baden bar, 1925.

Two examples of the developing anti-tradition in art: at the right, Unique Forms of Continuity in Space (1913), by the Italian Futurist Umberto Boccioni; opposite is Meret Oppenheim's fur-covered teacup, hit of a 1936 Surrealist show in New York.

The great depression of 1929–1932 brought this outburst of self-indulgence to a sudden halt. But the kind of life which the 1920s had created did not disappear without a trace. It was to revive on an even grander scale amid the affluence and uncertainty of the 1960s.

CULTURAL NIHILISM

From 1900 onward a great variety of ideologies spread in Europe which called for the destruction of the whole cultural heritage of the West in order to release man from the burden of the past and restore to him creative freedom. A kind of self-conscious barbarism took hold of the fringes of the Western intelligentsia, of which a typical expression was Futurism, a movement formed in Italy shortly before World War I. Its celebrated Manifesto of 1909 was not only a statement of literary principles, but an appeal for the annihilation of Western culture:

1. We shall sing the love of danger, the habit of energy and boldness.

2. The essential elements of our poetry shall be courage, daring and rebellion.

3. Literature has hitherto glorified thoughtful immobility, ecstasy and sleep; we shall extol aggressive movement, feverish insomnia, the double quick step, the somersault, the box on the ear, the fisticuff.

4. We declare that the world's splendour has been enriched by a new beauty; the beauty of speed. A racing motor-car, its frame adorned with great pipes, like snakes with explosive breath . . . a roaring motor-car, which looks as though running on shrapnel, is more beautiful than the Victory of Samothrace.

5. We shall sing of the man at the steering wheel, whose ideal stem transfixes the Earth, rushing over the circuit of her orbit.

6. The poet must give himself with frenzy, with splendour and with

lavishness, in order to increase the enthusiastic fervour of the primordial elements.

7. There is no more beauty except in strife. No masterpiece without aggressiveness. Poetry must be a violent onslaught upon the unknown forces, to command them to bow before man.

8. We stand upon the extreme promontory of the centuries! . . . Why should we look behind us, when we have to break in the mysterious portals of the Impossible? Time and Space died yesterday. Already we live in the absolute, since we have already created speed, eternal and ever-present.

9. We wish to glorify War—the only health giver of the world—militarism, patriotism, the destructive arm of the Anarchist, the beautiful Ideas that kill, the contempt for woman.

10. We wish to destroy the museums, the libraries, to fight against moralism, feminism and all opportunistic and utilitarian meannesses.

11. We shall sing of the great crowds in the excitement of labour, pleasure and rebellion; of the multi-coloured and polyphonic surf of revolutions in modern capital cities; of the nocturnal vibration of arsenals and workshops beneath their violent electric moons; of the greedy stations swallowing smoking snakes; of factories suspended from the clouds by their strings of smoke; of bridges leaping like gymnasts over the diabolical cutlery of sunbathed rivers; of adventurous liners scenting the horizon; of broad-chested locomotives prancing on the rails, like huge steel horses bridled with long tubes; and of the gliding flight of aeroplanes, the sound of whose propeller is like the flapping of flags and the applause of an enthusiastic crowd. . . .

Come, then, the good incendiaries, with their charred fingers! . . . Here they come! Here they come! . . . Set fire to the shelves of the libraries! Deviate the course of canals to flood the cellars of the museums! Oh! may the glorious canvases drift helplessly! Seize pickaxes and hammers! Sap the foundations of the venerable cities!°

The Futurists welcomed the Bolshevik Revolution in Russia and the Fascist one in Italy—not out of any sympathy for totalitarianism, but because these events portended the destruction of what they hated most: bourgeois values and the bourgeois way of life.

In the nineteenth century the Western class structure in its classical (and vastly oversimplified) form could be likened to a pyramid of three layers: on top, a small élite of wealthy landowners and capitalists, who worked little and earned much; below them, a thicker layer of the middle class, which both worked hard and earned well; and at the base, the most numerous element, the manual workers and peasants, who worked much but received little in return. In the twentieth century this pyramid has flattened at the top and narrowed at the bottom: the proportion of the idle rich and indigent poor has decreased, swelling correspondingly the interstitial middle layer.

But this middle layer is no longer the old bourgeoisie. It is a new estate whose

The Rise of the Salaried Estate

°Cited from Joshua C. Taylor, *Futurism* (1961).

distinguishing trait is that it derives its living from salary, the economic sinew of modern industrial society. Now whether one draws a six-figure salary, supplemented by a commensurate bonus, as company director, or a four-figure wage as factory foreman, makes, of course, a vast difference in the style of life. But the difference is less fundamental from that which had distinguished the old-style capitalist and the wage earner in the nineteenth century. The salaried estate is an open one, qualifications being the prime criterion for movement up the career ladder—for which reason some sociologists speak of the modern ruling class as a "meritocracy," an aristocracy of merit. Being open to talent, it does not provide the kind of security which the owner of capital had enjoyed. Even the highest-paid executives are dependent on the good will of the board of directors, and are liable to be fired at a moment's notice. They are constantly threatened from below by competitors for their positions; nor can they assure the future of their children. In this respect those at the top of the meritocracy are in no better position than those at its bottom. The reverse of social mobility is social insecurity.

The topmost layer of the modern business world consists of hired managers. As we have pointed out earlier, the tendency of modern business enterprise has been to become public. Family resources have seldom sufficed to finance the increasing costs of modern technology, with the result that major enterprises have found it necessary to issue stock. Once they do so, they place themselves under the scrutiny of shareholders and government bodies. They must assure the public that they are managed in the most efficient manner, and this they can do only by engaging the services of specialists, that is, salaried managers. The importance of managers in the modern world is so great that one American writer, James Burnham, even speaks of the occurrence of a "managerial revolution." The category of independent businessmen and self-employed has been steadily diminishing in the more advanced industrial countries. In Germany in 1870 they constituted 26 percent of the gainfully employed, and in 1939 only 14 percent. In Great Britain they decreased from 6.7 percent (1911) to 4.9 percent (1951); over the same period the percentage of managers and administrators has grown from 3.4 percent to 5.5 percent. The same tendency may be observed in other countries with developed industrial economies.

The descent of the capitalist proprietors into the ranks of the white-collar class was accompanied by a simultaneous rise in the social status of the higher echelons of the working class. The word "proletariat," frequently applied in the nineteenth century to manual workers, derives from the Latin *proles*, meaning "offspring"; it had been originally used for the lowest strata of the population of ancient Rome which had nothing to offer the state save their children. Already in the nineteenth century the situation of the manual worker in advanced industrial countries improved to the point where he ceased to be a proletarian in the original sense of the word. The rise in real wages brought about by a lowering of prices on basic commodities and the improvement in skills, as well as increased security due in part to unionization and in part to national welfare schemes, tended to transform the upper layers of the working class into a petty bourgeoisie. This fact was noted by the anarchists, and caused them to dismiss the European worker as a potential revolutionary.

In the twentieth century this tendency of labor *embourgeoisement* has been accelerated. Under modern industrial conditions machines are increasingly taking over functions previously performed by manual labor. Industry therefore needs proportionately fewer manual workers and more supervisory and administrative personnel. In countries with advanced economies the number of workers in the traditional sense of the word is therefore decreasing. German industry, for example, had in 1880 9.5 million workers and 0.5 million white-collar employees. In 1953 it employed 12 million workers and 4 million white-collar personnel. The ratio of manual workers to white-collar ones thus dropped from 19:1 to 3:1. A considerable part of those classified as white collar was drawn from the layer of skilled workers and craftsmen, or their children. In Great Britain between 1911 and 1951 the proportion of persons classified as manual workers decreased from 80 percent to 70 percent of all employed, while that of administrators, clerical workers, foremen, and inspectors doubled. The increase everywhere is greatest in the category of clerical help—testimony to the growing bureaucratization of modern life. Taking the advanced industrial economy as a whole, there is a visible shrinking in the number of persons engaged in production and a corresponding growth of those engaged in services of all kinds. In the contemporary United States the latter actually outnumber the former.

The group that shifts constantly from the productive to the service sector of the economy is no longer a "working class" in the traditional sense of the word; nor, for that matter, is the well-paid manual worker. Its manner of living is in no way distinguishable from that of the older petty bourgeoisie: its members own savings and property, usually a house and a car, enjoy regular vacations, and send their children to secondary schools and even to universities. With the rise in living standards and social status, the industrial worker rapidly sheds the proletarian mentality. Surveys conducted in Germany after World War II reveal that only a small minority of contemporary German workers think of themselves as workers: the vast majority, when asked what they were, identified themselves by their specific vocation; many did not even know what the word "proletarian" meant. If this holds true in a country which had the most highly developed socialist movement in the world, it is even more so in countries like the United States and Great Britain, where socialism had never struck deep roots. Today the self-awareness of the workers as a class apart still persists only in those countries (e.g., France and Italy) where social legislation had come relatively late and the worker had not yet become fully integrated into national life.

While, as we have noted, capital in the twentieth century witnessed a calamitous collapse, salaries and wages held their ground and made some gains. From 1914 onward they began to rise, keeping pace with prices even during the most extreme inflations. In the 1920s workers were relatively better off than professional people and self-employed; and apart from the disastrous period of unemployment in the early 1930s, the living standards of those depending on salaries and wages have everywhere in the Western world shown a steady improvement.

In this manner the decline of the middle class has been accompanied by the ascent of a new class, that of white-collar employees. The propertied have yielded to the salaried.

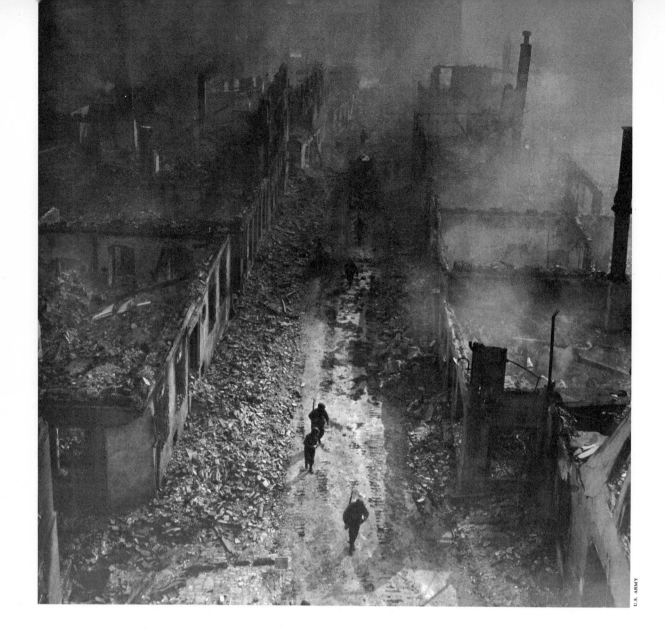

18

World War II

The origins of World War II are easier to ascertain than those of World War I: it was brought about by the man to whom the Germans had entrusted their destiny. "The Second World War was Hitler's personal war in many senses. He intended it, he prepared for it, he chose the moment for the launching of it; and for three years, in the main, he planned its course."°

During the first two years of his chancellorship, Hitler pursued a relatively cautious foreign policy so as not to alarm Britain and France until he had solidified his grip on Germany and made progress with the secret rearmament program. He withdrew from the League of Nations and on every possible occasion fulminated against the "Versailles *Diktat*," but he acted prudently. A nonaggression pact which he signed with Poland in 1934 was generally interpreted as a sign of peaceful intentions, although in fact it served as the first step in the isolation of France.

Hitler made his first overt aggressive moves in 1935. In March of that year he formally denounced the disarmament clauses of the Versailles Treaty and introduced compulsory military training. This measure did not produce abroad the expected violent reactions. Indeed that very year Britain signed with Germany a naval agreement which, by establishing ratios of naval power between the two countries, implicitly legitimized Hitler's breach of the Versailles Treaty. Emboldened, Hitler a year later sent German troops into the demilitarized zone of the Rhineland. Again nothing happened, although by so doing he had knocked out another prop of the French security system.

There is general agreement among historians that the years 1935–1936 offered the last chance to stop Nazi expansion short of general war. Had France displayed the same intransigence toward Nazi Germany that it had shown toward the Weimar Republic, Hitler would have had to retreat. We know now that German troops marching into the Rhineland had orders to pull back in the event of French countermeasures. The impunity with which Hitler violated the Versailles Treaty gained him immense prestige in Germany and vastly increased his self-confidence.

Behind Allied inaction lay the mood known as "appeasement." It was a crucial element in the chain of events leading to World War II, and played indirectly a major part in the conduct of international relations in the decade that followed the war. To "appease" meant yielding to the demands of the dictators in the belief that once these demands were satisfied the dictators would settle down and turn into good members of the international community. This belief rested on the assumption that the totalitarian dictators were at bottom motivated by a sense of self-interest and self-preservation. By their upbringing and experience the appeasers were unequipped to appreciate the self-destructive nihilism inherent in the totalitarian psyche.

°H. R. Trevor-Roper, *Hitler's War Directives, 1939–1945* (1964).

As the Nazi tide was rolled back across Europe in the last year of the war, the pattern of destruction by shellfire, bombing, and demolition mounted with grim regularity and precision. Here, American troops take what is left of a small German city in April, 1945.

The principal and universal element behind appeasement was pacifism. World War I had settled nothing, and had obliterated without trace that romantic militarism which had pervaded European youth in 1914. There was widespread expectation that another world war would be infinitely more destructive, particularly for the civilian population. Anything seemed preferable to fighting. The pacifistic mood of the time is well reflected in the amazing resolution adopted by the Oxford Union, the university's main political society, one month after Hitler's advent to power: "This House will under no circumstances fight for its King or country." Many of the appeasers wanted to meet hatred with love and rejected war even in self-defense. Antiwar sentiment also pervaded much of German public opinion. Hitler's early popularity at home derived in large part from the fact that he achieved his aims by diplomatic pressure and not by recourse to arms.

Pacifism was reinforced by additional factors, especially influential in Britain, where appeasement was most rampant. One was a feeling of guilt about Versailles. In the 1930s the passions of the immediate post-World War I years were spent, and the terms imposed on Germany appeared unduly harsh. Hitler took full advantage of these guilt feelings, and for some time disguised his aggressive moves as efforts merely to rectify the injustices of Versailles. By so doing he gained favor with many people of liberal and socialist convictions who had no sympathy whatever for nazism. Another factor was anti-communism. Hitler's successful pose as a crusader against the Communist threat neutralized the conservative, nationalistic circles in Britain and France who otherwise would have opposed German expansion. And, finally, a small but influential group wanted to appease Hitler because it admired nazism for the sense of purpose and the dynamism which it had seemingly given Germany, as well as for the effective manner in which it had dealt with unemployment.

In England the Conservative and Labour leaderships alike were addicted to appeasement. Both parties rejected a major rearmament effort long after it had become apparent that Germany was arming at full speed. The only prominent voice raised against the follies of appeasement and unilateral non-armament was that of Winston Churchill. He warned that unless Britain matched German military expenditures, it would lose air and naval superiority and become a helpless victim of Hitler's blackmail. He also courageously condemned diplomatic concessions to Hitler as whetting his appetite and encouraging him to further aggression. But Churchill had the reputation of a troublesome eccentric. He was remembered chiefly for the fiasco of the 1915 Gallipoli campaign and for his poor performance as Chancellor of the Exchequer. He was consistently kept out of office and ignored. As late as 1938 Britain's expenditures on armaments were only one-quarter those of Germany.

France had fewer illusions about the Nazis, but without British support it could not stand up to them. Hitler revealed how tenuous its international position was by his pact with Poland and remilitarization of the Rhineland. France was further weakened by internal dissent. In the 1930s the traditional rivalry between Republican and Conservative blocs was exacerbated by the emergence in each of extremist wings: a Communist bloc on the left, and a Fascist one on the right. Shortly after Hitler had marched into the Rhineland, France was paralyzed by the worst general strike in its history and seemed to teeter on the brink of civil war. This danger was averted by the formation in June, 1936, of a coalition government consisting of socialists and Communists, headed by Leon Blum. Blum's cabinet passed a number of long-overdue social reform measures, which alarmed the Conservatives. Under the slogan "Better Hitler than Blum" some right-wing circles in France began now openly to flirt with the Nazis. The Nazis fanned these sentiments by generously bribing susceptible politicians and journalists.

The fearful, accommodating foreign policy of the Western democracies had as one of its by-products the emergence of a coalition of authoritarian states led by Nazi Germany.

In October, 1935, Mussolini launched an unprovoked attack on Ethiopia, the last major independent state on the African continent. The League of Nations, in one of its more determined efforts, condemned Italy as the aggressor and voted to impose on it economic sanctions. Great Britain strongly denounced the Italian move, and even sent naval units to the Mediterranean. But Mussolini simply disregarded these threats and continued his campaign until all Ethiopia was in his hands. The attempted collective security measures proved too weak to halt Fascist aggression (the economic sanctions were never really enforced) but just irritating enough to push Italy into Germany's arms. Before long the two countries established close diplomatic links. Mussolini spoke of Rome and Berlin as forming a political "Axis." The term caught on and was subsequently applied to the whole anti-democratic, totalitarian bloc. The League of Nations suffered a grievous loss of prestige in the Ethiopian crisis and never recovered even that limited influence it had enjoyed until then.

The Ethiopian war was barely over when a civil war broke out in Spain. A group of conservative Nationalists, led by General Francisco Franco, invaded Spain from Morocco with the purpose of overthrowing a left-wing Popular Front

Picasso was moved to paint Guernica *(1937) by Nationalist terror bombing of civilians in the defenseless town during the Spanish Civil War.*

government, containing Communists, which had recently won the elections. The war was conducted with great savagery. Nazi Germany and Fascist Italy immediately aligned themselves with the Nationalists and sent them troops and equipment. The Soviet Union, on its part, came to the aid of the Republicans. The Western democracies sought to maintain and enforce neutrality. The war ended in March, 1939, when the Nationalists and their Nazi and Fascist allies captured Madrid.

Germany also managed to bring to its side Japan, which was increasingly moving in the direction of authoritarianism. In November, 1936, Germany and Japan signed the so-called Anti-Comintern Pact, ostensibly directed against the Communist International but actually designed as a vessel for a new coalition of powers in Europe and Asia. Italy signed a year later. (In 1941 the pact was renewed, and eleven other countries became signatories.)

Thus, while the democracies were ineffectually trying to preserve peace at any price, a group of expansionist countries formed a counter-alliance. Its leader, Hitler, played with consummate skill on foreign opinion, making demands that sounded limited and reasonable, but which were always coupled with threats of dire consequences if not met. The governments of England and France were confronted with a succession of artificial crises where the alternatives were either sacrificing a little (usually the property of third parties) or risking all-out war. The successes of Nazi diplomacy lay in its knowledge of precisely how far to push blackmail before its victims rebelled. Its crowning achievement was the Munich agreement of 1938.

Armored Japanese officers in Shanghai in 1932, during one of the "incidents" the Japanese used as pretexts to attack and carve up China during the 1930s.

On November 5, 1937, Hitler gathered around him the chiefs of the armed forces and outlined to them his long-range plans. One of those present, Colonel Friedrich Hossbach, took down the gist of Hitler's remarks. His record, the so-called "Hossbach Minutes," discovered after the war, represents a key document in the understanding of events leading to World War II. Hitler began by expounding his basic political ideas as he had formulated them in *Mein Kampf*: that the 85 million Germans had to acquire additional "living space" or face extinction. This space lay in Europe, not overseas: here alone were the raw materials and foodstuffs that Germany needed. Since history showed that space could be acquired only by violence, war was inevitable, the only question being when and under what conditions it should break out. Germany would attain the peak of military strength in 1943–1945, and this was the latest date for launching war, although it could begin earlier. In any event, the immediate task was to destroy Austria and Czechoslovakia so as to protect Germany's flank for the critical operations in the West.

These remarks are the earliest indication of Hitler's resolve to gamble for the control of Europe: in a sense they mark the beginning of World War II. But this intention was not apparent at the time, because Hitler cleverly camouflaged his assault on Austria and Czechoslovakia with slogans of national self-determination. All he wanted, he proclaimed, was to bring into the Reich the Germans who against their will had been separated from it: the Austrians and the German minority in the Sudeten region of Czechoslovakia. The deception worked. Two weeks after the talk recorded by Hossbach, Hitler invited to Germany British Foreign Secretary Lord Halifax, a leading appeaser. He warned Halifax that Germany had some outstanding issues to settle with its eastern and southern neighbors. Halifax let Hitler understand that Britain was not committed to the *status quo* in that part of the world, and would not object to a "peaceful" solution of the nationality problems there. Hitler correctly interpreted this statement to mean that Britain would not intervene.

In February, 1938, on the eve of the assault on Austria and Czechoslovakia, Hitler created a High Command of the Armed Forces to replace the Ministry of War, staffing it with loyal supporters. This measure severely limited the traditional autonomy of the German General Staff, and completed the *Gleichschaltung* of the country's institutions (Chapter 16). It assured Hitler of control of the army in the event of war.

The Austrian Republic was brought down in March, 1938, by the combined pressures of Germany from without and a Nazi "Fifth Column" from within. It was then fused with Germany into a Greater Reich. Hitler's claim that the political union (*Anschluss*) of Austria with Germany expressed the wishes of its population was given credibility by the hysterical welcome accorded Nazi troops, and by the zeal with which the populace of Vienna took to abusing its Jews.

Hitler was prepared to move immediately against Czechoslovakia, but here the difficulties were much more formidable. The Czechs, unlike the Austrians, wanted no dealings with the Germans and were prepared to resist them: their military equipment was first-rate, and they commanded excellent fortifications. Furthermore, Czechoslovakia had firm guarantees against external aggression from France, dating back to 1924–1925, so that an assault on it was likely to

Prime Minister Chamberlain on his return from Munich, waving the agreement that meant "peace with honour."

bring on a general war. Taking these factors into consideration, German generals opposed Hitler's designs: the *Wehrmacht*, in their opinion, was not yet ready to fight. But their advice was ignored, for Hitler felt confident he could have his way without recourse to arms.

In the spring of 1938 the Nazis began to stir up trouble among the 3 million Germans inhabiting the Sudeten region. Prague was prepared to go far in meeting the Sudeten Germans' demands for autonomy, but each time it made a concession the stakes were raised and more civil disturbances followed. Hitler, declaring "intolerable" alleged Czech persecution of the Sudeten Germans, threatened to intervene on their behalf. In September, 1938, war seemed imminent. The Germans carried out large-scale maneuvers along the French frontier, the French ordered a partial mobilization, and the Czechs made ready to fight.

How far Hitler was prepared to carry out his threats will never be known, because he was spared the necessity of a decision. At the critical juncture, as he was weighing the risks involved and contending with his own recalcitrant generals, Britain unexpectedly came to his aid. The Conservative Prime Minister Neville Chamberlain, although completely without experience in foreign affairs, believed himself destined to spare Europe another world war. He simply could not allow that the disagreements with Germany were insoluble. "How horrible, fantastic, incredible, it is that we should be digging trenches and trying on gasmasks here because of a quarrel in a faraway country between people of whom we know nothing," he exclaimed in a radio address at the height of the Czech crisis.

Encouraged by other appeasers, Chamberlain approached Hitler with a request for a meeting, hoping by a person-to-person discussion to solve once and for all the outstanding issues arising from Germany's claims. In negotiations held at Munich, later joined by Mussolini, he and the French Premier Edouard Daladier agreed to persuade Czechoslovakia to yield the Sudetenland to Germany. As Churchill protested in dismay, "the German dictator, instead of snatching the victuals from the table, has been content to have them served to him course by course." But Chamberlain thought otherwise, and so did the English public, which gave him an enthusiastic welcome when he returned home waving the Munich agreement and claiming that he had gained "peace in our time." For in return, Hitler had pledged not to make any further territorial claims in Europe.

Churchill was much closer to the mark when he described Munich as a "total and unmitigated defeat." Hitler was once more proved right in his tactics of blackmail and triumphed conclusively over his internal opponents. Henceforth his self-assurance knew no bounds, nor did his contempt for the democracies. French diplomatic guarantees became worthless, and the system of alliances which France had built up so assiduously in the 1920s in Eastern Europe crumbled: after Munich that area fell into the Nazi sphere of influence. Munich, as we shall see, also brought about a disastrous reorientation in Soviet foreign policy.

Barely one month after the signature of the Munich agreement, in total disregard of his pledges, Hitler ordered the German army to occupy the remainder of Czechoslovakia. The republic, shorn of its fortifications by the loss of the Sudetenland, could offer no resistance and capitulated (March, 1939).

As soon as he was installed in Prague, Hitler began to apply pressure on Poland, demanding Danzig and a corridor linking Germany with East Prussia. The Poles refused to bargain on these matters. This time the Western democracies came to the aid of Hitler's intended victim. Chamberlain, deeply offended by Hitler's breach of promise not to demand additional land in Europe, on March 30, 1939, wrote out with his own hand a guarantee to Poland, pledging Britain's entry into war in the event of a German attack on it. The French endorsed this pledge. But Hitler doubted that these pledges would be honored should he succeed in smashing Poland with one quick blow. On April 3, 1939, he issued secret orders to prepare the invasion of Poland.

Like almost everyone else, Stalin at first misunderstood Hitler and underestimated his aggressive intentions. In 1932 he had German Communists fighting the Social Democrats and thus indirectly helping the Nazis, and in 1933 he had declared publicly his intention of keeping out of European conflicts. But by 1934 he seems to have realized his mistake. Hitler's threats of an anti-Communist crusade, and later (1936) the conclusion of the Anti-Comintern Pact with Japan, posed a direct threat to the Soviet Union. Russia was diplomatically isolated, and in the event of a combined Nazi-Japanese attack could count on the support of no major power.

From 1934 on, Stalin took measures to overcome this isolation. In September of that year the Soviet Union joined the League of Nations, which it had previously denounced, and there became an ardent advocate of disarmament and collective security. In May, 1935, it signed mutual defense treaties with France and Czechoslovakia.° In the summer of 1935 the international Communist movement was instructed to enter into working alliances—Popular Fronts—with

The Nazi-Soviet Pact

°By terms of the treaty with Czechoslovakia, Russia was required to come to its aid only if France did likewise. The French betrayal of its ally at Munich thus absolved Russia, which in any event had no common frontier with Czechoslovakia.

socialist and liberal groups as a means of preventing Fascists and Nazis from coming to power. There is also reason to believe that the great Soviet purges of 1935–1938 were connected with the international situation, serving to eliminate rivals for power in the event of war and internal anarchy.

Western appeasement of Hitler aroused Stalin's suspicions. He began to think that it was part of a deliberate plot on the part of England and France to buy their own safety by deflecting Hitler's ambitions from the West to the East. The Munich agreement and the subsequent unopposed German occupation of Czechoslovakia seemed to confirm these suspicions. Stalin appears to have concluded that Eastern Europe had been conceded to Hitler as a springboard for an attack against Russia. If one keeps in mind that early in 1939 Soviet and Japanese troops were actually shooting at each other along the Mongolian border, Stalin's alarm becomes readily understandable. He now decided to extricate himself from his predicament by turning the tables on the Western democracies: instead of having them sit back and watch Russia being torn to pieces by Germany and Japan, he would make common cause with the Axis powers and enjoy the spectacle of a destructive war among the "capitalist" countries.

In March, 1939, a few days after Nazi troops had marched into Prague, Stalin made a speech in which he dropped hints that he was ready to come to an understanding with Germany. To Hitler, Stalin's overture presented another one of those unexpected gifts which he had come to view as signs of heaven's special favor. An agreement with Russia seemed to reduce even further any possibility of England and France risking a general war over Poland. The hint was therefore immediately taken up in Berlin, and soon Nazi and Soviet diplomats were engaged in secret negotiations. Overtly, Stalin made simultaneous approaches to the Western powers, but there can be little doubt that by this time he no longer had any intention of coming to terms with them and used these negotiations only as a means of exerting pressure on the Nazis.

As a price for his acquiescence in the Nazi destruction of Poland, Stalin demanded Poland's eastern regions as well as recognition of a Soviet "sphere of influence" over Finland, the Baltic states (Estonia, Latvia, and Lithuania), and Bessarabia. These were steep demands, but from Hitler's point of view there was no point in haggling over them, since ultimately he intended to conquer the Soviet Union anyway. The two powers signed a nonaggression pact, which on August 27 was announced to an unsuspecting world. The most important provisions, namely those calling for the partition of Poland and the division of Eastern Europe into spheres of influence, were not revealed, being incorporated in a secret part of the treaty.

Such was perhaps the most bitter fruit of appeasement. With the assurance of Soviet neutrality, Germany felt free to launch its projected attack on Poland, and thereby risk World War II.

Blitzkrieg The disarmament imposed on Germany by the Versailles Treaty had turned out to be a blessing in disguise for the Germany military, because once rearmament got under way they could immediately proceed to raise the most up-to-date armed force. In the 1920s, preparing for this eventuality, the German General Staff had studied carefully the lessons of World War I. Impressed by the possibilities inherent in mechanized warfare which the British had introduced but only partly exploited in the Somme offensive and at Cambrai, it decided that the future German army would be built around a nucleus of armored and motorized divisions operating with close tactical air support. The function of these mechanized units would be to break through enemy lines, spread out behind them, and form vast "pincers" isolating and trapping large enemy units. This strategy—blitzkrieg or "lightning war"—was ideally suited for a country with enormous technical resources and superb discipline but short of the raw materials essential for a protracted war of attrition.

If the Germans based their new strategy on that invented by the Allies, the Allies, in turn, adopted the defensive strategy that the Germans had put to good use during much of World War I. France, bled white and suffering a declining birth rate, could not afford another carnage. It decided therefore to post its forces behind the fortified Maginot Line, extending along the Franco-German frontier, and let the Germans do the attacking. Britain, once it began to rearm in late 1938, put its major effort into the air force. The military leadership of both countries was utterly second rate.

In the early hours of September 1, 1939, the Germans launched their attack on Poland. The first battle test of the new *Wehrmacht* exceeded all Nazi hopes. Slashing from the north, west, and south, the mechanized divisions cut through Polish defenses, and on the sixth day reached the suburbs of Warsaw. Those Polish units that had extricated themselves from German encirclements, as well as those that had not yet fully mobilized, retreated to the east, to make a stand in the wooded and marshy terrain there. But their hopes of resistance ended on September 17, when Russia sent troops into eastern Poland to claim territories accorded it by the secret agreement with Germany. Polish units were disarmed,

A German photograph, taken in Warsaw, shows Polish Jews being rounded up at gunpoint for transport to death camps.

and the officers sent to prisoner-of-war camps, where many were later massacred by Soviet police squads. Simultaneously, Soviet troops occupied strategic bases in the three Baltic republics.

Triumphant in the East, Hitler had an unpleasant surprise in the West. Two days after the invasion of Poland, Britain and its empire, followed by France, declared war. After the crushing defeat he had inflicted on Poland, Hitler hoped that France and Britain would change their minds and come to terms—a hope sustained by the fact that the Allies made no move to come to Poland's aid militarily, although the German frontier in the West had been only lightly defended. But the days of appeasement were over, and Hitler's peace offer made in early October was rejected.

Stalin too had a shock. The rapidity and finality with which the Germans had disposed of Poland had robbed him of a long period of grace on which he had counted and revived the possibility of collusion between Hitler and the Western democracies. To mollify Hitler he himself now began to pursue a policy of arrant appeasement. In October, 1939, Stalin informed the Nazis that in his view "a strong Germany was the absolute prerequisite of peace in Europe" and that "the Soviet Union could not give its approval to the Western powers creating conditions which would weaken Germany and place it in a difficult position." Communist parties abroad were accordingly instructed to defend the Axis cause. More concretely, Stalin signed with Germany a supplementary trade agreement, which had considerable influence on the subsequent course of the war. By its terms Soviet Russia undertook to supply Germany with scarce raw materials from its own territory and to facilitate for it the transit of strategic goods from the Middle East and East Asia. This accord enabled Nazi Germany to break the naval blockade that Britain had imposed on it in September, 1939. Henceforth, Soviet Russia regularly supplied Germany with grain, oil, phosphates, manganese, chrome, iron ore, and many other minerals, and arranged abroad for the purchase and shipment of natural rubber and materials used in the manufacture of synthetic rubber. In the first year of the treaty the Soviet Union shipped to Germany 1 million tons of cereals and sufficient quantities of oil and rubber to create there a large strategic stockpile, essential for the conduct of mechanized warfare. Soviet economic assistance to Germany in the first twenty months of World War II was of such dimensions that according to the historian who has investigated it, "it leaves open the question of whether without Soviet aid, particularly in the matter of oil supplies and rubber transit, the German attack in the West in 1940 could have been as successful as it was, and the attack on the Soviet Union [in 1941] would have been possible at all."[*]

In October, 1939, in accord with the secret clauses of the Nazi pact which had placed Finland within the Soviet sphere of influence, Stalin began to press the Finns for territorial concessions. When Finland resisted, the Russians attacked. The campaign went badly for the Russians, confirming European opinion in its low estimate of their fighting capacity. In the end, however, Soviet superiority in numbers (100 Red divisions against 3 Finnish ones) asserted itself, and the Finns had to capitulate (March, 1940).

In the West the winter and spring of the first year of war passed without

[*] Gerhard L. Weinberg, *Germany and the Soviet Union, 1939–1941* (1954).

action, in what came to be known as the "phony war" or "sitzkrieg"—"sitting war." The only important engagement occurred in Scandinavia. The British and the Germans simultaneously tried to seize Norway, but the Germans got there first with larger forces, occupying Denmark on the way (April, 1940).

Having eliminated all danger in Eastern Europe, Hitler was ready to tackle his original and principal objective, France. The strategic plan that the General Staff proposed and he accepted called for an ingenious reversal of the Schlieffen Plan (Chapter 11). This time the right wing, sent into the Low Countries, was to be a weaker, diversionary force. Once a major Allied force had rushed into Belgium to intercept it, the German left, containing the bulk of the armored and motorized divisions, was to strike westward and cut off the Allies.

The German offensive opened on May 10, 1940. Belgian fortresses were captured in a matter of hours by specially trained parachute units. The Dutch were given an ultimatum to surrender, and when they failed to capitulate in time, German bombers leveled Rotterdam, killing in the process 40,000 civilians. Refugees seeking to flee the zone of combat were deliberately machine-gunned from the air to create chaos, clog the roads, and hamper reinforcements.

As the Germans had anticipated, the Allies immediately dispatched strong infantry forces and much of their armor into Belgium. A week later Nazi mechanized armies concentrated in the west broke across the supposedly impassable Ardennes forest near Sedan and raced behind the Maginot Line for the Channel. The Allies had no reserve force to stop them. Five days later Nazi armored units reached the sea, cutting off the Allied army in Belgium. This done, the Germans wheeled south. Subsequently, the British managed to evacu-

ROGER SCHALL

As French resistance collapsed Paris was declared an open city to prevent its destruction. The occupying German forces emphasized the debacle by parading past the Arc de Triomphe.

Churchill inspecting the ruins of the House of Commons, wrecked by the Luftwaffe in 1940. "We shall not fail or falter," he promised; "we shall not weaken or tire. . . . Give us the tools, and we shall finish the job."

ate nearly their entire trapped Expeditionary Force, plus a considerable French contingent—338,000 men in all—through Dunkirk, but most of their equipment had to be left behind. The French army collapsed. On June 13–14 the Germans entered Paris, and shortly after France signed an armistice. The country was divided into two zones: the northern one was placed under German occupation, and the southern one was established as a satellite state ruled from Vichy by the senile Marshal Pétain. At this point (June 10) Mussolini, "rushing to the aid of the victors," declared war on France and Britain.

Britain was left alone to face the Axis powers. Had it made peace—as it could have—all of Europe would have been at Hitler's feet. But Britain, which had made concessions to Hitler when it had been in a position of strength, refused to do so when its prospects seemed hopeless—a reversal which Hitler could never quite comprehend.

In May, 1940, the prime-ministership in Britain had been entrusted to Churchill, the only man of sufficient stature to lead the country in the hour of its mortal peril. His youthful self-confidence and pugnacity, his honest warnings, his Gibbonian rhetoric, so dissonant during the years when Britain had sought "normalcy," were just what was needed by a nation left virtually unarmed to face the most powerful military force in the world. Churchill never wavered in his determination. Britain, he announced, would fight "if necessary for years, if necessary alone" until Germany gave up all its conquests. With the backing of his cabinet he rejected out of hand Hitler's second peace offer, made after the collapse of France.

Confronted with this intransigence, Hitler issued on July 16, 1940, orders for "Sea Lion," the invasion of the British Isles. The first phase of the operation was to secure mastery of the air, essential for the safe transport of the invasion force across the Channel. There could be little doubt that once the Germans secured a beachhead they would quickly conquer the British Isles, for Britain had no army left with which to oppose them.

Early in August the *Luftwaffe*, the German military air arm, launched its offensive against the Royal Air Force (RAF). For the next two months the air space over Britain was the scene of the greatest aerial battle in history. The RAF proved a tough nut to crack. Its main fighter plane, the Spitfire, had a slight edge over the German Messerschmitt, and so did the morale and training of its pilots. The RAF also had at its disposal a valuable defensive weapon: a chain of radar stations strung along the coast which, by giving timely warning of the approach of enemy squadrons, enabled it to make maximum use of its equipment. In the Battle of Britain the RAF managed to destroy on the average two German planes for each plane that it lost. At the beginning of September the *Luftwaffe*'s losses grew so high that it changed its tactics: instead of daytime attacks on air installations, it carried out nighttime attacks on cities. The intention was to break civilian morale and force Britain to make peace. For months London was subjected to nightly incendiary raids that destroyed large parts of the city. But British morale was not broken, and the RAF continued to exact a heavy toll of the raiders. In the end the bombing of cities proved a costly mistake, for it diverted the *Luftwaffe* from its primary task, that of gaining mastery of the air.

The crossing of the Channel could be effected, at the latest, in September, after which the weather became too unpredictable. Having failed to destroy the RAF by mid-September, Hitler ordered Operation Sea Lion indefinitely postponed. He had lost the Battle of Britain: Nazi Germany had suffered its first defeat.

At the end of 1940, notwithstanding the failure of the aerial assault on Britain, Hitler was at the peak of his power. Yet he could not rest on his laurels. His power derived from a five-year priority in armament, but the gap between German and foreign military power was bound to narrow: everyone was arming now, including the United States, which in 1940 made large appropriations for defense and introduced America's first peacetime military conscription.

The War Becomes Global

In other words, Hitler had to act while he still held his great advantage. He had a choice of options. His first instinct was to form a grand coalition to carve up the British Empire. In September, 1940, while the *Luftwaffe* was softening Great Britain for the kill, Germany concluded with Italy and Japan a Tripartite Pact dividing Asia and Africa into spheres of influence: Italy was to have the Mediterranean, Japan southeast Asia, while Germany reserved for itself central Africa. Hitler then turned to Soviet Russia, offering it as its share of the spoils territories in the Middle East, namely Iran, Afghanistan, and India.

By approaching Stalin only after the Tripartite Pact had been concluded, Hitler committed a major blunder. Stalin was offended at being treated like a second-class ally, and immediately became suspicious of Hitler's motives. Doubts seem to have arisen in his mind whether Hitler was not deceiving him as he, Stalin, had deceived England and France in 1939—that is, whether Hitler was pretending to seek an alliance with Russia while in reality forming behind its back an anti-Russian coalition. Stalin was particularly disturbed by aggressive

German and Italian moves in southeastern Europe, which he regarded as lying within his own sphere of influence. In October, 1940, the Italians launched an attack on Greece, and the following month the Germans pressured Hungary, Romania, and Slovakia into joining the Tripartite Pact. Thus the Axis partners obtained hegemony in the Balkans and established a potentially dangerous base on Russia's southwestern flank.

In secret negotiations conducted in October-November, 1940, the Russians expressed their willingness to join the Tripartite Pact, but insisted on the recognition of some of their rights in the Balkans. Hitler quickly lost patience with Stalin's reservations. He now began to contemplate the possibility of postponing the final assault on Britain and its empire, concentrating instead on the unavoidable destruction of the Soviet Union. When, at the end of November, Stalin formally demanded Bulgaria and the Turkish Straits as his price for joining the Tripartite Pact, Hitler did not trouble to reply. Instead, on December 18, 1940, he gave instructions to prepare for Operation Barbarossa, the invasion of Russia.

The strategy of the projected Russian campaign was to launch a lightning offensive that would bring German armies in eight to ten weeks to the banks of the Volga. German units were to conduct "daring operations led by deeply penetrating armored spearheads" that were to encircle and trap enemy forces, as they had done the preceding spring in France. The territories conquered west of the Volga were to provide Germany with abundant foodstuffs, raw materials, and slave labor, transforming German-dominated Europe into a self-sufficient, impregnable fortress. Areas east of the Volga were to be left to the Russians. Having destroyed the Red Army, Hitler intended to turn southward and take over the Middle East and North Africa.

The assault on Russia was conceived not merely as a war of conquest; it was to be a war of extermination, the first phase in clearing Eastern Europe of the "inferior races" for subsequent German settlement. The instructions given the *Wehrmacht* were unlike those ever given a European army. It was not only to destroy the enemy's armed forces but also to kill any and all "intellectuals" and "Communists" that fell into its hands. Two months before the invasion Hitler told his generals:

> We must abandon the point of view of soldierly comradeship. The Communist never was and never will be a comrade. This is a war of extermination. . . . We do not wage war to preserve the enemy. . . . Bolshevik Commissars and the Communist intelligentsia must be exterminated. The new states [of Eastern Europe] must be socialist but they must not have their own intelligentsia. A new intelligentsia must not be allowed to emerge. We must fight the poison of sedition. This is not a matter for war tribunals. The leaders of the troops must know what the issues are. They must lead the struggle. The troops must defend themselves with the same means with which they are attacked. . . . The fight will be very different from that waged in the West. In the East, toughness [now] means mildness in the future. The commanders must demand sacrifices of themselves to overcome their scruples.

The army issued appropriate directives to its forces, stating in addition that

AXIS EXPANSION
1936-1942

Allied powers
Axis powers
Axis allies
Neutral countries
Areas annexed by Russia, 1940
German diplomatic gains, 1936-1939
Areas occupied by Germany
Areas controlled by Vichy France
German lines of invasion
Maginot Line

IRELAND

UNITED
KINGDOM

London

NORTH
SEA

ATLANTIC OCEAN

Dunkirk
Rotterdam
NETH.
Brussels
BEL.
Cologne
Sedan LUX.
RHINELAND
Paris

FRANCE

Vichy
Lyons

SWITZ.

SPAIN

Madrid

CORSICA

ITALY

SARDINIA

Rome

Operation Torch
Oran
Algiers
Tunis

SICILY

ALGERIA

TUNISIA

Tripoli

NORWAY

Narvik

Trondheim

Bergen

Oslo

Kristiansand

SWEDEN

Stockholm

DENMARK

Copenhagen

BALTIC SEA

Hamburg

Berlin

GERMANY

Dresden

Munich

Vienna

AUSTRIA

SUDETENLAND

Prague

CZECHOSLOVAKIA

HUNGARY

Budapest

Belgrade

Sarajevo

YUGOSLAVIA

ALBANIA

GREECE

Athens

CRETE

FINLAND

Helsinki

Leningrad

ESTONIA

LATVIA

LITHUANIA

Memel

EAST
PRUSSIA

Danzig

Warsaw

POLAND

Krakow

Brest Litovsk

Kiev

BESSARABIA

ROMANIA

Bucharest

Odessa

BULGARIA

Sofia

Istanbul

Ankara

TURKEY

U.S.S.R.

Moscow

Smolensk

Minsk

Kursk

German front, Nov., 1942

Kharkov

German front, Dec., 1941

Stalingrad

Rostov

Sebastopol

BLACK SEA

MEDITERRANEAN SEA

CYPRUS

SYRIA

IRAQ

LEB.

PALESTINE

TRANS-
JORDAN

SAUDI-
ARABIA

Tobruk

Alexandria

El Alamein

LIBYA

EGYPT

"as a rule, the use of arms against Soviet prisoners of war is legal." In other words, the Germans about to enter Russia were given the explicit authority— indeed, they were told that it was their patriotic duty—to kill anyone whom they considered to be or chose to define as being a "Communist" or an "intellectual," as well as all captured enemy soldiers.

Stalin had ample warning of German invasion plans from his own and British and American intelligence services, but he chose to ignore them, for he admired Hitler and thought he could trust him. Instead, he continued his policy of appeasement, delivering to Hitler strategic supplies and even turning over to him the German Communists who had sought refuge in the Soviet Union.

Hitler was so certain of his ability to quickly dispose of the Red Army that he discouraged the Japanese from joining him in the projected invasion, and egged them on instead to attack British possessions in southeast Asia. In April, 1941, the Japanese signed with the Soviet Union a neutrality pact that subsequently proved of utmost value to both parties.

The German offensive against Russia was originally scheduled for mid-May, 1941, but it had to be postponed by a month. The Italians bogged down in Greece, and in April Hitler sent troops to bail them out. In the process the Germans also invaded and occupied Yugoslavia.

On June 22, 1941, 145 Nazi divisions, 20 of them armored, plunged into Soviet territory. The Russians were not prepared for the attack, and had not even fully mobilized. Nazi armored divisions pushed forward according to plan, encircling large Soviet contingents and capturing prisoners by the hundreds of thousands. Within six weeks the road to Moscow lay open. But Hitler, intending to avoid Napoleon's mistake, decided to postpone capture of the capital in order first to destroy what was left of Soviet armies and industrial resources in the northern and southern parts of the country. Overruling the General Staff he ordered at the beginning of August a temporary halt in the advance on Moscow. One part of the center force was to turn northward, take Leningrad and link up with the Finns, and another to veer southward and join up with the armies operating in the Ukraine. The northern operation did not gain its objective, for Leningrad held out, and in the end was never captured. But in the south, near Kiev, the Germans trapped an enormous Soviet force. They also succeeded in capturing the great industrial area of the Donbas.

Hitler's decision to postpone the capture of Moscow gave the Russians two months in which to raise fresh troops in the east and organize their defenses. It also forced the Germans to open the drive on Moscow at the onset of the winter, for which they had made no provisions. The offensive resumed early in October. On December 2, in savage fighting, the Germans penetrated the suburbs of the city, but here they were stopped. By now winter had set in: German soldiers were exhausted from half a year of continuous combat and froze in their summer uniforms; their motorized equipment stalled for lack of antifreeze. On December 5–6 the Russians, who had secretly brought fresh troops from Siberia, unexpectedly counterattacked. Hitler gave strict orders not to yield any ground, but the order could not be obeyed, and in the middle of January, 1942, the *Wehrmacht* retreated, digging in a hundred miles west of Moscow. Hitler, infuriated by the reverse, sacked his top officers and assumed personal command.

On the Russian side, the Nazi invasion produced a tremendous surge of national sentiment. At first the population offered no resistance to the Germans, and in some areas even welcomed them. But as soon as the *Wehrmacht* and SS began to shoot civilians and prisoners, resistance stiffened. Russians who faced death at Nazi hands for their party or administrative connections fled to the forests and formed partisan detachments, joined by patriotic youths and soldiers who had escaped capture. Surrounded Soviet military units often refused to capitulate, fighting to the last man. Stalin, in his propaganda, abandoned all pretense of defending communism, and frankly exhorted the nation to fight for "Holy Russia." All these developments proved an unpleasant surprise to the Germans, for the miserable showing the Red Army had made in the war with Finland led them to expect a rapid collapse of Russian morale.

Immediately upon the German attack on Russia, Churchill offered the Soviets British friendship and help. The United States, too, though still neutral, made no secret of its sympathies. President Roosevelt realized the grave danger that the Axis powers presented to American security, and did all he could to assist those who resisted them. In the summer of 1941 Congress extended to the Soviet Union the benefits of the Lend-Lease program, enacted in March, by virtue of which American war supplies were sent to anti-Axis powers. In August, 1941, Roosevelt and Churchill issued the Atlantic Charter, which proclaimed the desire of their respective countries to assure all nations of self-determination. Communist parties the world over changed their propaganda and exhorted freedom-loving peoples to fight the Nazis. Thus, something like an anti-Axis alliance began to take shape.

This alliance became a reality on December 7, 1941, when the Japanese launched a surprise attack on Pearl Harbor, and thereby brought the United States into the war.

KYODO PHOTO, TOKYO

At a ceremony in Tokyo, the Japanese Foreign Minister offers a toast to the Axis Tripartite Pact, signed in September, 1940. At right are German and Italian ambassadors. The officer in uniform at center is General Hideki Tojo, the War Minister, who led Japan into the war in December, 1941.

"Battleship Row" at Pearl Harbor, as photographed from a Japanese plane during the surprise attack on December 7, 1941. Fuel oil gushes from the torpedoed ships; at lower left the stricken Oklahoma *is about to capsize.*

The Pearl Harbor attack culminated a decade of Japanese expansion. Suffering from overpopulation and a shortage of raw materials for its industries, Japan in 1931 had begun to penetrate China, placing under its control Manchuria and much of the Chinese coastline. This expansion met with opposition from liberal circles in Japan, but the voice of the liberals grew fainter as the country came under the domination of military and industrial groups sympathetic to European Fascists and Nazis.

The defeats which the Nazis had inflicted on the great imperial powers—Britain, the Netherlands, and France—opened for the Japanese expansionists unprecedented opportunities. Southeast Asia, with its rich natural resources of rubber, tin, oil, and so forth, on which they had long cast a hungry eye, suddenly was available for the taking. The Germans encouraged the Japanese to move into these regions, but the Japanese hesitated, afraid of the reaction of the Soviet Union and the United States.

Anxiety about Russia evaporated in 1941. At the end of that year Russia seemed to be breathing its last, and certainly was in no position to thwart Japanese expansion. But the United States was another matter. It had made it clear that it would not tolerate Japan's expansion indefinitely, and for some time fear of its great might paralyzed Japanese will. In the late summer of 1941, however, tentative offensive plans were drawn up. Not even the most sanguine Japanese militarists hoped to bring the United States to its knees, let alone occupy it. What was considered feasible, however, was a series of lightning strikes leading to the seizure of European and American colonial possessions in southeast Asia, and their integration into an impregnable realm modeled on

Hitler's "Fortress Europe." The plan had one hitch: it required the elimination of the United States Pacific Fleet. The more militant Japanese hoped to dispose of this difficulty by a surprise blow that would neutralize American naval forces in the Pacific. Having completed their conquests, they intended to open negotiations with the United States.

In November, 1941, under pressure from moderate elements (among them, the emperor), the Japanese opened final talks with Washington. It was agreed that if the United States gave indications that it was prepared to acknowledge Japan's hegemony in East Asia, the projected assault on the U.S. fleet would be called off. But Washington refused to make concessions and continued to insist on Japanese evacuation of China. On December 1, 1941—as German troops were penetrating the suburbs of Moscow—Tokyo decided to go to war.

The United States Navy, having broken the Japanese diplomatic code, was in a position to listen in on many of the discussions on the other side. Nevertheless, through negligence, it failed to take the necessary precautions. As Japanese bombers, brought to the proximity of Pearl Harbor by carriers, struck, no fighters rose to intercept them. (A message alerting Pearl Harbor had been sent to Honolulu by a commercial radio agency; the dispatcher carrying it to the base was caught by the air raid while pedaling there on his bicycle.) In the raid two battleships were sunk and five others damaged, but fortunately no carriers were in port. Shortly after Pearl Harbor, in a succession of superbly executed campaigns, the Japanese conquered the Philippines, Malaya, the Dutch East Indies, New Guinea, and a chain of strategic islands to the east. The democracies suffered now yet another defeat, as disastrous as that which the Nazis had inflicted on them in France.

The debacle notwithstanding, Churchill at once recognized Pearl Harbor as the death sentence of the Axis. A few days after the Japanese attack, Germany, with incredible recklessness, declared war on the United States. This meant that the Axis powers now confronted the combined forces of the United States, Great Britain, and the Soviet Union—a combination which nothing could vanquish.°

The Nazi "New Order"

In the winter of 1941–1942 Hitler, considering the war as good as won, set into motion the first measures toward the "New Order"—a Europe refashioned according to the racial hallucinations which he had first experienced in his Vienna days.

His authority in Germany was total. In 1942 the docile Reichstag voted him the right to deal with any German as he saw fit (see Chapter 16); and there certainly was no limit to his authority over the inhabitants of the conquered territories. Only in the statellite countries—Hungary, Romania, Bulgaria, southern France—were there still some centers of independent power, as there were in Italy and Spain, but they were generally friendly to the Nazis.

As the war progressed, power increasingly fell into the hands of the SS and the Gestapo, both headed by Himmler. Disgusted with the *Wehrmacht*, Hitler even built up during the war an independent SS armed force. The SS and the Gestapo initiated throughout Europe a rule of terror. Persons suspected of any political

°The Soviet Union, on its part, did not declare war on Japan; nor Japan on Russia. Russia entered the war in the Pacific only in August, 1945, when it was for all practical purposes finished (see below).

misdemeanor, actual or potential, were sent to concentration camps, where they were placed at the mercy of their guards. In the Eastern territories, notably Poland and Russia, the Gestapo arrested from previously prepared lists numerous intellectuals, such as professors and well-known writers, and had them shot. The SS was specifically assigned the task of massacring European Jewry. Its device—"Faith is our honor"—absolved it from all moral responsibility save obedience to the Führer.

To convey the mentality that lay behind the unspeakable atrocities committed by the SS, we can do no better than cite the words that Himmler addressed to a gathering of its officers in 1943:

An SS man must adhere absolutely to one principle: he must be honorable, decent, faithful, and comradely to members of his own race, and to no one else. What happens to the Russians, what happens to the Czechs is to me a matter of total indifference. . . . Whether other nations live well or die of starvation interests me only in so far as we need slaves for our culture—other than that, it holds for me no interest. Whether during the construction of a tank trap 10,000 Russian women die of exhaustion or not, interests me only in so far as the tank trap for Germany has been constructed. We shall never be tough and pitiless where it is not necessary, that is clear. We Germans are the only nation in the world with a decent attitude toward animals; we shall also be decent toward these human animals. But it is a crime against our own blood to worry about them or to bring ideals to them so that our sons or grandchildren have more trouble with them. When someone comes to me and says: "I cannot build tank traps with women and children, that is inhuman, they will die," I shall say to him: "You are the murderer of your own blood, because if the tank trap is not built, German soldiers shall die, and they are the sons of German mothers. That is our blood." That is what I would like to inculcate in the SS . . . our care, our duty, is our people and our blood. . . . Everything else is of no importance . . .

I turn now to the evacuation of Jews, to the extermination of the Jewish people. This is one of those things that are easily said: "The Jewish people will be exterminated," a party member says, "of course, it says so in our program, we shall eliminate, exterminate the Jews." And then they all come, the brave 80 million Germans, and each one of them has his decent Jew. Yes, of course, the other Jews are swine, but this one is a first rate Jew. Of all those who speak so, none has witnessed it, none has experienced it. Most of you know what it means when 100 corpses lie next to each other, or 500, or even 1000. To experience this, and—apart from human weaknesses—to remain decent, that has made us hard. This is a glorious page in our history. . . .

The "glorious page" in German history began in late 1941 when Jews in German-held territories were herded into walled ghettoes and required to wear the Star of David. After the attack on Russia the Nazi leaders decided to commence the physical annihilation of the 11 million European Jews. At a conference held in January, 1942, at Wannsee, a suburb of Berlin, it was resolved to begin the

Rentabilitätsberechnung der SS über Ausnützung der Häftlinge in den Konzentrationslagern	Table of profits (or yield) per prisoner in concentration camps (established by SS)
Rentabilitätsberechnung	**Rental accounting**
Täglicher Verleihlohn durchschnittlich RM 6,–	Average income from rental of prisoner, per day RM [Reichsmark] 6.00
abzüglich Ernährung RM –,60	Deduction for nourishment, per day RM 0.60
durchschnittl. Lebensdauer 9 Mt. = 270 x RM 5,30 = RM 1431,–	**Average life expectancy:** 9 months: 270 [days] by RM 5.30 = RM 1431.00
abzüglich Bekl. Amort. RM –,10	Minus amortization on clothing RM 0.10
Erlös aus rationeller Verwertung der Leiche:	Profits from rational utilization of corpse:
1. Zahngold 3. Wertsachen	1. Gold teeth 3. Articles of value
2. Kleidung 4. Geld	2. Clothing 4. Money
abzüglich Verbrennungskosten RM 2,–	Minus costs of cremation RM 2.00
durchschnittlicher Nettogewinn RM 200,–	Average net profit RM 200.00
Gesamtgewinn nach 9 Monaten RM 1631,–	Total profit after 9 months RM 1631.00
zuzüglich Erlös aus Knochen und Aschenverwertung.	This estimate does not include profits from [sale of] bones and ashes.

deportation of Jews to special camps where they were to be most expeditiously and economically put to death.

The mass murder of Jewry was carried out with the precision which had always been the special pride of Germans. It was murder refined in an industrial, technological age, with bureaucratic procedures, careful accounting, a complex transport system, and maximum use of the human by-products. In 1940–1941 a number of new concentration camps were constructed, among them several designated as "extermination camps," which were in fact giant slaughterhouses. The largest of those was at Auschwitz, in the industrial region of Silesia; there were four others, all on the territory of what had been Poland.

Shortly after the Wannsee conference, special detachments of the SS began to round up Jews for what was euphemistically called "evacuation." The victims were merely told they were being shipped to points east, where they would be relocated and suitably employed. The shipment was done in cattle cars, into which the Jews were herded without food or water. Many died in transit. Upon reaching their destination the "transport" was at once divided in two parts. One group, consisting of able-bodied men and women, was sent to production centers to perform heavy labor on substandard food rations. The intention was literally to work them to death. When they collapsed from exhaustion, malnutrition, or disease, they were returned to the extermination camp for slaughter. The other group, that judged unsuited for work—it included all children and elderly—was sent directly to the gas chambers. To lull suspicion these chambers were disguised as shower rooms. The victims were told to undress and wash. As soon as they had filled the purported shower room and the guards had bolted the doors, poison gas was injected. For 15 or 20 minutes the condemned would choke amid inhuman struggles and shrieks. Once silence descended, the doors were unlocked and detachments of prisoners removed the corpses to search them for hidden valuables and to remove gold tooth fillings. Finally, the remains were cremated.

The operation was carried out with such efficiency that at Auschwitz alone 10,000 persons could be disposed of without trace each day. At this camp 2.5

The SS bureaucracy worked out this table (translated, right) as a model for profitable, organized murder of slave labor.

Victims of starvation at Gusen, a Nazi concentration camp in Austria, photographed after the camp was liberated by Allied troops in the last month of the war.

million persons, nearly all Jews, perished from gas poisoning, and an additional half million died from malnutrition and torture. To break the monotony of the daily slaughter, the Nazis invented ever-fresh methods of inflicting pain and humiliation. Only a diseased mind could even conceive of the variety of sufferings that the perverts of the SS devised for its innocent and helpless victims.

On Russian territory the Nazis did not bother to establish extermination camps. There, detachments of the SS, operating with the assistance of Ukrainian or other auxiliaries, rounded up the Jewish inhabitants in towns and villages, herded them into a nearby ravine or forest, and mowed them down with machine guns. Outside large cities giant pits were dug; the victims, lined up at the edge and shot, fell directly into their mass graves. In Kiev alone over 30,000 Jews were massacred in such a manner in a single day. The German army occasionally protested against these slaughters as dishonoring its name, but by and large it either turned its back on them, or, if required, lent a willing hand.

Between 1941 and 1945 the Germans killed an estimated 6 million Jews, a quarter of them children. This crime has no precedent in human history. Every period has had its massacres, and every nation has been guilty at some time of spilling innocent blood. But never before had a whole ethnic or racial group been condemned to die, for no reason and without possibility of reprieve, and the sentence carried out in so meticulous and cold-blooded a manner. Little was done to rescue those destined to die, and in the United States and Great Britain there was even a tendency to discount news of the massacres which was leaking out of occupied Europe. There were only a few honorable exceptions to the prevailing indifference. The Danes, having gotten wind of the deportation orders, ferried most Danish Jews to neutral Sweden. In Hungary, Horthy stanchly refused to condone deportation proceedings, and by his dilatory tactics saved the lives of some 200,000 Jews; another 200,000 perished in 1944, after the Germans had occupied Hungary. The Bulgarians resisted to the end German pressures to hand over their Jews to the SS, and so, in large measure, did the Italians.

It has been estimated that some 50,000 persons directly participated in the Jewish slaughters. After the war only a fraction of these was ever brought to trial, and only some 500 executed. Most of the remainder quietly slipped back into civilian life in Germany and Austria.

In addition to the Jews, other groups were subjected to mass murder. Three million Russian prisoners of war never returned home. A program of mercy-killing of demented and incurably sick persons, including Germans, claimed over 70,000 victims before it was restrained in 1941. Countless partisans were shot in Poland, Yugoslavia, and other parts of German-occupied Europe.

The Germans intended by this insane terror to assure their hold on the Continent and lay the foundations of a new Germanic civilization.

Upon its entry into the war the United States confronted two major decisions: whether to assign priority to the defeat of Japan or of Germany, and how to define its war aims.

The Grand Alliance

The first of these two issues was taken up during joint American and British staff talks held in early 1942. Here it was decided to recommend that priority be given to the European theater. Germany was by far the most powerful of the Axis partners, and if allowed to consolidate its hold on the Continent could transform it into a fortress that no subsequent effort would be able to reduce. Japan, on the other hand, was considered unable to withstand for long an Allied assault, once Germany was defeated. This decision was undoubtedly a correct one, as subsequent events demonstrated.

The second question was resolved in a manner that has since aroused much controversy. At a conference held in Casablanca in January, 1943, Roosevelt and Churchill agreed to pursue the war until the unconditional surrender of Germany and Japan. A few months later Stalin endorsed this declaration. The demand for unconditional surrender has been criticized on the grounds that it disheartened anti-Hitler opposition in Germany and needlessly prolonged the war. However, it is difficult to see how the Allies could have done otherwise. The alliance that the Western democracies had struck with the Soviet Union, Hitler's recent ally, was highly artificial, and there was a real danger that it would fall apart. Had the door been left open to a negotiated peace, Hitler would have gained the opportunity (on which he counted) of sowing suspicion among his enemies and dividing them. The unconditional surrender formula, which committed the three Axis powers to fight to the end, eliminated that opportunity and undoubtedly cemented the fragile anti-Axis partnership.

The immediate task of the Western powers was to bring relief to the hard-pressed Russians. Stalin wanted them to open at once a "second front" to divert German forces, but this was clearly impossible for some time to come. Britain and the United States were only beginning to build up their armies, and lacked the forces with which to assault the heavily fortified Atlantic shores of Nazi

An Allied convoy on the "Murmansk Run," delivering arms to Russia, under attack by German bombers in September of 1942.

Europe. Stalin, who had little understanding of amphibious operations, found these explanations lame, and never ceased to suspect that his allies were deliberately delaying the second front to bleed Russia. It was only natural for him to think so, for this is very likely what he would have done—indeed, what he did do in 1939–1941—when in a similar position. His morbid distrust was merely a counterpart of his infinite duplicity.

For more than two years after the Nazi attack on the Soviet Union, the Western Allies could only help the Russians indirectly, by delivering war supplies and by attacking and destroying from the air the German war potential.

The greatest contribution the United States could make to the Allied cause was to put to military use its vast industrial plant. This was done immediately upon America's entry into the war. President Roosevelt pledged to make his country "the arsenal of democracy," and American production of armaments indeed grew at a staggering rate. One year after Pearl Harbor it equaled that of Germany, Italy, and Japan put together, and by 1944 it was double that. An important share of this output went to the Soviet Union in the form of Lend-Lease. During World War II Russia received from the United States over 400,000 trucks, 12,000 tanks, 14,000 planes, and an immense quantity of other goods, totaling 17.5 million tons. The motorized equipment was of particular value to the Red Army, putting it for the first time on wheels, and enabling it to mount large-scale offensive operations. In the later stages of the war, thanks in part to

Lend-Lease, the Russians enjoyed a pronounced superiority in matériel over the Germans.

While vastly increasing their own war productivity the Western Allies made a determined effort to reduce by means of aerial bombardment that of Germany. Strategic bombers carried out intensive raids on German industrial and urban centers, gutting large areas of the country. In May, 1942, the British carried out the first 1,000-bomber "saturation raid," against Cologne. In the spring of 1943 the Ruhr was heavily struck. In July, 1943, a series of incendiary raids leveled Hamburg. By and large the strategic bombing effort suffered from lack of consistent purpose, indiscriminate bombing of cities alternating with precision attacks on selected industries. By dispersing their plants the Germans managed to maintain high levels of productivity, at any rate until the summer of 1944.

Naval operations, carried out jointly by American and British forces, were a vital episode in the Second World War, as they had been in the First. Fortunately for the Allies, the Nazis began large-scale constructions of submarines late in the war (Hitler had little confidence in naval warfare) and they never had enough of them. Nazi submarines achieved their greatest successes in 1942, when they sank over 8 million tons of shipping. To fight them the Allies began to employ with excellent results small aircraft carriers and radar-equipped long-range bombers capable of spotting submarines at night and in cloudy weather. Early in 1943 Allied aircraft were destroying submarines at such a rate that in May the Germans had to withdraw them from the Atlantic. The "snorkel" device, which permitted the submarines to remain submerged for long periods and thus to escape detection from the air, came too late to affect the outcome. By the spring of 1943 the Allies had conclusively won the Battle of the Atlantic.

The Axis Powers Rolled Back

The second half of 1942 proved to be the decisive period of the war as far as land operations were concerned. Until then the initiative had lain in the hands of the Axis powers; now it passed into those of the Allies. Between June, 1942, and January, 1943, the United States, Great Britain, and Russia each in turn dealt the enemy a crushing defeat. The three decisive battles, in chronological order, were Midway, El Alamein, and Stalingrad.

In the spring of 1942 the Japanese controlled an enormous empire with a diameter of some 5,000 miles, a population of 450 million, and a self-supporting economy. Out of this territory they sought to create a community of interest, an empire to which they gave the catchy name of "Greater Asian Co-prosperity Sphere." Under the slogan "Asia for the Asians," they made a strong appeal to anti-European national and racial sentiments. They liquidated the old imperial administrations and replaced them with puppet governments staffed by native nationalists. The elements that collaborated with them provided the cadres from which, after the war, came the leadership of the anti-Western nationalist movements in this part of the world.

Having achieved their immediate objectives, the Japanese were anxious to assure the maximum security for their empire. Their predicament was not unlike that which had confronted Hitler after the fall of France: they too had to keep on moving and expanding while the odds were in their favor. They now decided to seize control of the eastern Pacific so as to deprive the United States of naval

Combat half a world apart: at right, British infantry seize a crewman of a disabled German tank at the Battle of El Alamein in North Africa. Opposite, a Japanese kamikaze (suicide) plane attempts to crash a U.S. carrier near the Philippines in January of 1945. It missed.

bases, and to sever its sea route to Australia. To this purpose they assembled in late May, 1942, a great fleet, including four of their six large, modern aircraft carriers. The mission of this task force was to lure what was left of the U.S. Pacific Fleet into combat, destroy it, and occupy the Aleutians and Midway.

The American commander, Admiral Chester Nimitz, had at his disposal a much smaller force, but he did have a unique weapon: knowledge of Japanese naval codes which enabled him to know enemy dispositions and intentions. In the first week of June the two fleets clashed in the vicinity of Midway in what turned out to be one of the decisive naval battles of history. It was a new kind of naval warfare, for the ships never fired at each other; fighting was done entirely by carrier-based bombers and torpedo planes. American pilots won a striking victory, sinking all four of the Japanese carriers. The United States lost one carrier, but it had four remaining and thirteen under construction, whereas Japan lagged hopelessly in the naval construction race. At Midway Japan lost air superiority over the Pacific, and in effect naval superiority as well. In August, 1942, an American force attacked and seized Guadalcanal. From there, under the brilliant leadership of General Douglas MacArthur and Admiral Nimitz, the Allies started the process of "island hopping" toward Japan. The Japanese henceforth went over to the defensive.

The British scored their victory in North Africa. Fighting in Africa had begun in the fall of 1940 with an Italian attempt to seize British possessions, Egypt,

496   WORLD WAR II

and the Suez Canal. British imperial forces soon repelled it, and in turn invaded Italian colonies. The Germans once more had to come to the aid of their embattled allies, dispatching there an élite "Afrika Korps" under Erwin Rommel, one of their ablest generals. In the spring of 1942 Rommel launched an all-out offensive on Egypt. The Italo-German force reached El Alamein, within 60 miles of Alexandria, where it was thrown back (October, 1942) by a British army under General Bernard Montgomery. The invaders were driven headlong into Libya. At this point another Allied force, containing large American contingents, landed in their rear in Algeria and Morocco. After six months of fighting, the Axis North African army capitulated: the Allies took a quarter of a million German and Italian prisoners (May, 1943). The southern flank of Hitler's Europe now lay exposed.

The most portentous of the three battles waged in late 1942 took place at Stalingrad. The importance of Stalingrad was not so much strategic as psychological. As at Verdun in 1916, the two sides decided here to make their supreme contest of will. After they were beaten, many Germans for the first time realized that the war was lost.

In the spring of 1942, when operations on the Russian front resumed, the Germans were in a favorable position. They controlled the principal industrial and agrarian regions of the Soviet Union. They had suffered less than a million casualties, while inflicting 4.5 million casualties on the Red Army. They also were entrenched in the close proximity of Russia's two major cities, Moscow and Leningrad.

In making strategic plans for 1942 Hitler decided once more to postpone the capture of Moscow, and to concentrate instead on seizing the Caucasus, where lay Russia's richest oil deposits. The spring campaign began well, and advance German units planted the Nazi flag on the Elbrus, the highest mountain of the Caucasian range. But they failed to reach the oil-producing areas, and worst of all, they could not reduce Stalingrad, whose capture Hitler had demanded. The more troops they sent against it, the more troops the Russians committed to its defense.° The fighting grew steadily in intensity and in the fall developed into a major battle. In house-to-house fighting, troops of the German Sixth Army conquered nine-tenths of the gutted town, but the Russians held on to what was left. Both sides fought with incredible heroism.

Suddenly, on November 19–20, the Russians launched a powerful counterattack, breaking through the Hungarian, Romanian, and Italian units guarding the flanks of the Sixth Army. The German generals pleaded with Hitler for permission to stage a breakout from the trap while there was still time, but Hitler insisted that the troops hold on to every inch of gained ground. Outnumbered, freezing, so short of food that some of them resorted to cannibalism, the Germans held out for two months. Then, at the end of January, 1943, the Sixth Army surrendered. The Russians captured 91,000 prisoners, 1,500 tanks, and 60,000 vehicles. In Germany the news of the surrender was met with three days of national mourning. To straighten out the front after the loss of the Sixth Army, the *Wehrmacht* had to retreat, giving up most of the ground conquered the preceding spring.

Hitler's reaction to the Stalingrad disaster was to proclaim "total war." The German economy, until then relatively unregulated, was fully centralized under the Minister of Armaments and Munitions, Albert Speer. With his efficient and ruthless management, Speer increased armament productivity by one-half in five months. Forced labor was impressed from conquered territories, and concentration camp inmates were mobilized. At the height of the war Speer had at his disposal between 7 and 9 million slave laborers. "Defeatism," which spread in Germany, was pitilessly prosecuted. Germans accused of it were hauled before "People's Courts" and usually shot, following a perfunctory trial.

After Midway, El Alamein, and Stalingrad, the issue could no longer be in doubt. The days of blitzkrieg were over, and the Axis powers had to brace themselves for a war of attrition that they could not possibly win. As Churchill put it cautiously in a speech delivered in November, 1942, the world was witnessing "not the end, not even the beginning of the end, but possibly the end of the beginning."

Victory   Hitler, however, meant to hold out to the last. He counted partly on Allied disagreements and partly on a new secret weapon, a ballistic rocket known as the V-2, which his engineers were developing under highest priority; the first of these were sent against London in September, 1944, causing severe damage and

---

°For Stalin, Stalingrad had a personal significance. The city was named for him because in 1919 he had played an active part in directing its successful defense against the Whites.

greatly demoralizing the war-weary population. But if he had to lose, Hitler was determined all Europe would go down with him.

On the eastern front the Germans undertook in July, 1943, one more major offensive to boost their sagging spirits. They sent 17 armored divisions against the Russian defenses in the Kursk area, with the intention of executing a pincer movement. But by now the Russians were familiar with blitzkrieg tactics. In the greatest tank battle in history they repulsed the attack, after which they pushed the *Wehrmacht* back two hundred miles. The best the Germans could henceforth hope for was simply to hold in the East. The Russians had twice the manpower, and two to three times the weapons and equipment, including tanks and planes. Wherever the Germans were forced to retreat, they looted that which was movable and dynamited or set on fire what was left, including ancient churches and historic monuments.

The Western Allies in 1943 adhered to the strategy advocated by the British and concentrated on the Mediterranean, the "soft under belly" of Nazi Europe. In July they sent an invasion force from North Africa to Sicily. Italian armies offered only token resistance. A few days after the invasion a bloodless coup in Rome overthrew the Fascist regime, and the new government immediately opened negotiations with the Allies. The Germans reacted by sending troops into Italy to prevent it from falling into Allied hands. After the arrival of the Germans, the Allies had great difficulty making further progress, partly because the terrain favored the defenders, partly because their leadership was poor and indecisive. It took them a whole year to reach Rome.

The main preparations of the Western Allies in 1943–1944 went into "Over-

The Anglo-American invasion of Normandy in June, 1944: American troops wade ashore from a landing craft at Omaha Beach, the most heavily contested of the D-Day landing sites.

lord," the projected cross-Channel invasion of France. The difficulties and risks attendant on such an operation were enormous. In anticipation of the landings the Germans had withdrawn from Russia some of their best units, assembling along the Atlantic shores 60 divisions, 11 of them armored. The Allies could throw against them in the first critical day of the invasion only 7 divisions: to bring such an army across the Channel required no fewer than 5,000 ships and 12,000 planes. Unless a solid beachhead was secured in the first few hours to permit the landing of reinforcements, the Germans could concentrate an overwhelming force at the landing point and throw the invaders back into the sea. Everything therefore depended on the strength and speed of the initial blow.

The Allied strategic plan was worked out by General Montgomery, who had been placed in charge of the invasion forces under General Dwight D. Eisenhower, the Supreme Commander of the Allied forces. His proposal was for a British force to establish a beachhead near Caen in Normandy, with the purpose of attracting to itself the main German counterattack. While the British held the ground, the Americans, who were to land nearby, were to make an end run, swinging around the Germans and heading straight for Paris.

German preparations for the invasion were hampered by disagreements and miscalculations. Whereas the generals wanted to place the main defense forces in northern France, Hitler insisted on protecting the whole length of the Atlantic coast. As a result, German units were thinly dispersed. Furthermore, the *Wehrmacht* was so certain the Allies would land their main army at Calais that it concentrated there its own main force, leaving Normandy relatively unprotected.

"D-Day" came on June 6, 1944. Despite some errors in navigation, which placed American units off course, beachheads were established and held. In the course of the first day 156,000 men were landed, some from the sea, others from the air. With remarkable speed Allied engineers constructed off the beachhead two artificial ports, known by their code name "mulberries," through which poured an endless stream of men and supplies. One week after D-Day the Allies had more troops in France than did the Germans. They also enjoyed complete mastery of the air. In late July the American forces broke through German defenses and made a dash for Paris, which they took a month later.

At this point some generals wanted to make a direct drive on a narrow front for the heart of Germany, but General Eisenhower decided on a slower, more cautious strategy involving a steady sweep through France along a broad front. There is reason to believe that this strategy gave the Germans time to fortify their frontier and needlessly prolonged the war.

After D-Day the Allied air forces could concentrate all their resources on the destruction of Germany. In a few months the bombers reduced substantially the still formidable German industrial plant: from the summer of 1944 on, German industry could no longer meet the requirements of the military. Particularly damaging were the raids on oil installations: they reduced oil production to the point where many German planes, tanks, and trucks could not operate for lack of fuel. Saturation raids against cities also continued at full force. An incendiary attack on Dresden in February, 1945, killed an estimated 135,000 persons.

In July, 1944, a group of anti-Hitler conspirators attempted to assassinate the Führer and enter into negotiations with the Allies. Involved in the plot were

VICTORY IN EUROPE
1943-1945

Allied powers

Axis powers

Axis allies

Neutral countries

Areas occupied by Germany

Allied lines of invasion

German front, Nov., 1942

Allied front, Dec., 1944

Allied front, May, 1945

ATLANTIC OCEAN

IRELAND

UNITED KINGDOM

London

NORTH SEA

NORWAY

Oslo

SWEDEN

Stockholm

BALTIC SEA

FINLAND

Helsinki

Leningrad

U.S.S.R.

Moscow

DENMARK

Copenhagen

ESTONIA

LATVIA

Riga

LITHUANIA

Memel

Smolensk

EAST PRUSSIA

Danzig

Minsk

Kursk

Calais

Hamburg

NETH.

Antwerp

Cologne

BEL.

LUX.

Berlin

Posen

Warsaw

Brest Litovsk

Stalingrad

Caen

Paris

GERMANY

Dresden

POLAND

Kiev

Orleans

Prague

CZECHOSLOVAKIA

FRANCE

Munich

Vienna

AUSTRIA

Rostov

SWITZ.

HUNGARY

Budapest

ROMANIA

Odessa

Marseille

Toulon

ITALY

YUGOSLAVIA

Ploesti

Bucharest

Sebastopol

BLACK SEA

SPAIN

CORSICA

Rome

Anzio

Belgrade

BULGARIA

Sofia

Madrid

SARDINIA

Naples

Salerno

ALBANIA

Istanbul

Ankara

TURKEY

Palermo

SICILY

GREECE

Oran

Algiers

Bizerte

Tunis

Athens

CYPRUS

SYRIA

IRAQ

ALGERIA

MEDITERRANEAN SEA

CRETE

LEB.

PALESTINE

TRANS-JORDAN

SAUDI-ARABIA

TUNISIA

Tripoli

Tobruk

Alexandria

El Alamein

EGYPT

LIBYA

conservative statesmen and high army officers, who had become convinced Hitler would bring about the total destruction of Germany. A briefcase containing a powerful bomb was placed in Hitler's headquarters. It exploded, but failed to kill Hitler. The Gestapo quickly rounded up and executed the conspirators. For Hitler's private enjoyment, moving pictures of the ringleaders were taken while they were being strangled to death, suspended from meat hooks.

In April, 1945, with the Russians, Americans, and British converging on Berlin, Hitler decided to commit suicide. Germany, he declared, having lost a unique chance at world mastery under his leadership, did not deserve any better lot than that which it now had in store: enslavement by the subhuman Russians and decadent Anglo-Saxons. In the same month, Mussolini, seeking to escape to Switzerland, was caught by a band of Italian partisans and shot. On May 7 a delegation of German generals appeared at General Eisenhower's headquarters and signed a surrender act.

The war in Europe over, the United States and Britain could now turn their undivided attention to the Pacific front. At the time of Germany's capitulation, American troops, having seized Iwo Jima and Okinawa, were at Japan's doorstep. The Allied command wildly overestimated the Japanese willingness and capacity to fight. It was thought, on the basis of the experience gained in reducing Japanese-held island fortresses, that an invasion and occupation of Japan would cost a million casualties. In fact, however, the Japanese in the spring of 1945 were desperately seeking a way out of the war, and were putting out in vain a succession of peace feelers. One of these, sent through the Soviet Union (then still at peace with Japan), Stalin never saw fit to forward to Washington.

This gross miscalculation explains the Allied political and military strategy in defeating Japan. Great pressure was exerted on Stalin to secure Russia's entry into the Pacific war, although no pressure was necessary, Stalin being most eager

Dresden was crowded with refugees fleeing the advancing Russians when some 900 British and American planes fire-bombed it in February, 1945. The dead are shown being collected for cremation pyres in the streets.

WALTER HAHN, DRESDEN

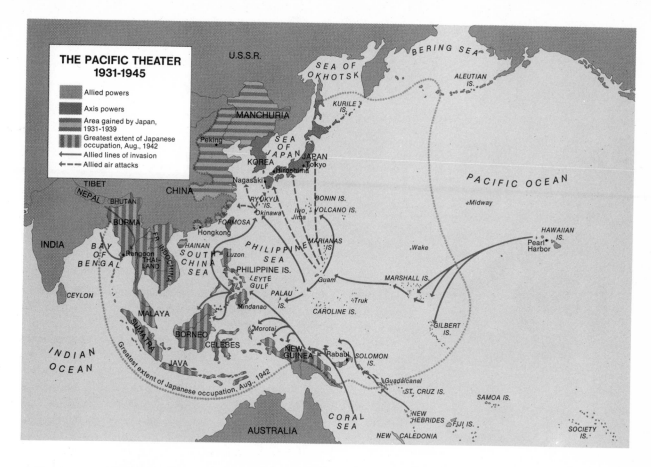

THE PACIFIC THEATER
1931-1945

Allied powers

Axis powers

Area gained by Japan, 1931-1939

Greatest extent of Japanese occupation, Aug., 1942

Allied lines of invasion

Allied air attacks

to do so anyway in order to profit from the collapse of the Japanese Empire. Furthermore, it was decided, after considerable deliberation, to subject Japan to bombardment by a new weapon, the atomic bomb. Work on this bomb had been carried out in utmost secrecy since 1942, when a group of physicists had set off in a laboratory a nuclear chain reaction. At first the possibility of dropping the bomb in an unpopulated place was considered, but uncertainty whether or not the bomb would go off induced President Truman to order its use against Japanese cities. In August, 1945, the two atomic bombs in the American arsenal were dropped, one on Hiroshima, the other on Nagasaki, causing 75,000 and 39,000 casualties respectively. Between these two atomic raids the Soviet Union declared war on Japan, occupying virtually without resistance Manchuria and Korea. Shortly afterward, Japan capitulated. A survey conducted after the war showed that Japan would have surrendered before the end of the year without an invasion, without the atomic bombs, and without Russia's entry.

The grim balance of World War II was 55 million dead, half of them civilians. Europe lay in rubble, many of its great cities leveled to the ground, its wealth and influence gone.

The War in Russia

NOVOSTI

I t was autumn, 1941, and the German panzer columns (right) were sweeping eastward along a 1,500-mile front, unchecked even by the first snows. Russian author Boris Pasternak was moved to write:

> Do you remember that dryness in your throat
> When rattling their naked power of evil
> They were barging ahead and bellowing
> And autumn was advancing in steps of calamity?

The Soviet Union was reeling under the onslaught of blitzkrieg, and as far as Adolf Hitler or the Western allies were concerned, it seemed on the verge of total disintegration.

Yet this was to underestimate the historic capacity of the Russian people to endure. For four years, while the greatest land war in history raged about them, they suffered brutality, starvation, and devastation. They met repeated defeat, yet they were never beaten. In time the war in Russia became "the Great Patriotic War," nurtured on ideals supposedly done to death by the Revolution. Officers led their men into battle (left) invoking images of 1812, of the great heroes of the Romanov epoch, of "Mother Russia."

On July 3, 1941, almost a fortnight after the German assault began, Joseph Stalin delivered his first wartime broadcast to the Russian people. In this historic speech, un-Stalinlike in its warmth (never before had he addressed the people as his "friends," his "brothers and sisters"), the Premier laid down the rules for total war. Above all, Stalin said, this was a "life-and-death struggle" against an enemy who meant to "destroy the national culture of the peoples of the Soviet Union. . . . The Red Army and Navy must fight for every inch of Soviet soil, fight to the last drop of blood. . . . All enterprises must intensify their work and produce more and more. . . ." There would be partisan war in the occupied areas "where intolerable conditions must be created for the enemy and his accomplices." Finally, there would be a scorched-earth campaign. "The enemy must not be left a single engine . . . , not a pound of bread nor a pint of oil. . . . All valuable property . . . which cannot be evacuated, must be destroyed."

Only last-ditch resistance outside Moscow and Leningrad, where they willingly traded lives at the rate of four to one, saved the Russians in 1941. Disaster threatened once again the next summer when the Germans resumed their offensive, this time angling southward toward Stalingrad and the oil-rich Caucasus. Hitler had predicted that in six weeks "the whole rotten structure will come crashing down." Fourteen months later his *Wehrmacht* and the Red Army were locked together in a death struggle at Stalingrad.

Stalin's collaboration with Hitler provoked a flood of intensely critical comment from foreign political cartoonists. England's David Low was struck by the cynical, even ludicrous, aspects of a deal between arch ideological enemies (right). Suggesting, as did a number of others, that Stalin was the dominant figure in the pact, a French commentator (opposite) saw Goering and Hitler—"Now you will pay us, eh?"—as whores nuzzling the Premier.

Depicting Europe under the pall of the combined visage of Stalin and Hitler (right), an American newspaper correctly forecast the events of 1939 and 1940, beginning with the joint dismemberment of Poland. Above, a Dutch cartoonist has Hitler and his henchmen (from the left, Goebbels, Ribbentrop, and Goering) dancing to a Russian tune.

Yesterday's Enemies

The Soviet-German nonaggression pact, signed in Moscow on August 23, 1939—even as an Anglo-French military mission was feebly promoting its own defense treaty a few blocks away—left the Western powers shaken and dismayed over what seemed a strange and cynical partnership. Moscow entered a *rapprochement* with Berlin anticipating a protracted, crippling war between the Axis and the Allies. It provided welcome breathing space when both Germany and Japan stood poised at the Soviet borders. Moreover, a secret protocol in the pact gave the Russians an equal share in carving out certain "spheres of interest" in Eastern Europe. As Foreign Commissar V. M. Molotov smugly observed on August 31, the day before Germany invaded Poland, "The political art in foreign affairs . . . is to reduce the enemies of one's country, and to turn yesterday's enemies into good neighbors."

Sixteen months after the start of the Soviet-German honeymoon, Hitler put his General Staff to planning Operation Barbarossa, the invasion of Russia. Every sign indicated it was coming. Yet Stalin chose to ignore warnings from Churchill and his own highly detailed intelligence reports. Shortly after midnight on June 22, 1941, a trainload of Russian wheat crossed the border into Germany in accordance with trade agreements concluded shortly after the nonaggression pact. At 3:15 A.M. 3 million German troops started into Russia.

Blitzkrieg

Ill-equipped and ill-commanded, Russia's soldiers and airmen paid a ghastly price on June 22. Battalions, regiments, whole divisions simply melted away under the shock of the German assault. "We are being fired on. What shall we do?" a beleaguered unit radioed. From headquarters came the reply. "You must be insane. And why is your signal not in code?" In some of the defensive positions no one had bothered to issue ammunition. Air force losses ran to better than 130 planes an hour.

Day after day the rout continued, with three great German army groups bearing down on the Ukraine, Moscow, and Leningrad. By mid-July the lightning thrusts of the German armor had carried it across the Dnieper, a leap of some 400 miles. Fresh reserves from Siberia were rushed in to counterattack, only to be sucked into the cauldron. Two entire Russian armies were encircled and destroyed at Smolensk on the road to Moscow and at Kiev in the Ukraine, the Germans collecting over 600,000 prisoners in the latter engagement. The low ebb came in early October when the Germans launched their decisive attack on Moscow. Briefly there was panic and "unauthorized withdrawals" of the Red Army. Party cards were burned in preparation for the occupation. But the Russians hung on through November and December, until the panzers bogged down in the cold and snow.

Villages put to the torch, groups of dazed peasants fleeing eastward, prisoners carried hundreds of miles in open freight cars to slave labor camps—this was blitzkrieg as recorded by German photographers in the summer and autumn of 1941. Opposite, a German antitank gun crew whoops in triumph after knocking out a Red Army tank. By the end of September the Germans had taken a toll of 2.5 million men, 22,000 guns, 18,000 tanks, and 14,000 planes. Still, the Russians kept on fighting. "There was resistance, always resistance, however hopeless," a German commented at the time. "A single gun, a group of men with rifles, a chap by the roadside with a grenade. . . ."

The New Order

At first parts of the Ukraine and Russia's newly acquired Baltic states welcomed the Germans with open arms. Smiling Ukrainian girls presented their liberators with food (above) and politicians, temporarily relieved of the Stalinist yoke, began planning nationalist governments.

For the conquered East, however, the Nazis specified a so-called New Order, based on unremitting exploitation of human and natural resources and the extermination of "undesirables." Nowhere was that special instrument of the Nazi regime—organized terror—applied with greater intensity. Slavs and Jews were *untermensch*, subhuman. A Nazi bureaucrat pronounced the official line: "The Slavs are to work for us. In so far as we don't need them, they may die. . . ." The best policy for the Ukraine, Hermann Goering declared, was "to kill all the men . . . and then to send in the SS stallions."

The Nazis wasted no time putting the New Order into effect. On the last two days of September, 1941, tens of thousands of Jews were killed at Babi Yar near Kiev. The scene at the right was repeated time and again in the Ukraine and White Russia, where roving SS squads massacred whole villages. Ultimately 3 million persons, mostly youths, were shipped to Germany as slave labor. In doing so, however, the New Order succeeded in spawning a formidable resistance movement.

510

A horse-drawn column of partisans, equipped with captured German weapons, returns from a raid in the Ukraine in 1941. In one four-month period the partizany wrecked a thousand German trains.

Mobilizing for Total War

Violence begat violence. Before long, propagandist Ilya Ehrenburg was inciting the Russian people to a vengeful crusade: "Let us not speak. Let us not be indignant. Let us kill. . . . If you have killed one German, kill another. There is nothing jollier than German corpses." The mood reached even into the intellectual community, culminating in the brutal chords of Shostakovich's *Leningrad Symphony* and in two of wartime Russia's popular poems, "Kill Him!" and "I Hate."

Stalin rapidly overhauled the Soviet military machine. The political warhorses were relieved of their commands (or shot for "treasonable activities") and replaced with such skilled officers as Vasili Chuikov and Georgi Zhukov, and even with some who had been in prison since the army purges of the late thirties. Drawing on seemingly limitless reserves, the Red Army mobilized a million men within a month of the invasion.

The evacuation of industry to the Urals and Siberia, one of the extraordinary feats of World War II, began at the same time. Steel mills, stamping plants, aircraft and tank factories were dismantled en masse and later reassembled at remote spots far to the east. In August of 1941, for example, one of the Soviet Union's largest tube-rolling mills was stripped down and shipped eastward in tens of thousands of boxcars. It was back in production in slightly over four months.

No person, no institution escaped service. Stalin "revived" the moribund Orthodox Church as a spur to patriotism, creating a government post jocularly known as the People's Commissar for God. Women by the thousands dug new coal mines to replace those lost in the Ukraine. Wives and daughters took over the nation's farms; lacking horses and tractors they often used cows as draft animals. Anticipating a long war, Stalin established a fertility prize, the Order of Motherly Glory, for those who bore more than seven children.

Reflecting and no doubt intensifying the national purpose, Soviet propaganda stressed the evil of the enemy and the need to destroy him rather than vague appeals to patriotism. An early example is the poster at right; the poster above, in which Hitler is greeted by the grim visage of defeat, appeared in 1943 as the tide was turning at Stalingrad. Below, models of the excellent T-34 medium tank take form on an assembly line east of the Urals. The Russian army and air force suffered terrible privations until the new factories and Lend-Lease shipments from Britain and America reached full stride in 1943. By the end of that year Soviet war plants were turning out tanks at the rate of over 2,000 a month.

Civilians dug hundreds of miles of trenches and tank traps around Leningrad. The inner perimeter, defended by troops under Marshal Zhukov, was never breached.

A dead child, a victim of the famine or the cold or the bombs, is borne by its parents to one of the common graves hastily prepared during the siege of Leningrad.

With the city's utilities smashed, women began drawing water from broken mains in the streets. Despite the hopeless outlook, looting and suicide—the symptoms of complete breakdown—never took hold.

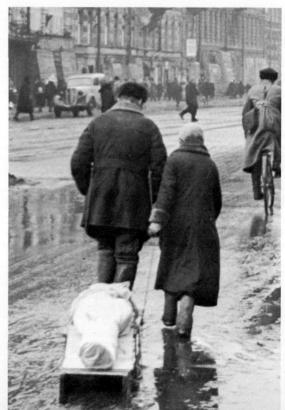

A People Besieged

Failing to take Leningrad by storm, the Germans determined to "hermetically seal" the city and starve it to death. When the noose tightened in September of 1941, three million people were trapped with about a month's supply of food. When the snows came people began consuming stray pets, hair oil, and homemade brews of furniture glue and wallpaper paste. At the height of the starving time deaths averaged between 3,500 and 4,000 a day. Men and women walking to makeshift factories collapsed and died in the streets, others went to sleep in the chill gloom of their homes and never awoke. Constant shelling and bombing (below) compounded the strain, but the city's nerve never broke. A factory official told British correspondent Alexander Werth of the will to resist: ". . . one day in December, in twenty degrees of frost, we had all our windows blown out by a bomb, and I thought to myself: 'No, we really can't go on. . . .' And yet, somehow—we didn't stop. A kind of instinct told us we mustn't—that it would be worse than suicide, and a little like treason." Finally, the Russians established a supply route across the ice of Lake Ladoga, the famous Ladoga Lifeline, but the siege was to last until January, 1944—over twenty-seven months in all—in which time an estimated one million Leningraders perished.

War of Attrition

Stalingrad: the name, like Verdun, stands for all of the horrors of war, for the ghastly expenditure of men and equipment, for the grave of an army. Here, from the end of August, 1942, until the following February, the armies flailed at each other in sewers, cellars, and bombed-out houses and factories. And always, as the opposing generals sought the decisive blow, the soldiers responded to their call for "one last heave." For the Germans, who had already lost one and a half million men in Russia, defeat in this place was the beginning of the end. In his diary an officer of the doomed German Sixth Army described the nether world of Stalingrad:

"We have fought during fifteen days for a single house, with mortars, grenades, machine guns and bayonets. Already by the third day fifty-four German corpses are strewn in the cellars, on the landings, and the staircases. . . .From story to story, faces black with sweat, we bombard each other with grenades in the middle of explosions, clouds of dust and smoke, heaps of mortar, floods of blood, fragments of furniture and human beings. Ask any soldier what half an hour of hand-to-hand struggle means in such a fight. And imagine Stalingrad; eighty days and eighty nights of hand-to-hand struggles. . . .

"Stalingrad is no longer a town. By day it is an enormous cloud of burning, blinding smoke; it is a vast furnace lit by the reflection of the flames. And when night arrives. . .the dogs plunge into the Volga and swim desperately to gain the other bank. The nights of Stalingrad are a terror for them. Animals flee this hell; the hardest stones cannot bear it for long; only men endure."

Laid out on the frozen earth (above), German dead await spring for a proper burial. At left, one of Stalingrad's "scorching, howling, bleeding nights."

The Road Back

Stalingrad was the turning point. Thereafter, except for a few brief detours, the road led inexorably to Berlin. Braced by its monumental victory on the banks of the Volga, and now armed to the teeth with equipment from the Western allies and the factories beyond the Urals, the Red Army was rapidly becoming the most potent ground force in the world. Before long, the Russians could muster 12,000 trucks to supply a single assault and at one point boast a superiority over the Germans of 5.5 times more men, 7.8 times more guns, 5.7 times more tanks, and 17.6 times more planes. In July of 1943, at the Kursk salient southwest of Moscow, this awesome new strength was exhibited: with immense tank formations using adopted panzer tactics and massed artillery (the "queen of battle" in Stalin's view) the Russians utterly annihilated the last great German offensive in the East.

By December of 1943 the Russians had established bridgeheads over the Dnieper and liberated two-thirds of German-occupied territory. Six months later they were across the Dniester and into Poland. Alternating offensives north and south in the last half of 1944, they swept into Romania, Hungary, Latvia, and Lithuania. By February of 1945, two years after Stalingrad, Marshal Zhukov stood poised on the Oder for the final drive to Berlin.

"Avenging Russia is advancing. . ." the poet Alexei Surkov wrote in late 1943, and indeed the Red legions advanced into Germany exacting "bread for bread, blood for blood." Revenge for Kiev, for Leningrad, for the murder camps where uncounted Russian Jews perished drove some of the troops. Others indulged in an orgy of rape and pillage for its own sake. Already a drama of infinitely greater impact had been played out in the "liberated" countries of Eastern Europe, where NKVD squads and special political action groups labored with ruthless efficiency to establish Stalin's own New Order.

"German towns are burning, I am happy," Ilya Ehrenburg announced as Red tank columns (right) ground through the snowy streets of the Reich. Ahead of them a mass of human flotsam fled westward in carts, or clinging to the sides of overloaded trains (left), or simply walking. Benumbed survivors of the Wehrmacht, *represented above in a captured German painting, dug in for the final, overwhelming attack on the Eastern front.*

The Victors

In mid-afternoon of April 30, 1945, after dictating his political testament and having a dose of poison distributed to his new wife, Adolf Hitler sat down on a sofa in the Chancellery *Führerbunker* and took a capsule of cyanide. On the following day, after nearly a week of the bitterest street fighting, a Russian soldier clambered atop the Reichstag and waved the hammer and sickle in a victory salute over the desolation of the Third Reich's capital (opposite). "Today is the first of May, a great holiday for our two nations," a surrendering German officer informed General Chuikov, one of the heroes of Stalingrad and now the conqueror of Berlin. "*We* have a great holiday today," Chuikov replied dryly. "How things are with you over there is less easy to say."

Soon the victory celebrations got underway in Moscow, with thousand-gun salutes; with Stalin praising the "small people, the little screws and bolts" of the invincible Soviet machine; with hundreds of German banners piled on the steps of Lenin's tomb; and, more ominously, with an endless procession of huge Stalin tanks passing in review. Yet no amount of exultation could obscure the scars of this most brutal campaign in history. At least 20 million Russians had lost their lives. Millions more were maimed, countless millions left homeless. A charred wasteland stretched from the Dniester to the Volga, from the Baltic to the Black seas.

Yet Russia had absorbed this frightful toll and emerged from the Great Patriotic War as the strongest power in Europe. It was the Russians who, in Churchill's charitable phrase, "tore the guts out of the German army." This they made manifestly clear during the proceedings at Yalta (above) and Potsdam. Indeed, Stalin's truculent behavior at the war's end gave reason to believe that the Soviets saw themselves as worthy challengers for the position of leading power in the postwar world. Already in the summer of 1945 the first confrontations, the probing tests, were taking place in the rubble of Germany.

19

—◈—

The Cold War

In dealing with international relations after World War II we run into a number of special difficulties. One is the scarcity of evidence. The great powers have so far made public only a fraction of the pertinent documents, so that our interpretation of post-1945 diplomacy must of necessity rest on much guesswork. In the second place, post-1945 events are part of our own time to such an extent that we are unable to view them as dispassionately as those of the more remote past. And, finally, there is a peculiar problem arising from the revolutionary changes that have occurred in the twentieth century in the nature of international relations. In modern times the customary distinction between diplomacy and warfare has become blurred. Since the *Weltpolitik* of Kaiser William II, but especially since the Bolshevik call for world revolution in 1917, international relations have increasingly tended to approximate the condition that Trotsky had defined as "neither war nor peace." The large powers, combined in vast blocs, contend against each other with as great determination as they would in war, using all available means short of direct military confrontation: hostile propaganda, sedition, economic warfare, rivalry over neutral states and outer space. This conflict, which has become a permanent feature of modern life, constitutes the Cold War. It reached the height of intensity during the first decade that followed World War II.

Signs of serious friction between the Soviet Union and the Western Allies manifested themselves while the war was still in progress. At first, during the early months of the Nazi invasion, Stalin showed every intention of accommodating his new allies. But once the Nazi drive on Moscow had been stopped and the United States had entered the war (these events occurred simultaneously, in the first week of December, 1941), his attitude visibly hardened. Unlike President Roosevelt, whose attention was concentrated on winning the war as quickly and expeditiously as possible, Stalin never ceased to think in long-range political terms. As early as January, 1942, he had warned Anthony Eden, the British Foreign Secretary, that after the victory he intended to press for major revisions of East European frontiers. The closer the moment of victory approached and the less Allied help he needed, the more uncooperative Stalin became. The evolution of his attitude can be traced in his wartime correspondence with Roosevelt and Churchill, whose tone, in the words of the historian Herbert Feis, gradually changed "from amiability—to reserve—to bluntness—to bold rudeness."

The Western Allies, and particularly President Roosevelt, were for a long time inclined to overlook Stalin's growing obduracy. They entertained considerable guilt feelings about the Soviet Union, not unlike those that Hitler's appeasers in the 1930s had experienced over Versailles. The record of Western hostility toward communism, and especially the Allied intervention in the Russian Civil War, troubled Roosevelt and some of his associates. They believed

Postwar Western Effort at Cooperation

The major upheaval of the Cold War in Soviet-dominated Eastern Europe took place in Hungary in 1956. Here, jubilant Hungarian "freedom fighters" pass a disabled Russian tank in Budapest; a few days later the reinforced Red Army crushed the revolt.

that by displaying patience and good will they could overcome what was regarded as Soviet Russia's understandable suspicion of the West and gradually draw it into responsible partnership with the United States and Great Britain in maintaining peace. Stalin, who had a totalitarian dictator's uncanny feel for the soft spots in the liberal conscience, fed these illusions. His quick mind and peasant gruffness as well as his democratic professions altogether charmed Roosevelt, who saw in the heroic Russian resistance to the Nazis ultimate proof of Stalin's right to speak for his people. In a radio address delivered on Christmas day, 1944, the President referred to Stalin as "a man who combines a tremendous relentless determination with a stalwart sense of humor." He added his belief that Stalin was "truly representative of the heart and soul of Russia" and that the United States would "get along very well with him and the Russian people—very well indeed."

Churchill had a more realistic estimate of Stalin and his government and no regrets about his role in urging Allied intervention in 1918–1920. But since he was certain that Russia would inevitably dominate postwar Europe, he was content with whatever concessions could be extracted from Stalin. After his plan for a major Allied invasion of the Balkans, intended to seize that area ahead of the Russians, had been vetoed by the United States, he made a secret agreement with Stalin dividing the Balkans into spheres of influence. But in general, his opinion carried less weight and did not vitally influence the major decisions.

Roosevelt, Churchill, and Stalin held during the war two major conferences, partly to coordinate military plans, partly to lay the groundwork for the postwar peace settlement. The first of these took place at Teheran (November, 1943). Here the basic positions were outlined and broad accord was reached on the principles on which peace was to be based. The second conference, held at the Russian resort of Yalta (February, 1945), produced detailed inter-Allied agreement on a number of outstanding issues. The three leaders decided at Yalta to divide Germany into occupation zones, and to take concerted measures against a revival of German militarism. In areas liberated from the enemy, it was agreed to apply the principles of the Atlantic Charter (Chapter 18), guaranteeing "the right of all peoples to choose the form of government under which they will live" by means of free democratic elections.

Stalin, however, was not content with such vague generalities. At Yalta he also demanded and received specific territorial and diplomatic concessions. Of these the most important concerned Poland. Stalin had no intention of giving up that part of Poland which he had secured in 1939 from Hitler. Under his pressure, Roosevelt and Churchill formally acquiesced to Russia incorporating this area, with the understanding that Poland would be compensated in the west at Germany's expense. Stalin, in return, promised "free and unfettered" elections in Poland, in which the leaders of the Polish government-in-exile, resident in London, would participate. In exchange for a promise to enter the war against Japan, Russia also secured territorial gains in East Asia, including a restitution of the "special rights" (i.e., a sphere of influence) that imperial Russia had enjoyed in Manchuria (Chapter 10). The Allies agreed on founding a United Nations Organization to take the place of the moribund League of Nations. In the United Nations Assembly the Soviet Union was promised three votes: one for itself, and one each for its constituent republics, Ukraine and Belorussia.°

Few international agreements have aroused such controversy as those reached at the Yalta Conference, once its secret clauses calling for territorial adjustments in Russia's favor had been revealed. Its critics charge that at Yalta the Western leaders made genuine concessions in return for worthless promises. In particular, they condemn the territorial awards that Roosevelt and Churchill made at Poland's and China's expense without the consent of the governments or peoples of these two Allied countries. Some critics attribute Western behavior to the physical debility of the President (he died three months after Yalta of a brain hemorrhage) and even to treason on the part of some high American officials (one of the members of the United States delegation, Alger Hiss, was indeed later convicted of perjury for denying connections with a Soviet espionage ring).

There is, however, no reason to suspect any foul play. The appeasement of Stalin was inspired by the same combination—an overwhelming desire for peace, an ignorance of history, and a constitutional inability to understand the totalitarian psyche—which a decade earlier had led to the appeasement of Hitler. Given the predisposition in his favor, it was a relatively easy matter for Stalin to extract concessions from the Allies. For, indeed, what was the surrender of some Polish or Chinese territory, or a couple of extra seats in the United Nations Assembly, in return for the Soviet Union's promise of full cooperation in the maintenance of peace?

No wonder the Allied delegations returned from Yalta in a jubilant mood. Harry Hopkins, Roosevelt's closest adviser, described the feelings that he and his colleagues shared at the conclusion of the Yalta negotiations as follows:

> We really believed in our hearts that this was the dawn of a new day we had all been praying for and talking about for so many years. We were absolutely certain that we had won the first great victory of the peace— and by "we" I mean *all* of us, the whole civilized human race. The Russians had proved that they could be reasonable and farseeing and there wasn't any doubt in the minds of the President or of any of us that we could live with them peacefully as far into the future as any of us could imagine.

According to Hopkins, the Western Allies' only worry was whether Stalin's successor would prove to be as "reasonable and sensible and understanding" as he had been. That Stalin, with his record, should have been able to persuade the President of the United States and his staff that he had any of these qualities must surely rank him as one of the greatest diplomats of all time.

As anyone even superficially acquainted with the history of the Communist movement might have anticipated, Stalin had no intention of honoring his Yalta pledges of "free and unfettered elections" in areas conquered by his armies. From the time it had dissolved the Russian Constituent Assembly (Chapter 12), the Communist leadership had never allowed itself to be constrained by respect for democratic institutions which, in its eyes, were merely instruments

The Stalinization of Eastern Europe

°By this arrangement, the Ukraine and Belorussia were and still are in effect represented twice: once through the Soviet delegation, and then again through their own. No other territories or countries enjoy a similar privilege.

of bourgeois exploitation. Stalin had made it very clear in his dealings with Hitler that he regarded Eastern Europe as lying within his sphere of influence. He certainly had no reason to give up, after having won a great victory over the Nazis, that which he had demanded and partly obtained from them in 1939 without losing a man. Stalin was much too realistic not to see that democratic elections would not yield him the majorities that he needed to secure a solid grip over this area. It had to be taken by force. To prepare for this eventuality Stalin formed in Moscow several "Patriotic" or "National Liberation" fronts, staffed with dependable Communists and fellow travelers from Eastern European countries, to serve as instruments for the eventual power seizure. These organizations had been created some time before the Yalta Conference convened.

The methods that Stalin employed in subjugating Eastern Europe closely resembled those that he and Lenin had employed in the course of eliminating internal opposition in Russia. They were later defined by a Hungarian Communist official as "salami tactics." Beginning with the broadest alliance of anti-Fascist parties, Stalin and his subordinates gradually sliced away from governmental power one party after another, until all that remained was its Communist core. This accomplished, Stalin got rid of Communists who had strong local roots and replaced them with those who had made their careers in Moscow. By the early 1950s, when the process was completed, the countries of Eastern Europe had been transformed into miniature versions of the USSR, or, as they came to be known, its "satellites."

The Stalinization of Eastern Europe began while the war was still in progress.

Truman and Stalin and their unruly "children," seen by the cartoonist Walt Kelly in early 1949, a period of tense East-West relations.

As soon as each country had been liberated by the Soviet army, the Moscow-based Fronts were brought in and established as provisional governments. In Warsaw, where a tremendous anti-German uprising of the underground Home Army erupted in August, 1944, while Soviet forces were approaching, Stalin ordered his troops to halt their offensive. Only after the Germans had slaughtered 200,000 inhabitants of the city and obtained the surrender of what was left of the pro-London Home Army was the Soviet advance resumed. In this manner Stalin let the Nazis liquidate the most serious threat to his power in Poland. By the time the Moscow-appointed "Committee of National Liberation" had entered Warsaw, there was no force left able to challenge it; indeed, there was virtually no city, for in the course of suppressing the uprising the Germans had dynamited and burned it to the ground.°

Initially, the provisional governments established by the Communists in Eastern Europe were coalitions embracing a multitude of socialist and peasant parties, including those representing the exile governments based in London. But it is worth noting that in all these coalitions the two key ministries—defense and security (police)—were from the beginning staffed by Communists. Sooner or later elections were held, as provided for by the Yalta agreement. In one or two cases they were indeed "free and unfettered." In Hungary the voters had an opportunity of giving a majority to the Smallholders party, a peasant group sympathetic to the West. In Czechoslovakia, where the memories of the Western betrayal at Munich were still fresh, the Communist ticket actually won a majority. But in most Eastern European countries the elections proceeded in an atmosphere of police intimidation, reminiscent of what had occurred in Nazi Germany in 1933. Candidates likely to pursue an independent policy, especially those affiliated with the London governments, were struck off the voting lists and personally harassed. When the Western Allies learned of these irregularities they protested to Moscow, but to no avail.

In 1945–1946 Stalin still maintained a pretense of coalition governments in areas occupied by his armies because he did not want to jeopardize the chances of those Communist parties which after the war had been invited to participate in ministerial cabinets in the West. Of these the most important were the Communist parties of France and Italy. At that time it seemed quite likely that these two organizations, in alliance with other left-wing groups, would win a parliamentary majority and come legitimately to power. But in early 1947 two events occurred which dashed this hope. One was the inauguration by the United States of the Truman Doctrine and the Marshall Plan (see below); the other was the dismissal of Communist ministers from coalition governments in France and Italy (May, 1947). Stalin now no longer had any reason to engage in the complicated and potentially dangerous game of coalitions. Everything dictated that he quickly consolidate his hold on Eastern Europe, for here disenchantment with Soviet Russia had begun to set in, and the non-Communist left was displaying an unmistakable yearning for closer links with the West. In 1947 Stalin

°During their alliance with the Nazis, the Russians massacred over 10,000 Polish officers whom they had interned in September, 1939. The bodies of the victims were unearthed by the Germans in the Katyn forest, near Smolensk. The Polish government-in-exile in London demanded a Red Cross investigation, causing Stalin to break relations with it (1943). This slaughter was intended to eliminate potential leaders of national resistance in Poland.

ordered the dissolution of the influential peasant parties in all countries occupied by his armies. The peasant leaders either fled abroad or suffered imprisonment and in some instances execution. The following year came the turn of the socialist parties. These were not outlawed but forced to merge with the Communist parties to form a common labor front, known by a variety of names (United Workers' party in Poland, Socialist Unity party in East Germany, People's Front in Hungary, etc.), in which the Communists controlled the key positions. These mergers were everywhere completed by the end of 1948. By then the one-party system was in operation throughout Soviet-controlled Eastern Europe.

The transformation of independent states into satellites was not accomplished without resistance. In Czechoslovakia the Social Democrats refused to merge with the Communists. The non-Communists in the Prague government also showed an alarming proclivity to seek United States economic aid. To nip in the bud this tendency toward independence, Stalin had the Czech Communists stage a *coup d'état*. In February, 1948, the Communists arrested the leading figures of the independent parties and established a one-party government.

In one country—Yugoslavia—Stalin's technique did not work, and he suffered a humiliating defeat. Here the liberation from the Nazis had been accomplished not by the Soviet army but by a local Communist partisan movement, whose members subsequently occupied major military and police posts. The head of the partisan movement, Joseph Broz, known as Tito, had been trained in Moscow and showed every intention of collaborating closely with the Soviet Union. But he was not willing to become a docile vassal of Stalin. In 1947–1948 a variety of conflicts developed between the two Communist leaders. They came to a head over the issue of economic planning, when Tito refused to subordinate the needs of the Yugoslav economy to those of the economy of the Soviet Union. Lacking an internal lever in the form of an army and police apparatus, Stalin had no way of forcing Tito out. In 1948 the quarrel broke into the open. Stalin excommunicated Yugoslavia from the Communist bloc, while Tito asked and received economic aid from the West.

To guard against a repetition of "Titoism" in his domain, Stalin inaugurated in 1948 a series of purges of the Communist apparatus in Eastern Europe. Communists who had been active in the partisan movement, who enjoyed strong local following, or who had resisted in any manner Moscow's pressures, were now ruthlessly weeded out. Between 1949 and 1952 a succession of mock trials took place in the satellite countries, in the course of which leading party and government officials confessed to the most outrageous crimes. Some were sentenced to long prison terms, others executed. Several of these "trials," notably that of the Czech Communists, carried unmistakable anti-Semitic overtones, for in his diseased imagination Stalin believed himself menaced by a world-wide Jewish plot.

Next to Poland, no single issue caused such bad blood between the West and the Soviet Union as the fate of Germany. It had been agreed among the Allies that as soon as feasible elections would be held in that country, the occupation zones merged, and a peace treaty signed. But the negotiations for a German peace treaty, which got under way in November, 1946, at once ran into snags, and after a while it became apparent that Stalin had no desire to settle the Ger-

The Berlin Airlift (June, 1948–May, 1949) delivered more than a million and a half tons of supplies to the blockaded city in 196,000 flights.

man question. Nor did he give any evidence that he intended to hold elections in his zone. To the Western Allies it was an urgent matter to put Germany on its feet as soon as possible in order to reduce the high costs of occupation and economic aid and to stabilize the political situation in the heart of the Continent. When it became obvious that Russia would indefinitely procrastinate on this issue, the three Western Allies merged their zones into one (1947). At the same time steps were taken to restore the German economy. In 1948 a reformed currency was introduced into West Germany, leading promptly to a revival of industry and trade.

To these measures Stalin responded with a determined effort to eject the Western Allies from Berlin and to consolidate his hold on East Germany. In the spring of 1948, without warning, he closed to Allied vehicles all land access to Berlin across the Soviet zone. The Allies asserted their rights in Berlin by undertaking a massive airlift. For almost a year, every day, a steady stream of transport and cargo planes supplied the blockaded city with all its necessities. Finally, in May, 1949, Stalin capitulated and lifted the blockade.

By then not only Berlin but Germany as a whole was split down the middle into two separate states. In the Western zone elections gave a majority to the Christian Democratic party headed by Konrad Adenauer, which formed a government of the German Federal Republic with residence in Bonn. The constitution of the Republic was based on that of Weimar. In the Eastern zone the Communists persisted in their refusal to hold elections, installing there instead a puppet Communist regime, modeled on those in their other satellites. The popularity of the German Democratic Republic may be gauged by the fact that from the time of its establishment until 1961 (when the construction of the Berlin Wall put an end to the population movement) 2,700,000 persons, or an average of 700 a day, fled from East to West Germany.

Once the countries of Eastern Europe had become full-blown satellites, their entire internal life came to be subordinated to Soviet interests. The economic development plans of each satellite had to be fully coordinated with the Soviet Five-Year Plan. The military and police security apparatus of each was integrated

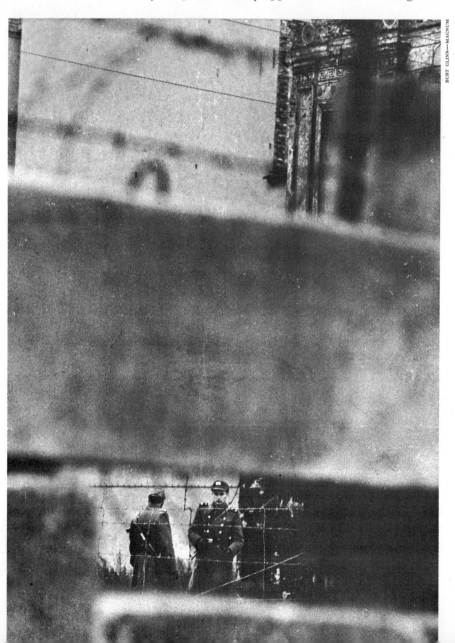

The Berlin Wall, erected in 1961, blocked the mass exodus from East Germany. These East German police of the large patrolling force were photographed through the barricade.

BURT GLINN—MAGNUM

with corresponding Soviet institutions; in the case of Poland the armed forces came directly under the command of a Soviet marshal. To ensure that none of the satellites defected despite these precautions, Stalin stationed in several of them a large Soviet army contingent.

The subjugation of Eastern Europe threw the Western Allies, and especially the United States, into a state of bewilderment. Unlike Stalin's earlier acts, his flagrant breaches of the Yalta agreements could not be explained by suspicion or ill-feeling arising from Western transgressions, real or alleged, dating back to the early years of Soviet history. What aggravated matters was evidence of Soviet expansionism in other parts of the world. In the summer of 1945 the Soviet government applied strong pressure on Turkey, coupled with military threats, to surrender territories adjacent to the Caucasus and to agree to a revision of the treaties regulating passage through the Straits. In early 1946 the Soviet army refused to evacuate northern Iran, which it had occupied during the war and promised to leave six months after the end of hostilities. In May, 1946, Communist guerrillas in Greece initiated a civil war against the duly elected, pro-Western government. A steady stream of anti-American invective in the Soviet press and radio depicted the United States as the successor of Nazi Germany and the main enemy of peace and freedom in the world.

The initial tendency in Washington was to respond to these acts with a show of firmness. President Truman shared neither his predecessor's sense of guilt nor his hopes about Soviet Russia, and in his dealings with Stalin he immediately adopted a resolute tone. Its monopoly of the atomic bomb appeared to assure the United States of an ultimate weapon should Soviet expansion ever directly menace its security. The American armed forces, which on the day of Japan's surrender had numbered 12 million men, were demobilized subsequently at a rate of a million a month, until nothing more than a skeleton army remained. To strengthen its position the United States conducted a series of atomic bomb tests in 1946–1947 in the Pacific, whose purpose was at least as much political as military, namely to impress Russia with the awesome destructiveness of this new weapon.

But neither verbal toughness nor atomic bomb demonstrations had any noticeable effect on Stalin, who calmly went on absorbing areas under his control and menacing areas outside it. Some circles in Washington, especially among the military, began now to urge a more forceful response, but the President and his foreign policy advisers preferred not to break openly with the wartime policy of great power cooperation as long as on some issues the Soviet Union continued to be cooperative.

One of these issues was the prosecution of the Nazis. In 1945 the Allies opened in Nürnberg, the city that had been used by the Nazis for their party rallies, a trial of the major war criminals. The testimony produced at the trial for the first time revealed to the general public the full horror of Nazi rule. The court sentenced the surviving Nazi government and military leaders either to death or long prison terms.

An even more important subject of agreement between West and East was the United Nations. This organization had first met in San Francisco in April, 1945.

Its structure and functions closely resembled those of the League of Nations, but with some significant differences. One was the participation in it of both the United States and the Soviet Union. Another was that in the Security Council —the institution specifically charged with the responsibility for maintaining peace—the five great powers had the right of veto. Both of these features made the United Nations more of an instrument of big-power politics than the League of Nations had been. This was not necessarily a fault, because it may well be argued that the weakness of the League derived from its unrealistic attempt to create a parity between great and small states. The Soviet Union from the beginning frequently availed itself of the veto right to kill resolutions that it disapproved, but it did actively participate in all the activities of the United Nations, and there was the hope that through its agency outstanding great power conflicts could be peacefully resolved.

The wartime policy of collaboration with the Soviet Union was finally abandoned only in February-March, 1947, when it gave way to the policy of "containment."

The theory of containment was first suggested in an 8,000-word telegram dispatched to Washington from the United States Embassy in Moscow in February, 1946. Its author, George F. Kennan, was one of the State Department's leading Russian specialists. Kennan argued that the Soviet Union's foreign policy was not significantly affected by the realities of the international scene; in other words, its policy was not a response to Russia's treatment by the great powers. Rather, it derived from internal traditions, particularly from a deep-seated sense of insecurity whose roots reached back to the Middle Ages, when Russia had lain exposed to the ravages of its nomadic neighbors. The expansion in which Russia had engaged since the end of the war was a natural consequence of its historical heritage. Kennan warned that Russia would maintain a relentless pressure on its neighbors, exploiting their internal weaknesses and divisions in order to conquer them. Russia was fundamentally committed to the view that no lasting peace between it and the rest of the world was possible. Given such an attitude, compromises and concessions could not mollify it, nor *ad hoc* emergency measures blunt its drive. In his subsequent writings Kennan argued that what was needed was an equally relentless and sustained counter-effort to "contain" the Soviet Union within its existing realm.

The views which Kennan articulated found support among the leading diplomatic and military figures in Washington, including Dean Acheson, an influential Undersecretary of State. They caused in time a complete reversal of earlier assumptions about the sources of Soviet behavior. Previously, Russia's obduracy had been interpreted as a reaction to Western wrongs; now it was explained as inherent in Russia's traditions and outlook. In 1948, surveying Soviet postwar policies, Acheson argued: "the direction and goals of Soviet action . . . were chosen and desired and were not forced upon her rulers as defensive measures . . . the main thrust of Soviet policy was self-generated and not a reluctant response to the acts or omissions of others."°

The event that decided the shift in American foreign policy was the economic crisis confronting Western Europe at the beginning of 1947. The winter that

°John C. Campbell, ed., *The United States in World Affairs, 1947–1948* (1948).

year was more severe than it had been in several decades. It destroyed fall-seeded crops and made extraordinary demands on the limited coal supply; Europe's scanty fuel reserves had to be diverted from industrial to consumer needs. The remaining dollar reserves, instead of being used for economic reconstruction, had to be spent on purchases of food and coal. Great Britain was in such straits that it had to curtail industrial production, even at the risk of mass unemployment. To save its economy from collapse the British government resolved to reduce its foreign commitments, and in particular to suspend the aid which it had been giving to Turkey and Greece to resist Communist diplomatic pressures and guerrilla warfare. On February 2, 1947, the British Foreign Office communicated this decision to the United States Department of State.

Britain's withdrawal from the eastern Mediterranean confronted the United States government with an urgent choice: whether to abandon Turkey and Greece to their certain fate, or to take on the international responsibilities traditionally shouldered by Great Britain. On the answer to this question depended the fate not only of the two Balkan countries but of Western Europe as well. In French national elections held in late 1946 the Communists emerged as the single most powerful party, while in Italy they were within a hairbreadth of an actual parliamentary majority. If Western Europe were allowed to suffer a serious economic depression, it was more than likely that Italy and France would come under Communist or Communist-dominated governments.

Confronted with this situation, President Truman initiated intense discussions involving high officials of the Department of State and the armed forces, and congressional leaders of both parties. The overwhelming consensus was that the United States had no choice but to confront the Communist threat and to declare its readiness to come to the aid of any and all countries menaced by it. The decision was inspired by a firm resolve to avoid the mistakes committed by the appeasers of Hitler, whose concessions and compromises had proved to encourage aggression.

On March 12, 1947, President Truman made his appearance before a joint session of Congress. He asked for an immediate appropriation of several hundred million dollars to provide assistance to Turkey and Greece. But in the course of his address he went beyond this request, outlining the basic principles of the containment policy, or, as it became subsequently known, the Truman Doctrine. He wanted a firm commitment of the United States now and in the future

> to help free peoples to maintain their institutions and their national integrity against aggressive movements that seek to impose on them totalitarian regimes. This is no more than a frank recognition that totalitarian regimes imposed on free people, by direct or indirect aggression, undermine the foundation of international peace and hence the security of the United States.

With Republican backing Truman received the appropriation for Turkey and Greece, and by implication, approval of his policy directives. Henceforth, containment became the official policy of the United States in its dealings with the Soviet Union and its satellites. The policy, however, was not entirely negative. It was designed not only to stop further Soviet expansion but also to remove the economic and social causes that facilitated it. To this end, the United States government launched in June, 1947, a program of economic aid known as the European Recovery Program, or Marshall Plan (Chapter 20).

The importance of the decisions taken in Washington in February-March, 1947, for the United States and the world at large, can hardly be overrated. The United States decisively and probably permanently broke with its traditional refusal to enter into peacetime alliances, committing itself to defend from external aggression a large number of countries extending from the northern tip of Norway to the borders of the Caucasus. This commitment was formally made in the North Atlantic Treaty, ratified by the Senate in July, 1949. By virtue of Article 5 of this treaty the signatories recognized that an armed attack on any one of them was an attack on all of them, and pledged themselves to come to the aid of the victim. A North Atlantic Treaty Organization (NATO) army came into being simultaneously. The United States dispatched its own contingents to the Continent to help its allies match the multimillion Soviet force stationed in Eastern Europe. Thus in 1947 the United States assumed nothing less than the responsibility, partly formal, partly moral, for safeguarding the external integrity of the entire non-Communist world—a responsibility that was bound in a thousand different ways to affect the life of the American people.

For Europe, the Truman Doctrine with its economic and military complements—the Marshall Plan and NATO—provided a unique opportunity for economic reconstruction. Shielded by the military might of the United States and assisted by its loans and grants, Europe made a spectacular recovery. By 1950 its production exceeded prewar levels, and the threat of economic collapse vanished. Western Europe was spared the fate of its Eastern half.

The Cold War Shifts to East Asia   Thanks to its "Eurasian" location Russia has the unique ability to engage in direct diplomatic and military activity in three of the world's major geopolitical areas: Europe, the Middle East, and the Far East. Already in the nineteenth century, having suffered a setback in one of these regions, the imperial government was observed to shift its attention to the others. Thus, the thwarting in the Crimean War of Russian ambitions in the Balkans was followed by an outburst of expansion in Central Asia; as soon as that had been checked by the British, Russia reverted to the Balkans and then to China and Korea.

This pattern recurred in 1948–1950. By then the Soviet drive in Europe, which at one time had threatened to bring the entire Continent under Russian domination, had been blunted all along the line. The Allied stand in Berlin and the emergence of a viable government in Bonn had stabilized the situation in Germany. Yugoslavia's defection from the Communist bloc had deprived the Greek guerrillas of their main base of operations and caused the civil war in Greece to collapse. Turkey, backed by the United States, refused to bow to Soviet demands. In France and Italy the Communists, having lost hope of coming legitimately to power, went over to sterile opposition. The good will that they had gained in Europe during the war, thanks to their partisan activities and the Russian stand against the Germans, eroded as it became obvious that the Communists had no real interest in economic and political reconstruction. In

1948, in a crucial Italian election on which the Communists counted to yield them a parliamentary majority, victory went to the liberal, pro-Western Christian Democrats; the Popular Democratic Front, sponsored by the Communists, won less than one-third of the vote.

In the Far East, by contrast, the situation looked promising. The defeats that the Japanese had inflicted on the Western imperial powers in 1941–1942 and those which the West in turn had inflicted on them in 1942–1945 had created in this area something approaching a political and military vacuum. Japan itself, ruled imperiously by General MacArthur, was closed to Soviet influence. But the whole eastern periphery of Asia, from Korea to Burma, was unsettled and vulnerable. Here a determined Communist drive seemed to offer excellent chances of success.

Although we have no documentary proof to this effect, it is fairly certain that sometime in the winter of 1947–1948 Stalin and the leaders of the local Communist parties decided to launch a coordinated offensive against Western and pro-Western governments in East Asia. The strategy adopted seems to have been fundamentally identical for all the countries concerned. Where the Communist movements were already well established and in control of some definite territory, they were to declare themselves the legitimate government and undertake a military campaign intended to conquer the rest of the country. Where this was not the case, they were first to form a National Liberation Committee, gain a foothold in some inaccessible area, and then go over to the offensive. The social base of these operations was to be the peasantry, but essential to their success was the sympathy of the urban intelligentsia and the neutrality of the middle class. For this reason the programs advanced by East Asian Communist movements at this stage were not Communist or even socialist, but rather broadly democratic and nationalistic.

Beginning with the spring of 1948 a succession of guerrilla movements erupted and spread in various regions of East Asia: in March in Burma, in June in Malaya, in September in Indonesia, in October in the Philippines. In China, where they had controlled since the 1930s territory in Yenan, near the Mongolian border, the local Communists in September, 1948, proclaimed the establishment of the North China People's Government. The same month, in North Korea, a Communist government installed by the Soviet army announced the creation of a People's Republic with authority over the entire peninsula.

Today, viewed from the perspective of decades, these events seem too closely timed to have been coincidental. But this was not seen then, the more so as East Asia, considered less important than Europe for Western security, was not so closely watched. It was only when all China came under Communist domination that the magnitude of the problem confronting the Western democracies in East Asia became apparent.

The Chinese Communist movement was, of course, pro-Soviet, but it was at no point a tool of Moscow. With its own army and administration it could maintain toward Russia an attitude of considerable independence. Its leader, Mao Tse-tung, enjoyed the same maneuverability toward Stalin as did Tito, something not true of Communist leaders who were placed in power by the Soviet army. Stalin must have sensed this fact and all along conducted in China a

An American soldier checks a rocket during NATO maneuvers in Germany.

U.S. infantrymen advance in Korea in 1951 as refugees flee the fighting zone—a scene as old as war itself.

double policy: he helped the Chinese Communists (for example, equipping them with captured Japanese weapons) but at the same time maintained friendly relations with the pro-American government of Chiang Kai-shek. Probably Stalin hoped that Mao and Chiang (himself a defected Communist) would eliminate each other and enable him to install in China a tractable Communist government of his own making.

The conflict between Chiang and Mao went back to the 1930s, and during World War II the two fought each other more doggedly than they fought their common enemy, the Japanese. After Japan's collapse the United States made several attempts to bring the two sides together into some kind of coalition government, but these efforts failed, and in the summer of 1947 full-blown civil war was in progress in China. The United States supported Chiang with money and weapons, while the Soviet Union increasingly and overtly backed Mao. After they had established the North China People's Government, the Communists made rapid progress in conquering the rest of the country. In October the Soviet Union let the Chinese Communists into Manchuria, which Russian forces had occupied by virtue of the Yalta agreement. The antiquated and corrupt government of Chiang collapsed under the combined onslaught of well-organized Communist armies in the countryside and pro-Communist intellectuals in the cities. In 1949 all China fell under Communist control and a Chinese People's Republic was instituted. Chiang, with the remainder of his troops, evacuated to the island of Formosa (Taiwan).

The Communist triumph in China was not only a major debacle for the United States, which had staked much on the Chiang regime; it was a portent of worse things to come. With a base in China the Communists could give direct support to the guerrilla movements in eastern and southeastern Asia and completely eject the Western powers from this area.

That the Communists meant to take advantage of this situation became apparent in June, 1950, when the North Koreans launched a surprise invasion of South Korea. Korea had been a Japanese dependency since early in the century. After the war it had been divided into two zones, separated by the 38th parallel: a northern zone, under Soviet control, and a southern zone, under that of the United States. As in the case of Germany, it had been agreed that as soon as conditions permitted, the Koreans would be given an opportunity to hold democratic elections and create a national government. But exactly as had occurred in Germany, the Soviet occupation forces refused to allow their occupation zone to vote, being well aware that victory would go to Syngman Rhee, the hero of anti-Japanese resistance and a stanch foe of the Communists. In September, 1948, the country split in two, each establishing its own government.

The establishment of the North Korean People's Republic, as in the case of the North China People's Government, was a prelude to a general offensive aimed at seizing the whole country. But in the case of Korea this offensive had to be somewhat postponed because South Korea still had a contingent of United States troops. At the suggestion of the Soviet Union, made in September, 1948, both occupying powers withdrew their armed forces. In June, 1950, the North Korean army, built up with Soviet help, struck. The Communists had good reason to expect that the United States neither would nor could defend Korea, for it had no forces able to come immediately to South Korea's aid. But, to their surprise, the invasion produced an instantaneous reaction in Washington. With the backing of the United Nations Security Council, which declared North Korea the aggressor, a token force was immediately dispatched to bolster the South Korean armies.°

By early September the small United Nations contingent in Korea was reduced to a beachhead in the southwestern corner of the peninsula. But just as victory seemed within sight, the North Korean drive ran out of steam. In mid-September General MacArthur launched a surprise landing operation in central Korea, compelling the Communist forces to withdraw or risk being cut in two. The United Nations army (consisting mostly of United States troops) now pursued the invaders northward, toward the Chinese frontier, MacArthur's intention being to reunite both parts of the divided country. As Allied troops approached the Yalu River, the Chinese armies intervened. In the ensuing seesaw battle the line was eventually stabilized along the 38th parallel. General MacArthur insisted on carrying the war into China by bombing Chinese air bases, but this permission was denied by President Truman, and MacArthur was eventually dismissed from his post.

The invasion of Korea was a major blunder on the part of the Communists. The United States and its Western allies might have tolerated guerrilla movements, especially those disguised as movements of national liberation, but they were not disposed to permit a brutal onslaught reminiscent of Hitler's blitzkrieg. In response to the Korean War, the United States undertook a major rearmament program. NATO forces in Europe were considerably bolstered, and it was decided to rearm Germany. In the Far East the United States signed in September, 1951, a separate peace treaty with Japan. The Asian guerrilla movements, which until then had been making good progress, were before long suppressed by the alerted national governments.

By the early 1950s the Cold War had reached a level of intensity at which the slightest provocation could have unleashed a thermonuclear conflict.†

The events that we have described produced in the United States a mood of confusion and frustration. As long as the country had been at war, the American public had been prepared to do whatever was needed to bring a military victory. It was not, however, prepared for the drawn-out contests of the Cold War in which the issues were vague and the methods of combat entirely unfamiliar. At first, Americans were told on highest authority that the United States and the Soviet Union would cooperate after the war as they had during the war. Then, scarcely two years after the Nazi capitulation, they were told on equally high

Domestic Repercussions in the United States

°The United Nations vote was made possible by a tactical mistake of the Soviet Union. In January, 1950, in protest against the presence of Chiang Kai-shek's representative, the Soviet delegation walked out of the Security Council. When, six months later, the Council voted on the resolution condemning North Korea as the aggressor, the Soviet representative was not on hand to veto it.

†It is now known that at the height of the Cold War the head of the British intelligence department charged with responsibility for neutralizing Soviet espionage activities, as well as a leading American specialist in the Foreign Office, were Soviet spies (both have since defected to Moscow). Through them Stalin must have been well informed of United States intentions—an invaluable asset in the Cold War competition.

authority that the Soviet Union represented a mortal danger to peace and freedom and had to be stopped from further expansion. The Communist subjugation of Eastern Europe and invasion of South Korea seemed to corroborate the new policy. Yet, when General MacArthur wanted to employ full force against China, which had intervened on behalf of the aggressors in Korea, he was unceremoniously fired. The confusion which these policy shifts in Washington engendered was compounded by two events that occurred almost simultaneously in 1949. One was the end of the American monopoly on atomic weapons. The explosion that year by the Russians of a thermonuclear device suddenly exposed the United States to a deadly danger from which it had considered itself immune. The other was the Communist victory in China, a country toward which the United States had a special sympathy, which it had aided in its struggle against the Japanese, and for the sake of which it had in 1941 refused to come to terms with Japan.

The anxiety that these rapidly succeeding developments produced enabled demagogic politicians to attract attention and improve their fortunes by blaming American reverses on treason. The most notorious of these was the Republican Senator from Wisconsin, Joseph McCarthy. In the summer of 1950 he publicly announced that he possessed a long list of Communists allegedly on the State Department payroll. He never produced this list, but went on to make wilder and wilder charges, claiming, among other things, that both the Communist victory in China and the Russian acquisition of atomic weapons were made possible by betrayal by United States officials. The image of a country infested with agents and spies seemed to many ill-informed people to provide an explanation for the puzzling events of the postwar era. McCarthy's demonstrated ability to cause the electoral defeat of candidates who had opposed him or his friends gave him immense power in Congress. This he used with utter recklessness to smear reputations and secure the dismissal from the government of persons he disliked. The Republican leadership did not much care for McCarthy's methods, but since they hurt the Democrats, it tended to look the other way.

In 1952 the country elected a Republican administration. The new President, Dwight D. Eisenhower, entrusted the conduct of foreign policy to John Foster Dulles, an experienced international lawyer. During the electoral campaign the Republicans had advocated a more dynamic policy abroad, urging that "containment" be replaced by "roll back." But, as we shall see, when subsequently the occasion to recapture territory from the Communists presented itself, it was not taken advantage of. In effect, the Eisenhower administration continued to adhere to the containment policy introduced by Truman. A tacit assumption of this policy was mutual recognition of the *status quo* established by 1947 between the Western and Eastern blocs.

The New Course in Russia   Stalin's postwar foreign policy, after its initial successes, had ultimately placed the Soviet Union in a position of isolation. His tendency to view the outside world in categories of white and black—those who obeyed Stalin and those who did not—forfeited to the United States leadership of the entire third, gray category, consisting of neutral countries uninvolved in the Cold War. Communist parties outside the Soviet bloc were reduced to the status of propaganda mouth-

"Over the East-West Wall": cartoonist David Low's 1954 comment on the Soviet "thaw" after Stalin's death. The gregarious housewife is Georgi Malenkov, briefly Stalin's successor.

pieces, as isolated from the societies in which they functioned as was the Soviet Union from the world at large.

Russia and its satellites lay supine at Stalin's feet. The police, to maintain its grip, carried out constant purges and arrests without rhyme or reason. Millions of people were confined in concentration camps, where they had to perform backbreaking labor and where many died from malnutrition or physical abuse. The old tyrant, completely out of touch with humanity, grew increasingly paranoid, sending to their death even his close relatives. Cut off externally from all contact with the rest of mankind, Russia, internally, hovered on the brink of physical and spiritual collapse.

In March, 1953, Stalin suffered a fatal stroke. Immediately, Lavrenti Beria, the head of the security police, made a bid for power, but he was thwarted by his colleagues in the Central Committee, arrested, and shot. The police, which in Stalin's last decade virtually administered the country, was subsequently reduced in power, and many of its camps were quietly shut down. The party now reasserted its authority. Between 1953 and 1955 a kind of "collective leadership" or leadership by committee emerged, in which two factions vied for control. One consisted of "conservatives," who wished to continue running the country much as it had been run under the late Stalin. The other, comprised of "liberals," pressed for a major reform of the existing system so as to return to that which had been in force in the early years of Stalin's dictatorship (1928–1933), before the senseless purges and indiscriminate terror.

Under conditions which remain obscure, but in which personal rivalries undoubtedly played as large a part as ideological considerations, the liberal wing triumphed. At the Twentieth Party Congress, held in 1956, the new leaders, at

In 1960 the peripatetic Khrushchev attended a United Nations session. Here he confers with Secretary General Dag Hammarskjöld (left center).

first cautiously and then with unexpected frankness, attacked Stalin and what they euphemistically called the Stalinist "cult of personality." The high point of the proceedings was a report delivered at a closed session by Nikita Khrushchev, the outstanding personality of the liberal faction. Khrushchev depicted Stalin as a demented despot who had killed thousands of good, loyal Communists, and would have killed many more if death had not intervened. Whether this information was indeed news to the Congress delegates, as their recorded expressions of indignation seem to indicate, may be doubted. But the shock of hearing these facts publicly conceded by the party leadership was indeed great. Khrushchev's report was subsequently read to party organizations throughout the country, producing general confusion.

The "de-Stalinization" launched at the Twentieth Party Congress was intended to clear the decks for a major reorientation of internal and external policy. The change was indeed bold, bolder than one might have expected from men who had spent their lives in the Communist apparatus. But it involved no basic change in the aims of either the Communist movement or of its institutions. The men who took over the reins of government had all been Stalin's men. Much as they may have resented Stalin's behavior toward them, they could not help but regard the world in his terms or they would not have survived as his close subordinates. Nothing comparable to even the moderate de-Nazification of post-Hitler Germany took place in post-Stalinist Russia. Except for Beria and a few of his closest henchmen, none of the persons involved in Stalin's acknowledged crimes was tried and punished. The apparatus of the party, police, and administration remained virtually intact; so did the constitution, which vested sovereignty in a self-perpetuating, oligarchical party organization; and so, finally, did the economic structure, by virtue of which that organization controlled the industrial, agricultural, and commercial wealth of the country.

Internally, the new course involved a certain measure of relaxation. To shake the population out of its lethargy, the Soviet government took steps to raise living standards above their bare subsistence level. It restored some intellectual freedom. It also made a rather ambitious attempt to assure the average citizen, previously left to the mercies of the secret police, legal protection in offenses of a nonpolitical nature. The cult of Lenin replaced the cult of Stalin, and a conscious effort was made to reinfuse the Communist movement with the enthusiasm of its early years.

The greatest change occurred in the realm of foreign policy. It was imperative for the sake of Soviet security to emerge from the self-imposed isolation in which Stalin had placed the country. The actual foreign policy directives that Stalin's heirs adopted between 1953 and 1956 are not known. But subsequent Soviet actions permit us to reconstruct in broad outlines their principal features.

There can be little doubt that the new Soviet rulers resolved to terminate the Cold War and thereby to break up the whole political and military establishment that the Western powers had formed while it was in progress. Relations with the West were to be normalized to the point where the latter would not feel threatened, and therefore would consent to dismantling its network of air bases and military outposts, dissolving NATO and other regional defense organizations, and slowing down the pace of armaments. To promote this end, Khrushchev advanced in 1956 a novel theory of "peaceful coexistence." According to this theory, the ultimate triumph of the Communist cause in the world does not require a general war. Instead, it can be brought about by a gradual shift of economic (and, implicitly, military) hegemony from the "capitalist" to the "socialist" bloc, and the disintegration of the former from the force of internal contradictions. Although the main purpose of the peaceful coexistence formula was and continues to be neutralization of the Western defense effort, behind it probably lay also a genuine realization that atomic warfare could destroy all life on this planet, and war therefore was no longer feasible.

The rejection of general war did not preclude the possibility, indeed the desirability, of local wars. The new Soviet regime, like its predecessor, declared itself ready to support "just wars," especially wars of national liberation. The stated intention of the Eisenhower administration not to participate in small "brush-fire" conflicts but to rely on what it called "massive retaliation" by atomic weapons encouraged Soviet leaders to believe that they could undertake and assist such actions with impunity.

Beginning in 1955 Khrushchev and his government carried out a series of measures designed to give credibility to the peaceful coexistence formula. They evacuated Soviet troops from Finland, signed a peace treaty with Austria, normalized relations with West Germany, and initiated a program of international economic and cultural cooperation. They also suspended the vituperative propaganda campaign against the United States and dissolved the Communist International (Cominform), which Stalin had revived in 1947.

An integral feature of the peaceful coexistence policy were personal encounters between Soviet leaders and their Western counterparts. In July, 1955, on Soviet initiative, the first "summit conference" took place in Geneva. In September, 1959, Khrushchev visited the United States and held a three-day private meeting with President Eisenhower at Camp David, in Maryland. The official communiqué issued on the completion of the Camp David talks affirmed the resolve of both parties to settle "all outstanding international questions . . . not by application of force but by peaceful means through negotiations."

While pursuing a *détente* with the West, the Soviet Union launched a vigorous diplomatic and economic drive to establish a foothold in the Middle East. This area had been neglected by Stalin, who preferred to expand in Europe and East Asia. But now there were excellent reasons for a resumption of an offensive in this region. During the postwar decade, Great Britain and the other colonial powers had withdrawn from most of their Middle Eastern possessions (Chapter 20), yielding to numerous young and unstable national governments. These were perennially short of money and arms, and liable to be won over by a power willing to supply both. Furthermore, the emergence of the state of Israel in 1948 had created in the eastern Mediterranean a permanent fulcrum of unrest. A determined drive in support of the Arab cause stood a good chance of winning the Soviet Union millions of friends in this important strategic region.

From 1955 on, Khrushchev, as head of the party, and Nikolai Bulganin, as head of state, undertook a series of visits to the Middle East, ranging from Burma to Egypt. "Bulgy and Khrushy," as they came to be known, behaved on these journeys like two experienced American campaigners, waving to the crowds, delivering flattering speeches, bowing to local divinities, and, above all, promising economic and other aid. That these promises were not empty became obvious in September, 1955, when Gamal Abdel Nasser, the dictator of Egypt, announced the conclusion of an agreement with Czechoslovakia providing for substantial military aid to his country. From then on, Soviet influence in the Middle East, especially in the Arab world, increased rapidly.

The new Soviet policy in the so-called "third world" called for cooperation with governments that in Communist parlance were clearly "bourgeois-nationalist." In a sense it involved a betrayal of the local Communist movements pledged to overthrow these regimes. This was a cruel decision to take, but it was worth the gamble because nowhere were the Communist movements strong enough to seize power on their own. On the other hand, they stood a good chance of success in a broad popular front involving socialists and nationalists and directed against the "imperialist" powers. Once the third world was won over, the United States would find itself as isolated as the Soviet Union had been under Stalin.

The third element in the new foreign policy was a massive modernization program of the Soviet armed forces. Although Stalin had authorized the manufacture of atomic weapons, he tended to think in nineteenth-century strategic terms of territory and manpower. His successors adopted a new strategy, consonant with the military technology of an age of atomic warheads and ballistic missiles. After Stalin's death the modernization of the Soviet army, navy, and air force along these lines proceeded at full speed. Its costs were so huge that the promise

A 1954 incident in the continuing war in Vietnam: prisoners repair road damage blocking a French column.

of a genuine improvement in the country's living standards could not be fulfilled.

The new foreign policy contained elements that were not fully compatible. The aggressive drive to penetrate the Middle East on the one hand, and the modernization of the Soviet military establishment on the other, were not likely to promote a *détente* with the Western powers. The arming of Egypt, and even more significant, the launching in 1957 of an artificial satellite (*sputnik*)— the by-product of an intense effort by the Soviet army to develop military missiles—alarmed the United States and induced it to launch a major missile program of its own. Nor did Khrushchev's frequent threats, sometimes ominously Stalinist in tone, help matters.

In a survey of this kind it is not possible to treat events of the most recent period. Suffice it to say that the policy of the United States toward the Soviet Union since 1956 has represented a continuation of "containment" as modified by "peaceful coexistence." The United States is still committed to thwart, by force of arms if necessary, any Communist expansion. But it accepts, even if only tacitly, the Soviet contention that an all-out war between Russia and America is unthinkable. Hence, confrontations between the two blocs are no longer direct, as they had been at the height of the Stalinist Cold War, but indirect, through the intermediacy of third parties. With the accession of President John F. Kennedy in 1961 the United States abandoned the strategy of "massive retaliation," developing instead a mobile armed force able to challenge Communist forces wherever they threaten legitimate governments. All East-West conflicts since

1956 have been of such an indirect character: the Vietnamese War, in progress uninterruptedly since 1946, the two wars between Israel and its Soviet-backed Arab neighbors (1956 and 1967), and the so-called Cuban missile crisis of 1962.[*]

Polycentrism   The liberal course adopted by the Soviet regime after 1953 had profound repercussions on the relations between Moscow, on the one hand, and the satellite countries and affiliated foreign Communist movements on the other. The monolith that Stalin had sought to fashion out of his domains, and to a large extent had succeeded in fashioning, revealed after his death serious internal fissures. De-Stalinization had the effect of widening them and causing a breakdown of the unity of the Communist bloc. The "socialist camp," once unanimous in thought and action, disintegrated into a loose alliance with several centers, several theories, and several strategies.

As soon as it had gained the upper hand in Moscow, the "liberal faction," headed by Khrushchev, began to introduce reforms in the satellites. As in the Soviet Union itself, the satellite governments reduced the power of the security police, released from jail and concentration camps many political prisoners, relaxed censorship, and permitted economic reforms. Among those freed from prison were Communist leaders who had been confined on Stalin's orders for nationalistic, "Titoist" tendencies.

In the Soviet Union the population appreciated such liberal measures. But in the satellites the relaxation of rule only released the pent-up hatred of the Communist regimes and of the Soviet army which stood behind them. Beginning with 1953 a series of uprisings, which startlingly recalled the revolutions of 1848, shook Eastern Europe: they involved the same social elements—intellectuals and workers—and the same ideologies—nationalism in combination with liberalism or socialism. Only this time the enemy was not the conservative monarchy with its church and nobility but the Communist dictatorship with its bureaucracy and police.

The first of these uprisings broke out in June, 1953, in East Berlin, where the construction workers engaged in building the monumental Stalin Boulevard rose up in arms. Before long the disturbance developed into a general anti-Communist revolt. Soviet armored units brought out to quell the melee were showered with pavement stones and rocks. It did not take them long, however, to restore order.

The resentment that smouldered throughout the satellite world erupted next in Poland. It began in Poznan, where in the summer of 1956 a large number of workers engaged in an illegal strike. As in East Berlin, what had begun as an industrial work stoppage quickly transformed itself into a broad protest movement against the Communist regime, with various disaffected elements gathering around the strikers. Fanned by intellectuals, the spirit of rebellion spread to other Polish cities and penetrated the party apparatus itself. In October, 1956, the Central Committee of the Polish Communist party fired from its membership the most notorious "conservatives" and elected as its First Chairman Wladyslaw Gomulka, a prominent Communist whom Stalin had jailed for his alleged nationalism.

[*] In Cuba, when a direct conflict between the United States and the Soviet Union seemed imminent, the Soviet Union quit the field.

The Soviet government did not quite know how to react to these developments. The liberal course taken by the Polish Communists was, of course, in line with the Soviet government's own desires. But in the satellites the conservatives were the very people who accepted subservience to Russia, whereas the liberals were nationalists and wanted genuine independence. Khrushchev and his colleagues procrastinated to see how things developed. When the appointment of Gomulka was imminent, the leaders of the Soviet government made a dramatic journey to Poland. To forestall a possible Polish break with the Communist bloc, they seem to have issued strong warnings, coupled with threats of military intervention. But Gomulka expressed his unflinching loyalty to the Communist bloc and readiness to accept Soviet guidance in foreign policy dealings. This prudence apparently saved the Polish Communist government from being overthrown by the Soviet army units stationed in Poland.

The greatest of the anti-Communist revolutions occurred in October, 1956, in Hungary. Here the party leadership was violently split between conservative and liberal factions, the latter demanding greater freedom and greater autonomy from Moscow. The quarrel among the leaders disorganized the party and state machinery and led to the collapse of authority. Soon throughout the country Communist offices were under attack. The population was particularly savage with the secret police, whose officials it sometimes literally tore to pieces. On a number of occasions Soviet army units came to the assistance of the Hungarian

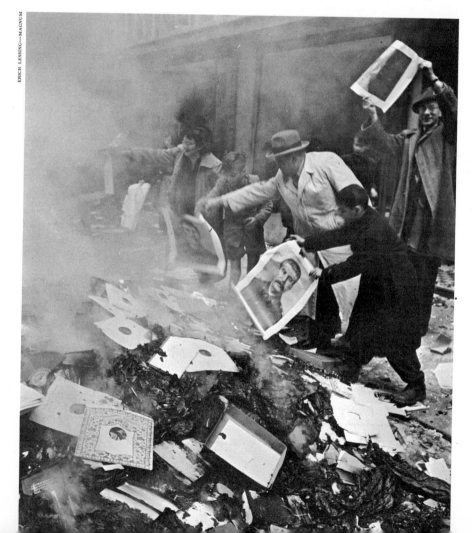

Hungarians burn pictures of Stalin and other Communist memorabilia during their abortive revolt in 1956.

police, but as the Hungarian army swung to the support of the rebels it had to ask for reinforcements. At the end of October a new liberal-national government headed by the Communist Imre Nagy came into existence. Nagy announced the abolition of the one-party system and Hungary's withdrawal from the Warsaw Pact, the Communist counterpart of NATO. As soon as a sufficiently strong Soviet army contingent had been assembled, it swung into action. A savage war ensued between Soviet divisions and the Hungarian army, supported by worker and peasant detachments. After the rebels had been crushed, a new Communist regime was installed. Nagy and the generals who participated in the uprising were subsequently shot, and many other Hungarians suffered imprisonment. Nearly 200,000 Hungarians took advantage of the revolution to seek refuge abroad.

After the suppression of the Hungarian uprising the situation in Eastern Europe stabilized. The failure of the United States to come to the aid of the East German and Hungarian rebels, despite its commitment to "roll back" communism, discouraged any thought of further armed action. The nationalists in these areas now preferred to concentrate their attention on slow economic, cultural, and political gains within the Communist framework. The Soviet Union demanded and obtained from its satellites subservience in all matters affecting foreign policy and military strategy. But it was not averse to a certain amount of internal liberalization and even nationalism, and it no longer insisted on economic mastery.

The loosening of control over the satellites was accompanied by a similar process within the international Communist movement. Leaders of Communist parties outside the Soviet bloc, especially in countries where they had a wide following, began to demand equality of status. In 1956 the head of the Italian Communist party, Palmiro Togliatti, called for frank recognition of the fact that the Soviet Union had no right to dictate policies to Communist parties abroad. "The Soviet model should no longer be obligatory," he said; "the complex of the system is becoming polycentric, and in the communist movement itself one can no longer speak of a single guide." The notion of "polycentrism" gradually gained acceptance, largely because of the general recognition that only by adopting utmost flexibility in dealing with local situations could the local Communist movements restore their waning fortunes.

Notwithstanding the violence in East Berlin and Hungary, and the relative emancipation of Poland, the relaxation of control over the satellites and foreign Communist parties proved on the whole successful. The satellite governments broadened their base of support, while the international Communist movement rid itself of the heavy onus of being a Soviet tool.

The fatal flaw in the whole post-Stalinist foreign policy was that it led to a violent clash between Russia and China which split the Communist movement in two. It is certain that Russia's rulers not only did not desire such a clash but sought at all costs to avoid it. But once it got under way, they were unable to stop it from taking its natural course.

Sino-Soviet friction may have existed earlier, but it became overt only in 1960. The Chinese Communists were watching with profound suspicion the Soviet pursuit of "peaceful coexistence," in particular as it affected relations between the Soviet Union and the United States. Being versed in Communist theory, the Chinese must have known what the concept meant and why it was invoked. But they seem to have suspected all along that behind the high-flown language of the new diplomacy the Soviet Union was arranging with the United States to divide the world into spheres of influence. What particularly chagrined them was Soviet readiness to negotiate with the United States limitations on the spread of nuclear weapons. In their view the inevitable outcome of the American-Soviet *détente* was the reduction of China to the status of a second-rate power.

The first open Chinese criticism of Khrushchev and his foreign policy followed the Camp David meeting. In early 1960 official Chinese organs stated that China did not feel bound by international agreements concluded without its participation. Next, they questioned the whole Soviet theory of "peaceful coexistence," restating the Leninist theory that communism could not triumph in the world without an ultimate and conclusive military conflict. In one particularly virulent statement the Chinese Communists asserted that a Third World War, involving atomic weapons, was not to be feared because it would cause the ultimate collapse of capitalism.

Gradually other sources of friction developed between the two countries. The Chinese resented the economic aid that the Soviet Union extended to India, partly because they had aggressive designs on that country (which they attacked in a brief war in 1959) and partly because such aid diminished whatever assistance the Russians could furnish them. Soon recriminations over frontiers also made themselves heard, the Chinese laying claim to all of Mongolia and even Central Asia.

As the conflict deepened, the Chinese advanced their own theory of Communist action. Following Lenin's tactics in 1900–1903 within the Russian Social-Democratic movement, they deliberately broke with the moderate (Soviet) wing in the Communist movement, accusing the Russians of having turned into Social-Democratic opportunists. The world, as Stalin had said, was indeed divided into two camps: the progressive and the reactionary. Soviet Russia had joined the latter camp, and was as much an enemy of the working class as was the United States. There was to be no peaceful cooperation with bourgeois national governments in the underdeveloped countries but a direct onslaught on them. The method advocated was guerrilla wars, based largely on the peasantry, which would isolate and bring down city-based governments, exactly as they did in China in 1947–1949. To wean aggressive elements away from Soviet influence, the Chinese leaders have sought everywhere to split the Communist parties and form small but dynamic organizations dedicated to their ideas. They have also aided, to the limit of their modest resources, guerrilla movements in various areas of the world, including Central Africa, the Middle East, and Vietnam.

The Sino-Soviet split derives from differences not of aims but of means. Nevertheless, given communism's stress on monolithic organization and unity of theory, it marks a very deep crisis in the movement. What used to be a conflict between two blocs—a Western and an Eastern—has turned into a more complicated struggle. This struggle is bound to affect profoundly the character of communism and its relations with the rest of the world, and may therefore be regarded as one of the most significant events of the twentieth century.

20

Europe and the World

V iewed on the scale of global history, the predominance of Western peoples and Western culture is a relatively recent phenomenon. Its origins date back to the end of the fifteenth century, when a sudden outburst of maritime exploration carried Europeans to the remotest parts of the globe and enabled them to link to themselves and to each other hitherto isolated communities and continents. The hegemony of Western nations in the post-Renaissance era derives from the fact that it is they who first made real the potential unity of the world. Later, thanks to the development in Europe of science and technology, Europe's leadership became virtually unassailable.

Natural and permanent as the hegemony of the West may have appeared when at its height in the nineteenth century, it is obvious today that it was neither. The attitudes, ideas, and techniques that had originally assured the West its preponderance could be learned by others and turned against it. Indeed, since the beginning of the present century the global position of Europe has steadily eroded. Around 1900 Western nations were still scrambling for the last unclaimed portions of Africa and Asia; half a century later they were abandoning with alacrity everything their ancestors had conquered since the fifteenth century. Today their direct political control is with a few exceptions (notably in the Soviet Union and South Africa) limited to Europe and to areas in which Europeans constitute an overwhelming majority of the population.

In a sense, therefore, one may speak of the four-centuries-old domination of the world by the West as finished. But such a statement calls for considerable qualification. Politically, the world hegemony of the West has indeed come to an end, and it is difficult to conceive how it can ever be restored. But economically and culturally the primacy of the West, far from being done for, has not even been diminished. Quite the contrary: by surrendering its political powers the West has succeeded in permeating other civilizations with its way of life to a far greater extent than before. The real Westernization of the world has taken place only after the West has given up its political hegemony over it.

The relationship between the West and the world at large is a subject of great subtlety which must not be dismissed with simplistic generalizations about the "end of imperialism." For better or worse, all modern culture is Western culture, and the contemporary non-European world, even when rebelling against Europe, is assimilating its values and copying its ways.

In this chapter we shall discuss two related topics: the withdrawal of the imperial powers from their colonies, and the adjustment of Europe to its changed position in the world.

Western authority in the colonies declined for two principal reasons: internecine conflicts among the imperial powers, and the emergence of a European-type nationalism among the native élites. The two factors reinforced each other, un-

The Causes of De-colonization

One example of the West's cultural influence is the new Indian city of Chandigarh, the capital of Punjab, whose public buildings bear the distinctive stamp of the Swiss-French architect Le Corbusier. This is the entrance portico of the Assembly building.

Thinly disguised and chanting "Africa for the Africans!" in unison, China's Mao Tse-tung (left) and Russia's Khrushchev enter the African power vacuum; a 1964 Dutch cartoon.

dermining among the subject peoples that awe of the white man which had furnished the psychological foundation of colonial rule.

The relative ease with which Europeans had conquered and subjugated overseas peoples was due not only to their military superiority but also to the absence on the part of the native peoples of an inner resistance to foreign rule. In their world, in which past and present generations mingled imperceptibly and magic permeated all life, the natives of Africa and Asia often regarded white men as a reincarnation of dead ancestors, come to provide help and protection. A French sociologist, having analyzed closely the mind of the inhabitants of Madagascar, concluded that the net effect of colonial rule was to make them totally dependent on their rulers. The natives, regarding their white conquerors from the beginning as superior beings because they were immune to magic, developed toward them a profound sense of inferiority. In actual practice, the psychological relationship between the domineering master and the subservient native resembles that established between Prospero and Caliban in Shakespeare's *The Tempest.*°

As long as the Western nations acted in harmony and beat down all opposition to their overseas expansion, this sense of awe, dependence, and inferiority remained intact. But at the beginning of the twentieth century it began to break down. The victory the Japanese gained over the Russians in the war of 1904–1905 made a tremendous impression on the non-Western world because it showed

°O. Mannoni, *Prospero and Caliban: The Psychology of Colonization* (1956).

for the first time that an Oriental people, properly armed and led, could humiliate a great Western power. So, to a lesser extent, did the stubborn Turkish resistance against Italy in the Tripolitan War (1911–1912). World War I, in which the white powers fought and slaughtered each other, and even had to import black troops to help them out, did little to enhance their prestige overseas. But nothing lowered this prestige more than the Second World War. The speed and almost contemptuous ease with which the Japanese disposed of Western armies and navies and seized Western colonial possessions irreparably damaged the reputation of the West throughout Asia. Europeans were now seen as having lost the "mandate of heaven." After the war it became simply impossible to re-establish Western authority in colonies that had been under Japanese occupation and difficult in those that adjoined them.

As Western prestige in the colonies waned, the sentiment of nationalism gained ground. Its leading exponents were intellectuals trained in Western schools, who in the course of their education had absorbed the European ethos with its stress on historicism, national culture, social equality, statehood, and other typical nineteenth-century ideas. Such intellectuals found themselves in a highly ambivalent situation. By virtue of their Western upbringing and outlook, they no longer fitted into the traditional society in which they were born; and yet, because of their race, they could not fully integrate into the ruling white society. To overcome its estrangement the native intelligentsia turned nationalistic, seeking on the one hand to sever its country's dependence on the imperial metropolis and on the other to transform its own peoples in accord with a Western model.

The colonial powers, of course, were not unaware that the education they were providing to the native élite could have such unwelcome consequences. But most of them continued to furnish education nevertheless: the British because they considered it necessary to train cadres of civil servants for ultimate self-rule, the French and the Russians because they hoped by its means to assimilate culturally their colonial élites. The Belgians and Portuguese followed a different policy, seeking to prevent the emergence of a native intelligentsia by confining education in their possessions to the elementary and vocational levels.

A powerful factor in the breakdown of the Western position in the colonial areas was also the anti-imperialist propaganda waged by the totalitarian powers. Both the Communists and the Nazis (and to a considerable extent the Japanese as well) vigorously attacked Western imperialism in Asia and Africa, although they engaged in far more brutal forms of domination along their own borders. This propaganda tended to lessen respect for Europeans and to intensify local nationalism.

Britain was the first imperial power to recognize the changes that had occurred in the spirit of its colonial peoples and to acknowledge the need for adjustments in its imperial constitution.

The Progress of De-colonization

In the 1920s and 1930s the idea of the empire was very much alive in Britain. The shrinking of its export markets, especially during the international depression, forced it to think in terms of maximum self-sufficiency. Free trade was given up and some external tariffs imposed (1932). The empire now appeared to provide a potentially gigantic internal market. In 1932, at the Ottawa Conference, Britain accepted the principle of imperial preference advocated earlier in the century by Joseph Chamberlain. By virtue of the Ottawa agreements, the Dominions agreed to offer advantageous terms for entry of British manufactured goods in return for preferential access to Britain of their foodstuffs and other raw materials. Thus, for the first time since protectionism had been abandoned a century earlier, the British Empire became something of a formal economic entity.

Simultaneously, the British government recognized formally what it had acknowledged informally for some time, namely that the Dominions were not bound by laws enacted in the British Parliament. The Statute of Westminster, passed in 1931, affirmed that Dominion legislatures enjoyed complete sovereignty. In this statute Britain and its Dominions were defined as "autonomous communities" within the British Empire, equal in status and "united by a common allegiance to the Crown." During the 1930s the term "British Commonwealth of Nations," as more accurately describing the new imperial arrangement, gradually superseded "British Empire."

The framers of the Statute of Westminster and the Ottawa agreements believed that they were laying the groundwork for a new and lasting kind of imperial relationship. Their expectation was that as the colonies inhabited by non-white peoples became politically and economically mature, they too would rise to the status of Dominions, and in time the whole empire would become transformed into a world-wide association of free and equal partners.

Under conditions other than those prevailing in the twentieth century, this noble vision might well have been realized. But it needed time, and time is something history rarely grants. The outbreak of World War II, less than a decade after the imperial reforms of 1931–1932, cut the ground from under the long-term program. Britain emerged from the war so impoverished that it could no longer afford to carry the financial burden of administering and defending most of its colonial possessions and therefore had to cut down drastically its imperial commitments.° Between 1946 and 1948 Britain pulled out from most of its Far Eastern and Middle Eastern possessions, proclaiming its intention of ultimately withdrawing from those remaining in Africa as well. This withdrawal was, on the whole, accomplished voluntarily and under the pressure of domestic economic considerations. But the speed with which the nationalist movement developed in the colonial areas after the war left no doubt that unless the British departed willingly, they would eventually be ejected. This consideration played no small part in Britain's resolve.

The critical decision concerned India, the keystone of the British Empire. During the war Indian nationalists of the Congress party showed disquieting sympathies for the Japanese and even a willingness to collaborate with their armies which had invaded and occupied a part of India. To prevent its defection, Britain promised to grant India independence after the war. In August, 1947, the promise was made good with the proclamation of the Indian Independence Act. The subcontinent subsequently split in two halves: a Hindu-dominated India, and a predominantly Muslim Pakistan. The cleavage occurred

°There is no better argument against the economic interpretation of imperialism (Chapter 10) than the fact that Britain sought colonies when it was rich and abandoned them when it became poor.

amidst mutual carnage between the two religious groups. In 1948 Ceylon and Burma also received independence. India, Pakistan, and Ceylon became Dominions within the British Commonwealth—a status that imposed no restrictions on their sovereignty, but allowed them to gather handsome benefits from trading within the pound sterling area.

While withdrawing from the Middle East, Britain also liquidated, though more gradually, its holdings in the eastern Mediterranean. The greatest trouble occurred over Palestine, which Britain administered under a League of Nations mandate (it had been taken from the Turks during the First World War). Since the early years of the century an increasing number of European Jewish Zionists had migrated to Palestine in the hope of establishing there a national home for themselves and their persecuted brethren. They purchased fallow lands from the Arabs and by dint of hard work and modern techniques transformed them into flourishing agricultural communities. In 1917, through the so-called Balfour Declaration, Britain pledged itself to assist the creation in Palestine of "a national home for the Jewish people." Later on, however, Britain found it difficult to honor this pledge because the Jewish influx inflamed Arab nationalists, who viewed the Jews not as refugees from Western persecution but as Western col-

Robert Capa photographed Israeli militia marching toward the front during the Palestinian War of 1948.

onists come to push them out of their ancestral lands. In view of the importance of Arab good will, Britain tried to thwart Zionist designs and restrict the flow of Jewish immigrants. After World War II and the unprecedented losses that they had suffered in it, the Jews became desperate for a place of refuge. They applied pressure on the British and, when this did not work, resorted to terrorism. In 1948 Britain announced its intention of withdrawing from Palestine. The United Nations voted a partition plan creating two states, one Jewish, the other Arab. The Arab countries rejected this plan and formed a coalition which invaded Palestine, seeking to occupy it and prevent the formation of a Jewish state. They were soundly beaten by an amateur Jewish army. The state of Israel, which came into existence in the midst of this war, has since been recognized by the whole international community, with the exception of the Arab countries.

During the course of 1947–1948 Britain liquidated the "imperial lifeline" that it had acquired with such effort during the preceding two centuries. The transfer of power to the local population occurred earlier than British imperial planners had anticipated, and for this reason in a number of areas such as India and Palestine it caused a collapse of public order. But on the whole the transition from colonial status to independence in the British Empire proceeded smoothly. Having trained honest and responsible civil servants in territories under their control, the British had officials to whom to entrust authority when the time came to withdraw. This was least true of Africa, which the British evacuated rather hastily in the 1950s, before such local cadres could be trained.

In the 1960s all that remained of the British colonial empire were strategic naval and air bases, and even these are now in the process of liquidation. The British Commonwealth survives essentially as the world's second largest trading area, enjoying preferential tariffs and employing the pound sterling.

With the exception of the United States, which in 1946 promptly granted independence to the Philippines, its one major colony, the other imperial powers surrendered their possessions much more reluctantly than did Britain.

The French Empire rested on very different principles from those of the British. Britain thought in terms of ultimate self-rule, whereas France thought in terms of ultimate assimilation. The ideal of French imperialists was not a commonwealth of many free and equal states but a single community of white, black, and yellow Frenchmen. Unlike the British, the French practiced little or no racial discrimination, regarding as one of themselves any person who had acquired French culture. These considerations explain why, if for the British the postwar transfer of sovereignty to the colonies involved advancing their timetable, for the French it involved abandonment of their whole conception of themselves as a world-wide, multi-racial civilization.

In 1946 the French government proclaimed the establishment of the "French Union" (*L'Union française*), which it defined as a voluntary association of France and its overseas territories. The idea behind the Union resembled that underlying the British Commonwealth. But France was not prepared to recognize the right of its possessions to self-rule, insisting that they exercise their political rights within the institutions of metropolitan France. Rather than constitute their own legislatures, the colonial areas were to send representatives to the French parliament.

This arrangement did not suit the nationalists in the major French possessions. They demanded self-rule, and when this was refused they took up arms. In 1946 a savage colonial war broke out in Indo-China (Vietnam), where the nationalist forces were directed by a veteran of the Communist International, Ho Chi Minh. In 1954 the French were defeated and forced to withdraw. Chastened by this experience, France in 1956 conceded independence to two of its North African colonies, Tunisia and Morocco. But in Algeria such a solution was thwarted by the objections of the large resident European population. When self-rule was refused to the Algerian Muslims, they launched a guerrilla campaign. An extremely brutal civil war ensued, whose repercussions even threatened to cause a breakdown of order in metropolitan France. In 1958 the French army in Algeria staged a coup which overthrew the Fourth Republic and brought to power General de Gaulle. De Gaulle originally won the sympathies of the army by intimating his support for a French Algeria, but as soon as he came to power he reversed his stand and offered the Algerians independence (1959–1962).

After withdrawal from its other colonies in Africa the French Empire dissolved into a trading community, loosely tied by allegiance to the franc.

The least enlightened colonial policy was conducted by the smaller European powers, such as Holland, Belgium, and Portugal. The Dutch, upon their return to the East Indies, encountered a powerful nationalist movement organized during the war by the Japanese occupants. In 1945 the local nationalists proclaimed the independence of Indonesia and launched a guerrilla campaign against the

Algerian nationalists, photographed in the capital city of Algiers, celebrate their independence from France in 1962.

MARC RIBOUD-MAGNUM

The anarchy in the Congo following the Belgian withdrawal was accompanied by a threat of famine. Here, a Swedish soldier attempts to maintain order at a UN food-distribution center in 1960.

Dutch. The latter at first tried to resist by force of arms, then sought a compromise by offering Indonesia something close to dominion status, but finally recognized their defeat and withdrew (1954).

The Belgians in the Congo conducted what is usually described as a paternalistic colonial policy. Their aim was to raise the material level of the native population but at the same time to prevent any political ambitions from striking root among them. In 1960, when the Congo appeared on the verge of a major revolt and the Belgians decided to evacuate it, there were in the entire area only a dozen or so natives with a college education. No wonder that the precipitous Belgian withdrawal was followed by anarchy. The Portuguese to this day pursue in their African colony of Angola a colonial policy generally similar to that of the Belgians.

The liquidation of the Italian and Japanese empires during the war, and of the British, French, Dutch, and Belgian empires after it, left only one major empire in the world, the Russian. In the Soviet Union the Russians constitute approximately one-half the population. They rule over 100 million non-Russians, originally conquered by the imperial government, including 45 million Ukrainians and 30 million Muslims. Soviet imperial policy, since the Revolution as before, follows the French model: it promotes the economic and educational progress of its subject peoples while depriving them of any meaningful self-rule. In the long run, the Soviet government expects its subject peoples to be assimilated and become Russified.

A Europe deprived of its colonies and wedged between the more powerful United States and Soviet Union no longer could afford the luxury of division into a multitude of sovereign, contending states. If Europe was to maintain its identity and avoid becoming a satellite of one or the other of its two giant neighbors, it had to unite.

The process of European integration, which began shortly after the end of World War II, was inspired by a political ideal—the United States of Europe—but it was launched on its way by economic exigencies. The post-World War II integration of Europe resembles closely the unification of Germany in the nineteenth century, where a customs union (*Zollverein*, Chapter 2) also preceded political union. In the catastrophic situation in which Europe found itself after the war, it became obvious even to the most unsentimental businessman that the retention of internal tariff barriers would fatally handicap European countries in any competition with the United States and the Soviet Union, each with the labor force, market, and capital of nearly 200 million people. As a result of this realization (and no little American prompting) the wheels of history, which for a century and a half had driven the countries of Europe further and further in the direction of political and economic self-sufficiency, unexpectedly reversed themselves. Europe today is more united than it has ever been since the emergence of the democratic national state at the end of the eighteenth century.

PHASE ONE: THE MARSHALL PLAN

The initial impetus toward economic integration came from the United States. It took the shape of a massive scheme of economic assistance, the European Recovery Program, popularly known as the Marshall Plan, which originated in the spring of 1947, a few weeks after the proclamation of the Truman Doctrine (Chapter 19). This was a time when the growing disenchantment with Soviet behavior had induced Washington to undertake a general reappraisal of its policy toward the Soviet Union and to assume world-wide responsibility for protecting the integrity and security of independent states from the Communist threat. General George C. Marshall, the Secretary of State, had returned in April from Moscow after another futile meeting of foreign ministers. He now became convinced that the Soviet Union not only had no desire to cooperate in promoting European economic recovery, but was interested in positively preventing such recovery in order to improve the chances of the Western European Communist parties. Marshall instructed the newly formed Policy Planning Council of the Department of State, headed by George F. Kennan, to formulate a broad proposal on how best to cope with the problems of the European economy and the attendant political dangers.

In their recommendations Kennan and his colleagues urged that the government be guided not by a desire to combat communism but by a desire to eliminate "the economic maladjustment which makes European society vulnerable to exploitation by any and all totalitarian governments." In other words, the need was not for stop-gap aid to neutralize momentary Communist influence, but for a long-range program designed to revive Europe economically. Essential to the success of such a program was active European participation and inter-European cooperation:

It would be neither fitting nor efficacious for this government to undertake to draw up unilaterally and to promulgate formally on its own initiative a program designed to place Western Europe on its feet economically. This is the business of the Europeans. The formal initiative must come from Europe; and Europeans must bear the basic responsibility for it. . . . The program which this country is asked to support must be a joint one, agreed to by several European nations. While it may be linked to individual national programs . . . it must, for psychological and political, as well as economic, reasons, be an internationally agreed program. The request for our support must come as a joint request from a group of friendly nations, not as a series of isolated and individual appeals.°

On the basis of these recommendations General Marshall, in an address at the Harvard commencement in June, 1947, issued an invitation to the European states to formulate a common recovery program to present to the United States government.

The offer was taken up promptly. The British, French, and Italian governments immediately instituted consultations, in which fourteen additional countries subsequently joined. (Poland and Czechoslovakia also expressed a desire to participate in these talks, but were prohibited from doing so by Stalin.) Before long the seventeen countries submitted a joint proposal scheduled for a four-year period and budgeted for $22 billion. President Truman requested this sum from Congress, which cut it down to $17 billion. During the four years that the European Recovery Program was in operation (1948–1952), the United States actually spent about $12 billion, half of which went to three countries (Great Britain, France, and Germany).

After the Marshall Plan had been authorized the participating countries founded an Organization of European Economic Cooperation (OEEC) to distribute Marshall Plan funds and to facilitate economic activity among member states. The OEEC became a rudimentary apparatus of economic coordination, an institution which, although not specifically designed for that end, taught the sovereign states to think and act in an all-European rather than a national fashion.

Aid under the Marshall Plan was extended in two forms, as outright grants or as loans. In general, funds for articles of immediate consumption, such as food or fuel, were given in the form of grants, while purchases of equipment were financed by loans. Private enterprise in both the United States and Europe was heavily involved. More than half the monies appropriated under the Marshall Plan were spent inside the United States, stimulating productivity and providing jobs during the period of postwar readjustment.

The results of the Marshall Plan were spectacular. Two years after its initiation the productivity of Western Europe exceeded its prewar average by 25 percent; at its termination, in 1952, productivity was twice that of 1938. The European dollar gap—the difference between dollars earned and dollars spent—was significantly reduced. In the remarkably short period of four years Europe, which had seemed on the verge of total economic collapse, had not only recovered but had launched what turned out to be the greatest boom in its history.

°Quoted in George F. Kennan, *Memoirs, 1925–1950* (1967).

Viewed from the perspective of its short-range interests, it was not to the advantage of the United States that Europe should recover its productive capacity or closely coordinate its economies. A vigorous, coordinated Europe was certain to become America's competitor in world markets. This was so obvious that a large part of the European public at first doubted the intentions of the United States, suspecting that its real purpose in launching the Marshall Plan was to seize control of the European economy. But in reality the thinking of American statesmen who had formulated and executed the plan was different. They acted on the sound commercial assumption that a prosperous neighbor was not only a competitor but also a customer; that is, that in the long run the United States stood more to gain from trading with a well-to-do Europe than from supporting a weak and dependent one. The fear of communism played its part, but it was not the main motive behind the European Recovery Program and does not vitiate the fact that the Marshall Plan was one of the most imaginative and constructive acts in human history, an instance of enlightened self-interest at its best.

PHASE TWO: THE COMMON MARKET

The Marshall Plan initiated Europe's economic *cooperation*; the next step was its economic *integration*. This was conceived in the shadow of the Marshall Plan, and saw the light of day in 1957 with the creation of the European Economic Community (EEC), better known as the Common Market.

The dream of a united Europe goes back to the medieval ideal of the restored Roman Empire; Napoleon played on it to justify his conquests, and so did Hitler. It was a genuine aspiration of those who loved Western civilization and feared its self-destruction from nationalistic conflicts. There had been a Pan-European movement during the interwar period, but the time then was not propitious, and its influence remained confined to a small body of visionaries. After World War II the movement revived. It now gained a number of proponents among eminent statesmen, including Winston Churchill, German Chancellor Konrad Adenauer, and several high French, Belgian, and Dutch officials. With this support a political movement aiming at a federation of European states actually got under way in 1948–1949. At this time, a Council of Europe was set up at Strasbourg to serve as the proto-parliament of a united Europe. But the movement for political consolidation never got far because of vehement British opposition. Britain still had a strong aversion to surrendering any part of its sovereignty and an equally deep fear of confronting a united Continent. Moreover, the Labour government, in power during the crucial years 1945–1951, had additional reasons for not wishing to become involved in a supra-national organization in which non-socialists would constitute a great majority.

Having failed in their political aspirations, the Pan-Europeans succeeded in their economic ones. The first genuine accomplishments achieved by the proponents of a united Europe came as an accidental by-product of Franco-German rivalry. The French viewed with mounting anxiety the rapid recovery of German industry after 1948. Initially, they proposed to control and limit the industrial productivity of Germany so as to prevent its eventual remilitarization, but this proposal was vetoed by the United States, which considered a strong German industry vital to the economic recovery of Europe. In 1950 the potential German military threat became acute, for in that year (the Korean War had just

A 1947 Russian cartoon, "The Modern Trojan Horse," sees American aid dollars threatening Europe's sovereignty.

broken out) the United States decided on rearming Germany. Although the new German divisions were to be integrated into NATO forces, from the French point of view the mere re-emergence of a German army was enough to raise frightening specters.

To deal with this problem French Foreign Minister Robert Schuman in 1950 formulated an interesting proposal. As a means of forestalling a future war between the two countries he proposed a merger of the French and German steel and coal industries, the two indispensable ingredients of modern military technology. His scheme called for the creation of a supra-national "High Authority," an administering body free from control or even influence by the governments of the two respective countries, which would direct the pricing, marketing, and distribution of their joint steel and coal output.

The Schuman Plan was ratified by the French and German parliaments. In 1951 Italy, Belgium, the Netherlands, and Luxemburg also subscribed to it. In this manner a six-nation European Coal and Steel Community came into existence, whose member countries agreed to transfer a small part of their sovereignty to the High Authority. Britain was invited to join the Community but declined.

The integration of the coal and steel industries worked so well for all concerned that in 1955 the six participating countries resumed negotiations to see whether they could not further expand their economic cooperation. These talks culminated in the signing of the Rome Treaty in March of 1957, establishing the European Economic Community. In the process of European integration the Rome Treaty represents the most important milestone. It made provision for

A series of talks between French President de Gaulle (at microphone) and West German Chancellor Adenauer (left) symbolized the postwar rapprochement *between France and Germany.*

ERICH LESSING-MAGNUM

the gradual elimination over a period of twelve to fifteen years of all tariffs among the six participating countries. When the process was completed, goods, capital, and labor were to move freely from one country to another, undeterred by frontiers. The Treaty of Rome laid the foundations of a free trade area inhabited by 170 million people—a market nearly equal to that of the United States. While doing away with tariffs among themselves, the signatories undertook to raise uniform tariffs for goods originating outside the EEC. In addition to a free trade area the six also agreed on several other joint ventures, including a common atomic energy effort (EURATOM).

Great Britain had a chance to become associated with the Common Market but once more decided against involvement in Continental Europe. The main reason for its decision was the obligation of states that joined the EEC to adopt common external tariffs. Acceptance of this obligation conflicted with Britain's commitment to extend preferential tariffs to its Dominions. It would have spelled the end of the whole idea of the British Commonwealth of Nations and transformed Britain into a purely European power. Britain was not as yet prepared to acquiesce to such a policy, so contrary to its entire historic tradition. Torn between its allegiance to the empire and its craving for access to the West European market, Britain opted for the empire (for the time being, at any rate).

Instead of joining the EEC, Britain hastily organized in 1959 a European Free Trade Association, consisting of, in addition to itself, Sweden, Norway, Denmark, Switzerland, Austria, and Portugal. The members of this association pledged themselves to abolish gradually all tariffs against each other, but they were not obligated to adopt common tariffs against non-members—a provision that left Britain free to retain its preferential tariffs for Commonwealth states.

The British decision not to join the Common Market was a major blunder that had dire consequences for Britain's economy. The Free Trade Association added only 38 million potential customers to Britain's market, whereas the EEC would have added 170 million. After ratification of the Rome Treaty, American capital shifted from the United Kingdom to Western Europe, where potential growth was much greater. The output of industrial goods and the exports of the Common Market countries indeed grew more rapidly than did those of the Free Trade Association. In the early 1960s, realizing its mistake, the British government applied for admission to the Common Market, but its application was vetoed by French President de Gaulle (in 1963 and again in 1967).

The success of the EEC inspired the establishment of two other free trade areas. The Communist countries had since 1949 a common economic organization (COMECON) originally created as a counterweight to the Marshall Plan. In 1960 the countries of South America formed the Latin American Free Trade Area. Neither of these blocs, however, has yet had much success, because the economies of their member states are neither as complementary nor as dynamic as are those of the West European economic community.

In the 1950s liberal political and economic doctrines, seemingly dead and buried during the interwar period, underwent an unexpected resurrection. The experiences with authoritarian regimes had a sobering effect on Europeans and made them more tolerant than before of the shortcomings of the liberal system. The

Neo-liberalism

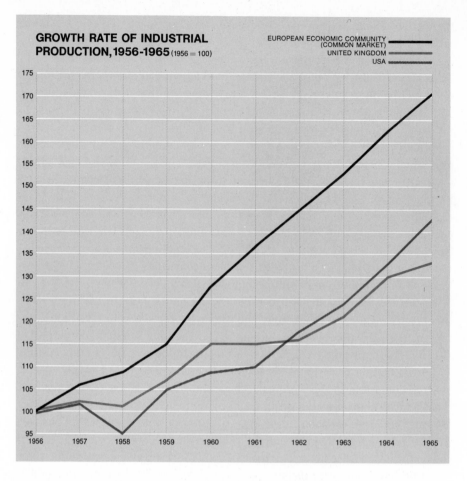

GROWTH RATE OF INDUSTRIAL PRODUCTION, 1956-1965 (1956 = 100)

EUROPEAN ECONOMIC COMMUNITY (COMMON MARKET)
UNITED KINGDOM
USA

United States, which in the immediate postwar years had had an overwhelming influence on Europe, encouraged and promoted this tendency. After the totalitarian "wave of the future" had receded, the older liberal values re-emerged surprisingly intact.

When we speak of a renascence of liberalism after World War II, we do not have in mind, of course, the classical, Manchester-type liberalism of the mid-nineteenth century (Chapter 2), but rather that liberalism modified by socialism which made its appearance later in the century (Chapter 9). This neo-liberalism adhered to the basic premises of the older doctrine—individualism, law, parliamentary institutions—but it no longer rejected state intervention. It regarded as essential government involvement in the life of society, especially in regulating its economic and social affairs.

After the immediate post-World War II anarchy had been overcome, the majority of voters in Western Europe expressed their preference for parties espousing such ideologies. In Germany and Italy—the two countries that had suffered most from the oppressive weight of regimentation—political power was entrusted to Christian Democratic parties. These were middle-of-the-road groupings committed to a modernized version of traditional liberalism. The Social Democrats, the principal opposition party in Germany, became hardly distinguishable from their rivals after 1959, when they formally disassociated themselves from Marxism and disavowed social revolution. In France the Fourth Republic that emerged in 1944 continued to suffer from the same parliamentary instability that had plagued its predecessor. In 1958, however, the military *coup d'état* originating in Algeria brought to power General de Gaulle, the leader of the Free French movement during the war. On de Gaulle's initiative, a new constitution was formulated which greatly strengthened the executive and introduced the American principle of direct popular elections for the Presidency. In its domestic politics the government of the Fifth Republic has shown itself to be fundamentally liberal. Finally, in Great Britain the Labour government which came to power in 1945 carried out an ambitious program of nationalization of heavy industry and social welfare. But as Britain's international economic position deteriorated, experimentation was abandoned, and succeeding administrations conducted a more moderate policy. The 1950s and 1960s thus have witnessed throughout Western Europe a re-emergence of political tendencies which had dominated before World War I. The basis of the neo-liberal state is an alliance of government and big business for promoting productivity and trade.

The revival of liberalism occurred against a background of unprecedented prosperity. After 1950 the economy of the West underwent an expansion that exceeded considerably anything experienced during the great boom of the nineteenth century. The annual rate of growth in the output of goods produced in the West (including the United States) had been 2.7 percent between 1870 and 1913; between 1950 and 1960 it averaged 3.9 percent. The growth was especially rapid among countries of the Common Market, showing during this period a rate of 4.4 percent in France, 5.9 percent in Italy, and an incredible 7.6 percent in Germany.°

This "economic miracle" had several causes. Among them were generous United States help in the form of loans and outright grants, the great reservoir of skills and the discipline of Western workers, and the expansion of the market by the reduction of tariffs. No little credit is also due to the farsighted steps begun during World War II to prevent another drying up of the sources of liquid capital such as had occurred in the 1930s. In 1944, at a conference held at Bretton Woods in New Hampshire, the Western Allies had established an International Monetary Fund designed as a pool from which member countries could buy gold or dollars in local currencies to overcome temporary disequilibriums in their balance of payments. Agreements of a similar nature entered into after the war stimulated the free flow of money. Thanks to these measures, world trade developed vigorously, nearly doubling in volume between 1948 and 1958. Increased trade meant increased productivity and this, in turn, meant increased employment. Thus the contraction of the world economy, which had begun in 1929 (Chapter 16), was now dramatically reversed.

Two additional factors influenced the spurt of the Western economy after the war: new techniques of economic control, and the emergence in Western Europe of a new business mentality.

During the depression of the 1930s much ingenuity had been exerted on finding means of alleviating unemployment. The most influential theoretical contribu-

° Figures from Angus Maddison, *Economic Growth in the West* (1964). In the period 1913–1950—an era of wars and depression—the over-all Western rate of growth had sunk to 1.9 percent.

tion to this discussion was that made by the English economist John Maynard Keynes. Keynes, whom we have encountered as a critic of the Versailles Treaty (Chapter 15), urged the government to intervene to promote full employment as soon as the natural operations of the market failed to do so. Among the steps he proposed were controls on interest rates on money, public work projects, and heavy government spending. The advice Keynes offered contradicted the traditional method of combating recession: limit spending and practice thrift. His advice was not taken in Britain at the time, though it had much influence on Roosevelt's New Deal. After the war Keynesian doctrines gained wide acceptance in both Britain and the United States. The two countries created elaborate mechanisms to keep a permanent check on the pulse of the national economy: as soon as that pulse slows down, the government intervenes, revivifying it by easing interest rates, or expanding credit, or lowering taxes, or increasing its own expenditures. When there is a danger of excessive inflation, the government reverses its policies. These techniques have helped substantially to reduce the business cycle and to save the economy from costly fluctuations.

On the Continent Keynesian methods gained less acceptance. Continental states, true to their tradition of centralism, have tended to adopt regular, over-all economic planning instead of manipulating money. None of the Western European states imitated the Soviet system of planning, with its firm production schedules. This system was quite inappropriate for countries that retained private enterprise and where the government could not command the entire national economy. In addition, the rigidity of the Soviet system was considered counter-productive. The model most widely adopted was that evolved in France in the 1950s. Its intention is not to direct from above the country's productive resources, but to make private business aware of general economic trends and thereby to induce it to think and plan its investments in line with the needs and tendencies of the national economy as a whole. The central organ of French planning, the *Commissariat du Plan*, although a branch of the government, has no executive authority: it advises (and given the power and wealth of the French government, its advice carries no mean weight), but it cannot command. On the basis of the French experience the other members of the Common Market group, as well as Britain, Sweden, Norway, and Austria, have introduced planning agencies.

The system of fiscal and budgetary control adopted by the United States and the United Kingdom, and the system of economic planning prevailing among the West European countries, have greatly enhanced the role of the state in the economic life of the West. The change is so great that some economists question whether the old term *capitalism* can be appropriately used today. They maintain that the modern Western economy is no longer capitalist in any meaningful sense, because it does not work for the free, competitive market. Rather, it is a mixed economy, depending on cooperation of the private and public sectors, without a clear line of demarcation between the two. Indeed, it is doubtful whether big business in the West could survive for long without government subsidies and other forms of assistance; nor is it conceivable that the state could manage an economy of such magnitude and complexity as that of the modern West without the help of private initiative. The mixed economy presently operating in the West may well provide the model for the world as a whole, replacing both the free, unregulated market economy of ideal liberalism and the fully regimented economy of ideal communism.

The other factor behind the economic boom of the 1950s and 1960s was a fundamental reorientation in the mentality of European business. Traditionally, European business enterprise had been more concerned with securing a share of the existing market than in expanding that market. This conservative policy contrasted with that pursued in the United States. The aim of business in the United States has been to enhance by all available means both the capacity and the desire of the consumer to buy. Among these means are full employment, high wages, liberal credit, and advertising. The American technique has been to place the maximum money or credit in the hands of the consumer and then to entice him to spend it on goods and services. By this method the United States has created an enormously productive economy, relying mainly on the domestic market (exports have always been secondary in the United States economy).

In the 1950s a similar philosophy began to permeate European business. A conscious effort was then made to increase the purchasing capacity of the working population. By pumping money into society through social welfare schemes, higher wages, and easier credit terms, the purchasing capacity of the average European has been considerably enhanced. The European consumer is today

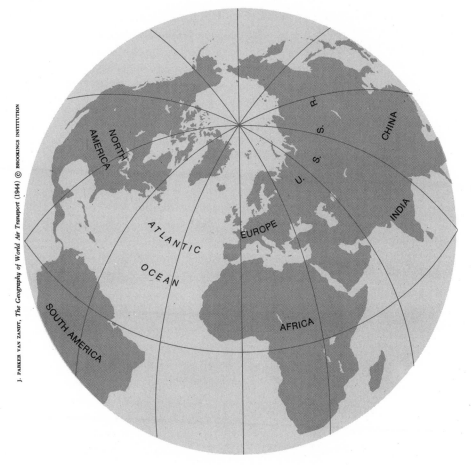

J. PARKER VAN ZANDT, *The Geography of World Air Transport* (1944) © BROOKINGS INSTITUTION

Europe's central position in what has been called the "principal hemisphere" is seen here. Within a hemisphere centered in northern France are 98 percent of the world's population, 94 percent of its industry, and the vast majority of its capital, natural resources, and management skills.

encouraged not to save but to spend. Much of the boom of the postwar Western European economy is due to the vast increase in the production of what is known as "durable consumer goods": automobiles, television sets, furniture, clothing, and so on. Many articles that had previously been confined to the middle class, notably the automobile, have now come within reach of the common man. This "Americanization" of the European economy has also had significant social consequences. With the spread of consumer goods an important distinction between classes—between those who have goods and those who do not—is disappearing. In its style of life postwar Western Europe is rapidly approaching the one-class pattern that has prevailed for some time in the United States.

The tempo at which its economy has developed after World War II has permitted the West to retain the international economic leadership that it had enjoyed at the height of the imperial era. The loss of colonies has had no appreciable effect on the position of the West in the world economy. With one-seventh of the world's population, Western Europe and North America produce 59 percent of the world's industrial goods, carry on two-thirds of the world's trade, and own three-quarters of the world's gold and foreign exchange. The rate of growth of the economies of the "underdeveloped countries" has been much slower, with the result that the distance between their standards of living and those of the West has tended to widen.

Concluding Remarks We have brought our narrative to a close with a discussion not of politics or of ideas but of the changes in the Western economy. The justification for this procedure is the fact that under modern conditions the economy is the single most powerful lever of history. Technology, capital, productivity, and marketing, with all that they involve, determine to a large extent how we live. They also provide a clue to the direction in which civilizations are likely to move in the second half of the twentieth century.

We have seen the West lose its global pre-eminence and almost simultaneously coalesce into a rudimentary supra-national bloc. In the postwar era the tendency everywhere has been for such large blocs to take shape, each united by political and economic interests and, to a lesser degree, by a common ideology. There is the Western bloc, consisting of two overlapping parts: the Atlantic community and the Common Market. There is also the Communist bloc, with its antagonistic halves: one under Soviet, the other under Chinese leadership. Other such entities are in the process of formation in Latin America and the Middle East. These blocs are in some measure supplanting the national state just as the national state in its time replaced the city-state and the feudal principality.

It is too soon to tell whether such blocs will solidify and become prevailing forms of political and economic organization, or turn out to be merely a transitional phase leading toward a single, world-wide community. In the long run the creation of a united world, in which people and goods will move as freely as they now do within the confines of the national state and free trade areas, appears inevitable. The process of world integration has been initiated by imperialism, and although imperialism itself appears a phenomenon of the past, the forces it has launched are irreversible. "Imperialism's one great achievement was to open up all parts of the world," writes William L. Langer, "and to set all humanity on the high road to eventual association and collaboration." And another historian, Herbert Lüthy, speaks of Europe's colonization of the world as "the painful birth of the modern world itself . . . the tumultuous and frightening genesis of a world which knows for the first time that it is one world and that its compass no longer stops at the edge of the visible horizon."

Whatever the future brings—many sovereign nations, several large supra-national blocs, or a United States of the World—it seems certain that the inter-dependence of the peoples of the world will continue to increase. Self-sufficiency can be purchased only at the cost of prosperity and in the long run is untenable. A division of labor has been taking place throughout the world since early modern times with a steady relentlessness that occasional reversals can delay but not prevent. Labor, goods, and capital are finding their way everywhere, seeking locations where they are most needed and most productive. The era of free trade inaugurated after World War II promises to cement the world market even more solidly than did the first great wave of free trade in the nineteenth century.

This means that human beings will be increasingly wrenched out of the security and isolation of their communities and thrown together—often in competition—with people whose cultures are altogether different from their own. We are already witnessing an expansion of the labor market that would have appeared fantastic fifty years ago, with Turkish workers operating machines in German factories, German stewardesses staffing domestic airlines in the United States, American workers drilling for oil in Arabian deserts, and Arab waiters serving tables in Swiss mountain resorts. The mobility of labor is bound to increase beyond anything known previously and to heighten the possibilities of conflict between nations and races.

In such a thoroughly intermingled world the need for liberal values will be greater than ever before. It will be imperative to learn respect for views and behavior other than one's own, to obey laws that make it possible for a variety of people to coexist in one community, to accept situations in which one does not have one's way in everything. Extreme authoritarian tendencies, such as National Socialism or communism, are not suited to the modern world. They are outdated survivals of an age when it still seemed possible for one person, or one nation, or one idea to transform life in its image. They are ideologies of peo-ple bewildered by modern life and anxious to do away with its inherent unpredict-ability. But life is too rich, too spontaneous to be held still. Nor is irresponsible anarchism the answer, for it undermines respect for law and institutions, without which coexistence of individuals and communities espousing differing interests and values is not possible. Only liberalism—with its tolerance and orderliness, with its mechanism for correcting outdated institutions and laws through demo-cratic elections, with its ability to balance the wants of the individual against the needs of the whole society—is a suitable system for the contemporary world. Under modern conditions the liberal way is not only the best way—it is the only way—to regulate human affairs.

Bibliography

§ INDICATES PAPERBACK EDITION AVAILABLE

EUROPE IN THE NINETEENTH AND TWENTIETH CENTURIES: GENERAL LITERATURE

COMPREHENSIVE SURVEYS

The New Cambridge Modern History, Vol. X: *The Zenith of European Power, 1830–1870* (1964); Vol. XI: *Material Progress and World-wide Problems, 1870–1898* (1962). The most recent attempt at a global history; Vol. X is better organized and altogether superior to Vol. XI.

POLITICS, DIPLOMACY, AND WARFARE

Clark, Grover, *A Place in the Sun* (1936). "This book is the result of an attempt to get, from the actual records, an answer to the question: Do colonies pay? Most emphatically, the answer is: No."

Craig, G. A., and Felix Gilbert, eds., *The Diplomats: 1919–1939*, 2 vols.§ (1953; 1965). Sketches of leading diplomatic figures of the twentieth century by diverse authors.

Falls, Cyril, *A Hundred Years of War*§ (1953; 2nd ed. 1961). The development of military technology and strategy from the American Civil War through World War II.

Fieldhouse, D. K., *The Colonial Empires* (1966). A general survey of Western imperialism since the eighteenth century; post-World War II developments briefly treated.

Fuller, J. F. C., *Armament and History* (1945). "A study of the influence of armament on history from the dawn of classical warfare to the Second World War."

Hawgood, J. A., *Modern Constitutions Since 1787* (1939). A survey of constitutional development in the West, by types of constitutional systems.

Ruggiero, Guido de, *The History of European Liberalism*, trans. R. G. Collingwood§ (1927; 1959). Surveys European liberal ideas and attitudes.

Taylor, A. J. P., *The Struggle for Mastery in Europe, 1848–1918* (1954). A controversial study of diplomatic history by an English historian.

Winslow, E. M., *The Pattern of Imperialism* (1948). A study of the theories of imperialism—its causes and significance.

ECONOMIC AND SOCIAL

Armytage, W. H. G., *A Social History of Engineering*, 2nd ed. (1961). How technology and technical innovation originate and how they influence history; with emphasis on Britain.

Ashley, Percy, *Modern Tariff History* (1904). The emergence of protective tariffs in Germany, the United States, and France.

Ashworth, William, *A Short History of the International Economy, 1850–1950* (1952). A succinct account of all branches of economic activity.

Birnie, Arthur, *An Economic History of Europe, 1760–1939*§ (1930; 1957). Brief survey, topical rather than regional, which emphasizes industrialism and industrial growth and their social aspects.

Bowden, Witt, Michael Karpovich, and A. P. Usher, *An Economic History of Europe Since 1750* (1937). A comprehensive survey which pays much attention to frequently neglected subjects, such as agriculture and Eastern Europe.

The Cambridge Economic History of Europe, Vol. VI: *The Industrial Revolutions and After*, 2 Parts (1965). The most up-to-date, authoritative treatment of Western economy since the mid-eighteenth century; partly topical, partly regional.

Cipolla, C. M., *The Economic History of World Population*§ (1962). An introduction to historical demography.

Clapham, J. H., *The Economic Development of France and Germany, 1815–1914*§ (1921; 4th ed., 1935). Comparative study of the two economies.

Condliffe, J. B., *The Commerce of Nations* (1950). The impact of the international economy on national economies in the nineteenth and twentieth centuries.

Derry, T. K., and T. I. Williams, *A Short History of Technology* (1961). A general introduction "from the earliest times to A.D 1900."

Dickinson, R. E., *The West European City: A Geographical Interpretation* (1951; 2nd ed., 1961). A historical survey of the Western city and its various types.

Glass, D. V., and D. E. C. Eversley, eds., *Population in History* (1965). A collection of essays dealing with various historic aspects of population growth and movement.

Landes, David S., *Unbound Prometheus: Technological Change & Development in Western Europe from 1750 to the Present* (1969). The story of the development of modern industrial technology.

Mumford, Lewis, *The City in History* (1961). The city from earliest times to the present, by a critic of modern industrial civilization and the sprawling megalopolis.

Palm, F. C., *The Middle Classes Then and Now* (1936). The bourgeoisie across the ages.

Rostow, W. W., *The Stages of Economic Growth*§ (1960; 1965). An attempt, by an economic historian, to provide a scheme of economic development valid for all countries.

Rudé, G. F. E., *The Crowd in History, 1730–1848*§ (1964). Analysis of crowd behavior on the basis of French and British experience.

Willcox, W. F., *International Migrations*, 2 vols. (1929–1931). Vol. I contains statistics, Vol. II, interpretation by country or ethnic group; the fullest account of modern population movements.

THOUGHT, SCIENCE, AND ART

Aron, Raymond, *The Opium of the Intellectuals*§ (1957; 1962). The myths of intellectuals: "revolution," "proletariat," "history," and so on.

Bowle, John, *Politics and Opinion in the Nineteenth Century*§ (1954; 1964). The ideological antecedents of twentieth-century politics: the Romantics, the Darwinists, the socialists, and extreme nationalists.

Caute, David, *The Left in Europe Since 1789*§ (1966). A sociological survey of radical movements and ideologies.

Cole, G. D. H., *A History of Socialist Thought*, 3 vols., (1953). A sweeping survey from the French Revolution to the outbreak of World War I.

Höffding, Harald, *A History of Modern Philosophy*, trans. E. B. Meyer, 2 vols.§ (1900; 1924). Vol. II deals with idealism and positivism in the nineteenth century; relatively non-technical.

McKenzie, A. E. E., *The Major Achievements of Science*, 2 vols. (1960). Stresses the nineteenth and twentieth centuries. Vol. I has a lucid historical exposition; Vol. II contains selections from original scientific writings.

Reichen, C. A., *A History of Physics* (1963); *A History of Chemistry*, (1963). Profusely illustrated brief introductions to the subjects.

Shryock, R. H., *The Development of Modern Medicine* (1936; 1947). Stresses social aspects of medicine.

Singer, C. J., *A Short History of Scientific Ideas to 1900*§ (1959; 1962). A comprehensive history of scientific thought, the latter part of which is devoted to the nineteenth century and the mechanistic outlook.

Singer, C. J., *A History of Biology to about the Year 1900* (1931; rev. ed. 1962). The evolution of knowledge about the nature of living things.

Whitehead, Alfred North, *Science and the Modern World*§ (1926; 1949). A popular exposition of the meaning of modern science by an eminent philosopher.

BRITAIN

Ashworth, William, *An Economic History of England, 1870–1939* (1960). A survey.

Briggs, Asa, *The Age of Improvement, 1783–1867* (1959). A topical description of England during its Industrial Revolution, stressing social and cultural subjects but also encompassing political history.

Carrington, C. E., *The British Overseas* (1950). Not so much a history of British empire-building as one of British colonization.

Checkland, S. G., *The Rise of Industrial Society in England, 1815–1885* (1964). The industrial sector of British society—the social history of all the elements involved in the industrial process, including inventors, businessmen, and workers.

Cole, G. D. H., and Raymond Postgate, *The British Common People, 1746–1946*§ (1947; 1961). The "people" here means the working class, whose social and political movements are traced.

Deane, Phyllis, and W. A. Cole, *British Economic Growth, 1688–1959* (1962). By economists using modern methods of analysis.

Ensor, R. C. K., *England, 1870–1914* (1936). A survey.

Knaplund, Paul, *The British Empire, 1815–1939* (1941). A survey of imperial history.

Lewis, Roy, and Angus Maude, *The English Middle Classes* (1949). A historical essay on the vaguely defined group.

Maccoby, Simon, ed., *The Radical Tradition, 1763–1914* (1952). Excerpts from English radical writings with brief commentaries.

Mowat, C. L., *Britain Between the Wars, 1918–1940* (1955). A comprehensive survey, with much attention to economics.

Schlote, Werner, *British Overseas Trade from 1700 to the 1930's* (1952). A statistical study.

Seton-Watson, R. W., *Britain in Europe, 1789–1914* (1937). British relations with the Continent, with emphasis on the "Eastern Question."

Taylor, A. J. P., *English History, 1914–1945* (1965). A survey.

Thompson, F. M. L., *English Landed Society in the Nineteenth Century* (1963). Deals with landed interests, often overlooked by historians emphasizing the moneyed middle class.

Thornton, A. P., *The Imperial Idea and its Enemies* (1959). Changing attitudes toward the empire in Britain, with emphasis on the past century.

Woodward, E. L., *The Age of Reform, 1815–1870* (1938; 2nd ed. 1962). A survey.

Young, G. M., *Victorian England*§ (1936; 2nd ed. 1953). An essay synthesizing the social and intellectual climate of England in the long reign of Queen Victoria.

FRANCE

Brogan, D. W., *France Under the Republic* (1940). A rambling, witty, idiosyncratic account of the Third Republic.

Cameron, R. E., *France and the Economic Development of Europe, 1800–1914*, 2nd ed., rev. and abr.§ (1961). Deals primarily with French banking and investments.

Cobban, Alfred, *A History of Modern France*, rev. ed., Vols. II and III§ (1957–1965). A survey from the rise of Napoleon I to 1962.

Plamenatz, J. P., *The Revolutionary Movement in France, 1815–1871* (1952). An essay on the republican, anti-monarchist ideologies and forces.

Priestley, H. I., *France Overseas* (1938). The growth of the French Empire in the nineteenth and early twentieth centuries.

Soltau, R. H., *French Parties and Politics, 1871–1921* (1930; 1965). The role of parties under the Third Republic.

Soltau, R. H., *French Political Thought in the Nineteenth Century* (1931).

Thomson, David, *Democracy in France Since 1870*§ (1946; 4th ed. 1964). Not a political history but an analysis of the interaction of conservative and revolutionary traditions in modern France, treated topically.

GERMANY

Craig, G. A., *The Politics of the Prussian Army, 1640–1945*§ (1956; 1964). The role of the military in German politics, and its disastrous consequences.

Hamerow, T. S., *Restoration, Revolution, Reaction*§ (1958). Argues that the triumph of anti-liberal forces in Germany between 1815 and 1871 was due primarily to the dissatisfaction of the lower classes with industrialism and the bourgeoisie.

Krieger, Leonard, *The German Idea of Free-*

dom (1957). Seeks to penetrate and explain the peculiarities of German political ideology.

Pinson, K. S., *Modern Germany, Its History and Civilization* (1954; 2nd ed. 1966). Concentrates on the post-1848 period.

Rosenberg, Arthur, *Imperial Germany: The Birth of the German Republic, 1871–1918*§ (1931; 1964). The internal history of Wilhelmian Germany and the reasons for its collapse. Should have been called: "The Death of Imperial Germany."

LOW COUNTRIES AND SWITZERLAND

Bonjour, Edgar, H. S. Offler, and G. R. Potter, *A Short History of Switzerland* (1952).

Edmundson, George, *History of Holland* (1922).

ITALY

Chabod, Federico, *A History of Italian Fascism* (1963). The title misleads, for this is really a general history of Italy from the end of World War I until 1949.

Clough, S. B., *The Economic History of Modern Italy* (1963). From the Risorgimento to the present.

Hughes, H. S., *The United States and Italy* (1953; rev. ed. 1965). Contains a great deal on the internal life of Italy.

Jemolo, A. C., *Church and State in Italy, 1850–1950* (1960). The crises in church-state relations from Risorgimento through most recent times.

Seton-Watson, Christopher, *Italy from Liberalism to Fascism, 1870–1925* (1967). A survey.

Smith, Denis Mack, *Italy; A Modern History* (1959). Italian political history, mainly from 1861 to 1925.

THE IBERIAN PENINSULA

Atkinson, W. C., *A History of Spain and Portugal*§ (1960). A survey.

Brenan, Gerald, *The Spanish Labyrinth*§ (1943; 2nd ed. 1950, 1960). An essay on the forces of Spanish history which pays much attention to social and economic subjects.

Carr, Raymond, *Spain: 1808–1939* (1966). A survey.

AUSTRIA-HUNGARY

Jászi, Oszkár, *The Dissolution of the Habsburg Monarchy*§ (1929; 1961). Emphasizes the Hungarian half of the empire.

Kann, R. A., *The Habsburg Empire* (1957). An inquiry, from the point of view of political science, of integration and disintegration of a multinational state on the example of Austria-Hungary.

Kann, R. A., *The Multinational Empire*, 2 vols. (1950; 1964). Nationality problems in the Hapsburg monarchy and the efforts to solve them between 1848 and 1918.

Taylor, A. J. P., *The Habsburg Monarchy, 1809–1918*§ (1941; 1965). A short survey.

Russia

Blum, Jerome, *Lord and Peasant in Russia*§ (1961; 1964). Agrarian conditions in Russia from earliest times to the emancipation of serfs (1861).

Florinsky, M. T., *Russia: A History and an Interpretation*, Vol. II: 1801–March, 1918 (1953). A detailed account by a historian critical of the imperial regime.

Kennan, G. F., *Russia and the West Under Lenin and Stalin*§ (1961; 1962). A history of Soviet Russia's relations with the Western powers, by a diplomat who at certain stages played a crucial role in shaping them.

Kornilov, A. A., *Modern Russian History from the Age of Catherine the Great to the End of the Nineteenth Century*, 2 vols. (1916–1917). An older account by a liberal Russian historian, almost exclusively devoted to internal policy.

Lederer, I. J., ed., *Russian Foreign Policy*§ (1962; 1964). A collection of papers dealing topically and regionally with Russian diplomacy.

Seton-Watson, Hugh, *From Lenin to Khrushchev*§ (1960; 1962). The history of Communism as an international movement, embracing the Soviet Union as well as Communist movements outside its borders.

Seton-Watson, Hugh, *The Russian Empire, 1801–1917* (1967). A general history which stresses successes and failures of "modernization."

Treadgold, D. W., *Twentieth Century Russia* (1959). The last decades of the imperial regime and the Soviet period, surveyed as an entity.

Wallace, D.K., *Russia*§ (1912). The *Times* correspondent describes turn-of-the-century Russia known to him from long residence. (The paperback version is abridged.)

Scandinavia

Arneson, B.A., *The Democratic Monarchies of Scandinavia* (1939). Some historical background, but concentrates on the twentieth century.

Hovde, B. J., *The Scandinavian Countries, 1720–1865*, 2 vols. (1943; 1948). An introduction to the emergence of modern Scandinavia.

Central Europe and the Balkans

The Cambridge History of Poland, Vol. II: *From Augustus II to Pilsudski (1697–1935)* (1941). A survey.

Davison, R. H., *Reform in the Ottoman Empire, 1856–1876* (1936). A history of the *Tanzimat* in the nineteenth century.

Halecki, Oscar, *A History of Poland*§ (1943; 1961; 1966). By a Catholic historian.

Lewis, Bernard, *The Emergence of Modern Turkey* (1961). The dissolution of the Ottoman Empire and the rise of the Turkish Republic.

Marriott, J. A. R., *The Eastern Question* (1917; 4th ed. 1940). The decay of the Ottoman Empire and international competition over its legacy.

Seton-Watson, R. W., *A History of the Czechs and Slovaks* (1943; 1965). A survey by a great sympathizer of the Czech Republic.

Seton-Watson, R. W., *A History of the Roumanians* (1934). A survey.

Stavrianos, L. S., *The Balkans Since 1453* (1958) A survey.

Wolff, R. L., *The Balkans in Our Time* (1956). Balkan history in the twentieth century.

CHAPTER 1. LIBERALISM AND CONSERVATISM: 1815–1848

Artz, F. B., *Reaction and Revolution, 1814–1832*§ (1934; 1957). A general survey, in the Harper Rise of Modern Europe series.

Bertier de Sauvigny, G. de, *The Bourbon Restoration* (1967). France from the fall of Napoleon to the July, 1830, Revolution, interpreted by a Catholic historian not unsympathetic to the Restoration government.

Bertier de Sauvigny, G. de, *Metternich and his Times* (1962). A sympathetic account.

Briggs, Asa, ed., *Chartist Studies*§ (1960). A collection of essays by different authors, mostly devoted to local activities of Chartist groups.

Burke, Edmund, *Burke's Politics*, ed., R. J. S. Hoffman and Paul Levack (1949). An anthology of his outstanding writings and speeches.

Butler, J. R. M., *The Passing of the Great Reform Bill* (1914). "More concerned with negotiations behind the scenes and effect of popular opinion, than with the course of events in Parliament."

Halévy, Elie, *The Growth of Philosophic Radicalism*§ (1928; 1955). Bentham and the Utilitarians.

Halévy, Elie, *History of the English People in the Nineteenth Century*§ Vol. II: *Liberal Awakening, 1815–1830*; Vol. III: *The Triumph of Reform, 1830–1841* (1926; 2nd ed. rev.). Britain between 1815 and 1841, by its outstanding French historian.

Hovell, Mark, *The Chartist Movement* (1918; 2nd ed., 1925). Despite its age, still not superseded.

Howarth, Thomas, *Citizen-King* (1961). The biography of the hapless Louis Philippe.

Hudson, Nora, *Ultra-royalism and the French Restoration* (1936). The rise and fall of the Right in Restoration France.

Johnson, D. W., *Guizot* (1963). An effort to redress the unfavorable prevailing view of the leading ideologist of the July monarchy.

Kissinger, H. A., *A World Restored*§ (1957; 1964). The efforts of Metternich, Castlereagh, and other participants of the anti-Napoleonic alliance to stabilize Europe, 1812–1822.

Magnus, Philip, *Edmund Burke, a Life* (1939). Biography of Europe's most seminal conservative thinker.

Mazour, Anatole, *The First Russian Revolution, 1825*§ (1937; 1961). An account of the liberal and republican officer uprising in Russia, the so-called Decembrists.

Nicolson, Harold, *The Congress of Vienna*§ (1946; 1961). By a participant in the Paris negotiations of 1919; hints at interesting parallels.

Packe, Michael St. John, *The Life of John Stuart Mill* (1954). The life and thought of the outstanding English nineteenth-century liberal thinker.

Phillips, W. A., *The Confederation of Europe* (1914). An account of the efforts made in 1815 and after to assure the "concert of Europe."

Pipes, Richard, ed. and trans., *Karamzin's Memoir on Ancient and Modern Russia*§ (1959; 1966). A translation and analysis of the most important Russian conservative document of the nineteenth century (1811).

Romani, G. T., *The Neapolitan Revolution of 1820–1821* (1950). Stresses the reasons for the failure of the Neapolitan rebels.

Webster, C. K., *The Congress of Vienna, 1814–1815*§ (1919; 1963). A diplomatic account.

White, R. J., *Waterloo to Peterloo* (1957). An essay in "suspended revolution"—social unrest in England after the Napoleonic wars.

Woodward, E. L., *Three Studies in European Conservatism* (1929). "Metternich, Guizot, [and] the Catholic Church in the nineteenth century."

(*See also* bibliography, General Literature—Politics, Diplomacy, and Welfare: Ruggiero.)

CHAPTER 2. THE BEGINNINGS OF INDUSTRIALIZATION

Ashton, T. S., *The Industrial Revolution, 1760–1830*§ (1937; 1964). A brief general survey.

Brady, Alexander, *William Huskisson and Liberal Reform* (1928). Not a biography but an analysis of the collapse of British mercantilism and triumph of liberalism, centered on the head of the Board of Trade.

Clapham, J. H., *Economic History of Modern Britain*, Vol. I: *The Early Railway Age, 1820–1850* (1926; 1939). A massive study of British industrialization at the time of its most dramatic progress.

Deane, Phyllis, *The First Industrial Revolution*§ (1966). The century 1750–1850 in the light of modern theories of economic growth.

Dunham, A. L., *The Industrial Revolution in France, 1815–1848* (1955). Stresses the causes behind the slow development of French industry.

Hammond, J. L., and Barbara Hammond, *The Town Labourer, 1760–1832* (1917; 1967). A devastating picture of living and working conditions of labor in England in the first phase of industrialization.

Henderson, W. O., *Britain and Industrial Europe, 1750–1870* (1954; 2nd ed., 1965). Deals with Britain's role in the development of the European economy.

Henderson, W. O., *The Zollverein* (1939). A history of the economic association which preceded and stimulated German political unification.

McCord, Norman, *The Anti-Corn Law League, 1838–1846* (1958). A fresh look at the League which endeavors, by pragmatic analysis of the evidence, to steer between liberal glorification and radical condemnation.

Mantoux, P. J., *The Industrial Revolution in the Eighteenth Century*§ (1927; 2nd rev. ed. 1961; 1962). The antecedents of nineteenth-century English industrialism.

Morley, John, *The Life of Richard Cobden* (1881). A detailed biography of the founder of the Anti-Corn Law League.

Singer, C. J., *et al.*, eds., *A History of Technology*, Vol. IV: *The Industrial Revolution, 1750–1850* (1958). A comprehensive survey of all branches of technological invention.

Thompson, E. P., *The Making of the English Working Class*§ (1963). The emergence of class consciousness among English labor in the first half of the nineteenth century.

(*See also The Cambridge Economic History of Europe*, Vol. VI, Pt. 1.)

CHAPTER 3. ROMANTICISM

Brinton, Crane, *The Political Ideals of the English Romanticists*§ (1926; 1966). The disillusionment of English Romantic poets with the French Revolution.

Brion, Marcell, *Romantic Art* (1960). A picture book with commentaries.

Chadwick, Owen, *The Victorian Church*, Pt. 1, 1829–1860 (1966). Religion and church in England and their problems.

Clark, Kenneth, *The Gothic Revival*§ (1928; 1964). An essay on early Victorian taste, with stress on architecture; confined to England.

Einstein, Alfred, *Music in the Romantic Era* (1947).

Gleckner, R. F., and G. E. Enscoe, eds., *Romanticism*§ (1962). The meaning of the term as interpreted by successive generations.

Halsted, J. B., ed., *Romanticism*§ (1965). A collection of excerpts by modern historians dealing with the meaning and significance of Romanticism.

Hugo, H. E., ed., *The Romantic Reader*§ (1957). Anthology containing excerpts on the idea of Romanticism, the Romantic hero, the artist, and other related subjects.

Royce, Josiah, *Lectures on Modern Idealism*§ (1919; 1964). A popular introduction to idealistic philosophy by a leading exponent of American pragmatism; originally delivered in 1906.

Stendhal, Henri, *Racine and Shakespeare* (1962). A contrast between the Classical and the Romantic, as seen by the French novelist.

CHAPTER 4. THE HIGH TIDE OF
LIBERALISM: 1848–1870

Bagehot, Walter, *The English Constitution* (1867). The classic summation of the English political system in the mid-Victorian era. (Available in several editions.)

Benson, E. F., *Queen Victoria* (1935). A brief biography.

Binkley, R. C., *Realism and Nationalism: 1852–1871*§ (1935; 1963). A survey, in the Harper Rise of Modern Europe series.

Eyck, Erich, *Bismarck and the German Empire*§ (1950; 1964) An abbreviation of a 3-volume German work by a historian somewhat critical of the Chancellor.

Friedjung, Heinrich, trans. A. J. P. Taylor and W. L. McElwee, *The Struggle for Supremacy in Germany, 1859–1866* (1935). The conflict between Austria and Prussia, by an Austrian historian of German sympathies; originally published in 1897.

Griffith, G. O., *Mazzini: Prophet of Modern Europe* (1932). "What has been attempted in the main is the setting forth of the development of Mazzini's inner life."

Hales, E. E. Y., *Pio Nono*§ (1954; 1962). A sympathetic view of the Pope and of the position of the Church in its struggle with the liberal, national state, by a Catholic historian.

Halévy, Elie, *History of the English People in the Nineteenth Century*§ Vol. IV: *The Victorian Years, 1841–1895* (1926; 2nd ed. rev.)

Howard, M. E., *The Franco-Prussian War* (1961). An account of military operations.

King, Bolton, *A History of Italian Unity*, 2 vols. (1899; rev. ed. 1912). A sweeping panorama of Italian political life from the fall of Napoleon to 1871.

Kitson Clark, George, *The Making of Victorian England* (1962). An effort to reinterpret the Victorian period in depth by using a variety of new methods, including statistical.

Longford, Elizabeth, *Queen Victoria* (1965). A full-dress biography, based on the queen's personal archives.

Mackay, D. C., *The National Workshops* (1933). The abortive socialist institutions set up in Paris in 1848.

Manuel, F. E., *The New World of Henri Saint-Simon*§ (1956; 1963). An intellectual biography of the thinker who exerted an enormous influence on French thought and politics of the mid-nineteenth century.

Mosse, W. E., *Alexander II and the Modernization of Russia*§ (1958). A brief survey of the reign which saw the most important liberal reforms.

Mosse, W. E., *The European Powers and the German Question, 1848–1871* (1958). The attitude of the other great powers toward the unification of Germany.

Namier, Lewis, *1848: The Revolution of the Intellectuals*§ (1944; 1964). Concentrates on the revolutions in Germany; reveals reactionary nationalist elements present in the German liberal movement.

Pflanze, Otto, *Bismarck and the Development of Germany*, (1963). Deals with Bismarck and his role in the unification of Germany, stopping with 1871.

Rath, R. J., *The Viennese Revolution of 1848* (1957). Emphasizes opinion.

Robertson, Priscilla, *Revolutions of 1848*§ (1952; 1960). A survey of the revolutionary year throughout Europe.

Salvemini, Gaetano, *Mazzini*§ (1910; 1957). His political thought and political action.

Simpson, F. A., *Louis Napoleon and the Re-*

covery of France (1923). The career of Napoleon III until the end of the Crimean War.

Simpson, F. A., *The Rise of Louis Napoleon* (1909; 3rd ed. 1950). The youth of Napoleon III.

Smith, Denis Mack, *Cavour and Garibaldi, 1860* (1954). Conflict between two political ideologies and personalities against the background of revolution in Sicily and Naples.

Smith, Denis Mack, *Garibaldi* (1956). "A great life in brief."

Temperley, Harold, *England and the Near East: The Crimea* (1936). The "Eastern Question" from 1839 onward, culminating in the outbreak of the Crimean War.

Thayer, W. R., *The Life and Times of Cavour*, 2 vols. (1911). A full-bodied life-and-thought, old but still not superseded.

Thompson, J. M., *Louis Napoleon and the Second Empire* (1955). Concludes "he was a man too small for the great things he set out to do."

Valentin, Veit, *1848: Chapters of German History*, trans. E. J. Scheffauer (1940). An abbreviated version of the standard German account.

Zeldin, Theodore, *The Political System of Napoleon III* (1958). An attempt to analyze the political techniques employed by Napoleon III.

(*See also* bibliography, General Literature—Britain: Young; and Russia: Kornilov.)

CHAPTER 5.   SCIENCE AND THE SCIENTIFIC OUTLOOK

Bagehot, Walter, *Physics and Politics* (1873). Politics seen from the point of view of Social Darwinism.

Becker, G. J., ed., *Documents of Modern Literary Realism* (1963). An anthology of writings by authors and critics of the nineteenth and twentieth centuries.

Berdiaev, Nikolai, *Leontiev* (1940). The life and thought of a Russian aesthete and enemy of industrial civilization.

Burrow, J. W., *Evolution and Society* (1966). The impact of Darwinian theories on social thought of the Victorian era.

Charlton, D. G., *Positivist Thought in France During the Second Empire, 1852–1870* (1959). Positivism and its influence on sociology, scientism, and literature.

Darwin, Charles, *On the Origin of Species by Means of Natural Selection*§ (1859). The classic statement of the theory of "natural selection." (Available in several editions.)

Darwin, Charles, *The Voyage of the Beagle*§ (1860). An account of the scientific journey which provided Darwin with evidence for the theory of "natural selection." (Available in several editions.)

Dostoevsky, Fedor, *The Diary of a Writer*, 2 vols. (1949; 1954). The political articles of the Russian novelist and conservative thinker.

Irvine, William, *Apes, Angels, and Victorians*§ (1957). Joint biography of Darwin and Huxley.

Kaufmann, W. A., *Nietzsche*§ (1950; 1964). A study of a leading critic of nineteenth-century civilization.

Marvin, F. S., *Comte* (1936; 1965). The philosophy of the founder of sociology.

Merz, J. T., *A History of European Thought in the Nineteenth Century*§ 4 vols. (1896–1914). A survey of scientific and philosophical thought in the age of positivism.

Sears, P. B., *Charles Darwin* (1950). An introduction to Darwin and Darwinism.

Woodcock, George, and Ivan Avakumovič, *The Anarchist Prince* (1950). The life of Peter Kropotkin, the Russian foe of Social Darwinism and the apostle of cooperation.

CHAPTER 6.   THE INDUSTRIALIZATION OF THE CONTINENT

Buer, M. C., *Health, Wealth and Population* (1926). An explanation of the population growth 1760–1815 in England and Wales in terms of rising living standards during the Industrial Revolution.

Feis, Herbert, *Europe, the World's Banker, 1870–1914* (1930). Europe's investments in its colonies and other economically underdeveloped countries.

Carr-Saunders, A. M., *World Population* (1936). A standard analysis of the problems posed by population growth in the modern world.

Clapham, J. H., *Economic History of Modern Britain*, 2nd ed., Vols. II (1932) and III (1938). The zenith of British industrial and commercial might and the beginning of the decline.

Hirst, M. E., *Life of Friedrich List* (1909). Still the only biography in English; includes selections from his writings.

List, Friedrich, *The National System of Political Economy* (1841). The classical modern argument for economic protectionism and national economic development.

Singer, C. J., *et al.*, eds., *A History of Technology*, Vol. V: *Late Nineteenth Century, 1850–1900* (1958).

Stolper, Gustav, *The German Economy, 1870 to the Present* (1940). Stresses the role of the state in German economy.

(*See also* bibliography, General Literature—Economic and Social: Ashley; Ashworth; *Cambridge Economic History of Europe*, Vol. VI; Condliffe; Glass and Eversley; and Landes.)

CHAPTER 7.   URBAN CULTURE AND THE MIDDLE CLASS

Banks, J. A., and Olive Banks, *Feminism and Family Planning in Victorian England* (1964). The domestic economics of the Victorian middle class.

Briggs, Asa, *Victorian Cities* (1965). An account of the life in several urban centers as an aspect of the total Victorian experience.

Briggs, Asa, *Victorian People*§ (1955; 1965). Biographical sketches of outstanding mid-Victorian figures intended to redress the prevailing unfavorable view.

Clephane, Irene, *Towards Sex Freedom* (1935). The social emancipation of European women, mostly before World War I.

Cruse, Amy, *The Victorians and Their Books* (1935). Literary history concentrated not on the writer but the reader; tells what was read in England in the first fifty years of Victoria's reign.

Dalziel, Margaret, *Popular Fiction 100 Years Ago* (1958). The literary tastes of the mass reading public in mid-Victorian England.

Dudek, Louis, *Literature and the Press* (1960). The effects of modern printing methods on culture in the English-speaking world.

Houghton, W. E., *The Victorian Frame of Mind, 1830–1870*§ (1957; 1963). The values and outlook on life of early Victorian England.

Lowndes, G. A. N., *The Silent Social Revolution* (1937). "An account of the expansion of public education in England and Wales, 1895–1935."

Morazé, Charles, *The Triumph of the Middle Classes* (1966). The European bourgeoisie during its zenith, 1780–1880.

Pevsner, Nikolàus, *High Victorian Design* (1951). The nadir of nineteenth-century taste, the Crystal Palace Exhibition of 1851.

Reitlinger, Gerald, *The Economics of Taste*, 2 vols., (1961; 1964). "The rise and fall of the *objets d'art* market since 1750."

Smiles, Samuel, *Self-help* (1859; 1959). From rags to riches to fame by way of honesty, industry, and thrift, as shown through examples of self-made men.

Sombart, Werner, *The Quintessence of Capitalism* (1913). The cultural background and the ethos of the European bourgeois.

Stutterheim, Kurt von, *The Press in England* (1934). Mostly devoted to the nineteenth and twentieth centuries.

Weber, A. F., *The Growth of Cities in the Nineteenth Century* (1899; 1963). The sociology of the modern city.

Wingfield-Stratford, Esmé, *The Victorian Tragedy* (1930). Victorian social life and values at mid-nineteenth century.

(*See also* bibliography, General Literature—Economic and Social: Dickinson; Mumford; and Palm.)

CHAPTER 8.   LABOR AND SOCIALISM

Berlin, Isaiah, *Karl Marx*§ (1939; 3rd ed. 1963; 1966). The man, his ideas, his achievements.

Bernstein, Eduard, *Evolutionary Socialism*§ (1909; 1963). The original statement of Marxist Revisionism.

Braunthal, Julius, *History of the International*, Vol. I (1967). Traces the history of the first two socialist internationals up to 1914; by a participant in the Second International.

Carr, E. H., *Michael Bakunin*§ (1937; 1961). A biography of the leading Russian anarchist.

Cole, G. D. H., *A History of Socialist Thought*, Vol. I: *The Forerunners, 1789–1850* (1953). A broad survey of modern socialist movements until the emergence of Marxism. Vol. II: *Marxism and Anarchism, 1850–1890* (1953). The conflict between Marx and Bakunin.

Cole, G. D. H., and A. W. Filson, *British Working Class Movements: Select Documents, 1789–1875*§ (1951). Excerpts from official reports, worker publications, and other sources bearing on the labor movement.

Gay, Peter, *The Dilemma of Democratic Socialism*§ (1952; 1962). Bernstein and Marxist Revisionism.

Hook, Sidney, *From Hegel to Marx*§ (1936; 1962). Philosophic and political radicalism as background to the emergence of Marxism.

Laidler, H. W., *Social-economic Movements* (1960). A general account of all the major and many minor socialist ideologies and movements.

Lichtheim, George, *Marxism*§ (1961; 1962). An introduction to Marxist theory.

McBriar, A. M., *Fabian Socialism and English Politics, 1884–1918*§ (1962; 1966). The role of Fabianism in the emergence of labor as a political movement.

Man, Henri de, *The Psychology of Socialism* (1927). By a disenchanted socialist.

Manuel, F. E., *The Prophets of Paris*§ (1962). Turgot, Condorcet, Saint-Simon with his disciples, Fourier, and Comte as social visionaries.

Marx, Karl, *Capital*§ (Vol. I, 1867, Vols. II–III, ed. by Engels, 1885–1894; Vol. IV, ed. by Karl Kautsky, 1905–1910). The main theoretical opus of Marx. (Available in several editions.)

Marx, Karl, and Friedrich Engels, *The Communist Manifesto*§ (1848). The prophecy of the imminence and inevitability of a Communist revolution. (Available in several editions.)

Maximoff, G. P., ed., *The Political Philosophy of Bakunin*§ (1953; 1964). An anthology of Bakunin's writings.

Mayer, Gustav, *Friedrich Engels* (1936). A biography of Marx's collaborator.

Mehring, Franz, *Karl Marx*§ (1935; 1962). An "official" biography, by the historian of the Second International.

Michels, Robert, *Political Parties*§ (1915). A study in political sociology revealing the bureaucratization of modern parties, including the Social Democratic.

Pelling, Henry, *The Origins of the Labour Party, 1880–1900* (1954; 2nd ed. 1965). Emphasis on political sociology: how the Labour party became a party.

Perlman, Selig, *A Theory of the Labor Movement* (1928). On the basis of historical evidence stresses the role of trade unionism and the gulf between laborers and socialist intellectuals.

Shaw, George Bernard, ed., *Fabian Essays in Socialism* (1889). The principal theoretical work of the Fabian socialists.

Sorel, Georges, *Reflections on Violence*§ (1908). A French syndicalist, who influenced Mussolini, stresses the need for the "myth" to keep the working class movement going. (Available in several editions.)

Webb, Sidney, and Beatrice Webb, *The History of Trade Unionism* (1894). The evolution of the trade-union movement in Britain by two leading Fabian socialists.

(*See also* bibliography, General Literature—Britain: Cole and Postgate; and Chapter 2: Thompson.)

CHAPTER 9. THE CRISIS OF LIBERALISM: 1870–1914

Chapman, Guy, *The Dreyfus Case: A Reassessment* (1956). An attempt to provide a balanced view of the issues and personalities.

Croce, Benedetto, *A History of Italy, 1871–1915*, trans. C. M. Ady (1929). A broad political and cultural analysis of Italy by a liberal historian.

Cross, Colin, *The Liberals in Power, 1905–1914* (1963). Emphasis on social legislation which laid the foundations of the welfare state.

Curtis, Michael, *Three Against the Third Republic* (1959). Sorel, Barrès, and Maurras.

Dawson, W. H., *Bismarck and State Socialism* (1890). An old account, still valid, of the ideas behind Bismarckian social measures and the whole modern welfare state.

Ensor, R. C. K., *England 1870–1914* (1936). A general survey.

Eyck, Erich, *Bismarck and the German Empire*§ (1959; 1964). A political biography.

Fischer, George, *Russian Liberalism from Gentry to Intelligentsia* (1958). From the middle of the nineteenth century to the Revolution of 1905.

Halévy, Elie, *History of the English People in the Nineteenth Century*§ Vol. V: *Imperialism and the Rise of Labour, 1895–1905;* Vol. VI: *The Rule of Democracy, 1905–1914* (1926; 2nd ed. rev.).

Hanham, H. J., *Elections and Party Management* (1959). "Deals solely with problems of the ordinary party politician and the growth of party organisation" in the era of Disraeli and Gladstone.

Hayes, C. J. H., *A Generation of Materialism, 1871–1900*§ (1941; 1961). A survey, in the Harper Rise of Modern Europe series.

Jellinek, Frank, *The Paris Commune of 1871*§ (1937; 1965). The story of the uprising of anarchists and Jacobins in the French capital during its siege by German armies.

Jones, Thomas, *Lloyd George* (1951). A biography of the man who first led and then wrecked the Liberal party.

Magnus, Philip, *Gladstone*§ (1954; 1964). The standard biography.

May, A. J., *The Hapsburg Monarchy, 1867–1914* (1951). A comprehensive survey.

Miliukov, P. N., *Russia and Its Crisis*§ (1905; 1962). Russia at the turn of the century as seen, at the time, by the leader of the Constitutional-Democratic party and an outstanding historian.

Monypenny, W. F., and G. E. Buckle, *The Life of Benjamin Disraeli, Earl of Beaconsfield* (1910–1920; 1929). The standard older biography.

Nowell-Smith, S. H., ed., *Edwardian England, 1901–1914* (1964). A collective work depicting various aspects of British life on the eve of World War I.

Pobedonostsev, K. P., *Reflections of a Russian Statesman*§ (1898; 1965). The political ideas of the man who most influenced the policies of Alexander III.

Pulzer, P. G. J., *The Rise of Political Anti-Semitism in Germany and Austria*§ (1966). Traces the emergence between 1867 and

1914 of anti-Semitic politics in German-speaking Central Europe, casting light on neo-conservative movements in general.

Robinson, G. T., *Rural Russia Under the Old Regime* (1932). Agrarian conditions and problems after the emancipation of the serfs.

Rogger, Hans, and Eugen Weber, eds., *The European Right* (1965). A collection of essays by diverse authors on conservative movements throughout Europe.

Somervell, D. C., *Disraeli and Gladstone* (1925). A double biography.

Venturi, Franco, *Roots of Revolution*§ (1960). The Russian social-revolutionary movement in the age of Alexander II.

Walkin, Jacob, *The Rise of Democracy in Pre-Revolutionary Russia* (1962). Stresses the forces tending toward greater democratization after 1861.

Weber, E. J., *Action Française* (1962). The story of the most aggressive neo-conservative group in Europe.

CHAPTER 10. DIPLOMACY AND IMPERIALISM: 1870–1914

Albertini, Luigi, *The Origins of the War of 1914*, trans. ed., I. M. Massey, 3 vols. (1952–1957). Vol. I: *European Relations from the Congress of Berlin to the Eve of the Sarajevo Murder*. Deals with the diplomatic antecedents from the Congress of Berlin (1878) to 1914; rather severe on Germany.

Bodelsen, C. A. G., *Studies in Mid-Victorian Imperialism* (1924). An intellectual history of the movement from "Little England" to "Greater Britain."

Brandenburg, Erich, *From Bismarck to the World War* (1927). Diplomatic history (1870–1914) concerned with the question of responsibility for World War I.

Brunschwig, Henri, *French Colonialism, 1871–1914* (1966). Stresses nationalism as a factor in French expansion and contrasts with British imperialism.

Clark, Grover, *The Balance Sheets of Imperialism* (1936). Shows the unprofitability of colonialism by means of statistics.

Craig, G. A., *From Bismarck to Adenauer*§ (1958). A brief, critical survey of German foreign policy and its lack of realism.

Hobson, J. A., *Imperialism*§ (1902; 1965). The classic argument for the economic interpretation of imperialism.

Hoffmann, R. J. S., *Great Britain and the German Trade Rivalry, 1875–1914* (1933). Upholds the thesis that Britain did not go to war for commercial reasons, but shows influence of economic fears on British opinion.

Hudson, G. F., *The Far East in World Politics* (1937). Great power activities in East Asia in the nineteenth and twentieth centuries.

Kipling, Rudyard, *Barrack-room Ballads* (1892). Sadistic, brawling verse meant to exult virility; reflects the mood of Social Darwinism and imperialism of the late nineteenth century.

Langer, William L., *European Alliances and Alignments, 1871–1890*§ (1931) and *The Diplomacy of Imperialism, 1890–1902* (1935). These two volumes provide a comprehensive survey of conflicts of the great powers and the formation of the principal alliances.

Langer, William L., *The Franco-Russian Alliance, 1890–1894* (1929; 1966). Supplements Langer's general studies (above) of diplomatic history of late nineteenth-century Europe.

Lovell, R. I., *The Struggle for South Africa, 1875–1899* (1934). Centers on Cecil Rhodes and the antecedents of the Boer War.

Lucas, C. P., *The Partition and Colonization of Africa* (1922). Devotes main attention to the late nineteenth-century "scramble."

Moon, P. T., *Imperialism and World Politics in the Nineteenth and Twentieth Centuries* (1919). Western imperialism in its final burst of expansion.

Petrovich, M. B., *The Emergence of Russian Panslavism, 1856–1870* (1956). The ideology behind Russia's push into the Balkans and conflict with Austria.

Saul, S. B., *Studies in British Overseas Trade, 1870–1914* (1960). Commerce within and without the empire as aspects of the emergent world economy.

Schmitt, B. E., *Triple Alliance and Triple Entente, 1902–1914* (1924). A brief account of the formation of the diplomatic alliances before World War I.

Sumner, B. H., *Russia and the Balkans, 1870–1880* (1937). From the antecedents to the consequences of the Russo-Turkish War of 1877.

Sumner, B. H., *Tsardom and Imperialism in the Far East and the Middle East, 1880–1914* (1942). Russia's contribution to the imperialist competition over land and influence.

Townsend, M. E., *The Rise and Fall of Germany's Colonial Empire, 1884–1918* (1930). From imperial indifference to imperial ambition to imperial collapse.

Wertheimer, M. S., *The Pan-German League, 1890–1914* (1924). The story of the powerful nationalistic and imperialistic lobby in Wilhelmian Germany.

Williams, Basil, *Cecil Rhodes* (1921). A biography of one of the leading British imperialists, by an admirer.

Woodward, E. L., *Great Britain and the German Navy* (1935). The "naval race."

(*See also* histories in modern diplomacy and imperialism listed in bibliography, General Literature—Politics, Diplomacy, and Warfare.)

CHAPTER 11. WORLD WAR I

Albertini, Luigi, *The Origins of the War of 1914*, trans. and ed., J. M. Massey (1952–1957). Vols. II and III.

Armeson, R. B., *Total Warfare and Compulsory Labor* (1964). "A study of the military-industrial complex of Germany during World War I."

Chambers, F. P., *The War Behind the War, 1914–1918* (1939). An account of home mobilization among the belligerents during World War I.

Cruttwell, C. R. M. F., *A History of the Great War, 1914–1918* (1934; 2nd ed., 1936). A general survey of all the fronts.

Falls, Cyril, *The Great War: 1914–1918*§ (1959; 1961). A general survey.

Fay, S. B., *The Origins of the World War*, 2 vols.§ (1928; 2nd rev. ed., 1938). Tends to be somewhat more generous to the German and Austrian side than most foreign historians.

Feldman, G. D., *Army, Industry, and Labor in Germany, 1914–1918* (1966). Social aspects of the German military effort.

Fischer, Fritz, *Germany's Aims in the First World War* (1967). On the basis of archival documents shows how broad and uncompromising were German ambitions.

Forster, Kent, *The Failures of Peace* (1942). "The search for a negotiated peace during the First World War."

Golovin, N. N., *The Russian Army in the World War* (1931). Not a military narrative but an analysis of the condition of the Russian armed forces.

Hašek, Jaroslav, *The Good Soldier: Schweik*§ (1930; 1962). The archetypal bewildered little man in World War I: a Czech recruit in the Austrian army.

Hemingway, Ernest, *A Farewell to Arms*§ (1929; 1967). World War I on the Italian front.

Kedourie, Elie, *England and the Middle East* (1956). "The destruction of the Ottoman Empire, 1914–1921."

Lee, D. E., ed., *The Outbreak of the First World War: Who Was Responsible?*§ (1958; rev. ed., 1963). A source book, with excerpts from differing points of view.

Liddell-Hart, B. H., *A History of the World War, 1914–1918* (1930). A survey by a leading British strategist.

May, A. J., *The Passing of the Hapsburg Monarchy 1914–1918*, 2 vols. (1966). Austria-Hungary during World War I.

May, E. R., *The World War and American Isolation, 1914–1917*§ (1959; 1966). The fight to keep the United States out of World War I, and its defeat.

Parsons, I. M., *Men Who March Away* (1965). British war poetry, 1914–1918.

Remarque, Erich Maria, *All Quiet on the Western Front*§ (1929; 1962.). This novel was the first to impress the broad public with the horror of modern warfare.

Renouvin, Pierre, *The Immediate Origins of the War (28th June–4th August 1914)* (1928). A balanced view of the question of origins and responsibility, rather severe on the Central Powers.

Ritter, Gerhard, *The Schlieffen Plan* (1958). A detailed analysis of the emergence of the plan, with documents.

Romains, Jules, *Verdun: The Prelude, the Battle* (1939). A novel, part of a cycle called *Men of Good Will*.

Tuchman, Barbara, *The Guns of August*§ (1962). An account of the opening phase of World War I.

Wegerer, Alfred von, *A Refutation of the Versailles War Guilt Thesis* (1930). A German response to the charge that Germany was the sole aggressor.

CHAPTER 12. THE RUSSIAN REVOLUTION

Borkenau, Franz, *World Communism*§ (1938; 1962). A survey of the activities of the Third International, by a one-time member.

Carr, E. H., *The Bolshevik Revolution, 1917–1923*, 3 vols.§ (1950–1953). Detailed, topical rather than narrative; sympathetic to the general course of Bolshevik policy.

Chamberlain, W. H., *The Russian Revolution, 1917–1921*, 2 vols.§ (1935; 1954). A general history stressing political and military events.

Daniels, R. V., *The Conscience of the Revolution*, (1960). The story of the opposition to the Bolshevik dictatorship within the party.

Daniels, R. V., *Red October* (1967). A narrative of the events leading to the Bolshevik seizure of power.

Degras, Jane, ed., *The Communist International, 1919–1943*, Vol. I: *1919–1922* (1956). Documents.

Denikin, A. I., *The White Army* (1930). By the commander of the principal anti-Bolshevik force, the Volunteer Army.

Deutscher, Isaac, *The Prophet Armed*§ (1954). The story of Trotsky's rise (1879–1921), by an ardent admirer.

Florinsky, M. T., *The End of the Russian Empire*§ (1931; 1961). Russia during World War I and the role of the war in causing the collapse of the old regime.

Katkov, George, *Russia, 1917* (1967). An investigation of the more obscure forces involved in the fall of the imperial regime, including German sedition.

Kerensky, Alexander, *The Kerensky Memoirs*, (1965). The autobiography of the last Prime Minister of the Provisional Government.

Kerensky, Alexander, and R. P. Browder, *The Russian Provisional Government, 1917*, 3 vols. (1961). A collection of documents bearing on the policies of the Provisional Government.

Nicholas II and Alexandra, *The Letters of the Tsar to the Tsaritsa, 1914–1917* (1929). A collection of private exchanges, miraculously preserved.

Pares, Bernard, *The Fall of the Russian Monarchy*§ (1939). By a British historian who was an eyewitness of the events.

Pipes, Richard, *The Formation of the Soviet Union*§ (1954; rev. ed. 1964). The history of the disintegration of the Russian Empire and the establishment of the multinational Communist state (1917–1923).

Radkey, O. H., *The Election to the Russian Constituent Assembly of 1917* (1950). An analysis of the voting and its results.

Reed, John, *Ten Days That Shook the World*§ (1919). A literary rendition of the Bolshevik power seizure, by a sympathetic American witness.

Schapiro, L. B., *The Communist Party of the Soviet Union*§ (1960; 1964). In view of the importance of the party, this is in effect a history of the Soviet Union and its government.

Schapiro, L. B., *The Origin of the Communist Autocracy*§ (1955; 1965). The story of the suppression by the Communist regime of internal dissent during Lenin's lifetime.

Sukhanov, N. N., *The Russian Revolution, 1917*, ed. Joel Carmichael§ (1955; 1962). A condensed translation of the 7-volume Russian work by a hostile socialist who was in the midst of the events.

Trotsky, Leon, *The History of the Russian Revolution*, 3 vols. (1932–1933). Not so much a historical study as a personal account by a leading actor.

Ulam, A. B., *The Bolsheviks* (1965). The rise of Bolshevism in the form of a biography of Lenin.

Wheeler-Bennett, J. W., *Brest-Litovsk*§ (1956; 1963). An account of the Russo-German peace negotiations after the Bolshevik power seizure.

Wolfe, Bertram, *Three Who Made a Revolution*§ (1948; 4th ed. 1964). The lives of Lenin, Trotsky, and Stalin before they became rulers of Russia.

Wrangel, N. E., *From Serfdom to Bolshevism* (1927). Recollections of the last commander of the White forces.

Zeman, Z. A. B., ed., *Germany and the Revolution in Russia, 1915–1918* (1958). Selected documents bearing on German-Bolshevik relations found in captured archives of the German Foreign Ministry.

CHAPTER 13. MODERN THOUGHT

Allen, G. W., *William James* (1967). A biography.

Ayer, A. J., *Language, Truth and Logic*§ (1936; 2nd rev. ed). An introduction to logical positivism.

Bergson, Henri, *Creative Evolution* (1907; 1944). The main work of the influential late nineteenth-century French philosopher, stressing difference between intelligence and instinct.

Cline, B. L., *The Questioners* (1965). An introduction to the history of the quantum theory.

Einstein, Albert, *Ideas and Opinions*§ (1954; 1960). An anthology of Einstein's pronouncements on men, politics, and scientific questions.

Frank, Philipp, *Einstein: His Life and Times* (1947). An intellectual biography, by a disciple and a leading philosopher of science.

Glover, Edward, *Freud or Jung?*§ (1950; 1963). Jung interpreted by a Freudian, with predictable results.

Heisenberg, Werner, *Philosophic Problems of Nuclear Science* (1952). The intellectual implications of post-quantum physics by a leading modern scientist.

Heisenberg, Werner, *The Physicist's Conception of Nature* (1958). A philosophic essay.

Hughes, H. S., *Consciousness and Society*§ (1958; 1961). Stress on innovations in the conception of man's place in the human environment, 1890–1930.

Infeld, Leopold, *Albert Einstein*§ (1950; 1953). An introduction to Einstein's theory.

Jacobi, Jolande, *The Psychology of C. G. Jung*§ (1942; rev. ed. 1963). By a follower.

James, William, *Essays on Faith and Morals*§ (1897). Representative selections.

Jones, Ernest, *The Life and Work of Sigmund Freud*, 3 vols. (1953–1957; § abr. Lionel Trilling and Steven Marcus, 1961). The author is the leading exponent of Freudian psychology in England.

Müller-Freienfels, Richard, *The Evolution of Modern Psychology* (1935). General introduction to various modern psychological schools.

Perry, R. B., *Philosophy of the Recent Past* (1926). Bergson, William James, and other thinkers of their time.

Planck, Max, *Scientific Autobiography, and Other Papers* (1949). By the discoverer of quanta; his philosophy of life and science.

Planck, Max, *Where Is Science Going?* (1932). Reflections on science and its place in modern life.

Rieff, Philip, *Freud*§ (1959; 1961). An introduction to Freud and his teachings.

Sartre, Jean-Paul, *Existentialism and Human Emotions*§ (1948; 1965). Popular exposition of existential philosophy by its most popular exponent.

Schrödinger, Erwin, *Science Theory and Man*§ (1957) [*Science and the Human Temperament* (1935)]. By a leading physicist, the author of the "uncertainty principle"; stresses the importance of chance in science and the flaws in common-sense causal thinking.

White, M. G., ed., *The Age of Analysis*§ (1955). An anthology of modern philosophic texts with brief introductions.

CHAPTER 14.   MODERN TASTE

Barr, Alfred, ed., *Masters of Modern Art* (1954). An introduction to Modernism in the visual arts.

Bowra, C. M., *The Heritage of Symbolism*§ (1943; 1961). Valery, Rilke, S. George, Blok, Yeats.

Collaer, Paul, *A History of Modern Music*§ (1961). An introduction.

Giedion, Sigfried, *Space, Time and Architecture* (1941; 4th rev. ed. 1962). Shows the interrelationship and purposefulness of modern art.

Haftmann, Werner, *Painting in the Twentieth Century*, 2 vols.§ (1961; new ed. 1965).

Hitchcock, H. R., *Architecture, Nineteenth and Twentieth Centuries* (1958; 2nd ed. 1963).

Humphrey, Robert, *Stream of Consciousness in the Modern Novel*§ (1954; 1962).

Joedicke, Jürgen, *A History of Modern Architecture* (1959).

Leymarie, Jean, *French Painting*, Vol. III: *The Nineteenth Century from David to Seurat* (1962). Classicism, Realism, and Impressionism, all richly illustrated.

Mackail, J. W., *The Life of William Morris*, 2 vols. (1899). A standard biography of the pioneer of modern design.

Madsen, S. T., *Art Nouveau* (1967). A survey of the decorative style popular at the turn of the century.

Pevsner, Nikolaus, *Pioneers of Modern Design*§ (1936; 1964). The origins, from William Morris to World War I, with stress on architecture and the applied arts.

Rewald, John, *The History of Impressionism* (1946; rev. ed. 1962).

Rewald, John, *Post-Impressionism: From Van Gogh to Gauguin*, Vol. I. (1956).

Salazar, Adolfo, *Music in our Time* (1946).

Wilson, Edmund, *Axel's Castle*§ (1931; 1959). A survey of Symbolic and post-Symbolic literature, 1870–1930.

CHAPTER 15.   THE TWENTIES

Birdsall, Paul, *Versailles Twenty Years After* (1941). Opposes the view that the Versailles Treaty was responsible for the collapse of peace in the 1930s.

Eyck, Erich, *A History of the Weimar Republic*, trans. H. P. Hanson and R. G. L. Waite, 2 vols. (1962–1963). Vol. I: *From the Collapse of the Empire to Hindenburg's Election*; Vol. II: *From the Locarno Conference to Hitler's Seizure of Power*.

Finer, Herman, *Mussolini's Italy*§ (1935; 1964). A survey of the history and life of Italy during the first decade of fascism.

Halperin, S. W., *Germany Tried Democracy*§ (1946; 1965). The Weimar Republic, a political history.

Link, A. S., *Woodrow Wilson* (1963). A biography.

Macartney, C. A., and A. W. Palmer, *Independent Eastern Europe* (1962). Eastern Europe between the wars.

Mamatey, V. S., *The United States and East Central Europe, 1914–1918* (1957). American diplomacy and the emergence of independent states on the ruins of Austria-Hungary.

Mowat, C. L., *Britain Between the Wars, 1918–1940* (1955). A survey.

Nicolson, Harold, *Peacemaking*§ (1919; 1965). Reflections on the Paris Conference by a diplomat-historian and a participant.

Rosenberg, Arthur, *A History of the German Republic* (1936; 1965). The Weimar Republic.

Rothschild, Joseph, *Pilsudski's Coup d'État* (1966). A monograph tracing the establishment of dictatorship in Poland (1926).

Walters, F. P., *A History of the League of Nations*, 2 vols. (1952). From its foundation to the end of World War II.

Wiskemann, Elizabeth, *Europe of the Dictators, 1919–1945*§ (1966). A brief survey of the destruction of democracy and the rise and fall of authoritarian states on the Continent.

CHAPTER 16. TOTALITARIANISM

Arendt, Hannah, *The Origins of Totalitarianism*§ (1951; 1966). Shows progression from anti-Semitism through imperialism to totalitarianism, concentrating on Soviet Russia and Nazi Germany.

Baumont, Maurice, J. H. E. Fried, and E. Vermeil, eds., *The Third Reich* (1955). The antecedents of nazism, its ascent and its manifestation, by an international group of scholars.

Bullock, Alan, *Hitler, A Study in Tyranny*§ (1952; rev. ed. 1964). A biography.

Carr, E. H., *History of Soviet Russia: The Interregnum, 1923–1924* and *Socialism in One Country, 1924–1926*§ 2 vols. (1954; 1961). Devoted to the struggle for succession and Stalin's triumph.

Cohn, N. R. C., *Warrant for Genocide* (1967). "The myth of the Jewish world conspiracy."

Conquest, Robert, *The Great Terror* (1968). The first full account of the detention, interrogation, exile, and mass murder perpetrated by Stalin in the 1930s.

Dallin,. David, and B. I. Nicolaevsky, *Forced Labor in Soviet Russia* (1947). A history of Soviet concentration camps by two Russian *émigré* socialists.

Deutscher, Isaac, *The Prophet Unarmed*§ (1959). The Trotsky-Stalin struggle in the form of a Trotsky biography.

Eschenburg, Theodor, *et al.*, *The Path to Dictatorship, 1918–1933*§ (1966). Essays by ten historians on the collapse of the Weimar Republic and the Nazi seizure of power.

Fainsod, Merle, *How Russia is Ruled* (1953; rev. ed. 1963). Soviet political institutions.

Fischer, Ruth, *Stalin and German Communism* (1948). A prominent one-time member describes the history of the German Communist party from its emergence until the late 1920s, when Stalin took over.

Ginzburg, Evgeniia, *The Wayward Path* (1967). Recollections of the Stalinist purges by a Communist, now living in Russia.

Hodson, H. V., *Slump and Recovery, 1929–1937* (1938). An economic analysis of the depression.

Khrushchev, Nikita S., *The Crimes of the Stalin Era* (1956). Khrushchev's "secret speech" at the Twentieth Party Congress, revealing facts about Stalin and his terror.

Orwell, George, *1984*§ (1949; 1963). An anti-utopian novel depicting life in an imaginary totalitarian state.

Reitlinger, Gerald, *The SS* (1957). Himmler and his apparatus of mass murder.

Robbins, Lionel, *The Great Depression* (1934). An economist's view.

Schoenbaum, David, *Hitler's Social Revolution*§ (1966). The Nazi policy toward various social groups before World War II.

Solzhenitsyn, Alexander, *One Day in the Life of Ivan Denisovich*§ (1963). A semi-fictional account of a Stalinist concentration camp by a Soviet writer speaking from personal experience.

Souvarine, Boris, *Stalin* (1939). A biography, ends in 1937.

Stern, F. R., *The Politics of Cultural Despair*§ (1961; 1963). Three sketches of German prophets of cultural nihilism as background to the rise of nazism.

Talmon, Jacob, *The Origins of Totalitarian Democracy*§ (1952; 2nd ed. 1965). Distinguishes between "liberal" and "totalitarian" democracies, and traces the latter in the thought of eighteenth-century believers in human perfectibility.

Wheeler-Bennett, J. W., *The Nemesis of Power* (1953; 2nd ed.). "The German army in politics, 1918–1945."

CHAPTER 17. THE DISSOLUTION OF THE MIDDLE CLASS

Brown, A. J., *The Great Inflation, 1939–1951* (1955). A rather technical discussion of what has happened to the value of money during 1939–1951, a period the author regards as "one of the greatest, if not the greatest" inflation in world history.

Burnham, James, *The Managerial Revolution*§ (1941; 1960). Asserts that managers are taking over the modern world.

Camp, W. D., *Marriage and the Family in France Since the Revolution* (1961). A statistical study of marital and familial institutions in France for the purpose of ascertaining the fate of both.

Djilas, Milovan, *The New Class*§ (1957; 1961). A Yugoslav Communist and friend of Tito depicts the emergence in Communist countries of a class of bureaucratic exploiters.

Graves, Robert, and Alan Hodge, *The Long Week-end*§ (1940). An amusing account of British life between the wars.

Hoggart, Richard, *The Uses of Literacy*§ (1957; 1961). The culture of the working class in the first half of the twentieth century as influenced by mass publications.

McGregor, O. R., *Divorce in England* (1957). Divorce legislation and incidence during the century following the easing of divorce procedures.

Marwick, Arthur, *The Deluge* (1966). The effects of World War I on British society, 1914–1920.

Mills, C. W., *White Collar*§ (1951; 1962). A sociological study of the American salaried class and its role in modern life.

Strachey, Lytton, *Eminent Victorians*§ (1918; 1963). A collection of four biographical essays intended to ridicule the Victorians by showing they were human after all.

Taylor, J. C., *Futurism* (1961). The artistic side of the Futurist movement.

Wingfield-Stratford, Esmé, *The Victorian Sunset* (1932). A social and cultural account of England 1870–1900, stressing the gradual erosion of Victorian values.

(*See also* bibliography, General Literature— Economic and Social: Palm; and Chapter 7: Lowndes.)

CHAPTER 18.   WORLD WAR II

Bettelheim, Bruno, *The Informed Heart* (1960). A psychologist's reflections on man, based on his experiences in Nazi concentration camps.

Broad, Lewis, *Winston Churchill*, 2 vols. (1958–1959). A biography, the bulk devoted to the years of World War II.

Chuikov, V. I., *The Battle for Stalingrad* (1964). Recollections of a Russian commander.

Churchill, Winston, *War Speeches*, 3 vols. (1951–1952).

Clark, Alan, *Barbarossa*§ (1964). The Russian-German war, 1941–1945.

Collier, J. B., *The Defence of the United Kingdom* (1957). The Battle of Britain and Hitler's invasion plans constitute a major part of this military narrative.

Dallin, Alexander, *German Rule in Russia, 1941–1945* (1957). Nazi occupation of Russia and its effect on the population.

Dark Side of the Moon, The (1946). Polish prisoners and refugees, interned in the Soviet Union, describe life in forced labor camps; with a Preface by T. S. Eliot.

Gehl, Jürgen, *Austria, Germany, and the Anschluss, 1931–1938* (1963). The antecedents of Hitler's annexation of Austria.

Gilbert, Martin, and Richard Gott, *The Appeasers* (1963). "British policy toward Nazi Germany" and its follies.

Greenfield, K. R., ed., *Command Decisions* (1959). An analysis of a number of crucial military decisions by the Allied and Axis powers during World War II.

Kogon, Eugen, *The Theory and Practice of Hell*§ (1950). A description of the Nazi concentration camp world by one who was an inmate for six years.

Langsam, W. C., *Historic Documents of World War II*§ (1958). A selection.

Milward, A. S., *The German Economy at War* (1964). The role of the economy in the German war effort.

Plievier, Theodor, *Stalingrad*§ (1948). A novel of the great battle, written by a German participant.

Poliakov, Leon, *Harvest of Hate* (1954). The Nazi genocide of European Jewry.

Reitlinger, Gerald, *The Final Solution*§ (1953; 1961). The murder of European Jews by the Nazis.

Rossi, Angelo, *The Russo-German Alliance, August 1939–June 1941* (1951). A diplomatic account.

Rothfels, Hans, *The German Opposition to Hitler* (1948; 1962). From the early 1930s through the July, 1944, plot.

Rowse, A. L., *Appeasement*§ (1961). An impassioned condemnation, by a historian who saw the appeasers in action at close range.

Royal Institute of International Affairs, *Documents on International Affairs, 1939–1946* (1958). Vol. I contains documents on the immediate antecedents of World War II; Vol. II is called *Hitler's Europe* and deals with the Nazi "New Order."

Royal Institute of International Affairs, *Survey of International Affairs 1939–1946* (1954). Vol. I, *The Eve of War, 1939*, describes the diplomacy of that year.

Sherwood, R. E., *Roosevelt and Hopkins*§ (1948; rev. ed. 1950; 1960). Offers many insights into U.S. policy during World War II.

Snell, J. L., *Illusion and Necessity*§ (1964). A diplomatic history of World War II.

Snell, J. L., et al., *The Meaning of Yalta*§ (1956; 1966). An attempt to clarify confusion about the controversial conference.

Sontag, R. J., and J. S. Beddie, *Nazi-Soviet Relations, 1939–1941* (1948). Documents, captured after the collapse of Germany, dealing with the origins and destiny of the Hitler-Stalin alliance.

Thomas, Hugh, *The Spanish Civil War*§ (1961; 1965). An account of the conflict in which the Nazis, Fascists, Communists, and Anarchists tried their strength, while the democracies watched paralyzed.

Trevor-Roper, Hugh, ed., *Hitler's War Directives, 1939–1945* (1964). Documents recording Hitler's grand strategy.

Weinberg, G. L., *Germany and the Soviet Union, 1939–1941* (1954). The Nazi-Soviet alliance.

Weiss, Peter, *The Investigation*§ (1966). A documentary play based on records of the trial of the guards who had served at Auschwitz.

Werth, Alexander, *Russia at War, 1941–1945*§ (1964). A historic account by a correspondent who had been an eyewitness.

Wheeler-Bennett, J. W., *Munich*§ (1948; 1966). The story of West's capitulation to the dictators in 1938.

Young, Peter, *World War, 1939–1945* (1966). A history of the major operations and engagements.

CHAPTER 19.   THE COLD WAR

Allulieva, Svetlana, *Twenty Letters to a Friend* (1967). Stalin and his domestic life, observed by his daughter.

Bor-Komorowski, Tadeusz, *The Secret Army* (1951). The story of the uprising of the Polish Home Army in Warsaw (1944) by its commander.

Brzezinski, Z. K., *The Soviet Bloc*§ (1960; rev. ed. 1967). A political history of the independent Communist states and satellites, and their relationship with the Soviet Union.

Davison, W. P., *The Berlin Blockade* (1958). The story of the Airlift to the beleaguered city.

Djilas, Milovan, *Conversations with Stalin*§ (1962). An intimate of Tito describes his experiences with Stalin and the Soviet ruling élite.

Feis, Herbert, *Churchill, Roosevelt, Stalin*§ (1957). A study of wartime diplomacy and the roots of the Cold War, centered on the three Allied leaders.

Fejtö, François, *Behind the Rape of Hungary* (1957). The subjugation of Hungary by the Communists and the 1956 revolt.

Jones, J. M., *The Fifteen Weeks*§ (1955; 1965). The formulation of the Truman Doctrine and Marshall Plan, by a State Department official who participated in the decisions.

Kennan, G. F., *Memoirs, 1928–1950* (1967). The recollections of a leading participant in the formulation of U.S. policy toward Soviet Russia after World War II.

Korbel, Josef, *The Communist Subversion of Czechoslovakia, 1938–1948* (1958). A Czech participant tells the story of the destruction of democracy in his country.

Kulski, W. W., *Peaceful Coexistence* (1959). Post-Stalinist Soviet foreign policy in theoretical and historical perspective.

Laqueur, W. Z., and Leopold Labedz, eds., *Polycentrism* (1962). The breakdown of the Communist monolith after the death of Stalin.

Lasky, M. J., ed., *The Hungarian Revolution* (1957). "The story of the October [1956] uprising as recorded in documents, dispatches, eye-witness accounts, and world-wide reactions."

Librach, Jan, *The Rise of the Soviet Empire*§ (1964; rev. ed. 1966). The expansion of the Soviet Union and the growth of its domain.

Mannoni, D. O., *Prospero and Caliban*§ (1956; 1964). A Freudian view of the effects of colonial rule on master and mastered.

Mehnert, Klaus, *Peking and Moscow*§ (1963; 1964). The historic antecedents of the Sino-Soviet rift.

Mikolajczyk, Stanislaw, *The Rape of Poland* (1948). The head of the Polish Peasant party tells of the Sovietization of Poland.

Price, H. B., *The Marshall Plan and Its Meaning* (1955). The origins, development, and results of the European Economic Recovery Program.

Seton-Watson, Hugh, *Neither War nor Peace*§ (1960). Reflections on the forces involved in the Cold War.

Spanier, J. W., *American Foreign Policy Since World War II*§ (1960; 2nd rev. ed. 1965). A comprehensive survey of the Cold War.

Truman, Harry S., *Memoirs*, 2 vols.§ (1958). Sheds light on the Cold War, its origins and development.

White, Theodore H., *Fire in the Ashes* (1953). A journalist's view of post-1945 Europe and America's role in rekindling the smouldering flame of life.

Zagoria, D. S., *The Sino-Soviet Conflict, 1956–1961*§ (1962; 1964). A Chinese specialist traces the origins of the rift.

Zinner, Paul, ed., *National Communism and Popular Revolt in Eastern Europe*§ (1956). Documents bearing on the 1956 upheavals in Poland and Hungary.

Zinner, Paul, *Revolution in Hungary* (1962). Hungary from the end of World War II to the revolt of 1956, based in part on interviews with refugees.

(*See also* bibliography, General Literature—Russia: Kennan.)

CHAPTER 20.   EUROPE AND THE WORLD

Graubard, S. R., ed., *A New Europe?*§ (1964). A collection of essays on European society and politics of the 1950s, with a look toward the future.

Haas, E. B., *The Uniting of Europe* (1958). The history of integration from 1950 to the Treaty of Rome (1957).

Harrod, R. F., *The Life of John Maynard*

Keynes§ (1951; 1963). By an eminent economist.

Henderson, W. O., *The Genesis of the Common Market* (1963). The antecedents of economic cooperation and integration from the eighteenth century to the formation of the European Economic Community.

Hutchison, Keith, *The Decline and Fall of British Capitalism* (1950; 1966). The British economy from 1880 to World War II.

Kitzinger, U. W., *The Politics and Economics of European Integration*§ (1963; 1965). An Englishman views (sympathetically) the emergence of the Common Market.

Shonfield, Andrew, *Modern Capitalism*§ (1965). Argues that the economy of the West is no longer capitalist; stresses the growing importance of the public sector.

Index

Asiento Treaty (*1713*), 48
Assembly, freedom of, 119
Assembly line, 160
Atatürk, Kemal, 418–419, 426
Atheism, 152, 229
Athenaeum, 73
Atlantic Cable, 181
Atlantic Charter (*1941*), 30, 485
Atom, 136; structure of, 369, 373–374
Atomic bomb, 374; against Japan, 503; in Soviet Union, 538; U.S. monopoly of, 531
Atomic energy, in united Europe, 561
Atonal music, 403
At the Races (Degas), 296; *illus.*, 298–299
Auber, Daniel, 103
Auderbrand, Philibert, 288
Au Moulin Rouge (Toulouse-Lautrec), *illus.*, 304–305
Auschwitz extermination camp, 491
Ausgleich, 130, 257–258
Australia, 175, 273, 322
Austria, 113, 121–122, 213, 219, 264, 271–272, 364; and Congress of Vienna (*1814–1815*), 27–29; Dual Monarchy in, 130–131, 257–259; ethnic groups in, 31, 128, 130–131 (*map*, 129); industrialization and, 57; under Metternich, 31; Nazi attack on, 475; Nazi party in, 445–446; revolution of *1848*, 107, 110–111, 128; and sphere of influence in Balkans, 267, 269; war with Piedmont, 121–122, 130; war with Prussia (*1866*), 126; in World War I, 315–322, 335, 414
Austro-German alliance (*1879*), 271
Austro-Hungarian Empire, 128–131, 331–332, 335; peoples of, 128, 257–259, 270; *map*, 129
Autarchy, and balance of trade, 437
Authoritarianism, 35, 116, 118, 359, 364
Avanguardisti, 429, 453
Avant-garde, 302, 310–311, 313; intellectuals in, 465; theater, 407; writers, 405
Avenue de l'Opéra (Pissarro), *illus.*, 290
Aviation, military, 335, 483; *see also* Bombings
Awakening Conscience, The (Hunt), *illus.*, 202
Axis powers, World War II, 473, 484, 495–496; expansion by (*1936–1942*), *map*, 485; *see also* Germany; Italy; Japan

B

Bach, Alexander, 130
Bach, Johann Sebastian, 401
Bacteria, 137
Baden, 127
Bagehot, Walter, 115
Bakunin, Mikhail, 229–230; *illus.*, 228
Bal à Bougival (Renoir), *illus.*, 300
Balance of trade, 437; *see also* Trade
Balfour Declaration (*1917*), 553
Balkans, 26, 47, 263–265, 284, 315–316, 322; great-power rivalry in, 267–269

Balla, Giacomo, 193; painting by, 193
Ballet Russe, 402
Ballet Seen from a Loge (Degas), 296; *illus.*, 297
Ballot Act, England (*1872*), 243
Baltic Provinces, 355; Hitler's aims in, 478
Balzac, Honoré de, 149; *illus.*, 149
Bank failures, *1930s*, 437
Bar at the Folies-Bergère (Manet), 293; *illus.*, 294–295
Barbarossa, Operation, 484, 507
Barbizon school of landscape painting, 80
Bartók, Béla, 403
Barzun, Jacques, 147
Bastiat, C. F., 57
Battle Symphony (Beethoven), 103
Baudelaire, Charles, 95, 105
Bauer, Bruno, 147–148
Bauhaus, in modern design, 400–401
Bavaria, 81, 112, 127, 364; Communists in, 423
Beckmann, Max, painting by, 465
Beethoven, Ludwig van, 77–79, 88, 103, 401
Behaviorist School, 379
Being and Time (Heidegger), 385
Belgium, 171, 173, 219, 233, 237, 278, 317–319, 329; colonial policy of, 555, 556; industrialization in, 46, 54, 155; in kingdom of Netherlands, 29; liberalism in, 25, 246; Nazi invasion of, 481; proclaims independence, 43
Bell, Alexander Graham, 157
Belle époque, la, 288–313
Belorussia, 261, 358–359
Bentham, Jeremy, 36, 57–58, 273
Bergson, Henri, 378–381; *illus.*, 379
Beria, Lavrenti, 444, 539–540
Berlin, 195; anti-Communist revolt in, 544; blockade of, in Cold War, 529; Congress of (*1878*), 264, 269; Reichstag fire (*1933*), 449; Russian capture of (*1945*), *illus.*, 521; Spartacist revolt in (*1919*), 423; *illus.*, 423; University of, 32, 86
Berlin Airlift, 529; *illus.*, 529
Berlin Wall, 530; *illus.*, 530
Berlioz, Louis Hector, 79, 103
Bernard, Claude, 144, 152
Bernhardt, Sarah, studio of, *illus.*, 206
Bernstein, Eduard, 236–237, 346; *illus.*, 226
Berry, Duc de, 32
Bessarabia, 478
Bessemer, Henry, 159
Bessemer converter, 159, 161
Biblical history, interpretation of, 147–148
Bill of Rights: U.S., 23
Biological sciences, 135, 137–139
Birth control, 173, 463
Bismarck, Otto von, 168, 233–234, 240, 252, 269–271, 284; *illus.*, 125, 253, 256; attack on Catholic Church, 123, 254; as Chancellor of German Empire, 127–128; in Franco-

Prussian War, 127; and Napoleon III, 127; and North German Confederation, 126–127; in power in Prussia, 125–127; and Schleswig-Holstein question, 126; and war with Austria, 126

Black Country, The (Meunier), *illus.*, 154

"Black Friday," London, 164

Black Lines (Kandinsky), *illus.*, 386

Black Shirts, Italy, 428

Blackstone, William, 22, 36

Blake, William, 88; paintings by, 84

Blanc, Louis, 110, 223, 229

Blitzkrieg, by German army, 478–479

Blok, Alexander, 404

Bloody Week, Paris (*1871*), 249

Blum, Léon, 473

Boccioni, Umberto, sculpture by, 466

Boer War, 279–281

Bohemia, 57, 111

Bohemianism, 224, 293

Bohr, Niels, 373; *illus.*, 375

Boileau, Nicolas, 67, 69, 75

Bolivar, Simón, *illus.*, 33

Bolivia, 162

Bollhagen, Otto, painting by, 186–187

Bolshevik Revolution, 342–345, 432, 467; *see also* Russian Revolution

Bolsheviks, 335–336, 347–355, 360, 362; *see also* Lenin; Marx; Marxism

Bolshevism, 347, 351, 358–359, 365; Lenin and, 347–349; *see also* Communist party

Bombings, World War II, 481, 495, 498–500

Bonald, Louis de, 24–25, 85

Bonaparte, Louis (king of Holland), 116

Bonaparte, Louis Napoleon, *see* Napoleon III

Bonaparte, Napoleon, *see* Napoleon Bonaparte

Bonheur, Rosa, 205

Bonnard, Pierre, 308, 313; paintings by, 308–309

Bosnia, 264, 269, 287

Boswell, James, 51

Boulanger, Georges, 250, 270

Boulanger, Louis, painting by, 149

Boulton, Matthew, 51

Boundary disputes, post-World War I, 417–419

Bourbon dynasty, 21, 28, 34, 39, 73, 76, 122

Bourgeoisie, 468–469; *see also* Middle class

Bowdler, Thomas, 201

Bowdlerizing, 201

Boxer Rebellion (*1900*), 257, 283; *illus.*, 283

Brahms, Johannes, 79, 401

Brazil, 33

Brest Litovsk, Treaty of (*1918*), 355, 413

Bretton Woods, N.H., Conference (*1944*), 563

Bridge building, 181; *illus.*, 181

Bright, John, 59

British Commonwealth of Nations, 552–554, 561

British Economic Growth, 1688–1959 (Deane-Cole), 64 n.

British Empire, dissolution of, 554

Broglie, Louis de, 375 n.

Brooke, Rupert, 326

Brothers Karamazov, The (Dostoevsky), 153

Bruant, Aristide (Toulouse-Lautrec), *illus.*, 306

Brunel, Isambard Kingdom, 181

Brusilov, Aleksei, 324

Buckle, Henry Thomas, 146, 152

Budapest, 195

Buddenbrooks (Mann), 407

Bulganin, Nikolai, 542

Bulgaria, 264, 269, 322, 335, 453; aid to Jews from, 493

Burckhardt, Jacob, 152

Burke, Edmund, 24, 36, 83–84

Burma, 281, 282, 553

Burne-Jones, Edward, 205

Burnham, James, 468

Burschenschaften, 32–33

Byliny, Russian heroic poems, 75

Byron, George Gordon, Lord, 70, 71–72, 73, 88, 90, 93; *illus.*, 72, 90, 93

Byzantine art, 397; revival of, 81

C

Cabet, Etienne, 222–223

Cab Horse, The (Bonnard), *illus.*, 309

Café-Concert aux "Ambassadeurs," Le (Degas), 288; *illus.*, 289

California, gold discoveries in, 163

Campbell, John C., 532 n.

Camp David talks (*1959*), 542, 547

Canada, 178, 273

Canning, George, 34, 36, 43

Canning industry, 160, 189

Cánovas, Antonio, 263

Cape Colony, 273, 279–281

Capitalism, 225–227, 236, 240, 364; new meaning of, 564; salaried class and, 467–469

Caporetto, Battle of, 335

Carbonari, 32

Carbon-filament lamp, 157

Carlsbad Decrees (*1819*), 33

Carlton Club, Torries and, 114

Carnap, Rudolf, 385

Carnot, Marie, 232

Carr-Saunders, A. M., 172

Cartels, 168–169, 186

Carthaginian Peace, The (Mantoux), 414

Cartwright, Edmund, 49

Casablanca Conference (*1943*), 493

Castlereagh, Robert Stewart, Viscount, 29–30, 33

Cathode rays, 370

Catholic Center party, Germany, 423, 425, 447, 449

Catholic Church, *see* Roman Catholic Church

Cavaignac, Louis Eugène, 110, 117

Cavour, Camillo, 120–123

484; in Stalinization of Eastern Europe, 526; Youth Movement among, 453

Comte, Auguste, 142, 145; *illus.*, 146

Concentration camps, German, 330, 491; *illus.*, 492; Russian, 362, 443, 539

Concert of Europe (*1815*), 29, 34–35, 43

Concordat of *1801*, 86

Condition of the Working Classes in England, The (Engels), 224

Congo, 556; manganese mining in, 160–161

Congress of Soviets, 351–354, 359

Congress of Vienna, *see* Vienna

Consciousness, concepts of, 378–379; states of, 405

Conservatism, 21, 23–26, 31–35, 43, 113, 240

Conservative party, British, 114, 242, 244, 420–421

Constable, John, 79–80; painting by, 100

Constant, Benjamin, 22–23

Constitution, American (*see* Federal Constitution, U.S.); Belgian, 43; French: of Year VIII, 118, 248; of *1848*, 117; of *1852*, 118; of *1875*, 248, 250; German Empire, *1871*, 126–127; Spanish, *1812*, 262; Russian, *1906*, 339–340

Constitutional Democratic party, Russia, 260–261, 356, 359

Constitutionalism, 113, 116, 131

Consumer goods, in European economy, 566; technology and, 189

Containment, U.S. policy of, 532–533

Continental system, 26–27

Contraceptives, 462

Conurbia, urban cluster, 197

Cooperative movements, 222–223

Copernicus, Nicolaus, 369, 373

Cornfield, The (Constable), *illus.*, 100

Corn Law (*1815*), British, 59–60; repeal of, 60–61, 65, 114

Corot, Camille, 80

Corsica, 222

Cort, Henry, 53

Cosmetics, use of, 210

Cosmopolitanism, 240

Cot, Pierre Auguste, painting by, 204

Cottage industries, 63

Cotton, American, 49; Egyptian, 162

Cotton gin, 49

Cotton textile manufacture, 48–52; British (*1772–1851*), *graph*, 49; calico printing machines, *illus.*, 60

Council of Europe, 559

Council of Four (World War I), 409

Courbet, Gustave, 149, 387; painting by, 150

Credit, post-World War II expansion of, 565

Crédit Foncier, 118

Crédit Mobilier, 118, 163–164

Crime and Punishment (Dostoevsky), 153

Crimean War, 132, 268

Criminal Law Amendment Act (*1871*), 234

Critique of Pure Reason (Kant), 82

Crompton, Samuel, 48

Cromwell (Hugo), 76

Cross and Cathedral in the Mountains (Friedrich), *illus.*, 99

Cruikshank, George, cartoon by, 93

Cry, The (Munch), *illus.*, 380

Crystal Palace, London, 176, 178, 186; *illus.*, 177

Cuba, 162

Cuban missile crisis (*1962*), 544

Cubism, 310–311, 395

Cultural revolution, 68, 87

Cultural values, urbanization and, 195

Culture, bourgeois, 198; mass, of 19th century, 213–215

Curie, Pierre and Marie, 371; *illus.*, 371

Currencies, gold-backed, 436–437

Czechoslovakia, 414; advanced economy in, 426; France and, 422; and Munich agreement, 474–477; Nazi attack on, 475; in post-World War II period, 527

D

Daily Mail, 215

Daimler, Gottlieb, 157

Dairyman's Daughter (Richmond), 213

Daladier, Edouard, 476

Dalton, John, 136

Danhauser, Joseph, painting by, 102–103

Dante Alighieri, 149

Dardanelles, 322

Darwin, Charles, 128, 139–143, 228, 382; *illus.*, 134

Darwin, Erasmus, 139

Darwin, Marx, Wagner: Critique of a Heritage (Barzun), 147 n.

Darwinism, 139–142, 146; natural selection and, 140–142; Social, 146, 186, 267; struggle for existence and, 140–141, 147; variants and, 140

Das Kapital (Marx), 226

Daumier, Honoré, 81, 105; painting and drawings by, 104, 118, 212

David, Jacques Louis, paintings and drawings by, 68

Dawes, Charles G., 425

Day of the God (Gauguin), *illus.*, 393

D-Day, *1944*, 500

Deane, Phyllis, 64 n.

Death of Sardanapalus, The (Delacroix), 95; *illus.*, 96–97

Death of Socrates (David), *illus.*, 68

Debussy, Claude, 401, 404

Decembrist uprising, Russia, 34–35

Decline of the West, The (Spengler), 336

De-colonization, causes of, 549–551; progress of, 551–556

Defence of the Realm Act (*1916*), British, 330

Defense of Usury (Bentham), 57

Deflation, in *1920s*, 420

in, 128, 447–453; National Labor Front, 452; Nazi totalitarianism in, 447–453; occupation of Poland, Norway, and Denmark, 480–481; overseas migration from, 175; post-World War II partition of, 528–529; post-World War II political parties, 562–563; reparations from, 413, 422–424; revolutions of *1848*, 107, 111–112; and Soviet alliance, 422, 477–478, 507; unemployment reduction in, 452; unification of, 123–128, 267, 269, *map*, 124; urbanization of, 62; and Versailles Treaty, 412–413; Weimar Republic, 423–425, 444; working class in post-World War II era, 469; world trade and, 169; in World War I, 315–335; in World War II, 471–493

Germinal (Zola), 62

Gestapo, reign of terror by, 489–490

Gide, André, 313

Gil de Castro, José, painting by, 33

Gilchrist, Percy, 159

Gioberti, Vincenzo, 85

Giovinezza, Italy, 429

Girodet, Anne Louis, painting by, 86

Gladstone, William E., 243–244; *illus.*, 245

Gobineau, Joseph de, 147

God, materialism and, 144; and Romantic impulse, 98

Goebbels, Joseph, 446, 450

Goering, Hermann, 510; *illus.*, 448, 506

Goethe, Johann Wolfgang von, 67, 69, 73, 88, 128; *illus.*, 73

Gogol, Nicolas, 74

Gold Exchange Standard, 436–437

Gold standard, 163; abandonment of, 437

Gomulka, Wladyslaw, 544

Goncharov, I. A., 151

Gotha Congress (*1875*), 233

Gothic Revival, 81; *illus.*, 80

Government, controls of, and liberal theorists, 23

Grand Alliance, in World War II, 493–495

Gray, Thomas, 73

Great Britain, 171, 195, 211, 213, 217, 219, 233; agricultural collapse in (*1870s*), 170; Anglo-German rivalry, 284–287; birth rate in post-World War I era, 463; and colonialism in Africa, 277–281; Common Market and, 561; and Congress of Vienna (*1814–1815*), 26–28; and Crimean War, 132, 268; de-colonization process and, 551–552; economic liberalism in, 57–61; foreign investments, 276; general strike (*1926*), 420, *illus.*, 420; gold standard abandoned, 437; impoverishment following World War II, 552; industrialization in, 35, 45–46, 155, 164–165; inflation in, 456–457; labor movement, 419–420; liberalism in, 25, 34–35, 39, 43, 243–244; mid-Victorian, 114–116; mutual defense treaties in World War I, 422; naval blockade, World War I, 413;

overseas migration from, 175; politics in interwar period, 420; in post-World War I period, 419–421; saturation bombings by, 495; self-employed in, 468; social unrest and reform, 19th century, 35–39; and trade overseas, 275; union of England and Scotland (*1707*), 47; urbanization of, 62; wartime taxation in, 456; in World War I, 319, 321–323, 328, 332, 335; in World War II, 470–483, 493–499

Great Depression, 437, 563; middle class in, 466; totalitarianism and, 432

Great Eastern, steamship, 181; *illus.*, 180

Great Exhibition (*1851*), 176, 178, 186; *illus.*, 178–179

Greece, 213, 265, 453; Italian attack on, 484; U.S. aid to, 533; uprising against Turks, 21, 33, 89, 133; War of Independence, 133; war with Turks, *1919*, 418–419

Greece Expiring on the Ruins of Missolonghi (Delacroix), 88; *illus.*, 89

Grenouillère, La (Monet), *illus.*, 389

Grimm brothers, 75

Gropius, Walter, 400; architecture by, 400

Guernica (Picasso), *illus.*, 473

Guilbert, Yvette, en diseuse (Toulouse-Lautrec), *illus.*, 306

Guilds, 54, 57, 65, 218

Guillaume, Albert, poster by, 188

Guizot, François, 41, 108, 110, 212; *illus.*, 109

Guys, Constantin, drawing by, 117

H

Habeas Corpus Act, 35

Haftmann, Werner, 394 n.

Hague Court, 415

Hahn, Otto, 374

Halévy, Daniel, 248

Halifax, Edward Wood, Viscount, 475

Hamburg, bombing of, 495

Hamilton, Alexander, 167

Hammarskjöld, Dag, *illus.*, 540

Hapsburg Empire, 128; Austrian, 31–32; dissolution of, 414

Hargreaves, James, 48

Harmsworth, Alfred (Lord Northcliffe), 215

Haussmann, Georges Eugène, 119, 291

Hayes, C. J. H., 193

Haystacks (Monet), 391, 396

Hazlitt, William, 92

Hearst, William Randolph, 215

Hebrides Overture (Mendelssohn), 79

Hegel, Georg Wilhelm Friedrich, 82–83

Heidegger, Martin, 384–385; *illus.*, 384

Heisenberg, Werner, 370, 377

Heliocentric theory, 369

Hellenistic Empire, 272

Helmholtz, Hermann von, 138

Hemingway, Ernest, 407

Henry IV (France), 291

emergence of the world market, 160–164; patterns of industrial development, 155 (*chart*, 165); population growth and migration, 172–175 (*graph*, 174); technological progress in last half of 19th century, 156–160; *see also* Industrialization

Industrial Revolution, 33, 45, 62–63, 105, 165

Industry, captains of, 186; consumer-oriented, 170

Inequality of Human Races, The (Gobineau), 147

Infeld, Leopold, 373 n.

Inflation, middle class and, 456–459

Ingres, Jean Auguste, painting and drawing by, 78

Intellectuals, Hitler's extermination policy toward, 484, 490; liberalism and, 23; migration of, from Russia, 362; positivism and, 146; and revolutions of *1848*, 107–109; of Russian minority groups, 261; socialism and, 220–221, 230, 237; in Spain, 263

Internal-combustion engine, 157

International Association for Woman's Suffrage, 211

International Monetary Fund, 563

International Postal Union, 415

International relations, *1870–1914*, 267

International trade, following World War I, 435–436; gold standard and, 436–437; and Great Depression, 437–438; prior to and following World War I, 162–163, 419

International Working Man's Association, 228

Interpretation of Dreams, The (Freud), 381

In the Conservatory (Manet), *illus.*, 292

In the Omnibus (Egley), *illus.*, 194

Introduction to Experimental Medicine (Bernard), 144

Investment banks, 163

Iran, Soviet army in, 531

Iraq, and Versailles Treaty, 415

Ireland, emigration from, 174; independence of, 421; insurrection in (*1848*), 114; nationalist movement, 243; potato famine (*1845*), 60, 175

Irish Home Rule party, 243

Iron deposits, German Empire, 165

Iron industry, 53, 159; British, 53; *illus.*, 63; *graphs*, 53, 169

Isabey, J. B., drawings by, 26

Isolationism, end of, 567

Israel, 553–554

Italy, 108, 110, 211, 213, 217, 220, 233, 270, 272; Austrian intervention in (*1821*), 34; boundary disputes, 418; Communist party in, 527, 534, 546; and Congress of Vienna (*1814–1815*), 29; "Corporate State" in, 429; fall of, in World War II, 499–500; fascism in, 426–429; and industrial progress, 47, 57; liberalism in, 251–252; migration from, 175; and Mussolini, 426–431; parliamentary regime in, 252; political parties in,

251–252, 426–429; postwar inflation in, 458; postwar politics, 562–563; revolutions of *1848*, 107, 110, 112; unification of, 120–122, 252, 267, 269; *map*, 121; and Versailles Treaty, 414; in World War I, 315, 319, 322, 325, 328, 335, 409; in World War II, 473, 484, 497, 499, 502

Iudenich, General, 356, 358

Iwo Jima, Battle of, 502

J

Jacobins, 249

James, William, 378–379; *illus.*, 378

Japan, 113, 131; Anti-Comintern pact with Germany, 477; as Axis partner, 474; attack on China, 488; expansion of in *1930s*, 488–489; in "Greater Asian Co-Prosperity Sphere," 495; MacArthur rule in, 535; Russo-Japanese War (*1904*), 284, 550; Sino-Japanese War of *1894*, 282; and Soviet Union, 486, 502–503; successes in Pacific, 489; in Tripartite Pact, 483; *illus.*, 487; Westernization of, 281; *see also* Pearl Harbor

Japanese art, influence of, 389

Japanese codes, breaking of, 489, 496

Jaurès, Jean, *illus.*, 216

Jazz Age, 465

Jesuits, expulsion of, from Prussia, 254; re-establishment (*1814*), 86

Jewish State, The (Herzl), 259

Jews, in Austria, 128, 258–259; emigration from Europe, 175; and Israeli state, 553–554; massacre of, in Nazi Germany, 451–452, 490–493; position of, in Russia, 260; and teaching of young, 212; *see also* Anti-Semitism

Joffre, Gen. Joseph, 320

Johnson, Samuel, 101

Joint-stock companies, 163, 169, 186

Joule, James, 138

Joyce, James, 407; *illus.*, 406

Jugendstil, 398

Jung, Carl, 384, 385; *illus.*, 383

Junkers, of Prussia, 123–125

Jutland, Battle of, 332

K

Kahnweiler, Henry (Picasso), *illus.*, 311

Kalevala, of Finland, 75

Kamikaze campaign, Japan, *illus.*, 496

Kandinsky, Vasili, 396; painting by, 386

Kant, Immanuel, 22–23, 82, 128; *illus.*, 82

Kapp *putsch*, *1920*, 424

Karamzin, Nicholas, 24

Katyn forest massacre, 527 n.

Kautsky, Karl, 237

Kay, John, 48

Keats, John, 69, 72 n., 73, 101, 105

Liquid fuels, 156

Lisle, Leconte de, 404

List, Friedrich, 167–168

Liszt, Franz, *illus.*, 102–103

Literature, drama and, 67–68, 75–76; liberalism in, 22; of mass culture, 214; modern, 403–407, 485; novel in, 74–75, 149–153, 207; poetry and, 67, 73–76; popular, 214; realism in, 148–151, 305; Romantic, 72–76; stream-of-consciousness technique in, 406–407

Lithography, 80–81

Lithuania, 415, 418, 478

Little Entente, 422

Littré, Maximilian, 145–146

Liverpool, 48

Living standards, industrialization and, 62, 64, 189; and mass culture, 215; and protective tariffs, 167; salaries and, 469

Livingston, David, 278

Lloyd George, David, 245, 322–323, 358, 409–412, 420, 456; *illus.*, 411

Locarno treaties, 422, 425

Locke, John, 81, 226

Logical positivism, 384

Lokal-Anzeiger, 215

Lombardy, 29, 112, 122

London, bourse, as central money market, 164; expansion of, *maps*, 197; Nazi bombing of, 482, 498–499

London Journal, The (Reynolds), 214

Lorraine, 159, 165, 270, 318–319; acquired by France, 421; ceded to Germany, 248

Louis XVIII (France), 39–40

Louis Philippe (France), 41–42, 81, 110, 116, 149, 209, 212; *illus.*, 42

Love and Pilgrim (Burne-Jones), 205

Lovely Day, A (Céard), 151

Lovett, William, 39

Low, David, cartoons by, 506, 539

Low Countries, and World War I, 409; *see also* Belgium; Netherlands

Lucca, 120

Lucinde (Schlegel), 208

Luddites, 65

Ludendorff, Gen. Erich Friedrich, 320, 328–330, 335, 425; *illus.*, 329

Ludwig I (Bavaria), 86, 112

Ludwig II (Bavaria), 81

Lueger, Karl, 258–259, 445

Luftwaffe, in Battle of Britain, 483

Luncheon of the Boating Party (Renoir), *illus.*, 301

Lunch Hour (Kollwitz), *illus.*, 190

Luther, Martin, 212

Lüthy, Herbert, 331 n., 567

Luxemburg, 317

Lyell, Charles, 139

Lyrical Ballads (Wordsworth), 73

M

MacArthur, Gen. Douglas, 496, 538

McCarthy, Joseph R., 538

McCormick, Cyrus, 178

Macedonia, 264–265

Mach, Ernst, 372

McKinley, William, 232

Macpherson, James, 73

Madame Bovary (Flaubert), 150

Maddison, Angus, 563

Magenta, Battle of, 121

Maginot Line, 422, 481

Magyars, 128, 130, 257

Mahmud II (Turkey), 133

Maine, Henry, 22

Maistre, Joseph de, 24–25, 85–86

Making of the English Working Class, The (Thompson), 64 n.

Malenkov, Georgi, *illus.*, 539

Malevich, Casimir, 396

Mallarmé, Stéphane, 403–404; *illus.*, 292

Malthus, Thomas, 139, 172–173

Malthusian League, 173

Man, capacity to control destiny and environment, 21; classicism concept of, 69; conservatists' pessimism about, 24; Enlightenment theory of, 176; Feuerbachian notion of, 144; and liberal ideology, 21, 24; materialist conception of, 143; positivism and, 142–143; Realism and, 148; Romanticists' concept of, 69, 148; skeletons of apes and, *illus.*, 143; 20th-century view of, 377–384

Man, Hendrik de, 221

"Managerial revolution," 468

Man a Machine (La Mettrie), 143

Man and Woman Gazing at the Moon (Friedrich), *illus.*, 99

Manchuria, 281, 536

Manet, Édouard, 293–294, 310; lithograph and paintings by, 249, 292–295

Manfred (Byron), 93

Manfred on the Jungfrau (Martin), *illus.*, 91

Manganese, 160–161

Manifesto of *1909*, 466

Mann, Thomas, 407

Mannoni, O., 550 n.

Man's League for Opposing Woman's Suffrage, 209

Mantoux, Étienne, 414

Mao Tse-tung, 284, 535; *illus.*, 550

Marne, Battle of, 320

Marriage, post-World War I views on, 460–461

Marshall, Gen. George C., 620

Marshall Plan, 527, 534, 557–559

Martin, John, painting by, 91

Marx, Karl, 42, 191, 223–228, 230, 234, 237, 382; *illus.*, 225, 229

Marxism, 85, 144, 220, 224–228, 233, 237,

Manifesto, 261; and Ottoman Empire, 131–133; political parties in, 260–261; Provisional Government (*1917*), 342–345, 348, 350–353; reforms of *1860s*, 131–133, 259; revolution of *1917–1921* (*see* Russian Revolution); takeover by Soviets, 354–355; and USSR, 359; and Versailles Treaty, 415; War Communism in, 360–361; and World War I, 315–325, 328, 333–335, 339, 344; *see also* Soviet Union

Russian Army, *see* Red Army
Russian motion pictures, 407
Russian music, 401–402
Russian Orthodox Church, 86
Russian poetry, 404
Russian Revolution, of *1905*, 344; of *1917–1921*, 169, 233, 338–365, 419–420; *illus.*, 338, 342, 354; *see also* Bolshevik Revolution
Russification, 261
Russo-Japanese War, 237, 261, 284, 319, 550
Russo-Turkish War (*1877–1878*), 264, 271
Rutherford, Ernest, 373, 375

S

SA, *see* Sturmabteilungen
Sabotage, industrial, 65
Sacre du Printemps, Le (Stravinsky), 402
Sadowa, Battle of, 126
Sainte-Beuve, Charles-Augustin, 208
St. Germain, Treaty of (*1919*), 415
Saint-Simon, Claude Henri de, 116–118, 209, 221–223
Salaried class, rise of, 467–469
Salazar, Antonio de Oliveira, 426, 431
Sand, George, 208–209; *illus.*, 102
San Stefano, Treaty of (*1878*), 269
Sant'Elia, Antonio, 176, 193; painting by, 192
Sarajevo, 315
Sartre, Jean-Paul, 385
Sassoon, Siegfried, 327
Savigny, Frederick, 85
Savoy, 121
Saxony, 165
Say, J. B., 57
Schelling, F. W. J. von, 82–83
Schiller, Johann von, 69, 73, 78, 128
Schlegel, August William, 73, 75, 93
Schlegel, Frederick, 69, 73, 88, 93, 208
Schleiden, Matthias, 137
Schleswig-Holstein, 126
Schlieffen, Alfred von, 318; *illus.*, 318
Schlieffen Plan, 318, 321, 481
Schönberg, Arnold, 403
Schopenhauer, Arthur, 152
Schubert, Franz, 78–79, 401
Schuman, Robert, 560
Schuman Plan, 560
Schumann, Robert, 78–79
Schutzstaffel Guards (SS), Germany, 451, 489–490

Schwann, Theodor, 137
Science, discoveries in first half of 19th century, 135–136; vs. experience, 369; philosophy and, 142–145; religion and, 147–148
Scientific culture, opposition to, 151–153; and realism in literature and art, 148–151
Scientific management, 160
Scotland, 212; union with England, 47
Scott, Sir Walter, 74, 135; *illus.*, 74
Seagull, The (Chekhov), 407
Sea Lion, Operation, 482–483
Sebastopol, 132
Second Empire (France), 116–119, 121
Second International, Socialists and, 235, 237, 347, 364
Second Republic (France), 110
Secularism, 87; education and, 240, 242, 246, 250
Sedan, Battle of, 248, 270
Sehnsucht, cult of, 98
Self-determination, national, 25, 34, 43, 113, 414, 417–419, 485
Self-Help (Smiles), 214–215
Sensible Etiquette of the Best Society (Ward), 203
Serbia, 211, 264–265, 269, 287, 315–317; Yugoslavia and, 414
Serfdom, 198, 226; in Russia, 132; *see also* Slavery
Seurat, Georges, 302, 392; painting by, 302–303
Severn, Joseph, 93, 105; painting by, 92
Sewing machine, 160
Sex, psychology of, 381
Sexual revolution, *1920s*, 461–462
Shakespeare, William, 75–76, 204, 550
Shaw, George Bernard, 235
Shelley Composing 'Prometheus Unbound' in the Baths of Caracalla (Severn), *illus.*, 92
Shelley, Mary Godwin, 75, 93; *illus.*, 75
Shelley, Percy Bysshe, 72 n., 73, 88, 93, 101; *illus.*, 92
Sherman Anti-Trust Act (*1890*), 169
Shipwreck, The (Turner), *illus.*, 66
Shirer, William L., 452
Shop Management (Taylor), 160
Sibelius, Jan, 403
Sicily, 499
Siegfried Line, 334–335
Siemens, Werner von, 156
Siemens-Martin open-hearth process, 159
Silas Marner (Eliot), 209
Silesia, 62, 165, 217, 418
Simplicissimus, cartoons, 278, 279, 424, 454, 458, 459
Sino-Japanese War (*1894*), 282
Sisley, Alfred, painting by, 388
Sismondi, Jean, 227
Six Acts, British (*1819*), 35
Skating (Manet), 293; *illus.*, 293
Slave trade, 47–48

Transylvania, boundary dispute over, 418

Treatise on Positive Philosophy (Comte), 145

Trevelyan, G. M., 207

Trevor-Roper, H. R., 471 n.

Trianon, Treaty of (*1920*), 418

Trieste, Italy, dispute over, 414–415, 418

Tripartite Pact (*1940*), 483

Triple Alliance (*1882*), 270, 272, 315, 322

Tripolitan War, 551

Tristan and Isolde (Wagner), 401

Trollope, Anthony, 150

Troppau Protocol, 33–34.

Trotsky, Leon, 349, 351–354, 356, 361, 439–441, 443; *illus.*, 353

Troupe de Mlle. Églantine (Toulouse-Lautrec), *illus.*, 307

Troyon, Constant, 205

Truman, Harry S., 503, 531, 533

Truman Doctrine, 527, 533, 557; *see also* Marshall Plan

Tunisia, 270, 555

Turgenev, Ivan, 151, 345

Turgot, Robert, 273

Turin, convocation in, 122

Turkey, 287, 322, 335; and the Balkans, 263–265; in Crimean War, 132, 268; dictatorship in, 426; Greek uprisings against, 21, 33–34, 89, 133, 418–419; intervention of army in political life, 265; reforms in, 133, 263; and Treaty of Paris (*1856*), 132; U.S. aid to, 533; war with Greece, 418–419; wars with Russia, 264, 269; in World War I, 409

Turner, J. M. W., 79–80; paintings by, 66, 101, 180

Tuscany, 120, 122

Two Sicilies, Kingdom of the, 120, 122

U

Ukraine, 261, 355, 358–359, 443

Ultramontanism, 86

Ulysses (Joyce), 406

Unemployed (Kollwitz), *illus.*, 436

Unemployment, industrialization and, 64; Keynes' theory of, 564; public works and, 118–119; relief payments and, 223; and World War II, 472

Union Act of *1840* (British), 273

Unique Forms of Continuity in Space (Boccioni), *illus.*, 466

United Nations Organization, 30; founding of (*1945*), 524, 531; and Korean War, 537

United States, aid to Soviet Union in World War II, 487; as "arsenal of democracy," 494; Cold War and, 537–538; "containment" policy of, 532–533; divorce in, 464; and European Recovery Program, 557–559; foreign aid as continuing policy, 533; gold standard abandoned, 437; Hitler declares war on, 489; industrialism in, 46–47, 54, 155; Italian immigrants in, 175; and Japa-

nese expansion, 488–489; and Korean War, 537; and League of Nations, 417; loans by, *1920s*, 436; in postwar European economy, 562–563; "massive retaliation" policy, 543; trade following World War I, 419; in World War I, 319, 333–334, 409–410; in World War II, 489–498

United States and Italy, The (Hughes), 252

United States Navy, World War II, 487–489

United States of Europe, 557

Universities, liberalism and, 32–33

Upper-middle class, 197; domestic help and, 201; family and, 200–201, 207; industrialization and, 199; money and, 203; morals and manners of, 198–203; of Paris, 293; reforms of in Europe, 198; sex attitudes of, 201–202; tastes of, 203–207; *see also* Middle class

Urbanization, 61–62, 87, 108, 173, 195–197, 227; *maps*, Europe in *1850* and *1910*, 166; middle class and, 197

USSR, *see* Soviet Union; Russia

Utilitarianism, 36–38

Utopian socialism, 223, 237

V

Valadon, Suzanne (Renoir), *illus.*, 300

Valery, Paul, 337

Van Gogh, Vincent, 392; painting by, 394

Vanished Supremacies (Namier), 109

Van Tieghem, Paul, 70

Venetia, 112, 122

Venice, Republic of, 29

Verdi, Giuseppe, 79

Verdun, Battle of, 323–325

Verlaine, Paul, 404

Verona, Congress of (*1822*), 34

Versailles, William of Prussia proclaimed Emperor at, 127

Versailles Treaty (*1919*), 409; German buildup after, 478–479; guilt about, 472; and League of Nations, 417; and postwar Germany, 424; provisions of, 412–415; and World War II, 471

Vichy government, 482

Victor Emmanuel II (Italy), 120, 122

Victoria (England), 114–115, 243; *illus.*, 115, 274

Vienna, Act of (*1815*), 29; Congress of (*1814–1815*), 21–30, 122; *illus.*, 27; uprising (*1848*), *illus.*, 106; and Versailles Treaty, 415

Vietnam War, 544, 555; *illus.*, 543

Vlaminck, Maurice, 313

Volta, Alessandro, 156

Voltaire, 75, 128

Voyage to Icaria (Cabet), 222

Vries, Hugo de, 142

V-2 rockets, 498

Vuillard, Edouard, 313; drawing and painting by, 238, 312

W

Wages, real, 217, 230–231
Wagner, Richard, 79, 103, 401
Wallace, Alfred R., 140
Wannsee, conference, 490–491
War, glorification of, 193, 467
War Communism (Russia), 360–361
War of *1870*, 414
Ward, Mrs. H. O., 203
Warfare, application of industrial methods to, 318–319, 335; depersonalization of, 326; submarine, 332–333, 495; total, 319, 358, 498; trench, 323, 327
Warsaw, destruction of, 527
Warsaw, duchy of, 28, 31, 260
Watson, John B., 379
Watt, James, 50–51
Wealth of Nations, The (Smith), 167
"Weavers, The" (Kollwitz), 191
Webb, Sidney and Beatrice, 235–236; *illus.*, 236
Weber, Karl Maria von, 79
Weber, Max, 242
Wedgwood, Josiah, 51–52
Wehrmacht, German, 478–479, 484, 504
Weimar Republic, 423–425, 444
Weinberg, Gerhard L., 480 n.
Weismann, August, 142
Wellington, Duke of, 103
West, as supra-national bloc, 549, 560, 566
West Germany, growth of, 529, 563
Westminster, Statute of (*1931*), 552
Westminster Review, 37
Westphalia, 217
What Is Art? (Tolstoy), 204
What Is Property? (Proudhon), 229
What Is to Be Done? (Lenin), 347
Where Is Science Going? (Planck), 376 n.
Whigs, British, 37, 60, 114
White-collar class, 217, 469
Whitney, Eli, 49
Wilberforce, Samuel, 141
Wilkinson, John, 51
William I (king of Prussia and German emperor), 124–128, 271
William II (Germany), 191, 257, 272, 285, 315, 317, 335, 365, 523; *illus.*, 256, 266, 286
William IV (England), 114
Wilson, Edmund, 367
Wilson, Woodrow, 331, 358, 409–410, 418; *illus.*, 409; and League of Nations, 415–417
Witte, Sergei, 170
Wittgenstein, Ludwig, 385
Women, emancipation of, 207–211, 460, 462, 463

Wool, 48
Woolf, Virginia, 405 n., 406
Words of a Believer, The (Lammenais), 122
Wordsworth, William, 73, 88, 101, 135, 176
World market, 160–164
World War I, Balkan front, 322; boundary disputes following, 417–419; breakdown of ideas in, 367; campaigns of, 319–325, 334–335; *maps*, 320, 324, 334; casualties, 325, 336 n.; divorce rates and, 463–464; on Eastern front, 322, 324–325, 334–335, 344, 357; *map*, 324; economic crisis following, 435–438; effects of, 336–337; inflation and, 456–457; Italian front, 325, 335; military preparations and plans, 317–319; mobilization on home front, 328–330; morale of troops, 326–328; outbreak of hostilities, 265, 315–317; peace initiatives, 331–332; peace finally obtained, 409–410; sexual morals and, 462–463; taxation in, 456; war at sea, 332–334; Western front, 321–327, 335, *map (1914–1917)*, 320; *map (1918)*, 334; Versailles Treaty and, 409–415
World War II, background, 471–503; decisive battles of, 495–496; end of, 503, *map (1943–1945)*, 501; Hitler's role in, 471–498; Lend-Lease and, 494–495, 509; naval operations in, 495–496; origins of, 446–447, 471; Pacific Theater, *map (1931–1945)*, 503; Pearl Harbor attack, 487–488; Popular Fronts in, 477–478; Roosevelt and, 487, 493–494, 564; Teheran and Yalta conferences, 524–525; war in Russia, 504–517; *see also* Axis powers; Stalin
Wreck of the Hope, The (Friedrich), *illus.*, 98
Wundt, Wilhelm, 145
Württemberg, 127
Wyatt, James, painting by, 80

X–Y–Z

X rays, 368, 370
Yalta Conference (*1945*), 520, 524–525, 531; *illus.*, 520
Yeats, William Butler, 404
Yellow journalism, 215
Young, Edward, 73
Young, G. M., 199 n.
Young Europe, international society, 120
Young Turks, 265
Ypres, Battle of, 321
Yugoslavia, dictatorship in, 426; German occupation of, 486; Stalin and, 528
Zemstva, 132–133, 340
Zinoviev, Grigori, 364
Zionism, 259, 553; *see also* Palestine
Zola, Émile, 62, 250; *illus.*, 250
Zollverein, customs union, 56, 167, 557; *map*, 56
Zurich, Treaty of (*1859*), 121